"Krebsz has provided a thorough and helpful reference book on all aspects of structured finance. For the layman, the opening chapters will provide a useful account of the processes and motivations behind structured finance products. For those involved in the ongoing management of data and risk processes, the detail in later chapters on systems and infrastructure available is unique and it is good to find all of this information in one place."

Faten Bizzari, Principal at Eastfield Capital Ltd

"Markus Krebsz has achieved a rare feat. He has written a book about securitization that is practical and useful for practitioners but at the same time provides enlightenment to the general reader.

When the structured finance markets froze up as a result of sub-prime contagion in July 2007, many practitioners walked away, assuming the game was over for good. But Krebsz, who has worked for a variety of global financial institutions, remained a firm believer, always confident the market would come back—albeit perhaps in modified form. He took advantage of the lean years to write this book.

The book provides real value-added for market practitioners of what is a mind-numbingly complex area, including easy-to-follow lifecycle charts of structured products, detailed checklists, graphs, and illustrations. In the second half he also talks you through how to use some of the new analytical and risk management tools available from Principia Partners, Bloomberg, and others.

Given the recent dribbles of new issuance, Krebsz was right to persevere with the market, and one of his main predictions (which almost verges on a plea) is that when securitization does fully return, it will be characterized by transparency, standardization, and simplicity—traits which seemed noticeable by their absence during the rapid growth years of 2003–07. In the introduction to his chapter on Bloomberg he reveals how the expected transformation of the market has been galvanized by the shift in power away from issuers and towards investors. Clearly, if the investors are in charge, they are going to be a lot more discriminating about what they actually buy.

Krebsz is a passionate believer in the need for a healthy securitization market. If all market participants and investors were to read, learn, and inwardly digest this book, common sense would doubtless prevail."

Ian Fraser, *Financial Times* correspondent and consulting editor at Bloomsbury Publishing's *Qfinance*

"... an authoritative text on the practicalities of securitization, providing a wealth of detailed information on the lifecycle of a typical deal. As the market for structured finance products comes gradually back to life, this book is likely to become a valuable reference for market participants."

Professor Alexander J. McNeil, Department of Actuarial Mathematics and Statistics, Heriot-Watt University

"This is a fantastically researched in-depth publication that I learned a great deal from reading and will continue to consult on an ongoing basis. No matter which angle you come from this should be a must-read for all market participants both old and new."

Martin Sampson, European ABS Business Manager, Bloomberg L.P.

"... a book that is both encyclopaedic in its coverage of the structured products business and a model of clarity of exposition."

Paul Wilmott, financial engineer and founder of Wilmott.com

The Chartered Institute for Securities & Investment

Mission Statement:

> *To set standards of professional excellence and integrity for the investment and securities industry, providing qualifications and promoting the highest level of competence to our members, other individuals and firms.*

Formerly the Securities & Investment Institute (SII), and originally founded by members of the London Stock Exchange in 1992, the Institute is the leading examining, membership and awarding body for the securities and investment industry. We were awarded a royal charter in October 2009, becoming the Chartered Institute for Securities & Investment. We currently have around 40,000 members who benefit from a programme of professional and social events, with continuing professional development (CPD) and the promotion of integrity, very much at the heart of everything we do. Additionally, more than 40,000 examinations are taken annually in more than 50 countries throughout the world.

The CISI also currently works with a number of academic institutions offering qualifications, membership and exemptions as well as information on careers in financial services. We have over 40 schools and colleges offering our introductory qualifications and have 7 University Centres of Excellence recognised by the CISI as offering leadership in academic education on financial markets.

You can contact us through our website *www.cisi.org*

Our membership believes that keeping up to date is central to professional development. We are delighted to endorse the Wiley/CISI publishing partnership and recommend this series of books to our members and all those who work in the industry.

As part of the CISI CPD Scheme, reading relevant financial publications earns members of the Chartered Institute for Securities & Investment the appropriate number of CPD hours under the Self-Directed learning category. For further information, please visit *www.cisi.org/cpdscheme*

Ruth Martin
Managing Director

Securitization and Structured Finance Post Credit Crunch

A Best Practice Deal Lifecycle Guide

Markus Krebsz

WILEY

A John Wiley and Sons, Ltd, Publication

This edition first published 2011

Registered office
John Wiley & Sons Ltd, The Atrium, Southern Gate, Chichester, West Sussex, PO19 8SQ, United Kingdom

For details of our global editorial offices, for customer services and for information about how to apply for permission to reuse the copyright material in this book please see our website at www.wiley.com

For other titles in the Wiley Finance Series please see www.wiley.com/finance

ISBN 978-0-470-71391-4 (hardback)
ISBN 978-0-470-66212-0 (ebook)
ISBN 978-0-470-66206-9 (ebook)
ISBN 978-1-119-97793-3 (ebook)

A catalogue record for this book is available from the British Library

Project management by OPS Ltd, Gt Yarmouth, Norfolk
Typeset in 10/12pt Times
Printed in Great Britain by CPI Antony Rowe, Chippenham, Wiltshire

Contents

APPENDIXES

Dedication

I am dedicating this book to my fiancée and partner Sally and my son Jimmy. My attention for them vanished when I went into "writing mode", and it is their patience, understanding, and support that helped me to keep going throughout and eventually—after 4 long years—to complete this project.

Our Jack Russell terrier Heidi has kept me fantastic company during protracted writing sessions (evenings and early mornings) and deserves a place here for her loyalty.

A big *Herzlichen Dank* to my parents Ursula and Hans who have supported me throughout my life and career and to my sister Michaela whose own perspective on life has helped me adjust the way I see things.

This book is dedicated to all of you—with love.

Preface

If you can't wait to delve into the substance of the book, I suggest you go straight to Chapter 1: Introduction. However, if you would like to find out more about the background to the book, why it was written, and how it evolved during writing (at the height of the credit crunch in a largely frozen structured finance market), then the preface to the book will paint the picture of my personal journey whilst writing—and pausing—and writing again about a market that was at the time of writing going through both major revolutionary and evolutionary changes, which served to set the backdrop to the book.

The original idea for this book dates back to early 2007 and, by the time the initial proposal was approved by my publisher, the structured finance markets had started to crumble—big time. Nevertheless, I continued working on an early draft until October 2008. Despite there being little new public issuance and virtually closed secondary structured finance markets, I still felt it right to continue.

However, the collapse of Lehman Brothers and its impact on global financial markets forced me to take a step back and give thought to some fundamental questions: given that the structured finance markets had since November 2007 dried up, with very limited public issuance and non-existent secondary-market trading, I wondered whether it would ever return and, if so, when. Seasoned market participants' view on this issue was clearly divided: some said "yes" (with some reservations), others said "no way" and decided on—or in many cases were forced into having—a career change, where anything other than structured finance would do.

If the market was not going to come back, then writing a book about it would be a waste of my time, the publisher's time and resources, and of course your time and money because there would be no reason for you to buy it? On the other hand, if it was going to return would there still be a need for such book and, if so, why?

Instead of writing about a subject I feel I know very well, I found myself researching many unknowns and uncertainties. For instance, what would the regulatory environment look like? Bad press, negative publicity, and increasing political global pressure seemed to be heavily focused on this particular market, and "securitization" was being likened to "subprime" by many people at that time. All of which was doing few favors for the majority of otherwise largely unaffected asset classes.

As a consequence of all this research, I concluded that the structured finance market would come back eventually, *but* it would not bear much resemblance to what it used to look like before mid-2007. In fact, fundamental changes would be necessary to get it back; otherwise, it would not return at all. The key areas I mostly expected to change were *standardization*, *transparency*, and *simplicity*.

Standardization

I expected everything to be much more standardized in terms of asset classes, pre-issuance and post-issuance information, deal reporting, and analytical approaches and models.

Transparency

Another area that I would expect to fundamentally change is the provision of transaction-specific information. This will include information on bond performance (e.g., details on such credit enhancement draws as monoline insurance wraps), such as underlying collateral information like loan-by-loan information. For the first time in this market, investors are now in the powerful position to demand performance-related information from issuers as a condition for them to return to the market and start investing again. What is more, issuers find themselves obliged to listen to investors' demands for this kind of information, or else they would be faced with a situation in which the majority of investors would be clearly reluctant to invest in issuers' products. Furthermore, many global initiatives by trade bodies such as AFME/ESF, SFIMA and many more—with input from Bloomberg and other third-party vendors—will help to set new standards and provide templates and best practice models for standardized deal information.

Simplicity

One of the key features of some asset classes was the complex nature of the structures. Deal structures had become overly complex for various reasons pre credit crisis, but going forward there will be no place in the market (or investor appetite) for deals that have been structured in such an opaque fashion. Some of these deals were structured intentionally to achieve artificial asymmetry of information, either by using structures that were so complicated that no one could *really* understand and follow them or by using "black-box" models that were nigh on impossible for investors to grasp—no matter how sophisticated they considered themselves. You may also call this "arbitrage on information"—more on this in Chapter 4 on sound practice principles.

The "box-to-line ratio"

When I first started as an apprentice and newbie in the structured finance market back in 2001, my then manager—who happened to be the senior risk manager for "special products"—occasionally used to decline credit approvals for instruments where the structural complexity was simply too unwieldy to quantify and the underlying risks too difficult to understand. He used to call this the "box-to-line" ratio; if there are too many "boxes" (i.e., too many counterparties performing different functions in the deal) and too many "lines" (i.e., too many multi-dimensional relationships between these counterparties), we should steer clear of the deal. In a sense, I guess he was right and, since investors will increasingly be required by law to rely on their own structural analyses rather than just on research provided by credit rating agencies, simplicity will be an important factor for the return of the future market.

Arbitrage mechanisms

"Arbitrage" has been inherent in many transactions and simply means that one or more counterparties to a transaction can (and will) profit from any imbalance in the transaction. Such imbalances can appear in many shapes and forms not all of which are necessarily detrimental:

- *Timing arbitrage*. Someone may receive funds that legally belong to somebody else but is contractually required not to pass these funds on immediately.
- *Informational arbitrage*. Somebody may have access to or simply has more information available than someone else and may be tempted to act on the basis of this knowledge. Such asynchronous information can make all the difference when executing a trade; the line between this and "insider trading"—which is illegal—can be thin.
- *Different regulatory treatments* (e.g., different regulatory rules used for banks using the standardized or foundation approach vs. the internal ratings based approach led to the application of different multiplication factors when calculating the required capital reserve). As a result one investor's strategy may be more focused on investing in higher grade assets (i.e., assets with investment-grade ratings) whereas others may be specifically looking to invest in lower grade bonds (i.e., with speculative-grade ratings). This is also occasionally referred to as "regulatory arbitrage", which can also occur as a result differences in legal jurisdictions and in cross-border transactions.

Declaration of "interest"

Finally—before bringing the preface to a close and jumping straight into the main body of this publication—let me declare my "interest" and make a "confession": you will see from reading the book that I strive to maintain a fair and constructive level of criticism concerning the rating agencies—at least, concerning the three major ones (i.e., Moody's Investor Services, Standard & Poor's, and Fitch Ratings).

First, you may be aware or have seen in my bio that I worked for Fitch Ratings from 2004 to 2006—first, as a performance analyst and, then, as a primary ratings analyst for corporate and infrastructure securitization. During little more than those 2 years I gained great insight into the credit rating agency business and was able to refine and polish my analytical skills. The atmosphere at Fitch was great and it was an interesting place to be and a great company to work for. I was also passionate about my work there and, hence, got pretty upset to see the demise of the agencies when they became scapegoats for the collapse of the market. Don't get me wrong, they for sure contributed to the collapse, but it was by no means their sole fault. After leaving Fitch, my passion for the structured finance market evolved and, whilst I still respect the work that is done by the agencies, I have also become one of their critics, albeit a measured one. Although critical, I still consider myself a "friend" of the agencies and hope some of my criticism will be read and interpreted as constructive rather than destructive. The service the agencies provide will continue for a long time, but the framework within which they operate has already changed and further changes are highly likely. So, please, when I criticize the agencies in the following pages, keep in mind that this criticism comes from passion for them rather than dislike of them.

Furthermore, note that all references to ratings apply (unless otherwise stated) only to the structured finance area, which differs considerably from how corporate ratings are assigned.

A second point you may pick up on is that I dedicate quite a few pages to Bloomberg and its services (Chapters 13 and 22). I can assure you this is not a marketing pitch for Bloomberg and (unfortunately) I will not get any commission for the number of times the firm gets mentioned in this book. However, I am happy to confess to being a Bloomberg beta-user and over the past 2.5 years have been in close discussions with the firm to develop customized solutions in collaboration with them for the structured finance market. Bloomberg has always been receptive and—more than once—came up with brilliant and innovative solutions that will benefit the structured finance market for years to come. Bloomberg has kindly supported my efforts by providing me with reprint licenses for a considerable number of screenshots and I am truly grateful for such support. Ultimately, I hope that you will be able to benefit from this symbiosis and end up using some or all of these tools in your day-to-day business.

Third, you may have noted that this book is published by Wiley under the umbrella of the Chartered Institute of Securities & Investment—CISI (*www.cisi.org*). I am an ordinary member of the CISI who sits on the Institute's Risk Forum and IT Forum Committees. Furthermore, I undertook the technical review for the CISI's *Risk in Financial Services* workbook and the senior review for both the CISI's *Operational Risk* (13th edition) workbook and the *IT in Investment Operations* workbook. In such capacities, I have been conducting volunteer and charitable activities for the CISI, but I am not an employee of the Institute. Having said that, I am a great supporter of what the CISI does and stands for and, hence, will recommend some of the Institute's other publications as and when applicable throughout the book.

Disclaimer

Before you rush off and try out the tools referred to in Part IV of the book (some of which are available for download on the companion website *www.structuredfinanceguide.com*), note that I will not assume any liability for using these tools. Although carefully written and developed, they rely to some extent on third-party applications (e.g., Bloomberg and Excel) and, hence, some of the code will naturally be subject to change.

For instance, whilst some old BBG code was based on "blpb" and "bdp", current codes use "bdp" and "bps" functions which make things considerably faster and more efficient. In addition, Bloomberg offers "code conversion tools" as part of its Excel plug-ins and you may need to tweak some of the downloadable files to get them working. Some of the suggested functionality (e.g., the "BBG Portfolio Uploader" or the "MTGE Bond List Generator") contains Bloomberg's proprietary code and macros, hence I will not be able to supply this as a downloadable file due to copyright and software licensing restrictions.

Nevertheless, I can direct you to the relevant function or function code which will enable you to download the newest version. Again, as functionality is constantly improving you may find that tools work slightly differently than described in the book. If you experience difficulties with any of the Bloomberg functions, I suggest you get in touch with the firm's helpdesk. Otherwise, check out the book's companion website *www.structuredfinanceguide.com* to look for updates.

The year of regulation: 2010

2010 turned out to be the year of regulation: the only things that remained static in the structured finance market were the constant regulatory proposals, impact assessments, the setting up of many working groups around the globe by various trade bodies, regulators, central banks, and the like, and the hundreds of working group meetings—all aimed at getting the market back on its feet.

Section 3.1 provides a brief, but by no means exhaustive, list of initiatives that will have a major influence in years to come (some, such as Basel III, until 2018 and beyond) and will determine the shape, look, and feel of the new market. Many of these initiatives were only set in stone in the second half of 2010 and some will undergo impact assessments before they take their final shape and became regulatory rule(s). So, you will have to forgive me if I cannot draw a more precise and more detailed picture of the future market landscape, simply because there are too many uncertainties in terms of practical implementation and actual impact on the market. Some of these initiatives will continue at least until 2012, so be wary of the muddied waters you will find yourself in if you work in this particular sector of the capital markets.

Conclusion

As of July 2010—3 years after starting to write this book—I can see the first clear signs of the structured finance market gently returning (at least some parts of it): there was some issuance of ABS notes in 2008 and 2009, approximately USD900bn of which was issued in the U.S. (representing a 50% increase over 2007 U.S. issuance levels) and around USD65bn was issued in Europe, which was 87% less than 2007 issuance volumes (*source*: AFME/ESF).

In stark contrast are the figures for European ABS issuance financed and retained by the European Central Bank and the Bank of England, who have since become two of the world's largest special investment vehicles (SIVs): around USD1,100bn of European ABS issuance in 2008 and 2009 was retained by the European Central Bank and around USD535bn by the Bank of England (*source*: CABS/Bloomberg).

Moreover, whereas the U.S. market has seen previous ABS investors recently returning to the market, Europe is still lacking a similar private investor base, meaning the pricing for European ABS remains expensive compared with pre–credit crunch levels. For instance, a AAA-rated auto loan ABS transaction priced at +5 to 10 basis points over the 1-month EURIBOR in Europe compares with a similar AAA-rated bond priced at +100 to 160 basis points over 1-month EURIBOR in the U.S.

By mid-June 2010 there appears to be a thin but healthy pipeline of transactions lined up for issuance in the second half of this year and 2011. What surprised me most is that one rating agency indicated that they have been asked (as of June 2010) to rate around 20 collateralized debt obligations (CDOs)—one of the asset classes that suffered the greatest losses during the credit crunch. However, they also made it pretty clear to me that, while these deals are CDOs in nature, the issuers requested the agencies call them anything but CDOs; so, instead, they will now be called either structured credit financing of corporate loans (old name CLOs) or structured project financing (previously these transactions were either called "synthetic CDOs" or "CDOs" or something similar). Not only does the market seem to be picking up in terms of issuance pipelines, but I also noticed recently an increased number of adverts for deal structurers, rating agency analysts, and other jobs that play a predominant part at deal lifecycle inception and early stages.

Only time will tell how large the future structured finance market will become and what it will look like, but I dearly hope that it will achieve organic but sustainable growth to maximize the benefits for the real economy (i.e., small businesses, firms generally, and ultimately individual consumers). I doubt it will ever reach the size pre credit crunch, but as my dear friend Nassim Nicholas Taleb (author of *The Black Swan*, *Fooled by Randomness*, and *Dynamic Hedging*) would suggest, too big is not beneficial and eventually doomed to failure—he was right about the 2007–2010 credit crunch.*

Markus Krebsz

* Just to clarify, Nassim Taleb says that the credit crisis has been predictable and, hence, was *not* a "black swan". Read more on this in *The Black Swan: The Impact of the Highly Improbable* (Second Edition, March, 2011), with a new chapter "On robustness and fragility" by Nassim Nicholas Taleb.

Acknowledgments

First, I extend my gratitude to Wiley's commissioning editor Jenny McCall who played a huge part in making this successful by encouraging me to finish the book over the past four years and the Chartered Institute for Securities & Investments for supporting this project.

I would also like to thank everyone who made my professional journey over the past two decades enjoyable—there are too many individuals to mention, but they will know when they read this.

Last but not least—thank YOU for buying this book and your interest and belief in the structured finance market. If you are working in this sector, please do your bit to represent it with the integrity it needs and the professionalism it deserves, particularly when you are dealing with "other people's money". This may be something that was often forgotten prior to the credit crunch but, nevertheless, is one of the most important foundations of this profession.

The following individuals (in alphabetical order) have all somehow inspired me or helped in their unique ways to make this book happen—although some may not even know they did. As such, I am privileged for having known them and grateful for having been able to work with them: Zeyn Adam, Marco Angheben, Patricia Perez Arias, Rui Barros, Faten Bizzari, Mark Bowles, Catriona Boyd, Dennis Cox, Frank J. Fabozzi, David Flett, Ciro Ferraz, Lillian Flores, Simon Furey, Charlie Genge, Jamie Harper, Usman Ismail, Mark Kahn, Chris Kilborn, Vas Kosseris, Vinod Kothari, Stephanie Kumar, Guillaume Langellier, James Leppard, Douglas Long, José Lourenço, Mitchell Maddox, Kerry McGrath, Doug McLean, Jean-Christian Mead, Ashley Meek, Ned Meyers, Gabriel Odediran, Graham Page, David Pagliaro, Stephen Peecock, David Pellatt, Lawrence Richter Quinn, Christina Reinke, Martin Sampson, Neil Shuttlewood, Lucy Smith, Neil Smith, Nassim Nicholas Taleb, Janet Tavakoli, Harry Thurairatnam, Gemma Valler, Gary van Vuuren, Colin Warschau, Rick Watson, Gerald M. (Jerry) Weinberg, Paul Wilmott, Jim Wilner, Debra Wilson, and Mi Zhou.

Hope you will enjoy reading this book as much as I did writing it.

ACKNOWLEDGMENTS

1 Introduction

1.1 SETTING THE SCENE: ABOUT THIS BOOK

First of all—and before I forget: *Thank you for buying this book.*—I much appreciate your interest and curiosity.

As the subtitle of this book implies, we will be taking a close look at a securitization and structured finance "deal". But, hang on a minute, there are so many different deals out there, spanning across many different asset classes as well as jurisdictions, so why are we looking at one "deal"?

The answer is simple: Our starting point for this journey is a generic deal, with no particular focus on asset class, deal structure, or jurisdiction. Based on the generics, I will guide you through along the way and would hope to develop your understanding so that you are equipped with the right tools, are able to ask the right questions, and consequently receive the appropriate answers.

Thinking about this introduction, I realized that there is really no such structured finance or securitization "college" or "university" course out there that would equip practitioners with the necessary tools and skills to just go away and structure or manage a deal throughout the transaction's lifecycle for their firms. Clearly, there are many independent providers of courses (including more recently the rating agencies themselves), but with those courses being more theoretical in nature and typically only lasting a short duration (i.e., 2 to 5 days), don't expect to walk away as a qualified structurer, underwriter, rating agency analyst, or securitization lawyer from such seminars.

Furthermore, a lot—if not most—of the practical knowledge and skills that are needed for these kinds of fairly complex activities are typically acquired over a long period of time on the job and by working with more experienced colleagues. However, as a direct consequence of the credit crisis, many banks and other financial institutions were forced to wind down some—if not the majority—of their structured finance-related business areas leading directly to a huge drain on experienced resource.

The knowledge in this book has been accumulated over at least 10 years including the "good" years, when this was a highly buoyant market as well as the four solid years of the 2007–2010 credit crisis—which many commentators referred to as the worst one of the last century. I am very grateful and indeed feel privileged to have been able to see both sides of the coin and to have been able to learn from both of them.

Whilst I can understand that some people may wish they could turn the clocks back pre crisis, when many institutions as well as individuals were doing very well, I can also understand an adjustment was probably overdue and with the crisis the pendulum had overswung. What we have seen since are many serious attempts to restore some kind of equilibrium. The danger here is of course that the securitization and structured finance market will be hit too hard with new regulatory requirements and essentially become prohibitively regulated.

Structuring a transaction can take anything from 2 to 6 months whereas the resulting structured finance deal is likely to be around for much longer—anything from 5 to 25 years, in extreme cases even considerably longer (usually due to specific legal or other requirements in certain jurisdictions).

The book's key aims are twofold:

- To provide a solidly grounded back-to-basics approach that allows you to gain a quick understanding of the underlying key principles and sound practices for conducting these types of transactions.
- To give you a tried and tested set of tools to get you started in the structured finance market.

Please note, however, that the market itself has always been—and continues to be—in constant flux and, more recently, it has become increasingly difficult—if not at times impossible—to keep up with global developments. This leads to a higher level of uncertainty in terms of the form and shape the future market will actually evolve into. Taking a more generic deal view helps here in ensuring that most of this will be applicable to you in one way or another, no matter whether you are based in Europe, the U.S., or Asia—as I take a global view here.

I personally hope that you get value out of the book. If you have any comments—good or critical—please feel free to send them to me via the book's companion website *www.structuredfinanceguide.com* or contact me at *www.markuskrebsz.info*

1.2 DIAGRAMMATICAL OVERVIEW OF DEAL LIFECYCLE STAGES

The following section provides a diagrammatical overview of deal lifecycle stages for a **generic** structured finance transaction. I emphasize the focus on generic as there may be slightly different steps depending on the asset class and jurisdiction that are involved. Figure 1.1 gives you a general overview of these deal lifecycle stages and also provide a roadmap to the book.

Following this overview you will find a more detailed roadmap (Chapter 2) dependent on the particular role you may currently be playing in the market (i.e., originator, issuer, deal structurer, arranger, lawyer, rating agency analyst, investor, portfolio manager, researcher, regulator, financial journalist, or other interested parties).

1.3 ROLE-BASED ROADMAP TO THE BOOK

Assuming that you are currently playing a particular role in the structured finance market, you would typically be more interested in certain areas and chapters more than others. Hence, I hope that you will find the following guidance with a focus on your particular area useful.

1.3.1 Originator, issuer, deal structurer, arranger

If you look at these roles logically, you may see that most of the chapters covering pre-close and at-close lifecycle stages are likely to be of most interest to these types of market players.

1.3.2 Investor, portfolio manager, asset manager

Equally, from an investor's, portfolio manager's, and asset manager's perspective anything post close of a transaction's lifecycle is likely to be most interesting for the analysis of transactions. However, in light of recent regulatory changes (e.g., requiring investors to undertake their own due diligence), some chapters on asset readiness are likely to be of interest to these roles too.

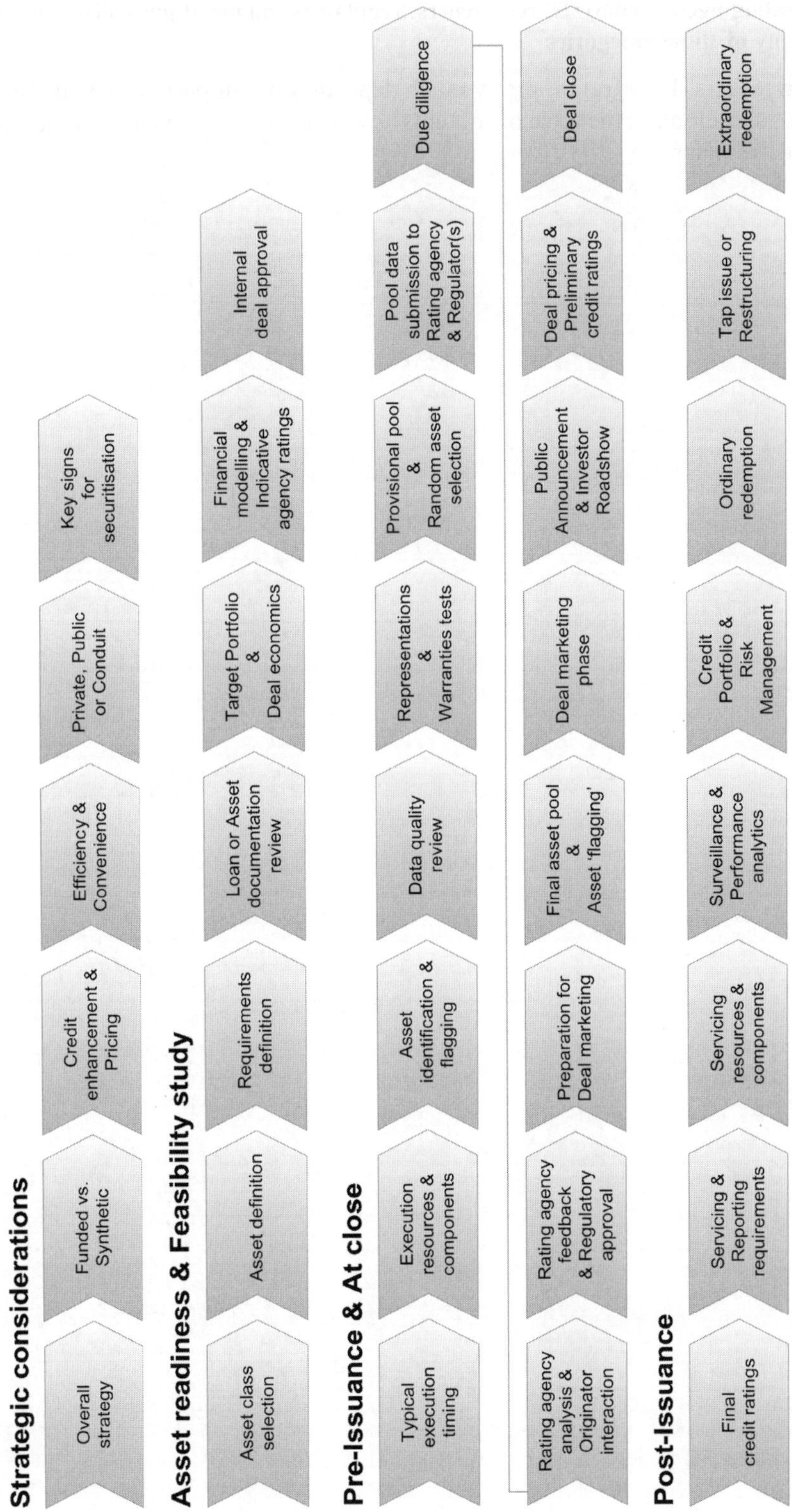

Figure 1.1. Generic deal lifecycle stages.

1.3.3 Lawyers, rating agency analysts, researchers, regulators, financial journalists and others that do not fit any of these categories

For the remaining readers, I'm afraid it pretty much depends what in particular you are after, so you are best advised to take a look in the table of contents as well as the comprehensive index at the back of the book to see if this helps.

Part I
The credit crisis and beyond

2

Looking back: What went wrong?

2.1 OVERVIEW

To answer the question, "Looking back: What went wrong?", the answer can be succinctly given as "Quite a few things actually."

But in all fairness, each of the following sore points on their own would probably not have led to the spectacular collapse of the structured finance market, in particular, and the global financial markets, in general. The combination of them, however, within the framework of globally operating and highly interconnected capital markets led to the chain of events that unfolded into the financial crisis 2007 to 2010.

This was then further exacerbated by a panicked reaction of the global financial regulators as well as market participants. For instance, the decision to withdraw formal support for Lehman Brothers in September 2008: I remember working for one of my clients who was at that time holding one of the largest portfolios of structured finance bonds—approximately 1,100 bonds worth around £45bn at the time—and many of these bonds were in one way or another exposed to Lehman credit risk as counterparties. The impact of Lehman's bankruptcy on those bonds as well as countless transactions where it acted as credit default swap (CDS) or interest rate swap (IRS) counterparty was almost impossible to assess—you can imagine the tension in the air; something I will never forget.

Some call this "the law of unintended consequences" and I guess they are right. These panicky decisions were taken in a matter of days—sometimes hours—and the only people involved were usually senior government officials, central bankers, and the CEOs of all the big banks affected—not necessarily best placed though to understand the potential impact of their decisions on the market, particularly the structured finance market.

I don't blame them: it's just the way things were in those days in many institutions: information would be filtered before it actually hit the top level and in many cases senior management would only get to see part of the picture—not always able to properly understand the implications of what they did get to see. Another example was a client who was sitting on a sizable structured finance portfolio for years with senior management blissfully unaware of what "assets" were sitting in its books.

In order to develop best practice principles for the market post credit crunch it is important to understand what went wrong and why? Once the shortcomings have been identified, we will be able to look ahead and understand the requisites so that a better and more robust market develops.

Before we delve deeper into this in Section 2.2, please note that we will be taking a closer view at areas that are of particular importance for securitization and structured finance only. If you are after additional sources and reports covering the whole financial market and not only this subsector, then please refer to this book's bibliography. Alternatively, search for "Financial crisis of 2007–2010" on Google which will help you identify the comprehensive coverage and the underlying problems that led to the credit crunch.

2.2 DATA, DISCLOSURE, AND STANDARDIZATION

When you as an individual are borrowing a substantial sum (e.g., for a mortgage) from your bank, the lender would like to become fairly comfortable that you will be able to repay the mortgage over the agreed period as well as ensuring that you have a sufficient regular income to service the interest payments for the term of the mortgage. You may call this process of gathering data and answers to relevant questions "due diligence".

In order to support such due diligence activities as well as subsequent risk analysis your lender will typically request a considerable amount of information (i.e., data) so that he can support his decision and justify whether or not you have the creditworthiness and financial standing to service your principal as well as interest payments.

Some of the data used by lenders would be information about your financial history and possibly the use of a "credit score" of some kind, which simply puts you into one of various categories which expresses your presumed current credibility based on your past financial performance. This credit score would then be used as a measure to forecast and predict whether or not you may be able to repay the mortgage over the term of the loan.

You would expect the same lender to be even more prudent when using substantially larger amounts of (not quite his own money) to purchase, say, AAA-rated prime U.S. RMBS tranches. Amazingly, this was not always the case with structured finance investments as many investors turned to the credit rating agencies for such assessment instead.

For starters, rating agencies would typically receive larger amounts of data which enables them to undertake detailed analysis. Some of these data would have been treated almost as proprietary by the originators of such instruments and hence they would not offer the same level of information to investors of their structured finance bonds. Furthermore, rating agencies would also request considerable amounts of historical data in order to model the future expected (rating) performance of these structured finance bonds. The difficulty here though is that it is fairly difficult—in fact, almost impossible—to model future performance based on historical information because

- A rating model will always be a "model" and never be able to reflect true reality. In fact, as my dear friend Nassim Taleb would put it: "Models are always wrong, but some are harmful." So please keep this in mind.
- People in the investment funds business know and understand this truth—hence they include a disclaimer in their prospectuses which states that "Past performance is no indication of future returns" which is not just a legal clause but a fundamental investment principle that should never be ignored.

Once the deals have been structured and issued to the market, there would be—depending on the asset class—considerable amounts of performance-related data (e.g., trustee, servicer, cash manager reports, etc.) available to investors. However, from an investor's perspective, it can be a lengthy and tedious process to lift this information from these reports and change it into a comparable, digestible, and easy-to-process format to support the investor's surveillance, performance, and risk analysis.

Even back in 2006 at the height of the market prior to its collapse there was a considerable amount of structured finance bond issuance in some asset classes which would report either in paper or near paper electronic format.

2.3 PAPER REPORTS

Paper reports can be sent by post or alternatively distributed as telefax. Paper reports do not generally provide an easy means of entering the information into a bank's or financial institution's proprietary performance analytics systems. You would literally need a team of "performance data coordinators" or similar who would lift (i.e., physically read) the information of these paper-bound reports and then enter them into the relevant systems. Even some of the rating agencies' surveillance teams would process paper reports in such a fashion. You can imagine that this is not the most efficient process and in some case it can take considerable time from the receipt of those reports until they finally appear (e.g., on the rating agencies' websites). Furthermore, if your institution has a file retention policy which, depending on the jurisdiction you are operating in, can be anything from 5 to 10 years after a transaction has matured (and some have maturity dates of 25 years or even longer), you will appreciate that the collection of various monthly investor reports for one single transaction can consume considerable storage space over the deal's life. Let alone if you have several dozen of these transactions in your portfolio. Fortunately, the parties involved have recognized these issues and electronic reports are becoming much more common.

2.4 ELECTRONIC REPORTS

Reports in electronic format are considerably easier to distribute and store, but it depends a lot on the format of these files whether they are actually easier to use than paper files.

The most common electronic file formats are portable document format (PDF) and tagged image file format (TIFF) files. TIFF is used to store images and in this context are in essence scanned paper documents which are easy to distribute, but are similarly annoying to paper reports when processing them, as they are typically not searchable. Assume you have a 250-page portfolio manager's report as a TIFF file and you are looking for certain key performance indicators: you will most likely have to flick through the pages on your screen to see whether you can find the data points you are after. Depending on the file format, you may be able to use optical character recognition (OCR) software in order to transpose such reports into an electronically readable format; but OCR software is usually not part of the standard desktop setup in a bank or financial institution.

Portable document files (PDF), on the other hand, are easily readable and electronically searchable and hence represent much better usability.

Both TIFF and PDF files have one major constraint: the data in these file formats are not easily exportable into Excel or similar programs and hence do not facilitate detailed analysis. Of course, you could use conversion software which transposes the information from PDF into Excel. In my experience, whilst such software may work with simple embedded PDF tables, it is not always possible to get the data into Excel without manual intervention.

Issuers of ABS deals are currently required to file their registration statements, current reports, and periodic reports in ASCII (American standard code for information interchange) or HTML (hypertext markup language). The SEC has in its proposed new ruling for ABSs (Release No. 33-197; 34-61858; File No. S7-08-10) suggested introducing a filing requirement in XML (extensible markup language) as an asset data file. XML is a machine-readable language and the SEC expects, by proposing this new disclosure requirement, that users of these data (such as investors) will be able to download this information directly into their proprietary spreadsheets and databases. As XML follows an open-format data structure, investors will be able to use off-the-shelf commercial software solutions to analyze it further or indeed are able to build their own analytical tools.

A key advantage of data in XML format is that the information can be processed automatically, without any great manual intervention. Further, it can also be "tagged" ensuring consistent structure of context and identity, which helps recognition and processing by a variety of analytical software.

2.5 DATA FEEDS

As an alternative to collecting individual files, and in particular if you are holding a large number of bonds (say > 500) and only have a limited amount of staff resources to look after the performance of such a portfolio, you may wish to consider a third-party vendor solution such as an automated data feed. Of course, such a service will usually come at considerable cost, but clearly can have additional advantages. These feeds can either come in the shape of an XML file which may be provided to you via FTP (e.g., ABSNet's "scheduled export") or you may be able to source the information directly into your proprietary applications via an application-programming interface (API), such as Bloomberg's desktop and/or server API. Alternatively, you may be able to download specific performance information in a digestible and easily processable data format (e.g., Excel or CSV) from the credit rating agencies; this could either relate to individual deals you hold or you may also be able to source benchmark information (e.g., Fitch's and S&P's credit card index data) so that you can compare the performance of your deal(s) against the performance of the whole market sector by benchmarking your transaction(s).

2.6 DEFINITIONS

Another problem that has affected the structured finance market in the runup to the credit crisis was the lack of standardization as well as the perceived complexity of the instruments due to the lack of clear definitions and use of jargon. Structured finance instruments can already be complex enough due to the nature of these deals, mainly caused by the number of structural features and various counterparties involved. In addition, the individual asset classes are not always as clearcut as you might expect; for instance, whilst some whole business securitization transactions may be considered (and rated as) commercial mortgage-backed securitizations, others may fall into the commercial asset-backed securitization or corporate and infrastructure securitization category and hence be subject to a different rating methodology with subtle differences that can impact the actual ratings.

In addition, structured finance practitioners were always quick in coming up with innovative structural features which would also require fancy jargon. Whilst some of this jargon may have been justified to describe these features in a brief fashion, to some extent this was also deliberately used to make the market look more opaque.

External credit ratings may also tempt their users in the investor community to directly compare them across different credit rating agencies (CRAs). For instance, take a AAA rating by Fitch and compare this against a AAA rating from Standard & Poor (S&P) and a Aaa rating by Moody's. Unless investors are aware of the fact that credit ratings cannot be compared or mapped between the different rating agencies, you are almost in a way tempted to compare both Fitch's and S&P's AAA with Moody's Aaa and may be misguided into thinking it is the same. Well, clearly it *is not*.

2.7 REPORTING STANDARDS

Unfortunately, whilst several attempts have been made to establish appropriate reporting standards across various jurisdictions as well as asset classes, prior to the credit crisis there were no real investor-centered reporting standards for the structured finance markets. Until recently, issuers were able to some extent to determine what kind of information they would like to provide and when. Yes, the rating agencies have run several initiatives during the past few years and some of these were more successful than others. Fitch ratings, for instance, introduced so-called "issuer report grades" (or IRGs) back in 2004 which would grade investor reports provided by issuers in the European structured finance market. IRGs would be assigned to each bond issuance on a scale from 5 stars to 1 star and the agency would also publish those IRGs on its website. Furthermore, Fitch would then provide an annually updated research paper which clearly showed that the IRGs improved over time, meaning that (some) issuers actually took note and were keen on having better IRGs than their competitors. Other issuers, however, were largely unimpressed and did not change their reporting template formats at all. This initiative, however, was a voluntary scheme and there was no obligation to follow or reflect the recommendations of the agency by those issuers which only achieved lower grades.

There have been other similar voluntary schemes by trade associations such as the European Securitisation Forum (ESF) in the past with some issuers signing up to those schemes, but no real governance around actual compliance with these initiatives.

2.8 UNDERWRITING STANDARDS

This is probably one of the areas where lack of standardization (and lack of any reporting of changes to those underwriting standards) has played a considerable role in the credit crunch. How can you increase your lending volumes in a bullish housing market with many first-time buyers and increasing competition of the retail banks fighting over customers? Well, you can reduce interest rates (some of these were deceptively called "teaser rates"), or you could ignore usual prudent requirements such as a 10% deposit, or you can increase your loan-to-value (LTV) ratios from conservative levels to up to 100% (something that has now, post credit crunch, been outlawed in the U.K.) or you can accept weaker types of collateral, or instead of having full financial documentation you could just ask your borrower to self-certify their income (another market practice that is now no longer permitted in the U.K.). You could extend a loan on a 10× income ratio basis rather than the usual 3.5× to 4× multiplier. All of these practices (and many more) were increasingly aggressively applied by banks and financial institutions in the runup to the credit crisis and in the daily fight for customers, revenues, and, ultimately, big juicy bonuses. Nice if you are one of the bankers at the receiving end of the bonus, but terrifying if you are one of those borrowers that have lost the roof over your and your family's heads. Lack of strong regulation and no market-wide minimum underwriting standards led to the numbers of delinquent mortgage loans, ultimately foreclosures, and personal bankruptcies rising to levels previously unheard of.

From an investor's perspective it is also pretty difficult—if not almost impossible—to assess whether the residential mortgage-backed transaction you are investing in will suffer in its performance due to changes in the originating institution's underwriting standards over time. Prior to deal inception you may get such information as part of the roadshow or pitch book and possibly as part of the rating agencies' pre-sale reports. However, once an RMBS deal has been issued to the market you would typically not find this kind of detailed level of information in frequent investor reporting. Again, if the rating agencies are aware of such changes to the originator institution they may refer to these in their ongoing performance updates, but at the time of writing this section (3Q09) there does not appear to be a consensus on how underwriting standards and changes to underwriting standards for originator institutions should be reported.

2.9 DUE DILIGENCE

The previous section leads us to some of the activities investors should undertake prior to purchasing new bond issuance. If you were to purchase a property, you would probably get a surveyor to look at the new house in question to ensure that it is structurally sound with no rising damp, etc. In addition, considering the fact that for most people a house purchase represents a significant investment, you would probably undertake your own research in terms of history of the property, neighborhood crime rates, environmental issues (e.g., what activities are undertaken in the nearby industrial estate, etc.). As it turned out during the credit crisis, it would appear that many investors in structured finance instruments did not undertake sufficient due diligence of the bonds they were investing in. The reason for this is twofold: first, only the most influential investors in the market would typically have been able to request information or receive answers to their individual questions on certain instruments. This is due to the fact that many originating institutions closely guard their proprietary information. For instance, they would not provide loan-by-loan information as they were concerned that this may give detailed insight into the bank's business model and origination practices. To be fair, some jurisdictions do not permit the release of such information and had originators done so, then they may have become legally liable under confidentiality agreements with their borrowers as well as bank secrecy laws. But, I suppose, if originators really wanted to provide this information to their investor pools, there are ways and means to overcome this limitation (e.g., by releasing some of this information anonymously).

Second, investors to a large extent believe that the rating agencies undertake sufficient due diligence activities and then rely on the assigned rating and the due diligence information provided as part of pre-sale rating reports. But, in contrast, rating agencies were always keen to stress that they do not really undertake "due diligence" activities; in fact, at least one of the rating agencies insisted that its analysts and documents would not even refer to due diligence, neither verbally nor in writing—they called it "servicer review" instead. These due diligence activities usually consist of a pre phase whereby the agency sends the originator an asset class–specific questionnaire, giving enough time to prepare and send the answers back to the agency. Subsequently, the lead analyst, a senior rating agency member, and the relevant surveillance or performance analyst will go to visit and further question the client about their response as well as the transaction itself. The asset originator's representatives during such due diligence meetings usually comprise the chief financial officer (CFO), the head of underwriting or origination, the head of risk, and other senior key members of staff. These meetings typically last between 2 and 4 hours and are sometimes complemented by a walkthrough of the origination/underwriting departments, similar business areas, and other facilities that may be of interest to the rating agency.

Given the limited time of this exercise and the ability of the originators to prepare for an agency's visit, it is questionable whether the rating agency analysts participating in these due diligence activities are always able to uncover thorny issues and then dig deeper into them. Furthermore, bear in mind that the originator is actually a paying client of the rating agency since he is the one who has requested the rating and is hence remunerating the agency for its work.

This raises another issue: like it or not, the rating agency's analysis is naturally in one way or another "conflicting" because it's the originator (hence the recipient of the rating) who pays the fees for receiving the rating. In comparison, there is actually not that much difference from a film company that, after producing a new blockbuster, asks a professional film reviewer to write a review for them and then pays the reviewer for receiving the review. It seems logical and realistic that this would naturally lead to a somewhat biased film review.

In all fairness, the rating agencies apply certain safeguards such as adherence to the IOSCO Code of Conduct for Credit Rating Agencies, but nevertheless the underlying issue of such a conflict of interest cannot be removed—unless it were the investors (instead of the issuers) who pay for the rating agency's analysis. This is actually how it used to be until the three big rating agencies' business models changed in the 1970s into today's "issuer pays" business model.

2.10 DEAL MOTIVES

The question as to what is the actual, real motivation behind a securitization transaction is one that has often been overlooked in the endless market discussions that followed the collapse of the structured finance market. Investors should not only ask themselves "what is in it for us?" when investing say £50m or even £100m into a new transaction, they should also ask "what is in it for them?", "them" being the originators of these assets and the issuers of the securities. In undertaking this quest they may discover that there is actually not always a plausible explanation as to why a deal has been structured and why the structured finance notes are issued.

2.11 ARBITRAGE

If that is the case, then I suggest the key drivers may be largely financially motivated, meaning the originator is keen on earning some excess amounts of money on what they would normally get out of the assets in question. In such case, one of the key drivers can be "arbitrage", meaning the originator's aim is to leverage an actual or perceived advantage it may have: this could be regulatory arbitrage (i.e., applying different rules for the purpose of calculating capital charges under the Basel 2 regime), informational arbitrage (i.e., having a deeper insight or more information on the underlying assets than the investors), technological arbitrage (i.e., having sophisticated models that give it a real or perceived analytical edge), or simply financial arbitrage (i.e., receiving a considerably greater cash flow from the underlying assets of what they are passing on to the investors in the structured finance notes issued).

2.12 RATING SHOPPING

Furthermore, if an investor is looking at a transaction that is rated by two credit rating agencies at AAA—say Moody's and Standard & Poor's but not by Fitch's—then investors would typically only look at the rating agency reports from the agencies that have rated the transaction in question. The lack of a Fitch rating would not necessarily indicate that Fitch has not been invited to look at the proposed transaction in order to assign a rating. What it could also mean is that all three agencies were originally instructed to rate this transaction. During or after the rating process, however, it may have transpired to the originator that by using Fitch's rating proposal the transaction may become more expensive due to the agency, for instance, requiring additional credit enhancement in order to support the transaction's capital structure and its final ratings. The originator in turn may feel that having credit ratings from the other two rating agencies at lesser (and cheaper) required credit enhancement may still be sufficient to satisfy investors—and hence may ask Fitch not to rate the transaction. In other words, the originator has selected the two agencies that are able to offer the best rating at the lowest (i.e., cheapest) required credit enhancement. Such behavior, in other words, is also called "rating shopping", as the originator is essentially selecting the rating agencies that are able to offer the cheapest ratings. You may think now that this is totally understandable behavior by both the issuer and the rating agencies, and I would agree—of course, it is. In fact, this happened often in the runup to the credit crisis—unfortunately, there are no statistics available as to how many times a rating agency was formally requested to rate a transaction—and was then asked not to assign it due to too stringent credit enhancement level requirements. The agencies themselves would be best placed to answer this particular question. However, future agency regulation may be able to take this factor into account and require agencies to keep and maintain these statistics. But there's something even simpler investors can do themselves—and I would encourage them to do so. Simply ask the agencies and/or the issuers.

If you are considering a transaction that has been rated by two agencies, then I suggest you ask the agency that appears not to rate this deal whether or not it was originally invited to rate the transaction. If they say that they had an original request but did not assign a rating, then maybe they are able to share with the investor, at least verbally, the reasons for not assigning a rating. I have seen credit departments that based their formal decline of an investment on a certain agency not rating a transaction instead of relying on the ratings from the other two that actually rate the deal.

2.13 OVERRELIANCE ON CREDIT RATINGS

Crucially, this issue brings us onto another topic closely related to the previous one: investors' overreliance on credit ratings.

Prior to the credit crisis, some less sophisticated investors happily used credit ratings and rating agency analysis (in particular, pre-sale, new-issue, and performance reports) in lieu of their own analysis. In doing so they essentially "outsourced" their in-house analysis to the rating agencies and may have in one way or another contributed to the credit crisis. In all fairness, even independent risk teams of more sophisticated investors would have had a fairly hard time to reason against or challenge front-office staff or portfolio managers by arguing that the deals they were purchasing were AAA-rated by three agencies. Based on the AAA rating there would not even have been a shadow of doubt whether or not the assigned ratings would actually be in line with the underlying risks.

However, what followed from mid-2007 to 4Q09 was the largest number of downgrades of AAA-rated securities on a scale that has never been seen before. Figures 2.1 and 2.2 visualize the sheer magnitude of rating changes from 2007 until mid-2010.

Figure 2.1 shows the number of downgrades experienced over each quarterly observation period from 1Q07 to 3Q10 inclusive (the number is given on the *y*-axis). These are tranche (not issue)

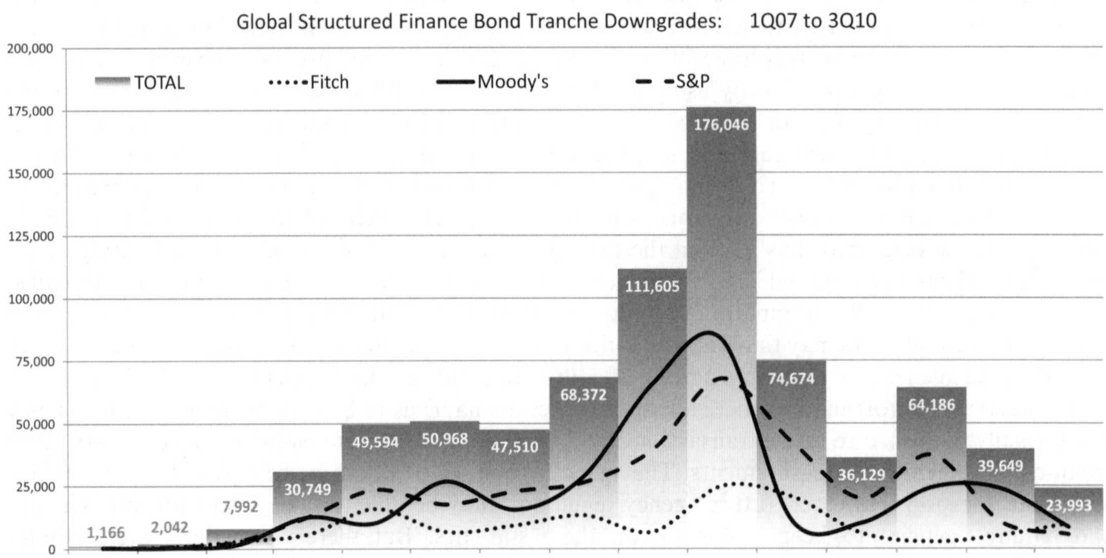

Figure 2.1. Number of downgrades from 1Q07 to 3Q10.
Source: Bloomberg Finance L.P. Copyright © 2011 Markus Krebsz, *www.structuredfinanceguide.com*. All rights reserved.

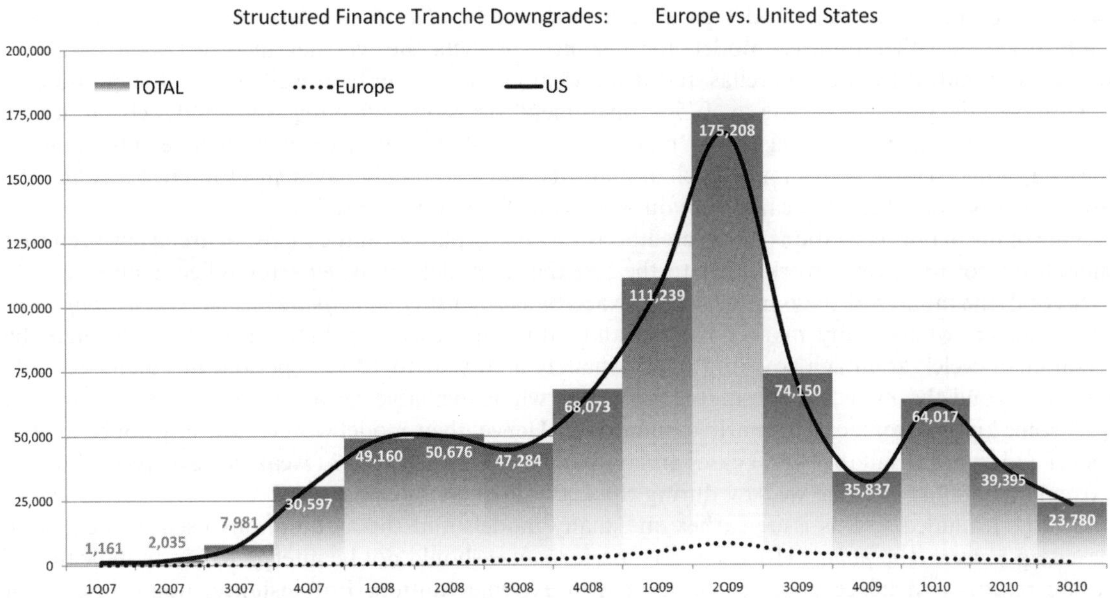

Figure 2.2. Structured finance tranche downgrades.
Source: Bloomberg Finance L.P.

downgrades and—as seen in late 2008 and particularly throughout the first half of 2009—some tranches may have been downgraded several times by the same rating agency.

In other words, if an individual bond tranche was downgraded by Moody's three times, by S&P twice, and by Fitch once, then this contributes six downgrades altogether to the count—although it's just been one bond tranche.

Sophisticated investor or not, if AAA ratings (or more generally investment-grade ratings) have been one of your key investment criteria, you would find that your portfolio's rating quality has significantly deteriorated since the beginning of 2007. However, any rating change on its own would not allow you to sufficiently assess the actual quality of the underlying securitized assets. As a consequence of the credit crisis, investors lost the confidence they previously had in the rating agencies—and rating agencies in turn found themselves exposed to significant pressure by the market at large and politicians and regulators, in particular—ultimately leading to new CRA regulation on both sides of the Atlantic, such as the SEC Rule 240.17g-5 in the U.S. and Regulation (EC) No. 1060/2009 in Europe.

2.14 MODELS, ASSUMPTIONS, AND BLACK BOXES

Many banks and financial institutions as well as credit rating agencies have extensively used financial models in order to undertake financial analysis. The suite of models would range from fairly simple financial models to structured cash flow models as well as more complex ratings models that would run Monte Carlo simulations for various stress scenarios.

Although considered as "sophisticated" tools by many market participants, four key issues with such models transpired fairly quickly during the credit crisis

First, a *"model" is always a model* and hence is naturally constrained by its capability to simulate "reality". As a matter of fact, even the most complex model that could, for instance, deal with several thousand or more different model parameters *will not be able to simulate reality*. Even the most sophisticated weather forecast model, for instance, predicts the weather incorrectly on occasion; but, never mind, there are umbrellas and if the weather gets really bad, well then just stay inside.

However, if you are basing a £75m investment decision—affecting somebody else's money (i.e., depositors' money)—purely on a "model" indicating that your investment will be "OK", meaning you should receive your money back at maturity and also timely payment of interest through the investment period, then all I can wish you is good luck—you may need it.

One of the major realizations of the credit crisis by many players in the financial arena has been that models do not necessarily work—due to the fact that a model can never truly reflect reality.

Second, the failures of these models were exacerbated by using *inadequate or incorrect assumptions*. For instance, whilst many market players and rating agencies may have applied a "through the (economic) cycle" approach covering approximately a 10-year to 12-year period, not many actually looked beyond that time horizon and closer at the whole available set of historical data to come up with some kind of worst case scenario assumptions. Hence, their model would naturally not be able to reflect and cater for suitable worst cases and only cover average periods of weak performance—but not extreme events like the one we saw during the 2007–2010 credit crisis.

Third—I alluded to this issue earlier on—many models and the assumptions used in them were based on *historic data points*. However, past performance should not be interpreted as an indicator of future returns and hence needs to be used with extreme caution. For instance, house prices can unfortunately go down as well as up, but that alone would not necessarily explain why some of those models have failed. You would need to be very careful and considerate in modeling, for instance, different borrower behaviors and also changes to the legislative environment to assess and understand that a homeowner with negative equity in his bank-financed property would in certain instances rather walk away from it than continue with his mortgage payments. We are almost talking about "behavioral modeling" now or at least applying some common sense to identify more uncommon scenarios.

Fourth, many financial models, particularly third-party vendor models—including the ones investors can download from the rating agencies—contain so-called *black boxes*, meaning some or all of the calculations are running in a locked-down back-end of the model whereby the user has only limited access to and no ability to understand the crucial calculations that are running in the background. In these instances, the model user would fill in a given form with various input parameters, and then start the model engine which, for instance, runs a selected number of iterations and maybe applies different stress scenarios only to return an output—usually some kind of report or dataset. Most of these models are not quite like an Excel spreadsheet where you could easily undertake a reconciliation, for instance, by looking at the actual formulae that are calculated. These black-box models are usually locked and not accessible for model users—hence, the calculations are not easily reconcilable. This in turn, however, increases user reliance on the model working as it is supposed to, but of course it can have hidden errors that are difficult to trace.

2.15 PROPRIETARY ANALYSIS

With the overreliance on credit ratings as well as extensive use of models, one balancing factor has often been overlooked: good old-fashioned analysis. In fact, this may be the new kid on the block once the credit crisis is overcome. Some banks, possibly the bigger ones and maybe more "sophisticated" investors have afforded themselves dedicated teams of credit analysts that have been doing as their name would suggest—analysis. In fact, lots of analysis.

Prior to and after the purchase of the bond an analyst would typically go through the relevant documents assessing the risks and rewards of each individual bond as well as of the institution's portfolio. These analysts would look into the relevant asset class, sector research, and available agency analysis, spend sufficient time to understand an individual deal structure as well as the available credit enhancement and other safeguards, and then, based on all these factors, come to an investment decision. Dependent on the size of the institution's bond portfolio, some companies would employ sector specialists who understand the intricate details of different asset classes. Some of these teams would almost be mirroring the structure of a rating agency, where you would find primary analysts responsible for the initial purchase and investment decisions as well as dedicated surveillance analysts who would be able to source relevant deal-specific performance information and, based on this, undertake relevant performance analysis.

Sadly, the majority of firms relied upon analysis either provided by rating agencies or, in addition, buyside and/or sellside research desks from the large investment banks. However, only an in-house analytical team can provide impartial and less biased analysis and, unfortunately, until now only a minority of firms afforded themselves such analytical teams.

2.16 RISK MANAGEMENT AND RISK MITIGANTS

In addition to having such analytical capabilities, many firms seem to have lacked qualified risk management practices which would enable them to challenge investment decisions taken by the front office or portfolio managers. We would expect that a firm's risk appetite and strategy would be able to translate into an internal risk policy as well as investment guidelines. These would then further be broken down into, for instance, asset class–specific, region-specific, or product-specific credit limits in order to support business growth in certain areas but also to limit exposure to certain assets.

In case of any potential investment decisions that would either lead to an actual limit excess or investment proposal outside the firm's credit policy or investment guidelines, robust risk management would need to be empowered to put its foot down and veto such investments if necessary. Alternatively, an active risk management function would be empowered to suggest suitable risk mitigants if necessary: for instance, the purchase of a more senior tranche with better credit enhancement levels, or a bigger potential investor base that would ensure a certain secondary market liquidity (assuming we are functioning in a fully liquid market).

2.17 SENIOR MANAGEMENT AWARENESS

Management reporting—or the lack of it—played to some extent a role in the recent credit crisis. This can be due either to limited systems capabilities which prevent a firm from producing relevant and appropriate reports of its structured finance portfolio, or management information is produced, but through the distribution channels up to senior management may be filtered and watered down. Consequently, when such reports finally reach a firm's board of directors, it is questionable whether this information still paints the full picture.

What's worse though is if senior management receives relevant and timely information and either ignores it or in some case misinterprets it (or simply does not understand the information given).

Example 2.1. To know or not to know?

For instance, a well-known financial institution with a considerable structured finance portfolio produced relevant information and then passed it on to senior management over the past 5 or 6 years at least prior to the credit crisis.

The same management was more than "surprised" to learn at the end of 2007 how large the firm's exposure to this market actually was—£45bn.

Not surprisingly, it eventually went under and was taken over by another financial institution. If you thought that due diligence during the acquisition would have revealed the size, make-up and risks of the structured finance portfolio—then, you are right, it did.

But, once again the senior management of the new firm failed to fully appreciate the implications of this book on its own portfolio and pressed ahead with the acquisition regardless. Ultimately, it was the shareholders as well as the government stakeholders (i.e., the taxpayers) who suffered due to the management of this firm getting it wrong. As far as I am aware, they did have *all* the information needed, but were either not able to understand it or (in their defense) maybe their hands were to some extent politically tied and hence they had to proceed.

There are clearly several factors (including board-level education) required in order to raise senior management awareness of the products and assets classes a company is exposed to, but even if any of those is failing it is not acceptable to excuse ignorance by the board.

2.18 LACK OF DRILLDOWN CAPABILITY AND GROUP-WIDE CONTROLS

Even if senior management is adequately informed of the structured finance portfolio it holds, understands the related risks, and is able to translate this into firm-wide investment strategy and risk policies, the lack of group-wide controls may in practice limit a company's ability to manage its structured finance portfolio risk appropriately. For instance, some sophisticated investors saw the problems in the U.S. subprime market coming, and those that were an active player in this area managed to withdraw from these particular asset classes. However, as a substitute some of these firms chose then to invest in AAA-rated CDOs of ABS instruments, because the spread for these instruments used to be better than for other AAA-rated structured finance bonds.

In doing so, they overlooked one minor issue, which would become a major disaster later on. These CDOs of ABS instruments contained to a large extent U.S. RMBS deals that were repackaged—with the underlying collateral actually being subprime mortgages. So, whilst they had a clear strategy to get out of the subprime market, in practice they still invested in the same asset class via repackaged transactions and, worse, may initially not even have been aware of it.

Another example is firms where the origination desk would carefully select certain assets for disposal (e.g., for pricing, risk, or diversification reasons), package them into structured finance bonds, and sell them to the market. Some of these tranches (the ones that didn't sell that well) would then be taken up by investment banks, repackaged into new structured finance instruments and sold to the market again. The originating bank investing into some of these "new" instruments would have unknowingly purchased some of their own assets which they wanted to dispose of in the first place. Due to the inability to drill down through some bonds into the actual underlying collateral, many firms increased their exposure to asset classes when the original intention was actually to reduce it.

2.19 MARK TO MARKET, MARK TO MODEL, AND PRICING OF ILLIQUID BONDS

In "normal" times where there is a fully liquid primary as well as secondary market it is fairly easy to price a structured finance instrument: you could either use electronic trading systems that match bid-and-offer prices or pick up the phone to brokers to collect some quotes. This changed totally during the credit crisis since secondary markets (largely) froze and for many structured finance bonds prices subsequently became unavailable. In such cases it does not make much sense to price an instrument at mark to market if there isn't any market. You could price "mark to model" but that only works under fairly normal market conditions as these pricing models are usually based on "normal" (i.e., functioning markets), but not for illiquid ones.

Equally, you may find it difficult to identify brokers that are willing to provide quotes if there is no trading activity and whilst such quotes are usually "indicative", you may find that if you wish to execute one of them, then the prices are considerably different from the actual quote.

Even worse, adverse market conditions forced many banks and financial institutions to undertake a "forced sale" which meant that more instruments flooded an already illiquid market, totally distorting the genuine prices that were out there—eventually freezing completely. An illiquid bond that does not sell due to the absence of a secondary market is difficult to price.

2.20 GOVERNMENT SALVAGE SCHEMES: WHAT'S NEXT?

With the liquidity crisis in mid-2007 leading into a full-blown credit crisis in 2008, central banks, financial regulators, and governments in the U.S., Europe, and Australia rallied to put a variety of government facilities in place to save the collapsing global financial markets. As a result, central banks put emergency lending facilities in place in order to keep the real economies afloat. Many of those schemes permitted the posting of suitable collateral, including highly rated structured finance bonds in return for cash or other means of short-term funding. Further schemes were established in and throughout 2009 which enabled some financial institutions to take some of their severely downgraded assets, sell them to special purpose vehicles (SPVs) and then in turn purchase (these better rated) structured finance bonds with the original lower rated collateral as underlying back from the SPV—instruments that are also known as "Re-REMICS" (resecuritization of real estate mortgage investment conduits).

By doing so, lower rated assets which would incur considerably higher capital charges were transferred into higher rated assets thereby reducing the required capital. In addition, whilst the original instrument would not be eligible for repos with the central banks, the higher ratings (mainly in the AAA and AA rating bands) would enable banks to post such Re-REMIC bonds as collateral with the lenders of last resort.

Although there have been benefits in doing this, the central banks unintentionally have become one of the largest "investors" in the structured finance market—which has put them into an awkward position: they do not really want to be seen investing at such large scales into these instruments.

As a consequence, central banks have been actively involved in discussions with market participants in order to understand how they can shift these exposures back to private investors—and, by doing so, breathe some life back into the market.

2.21 RE-REMICS: PRIVATE VS. PUBLIC RATINGS

Up to this point, we have only really considered what was happening during the credit crisis. We have heard about the Re-REMICs which have been issued by banks to themselves for the purpose of capital reduction and in order to post these new bonds as collateral with the central banks. In order to be able to post those bonds as collateral, central banks require certain minimum ratings—usually somewhere in the AA to AAA rating bands. However, the central banks do not require a public rating, whereby the agency's analysis is published in a so-called pre-sale or new-issuance report; in fact, they are quite satisfied with what is known as a "private rating". Such private ratings are typically issued in the form of a private rating letter, which is simply a letter from the rating agency to the originator stating the capital structure of the new Re-REMIC, the ratings for each tranche, and some boiler plate language.

There's usually no word of the analysis undertaken and the outcome of this type of analysis, and why would there be? The originator at the point of issuing the Re-REMIC bonds only really cares about the ratings (which are part of this private rating letter) and happily passes this information on to the central bank which accepts such private ratings as proof that the rating agency has undertaken appropriate analysis to arrive at the appropriate rating for this bond. So far, so good, but this becomes a slightly different scenario at a future point in time when originators may be required to take such repoed bonds back onto their balance sheet and when originators in turn may wish to sell those bonds on to investors.

In light of all current initiatives going on in this market in terms of transparency and provision of sufficient information, investors will likely refuse to purchase such Re-REMICS on the back of the private ratings. In fact, they may require a full-blown rating report to understand the outcome of the agency's analysis and how this has been translated into the relevant ratings—and they may insist on seeing public ratings. I would hope that the agencies have been applying the same rating methodology when they assigned the original private ratings—in fact, that is my understanding from conversations with them—but only time will tell.

2.22 CONCLUSION

So, in a nutshell, these are some of the major shortcomings that led to the collapse of the structured finance market prior to and during the credit crisis. There are certainly many more areas that should be subjected to a thorough review and discussion and they will no doubt be covered in other books and publications.

3

Looking ahead: What has happened since?

3.1 CURRENT INITIATIVES: AN OVERVIEW

Taking all the weaknesses mentioned in Chapters 1 and 2 into account, the European Securitization Forum (AFME/ESF) as well as the Financial Stability Forum, the Bank for International Settlements (BIS), the European Commission (EC), the International Organization of Securities Commission (IOSCO), the Committee of European Banking Supervisors (CEBS), the Committee of European Securities Regulators (CESR), the European Central Bank (ECB), the Bank of England, European Union national regulators, and the U.S. Securities and Exchange Commission (SEC) have been contributing to a global initiative to restore confidence in the securitization markets.

These recommendations are as follows:

1. Increase and enhance initial and ongoing pool information on U.S. non-agency RMBS and European RMBS into a more easily accessible and more standardized format.
2. Establish core industry-wide market standards of due diligence disclosure and quality assurance practices for RMBS.
3. Strengthen and standardize the representations and warranties as repurchase procedures for RMBS.
4. Develop industry-wide standard norms for RMBS servicing duties and evaluating servicer performance.
5. Expand and improve independent third-party sources of valuations and improve the valuation infrastructure and contribution process for specified types of securitization and structured products.
6. Restore market confidence in credit rating agencies by enhancing transparency in the rating process.
7. Establish a global securitization markets group to report publicly on the state of the market and changes in market practice.
8. Establish and enhance educational programs aimed at directors and executives with oversight over securitized and structured credit groups, as well as investors with significant exposures to these products.

For a comprehensive list of legislative and regulatory initiatives see Section 5.1.6.

4

Sound practice principles

This chapter introduces sound practice principles for the structured finance market and subsequently applies those throughout the generic deal lifecycle chapters that will follow.

You may have noticed that I prefer calling these "sound" rather than "best" practice principles—although the book's subtitle calls them "best"—but that refers to marketing. I guess there are different ways of doing things and I would not like to suggest that any of the principles that follow are the best ones around—but they are what I consider to be at least sound.

Furthermore, what's best for one may not be best for another: due to the sometimes polarized nature of the various key players (e.g., originators, investors, trustees, and other counterparties to transactions), we may always need to consider a certain tradeoff and find a balanced but still agreeable approach.

For instance, from an investor's perspective I would always ask for as much information from the originator as possible if I were to invest in a particular transaction. But from the originator's perspective I would be reluctant to release more information to investors than really needed in the originator's view. Such contravening attitudes will always exist in this market and I am not on a quest to overcome those.

What I would hope instead is that the following principles are sufficiently sound to support the rise of a new and improved market, each being equally pragmatic enough so that market participants can actually implement them. And, yes, once you have read them, you may ultimately disagree with my opinion, but at least, I hope, they will give you food for thought. Any feedback on these points is welcome and if you have any questions, comments, thoughts, or other feedback please feel free to contact me via *www.markuskrebsz.info* or the book's companion website *www.structuredfinanceguide.com*.

One final comment before outlining those principles: most of them are written with new issuance in mind, as it will be fairly difficult for market participants to implement some of these for existing legacy transactions. This is for various reasons: one, for instance, being transactional counterparties such as trustees who will have to adhere to legal requirements and hence are not likely to change (or in fact often legally restricted to change) the deal-specific information they are supplying.

Furthermore, most originators (which are typically banks and other financial institutions) have over the past 3 years since the crisis almost completely immersed themselves in their own problems. In addition, many of these firms were forced to considerably reduce the staff as well as proprietary expertise working in these business units—hence they were, and some still are, overworked and understaffed. Consequently, they are not best equipped to fix the issues with all of the legacy bonds that are still outstanding.

However, I would hope that these principles can and will be applied to new issuance—some of them will have to be applied in one way or another simply because they form part of regulatory requirements. Others may be voluntary to some extent, but as long as there is mutual benefit to originators as well as investors, I would think that common sense would prevail—something that seems to have disappeared in the runup and during the credit crisis—and that originators as well as investors will not deliberately cut corners to save a few thousand pounds from their own pocket here and there and for the short term—only having to rely on the taxpayer in the long run. This is a sure way to bring the whole market into disrepute and I would hope that after the rise of the "new" market a similar global catastrophe can be avoided.

4.1 DATA

Data are what transactions ultimately come down to, not only in structured finance but even more so for most financial market products. Data equate to knowledge and if you have data then you are at least enabled to analyze the deal they relate to.

Without the relevant data, you will not know very much about the particular transaction. And data are to some extent what has been missing in the runup to the credit crisis—at least, sufficiently granular data.

Surely, deal information was generally available—but it was either not easily accessible (e.g., residing on password-protected websites), delivered in an outdated way (e.g., by post or fax) in a non-digestible format (e.g., paper or image files), in a difficult-to-transpose file format (e.g., PDF or TIFF), on a deal-by-deal basis only (e.g., you would only receive information for the deal you hold, and not for all deals issued by the same originator), and finally with market data difficult to get hold of.

The following rules will hence all be based on the shortcomings observed—with the hope that this will help investors to get sufficient data to support their own analysis and in doing so, helping to kick-start the market again, enabling further bond issuance.

4.1.1 Access: Open source

Principle 4.1. Open source data access

All deal data should be freely and openly available to everyone interested in either a specific transaction they invest in or similar transactions by the same issuer.

As simple as this principle may sound, in the past this was not always the case. Access to deal information has been limited to, for instance, investors that are actually participating in a particular transaction. One of the ways this was controlled and monitored was by giving investors access to password-restricted websites. As a result, potential investors, particularly secondary-market investors, would not have been able to access the necessary information, unless of course they could actually purchase the bond in question.

Equally, investors may have been provided with deal-specific information that refers to the particular bond issuance they are investing in; however, they may have been refused information to other similar transaction information by the same issuer. This, however, would prevent these investors from undertaking their own peer-to-peer analysis of their particular transaction compared with the other ones in the same series.

In order to support a transparent market, everyone—no matter whether primary-market or secondary-market investors or any other interested party—will need to be able to access the same information, hence this first principle.

4.1.2 Information asymmetries

Principle 4.2. Removal of unnecessary information asymmetries

If there is no substantial reason (i.e., show-stoppers for certain deals due to banking secrecy laws) then informational asymmetries need to be eliminated.

There used to be an imbalance in terms between who would be provided with what level of information as part of a transaction. Whilst originators were happily providing rating agencies with loan-level information (in return for getting the deal rated), investors would—in the majority of cases—only be provided with loan stratifications and other accumulated information.

Clearly, there may be individual circumstances where it is only possible to provide data on a cumulative basis: namely, legal requirements or certain jurisdictions (e.g., Germany) in which it is not permitted to pass on loan-level data to investors in order to comply with bank secrecy and data protection rules.

However, in these cases, there may be ways and means of overcoming these legislative limitations; for instance, by removing borrower names and addresses and replacing them with unique loan identifiers and simply providing the postcode instead of the borrower's full address.

Similarly to Principle 4.1, it is important to allow the market at large (i.e., primary as well as secondary investors and any interested party) to access the same information at the same time—in doing so information asymmetries and resulting unnecessary disadvantages caused by them will be removed and the market will become more of a level playing field for all the participants—no matter how big or small (or how influential) they are.

4.1.3 Data formats

Principle 4.3. Provide electronic reports in usable data file formats

Deal-specific data need to be supplied electronically (i.e., not printed papers or by fax) and the electronic file format (e.g., Excel or XML) will enable easy and efficient processing of this information laying the foundation for further thorough and timely analysis.

The rationale for this principle is that whilst most investors have different processes and procedures, most of them will want (and in fact are going to be required by some of the new regulations) to undertake their own analysis.

This could mean automatically loading the data that they receive from originators/servicers/trustees into their proprietary systems for automated processing. Or, alternatively, smaller firms in particular may just want to transfer the data they receive into an Excel spreadsheet to undertake a few specific calculations as part of their analytical framework.

If the information is already available in Excel or, alternatively, easy to migrate into the desired format, then analysts are able to do their work efficiently and are also able to produce timely analysis.

If, on the other hand, the data received need to be—in some cases—manually transposed from one format (i.e., paper or printout of a TIFF or PDF file) into another, then analysts are more likely to spend time on migrating or copy and pasting data than actually interpreting the data.

The same principle applies, by the way, not only to buyside investors, but also for rating agencies' surveillance and performance analytics teams. Even in late 2006, rating agencies would still receive transaction reports in paper and other not easily digestible formats making surveillance analysts' professional lives somewhat more difficult than necessary and in some cases also unwittingly delaying the agencies' regular deal performance updates. This may also have been a contributing factor to delayed rating decisions, and overcoming this barrier could bring about an increase in timelier rating actions—something the rating agencies have been criticized of for some time.

4.1.4 Data delivery

Principle 4.4. Automated, timely data dissemination and alerts

Once data/deal information is available then ideally market participants should receive this information in a timely fashion or, alternatively, should be aware of where they can get the relevant information.

Granted, this principle readily assumes that deal-specific information will be supplied in an electronic format rather than by paper or post. But it goes further: it suggests that originators/servicers/trustees actively inform investors that new information has become available rather than having investors looking for it. In doing so, the market at large is informed at the same time that new deal-specific performance information has become available.

In coming up with this principle, I fully acknowledge that this may currently have some technical restrictions, but there are several pragmatic ways and means that market participants can achieve this. The market at large could club together and establish (and also fund) a data portal that provides this information and would give investors the opportunity to sign themselves up to receive frequent updates for the deals relevant to them. Or, alternatively, third-party vendors such as ABSnet, Bloomberg, Intex, and others could amend their current system functionalities. Bloomberg, for instance, currently permits investors to conveniently upload a list of bond identifiers for all their holdings (a so-called "portfolio") and then distributes real-time updates (in the form of email alerts, messages, pop-up windows on the Bloomberg Professional terminal, etc.) when new investor reports or trustee notices for such transactions become available.

Equally, investors can subscribe to the various email alert functions of rating agencies but this still requires considerable manual intervention and fine-tuning in order to maintain these alerts, particularly when you are looking after larger portfolios (500+ bonds).

4.1.5 On deal level

Principle 4.5. Where possible, deal information needs to be at a loan-by-loan level

Unless there are certain legal restrictions or requirements by data protection and bank secrecy rules, the market should be supplied with loan-level data reporting.

Many market participants see this as a crucial requirement in order to get both primary issuance and secondary-market activities post credit crunch back to trading. It's also probably the principle where issuers and investors tend to disagree most. It is not always clear why issuers are so reluctant to produce this information and to supply it on an ongoing basis—they are doing this already in order to provide it to the rating agencies. They in turn use the information to in essence rerun their models based on such changed portfolio information. Until recently, however, investors could consider themselves privileged if they were given this information without considerable effort and individual negotiations with the issuers. Of course, there's always been the bargaining where (usually one of the larger) investors could make their investment in a transaction subject to the provision of loan-by-loan information. However, even with the provision of this detailed information, some of these investors became unstuck during the credit crisis as they were not able to pass on this information (which was usually kept under close guard and strict non-disclosure agreements) to potential buyers of such tranches (which ties in with Principle 4.2).

As mentioned earlier, the information is already there, readily available as issuers are frequently providing the rating agencies with (anonymous) loan-level reports hence the additional cost in distributing this already existing information should be negligible.

Of course, if this information is supplied to the market at large, it will be up to individual investing firms to decide whether or not this is a suitable piece of additional information or if they are satisfied with portfolio-level cohort information. The key here is market enablement: without it nobody will be able to undertake such analysis but with it at least there is a real opportunity for interested and capable investors to sift further through this information and come to their own conclusions.

Ideally, this information would need to be available from a centralized portal. Bloomberg, a private and subscriber-only data provider, already provides for most of the U.S. transactions and for the majority of European transaction loan-level information. Bloomberg has built some great analysis features around what's there already (more on these features in Part III: Toolbox and Chapter 22).

4.1.6 For the market at large

Principle 4.6. Market data need to be freely and openly available to support benchmark analysis

Again, the data should be available to primary-market as well as secondary-market participants in order to be useful in supporting peer-to-peer analysis between existing transactions as well as new issuance. The level of information that is suggested would in particular look at

- *Spread data* for ABS, CMBS, RMBS for both Europe and the U.S. for different rating buckets (e.g., AAA, BBB, subinvestment grade) and different maturity bands (e.g., 1–3, 3–5, 5–10 and 10+ years).
- *Prices* for ABS, CMBS, RMBS for both Europe and the U.S. for different rating buckets (e.g., AAA, BBB, subinvestment grade) and different maturity bands (e.g., 1–3, 3–5, 5–10 and 10+ years).
- *Total return benchmark* data for ABS, CMBS, and RMBS for both Europe and the U.S.
- *Index data* such as securitized index option-adjusted spreads, pan-European fixed and floating rate index prices, ABX HE and CMBS prices, and PrimeX.ARM and PrimeX.FRM prices.

One source of this information is the AFME/ESF's *Securitisation Monthly Data Supplement*, which you can find on AFME's website *www.afme.eu* and then in the section "Positions and publications/reports". This is further complemented by AFME/ESF's quarterly market reports.

Until recently, it has been fairly difficult to get benchmark information for transaction and whole asset class sectors. Of course, sellside analysis has been around for years, but was only available to selected investors (usually larger ones with the relevant capital backing them—making them more influential).

For the past 5 years, rating agencies have been aiming to provide peer-to-peer analysis (but not necessarily sufficient underlying data) to investors; however, most of this information requires subscriber access and hence is only available to investors who are willing to pay considerable annual subscription fees.

More recently, with all three agencies' reputations suffering, many investors chose to some extent to ignore their analysis—which is a shame because the quality and volume of freely available information from the agencies has actually improved since the onset of the credit crunch.

Bloomberg has done a brilliant job over the past couple of years as they realized that the structured finance market was almost completely turned upside down: as it evolved into a much more "investor"-centric market, Bloomberg foresaw investors' needs for portfolio management and benchmarking tools that can support investors' surveillance and performance analytics activities.

Furthermore, Bloomberg has also been heavily investing in building customized applications and tools that can lift information automatically from investor reports and make it available via the Bloomberg terminal—also permitting exporting deal-specific as well portfolio-specific information straight into Excel. In addition, this permits Bloomberg users to build customized Excel spreadsheets sourcing selected deal information dynamically into them or even using the Bloomberg desktop or server API directly in other database applications (e.g., access databases).

Finally, Bloomberg offers since March 2010 *click-through transparency* which enables users to click on a selected key performance indicator on the Bloomberg terminal and the relevant investor report containing the source data will open up automatically, with the relevant performance parameter or value already selected and highlighted in the report. This feature is not only available for U.S. and European RMBS transactions, but also for auto loans and credit card receivables transactions and includes 5 years of historical data in the collateral performance (CLP) function for auto loans as well as links to the prospectus of any new credit card receivables trust.

These are all exciting new developments which have brought a level of investor transparency (at least if you have access to a Bloomberg terminal)—something we would have been dreaming of only a few years ago.

4.1.7 Industry data portals

Principle 4.7. Provide information via freely accessible and open industry data portals

Whilst the initial establishment of such a portal can be costly, the ongoing maintenance expenses should be manageable and one solution may be that the costs for such a service are pooled and covered by the issuers. Such portal(s) would benefit not only issuers, but also investors, the market at large, and indirectly the global economy.

In line with Principle 4.1, ideally it is important to have a known access point or, if it is for whatever reason not possible to have such a point, several industry portals where market participants can source the relevant deal information in order to support an informed analysis and decision-making process.

Several ideas in this direction were developed in close coordination with market participants during the credit crisis and, as a result, the following industry portals have been established.

Global ABS Portal

Global ABS Portal's aim is to promote transparency in the structured finance market and can be accessed at no cost by visiting *www.globalabsportal.com* and requesting free user credentials and a password (you will be asked to accept a "licensing agreement" but use of the portal is free).

This portal enables you to access only the most recent investor reports and original offering circulars (OCs) for public European securitization transactions. Global ABS Portal's aim is to provide a free centralized access point for public deal information enabling easy access for investors and regulators alike.

Prior to the establishment of this portal the allocation of deal-specific information was only available via commercial vendors; hence, this is a great step towards more transparency and simpler access to deal-related information.

The original OCs and the remittance reports via Global ABS Portal and the information on the portal are updated in real time (i.e., as soon as new reports become available). If you require more detailed information (e.g., access to the whole history behind these reports) then you may need to consider commercial services such as Lewtan Technologies' ABSnet (who is the private vendor behind this portal) or other third-party vendors such as Bloomberg and Intex.

This particular initiative helps to bridge the gap between Europe and the U.S., which uses the SEC's EDGAR database to provide similar information on U.S. transactions paired with increased disclosure requirements under RegAB.

From EDGAR to IDEA

The SEC has recently been modernizing its system for public disclosure. The agency's current EDGAR database—which stands for electronic data-gathering, analysis, and retrieval system—will be succeeded by a newer system—IDEA—giving investors faster and easier access to financial filings on public companies and mutual funds.

IDEA, which stands for interactive data electronic applications, is based on new database architecture and built from scratch by the SEC.

The changes enable a transition from collecting forms and documents to making the information freely available to investors. The new system will also provide current information in a format that is easy to access, collate, sift through, and compile into new reports.

Most SEC filings have used the previous EDGAR format, which has limited use by investors and others who want to examine information about public companies to viewing one form at a time.

From 2011 onwards, the SEC wants U.S. companies to provide financial information through interactive data as well as mutual fund information filed through interactive data, which uses tags to identify contents in companies' disclosures making internet searches about publicly held companies and mutual funds simpler and more comprehensive. It also allows information to be more easily downloaded into Excel spreadsheets and to feed this into external databases enabling peer-to-peer comparisons.

Despite this, and throughout the transition, companies can continue using EDGAR and filings will remain available as archives of past years.

Users can search information collected by the SEC in several ways:

- Company or fund name, ticker symbol, CIK (central index key), file number, state, country, or SIC (standard industrial classification)
- Most recent filings
- Full text (past 4 years)
- Boolean and advanced searching, including addresses
- Key mutual fund disclosures
- Mutual fund voting records
- Mutual fund name, ticker, or SEC key (since February 2006)
- Variable insurance products (since February 2006).

Custom searches:

- Confidential treatment orders
- Effectiveness notices
- SEC central index key (CIK)
- Daily filings.

You can find more information about EDGAR as well as its successor IDEA at the SEC's website: *http://www.sec.gov/edgar.shtml*

Irish Stock Exchange

Irish Stock Exchange transparency initiative

Some of the stock exchanges that—due to taxation laws, jurisdiction, and regulation—are more involved in the structured finance market than others have realized that they can play a vital part in increasing transparency and providing all of the transaction documentation of deals that are listed by them on the exchange's website. This is with a view to overcoming the previous lack of a centralized information repository that can be used by issuers and investors alike and hence can help in decreasing the perceived opaqueness of the structured finance market going forward.

An example of such an exchange-driven project is the development of a transaction data portal by the Irish Stock Exchange which you can visit at *http://www.ise.ie/app/specSecList.asp*.

The portal is in essence an enhancement to the exchange's website providing more information on issued securities as well as deal-related information. This offering is available to all issuers whose securities are listed on the Irish Stock Exchange enabling them to publish electronic versions of investor reports, transaction documents, and other related financial information on the site. Typical information that can be found encompasses trust deeds, agency agreements, subscription agreements, servicing agreements, sale agreements, security agreements, investment or collateral agreements, swap documentation, post-issuance reports, collateral reports, and so forth. "Financials" can include annual financial statements, half-yearly financial statements, quarterly financial statements, and so on.

The use of this functionality by originators and issuers, however, incurs a cost and there is no listing requirement that would make it obligatory to provide this information. Consequently, some originators may wish to use this facility whilst others may decide not to participate.

4.2 DEFINITIONS

Whilst Principles 4.1–4.6 were mainly focused on data and the methods of providing this information, the following principles will suggest improvements for the overall market framework and how some of the current complexities can be removed to make this a generally simpler and transparent market that is easier to understand and analyze.

4.2.1 Simplifications

Principle 4.8. Securitization and structured finance is complex enough and often unnecessary; let's help make it simpler

There is really no need for adding further layers of complexity and artificially making this market more opaque. Instead, market participants have to aim at finding common ground and developing simplified definitions that will increase true understanding of the underlying instruments.

Structural simplicity should also be the guiding principle for new transactions and will also help to increase overall transparency (see Principle 4.9).

Market participants, particularly investors since January 1, 2011 (for deals issued on or after this date) are required to undertake their own due diligence and reduce their reliance on, for instance, credit ratings in their investment decisions.

If issuers want to support investors' analytical efforts and ultimately place their issuance in the market, they need to strive to remove any unnecessary opaqueness and complexity and facilitate investor analysis and due diligence. Structured finance instruments are not (any more) the place to hide underlying collateral or loans in a way that does not lend itself to simple and straightforward analysis. Previous deal features such as black boxes of bundled loans for which only certain aggregated parameters, such as weighted average rating or sector and industrial distribution come to mind, will not sit comfortably in a new transparent market.

Similarly, structural features—for instance, contractual subordination of senior tranches to mezzanine and junior tranches that would only become apparent after instructing a lawyer to wade through 200 pages of legal documentation—will not fit very comfortably into a post-credit crisis world. In fact, I would hope and expect the rating agencies to pick up such issues and—whilst they may not be sufficiently severe to prevent AAA ratings for senior tranches—I certainly hope to see warning messages referring to such deal features in rating agencies' analytical narratives. If so, then this is clearly one of the areas where investors can derive real value from the agencies' analyses—not from the rating designators themselves.

4.2.2 Transparency

Principle 4.9. Increased transparency is one of the key factors that can help in overcoming the shortcomings that led to the credit crisis

Transparency can have many angles: data, performance, counterparty information, etc. and forms the basis for proprietary and independent analysis by investors. The more transparent a market is the less will you see arbitrage due to informational asymmetries.

Transparency (and translucency) in the real world is the physical property of allowing the transmission of light through material. In simple terms you would consider this as "see through". If you translate this to the structured finance and securitization market, then a transparent market is one in which every participant generally knows

- What products are available?
- At which price?
- And where?

Transparency and the availability of key information that follows from it are key to enabling *informed* decision making—such as whether to buy or sell a particular bond now.

On the other hand, without the available information, investors will have to make assumptions on missing pieces of information. The more information that is missing, the more assumptions that are needed. However, it is not the best basis on which to make informed investment decisions, for example, when you do not know the credit quality of the underlying collateral. In fact, all it can then be is a best guess which sometimes may turn into a gamble.

In conclusion, transparency is vital for robust functioning where decisions are based on hard facts (i.e., available information) rather than soft views or "opinions".

4.2.3 Standardization

> **Principle 4.10.** New standards that can ideally be applied across borders and for all players in the market need to be used wherever feasible
>
> Standardization helps the "new" market and future issuance to gain momentum and is a simple objective all market players should strive for.

From an originator's perspective, increasing the level of standardization can make future issuance considerably cheaper due to repeat application of templates and less tweaking and customization of the required infrastructure.

Investors would also greatly benefit from standardization as this will enable comparative, peer-to-peer, and benchmark analysis, which otherwise is not easily achievable and sometimes not possible at all. There are many ways of increasing standardization.

Standardization of asset classes

Asset classification for structured finance bond instruments can be tricky but can also have far-reaching consequences. For instance, whether a transaction is classified as a whole business securitization (WBS) or a commercial mortgage-backed securitization deal (CMBS) will dictate which rating methodology is used by the agency in order to assign the ratings. Not only that, but there may even be different analytical teams for such a deal subject to which asset class it is thought to belong. More perversely, you could have one agency rating a transaction applying to its WBS criteria whilst another may treat the transaction as a CMBS deal and hence use CMBS rating models, arriving at considerably different ratings. What a fine mess ...

The following principles will suggest further ways for more market standardization.

4.3 STANDARDS

4.3.1 Underwriting standards

> **Principle 4.11.** Underwriting standards are a major driver of underlying asset performance and need to be fully disclosed throughout the life of a deal and in particular when they have been changed
>
> Originators should provide complete deal transparency on the underwriting standards they use and indicate any changes to underwriting standards throughout the life of outstanding transactions.

Underwriting standards are representative of the originator's operational framework within which the securitized assets (e.g., personal loans, mortgages, etc.) have been originated. In a way, they are the "oil" for the "engine" of structured finance bonds. Although these standards will be internally translated into the originator's operational model and translate into more detailed rules and procedures, externally they can help investors to understand *how* these assets have been originated and if and how prudent the originator acts throughout the underwriting process.

Whilst it is quite usual to present underwriting standards during deal roadshows and in the pitch book prior to the transaction's close, it is currently not common market practice to inform investors either within servicer reports or, ideally in an issuer's stock exchange notice, of changes to the underwriting standards throughout the transaction's life. However, depending on the deal's structural features (i.e., revolving or static pool, etc.) changes to these standards can have a crucial impact (positive as well as negative) on the performance of the underlying pool itself or on the payment streams that come from the underlying assets. Either way, though, investors ought to recognize these changes if and when they happen and not after the transaction's cash flows have been impacted; hence, it would be sensible (and desirable from an investor's perspective) to provide a "change log" of underwriting standards to investors, assuming the originator maintains this information and can retrieve it.

If this information is stored, then the issuer may wish to consider including the following information in its investor reporting:

- The current, underwriting standards, loan documentation, and terms and conditions (T&Cs) used
- Previous underwriting standards, loan documentation, and T&Cs used and during which period
- Percentage breakdown of the securitized loan portfolio by underwriting standards used to originate these loans.

4.3.2 Reporting standards

Principle 4.12. Standardize the investor reporting of transactions as much as possible

Investor reports need to be standardized as much as feasible in order to enable investors to undertake their own analysis. Standardization of investor reports across asset classes and regions will to some extent remove the complexity of such analysis and in turn help to increase transparency.

Historically (i.e., prior to the credit crunch), investors tended to use several tools in order to undertake comparative or peer analysis for their bonds:

- *Credit ratings*. Bonds would be benchmarked against a rating category level whereby some investors only worried whether or not Bond 1 had AAA ratings and how this would compare with Bond 2 that was also rated AAA. By doing so, investors overlooked the fact that the AAA rating is in essence a rating cap which consequently can lead to inconsistencies in the AAA rating sphere. If the cap did not exist, some of those bonds' ratings may actually be relatively weaker than others despite all of them carrying AAA ratings. The AAAs at the top of a capital structure and sitting in the waterfall above other structurally subordinated AAAs are also commonly known as "super senior" tranches.

  However, after the credit crisis, the whole rating spectrum for structured finance bonds has been heavily scrutinized by the agencies and almost every SF rating that was ever assigned to a structured bond was subject to analysis and, subsequently, a very large proportion of bonds were downgraded. Which makes me wonder whether the way ratings that were incorrectly used and interpreted could actually apply nowadays? I am not sure and I would certainly not recommend or encourage the use of ratings in such a way.

- *Pricing*. Another bond parameter that used to be deployed in order to benchmark bonds against each other was pricing information. In fact, it was pricing information paired with the available ratings whereby people tried comparing a AAA-rated U.K. non-conforming bond with the pricing of a similarly rated bond instrument in the same asset class to figure out which one would be the "better" investment. Whilst the wider price for one of them would indicate that there is intrinsically more risk involved, hence the bond with the "better" pricing has got a "weaker" AAA rating, investors would probably still go for the bond with the higher "return" profile since the AAA rating gave them a certain kind of security. With trading activities almost completely ceasing during the credit crisis, price information disappeared—there were no prices for most instruments—and hence there was no sure way of benchmarking such bonds.

You may now wonder how these issues relate to reporting standards. Well, think about the following. With the lack of any other tools such as rating and pricing information, is there any other way in which investors can benchmark transactions, can undertake peer analysis and filter out the wheat from the chaff? Yes, possibly, but this will require investors doing their homework and executing their own analysis. But, what can support this kind of work?

Good solid, standardized investor reports with a market-wide agreed format that allows direct side-by-side comparison of transaction performances.

Market participants have been working hard and long over the past 3 years to develop standardized templates for generic asset classes that can be adjusted to reflect differing regional requirements. This involves an ongoing dialogue between the key recipients and users (investors) of these reports and the providers (originators and issuers) co-ordinated by a trade body such as the European Securitization Forum (now part of AFME).

Granted, it is difficult to change the reporting format for existing legacy structured finance transactions—but actually not totally impossible. The focus, however, should be on new transactions entering the market and I would hope that issuers wherever available use industry-wide standardized investor-reporting templates. If they warm themselves to this idea and investors utilize this information in order to benchmark the transactions they are looking at buying based on the information that will be available to them—including loan-level data—then we will encounter a much more transparent market.

4.3.3 Representations and warranties

Principle 4.13. Representations and warranties (R&Ws) should conform to a market standard with deviations clearly identified

With transparency in mind, there should be a defined set of R&Ws signed up to by as many issuers as possible. Investors in turn will need to know which R&W features are captured by such standards. As a result, issuers and investors will develop a common understanding of and basis for R&Ws, which can help restore confidence in the market.

Deviations from the R&W standard are of course possible and in fact sometimes necessary due to certain features of underlying assets, and standard R&Ws are not meant to limit or prohibit the securitization of assets that do not conform with those standards. *But*, it is crucial that deviations of individual transactions from the standard are clearly earmarked.

Representations and warranties should conform to a market standard adhered to by originators. Any deviations from such a standard R&W agreement should be clearly earmarked to the investors and the reasons for such deviations should be explained in the deal documentation.

It is then up to the investors whether such deviations are acceptable or not and, if so, to understand whether they have been appropriately reflected in the transaction's pricing.

In fact, this is another documentation feature that helps to facilitate investor due diligence and allows them to undertake more efficient analysis. Furthermore, it supports side-by-side comparison of different transactions' OCs—something that is otherwise not always that easy.

4.4 INVESTOR FOCUSED

4.4.1 Government facilities

Principle 4.14. Government facilities/salvage schemes are meant to tie over the market through the credit crisis in the short to medium term

Long term it is important for the market to come back eventually and rebuild trust into its private counterparts.

Government salvage schemes have been vital in dampening the effects of the global financial crisis; however, they cannot and will not be able to keep the market on life support over the longer term. Central banks have become the biggest "investors" in structured finance instruments, but longer term this will not be sustainable.

Hence, it is important that all private players eventually get back onto the pitch and start trusting each other again. As the 2010 sovereign crisis showed, even the financial capabilities of governments, central banks, and sovereigns are somewhat restricted and cannot be used indefinitely.

4.4.2 Private investors

Principle 4.15. Originators are well advised to keep private investors in mind when issuing new bonds (such as Re-REMICS) even if these instruments will be used in the short term to access government salvage schemes and central banks' repo facilities

By structuring with long-term focus on the private market they may become more expensive to execute but will not require further restructuring (i.e., become more sustainable).

In the short term such an approach may be slightly costlier inasmuch as this would require adhering to the new investor-reporting templates as well as considerably more detailed transaction reporting. Granted, such deals may take a little longer to structure. Assuming that governments as well as central banks will eventually terminate the existing emergency schemes with the hope and intention to move the market back to private investors, it should be much easier and more efficient to move such properly structured and documented deals back to private investors without further restructuring.

In fact, the changed investor requirements for increased due diligence may render it otherwise impossible to transfer such deals back to the private market if the overall documentation is insufficient.

4.4.3 Incentive alignments

> **Principle 4.16.** Incentives between originators and investors need to be better aligned
>
> This aims at removing imbalances which may mean that investors are overexposed to potential losses throughout a transaction's life whilst the originator is profiting at the outset of a transaction and then has no real economic benefit to ensure that the deal performs well.

Originators and underwriters have mostly been compensated in the structured finance market at the inception of a transaction following the initial purchase of the assets by the SPV and ultimately the investors. However, following this initial sale the ultimate benefits (and sometimes burden) of such an asset sale lie with the investors only. Subsequently, regulators around the globe have demanded a better alignment of incentives including the requirement that originators maintain some "skin in the game"—in other words, retain an economic interest in their transactions (see Section 4.5.1).

Furthermore, and particularly from an investor's perspective, it is important to understand the motivation for the originator(s) to securitize as well as the underlying deal drivers (see the following section).

4.5 MOTIVATION AND DEAL DRIVERS

4.5.1 Arbitrage

> **Principle 4.17.** Issuers need to avoid what may be conceived by investors as malicious (albeit lawful) arbitrage and investors must understand the benefits and drawbacks of arbitrage mechanisms
>
> Of course, when you enter a securitization deal, or indeed any other commercial transaction, there will always be a commercial element focused on making profit—because that is what banks and all businesses do. However, if arbitrage becomes the main deal driver, then you may question whether this is something you want to participate in—either as issuer or investor.

Arbitrage (i.e., active deployment and use of differences in the level of available information, different regulatory treatment, adding additional layers of complexity for complexity's sake, rating arbitrage, etc.) should be avoided by originators *if it may be conceived by investors as malicious practice.*

Investors, as part of their due diligence activities and investment analysis, should ask themselves *What's in it for my firm/me?* and *What's in it for their firm/them?* and see whether they can identify disadvantageous arbitrage mechanisms that may suggest the need to delve deeper into the rationale of a transaction prior to any investment decision.

If so, they may wish to raise their concerns with the originator prior to investing in such a transaction and only proceed once they have received satisfactory responses or clearances—otherwise they may be better off staying away from such an investment.

Whilst the majority of deals issued in the market are driven by genuine reasons, there have also been some cases where assets are securitized for no apparent reason or reasons given that do not seem plausible. Take the whole exotic assets. By the way, if you remove the "e" of "exotic" and then swap the "t" and "x", you will get "toxic"!—funny coincidence how closely related these two words are—as may also be the asset types described by them: such as CDO of ABS, CDO of CDOs (CDO^2 also known as "CDO squared"), CDO of CDOs of CDOs (CDO^3 also known as "CDO cubed"). Try to understand why those deals were structured and see whether you can find any *real justification* behind them? Can you see any? I can't.

Granted, these structures permitted the pooling of (in some instances already pooled) structured finance bonds, inclusion of other finance instruments, increasing the complexity, and—by discouraging/preventing drill-down into the underlying assets (not the underlying SF bonds)—increasing leverage to these investments. Smack on top a couple of AAA ratings and everybody is happy—until these monstrous structures default. But the real drivers for executing these highly complex and opaque transactions in the first place

- From an originator's perspective, they were earning more money.
- From the perspective of counterparties involved in structuring such vehicles (such as law firms, rating agencies, trustees, collateral managers), they were earning more money.
- From an investor's perspective, I am actually not so sure: maybe the ultimate desire was to be seen by the market as "hip" or part of the "in crowd", being a "sophisticated" investor because you are investing in "sophisticated" instruments, or "diversifying" your portfolio (by adding risk that no one really understands) or getting "access to a new fancy structure" but overlooking the fact that there was a greater chance of not getting your money back.

Beware of unexplainable "arbitrage" in any shape or form (i.e., without any obvious purpose). Arbitrage can come in many forms or shapes, it is for you to figure out whether there is real justification behind it or if it looks plain "dodgy":

- *Informational arbitrage*. This is where the originator has considerably more information on the actual performance on the underlying assets (as they originated and are holding them and have the relevant information at hand), but is not willing to give away too much of this information. For instance, if you participate in a collateralized loan obligation (CLO) transaction containing say 150 corporate loans ranging from £1m to £50m each, then I guess it would be nice to know quite a few details including the names (if permissible under bank secrecy and data protection laws, etc.) of those borrowers as well as corporate rating (if any), sector or industry, country, etc. However, if you are only given high-level cohort data with limited information then I guess you may consider this as a form of informational arbitrage.
- *Regulatory arbitrage*. This happens when two counterparties (i.e., the seller and buyer, or issuer and investor) are subject to two different regulatory regimes (e.g., the standardized approach and internal ratings–based approach under Basel 2) and hence may profit from either clever structuring activities or, alternatively, transfers of differently rated risks from one to another. Equally, issuers are likely to choose cost-efficient jurisdictions where it can be easier and quicker to set up special purpose vehicles—and in many instances this will also include local tax regimes that encourage the establishment of such vehicles in these countries.
- *Rating arbitrage*. See Section 4.5.2 for "rating shopping" which in essence can also be another form of arbitrage.

4.5.2 Rating shopping

Principle 4.18. Active "rating shopping" by issuers is legitimate but represents another form of arbitrage and should be avoided

Investors should tread carefully if they suspect "rating shopping" and factor this into their own analysis.

Whilst rating shopping is not unlawful, it is questionable whether it is ethical and morally right—hence issuers are well advised to avoid it. Similar to other forms of arbitrage, investors who detect rating shopping are well advised to stay clear from the respective transaction and may raise their concern with the originator. If they decide to still go ahead with their investment, they should factor the presence of rating shopping and the impact this may have on the investment into their analysis.

From an originator's perspective, rating shopping may be attractive as it can enable the reduction of funding costs by squeezing the level of credit enhancement required by the rating agencies for a given rating level. However, from an investor's perspective, this is not wanted behavior since it can also erode credit enhancement at the outset which would have otherwise been factored into the final ratings of the respective transaction.

Similarly to other forms of arbitrage, it is of course up to the investors whether or not they wish to financially support watered-down credit enhancement provisions and to analyze whether or not the benefit of such a consequently cheaper transaction will be passed on to the investor by the originator—which I personally doubt.

Since this is not always a visible activity, it may be worth the rating agencies considering whether they would like to publish if they have been asked to assign a rating but in the end did not for the reasons that their credit enhancement requirements would not be met. This would certainly prevent investors from having to contact the agencies and find out whether or not they were initially asked to participate in the rating process but did not end up assigning final ratings and, if so, why—something I found is worth doing.

If you are an investor and notice that a deal is only rated by one agency or two, I would strongly recommend you seek to clarify with the other two (one) agencies that do not rate the deal if they were originally approached by the originator and, if so, why they did not assign final ratings—you may be surprised by the answer.

Of course, this only applies to investors who feel reliant on rating agency analysis. However, some investors feel, particularly after the credit crisis, that they should be placing less reliance on credit ratings than they used to and hence they may not necessarily care so much about the actual ratings and whether there has been an element of rating shopping. If you are still heavily reliant on credit ratings then have a look at Principle 4.20—which looks closer at reducing the overreliance on credit ratings.

4.5.3 Risk transfer and "skin in the game"

Principle 4.19. Securitizers need to maintain an economic interest in their transaction (i.e., have some "skin in the game") in order to ensure a better incentive alignment between originators and investors

No matter how this is achieved (either by retaining a "vertical slice" or by means of an "originator interest"; see "Retention mechanism" in the glossary) originators should not be permitted to hedge this retained risk or erode it over time by having accelerated redemption features that would reduce faster than investor risk. The idea is to have effective economic interest throughout the life of the transaction.

As mentioned in Section 4.4.3, by making sure that the originator maintains an economic benefit (or potential burden) in his own transactions is an important means of ensuring that incentives are better aligned. Equally, this means that originators remain to some extent exposed to their own deal's risks of not performing well.

Pre crisis, originators would typically aim to transfer as much of a transaction's risk to the investors as possible—mainly to maximize the economic benefit of the transaction (and minimize the incurred costs) and also to free up sufficient capital which would then be available for funding the originators' other regular business activities. Yes, there may have been the retention of the first loss or equity piece in transaction, but the risk related to them was in many cases also transferred, hedged, or somehow mitigated. Ultimately, this meant originators did not maintain much of the economic benefit in transactions and in one way or another transferred the risk away from themselves.

4.6 ANALYSIS

Whilst the previous principles were mainly centered around data, standards, deal motivation, and overall drivers behind structured finance deals and hence mainly affected the issuers of such transactions, Section 4.6.1 has its main focus on analysis and, consequently, the investors who undertake this kind of research.

4.6.1 Reduced overreliance on credit ratings

Principle 4.20. Overreliance on credit ratings must be reduced and investors need to undertake their own analysis and due diligence instead

Of course, investors can (and should) look to the credit rating agencies to see what and how they are analyzing structured finance instruments that are rated by them, but the key is to focus on the **narrative of the agencies' analyses** and *not* the designatory rating letters (i.e., the AAAs and BBBs, etc.).

Since the beginning of the credit crisis there have been repeat market, regulatory and political initiatives to reduce investor overreliance on credit ratings. I've given a number of lectures and seminars on the topic "the risk of overreliance on ratings" and "risky ratings", etc. and the response from the market and participants has been overwhelming and, honestly, at times shocking. I usually tend to do these sessions in a survey-style lecture where I ask questions and the audience is given time to think about the answers and then respond. The feedback from the audience—all from the financial sector including banks, insurance firms, asset and fund managers, and the occasional central banker or regulator—has often really surprised me in terms of the misconceptions about credit rating agencies that have been prevalent in the market.

Furthermore, investors are encouraged to take a more active role in challenging rating agency opinions as well as the underlying methodologies, rating criteria, and model assumptions the agencies use. For some investors this may require education as well as emancipation from a previously passive role into taking more active responsibility for the assets they invest in.

In order to reduce the risk of overreliance on ratings, investors ought to understand not only what ratings are and what they can tell someone—but also what are the ratings' limitations.

In general, and according to the agencies' own words, ratings are an expression of the agencies' "opinion on the relative ability of an entity to meet financial commitments." Hang on, let's look further and ask what actually is an "opinion"? Well, according to the *Oxford English Dictionary*, an "opinion" is a "view not necessarily based on fact or knowledge".

Oops! If ratings are not necessarily based on fact or knowledge, what are they actually based on? Well, having worked for one of the agencies I am happy to state that a lot comes down to expertise, in-depth discussion in rating committees, as well as thorough analysis of historical data and sometimes lengthy internal deliberations and discussions.

But, of course, there will also be elements of "feeling" (which is not always a bad thing, see "gut feeling" in Section 4.6.3) and internal politics (you will find this naturally in any firm where more than one human being works together and have to make hard decisions). Hence the political element is in practice not avoidable but may be limited. Lastly, albeit to a lesser extent, commercial interests may—but should of course not—play a role (knowing that someone, typically the originator, will "pay" for the rating). So, we have all these individual contributors that are somehow reflected in, say, a AAA rating. Yet, many investors have been almost solely relying on the rating when buying fancy instruments such as a CDO squared or CDO cubed, etc.—this has turned out to be a dangerous practice and the market has paid the price for it.

Now that we know what a rating represents, can we still derive some value from it? In short, yes, we can. But you will need to look beyond the rating letters and understand which risks can or cannot be captured by ratings. Given that ratings are in fact "credit ratings", it is important to know that they are naturally limited and can capture "credit risk" only.

This means that other risks, such as market risk, operational risk, liquidity risk, volatility risk, etc., which can cause—very similar to credit risks—investors to lose money (as evidenced during the credit crisis) are *not* captured by credit ratings. This is a very important fact which has unfortunately often been overlooked.

Furthermore, something that is rated AAA by S&P and Fitch, and Aaa by Moody's can look deceptively the same—unless you are aware of the subtle differences—and hence may lead investors to conclude that the ratings must be the same since the instrument in question is in essence AAA-rated by all three agencies. But, beware, that is not the case for the following reasons:

- *Different rating methodologies*. Rating agencies use two fundamentally different rating approaches. Fitch and S&P use the probability of default (PD) methodology in order to assign their ratings. In doing so, both agencies look at the "first dollar of loss" and try to determine what the ultimate default risk is. In contrast, Moody's is trying to express the amount of net loss suffered in its ratings which is derived by multiplying the probability of default (PD) by the loss-given default (LGD) resulting in the expected loss (EL). These are two fundamentally different rating approaches, yet the actual ratings can look very similar—which may confuse users who are not aware of such subtleties.
- *Different rating scales*. As a direct result of these differences, Moody's lowest rating is C whereas Fitch and S&P have D as the weakest rating on their long-term rating scales. The way I tend to remember this difference (and teach that in my seminars and courses on credit ratings) is that Moody's has got a "D" in its name but not in its rating scale.
- *Different probability of default curves*. Given that Moody's as well as Fitch and S&P use probability of defaults (PDs) in their rating methodologies, we would expect that at least these PDs would be the same across agencies, but, beware, they are not. Each agency calculates its own PDs based on huge volumes of historical information available to the agency from different sources. Whilst the PD curves are very similar in investment-grade rating categories and for 1-year PDs, they tend to differ quite a bit over a 10-year horizon as well as in the speculative-grade rating band.
- *Intrinsic rating "cap" or "ceiling"*. Take so-called "super senior" tranches as an example: these tranches are typically the most senior tranches in structured finance bonds where several bond tranches have been rated AAA or Aaa. Take a capital structure as an example where Tranche C is AAA-rated, Tranche B is AAA-rated and Class A sitting on top of the "waterfall" (i.e., the cash flow distribution throughout the SF structure) is also rated AAA. Tranche C is subordinated and providing credit enhancement to Tranche B and Tranche A, equally Tranche B is subordinated to Tranche A and also providing credit enhancement to Tranche A. Hence Tranche A is called 'super

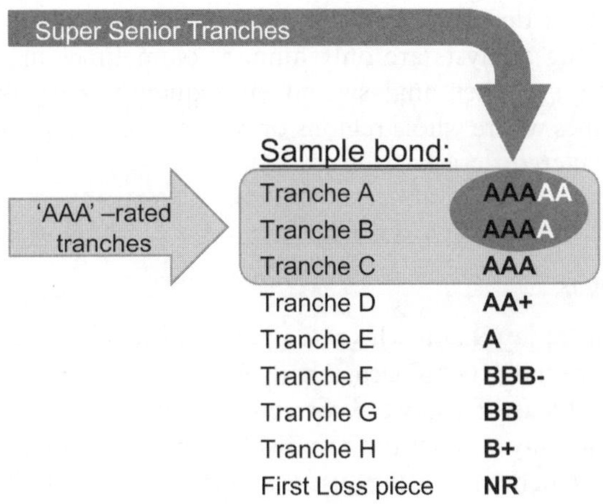

Figure 4.1. Super senior tranches.
Source: Copyright © 2011 Markus Krebsz, *www.structuredfinanceguide.com* All rights reserved.

senior" in relation to the other senior Tranches B and C. We may argue that Tranche A, which is AAA-rated, has now, of course, a much better standing as a result of the subordination and additional credit enhancement than the other two AAA-rated tranches. Really, you could almost say that Tranche B is "AAAA-rated" and hence Tranche could be "AAAAA-rated". Unfortunately, a rating better than AAA does not exist in the agencies' rating scales and hence, like it or not, there is a natural cap on ratings, with the cap level set at AAA. Figure 4.1 illustrates this example. Fair enough, but if you are an investor who is faced with having to make an investment choice of £75m for two SF bond tranches, both of which are rated at AAA/Aaa, which one are you going to go for? Well, quite frankly, without any further information probably none of them (I would hope)—until you have undertaken further analysis.

- *Analysis vs. rating*. Given that ratings on their own cannot tell us a lot, it is much more important to look beyond the ratings and understand the analysis (and to be more specific, the actual analytical narrative) that was undertaken by the agencies. A good starting point here is the agencies' pre-sale and new-issuance reports, but these are only typically published at issuance of a transaction and maybe at the point when an originator decides to issue further "taps" to an existing transaction. Investors also need to understand the agencies' rating criteria which has become pretty difficult during the past 2 years since almost all of them have been completely revised—some of them more than once during a relatively short period of time. In addition to these reports investors also ought to read any deal performance-related analysis and, for the more generic asset classes (such as auto loans or credit card receivables securitization), agency indexes which enable benchmarking as well as peer-to-peer analysis. So, there is a plethora of material available from the agencies and their quality has considerably improved since the credit crisis started and most of this is well worth taking a closer look at.

In conclusion, keeping these points in mind, it is of utmost importance that investors fully appreciate the limitations of credit ratings and also develop approaches to—at least to some extent—overcome them.

This includes seeking an active dialogue and discussion with the agencies to further understand their analysis. Investors should also not shy away from challenging the agencies on some rating decisions if they feel rating actions (e.g., a downgrade of a certain bond), are not explainable by applying the agencies' rating criteria: rating analysts are only humans (sometimes under immense pressure) and they can (and do infrequently) get their analysis and, subsequently, the published ratings wrong. This holds particularly true in times where whole regions or whole asset classes are impacted by bulk rating changes—such as during the credit crisis.

Challenging rating decisions

Whilst consulting with one of my clients who was an investor in a huge portfolio of approximately 1,500 SF bonds totaling around $100bn occasionally we saw hastily made rating changes, some of which appeared wrong—at least if you were correctly applying the agencies' own rating criteria. In such cases, we would usually contact the responsible analyst(s), discuss their rationale for the rating change and clarify which criteria they used, and then talk them through why we disagreed with them and where we felt their rating was incorrect.

The analyst(s) would then make their excuses, but equally would revisit their decision and, if they recognized they made an error, would remedy their mistake.

Such an approach is of course only feasible if your in-house analytical team is suitably staffed, with the relevant deep-level knowledge and expertise, as well as sufficient time to question the agency's analysis—more on this in Principle 4.21.

4.6.2 Increased proprietary analysis

Principle 4.21. Investors in structured finance need to increase the level of proprietary analysis with an aim of thoroughly *understanding* what they are actually investing in

The key focus here is on *understanding* the relevant risks and rewards of the transactions you are considering investing in. From an investor's perspective the key questions that need to be addressed and answered in such an analysis are:

- Will I get my (or worse, someone else's) money back and if so when (i.e., timely, or ultimate, repayment of principal)?
- What will be the reward for putting my money to work and when will I get this (i.e., timely payment of interest?).

Two simple questions which *need to be answered* and an understanding of transactions should ensure that you get the answers. If you don't like the conclusion then you should seriously consider either hedging yourself to cover remaining uncertainties or, alternatively, *don't touch* such an investment. It is as simple as that!

Outsourcing analysis (e.g., to the credit rating agencies) and sole reliance on third-party recommendations is not a suitable approach when investing say $50m of $100m of (what's usually) someone else's money into capital markets instruments—no matter if they are complex structured finance bonds or plain vanilla corporate bonds. In fact, under the new Basel II/III and CRD rules, investors may attract considerably higher capital charges to their investments if they are failing to conduct the necessary due diligence which is part of the investor's analysis.

Understanding is the key word, and it does not simply cover the bond instruments you are investing in, but goes much further: it also ought to include the asset classes your firm is investing by undertaking sector-related analysis. You ought to know the current issues that make a certain asset class tick and, more importantly, know the key performance indicators (KPIs) that can severely impact the performance of such instruments.

The subprime crisis is a good example: you ought to know the local/regional market, including the origination process for the assets that are being securitized starting with mortgage brokers and individual loan-underwriting practices. Then further up in the "value chain" you need to be familiar with the banks' practice in pooling and packaging these loans into bonds. In addition, you need to understand the nature and behavior of the underlying assets and what factors can impact their relative value, such as property price volatilities, recognizing that house prices have historically gone up for a long time, *but* can of course equally go down as well. Furthermore, you ought to understand the underlying product's features (e.g., rate reset mechanisms that may negatively affect the interest rate the borrower has to pay). You ought to understand potential borrower behaviors in certain markets (e.g., people walking away from their house if they have negative equity without any further detrimental implications on their financial status) and so on.

If you are referring to rating agency analyses, then you ought to understand what methods and criteria have been used by them, you ought to see whether this has consistently been applied for the bond(s) you are looking at or whether there are any deviations from the published methodology, and, if so, how the agencies explain those differences.

Furthermore, and this applies to many areas in life, you ought to look not only for what's visibly there, but also *what may be missing*: are there any gaps in the analysis, any points or scenarios that have not been covered, or any outstanding questions, either blindingly obvious ones or more subtle questions that have not been answered?

4.6.3 Models, assumptions, and common sense

Principle 4.22. Models and assumptions are what their name suggests. They are not a true reflection of reality and never will be

"Gut feeling", "instinct", and "common sense" are probably even more important than models and should be factored into your analysis.

Users of rating, cash flow, risk, earnings, econometric, financial and similar models will have to apply extreme caution when using such instruments to estimate whether or not they will experience losses with their investments.

Heavy use of models should always be balanced with common sense (some of the more experienced risk managers may also call this "gut feeling"). If something smells "fishy", even if it is difficult if not impossible to quantify how bad it smells, then there is probably something wrong with it—hence you are well advised to look very closely, think very carefully, and occasionally may even conclude that your firm (and you) are better by *not touching* conspicuous-looking investments.

Common sense is unfortunately not so common and it is fairly easy to move the responsibility for making a decision to a model of some kind or to a third party: if anything goes wrong with the investment, well it was simply all the "fault" of the model; and, even if the model has worked perfectly, well then maybe the assumptions (i.e., the model's parameters) were set wrongly.

That may be fine if you are looking at the weather forecast where even highly complex models and considerable computational power behind such calculations get the weather on occasion wrong. In the worst case, if it does go wrong, you may get wet—or become the next Michael Fish, a British weather forecaster famously known for failing to predict the Great Storm in the U.K. in 1987.

In contrast, if you are an investor who is investing 5% of your $50bn portfolio in various CDOs of ABSs where the underlyings are largely U.S. RMBS subprime bonds and you are experiencing losses for a large chunk of this $2.5bn investment, I guess it becomes slightly more difficult to blame the model or the even the market for the mess you "suddenly" find yourself into. Granted, there are catastrophic events that are clearly unpredictable: think of September 11 or the devastating tsunami in December 2004.

But in the case of the subprime crisis, there were people out there warning for considerable time prior to it happening and some of my clients who invested heavily in those subprime assets managed to get largely out of this asset class prior to the collapse of the market. Or think of the demise of the monoline insurance companies such as AMBAC, CIFG, FIGC, FSA, and MBIA: Bill Ackman, who is the now famous major investor, founder and CEO of hedge fund Pershing Square Capital Management LP has criticized the monoline business model for years—and as it turned out in 2008/2009 he was right—and also earned considerable amounts of money by shorting MBIA as well as other monolines.

Good for him, but he only succeeded because he did not follow the herd, did not listen to the rating agencies who all rated the monoline insurers until 2009 at AAA/Aaa, and let us not forget, he did his own thorough analysis and even published his analysis, including his model, on the internet for people including the regulators to review and comment on.

On the one hand, he was heavily criticized by some market participants yet equally strongly celebrated by others—at least he had a very clear view and understood the market (or has been very lucky)—that's what set him apart and sets a good example of how common sense can prevail above all the models, assumptions, and other fancy "tools" that in the end were all proven inappropriate, or worse, flawed.

4.6.4 Risk management and risk mitigation

Principle 4.23. Complex instruments, such as structured finance bonds, require a robust risk management environment that can challenge the front office

Risk management should be positioned to enable business (i.e., front-office) activities, but equally empowered to ensure that a firm's overall risk strategy and risk appetite are properly addressed and enforce that the firm's investments fully comply with the company's risk policies.

Disagreements between risk management and the front office do, of course, happen, in fact they are healthy, but firms need to have proper escalation routes up to top management in place so that such differences can be amicably discussed, addressed, and hopefully overcome. Where possible, risk management needs to be able to put certain risk mitigants in place, such as investment limits on asset classes, regional exposures, and maturity profiles of the relevant books, etc.

"Box ticking" is not enough

One of my clients combined the portfolio management with the "risk management" function, meaning there was no business challenge whatsoever and the head of front office had an almost completely free reign.

Even when the firm went through a major acquisition and a subsequent integration and restructuring process, the "new" risk management function was literally just there to "tick" internal as well the regulator's "boxes" and to essentially "rubberstamp" any of the bank's investments without any real challenge. Pretty scary to observe but I am convinced this has happened in many other firms, too.

For anyone working in the risk management area—or any area—of a financial institution (and that is most if not all) I warmly recommend the Chartered Institute for Securities and Investments' *Risk in Financial Services* book. Structured and laid out as a workbook for CISI qualifications it provides a broad understanding of the general principles of business risk, the key risks that arise within the financial services industry, the influence of corporate governance, regulation and codes of conduct, and the approaches that are typically used to identify, reduce, and manage specific aspects of risk. Although strictly speaking a workbook, it also makes an ideal succinct desktop reference guide, capturing credit, market, operation, liquidity, investment risk, and enterprise risk management (ERM)—I warmly recommend it to you and if you are interested then you can order it directly from the CISI's website: *www.cisi.org*.

Part II
Deal lifecycle

5
Strategy and feasibility

5.1 STRATEGIC CONSIDERATIONS

A company's strategy and how this translates and has been implemented into its business model should be key drivers in determining and steering the firm's future. Hence, securitization deals, particularly since they typically involve large amounts of money (usually several hundred million but occasionally going into several billion dollars), should form an integral part of an originator's strategic considerations.

This chapter covers the following questions that an originator or financial institution that chooses to use securitization may wish to consider in more detail as part of its strategy:

- What are the strategic considerations that need to be taken care of?
- What drives deal structures?
- What are the key signs that would indicate that an institution may securitize its assets?
- What is key to issuing a successful deal?

5.1.1 Overall strategy

Business model

Given that typical securitization structures usually carry a maturity of a minimum of 5 years (shorter maturities are possible but may not be economically viable), a bank or financial institution considering securitizing its assets would need to give careful consideration to how this can fit into the overall business model. Most banks have a short-term (1-to-2-years) and long-term (5+-year) strategy in place and any future securitization transaction should be analyzed for its strategic fit.

Part of such analysis should consider whether the anticipated securitization transaction is more of a tactical nature (i.e., a one-off deal) or whether "securitization" itself is thought of as a strategic solution to address particular needs on an ongoing basis (i.e., repeat issuance).

The answer to this question may have far-reaching implications and can lead to building a strategic securitization platform which would typically be reflected in the bank's organizational structure, systems, and synergies which could be realized as part of such a strategic approach. Ideally, these decisions should be driven and made by top management, typically the chief financial officer or group finance board members and in close co-operation with all relevant divisional heads.

Origination

For instance, if a bank was to plan to securitize its loans to small and medium enterprises (SME loans), it could be that a larger number of these particular loans (but with relatively small loan balances) are originated by the bank's retail business banking unit whilst a smaller number of loans (with usually considerably higher loan balances) are originated by the bank's corporate business banking unit. Furthermore, the loans may be originated by using slightly different underwriting standards with different loan documentation, managed by different loan-servicing teams (i.e., regional centers vs. a centralized loan-processing team) and maintained in entirely different IT and booking systems which increases the overall complexity of such transactions. In such a scenario, careful thought should be given at an early stage whether if would be advisable to securitize these loans as part of a cross-divisional transaction or if it would be easier to utilize the portfolio of only one business division at a time.

A bank's or financial institution's origination activities and asset churn rate can give a good indication of the originator's future asset pools and potential portfolio concentration that may require either a synthetic risk transfer via a synthetic structure or, alternatively, the true sale via a funded transaction.

From the originator's perspective, it is certainly worth spending some time at an early stage to decide or at least have a strategic view on the anticipated and most likely origination frequency. This decision in principal can have far-reaching implications in terms of the overall setup of the originator's deal platform. An integrated approach whereby the originator is using various available resources within existing departments can work for a one-off deal structure.

In contrast, if the originator was to go for a more strategic securitization platform, it is certainly worth considering establishing a dedicated securitization program that can operate to an extent in parallel with the originator's existing divisions. This would also allow the originator to provide and allocate dedicated resource, such as program and project managers, business analysts, and subject matter experts with the key objective of getting the deal structure established as quickly as possible and with minimal impact on the existing business and processes.

5.1.2 Funding sources

At times when short-term as well as longer term markets—not only for structured finance but any kind of intrabank tradable vehicles—have dried up, liquidity and funding in a wider sense has become one of the scarce resources for banks and other financial institutions. This is even more of a concern as banks need funding to conduct their business on an ongoing basis.

In the past so-called "funding gaps" were easily overcome by using readily available assets with predictable cash flows in order to fund the business. The lack of liquidity and the repercussions on funding require financial institutions to tread carefully and use methods to source funding as efficiently as possible.

Liquidity and funding

The credit crisis with its far-reaching implications for the global financial markets has put the liquidity and funding strategy on the top of the agenda of most banks and financial institutions. Funding gaps, the difference between deposits raised and funds provided, have widened considerably for many institutions. This widening was further magnified by the maturity mismatch of short-term financing and long-term lending to off-balance-sheet activities, asset-backed commercial paper (ABCP), and structured investment vehicles (SIVs).

Funding source diversification

Securitization vehicles can be used by originators to diversify their funding resources. Essentially, if an originator has many similar types of assets (e.g., mortgages with a statistically predictable stream of cash flows), he can bundle and package these assets into a securitization transaction. By securitizing these assets, the originator will bring some of the cash he would be receiving over time during the life of the underlying pool forward and will receive funds now.

Of course, he will need to pay sufficient spread to the noteholders and eventually return their money when he passes the cash flows from the underlying mortgages through to the noteholders. However, by means of securitization, the originator can receive an initial cash flow at the time of closing the securitized deal, when otherwise he would need to wait for many years to receive the equivalent cash.

Investor focus

The *crucial questions for noteholders*—which are essentially investors in the assets provided by the originator—are, of course:

(1) Will I receive (timely) interest for providing funds to the originator and what is the likelihood of doing so (or not doing so)?
(2) Will I get my principal funds back (in an equally timely fashion)—and when and what is the likelihood that some or all of the funds will be returned (or lost)?

Funding mix and repo tool

Furthermore, rather than having to rely on one or few sources of funding (e.g., by means of customer deposits), an originating bank can diversify its funding mix.

More recently, particularly since the onset of the credit crisis and provision of various special lending schemes (SLSs) by central banks around the globe, originators/issuers have used the issuance of bonds as an active tool to access these schemes and as a repo tool. Having said that, central banks have been restricting these schemes since September 2008—as many banks issued sizable new securitization deals which were never really intended for issuance into public markets and only served to access central banks' funding schemes. These issuances, however, have cut some corners in terms of underlying collateral and transaction reporting provided, leading to lower quality transactions than prior to the onset of the credit crisis—which did not go unnoticed by the financial regulators.

Liquidity tool

In addition to diversifying a bank's funding base, securitization can also be used as a liquidity tool: Assets that are otherwise considered as relatively illiquid (e.g.,non-performing or sub-performing loans, NPLs), can be removed from an originator's balance sheet and placed into a securitization and hence provide liquidity.

Equally, real estate assets which the originator would like to retain for future use could be sold to an SPV and, once sold, can be leased back from the SPV—hence called a "sale-and-lease-back" transaction.

Suitable and eligible securities, including highly rated asset-backed or mortgage-backed transactions, can be used as a short-term liquidity tool as part of repurchase agreements (repos) with central banks or other banks who wish to enter such deals: Due to the short-term nature of repos, such an exchange of assets should not be considered as a proper funding mechanism, it is more a short-term measure to overcome periods of limited liquidity.

5.1.3 Asset and liability management

The bank's funding base and its liquidity strategy are direct determinants of its asset-and-liability management. Prior to the credit crisis banks holding large portfolios of asset-backed and mortgage-backed assets would normally be well placed to manage their own funding requirements. By holding different types of ABS/MBS bonds on either trading, available-for-sale, and banking books as well as in off-balance-sheet vehicles, they could have profited from higher yields than for cash or near-cash funds.

Equally, if and when the need arises to turn more of these assets into cash, there was a happy and willing secondary market to purchase these bonds in return for cash. However, with the onset of the credit crisis this changed completely: the secondary market disappeared for a considerable period of time (only showing the first signs of coming back in mid-2010) and liquidity subsequently dried up.

Only the intervention of the Federal Reserve Bank in the U.S., the European Central Bank, and the Bank of England and the establishment of innovative new money market instruments allowing banks to pledge mortgage-backed securities within certain criteria contributed to bringing the global capital markets back to life. The overhaul of these central banks' monetary instruments permitting ABS and MBS instruments led to new tools for asset-and-liability management such as repo agreements and other innovative funding strategies.

5.1.4 Regulatory capital management

By transferring the assets and some of the risk associated with them away from their balance sheets, banks free up regulatory capital.

The reduction of capital charges became an increasingly important issue during the credit crisis: many banks who have been acting as institutional investors are holding ABS/MBS portfolios that were originally mostly rated at AAA or similarly high ratings which would have attracted fairly small capital charges.

Many of these ratings, however, changed substantially during the credit crisis when credit rating agencies overhauled their rating methodologies and assumptions for most structured finance asset classes by using much more conservative rating approaches.

As a direct consequence of these model and criteria revisions, a large number of assets with previously high-quality ratings (e.g., AAA and AA) were suddenly downgraded in many cases to speculative grade ratings (i.e., to BBB and below).

Subsequently, capital charges rose exponentially making those transactions economically unfeasible for the institutions affected. Whilst there was plenty of supply of these assets in the market, the demand from investors had completely dried up and the structured finance markets stalled. Under normal market conditions, affected institutions would have sold these assets, bearing in mind that most of these transactions were robustly structured and providing a considerable level of credit enhancement—but, still, the ratings would now make them economically unattractive to hold.

Improve key financial ratios

By reducing the total assets of the originator, securitization clearly improves return on assets (ROA) and economic value added (EVA). For banks, the positive impact also affects return on equity (ROE).

5.1.5 Efficiency

In terms of efficiencies and economies of scale it is worth establishing at the outset prior to issuing any bonds whether the originator wishes to issue either as a one-off (i.e., a tactical deal) or whether there is sufficient need going forward as well as potential benefit justifying an ongoing issuance process (i.e., taking a long-term view which would justify building a strategic securitization platform that is capable of supporting ongoing issuances for different asset classes).

Typically, a tactical solution will usually be cheaper; however, economies of scale can usually be more efficiently realized via a strategic platform.

5.1.6 Legislation and choice of jurisdiction

One of the key drivers behind any securitization transaction is legislation and the regulatory environment: If you or your firm considers structuring a transaction, you need to be aware of applicable laws and security regulation that may impact your transaction. This holds particularly true for a post–credit crisis market.

During and following the credit crisis, the structured finance market has been in the media spotlight receiving considerable attention from politicians, multinational bodies, and the general public. Ultimately, many of these discussions led to numerous legislative initiatives, particularly by the EU but also in the U.S. As a result of these discussions, the market has seen considerable regulatory changes since 2009, which are likely to continue until 2011/2012:

- *Basel II and revisions to the Capital Requirements Directive*
- *Basel III*
- *Capitalization*
  - Basel Committee on Banking Supervision, consultative document "Proposal to ensure the loss absorbency of regulatory capital at the point of nonviability" (October 1, 2010)
  - European Commission, Directorate General Internal Market and Services, "Roundtable on debt write down as a resolution tool" (September 10, 2010)
- *Corporate governance*
  - CRD II provisions relating to remuneration, parliamentary press release
  - FSA CP 10/19 Revising the Remuneration Code (proposals to implement CRD II in the U.K.)
  - EU Green Paper on Corporate Governance
  - FSA/FRC DP 10/3 Enhancing the Auditor's Contribution to Prudential Regulation
  - FSA CP 10/3 Effective Corporate Governance (Significant Influence Functions and the Walker Review):
- *Dodd–Frank Wall Street Reform and Consumer Protection Act*
  - *Asset-backed securities*
    - §621: Propose rules prohibiting material conflicts of interests between certain parties involved in asset-backed securities and investors in the transaction
    - §941: Propose rules (jointly with others) regarding risk retention by securitizers of asset-backed securities, and implementing the exemption of qualified residential mortgages from this prohibition
    - §942: Propose rules regarding the reporting obligations of ABS issuers that, prior to enactment of the Act, were not required to report under section §15(d) of the Securities Exchange Act
    - §943: Adopt rules regarding the use of representations and warranties in the asset-backed securities market
    - §945: Adopt rules regarding asset-backed securities' issuers' responsibilities to conduct and disclose a review of the assets
    - §621: Adopt rules prohibiting material conflicts of interests between certain parties involved in asset-backed securities and investors in the transaction
    - §941: Adopt rules (jointly with others) regarding risk retention by securitizers of asset-backed securities, and implementing the exemption of qualified residential mortgages from this prohibition.
  - *Credit ratings*
    - §932: Complete process for establishing new Office of Credit Ratings
    - §932: Appoint director of new Office of Credit Ratings

§932: Begin publishing reports the Commission receives from NRSROs on certain employee departures
§932: Propose rules regarding NRSRO reports of internal controls over the ratings process, preventing sales and marketing activities from influencing the production of ratings, providing for a report to the Commission and "look-back" when an entity subject to a rating employs a person who previously worked for the NRSRO
§932: Propose technical amendments to NRSRO Rules to conform text, terms and definitions in the Rules to amendments to text, terms, and definitions in the Securities Exchange Act of 1934 (e.g., changing "furnishing" information to the Commission to "filing" information with the Commission)
§932: Propose rules regarding transparency of NRSRO ratings performance
§932: Propose rules requiring certain steps be followed when adopting or revising credit ratings procedures and methodologies, and providing for disclosure of certain information to accompany the publication of a rating
§932: Propose rules requiring third parties retained for the purpose of conducting due diligence related to asset-backed securities, to provide a certification containing specified information to the NRSRO that is producing a rating for the ABS
§932: Propose rules establishing fines and other penalties for certain violations of law
§936: Propose rules establishing training, experience and competence standards and a testing program for NRSRO analysts
§938: Propose rules regarding ratings symbols
§939A: Review of existing references to credit ratings in statutes and regulations; propose revisions to rules that contain references to credit ratings
§932: Adopt rules regarding NRSRO reports of internal controls over the ratings process, preventing sales and marketing activities from influencing the production of ratings, providing for a report to the Commission and "look-back" when an entity subject to a rating employs a person who previously worked for the NRSRO
§932: Adopt rules establishing technical amendments to NRSRO Rules to conform text, terms and definitions in the Rules to amendments to text, terms, and definitions in the Securities Exchange Act of 1934 (e.g., changing "furnishing" information to the Commission to "filing" information with the Commission)
§932: Adopt rules regarding transparency of NRSRO ratings performance
§932: Adopt rules requiring certain steps be followed when adopting or revising credit ratings procedures and methodologies, and providing for disclosure of certain information to accompany the publication of a rating
§932: Adopt rules requiring third parties retained for the purpose of conducting due diligence related to asset-backed securities, to provide a certification containing specified information to the NRSRO that is producing a rating for the ABS
§932: Adopt rules establishing fines and other penalties for violations of law
§932: Publish a report summarizing NRSRO inspections, findings, responses, and evaluating appropriateness of responses
§936: Adopt rules establishing training, experience and competence standards and a testing program for NRSRO analysts
§938: Adopt rules regarding ratings symbols
§939(h): Report to Congress on standardization within certain elements of the credit rating process
§939A: Report to Congress on review of existing references to credit ratings in statutes and regulations; adopt revisions to rules in accord with review

— *Derivatives*

§712: Propose rules, jointly with the CFTC, further defining key terms used in the Act

§§763 & 766: Propose rules on trade reporting, data elements, and real-time public reporting for security-based swaps

§763: Propose rules regarding the registration and regulation of security-based swap data repositories

§763: Propose rules regarding mandatory clearing of security-based swaps

§763: Propose rules regarding the end-user exception to mandatory clearing of security-based swaps

§763: Propose rules for clearing agencies for security-based swaps

§763: Propose rules regarding the registration and regulation of security-based swap execution facilities

§764: Propose rules regarding the registration and regulation of security-based swap dealers and major security-based swap participants

§719: Report to Congress, jointly with the CFTC, on a study regarding the feasibility of requiring the derivatives industry to adopt standardized computer-readable algorithmic descriptions

§765: Adopt rules regarding conflicts of interest for clearing agencies, execution facilities, and exchanges involved in security-based swaps

§712: Adopt rules, jointly with the CFTC, defining key terms used in the Act

§763: Adopt anti-manipulation rules for security-based swaps

§§763 & 766: Adopt rules on trade reporting, data elements, and real-time public reporting for security-based swaps

§763: Adopt rules regarding the registration and regulation of security-based swap data repositories

§763: Adopt rules regarding mandatory clearing of security-based swaps

§763: Adopt rules regarding the end-user exception to mandatory clearing of security-based swaps

§763: Adopt rules for clearing agencies for security-based swaps

§763: Adopt rules regarding the registration and regulation of security-based swap execution facilities

§764: Adopt rules regarding the registration and regulation of security-based swap dealers and major security-based swap participants

— *Market oversight*

§929W: Propose revisions to rules regarding due diligence for the delivery of dividends, interest and other valuable property to missing securities holders

§956: Propose rules (jointly with other regulators) regarding disclosure of, and prohibitions of certain, executive compensation structures and arrangements

§916: Adopt streamlined procedural rules regarding filings by self-regulatory organizations

§929W: Adopt revisions to rules regarding due diligence for the delivery of dividends, interest and other valuable property to missing securities holders

§956: Adopt rules (jointly with others) regarding disclosure of, and prohibitions of certain, executive compensation structures and arrangements

- *Financial stability and systemic risk*
  - — Proposals to strengthen financial supervision in Europe
  - — Community macro prudential oversight of the financial system and establishing a European Systemic Risk Board

- Public Consultation regarding an EU framework for Cross-Border Crisis Management in the Banking Sector
- New framework to increase transparency and ensure coordination for short selling and Credit Default Swaps
- SIFI Capital Charges: Group of Governors and Heads of Supervision announce higher global
- minimum capital standards, September 12, 2010:
- ECB paper: Financial Stability Review June 2010:
- Debate and future outcomes on "Breaking up the Banks" (UK) Consultation: A new approach to financial regulation: judgment, focus and stability.

- *Financial resource*
  - Consultative proposals to strengthen the resilience of the banking sector announced by the Basel Committee, December 17, 2009
  - June 18, 2010 Press Release—Adjustments to the Basel II market risk framework announced by the Basel Committee
  - July 16, 2010 Press Release—Progress on regulatory reform package: Basel Committee press release
  - July 26, 2010 Press Release—The Group of Governors and Heads of Supervision reach broad agreement on Basel Committee capital and liquidity reform package
  - Annex to July 26, 2010 Press Release—Broad agreement on main elements of the design of Basel III as announced by the Group of Governors and Heads of Supervision
  - Group of Governors and Heads of Supervision announce higher global minimum capital standards, September 12, 2010.
- *Market infrastructure*
  - OTC derivatives and market infrastructures
  - "Short Selling and certain aspects of Credit Default Swaps"
  - CCP Regulation: EC Consultation on EU Legislation on Derivatives and Market Infrastructures
  - Securities Law: EC Consultation on EU Legislation on Legal Certainty of Securities Holdings and Dispositions
  - UNIDROIT Convention on Substantive Rules for Intermediated Securities (aka "Geneva Securities Convention")
  - Withholding Tax Collection Procedures: EC Recommendation on Withholding Tax Relief Procedures
  - OECD Consultation (aka "Implementation Package") on Improving Procedures for Tax Relief for Cross-Border Investors.

It is important that you become or are already aware of the legal and regulatory changes that have an impact on the market and/or jurisdiction in which you are operating and conducting business. Ideally, such awareness should not only include legislation that has already been passed by law-makers but also consider proposed new regulation that is anticipated to be passed in the near term. If your firm is not fully aware of these changes, then there are several different ways enabling you to understand what will impact your firm and the market going forward. You could either pay "experts" in this area of the market (e.g., a securitization lawyer or a capital markets or securities consultant who is familiar with the market and has relevant insight—both of these options are likely to be expensive). Alternatively, you may wish to consider joining one (or more) of the following professional associations:

- *ASF, the American Securitization Forum.* This forum is the securitization industry's unifying forum, converting ideas into action to enhance and improve the securitization market. Its membership encompasses all aspects of the industry, including issuers, investors, financial intermediaries, rating agencies, legal and accounting firms, trustees, servicers, guarantors, and other market participants. The ASF advocates the securitization industry's interests in various market practice, legal, accounting, tax, regulatory, legislative, and policy issues. The forum builds consensus, coordinates advocacy efforts, and informs and educates the securitization community and related constituencies on issues of broad importance to the industry. Important issues for the ASF include bank capital adequacy regulations, accounting standards governing the recognition, de-recognition, and consolidation of assets conveyed to securitization vehicles, federal securities' registration, disclosure and reporting rules, legal investment laws and restrictions, and a host of other topics that present challenges and opportunities to the domestic securitization market and its participants. The ASF is also committed to providing substantive and timely informational and educational programs of value to U.S. securitization market professionals. It offers a unique opportunity for its members to participate meaningfully, with a diverse range of professional colleagues and peers, in shaping the future of the financial market. Visit the ASF at *www.americansecuritization.com*.

- *The European Securitisation Forum (now known as AFME/ESF)*. This forum addresses financial markets policy issues relating to securitization, development of best practices, and member education. Membership comprises securitization arrangers, issuers, investors, credit rating agencies, law and accounting firms, trustees, servicers, data and other service providers, stock exchanges and other market participants. AFME/ESF seeks to build consensus within the industry on issues of broad importance to the participants involved; to advance AFME/ESF's substantive positions by interacting with appropriate governmental, regulatory, accounting, legislative, and other policy-making bodies at the EU, national, and international levels; to educate the securitization community and related stakeholders about the benefits of, and market developments in, securitization; to conduct substantive, high-quality conferences, workshops, and educational programs; to provide member firms with a forum to identify, raise, and discuss industry issues and concerns; to eliminate inefficiencies in market practice and regulation; to facilitate the development of best practices and industry standards; to contribute industry expertise to facilitate an informed debate about regulation; and to serve as a resource for policy makers, media, and private individuals seeking to understand the securitization markets. Initiatives are generated by the members, approved by the division's board, and carried out by AFME staff with input from AFME/ESF working groups. The projects take a variety of forms, from informal discussion groups to formal responses to government consultations.
- *AFME, the Association for Financial Markets in Europe*. This association promotes fair, orderly, and efficient European wholesale capital markets and provides leadership in advancing the interests of all market participants. AFME was formed on November 1, 2009 following the merger of LIBA (the London Investment Banking Association) and the European operation of SIFMA (the Securities Industry and Financial Markets Association). AFME represents a broad array of European and global participants in the wholesale financial markets, and its 197 members comprise all pan-EU and global banks as well as key regional banks, brokers, law firms, investors, and other financial market participants. AFME provides members with an effective and influential voice through which to communicate the industry standpoint on issues affecting the international, European, and U.K. capital markets. AFME is the European regional member of the Global Financial Markets Association (GFMA). For more information, visit the AFME website *www.AFME.eu*.
- *ASIFMA, the Asia Securities Industry & Financial Markets Association*. This is a broadly based professional advocacy organization that seeks to promote the growth and development of Asia's debt capital markets and their orderly integration into the global financial system. ASIFMA works to develop more open domestic capital markets, more standardized market practices, and

a more stable and transparent regulatory environment, which will help mobilize and redirect the region's considerable financial savings to support Asia's continued economic growth and development.
- *BBA, the British Bankers' Association.* This is the leading association for the U.K. banking and financial services sector, speaking for over 200 banking members from 50 countries on a full range of U.K. and international banking issues. All the major institutions in the U.K. are members of the Association as are the large international EU banks, U.S. banks operating in the U.K., as well as financial entities from around the world. The integrated nature of banking means that BBA's members engage in activities ranging widely across the financial spectrum encompassing services and products as diverse as primary and secondary securities trading, insurance, investment bank and wealth management, as well as conventional forms of banking. The BBA's website is *www.bba.org.uk*.
- *GFMA, the Global Financial Markets Association.* This association joins together the common interests of hundreds of financial institutions across the globe. GFMA's mission is to develop policies and strategies for global policy issues in the financial markets, thereby promoting co-ordinated advocacy efforts across its partner associations. GFMA is partnered with the Association for Financial Markets in Europe (AFME), the Asian Securities and Financial Markets Association (ASIFMA), and, in the U.S., the Securities Industry and Financial Markets Association (SIFMA). Visit *www.gfma.org* for more information.
- *ISDA, the International Swaps and Derivatives Association.* This associaion was chartered in 1985 and has over 820 member institutions from 56 countries on 6 continents. Members include most of the world's major institutions that deal in privately negotiated derivatives, as well as many of the businesses, governmental entities, and other end-users that rely on over-the-counter derivatives to manage efficiently the financial market risks inherent in their core economic activities. Since its inception, ISDA has pioneered efforts to identify sources of risk in the derivatives and risk management business and reduce them through: documentation that is the recognized standard throughout the global market; legal opinions that facilitate enforceability of agreements; the development of sound risk management practices; and advancing the understanding and treatment of derivatives and risk management from public policy and regulatory capital perspectives. See *www.isda.org* for more details.
- *SIFMA, the Securities Industry and Financial Markets Association.* This association brings together the shared interests of hundreds of securities firms, banks, and asset managers. SIFMA's mission is to support a strong financial industry, investor opportunity, capital formation, job creation, and economic growth, while building trust and confidence in the financial markets. For more information, visit *www.sifma.org*.

You may wish to check with the relevant organization whether your firm is already a member—most of these organizations finance themselves via an annual fee paid by the association's member firms. These fees, however, are small compared with the first option. Furthermore, many associations have several committees and/or specialized working groups tailored towards the functional role of the attendees (e.g., investor, originator/issuer, servicer, data provider, etc.). These groups are taking the lead in market initiatives and hence are more aware of all legal and regulatory issues that impact their subject area, and members are usually actively involved in shaping any new legislation.

A downloadable blank template of Table 5.1 is available on the book's companion website (*www.structuredfinanceguide.com*), which you can use for discussions with law firms in case you consider a jurisdiction that is not mentioned below.

Table 5.1. Legal considerations and jurisdiction: United States

	Overview and legal regime
Transaction types	Continuing securitization activities during the credit crisis, particularly credit cards and trade-receivable deals. Increasing activity in credit derivatives and repurchase agreements (repos)
Industry sectors	Securitization is a well-established tool for banks, financial institutions, funds, and corporates to manage funding, liquidity, and credit risks
Governing laws	No single state or federal statutory authority. Subject to the nature of transactions, several U.S. state or federal laws may be applicable
Regulation	Securities and Exchange Commission, Board of Governors of the Federal Reserve, Department of the Treasury, Internal Revenue Service (IRS), Office of the Comptroller of the Currency, to name a few
	Main drivers
Accounting standards	FIN 46, FAS 140
Economic/Capital charges	Non-recourse sale of assets: no capital charges incurred by the seller. Going forward and subject to new regulation, originators will be required to retain a percentage of the assets and retain an economic interest—which would incur capital charges
	SPV setup and governance
Form and setup	Subject to federal laws in which the SPV will be established (i.e., State of Delaware, State of New York). This will have implications on applicable tax laws and bankruptcy status of the SPV
Legal status of SPV	Limited liability partnership (LLP), limited liability company (LLC), limited partnership (LP), corporation, statutory trust Typically, an orphaned entity with minimal capital which is formed specifically for the purpose of the structured transaction
Ownership	—
Regulatory/Governance	—
Establishment	Depending on the nature (cross-border) and the investor base (U.S./non-U.S., both) Cross-border/Non-U.S. investors Non-U.S. SPV (i.e., Cayman Island, Ireland, or Jersey/Channel Island SPVs) if the transaction is intended as a cross-border deal Cross-border + U.S. investors Joint co-issuance of securities by a U.S. SPV and a non-U.S. SPV (see above) Due to U.S. taxation law, this is usually set up as a U.S. SPV (Delaware, LLC) with the membership interest owned by the non-U.S. SPV

(continued)

Table 5.1 (*cont.*)

	SPV setup and governance
Bankruptcy remoteness	Typically achieved by strictly limiting the SPV's permitted activities in its legal documentation and contractual agreements Furthermore, corporate actions such as filing for voluntary bankruptcy as well as contractual amendments could be made subject to the vote by an independent director of the SPV Inclusion of non-petition covenants by counterparties to the transaction
Legal separation	Via "true sale" and ensuring that assets sold to the SPV cannot be considered as a secured loan Operation of the SPV separately from the originator/seller of assets to avoid potential consolidation by a bankruptcy court
	Synthetic structures
Availability	Yes, synthetic structures are possible and frequently seen in the U.S.
Common structures	Documentation is usually either as credit default swaps or total rate of return swaps
Rationale for synthetic deals	Cost-efficient relief of regulatory capital. No disposition of assets by the originator and acquisition of those assets by the investor necessary in order to achieve a synthetic risk transfer via CDS
	Bond instruments
Issuance	Both, public and private issuance can be seen Private issuance can be via private placement under Section 4(2) of the 1933 Securities Act which exempts the issuer from registering an issue that does not involve a public offering Alternatively, issuance under Rule 144A gives issuers more flexibility with regard to secondary-market trading activities provided that the counterparties involved are "qualified" and "institutional" investors Public registration provides more liquidity to the securities due to access to a wider investor base and allows investors to resell without any further restrictions—as may be the case with private placements under Rule 144A
Exchange (if public)	Highly rated instruments may qualify for registration on form S-3 (SEC) allowing quick processing and registering of the securities
Listing documentation	—
Share capital	—
Security constitution/ documents	Indenture, which includes amongst others • Terms of reference for the transaction • Includes legal language creating security interest over the underlying collateral • Waterfall of payments • Documentation of the control and voting rights

	Assets and receivables
Typical asset classes	Most common asset classes are mortgages, credit card receivables, trade receivables, auto loans, and leases
Transfer (from originator to SPV)	Two-step sale to ensure sale process is classed as "true sale" (3) Originator sells assets to SPV specifically organized to purchase these assets (4) Purchasing SPV sells assets to SPV which issues debt certificates/notes to the investors
Exclusions	Securitization of some assets for which it is difficult to establish security over the underlying collateral (e.g., because there are different state laws applying to the creation of security) may prohibit issuance from an economical perspective
Perfection	—
Restrictions	The originator may be prohibited either by contractual obligations or state law
Recharacterization	"True sale" status needs to be confirmed, ideally by a law firm that is familiar with the underlying transaction and maybe by means of producing a "true sale" legal opinion
Unwinding	—
	Security creation
Security types and perfection requirements	Perfection of the security interest in the SPVs financial assets The perfection method varies depending on the underlying collateral and could, for instance, be achieved by filing financial statements in the relevant jurisdiction
	Other factors
Sovereign rating ceiling	There may be sovereign rating ceilings in the rating agencies' criteria that could limit the maximum rating that can be achieved for a securitization transaction
Tax implications	The transaction is likely to be subject to U.S. federal income tax issues which may impact the SPV, the sponsor, and the investor in such transactions. This taxation depends on various factors such as the type of receivable, nature of pool (fixed or floating), location of the SPV (onshore/offshore), terms of the SPV's securities Transaction may also be subject to withholding taxes and other taxes Material entity-level tax on the SPV may represent a material tax burden rendering transactions economically unfeasible and hence this should be carefully looked at early in the transaction.

5.1.7 Platform: Tactical vs. strategic

Decisions concerning the origination frequency will also have a direct impact on the actual scope of the securitization platform (if any). Whilst one-off deal structures can be successfully integrated and run within existing functions and departments, repeat issuance can quickly become a constraint on the day-to-day business and work flow. Consequently, a strategic securitization platform may justify the establishment of a dedicated securitization unit that has the necessary staff with the relevant skill sets.

5.1.8 Investor considerations

Investor consideration should be a core element of any bank's or issuer's securitization strategy. Issuers need to treat investors as their "clients", meaning the client has needs and only sufficient catering for those needs will enable issuers to place their product (i.e., the structured finance bond) with those investors.

Prior to the credit crisis, transactions used to be heavily oversubscribed and issuers would typically have no problems in selling and managed to place all bond tranches, typically with ever tightening spreads, across the whole capital structures with investors. If investors were careful and requested more information from issuers, the issuers would argue that the transaction was oversubscribed and hence the investor would need to make her mind up quickly, even without some of the information that the investor would deem necessary to commit to the transaction.

From an investor's perspective, structured finance investments can offer amongst others the following benefits:

- *Diversification.* As with other pooled financial instruments, ABS/MBS bonds provide investors with exposure to a diversified pool of underlying retail, corporate, or real estate assets. Rather than having to build up a diversified portfolio on their own, investors have the ability to pick and choose bonds with certain attributes, such as a certain number and/or selection of industries, geographic areas, and different maturity profiles. These portfolios are typically already in existence and don't require prolonged ramping up. Furthermore, at least prior to the credit crisis, investors were literally spoilt for choice with a wide-ranging variety of asset classes to pick and choose from.
- *Additional protection mechanisms.* In addition to a standalone loan portfolio, SF instruments typically offer additional protection mechanisms that are built into the structure, such as legal safeguards and various ways and means of credit enhancement.
- *Ability to address different types of investors.* Given that such instruments are usually broken down further into different tranches that carry different levels of ratings, such instruments naturally attract a wider ranging investor audience than just a simple portfolio of loans. Consequently, there are investors who are either more risk-averse in their investment scope (or limited by investment guidelines and policies) and hence prefer AAA-rated super senior tranches. Equally, other investors may prefer slightly riskier investments with a better return profile and, hence, may opt for mezzanine tranches with better spreads but still relatively stable investment-grade ratings down to BBB−/Baa3.
- *Wider pricing.* ABS/MBS bonds generally price wider than comparably rated corporate bonds which can given them more attractive risk-adjusted returns. Pricing evolution for various asset classes and geographical regions since the beginning of the credit crisis can be found in AFME/ESF's monthly and quarterly data reports.
- *Ratings stability—will it return?* Historically and prior to the credit crisis, structured finance ratings, at least for the higher rated instruments (i.e., AAA to A) used to be generally stable and showed a fairly low rating volatility compared with corporate bond instruments, due to built-in credit and other structural enhancements. This, however, changed dramatically during the credit crisis when

the market saw for the first time bulk downgrades of AAA-rated SF instruments, sometimes bond downgrades by up to 14 notches (i.e., for some CDO of ABS deals) in a single rating action. Since early 2011, the market has seen these bulk actions largely disappear and deals that have previously been placed on rating watch negative were mostly removed from watch and the ratings were affirmed (and some downgraded). Whether or not these rating changes have always been justified or were to some extent driven by the pressure on the agencies and the newly introduced European regulation, structured finance ratings have undergone a global-scale "detoxification" program. As a result, such revised ratings reflecting more stressful assumptions and factoring in more macroeconomic factors should in theory have become even more stable after the credit crisis. In practice, only time will tell whether this holds true.

5.1.9 Publicity

Prior to 2007, many originators were keen on getting innovative deals and structures issued in the market, maybe in order to signal a certain "sophistication" on their behalf or maybe they were more scared of "losing out" and "falling behind" by not participating in the ever growing securitization market.

This changed rapidly after 4Q07 when the first quarterly and annual results were published and banks were forced to disclose the impact of the credit crisis on these positions.

Since then, at least for the short term, many banks wished that they had stayed away from this particular market, or at least that they had invested less aggressively into subprime, CDO of ABS, CDO^2 and monoline-wrapped deals—just to name a few asset classes which had received the brunt of negative publicity.

5.2 KEY SIGNS FOR SECURITIZATION

How can the need for securitization by a financial institution be identified? There are some telltale signs which can help to identify the need for securitizing and optimizing an originator's funding strategy. Section 5.3 discusses a selection of key indicators for securitization such as:

- Reliance on one funding source
- Poor return on asset ratio
- Poor return on equity ratio
- Candidate for share buyback
- Poor Tier 1 ratio
- Liquidity need (e.g., asset growth outstripping growth in deposits)
- Merger and acquisition candidate
- Specific business area that is capital constrained internally
- Need to free up capital in order to book new business.

5.3 DEAL STRUCTURE TYPE

The deal structure is one of the points that require careful consideration at an early stage of the transaction as it is typically not possible to change the transaction structure after the deal has closed.

When looking at the proposed deal structure, you should be looking closely at the impact the structure will have on the following areas:

- Cost (of setting the particular structure up and maintaining it over the life of the transaction)
- Tax implications (translating into costs and potentially other restrictions)
- Investor appetite for particular structures
- Regulation (such as Basel III which will place certain restrictions and limitations on deal structures and the use of multiple tranches)
- Setup of the SPV (onshore/offshore/trust, etc.).

5.3.1 True sale

"True sale" is at the heart of the matter of many (but not all) securitization transactions and means that the right of ownership on the underlying assets has been legally transferred from the originator to the special purpose vehicle that looks after the assets on behalf of the investors. This is not merely a physical transfer of assets and, if executed properly, puts the investor into the position of a secured lender.

The true sale of assets to the SPV is meant to ring-fence these assets and achieve so-called "bankruptcy remoteness" of the asset pool in case the originator defaults. Although such remoteness from bankruptcy may be achieved by ensuring independence of the SPV from the originator, in practice this has been thrown somewhat into doubt during the credit crisis as the true sale status has been challenged in some federal courts in the U.S. Time will tell whether bankruptcy remoteness can hold up to what it claims to be. Structural features such as the ability to repurchase assets from the SPV by the originator to increase credit enhancement level in order to prevent assets from going into default may be interpreted by courts as measures contradictive to a true sale.

The true sale is typically confirmed by a strong legal opinion confirming the a true sale has been executed and that the assets are now bankruptcy remote. However, as with most legal opinions, they are "just" an opinion. More importantly, most legal opinions have not been tested in court to see whether they uphold what they are claiming. Somewhat, I expect this to change as a byproduct of the credit crisis where foreclosed borrowers may contest bankruptcy proceedings by servicers and trustees (on behalf of the SPV).

In conclusion, true sale is at the heart of the matter in order to get a securitization deal up and running and working smoothly throughout its life. However, originators need to tread carefully in ensuring that the transferred assets are ring-fenced from further originator interaction and need to carefully balance any structural feature that may threaten the true sale claim.

5.3.2 Funded structures

The crucial point in defining the ABS structure is to match the cash flows generated by the underlying assets with the cash flows required to service the notes issued. There are two basic ABS structures:

- *Revolving structure*. This means the principal generated by the short-term assets is used to purchase new receivables during a specified period of time and is applied afterwards to repay the bonds. A further evolution of the revolving structure is the *master trust structure* developed in the U.K. market which consists in transferring to the trust a portfolio much larger than the issued ABS, thus allowing greater flexibility in defining the notes repayment profile (hard-bullet payment).
- *Pass-through structure*. This means the principal payments generated by the assets, instead of being applied to purchase new assets, are passed through to investors to repay gradually the outstanding amount of the ABS.

5.3.3 Funded revolving structure

In general, the revolving structure is applied when a pool of underlying short-term assets is used to back a longer term structured finance bond. Such "revolvers" as they are also referred to usually incorporate two periods:

- *Revolving period.* During the revolving period the principal under the ABS remains outstanding in full and the revenues generated by the underlying assets are used to pay interest to investors, to pay the SPV expenses, and to absorb losses. On the other hand, the principal payments generated by the underlying assets are used to purchase new assets for so-called "replenishments" of the underlying pool.
- *Accumulation period.* At the end of the revolving period the principal payments generated by the underlying assets are deposited into a reserve account. The funds accumulated in the reserve account are applied to pay the structured finance bond at its maturity through a soft-bullet payment or through regular instalments (sometimes also referred to as "controlled" or "scheduled" amortization).

Typical features in these structures are early-amortization triggers, protecting ABS investors from adverse events that could impact the ABS principal. Early-amortization triggers define the so-called "trigger events" (e.g., bankruptcy of the originator, deterioration of underlying assets' performance, etc.) that trigger the amortization of the bonds on a passthrough basis (all the principal payments generated by the underlying assets are passed through to investors to pay down the structured notes). The early-amortization events could occur at any point in time during the revolving period or the accumulation period.

5.3.4 Funded pass-through structures

Pass-through structures are normally used to securitize assets with longer maturities (e.g., mortgage loans, auto loans, etc.) and a common characteristic of underlying assets with longer maturities is that borrowers often prepay (i.e., to exploit market situations where interest rates are falling to refinance their liability).

From the point of view of the ABS investors, this means that they receive back the principal much earlier than expected while interest rates are falling, thus exposing them to a potential reinvestment risk.

A key element for the investors (and for the price of the ABS) will therefore be the expected prepayment rate of the underlying asset pool. The arranger of the securitization and the rating agencies will assume a constant prepayment rate (CPR) over the life of the transaction in their cash flow models.

5.3.5 Funded vs. synthetic transactions

An originator's goals are major drivers for the type of securitization transaction as funded, while synthetic deal types can have relative advantages or disadvantages when comparing them. This section provides an overview of these differences in discussing financial benefits, regulatory issues, and operational differences and looks at other considerations, such as structural implications and offering methods. Furthermore, we will take a closer look at the relative differences for each of these areas.

Financial benefits

Funded transactions offer a high *funding benefit* whilst synthetic transactions do not provide any funding diversification and are purely a transfer of risk. In addition, funded transactions use many different sources of funds for the purpose of the transaction and therefore help to diversify the funding basis of an institution.

The *fixed costs* involved in setting up a transaction, including the setup of a special purpose vehicle (SPV) as well the fees incurred by underwriting, legal review, and transactional audits in addition to rating agency fees, etc. are relatively higher than for a synthetic deal. In addition, costs to transfer the assets to the SPV and to set up the deal's operational framework add to the overall fixed cost for funded transactions. In comparison, synthetic transactions require no SPV setup costs, the assets remain on the balance sheet of the originator which means a lean operational framework, and the fixed costs are therefore relatively lower.

Whilst this fixed cost differential on its own can make a considerable difference on a pure fixed cost basis only, the overall impact on the *cost per basis point (bp) of capital freed* is relatively smaller. When measured on a cost per bp of capital freed basis, funded transactions would appear to be slightly more expensive, due to the higher fixed cost; however, this can typically be set off by the higher amount of capital that can be freed up with these structures. Synthetic transactions have fewer of these costs, but are also freeing up no capital in turn.

Regulatory issues

From a regulatory perspective, both types of transactions, funded as well as synthetic, need to be approved by the regulator (FSA) so there are no differences in terms of *registration.*

In terms of *risk transfer*, when securitizing a discrete pool of assets, the originator in most cases would keep the so-called first-loss piece on its book and under new regulation from January 2011 onwards is actually required to retain at least 5%.

Whilst he would keep the bond for the first-loss tranche for a funded transaction, he would equally keep the first-loss piece of synthetic transaction, either by transferring only the risk for higher tranches via credit default swaps (CDS) or similar instruments to investors.

This means that there is no distinction between funded or synthetic transactions; however, it also means that only the catastrophic risk for the securitized portfolio is transferred and not the risk that comes within the originator's normal day-to-day operations.

Operational differences

Another key difference between funded and synthetic transactions is the impact on the *systems requirements* in order to manage and support these transactions. Operational requirements for funded deals are challenging: the originator has to be able to isolate the assets from its own assets in the systems, enable the true sale to another entity (special purpose entity), track and distribute the cash flows received from these assets, and provide in-depth reporting for investors and rating agencies. I once worked on a securitization project for a large U.K. bank which established and built a strategic securitization platform literally from scratch. As a large-scale project, this involved a large number of staff (literally hundreds) across all divisions and levels of management. Whilst the initial work was more a project-type environment, which on its own can be a challenge to get employees (a scarce resource) either seconded or find suitable contractors, this can change naturally over time into a more business-as-usual work environment.

The initial setup of such new functions and departments can take considerable time—in the instance of this particular originator it took about 2 years for the first transaction to be placed. Synthetic transactions put much fewer constraints on system requirements as the assets remain on the originator's balance sheet and cash flow tracking and reporting can potentially be done by enhancing the existing system infrastructure rather than building a completely new platform. Consequently, structuring a synthetic transaction and placing it within the markets is usually considerably quicker than structuring and placement of a funded transaction.

Systems requirements are only one component that has an impact on the *execution timeframe*. The systems together with the condition of the actual loan files and the data and information requirements of the rating agencies are the biggest contributor to delays in funded transactions. Furthermore, the assignment language in loan terms and conditions can also play an important role and lead to further delays.

Prior to the credit crisis, placing a new transaction into the market by a first-time issuer could easily take 6 to 8 months for an established asset class and potentially longer for a new asset class entering the market. Established issuers who knew what was expected from them could close a deal within a 4-to-7-month window. Mainly due to lesser systems requirements but also due to reduced legal deal documentation, synthetic transactions are typically quicker until close than funded transactions and the execution timeframe for such deals would be in the region of 2 to 5 months. Generally, the rating agency requirements used to be the biggest obstacle for such deals. And if an agency happened to review and redefine its current model and the relevant assumptions, the close of any transaction affected by such rating criteria changes—funded and synthetic—could easily be delayed another month or two.

Although issuance of some asset classes such as student loans, credit card receivables, and a few RMBS deals continued during the credit crisis, I expect that any future large-scale issuance in the near term (i.e., the remainder of 2011 and beyond) could take longer for the following reasons:

- Increased requirements by rating agencies as well as regulators may take longer to reflect in the relevant systems. There have been various global initiatives for greater transparency since the credit crisis started resulting in greater investor as well as rating agency appetite for information and data on the assets that are securitized. Naturally, this means that originators will have to first locate and then query more information from their source systems that are used to service these assets on a day-to-day basis. Some originators may even find that, whilst previously they could have easily securitized some of their assets, now there may be greater restrictions on doing so; either because the additionally required information is not available or not sufficient to support any new transactions.
- Lack of staff experienced in origination and structuring as a result of many banks and financial institutions essentially closing their structuring departments down. It will take some time to replace these employees and new starters will naturally take some time to familiarize themselves with the originator's products and systems.
- Lack of analytical staff to conduct the primary rating analysis at the credit rating agencies. All the major agencies reduced their staff volumes considerably from late 2007 and furthermore throughout 2008/2009 to reflect the state of the structured finance market with regard to new issuance. Again, it will take some time to rebuild these analytical teams if and when the market kick-starts again at a larger scale. In addition, the agencies may find it more difficult to hire new staff since the agencies' reputation has rightly or wrongly suffered greatly during the credit crisis.
- Many banks and financial institutions either closed their structured finance fixed income operations completely or reduced the number of staff considerably. Prior to the credit crisis, traders and sales departments had well-established and widespread contacts and could therefore market and place a trade fairly quickly. This also meant that most deals were heavily oversubscribed and investors could consider themselves lucky if they were able to participate in the transaction. As a direct consequence of the credit crisis, many of these informal interbank contact networks have disappeared together with the fixed income traders and people that were a crucial part of it. Naturally, once the market returns, it will take some time to re-establish these networks and originators,

issuers, and investors who have afforded themselves the "luxury" of keeping the majority of the structured finance trading desk alive will clearly have a competitive advantage.

- Senior management's confidence and support for the structured finance–related business lines has been severely dented during the credit crisis and many institutions will take quite some time to realign their structured finance business lines and redefine their strategy with regard to this business area going forward. Anecdotal evidence suggests that there has been an ongoing educational process with regard to these asset classes extending to the top of all those banks and financial institutions that have been involved in many kinds of structured finance deals, particularly the more riskier ones. As the Head of Risk, Treasury at one large U.K. financial institution and one of my clients puts it: "Senior management and the board have learnt in the last year or so more about structured finance and securitization than they have ever dreamt about or wished for." I hope that these experiences have not always been negative, but on the positive side may have proven the need of independent institutionalized risk management departments that question, challenge, and contest the analytical work of the rating agencies and that have the power, encouraged by top senior management, to turn down deals (and therefore potential business and profit) if they feel that short-term profits may be eliminated by longer term deterioration and potential writedowns and losses.

5.4 ASSET CLASSES

Securitization and structured finance are generic terms, which are applied interchangeably to several asset classes. The classification of structured finance bonds (i.e., the "asset class") is typically based on the underlying assets or instruments that have been securitized. These include asset-backed securities (ABS) and mortgage-backed securities (MBS), collateralized debt obligations (CDO) in the widest possible sense, synthetic securitization (credit derivatives), operating assets ("whole business securitisation"), future flow ("revenue-based"), and finance and structured credits—which securitizes one or more of the other asset classes mentioned in this paragraph.

The proper categorization of a given transaction into the right asset class category is important as the following areas, amongst others, are based upon the asset class and can be fundamentally different for a transaction that would fall into a different asset class category:

- *Feasibility and asset readiness studies undertaken by the originator.* The originating institution would typically have certain pools of assets in mind when considering a securitization. This would then, for instance, drive the selection of rating agency and investor report data templates that need to be applied to rate a particular asset class. Even if the anticipated asset class for a transaction has been identified, there will still be differences in terms of the chosen funding profile (i.e., there are different sets of data necessary for funded transactions than for synthetic transactions).
- *Legal counsel selection.* Seasoned originators may pick the law firm to work with on legal opinion based on such things as fee schedules, previous experience, an already established relationship, and on the experience of the particular law firm with certain asset classes. There is not much point in selecting a firm that is not familiar with the particular asset class considered for securitization as this can slow the overall process down considerably. Ultimately, law firm selection can also have an impact on the overall quality and robustness of the legal opinion.
- *Investor interest and appetite.* Investors may be looking for particular assets to enhance or diversify their portfolio and therefore will be more concerned with particular asset classes.
- *Applicable rating methodology, agency model, and analysis.* These are heavily determined by the asset class.
- *Market benchmarks for new transactions.* Any new deal should and will be compared by market participants against similar existing deals from the same or a different originator.

- *Third-party vendor treatment*. The asset class defines how a new transaction is treated by third-party vendors such as ABSnet, Bloomberg and Intex. Based on the classification, these vendors will use predefined templates to provide performance data for these assets to the market.
- *Investor-reporting templates*. More recently there have been attempts to establish generic (but also asset class and jurisdiction-specific) templates for investor reports. One of the requirements for using such templates is that the asset class is properly specified and assigned.

Asset class identification

You might now wonder how to select asset classes and then assign them to a new transaction? A key factor in selecting the relevant asset classes is the underlying type of assets as this can help to distinguish which kind of asset class category a certain deal will belong to.

The truth is, there is no simple answer. Most deals can be clearly categorized into existing asset classes: an underlying pool with residential mortgages will most likely belong to RMBS, if the underlying are non-conforming loans in the U.K.; this would then mean it's likely to be called a "U.K. non-conforming RMBS" deal or something along those lines. Similarly, if the underlying are personal and auto loans originated in Spain, then this would fit best into the "Spanish consumer loan ABS" category.

It certainly becomes trickier when the underlying are a combination of U.K. property ("PropCo") and an operating company ("OpCo")—this could then in some instance be a "U.K. whole business securitization" or a "U.K. CMBS transaction". The key difference here would be, for instance, the treatment by the rating agencies which could either rate such a transaction according to the agency's whole business securitization criteria or, alternatively, by applying the agency's CMBS rating criteria.

It becomes even more complex and confusing when the transaction falls into the collateralized debt obligations sphere (CDO) where the underlying assets can be anything from small to medium enterprise loans (SME CDO), corporate loans (CLO), synthetic notes (CSO), synthetically transferred risk by using credit default swaps (synthetic CDO), hedge funds, or other fund-type obligations (CFO).

This can be further complicated by using structured finance instruments (such as any or all of the above), as the underlying assets are then repackaged into new complex structured credit vehicles, such as ABS (CDO of ABS), CMBS (CRE[1] CDO), CDO, CDO^2 (or "CDO squared"), CDO^3 (or "CDO cubed"), etc.

During the financial crisis, most if not all new issuance of these complex structured credit products disappeared and many investors abstained from anything that had a "C" and an "O" in the asset class description. However, during the second half of 2010, there appears to be a pipeline of around 20 or so transactions which would previously have fallen into one of these asset class categories. Having said that, these new instruments appear to be more robustly structured and are no longer called "CDOs": the market term is now simply just "structured corporate credit" or "structured project finance" (or something along these lines), but principally the underlying mechanics for these new instruments are the same as for CDOs.

Rating agencies need to identify the asset class at an early stage in the rating process in order to assign any deal that is going to be structured to the relevant analytical department. Once identified, the pre-sale and new-issuance reports will state which asset class such deal belongs to and many market participants use this as a guideline for benchmarking the transaction against existing ones.

Borderline cases, for instance, "whole business securitization" deals that could either be rated by using a more corporate-type analysis or, alternatively, a CMBS methodology can lead to interesting differences in rating methodologies used by different agencies and, potentially, to so-called "split

[1] CRE CDOs = collateralized debt obligations with commercial real estate (i.e., commercial mortgage-backed securitization transactions as underlying assets).

ratings". This would mean that one or more tranches in such a transaction are rated differently by two or more agencies.

Having said that, in practice, originators try to avoid any new issuance with split ratings in order to prevent investor confusion and would rather increase the level of credit enhancement so that the final ratings by all three agencies are on a comparative level.

Split ratings become much more common during the life of a transaction, for instance, when one agency acts more quickly and downgrades one or more tranches whilst the other agencies are keeping the ratings unchanged. Some of these split ratings affected whole asset classes during the credit crisis since agencies undertook many bulk reviews for certain asset classes and subsequently changed the ratings for many deals.

5.5 PRIVATE ISSUANCE, PUBLIC ISSUANCE, OR CONDUIT FINANCING

There are various ways of issuing securitized assets via a bond structure to the markets. They include private issuance, publicly issued notes, or short-term issuance of commercial paper via a conduit vehicle.

A securitisation can be implemented by either issuing ABS directly to the investors through the SPV or by using a conduit managed by a financial institution, which purchases assets for a number of sellers and funds these purchases by issuing ABS into the market.

A further alternative is represented by a private ABS, whereby the ABS issued by the SPV is not sold on to the public but to one or more specific investors.

Table 5.2 compares the advantages and disadvantages of the three funding alternatives from the originator's point of view.

5.6 CREDIT ENHANCEMENT AND PRICING

5.6.1 Definition and sizing

Any structural feature or counterparty that is used as part of a structured finance transaction to enhance the pure credit quality of the underlying assets to the level of the desired ratings can be described as "credit enhancement" or "credit enhancers" (in the case of a counterparty).

The purpose of credit enhancement is twofold: absorbing losses on the assets that are financed via the transaction and enabling the originator/issuer to structure the transaction so that, as a result of these activities, the resulting different bond tranches carry different risk, which is expressed by different pricing, different ratings, and different investor types for the resulting tranches. This activity is also known as "tranching" or "sizing the credit enhancement and capital structure".

The size of the credit enhancement is determined to absorb expected losses that assets could experience during the transaction's lifecycle and therefore serves as a cushion put in place to protect investors against such losses. The rating agencies' rating criteria play a key role in determining the size of the required credit enhancement and the higher the quality of the required rating for a particular tranche, the greater the protection required.

Credit enhancement is sized to protect investors from expected losses, which in turn can arise from a variety of risks, such as commingling risk, setoff risk, servicer and other counterparty risk, risk of cash transfer delays, etc.—to name a few.

In practice, a particular deal's credit enhancement is usually a combination of several forms of different credit enhancement mechanisms. Given that this is something the originator needs to provide for as part of structuring the transaction, credit enhancement is also a reflection of the specific

Table 5.2. The three funding alternatives from the originator's point of view

	Multi-seller conduit	*Public ABS*	*Private ABS*
Pros	▲ Can handle smaller size transactions (€250m) ▲ Proven track record: price, structure, execution ▲ Established investor and rating agency relationships ▲ Easy and fast to execute; no rating required with bank's conduit programs ▲ No seller name in the market, only vehicle name ▲ Black-box AAA/Aaa term funding through the conduit	▲ Large size (up to €2–3bn) ▲ "Halo effect" of AAA issuer in the market; public perception of the originator ▲ Diversification of the investor base; wider distribution than private ABS ▲ Tightest pricing ▲ Term funding; no price risk	▲ Can handle smaller size transactions (€250m+) ▲ Lower transaction costs (no SEC registration) ▲ Disclosure to a limited investor group
Cons	▼ Need liquidity (backstop purchase commitment) ▼ Market practice is 364-day commitment ▼ Seller rating downgrade trigger ▼ Banks have a limited group capacity ▼ Price risk; weighted average funding cost plus spread	▼ Minimum size (€250m+) ▼ Requires SEC registration ▼ Disclosure of portfolio data to public ▼ More detailed reporting requirements ▼ Longer execution time ▼ Significant rating agency involvement	▼ Higher spreads than public market ▼ More limited investor base than public market ▼ More detailed reporting requirements ▼ Longer execution time

characteristics of the securitized assets, the overarching goals of the securitization sponsor, and last but not least the requirements of the rating agencies.

Although rating agencies are keen to stress that they are not actively consulting and structuring on behalf of the originator, they play a key role in sizing the credit enhancement by means of an iterative process whereby the originator provides the transaction's details and credit enhancement and the agencies model the transaction and then give their feedback to the originator on whether the enhancement provided is sufficient for the relevant rating band. If not, the originator would then have to try and understand what is needed in order to satisfy the agencies' rating requirements and provide the additional level of credit enhancement in order to address the unfavorable eventualities that could adversely affect the bond over the deal's life.

Internal and external credit enhancement

Internal credit enhancement means that it is provided within the structure by the originator or through internal mechanisms as part of the actual deal structure. Internal credit enhancement can further be separated into

- *Hard credit enhancement.* This is usually static (i.e., does not change) and exists from the inception of the transaction. Due to its static nature it is not expected to "disappear" when it's needed most (i.e., when problems with the underlying assets arise, cash flows from the asset dry up, and the investors then have to rely on protection provided by the structure itself). Typical examples of such hard credit enhancement are

  - *Subordination*
  - *Overcollateralization*
  - Static or fixed *reserve funds* or *cash collateral accounts*
  - *Trigger events*
  - Maintenance of *certain financial ratios*
  - *Insurance cover* provision on the underlying assets, such as mortgage payment protection.
- *Soft credit enhancement.* This is usually of a dynamic nature, it can change frequently, and it may start with a minimum requirement and will be built up over the life of the transaction. Due to its changing nature it can potentially "disappear" when it's needed most and the availability of it should be monitored carefully. From an analytical perspective, it makes sense to assume this kind of credit enhancement is not available and hence ignore it in the analysis when looking to invest—and by doing so removing any reliance on it. Examples of soft credit enhancements found across a wide range of structures are
  - *Excess spread*
  - Dynamically reducing *reserve funds* or *cash collateral accounts.*

External credit enhancement, in contrast, is provided outside the transaction's structure itself and usually by counterparties or guarantors other than the originator. Section 5.6.2 takes a closer look at both types of credit enhancement.

5.6.2 Internal enhancement

Commonly used types of internal credit enhancement for a variety of asset classes are

- *Subordination.* Subordination assigns a different ranking order to issued note obligations which are all secured by the same pool of underlying assets. This ranking determines how losses experienced in the asset pool are distributed to the various note tranches. This means that junior tranches would usually be hit first by losses (hence they are also commonly referred to as "first-loss tranches") which, after the junior tranches have been eroded, may "eat" further into the capital structure and also incur losses for the mezzanine and, in extreme cases, also for the senior noteholders.

  Subordination, expressed by different note tranches as part of the same issuance, usually also impacts the allocation of cash flows (the so-called "waterfall") which are generated by the underlying assets in order of note seniority. This would, for instance, mean that senior tranches receive the cash flow generated by the underlying assets first and subordinated bond tranches will profit from cash flows last. Equally, loss absorption by the note structure would impact the first-loss tranche initially and then the junior notes next and the senior notes last.

  Originators tend to hold the equity or first-loss tranches, which are the most junior tranches in the majority of transactions. These tranches serve as an incentive for the originator to assure that the transaction is performing according to expectations, as losses will impact them (i.e., the originator's first). This is, however, no guarantee that the transaction will actually perform as expected.

  Timely subordination is usually a consequence of the transaction's legal documentation, whereby some payments are subject to certain conditions being met or otherwise may be delayed until a breach of those conditions has been remedied. From an investor's point of view it is important to know, for instance, whether the senior tranches you are investing in are subject to timely subordination, which may disadvantage you compared with mezzanine and/or junior noteholders, even if you are structurally a holder of a senior note tranche.

  Structural subordination is where the chosen structure determines the actual structural position of noteholders—in other words, are you a senior noteholder (i.e., at the top of the structure, enjoying the highest ratings and the greatest credit protection) or a junior note investor (i.e., sitting structurally at the bottom with limited credit enhancement and the lowest ratings)? In this context, it is also important to be able to distinguish between both forms of subordination. The following structure serves as an example:

Class A	(AAA-rated)	
Class B	(BBB-rated)	(*structurally subordinated* to Class A)
Class C	(B-rated)	(*structurally subordinated* to Class A and Class B)

Class A will receive principal repayments first, then Class B, then Class C. *But*, Class C will receive interest payments first, then Class B, then Class A, which means that interest payments in this structure would be in "reverse sequential" order; or, in other words, interest payment for Class A notes is *timely subordinated* to interest payments of Class B and Class C.

The key benefits of subordination are that it is typically available as soon as the deal has been established and the issuance is closed. Furthermore, it is usually static and is not linked to the performance of the underlying assets or the performance of the originator/issuer and as such provides fairly stable protection.

Due to the way this type of credit enhancement is calculated, certain structures have growing subordination levels relatively over time when some of the senior tranches are paying down. Whilst the provided levels of subordination—which are typically expressed as a percentage—do not change, the relationship of the available tranches to each other changes when tranches within such structures are paid down or redeemed and consequently *relative subordination* or *relative credit enhancement in %* may change (i.e., increase).

Whereas some forms of credit enhancement (e.g., "excess spread") may be made available on a "use it or lose it" basis at a certain interest payment date (IPD), subordination is constantly available throughout the life of the transaction.

- *Reserve accounts*. These accounts provide a liquid source of protection within a structure that either already holds at transaction close a predetermined amount of cash (or cash-near liquid instruments) or serves to redirect part of interest and/or principal receipts from the transaction's waterfall and accumulate them in the relevant "reserve ledger" or reserve account.

  The purpose of this account is to park funds until they either need to be used to make up—depending on the individual structure—interest or principal shortfalls on the notes or, ultimately, if they have not been utilized, they can be returned to a predetermined counterparty other than the noteholders, typically the originator. Such reserve accounts can either be prefunded by utilizing some of the proceeds from the note issuance at outset of the transaction that are put aside as cash. Alternatively, the structure may have a ramp-up period, typically 6 months to 1 year, during which cash collateral—likely to be funded by all or some excess spread payment—can build up within the dedicated reserve account.

  On the occurrence of certain trigger events that are, for instance, linked to the servicer's credit ratings or the performance of the underlying collateral, the reserve account may be contractually required to increase further to cover the additional risk that may arise from a weaker servicer or decreasing asset performance. Equally, if a transaction amortizes, issuers may be permitted to release some of the cash held in the reserve accounts, which means that this cash is then leaving the structure and will no longer be accessible to noteholders.
- *Overcollateralization*. This occurs when the value of the underlying assets exceeds the face value of the issued notes. For instance, if the value of the underlying securitized asset pool is £550m, but the notional value of the outstanding notes at issuance is only £500m, this means that the securitized assets of £550m were essentially purchased at a discount of 10% and the transaction is in essence overcollateralized by 10%, meaning 110% assets compared with 100% issuance. The overcollateralization rate (OC) in this example is 110% or 1.1× (= 110/100 and also = 550/500). Such a level of

overcollateralization reflects the level of expected losses for this pool of assets and is also an expression of expected deal expenses.

OC within a structured transaction is meant to absorb losses second in line after excess spread (which is usually the first line of defense) but prior to passing on any losses to the noteholders. The amount of OC provided is usually fairly small (since the provision of it can be quite expensive for originators/issuers who could use the collateral utilized for the resulting overcollateralized part more efficiently in similar transactions). Furthermore, junior noteholders are the ones who benefit most from the availability of overcollateralization (as second line of defense) given that they themselves are the third line of defense—in the form of subordination they are providing to mezzanine as well as senior noteholders.

Overcollateralization can be fully funded at deal inception or can be structured in a way that it builds up (or decreases) over time throughout the life of the transaction. Due to such built-in fluctuations as well as the nature of the underlying collateral (which is usually a dynamic pool of assets) the overcollateralization rate in transactions will usually vary over time.

In order to protect investors from disadvantageous changes, many transactions contain certain OC triggers that ensure that a minimum level of OC is maintained and if the level falls below the trigger level, early amortization of the transaction may be initiated.

- *Trigger events.* Trigger events are another important structural feature: the occurrence of specified trigger hits such as exceeding pool concentration limits (e.g., TOP 5 borrower or industry concentration) or deterioration of the underlying pool quality (e.g., for rising delinquencies, losses, and defaults) triggers subsequent events. Such trigger events can be as far reaching as cash flow redirection within a deal structure or even early amortization and wind-down of a transaction.

  It is therefore important that such triggers and also the non-occurrence of trigger events are frequently reported as part of the transaction's regular investor reporting.

  Trigger events that are defined by the transaction's legal documentation and that impact the transaction in case of a trigger hit are sometimes referred to as "hard triggers". In addition to these hard triggers, sophisticated investors may also use "soft triggers" internally, which have no direct impact on the transaction itself but can serve more as an internal early-warning mechanism. These soft triggers can be extremely useful for surveillance and performance analysis undertaken by investors: for instance, if a performance indicator came within, say, 25% (the soft trigger level) from the transaction's hard-trigger level (e.g., cumulative losses), then the investor may wish to consider some action for this particular bond.

  Rating agencies also use soft triggers in their surveillance and performance analysis function to identify potential problems early, before any hard trigger will be hit, and would then place a transaction on rating watch negative while further investigating the reasons for these performance outliers.
- *Minimum debt or interest service coverage levels (DSCR or ICR) and other financial ratios.* These levels measure, over a specified period of time (3-month DSCR, 1-month DSCR), if the cash flows generated by the underlying assets exceed the interest or debt service requirements of the securitization transaction. The actual coverage ratio is then compared against the expected ratio for the same period of time, which enables rating agencies as well as investors to monitor the performance of the transaction and, in case of adverse performance, trigger certain events such as early amortization of a transaction.
- *Subordinated loan(s) provided by the originator.* As part of the actual transaction structure these loans can also serve as internal credit enhancements to a securitization. Such loans could, for instance, serve to provide an initial amount to fund a transaction's reserve account at the outset of the deal which would usually contribute to the deal's total credit enhancement. Typically, these funds are either repaid once the transaction has redeemed, or once sufficient funds have been

generated and a portion of the cash flows generated after close of the deal have been accumulated in the reserve account which permit early redemption of the originator's funds.

- *Excess spread.* As mentioned in the overview section on credit enhancement, excess spread is a dynamic form of soft credit enhancement that by its nature will likely change from one interest payment date (IPD) to the next. Excess spread is in essence the difference between revenues generated by the securitized assets—usually interest cash flows—and the transaction expenses, such as interest payable to the noteholders, servicing and operating fees, and losses on the underlying assets, etc.

  Securitized assets generate revenue streams, normally either in the form of pool interest or rental payments. These revenue streams generated by the underlying assets and prior to any deduction or diversion of this spread can be considered as *gross yield.* These cash flows are then used to cover the operating expenses of the special purpose vehicle and the coupon payments to the noteholders of the bond. In addition, fees payable to transactional agents such as the servicer of the assets, swap providers, providers of liquidity facilities, and others can be paid by utilizing some of the available excess spread. The deduction of these running costs for a transaction leads to the so-called *base rate.*

  In addition to covering the transaction's running costs, depending on the individual structure, these revenues can also be used to absorb eventual losses in the assets (e.g., defaults) or to cover shortfalls during asset liquidation.

  Given the frequently changing nature of excess spread, it is therefore considered as dynamic credit enhancement, meaning that there can be some excess spread available, but equally it could disappear when needed most. Consequently, from an investor's perspective, it is recommended to ignore excess spread for the purpose of calculating a transaction's total credit enhancement, unless the excess spread is collected and trapped in the transaction's reserve account. Dependent on the individual structure, the rating agencies also tend to ignore excess spread in their credit enhancement calculation.

  From a performance analysis perspective, however, it is useful to know the level of excess spread produced by the underlying assets as this would usually indicate whether the assets are performing well and, hence, excess spread can serve as a key performance indicator (KPI) for the overall quality of the underlying assets, which directly impacts collateral performance.

5.6.3 External credit enhancement

Commonly used types of such external enhancement are *guarantees*, *surety bonds*, or *letters of credit* which are provided by a counterparty—sometimes referred to as a "credit enhancer"—such as a bank, insurance company, or monoline insurer. This kind of guarantee can either apply to all tranches of a securitization or, more typically, only to one particular tranche. The rating of a guaranteed bond tranche is normally directly linked to the rating of the credit enhancer. As a consequence of the bond rating linkage to the counterparty rating, any rating action or volatility in the quality or performance of the credit enhancer may have a direct impact on the rating of the enhanced bond.

5.7 ASSET READINESS AND FEASIBILITY STUDIES

What can be securitized?

Generally speaking, any type of asset that meets the following criteria can potentially be used to securitize a transaction:

- *Asset transfer*. This is the ability to transfer the legal ownership of the assets from the originator to a special purpose vehicle (SPV) so that the ABS investor can benefit from such an asset transfer. This asset transfer can either be undertaken as a true sale whereby the assets are removed from the normal operations of the originator and its balance sheet and are placed with the SPV. Alternatively, in case of a synthetic securitization, the assets will remain on the originator's balance sheet and within the originator's normal operations; however, the credit risk for these assets will be transferred by using credit derivative instruments such as credit default swaps. In both cases, the ownership to either the assets themselves or asset-related risk and cash flows are transferred to investors.
- *Predictable stable cash flows*. The expected cash flows generated by the assets that are transferred need to be stable and predictable, at least with some extent of certainty. Of course, pool characteristics can change during the life of a transaction and the historic performance of similar assets are not a guarantee for future performance. However, properly structured deals should produce predictable and sufficient cash flows over the transaction's life. Additional structural features, such as replenishment periods, overcollateralization, reserve accounts, principal deficiency ledgers (PDLs), etc. are therefore built into most transactions to either trap surplus cash when it is available or permit the originator/collateral manager to replace insufficient assets with assets that produce better cash flows.
- *Historical data and proven performance track record*. This last point is not to be underestimated since it is only possible to determine the previous point (i.e., the predictability of stable cash flows) if there are sufficient historical performance data available. Historical performance data are needed as input parameters for the chosen (rating) methodology which is used to determine and quantify the intrinsic credit risk in such a transaction. Prior to the credit crisis, rating agencies would feel comfortable with a minimum of 3 years of historical data for established assets classes and known originators. If a deal entered new asset class territory or was structured by a previously unknown originator, agencies were more careful and would ask for a minimum of 5 years of historical data. The obvious danger with limited periods of data is that they would cover only part of the economic cycle—not a full one.

Why are asset readiness/feasibility studies useful?

Assume that a financial institution has fairly new systems to manage its assets efficiently, which were custom-built to securitize and therefore contain all the relevant asset and pool information in order to accommodate such transactions.

Unfortunately, in most cases, the infrastructure of banks and originators is usually not the most modern and their "legacy" general ledger and account management systems could easily date back to the 1970s. Mix this with many institutions that have grown over time by merging with or taking over some of their peers and have never managed to fully integrate their IT systems into one structure. As part of these mergers, some banks have taken the strategic decision to continue with both brands, which usually means they are also using different systems to manage the assets, different underwriting criteria, and their terms and conditions may also differ between these brands.

For instance, small-and-medium-enterprise (SME) loans which are, by their very nature, cross-divisional assets (e.g., looked after by both the bank's retail business banking departments as well as the originator's corporate division for larger loans) can span across divisions as well as different brands within a financial institution group.

Furthermore, the bank may not internally have a clear definition of "SME customer" and "SME loan" let alone the different external definitions that may apply to such assets: for instance, Fitch, Moody's, and Standard & Poor's all have slightly different definitions for SME loans and there's also a definition by the Competition Commission in the U.K. that defines SME-type customers for the larger four banks. Combine this with the fact that rating agencies require considerable levels of details in terms of asset and pool data with slightly different data requirements for cash than for synthetic transactions. This is why any asset readiness and feasibility study is useful and should start at the outset by addressing the following questions.

Questions concerning the rating agencies

— What are the rating agencies' current requirements for this particular asset class and are they expected or known to change over the next half-year period?
— If the rating agencies' requirements are known to change, is there a way to get clarity from the particular agency with regard to these changes and is it possible to assess the impact on the rating methodology and model assumptions for this kind of deal?

Questions concerning the assets

— How are the underlying assets to be defined and are there potentially differing definitions?
— What are the minimum data requirements that are needed to manage the assets?
— Which systems are used to account for these assets and which of them is considered to be the "golden source"?

Questions concerning legal aspects

— What are the current underwriting standards including the relevant documents that could evidence them?
— Have there been changes to standards (as well as to terms and conditions) and, if they have changed, have they been documented?
— Is it possible to identify customers and or assets that relate to specific underwriting standards?

Questions with regard to divisional reach

— How many divisions are involved (retail/corporate/business banking)?
— Are all of these divisions using the same systems and datawarehouses or are you looking at many differing sources of asset information?

Questions concerning deal economics

— How granular is the portfolio that will be securitized and how can it sensibly be broken down?
— What are the anticipated transaction costs (one-off and annual maintenance) and are there ways to make the transaction more economical?

5.7.1 Asset class selection

Each of the following structured finance asset classes (see Table 5.3) produces slightly different results in terms of funding costs, capital release, and profit and loss account impact.

Residential mortgage-backed securitizations (RMBS)

RMBS deals provide the lowest cost of funding and a medium capital release (due to the 50% risk weighting). These transactions can produce a positive impact on P&L either on the year of sale or through the life of the transaction. Prior to the credit crisis, RMBS enjoyed a significant and growing

Table 5.3. Structured finance asset classes

	Cost of funding	*Capital release*	*Profit and loss*
Residential mortgages	L	M	+
Commercial mortgages	M	H	+
CDOs/CBOs	H	M	+/−
Leasing	M	M	+
Consumer loans and credit cards	L	H	+
Real estate	M	H	+/−
Non-performing loans	H	H	−

High = H, medium = M, low = L.

liquidity on the secondary market and the level of liquidity seen before is expected to return—eventually.

The key advantage of RMBS (bar Alt-A and subprime) is that they provide the highest certainty in terms of results (cost, tranching, distribution) and overall success and visibility. On a funded basis, RMBS deals can achieve low cost of funding and a potentially high capital release.

Commercial mortgage-backed securitization (CMBS) transactions

CMBS achieve potentially high capital release at a cost slightly higher than that of more granular portfolios (i.e., residential mortgages, consumer loans, etc).

These factors are driven by the actual quality and diversification of the underlying real estate portfolio. Good and detailed property information are key to getting good results from rating agencies.

Secondary-market liquidity is more limited than for RMBS deals and CMBS suffered most during the credit crisis as corporates' financial performances were dented, affecting the cash flows of CMBS deals. Due to the size of the transactions and the values of the underlying properties and/or lease contracts, many CMBS deals have a substantial refinance risk at the end of their deal maturities which could increase funding pressures when a CMBS deal is to be refinanced.

Securitisation of corporate loans and bonds (CDOs and CBOs or structured corporate credit)

These types of transactions can both release capital and reduce economic risk. Their impact on the profit and loss account depends largely on the portfolio's composition and the average rating—which means it can increase as ratings are downgraded.

At present they are expensive asset classes to securitize because of the recent corporate defaults and uncertain economic outlook, but they are certainly worth considering both on a funded and unfunded basis.

Leasing

Leasing transactions can bring a significant capital release. Their requirement is a medium cost of funding and, largely, a positive impact on an originator's profit and loss account.

Leasing securitizations are among the most popular asset classes in Italy as originators are permitted to include any type of lease (auto, equipment, and real estate).

Consumer loans and credit cards (consumer and credit card ABS transactions)

Consumer ABS and credit card receivables transactions permit a high capital release and are typically very competitive in terms of the required cost of funding. Furthermore, they have a positive impact on the originator's profit and loss account. Due to the relatively short life of the underlying assets, most of these transaction types have a revolving pool.

Real estate

Securitization can be an efficient fund-raising tool for real estate portfolios. It can also provide capital release under certain assumptions and it is worth pursuing as part of a firm's wider real estate initiative/strategy.

"Non-performing" loans (NPLs)

Securitizing NPLs is a fairly expensive exercise but at the same time provides real risk transfer and capital release.

5.7.2 Asset definition

A simple question such as "How do you define your assets?" can cause quite a headache and may take considerable time to answer. Take SME loans, for instance, and ask yourself and colleagues which internal criteria would need to apply to say that a particular loan is SME and not classified as another product.

Furthermore, it's also advisable to have a look at the market and existing similar transactions (i.e., SME CDOs) to understand how these loans are identified. Last but not least, I recommend asking the rating agencies for their definition. You may be surprised to find they are all slightly different, typically taking the size of the firm, number of employees, and annual turnover into account.

Once the necessary background information has been collated it is well worth considering getting a product view—which is a reflection of internal products and external rating criteria—signed off by the project team that looks after this potential future securitization. This clarity is needed since all subsequent analysis will be based upon this particular definition. How else would someone be able to say it is feasible to securitize a certain pool of loans, if it is not clear which product(s) you are analyzing as part of this feasibility and asset readiness study. Table 5.4 links firms' objectives with solutions and the rationale for choosing a particular asset class.

5.7.3 Requirements definition: Checklist

The following is a list of generic questions and areas which may be considered as part of any securitization project within a bank/financial institution. Given that a securitization can also be treated as a large-scale, sometimes even cross-divisional project, an early impact assessment of the areas discussed can help avoid costly delays or "scope creep" at a later project stage. Whilst some of these areas will certainly be of interest, others may be simply disregarded in certain instances.

In order to support an assessment of whether or not it is worth securitizing certain assets it is useful to understand the underlying products' features in detail in order to grasp the suitability of the assets to be securitized.

This work stream is usually done as part of the asset readiness or feasibility study and the detailed information gathered during this process helps build a useful reference point and data repository of a firm's products.

Table 5.4. Asset selection vs. firm's objectives

Objective	*Solution*	*Rationale*
Achieve maximum capital relief	• Corporate loans • Commercial mortgages • Real estate owned • Credit cards • Consumer loans • Non-performing loans	Assets are 100% risk weighted vs. 50% for residential mortgages
Reduce funding costs to a minimum	• RMBS • Credit cards	RMBS and credit card ABS securities are the most efficiently priced securities
Maximize the amount of funding/liquidity	• RMBS	RMBS is the largest and—was prior to the credit crisis—the most liquid structured finance market
Business-specific capital constraints	• Project finance	Assets which are perceived by an institution as profitable but higher risk
Maximize the positive impact on the profit and loss account	• 100% risk-weighted assets (e.g., corporate loans, commercial mortgages, real estate owned, credit cards, consumer loans, and non-performing loans) • High-yielding assets	The higher the risk weight, the better the impact on regulatory capital and thus on ROE High-yield assets achieve at deal close an upfront gain on true sale in the securitization transaction

In addition, please note that some of these questions cover areas rating agencies would also look at as part of the agencies' due diligence activities. Given that there are likely going to be specific legal requirements under the revised capital requirements framework and Basel III for investors' due diligence along the same lines, many of the following questions could form part of investors' due diligence activities and, hence, it helps by looking at them and gathering the answers to those questions in advance. Possible due diligence questions in Section 5.7.11 are identified by the DDQ prefix.

It is also noteworthy that the following list was compiled against the backdrop of U.K. jurisdiction—other jurisdictions may likely have slightly different requirements.

5.7.4 High-level cost and benefit analysis

Gathering the following information is useful not only in order to undertake a high-level cost–benefit analysis, but some of the discoveries can help determine whether you, for instance, are looking at a revolving pool or a static pool and whether there is sufficient investor interest for a particular transaction structure.

Customer volumes

The number of customer accounts as well as account turnover, retention, historical account deletion, and forecast customer growth are important in order to understand the firm's underlying business model and, consequently, its enablement to originate sufficient assets—as customer accounts are the basis for the firm–customer relationship.

(DDQ) *What are the projected customer volumes and account volumes involved or anticipated?*

Product or asset volumes

When looking at a firm's products or originated assets that may be targeted for securitization (e.g., the bank's current pool of issued credit cards), we ought to understand the current number of issued credit cards, the firm's strategy for this product going forward, and the projected and anticipated credit card issuance over time.

(DDQ) *What are the firm's products, origination process, and product strategy?*

Similar structures from competitors

Firms operating in the same jurisdiction with a comparable business model and an equal client base are likely to experience similar challenges—and may even be able to overcome the same issues by utilizing structural features that have already been proven to work. For instance, HSBC issued a so-called "hybrid covered bond" structure in 2006 that enabled it to issue either covered bonds or residential mortgage-backed securities (RMBS) by utilizing the same special purpose vehicle (SPV) but addressing two different investor bases. At around the same time, Barclays issued a RMBS transaction in the U.K. that utilized a so-called "yield supplement reserve mechanism"—a structural feature enabling the originator to securitize lower yielding mortgages which had the yields enhanced by subsidizing these low-yielding mortgages. The method of supplementing these mortgages originated from the U.S. where it was a frequently observed structural enhancement method for low-yielding auto loans, hence a different asset class compared with RMBS. However, at the same time, another major bank was looking at how they could securitize a pool of mortgages either as part of a RMBS deal or a covered bond instrument. In addition, most of these loans were originated in a highly competitive (i.e., low-yielding) lending environment. As a solution to these particular issues, the bank combined the hybrid covered bonds with the yield supplement reserve feature. In doing so, the firm could lever off the rating agencies' analytical familiarity with both features, albeit they were previously separately applied.

(DDQ) *Do competitors offer solutions that can be borrowed and enhanced?*

Time to market

It is important to understand how long it will take to bring a new product to market and how long it will take to ramp up a pool of considerable size.

(DDQ) *For new products or enhancements to products/services what is the projected time to market?*

Phased delivery

Take the implementation of Basel III as an example: implementation of the new rules has a given timeline between 2013 (2011 with various observation periods to collate data) and 2018. The different milestones lend themselves to a phased delivery for the implementation of Basel III which in turn permits the users to prioritize throughout the development lifecycle.

> **(DDQ)** *Are there any phasing considerations or opportunities, a ramp-up phase, pooling of different assets, and a certain order or prioritization.*

Tactical or strategic solution

This depends pretty much on the requirements of the individual firm: maybe there is a need for a "quick fix" (i.e., is there a specific problem that needs to be addressed right now?), or are we expecting to see problems in the future, for instance, due to new forthcoming regulation or has the firm chosen to actively add a new asset class to its portfolio and hence will need to identify (and eventually address) the strategic needs going forward by means of a strategic solution.

> **(DDQ)** *How does the phased delivery impact various stages of the development, product, or deal lifecycle and is there a breakdown into a tactical vs. a strategic solution (which may have conflicting requirements on key resources)?*

5.7.5 Regulatory issues

Consumer Credit Directive (CCD)

Take the combined loan book of a bank which would typically contain anything from one million loans upwards. Assume they are all originated within the same geographical area or jurisdiction and during a certain origination timeframe. You ought to understand which kind of legislation—for instance, either the Consumer Credit Act 1972 or the Consumer Credit Directive 211 (which came into force on February 1, 2011 in the U.K.)—would apply to these loans.

If so, then we would hope that the bank's account management as well as management information system flag individual accounts, loans, etc. in order to identify which different legal principles apply.

> **(DDQ)** *Should any distinction be given between products that are Consumer Credit Act–regulated and those that are not?*

Mortgage Code of Business

Similar to the previous point, an originator ought to know—and record in its systems—whether or not a mortgage has been originated in accordance with the Mortgage Code of Business (U.K.). The rationale here is that the Mortgage Code of Business (or similar business codes for other asset class/ jurisdictions) in itself represent a minimum underwriting standard and adhering to these origination standards will ensure the mortgages in question are better quality.

(DDQ) *Should any distinction be given between those secured products that are CP186-regulated and those that are not (MCOB = Mortgage Code of Business)?*

Data Protection Act

Data protection is one of the key issues when considering a particular securitization structure. After the credit crunch the term "loan-by-loan" data has become one of the buzz words, at least from an investor's perspective. However, originating institutions as well as data protection officers are not too keen on the provision of this information, with the first claiming this may give away too much information about a firm's business model and origination practices whereby the latter claim that borrowers' details ought to be protected. So-called "true sale" transactions—whereby a whole pool of mortgages is lifted from a bank's balance sheet and sold to a special purpose vehicle—may not be permitted in certain jurisdictions and may require a synthetic risk transfer to the SPV instead. Synthetic deals enable issuers to maneuver inside data protection laws, but of course this is one of the crucial areas that will drive a transaction's structure and hence ought to be considered at an early stage in a potential deal's lifecycle.

(DDQ) *Has sufficient thought been given to Data Protection Act expectations?*

Regulator's expectations

Equally, originators ought to consider at an early deal stage whether any forthcoming new regulatory requirements have been considered and the potential impact of the planned transaction. In Europe, for instance, additional regulations such as the Transparency Directive, Markets in Financial Instruments Directive (MiFD), Prospectus Directive, etc. spring to mind as regulations having an impact on the transaction's documents, listing, and conduct of its roadshows.

As of late, there has been a raft of new regulatory proposals with a particular focus on the securitization and structured finance market. These include New Basel III requirements, Capital Requirements Directive, due diligence requirements for investors, capital retention rules for originators, investor reporting, rating agency regulation, etc.

If your firm is currently considering structuring and issuing new deals, then this is certainly an area where I would suggest early consultation with either a law firm that specializes in this area or even trade associations such as the American Securitization Forum (ASF) or European Securitization Forum (AFME/ESF).

(DDQ) *Has due attention been given to any new regulations that may be in the pipeline?*

5.7.6 Third-party interfaces

Although I mentioned this already earlier, I cannot stress enough that data and an efficient exchange of deal-specific information are crucial for financial instruments, not only structured finance bonds. However, due to the complex nature of some of these structured transactions and investors needing to be able to undertake their own analysis in addition to what the credit rating agencies are doing, third-party interfaces play an important part in exchanging this information.

Credit rating agencies

Throughout the lifecycle stages of a transaction, credit rating agencies require very detailed information from the originators. The rating agencies have different data templates for different asset classes ranging from pre-deal minimum requirements which gives the agencies an idea of what the originator's provisional pool looks like and enables them to undertake their initial analysis. This is then followed by further data templates with a slightly different focus which some of the agencies require at the close of the transaction, mainly to confirm that the final pool cut meets their rating criteria and does not differ considerably from what they were originally presented with. From an originator's perspective, it can be beneficial to request the agencies' templates for "investor reporting" prior to the deal close: this way originators can understand the agency's investor-reporting requirements prior to issuing the bond and will be able to source relevant information parallel to structuring the transaction. Some of my clients were surprised to discover that investor-reporting requirements may differ from the agencies' rating requirements. Managing these differences and the impact this has on the originator's issuance platform can cause some headaches, particularly if left unattended until after the deal has closed.

(DDQ) *Are the requirements likely to have an effect on data transmitted to credit rating agencies?*

Others

Rating agencies are not the only recipients of data. Once the deal has been issued, the key recipient of this information shifts a little away from the agencies and more towards investors. There are wide differences of how good (or bad) originators can present and disseminate the performance data for their transactions. When assisting originators in developing their investor reporting I had a German client who started off with 4-to-6 pages of information on their monthly report (this was for an auto loans transaction issued by a German car manufacturer), but after collaborating with and developing the investor reporting for them, the new report contained 21 pages and they were proudly saying that this superior report was now representative of the high-quality cars they produce.

(DDQ) *What impact might the change have on other external agents (e.g., trustees, SPV management, etc.).*

5.7.7 Requirements checklist

Banks, brands, and legal entities

Information available on the underlying assets will depend on the jurisdiction in which the originator operates, the different brands, and the various subsidiaries and legal entities involved. All these would typically use different underwriting standards when dealing with borrowers as well as different systems. For instance, even mortgages from the same originator within the same country can differ if different brands are used. This will need to be reflected in the transaction documents as well as in the technical implementation of the chosen platform that handles the individual issuance.

Domestic and/or overseas banks

It is certainly feasible to issue a bond that includes cross-country collateral and, in the past, we have seen pan-European CMBS deals that contain loans from several countries in Europe. In such a case you will find that the available information on the underlying collateral can differ and, hence, an additional layer of complexity is added to such deals.

> **(DDQ)** *Do the requirements apply to domestic (U.K.) and overseas banks and a cross-country collateral pool?*

Legal entities

Equally, different legal entities within the same issuance can add additional challenges as, for instance, originators may be faced with different sets of underwriting standards which then in one way or another may impact the performance of such blended pools. As an example, take the Royal Bank of Scotland Group in the U.K. which frequently securitises assets from both the NatWest and the RBS heritages. Not only have both entities different underwriting standards, but they are also using different account management systems in their branches with electronic storage of different data points and key performance indicators that cannot simply be mapped across at the group level. This adds a considerable layer of complexity when combining the relevant data sets from both legacies in order to issue one large transaction.

> **(DDQ)** *Are there any specific requirements or exceptions for banks and legal entities?*

Jurisdictions

Legal requirements are one of the key drivers that dictate how a firm can conduct its business including, for instance, loan documentation, contract language, availability and treatment of collateral, ability to cross-collateralize and offset, and the storage and protection of customer data. This will of course differ considerably within different jurisdictions. Hence, jurisdiction should be considered at an early stage in the feasibility to assess whether there are any "show-stoppers" that could prohibit the securitization of certain assets. Furthermore, I recommend consulting a member of your firm's in-house legal counsel at an early stage, ideally as part of the asset readiness and feasibility study to ascertain that crucial legal questions with regard to the jurisdiction have been addressed.

> **(DDQ)** *Which jurisdiction governs the transaction's requirements?*

Brands

If a firm is considering securitizing multi-brand products, it is worth considering each individual brand as an individual firm with its own underwriting standards and other distinct differences. Although the firm may perceive that all its brands are using the same standards, contractual and legal documentation, and the same origination work flow, the devil is almost certainly in the detail and you are well advised to assume that two different brands (e.g., NatWest and RBS) are much like two different firms.

> **(DDQ)** *Are there are specific requirements or exceptions that apply to specific brands?*

5.7.8 Products

One of the keys to any structured finance transaction is, of course, the underlying assets which will serve as collateral and produce the relevant cash flows. Broadly speaking, there will be requirements for the different types of products, be it mortgages, credit card receivables, auto loans, or even aircraft ticket receivables.

Product types

Driven by the anticipated asset class (e.g., mortgages), it is important to form an early view on which mortgage types are to be potentially included in the new transaction. This is, of course, largely driven by the various product features of those mortgages. Features that come to mind are product maturity, interest type (i.e., fixed or variable), actual interest rate, first or second lien, low or high values, secured or unsecured, interest only or interest and principal repayment, prime or non-conforming, etc.

(DDQ) *Which specific product types are impacted? Are there are any exceptions?*

Purpose of account identifiers

Whilst a fairly technical question, the answer may provide a rough guide which could naturally be used to identify certain pools of a potential asset. For instance, if a firm uses a 10-digit account number system where the current account shows a 3XXXXXXXXX, savings accounts a 4XXXXXXXXX, mortgages a 5XXXXXXXXX, and so on, such logic can help to speed the selection process up for certain assets (e.g., mortgages), and, moreover, can be used to support early-deal economic analysis of a firm's product suite.

(DDQ) *Are there any specific rules or exceptions relating to the purpose of account codes?*

Cross-products

Some products may permit cross-collateralization, whereby collateral pledged by one borrower can be used for Loan 1 and for Loan 2 of that borrower. This is likely to have implications if certain collateral for a borrower's mortgage, which is expected to be securitized, also legally serves as collateral for, say, the borrower's business account, which will not form part of any securitization.

(DDQ) *Are there any requirements across products and account types?*

Business vs. personal loan products

In addition, it is useful to understand whether or not loan products are treated as a business or personal loan. Personal loans would normally be captured under the Consumer Credit Act (CCA) in the U.K. or a similar legal rule. Business loans, on the other hand, are not required to conform with consumer credit regulation and, hence, the loan documentation may not be comparable.

> **(DDQ)** *At a more generic level, do the requirements apply only to personal products, only to business products, or to them both?*

Channel

Financial products can be distributed, sold, and delivered via different channels (i.e., either in person in the bank branch, via telephone or internet, or via third-party agents or introducers on a commission basis). These intricate details, in terms of product sales and delivery channels, can have a significant impact on loan origination and underwriting—and subsequently on actual pool performance. It helps keeping this information at hand as rating agencies are keen to understanding how (and maybe how aggressively) these products were originated, which ultimately may also impact the performance of these products—just think of subprime mortgages as a negative example.

> **(DDQ)** *Are the requirements applicable to all products, regardless of delivery channel, or should any exclusion/differentiation be made (e.g., internet/phone sales, as opposed to branch sales)?*

Secured or unsecured products

From a deal-structuring and investor perspective, this is certainly one of the most important questions that needs to be addressed in a firm's systems: Is the underlying credit to the borrower secured by suitable collateral or is it completely unsecured? And if a borrower's obligation has been secured, how valuable and easy to liquidate is the collateral in question.

> **(DDQ)** *Are there any requirements that need to distinguish between secured and unsecured products?*

Secured products

Secured products, due to their nature, usually possess a higher degree of complexity normally involving counterparties other than the originator and lender. Typically, there will be a security provider (which may or may not be the borrower himself). Furthermore, there will be other contractual agreements in addition to the loan contract, such as security or collateral pledges, (mortgage) insurance policies, etc.

In the case of second-lien loans there may be other preferential creditors that may be able to claim security before the originator and such terms and conditions may spoil the feasibility of securitizing such second-lien loans.

> **(DDQ)** *Are there any requirements that need to be considered for mortgages and other secured non-mortgage products, for instance, cases where the securitization of such secured loans is prohibited?*

Interest rate types

As innocent as this may look, the interest payment nature on the underlying collateral that is considered for securitization is likely to be a key driver for the transaction.

First of all, it's important to understand the interest payment cash flows and the type of interest rate (i.e., fixed or floating) to understand the pool's capability to generate sufficient interest payment cash flows throughout the life of the transaction.

Second, if a considerable portion of the underlying pool carries fixed rate arrangements, it is equally important to understand how these fixed rate payments are impacting the cash flow profile and to understand the risks that may arise when fixed rate arrangements change back to variable rate loans.

The knowledge gained as part of such analysis may then feed back into structuring the transaction, particularly if such interest rate risks need to be reduced or eliminated by deploying one or several interest rate swap arrangements.

Base rate–related rates

It is crucial to know and understand the implications of the underlying collateral's interest rate profile, particularly the base rates that are used to calculate the interest (e.g., the Bank of England base rate). This then needs to be compared against the interest that will be paid to the noteholders and the rate that is used as the basis for noteholders' interest (such as LIBOR or EURIBOR, etc.).

Consequently, if there are any major differences between these different interest rates, an originator/issuer may wish to consider using a swap counterparty to hedge the risk arising from these differences.

Furthermore, assume that there is a considerable proportion of mortgages that have normally insufficient yield (e.g., due to aggressive lending practices undercutting the competition by applying so-called "teaser rates" or there are low-yielding mortgages for other reasons), issuers may then consider structural features, such as yield supplement reserve mechanisms that would enable them to securitize these assets as well.

(DDQ) *Are there any specific requirements or exceptions for base-related rates?*

Fixed rates

Equally, if a large portion of the underlying collateral has fixed interest rates, but the structure issues "floating rate" notes, the issuer may wish to consider arranging for an interest rate swap that transfers the fixed interest received on the underlying mortgages into floating interest payments for the investors and thereby protecting against the risk that arises from interest rate–type mismatch.

(DDQ) *What is the proportion of fixed and floating rate assets in the underlying pool?*

Negotiated rates

Negotiated interest rates are typically either a fixed or variable interest rate that is considerably below the usual market level. Whilst the reasons for offering these rates to clients or companies may vary, the underlying rationale is either to build up a new client relationship with the hope that further (more profitable) client business is to follow, or simply to maintain an ongoing relationship with what could be considered a strategic client. Either way, these arrangements need to be captured and catered for properly when structuring transactions.

(DDQ) *Do any of the accounts or products allow negotiated interest rates (i.e., rates specific to a given account)? Are there any specific requirements or exceptions?*

Differential rates

Sometimes banks offer rates that differ from standard interest rates on a large scale (e.g., for different brands or as part of certain marketing campaigns which can affect a large number of accounts). In such a case, it is important from the originator's/issuer's perspective to be able to distinguish between them, particularly accounts for which such special arrangements are to be securitized, either in part or as a whole.

(DDQ) *Are different rates (i.e., other than standard rates) to be considered due to different branding or a product offset (e.g., offsets can have the ability to have different interest rates for accounts within offset arrangements) and how can they impact the transaction?*

Account features

Ownership

Account ownership is more of a theoretical question and usually not of much relevance for securitizations deals. However, from an originator's perspective, it is still important to understand who the account owners are and whether or not it is feasible (and permitted) to securitize their accounts.

(DDQ) *Are there specific requirements for single and jointly owned accounts?*

"Dormant, bad, and doubtful" (D,B&D) accounts

Not every account that is held by a bank or financial institution is active in the sense that normal payments are routed through it and that it has an account holder that uses it for the purpose it was originally opened. Some accounts are inactive or dormant simply for the reason that the account holder forgot about it or in some cases has deceased. In other instances accounts may be exposed and used for dubious activities (i.e., money laundering) and hence may be classed internally as "doubtful". Equally, some accounts may fall into arrears with their mortgage or other payments and such an account, at least from a securitization perspective, could be considered as "bad" and not securitizable (unless it is a securitization of non-performing loans, short NPLs).

(DDQ) *Any there any rules or exceptions relating to D,B&D accounts?*

5.7.9 Customers

Retail and corporate clients

This somewhat links back to products, which are of course subscribed to by the originator's customers. So, we would be looking at certain profiles of the borrowers and attributes that may provide important clues about the borrower's payment behavior, etc.

Personal/Non-personal

Do the requirements apply to personal and non-personal customers, for instance, for an SME-type transaction and would only the company's account be included in the securitization transaction and not the borrower's personal bank account?

> **(DDQ)** *What is the customer breakdown in terms of Personal and Corporate accounts?*

Customer relationship and account type

Are there any account specifics and exceptions for different customer types?

> **(DDQ)** *Are there any specific account features that would disallow the securitization of particular loans or receivables (e.g., owned, joint owned, authority to operate, related, account of minors, students, offshore accounts, etc.)?*

Corporate entities

> **(DDQ)** *Are there any distinctions to be made for customers that are sole traders/partnerships/limited companies/SMEs/large enterprises/international enterprises?*

5.7.10 Access controls, auditing and security controls

The following areas should be considered for both: a tactical and a strategic securitization platform. It may be useful to at least give some thought to them during initial business analysis but, to be honest, it's probably sufficient to defer detailed consideration until the functional design is carved out.

Access and control rights

> **(DDQ)** *What do specific access controls and rights to the securitization systems look like?*

Auditing

> **(DDQ)** *Will auditing of the system be necessary and, if so, what are the auditing requirements?*

Chinese walls

> **(DDQ)** *How do Chinese walls and access policies need to be implemented in the securitization platform?*

5.7.11 Non-functional requirements

The following are lists of a few non-functional requirements that are nonetheless important features for consideration and hence should be looked into at an early stage of building a securitization platform and structuring transaction.

Response time

> **(DDQ)** *What response times are required for any online components and to produce ad hoc reports?*

Availability

> **(DDQ)** *What system availability is required? Is existing back-office availability acceptable? Or is there a requirement for a true 24 × 7 availability?*

Data retention

> **(DDQ)** *What are the data retention requirements, as some information may need to be stored (or be retrievable) for anything between 7 and 30 years?*

5.8 DOCUMENTATION REVIEW

The following questions should be considered as part of a legal review of the current documentation (i.e., the terms and conditions, or T&Cs, used by the originator). The objective of this exercise is to identify any limitations that would restrict the ability to securitize. A firm's in-house legal counsel is most likely to be best suited to undertake this review; however, it may also involve business analysts who could assist in sourcing the relevant documentation. Please note that whilst the following questions serve as an example, they have been part of an actual legal review undertaken by an originator in the U.K. with its focus on loans originated in England, Scotland, and Wales. Assets originated in other jurisdictions may require a different scope or a review of additional documentation, subject to the relevant region or country in question.

Sampling and irretrievability

The following questions require assessment of the currently used loan documentation. Furthermore, I recommend undertaking a sampling of loan documents to review to discover how the actual loan documentation is used in live loan documents.

Whilst there are no clear rules for this sample review, I suggest pulling a fair (maybe around 100) number of loan documents from the originator's branch network or central loan-processing center or both. Anecdotal evidence suggests that even with the utmost due care an originator sampling its documents may find that there can be a small number of cases where actual loan documents are irretrievable. A high percentage of irretrievable loan documents, as a rule of thumb greater than 20% (or 5 loans out of a sample of 25) where the physical loan files could not be located should give the originator some concern. For instance, rating agencies, as part of their own due diligence analysis may look into loan retrievability and, if coming to the same conclusions, may find the transaction cannot be rated due to a lack of sufficient available loan documentation.

It could be argued that it may be worth investing money and resources on improving an originator's file retention and archive system first even before considering securitizing a loan book where 20% of the loan documents cannot be found.

Explicit prohibition of securitization

(Q1) *Are there any terms and conditions for each product by each brand which are considered as part of this asset readiness/feasibility study that would explicitly prohibit securitization?*

The rationale for this question is to assess whether there are any generic terms and conditions used for either particular brands or particular products where securitization may be explicitly prohibited by the contractual documentation. In addition, it is also a valuable exercise as part of such legal review to assess which terms and conditions actually contain transfer provisions and therefore already anticipate potential asset transfers as part of securitization activities.

Transfer of rights

(Q2) *Do terms and conditions in customer loan contracts for all jurisdictions allow securitization by the transfer of rights to other parties on a loan-by-loan basis?*

The transfer of rights covers the transfer to other parties, rather than the ability to assign loans which is covered in a separate question.

The purpose of this question is to look from a legal standpoint at situations whereby the terms and conditions permit borrowers to add another party to the loan contract without the agreement of the lender or originator. For instance, this situation could occur where a borrower becomes married and would like to add his spouse to the loan agreement. If the terms and agreements of the loan arrangement allow borrowers to make such changes to the loan, these loans would become more difficult to securitize as this actual right would continue post securitization. Consequently, this may also inhibit and limit enforcement rights under the loan or mortgage agreements in case the borrower were to go into default.

The originator's expectation in this case was that these transfer rights would not exist; however, only an actual legal review of the terms and conditions used by its loan origination units could help clarify the situation and answer this question.

In this instance, the security documents specified that a borrower could not grant a disposition over the particular property and assign any rights without consent. The legal review further detailed that a borrower would either need to go through a procedure whereby he would redeem the outstanding loan and then reapply or, alternatively, use a formal "transfer of title" application for some of the originator's other brands.

Confidentiality and data protection

> **(Q3)** *Are there any clauses with regard to confidentiality or data protection which would prevent securitization?*

Multiple group companies and offset arrangements

> **(Q4)** *Is there more than one company of the same group involved in the (loan) product that is expected to be securitized in the relationship with the individual borrower?*

Some loan accounts offered by banks could in fact involve more than one originator. For instance, several mortgage offset accounts in the U.K. are actually managed by two companies whereby one company undertakes the initial origination and the account is then serviced by a second company.

Other possible scenarios are constellations whereby a customer has a current account relationship with one bank as part of a group (e.g., NatWest, which is part of the Royal Bank of Scotland Group) and a mortgage loan account with Direct Line mortgages which is also part of the same banking group. There may be offset arrangements in place whereby the banking group could utilize funds from a customer's deposit account in one subsidiary to offset with loan obligations of the same customer in the other subsidiary. This pretty much depends on the individual terms and conditions.

Non-standard agreements

> **(Q5)** *How are non-standard agreements (e.g., loans where the terms and conditions have been altered, amended, or shortened from the currently used version) to be treated?*

This is a broad question but can have far-reaching implications. In order to be able to formulate an answer, the originator would need to be able to identify any changes that have been made by the relationship managers to the loan documentation (e.g., by having a flag in the bank's systems that identifies standard vs. non-standard agreements). Alternatively, if it is not possible to identify such loans, the originator may be able to take a random sample of loan documents, assess the sample for standard vs. non-standard documentation, and, based on this file assessment, determine the ratio of standard to non-standard documentation and apply this ratio to the portfolio.

Consumer Credit Act (CCA) regulation

> **(Q6)** *Are some or all of the loans to be securitized regulated by the Consumer Credit Act in the U.K. or by similar regulation in other jurisdictions?*

This question aims to identify whether U.K. loan documentation is regulated under the Consumer Credit Act and whether it is in compliance with the CCA Agreements Regulations 1983 (as amended).

This may not require a detailed analysis of loan documentation, but could assess whether the various subheadings are in the right order and there are no obvious intersperses.

The rationale for this loan documentation review is to ensure a high level of compliance with the CCA regulations as non-compliant agreements will only be enforceable with a court order and place a considerable restriction on the enforceability of the loan.

Product features

> **(Q7)** *Are there particular product features that could have an impact on the ability to securitize these particular products?*

Examples of such restrictions are the Small Loans Guarantee Scheme to SME customers in the U.K., whereby banks provide the banking facilities and loans which are guaranteed by the government in order to support economic growth. Such an obligation would need to be excluded from any forthcoming securitization transaction.

5.9 TARGET PORTFOLIO AND DEAL ECONOMICS

Portfolio breakdown

The following lists how an originator's portfolio could typically be broken down in order to grasp the portfolio's particular characteristics and to assess whether they are suitable for a potential securitization transaction. The example used is a SME CDO.

Sample breakdown

- Breakdown by product (e.g., different loan or mortgage type)
- Breakdown by relationship management responsibility (e.g., retail business banking vs. corporate business banking)
- Breakdown by country code
- Breakdown by incorporation (i.e., incorporated vs. not incorporated)
- By collateral (i.e., unsecured vs. secured loans)
- By type of collateral or security held
- By Standard Industry Code (SIC)
- By loans subject to the Credit Consumer Act (CCA)
- By loan size, broken down into the following buckets: £0–<£25,000, £25,000–<£1m, £1m–<£5m, and >£5m.
- By initial loan term, broken down into 0 to 1 year, 1 to 2 years, 3 to 4 years, 4 to 5 years, and 5+ years
- By loans subject to offset arrangements within different banking divisions
- By drawn and undrawn balances
- By repayment type (structured, amortizing or, bullet repayment)
- By legal entities (of that bank or a financial institution)
- By interest profile (i.e., fixed or floating)
- By interest margin
- By refinance rates

- By loan documentation (i.e., standard loan documentation vs. loans potentially subject to challenge)
- "Scheme flags" (e.g., for small loans guarantee schemes that are guaranteed/protected by the government and hence would need to be identified and excluded from the pool that is to be securitized)

All information should be by total number of loans in each category and by the accumulated total loan balances for each category.

Deal economics

The economics of a new transaction are driven by many factors, Basel II (and going forward Basel III) being a major one: this considers many individual factors for the calculation. As a consequence, assessing the impact of Basel II/III can only really be done on a case-by-case basis; however, the following parameters influence the regulatory capital charges:

- Applicable Basel II/III calculation rules (e.g., standardized approach vs. internal ratings–based approach or IRB)
- Asset class of the underlying collateral
- Capital structure
- Collateral quality (rating)
- Pool quality (granular vs. concentrated)
- Credit risk estimates (expressed by probability of default, PD, and loss-given default, LGD)
- Performance analytics processes
- Translation, interpretation, and implementation of regulatory policies (retention rules and regulatory treatment of securitization exposures)
- Investor risk desire/appetite
- Market conditions (risk-averse environment)
- Opportunity costs (i.e., regulatory capital costs for similar risk exposure alternatives)

To make it more complex, Basel III will be coming into play from early 2011 with various impact assessment and calibration exercises and properly from 2013 with a phased implementation until 2018.

The key Basel III features impacting securitization and structured finance transactions are as follows:

- Effective from December 31, 2010, capital charges for banking book securitization exposures have increased and banks are only permitted to invest in securitizations if the originator or arranger retains 5% of the risk, unhedged, for the life of the deal. If they do not comply with this requirement, additional risk charges will apply immediately (i.e., there is no remediation period to rectify) and the application of these risk weights may in some instances render such investments economically not feasible. Corporate loans held in the banking book will otherwise not be affected.
- Since December 31, 2010, capital charges have increased materially for banks across their trading books. Among other changes, banks are now subject to new "stressed" VaR models, increased counterparty risk charges, more restricted netting of offsetting positions, increased charges for exposures to other financial institutions, and increased capital charges for securitization exposures. Changes to the VaR models alone may double, triple, or even quadruple regulatory capital charges for loans and bonds that are "warehoused" in a bank's trading book pending syndication, depending on the bank's risk management practices and other factors.

New investor requirements

Paragraph 4, Article 122a of the Capital Requirements Directive details the new requirements for investor due diligence and with non-compliance increasing risk weights further.

Since January 1, 2011 investors are required to

- Have a comprehensive and thorough understanding of their individual securitization position including
  - —the risk characteristics of the individual tranche
  - —the risk characteristics of the underlyings
  - —the originator's or sponsor's reputation and loss experience
- Have disclosure by originator, sponsor, or original lender of the retention of net economic interest including an understanding of the due diligence statements and disclosures
- Understand the valuation methodologies and ensure the independence of the collateral valuers
- Understand all structural features that can materially impact performance
- Regularly undertake their own stress tests
- Take due care to validate and understand the relevant model methodologies, assumptions, and results.

Practical issues

The Committee of European Banking Supervisors (CEBS) consultation paper on the guidelines of Article 122a (CP40) states that "the intensity of the due diligence process may vary" depending on whether the investments are part of a trading or banking book. The key argument here is whether or not threshold due diligence requirements should apply to the trading book which, if this is the case, would contrast with the use of the trading book as an effective risk management tool. There appears to be an inconsistency between the CP40 guidance and the actual Article 122a requiring further clarification by CEBS.

It may also be difficult in practice for institutions to "justify" to regulators if and how trading book positions are held with an intention to trade, but as a result of adverse market conditions may actually not be tradable.

Reducing overreliance on credit rating agencies vs. new regulatory requirements

Industry guidelines to reduce overreliance on credit rating agencies were jointly published by AFME/ESF, the European Fund and Asset Management Association (EFAMA), and the Investment Management Association (IMA) in December 2008. They suggest that asset managers investing in structured credit products (SCPs)

- Have an obligation to act professionally and in the best interests of their clients requiring
  - —competent and diligent staff
  - —well-articulated investment processes
  - —risk analysis commensurate with the complexity of the structured product invested in and the materiality of the holding
  - —monitoring whether any determinations, opinions, or assumptions remain valid during the transaction's life
- Understand the limitations to any credit ratings and address the risks arising given that credit ratings are
  - —incomplete descriptions of riskiness
  - —of a one-dimensional nature

— unable to capture risks other than credit risks (such as liquidity, market, and operational risks)

- Understand the methodologies and competences of rating agencies
- Acknowledge that significant areas of information are not available to those relying on credit ratings including
  — expected loss distributions
  — probabilities of default
  — differences in credit assessment criteria
- Understand that credit ratings should not be the decisive factor in investment decisions.

However, this contrasts with some of the new regulation, particularly around "stress testing" suggesting that investors relying on CRA financial models cannot simply use the outputs but are also required to run the actual models themselves. Such models are not always made publicly available and, moreover, it may prove difficult to validate the agencies' assumptions that are used in structuring these deals.

Penalties for non-compliance

Failure to comply with these new requirements can lead to high penalty charges by applying additional risk weights, currently proposed to be of no less than 250% of the original risk weight.

For instance, if the original risk weight is 10%, the new risk weight would be at least $10\% + (250\% * 10\%) = 35\%$.

The (proposed) impact of non-compliance and the additional risk weights that will be added as a consequence are given in Table 5.5 (examples are based on an original RW of 10%).

In conclusion, whilst it was fairly simple to undertake and determine the economic impact of securitization transactions prior to the credit crisis, it has now become an art to figure out what the real benefit is. There are ways and means of calculating the economic benefit, but this is best done on a case-by-case basis and, unfortunately, I am not able to provide you with a template-style answer.

However, it is important to recognize that Basel's risk sensitivity is one of the key drivers of capital dynamics, and subtle nuances in a deal's capital structure can a have sizable impact on the regulatory costs.

5.10 INDICATIVE RATING AGENCY AND FINANCIAL MODELING

A crucial component of completing a securitization, especially for a first transaction, is maximizing the portion of the AAA rating from the rating agencies. Some of the issues that the rating agencies address are given in Sections 5.10, 5.11, and 5.12.

5.10.1 Operational history

For a new ABS issuer, rating agencies will first look to operational history. A greater degree of historic arrears and performance information will help to improve credit enhancement levels (by reducing the level of assumptions the rating agency would otherwise make instead of missing information). Three years of historic information is typically the minimum, 5 years is OK, 10 years is better, and anything above 15 years is fantastic, since it shows the performance through a full economic cycle.

The agencies will also look to establish the issuer's long-term viability as a servicer by examining its management expertise.

Table 5.5. Non-compliance and risk weights

Non-compliance to	*Additional risk weight* (%)	*New risk weight* (%)
Ensure disclosure by originator, sponsor, or original lender of the retention of net economic interest	1,000	110
Monitor (undertake surveillance) the ongoing performance of securitization positions	750	85
Stress-test securitization positions	500	60
Understand, analyze, and record (i.e., undertake due diligence) of		
—the risk characteristics of individual securitization positions	250	35
—the risk characteristics of underlying exposures	250	35
—the reputation and loss experience in earlier securitization transactions of originators and sponsors	250	35
—statements and disclosures made by originators or sponsors about due diligence on securitized exposures	250	35
—collateral valuation methodologies used to value collateral that supports the transaction	250	35
—structural features of the securitization that can impact the transaction's performance	250	35
For multiple breaches: Risk weights are additive, but capped at	max. 1,250	135

5.10.2 Operating procedures

Credit rating agencies will want a detailed understanding of your credit procedures, including:

- Loan/Card-underwriting criteria and approval process
- Terms of the loans
- Credit monitoring and collection procedures
- Delinquency and charge-off policy.

5.10.3 Differences in rating approaches

Credit enhancement is determined by the rating agencies, after evaluating the current, historical, and future performance of the pool of assets backing the structured finance bond. To establish its size, though, the rating agencies use different approaches.

Moody's, for instance, applies the expected loss (EL) approach, where they determine the expected losses in the pool under various scenarios. Under this approach, the expected severity of loss to investors as well as their frequency or probability of occurrence is determined. The rating agencies simulate the expected cash flows that the pool could generate, determining the potential losses that it could accumulate.

Some go further by linking the expected loss to the level of reduction of the internal rate of return (IRR) of the bond: the higher the IRR reduction, the lower the bond rating.

Other rating agencies base their assessment on the so-called weak link approach: under this methodology, the rating agencies look at the confluence of different entities and assets in the structure and determine where the structure could "break" (i.e., the weakest link in the chain of assets, counterparties, and entities). The final rating of the security can never be higher than the weakest link in the structure. On that basis, the rating agency could determine the probability of first-dollar loss, which is a methodology used by Standard & Poor's as well as Fitch's.

It is also important to understand that more often than not an asset-backed security is rated by at least two rating agencies. Each of them may use a different approach to derive the ratings and may focus on different factors or weigh the same factors differently to determine the performance under stress scenarios and related expected loss.

The credit enhancement which the respective asset-backed security carries is the highest required by any one of the rating agencies in order to achieve the desired bond rating. In this respect, it is worth investigating any split ratings that exist, especially on lower rated tranches of the securitization bonds.

5.10.4 Ratings mapping

In order to understand an originator's or issuer's internal rating system, rating agencies will analyze how closely the rating system aligns with the agency's own public credit rating scale. This analysis typically results in the credit rating agency mapping table. Although the agency may, as part of this exercise, share this information freely with the originator or issuer, it is typically not published as part of the agency's rating analysis as it represents proprietary information for the bank.

Ratings mapping exercise

Areas that are investigated as part of the agencies' mapping exercises are as follows:

- Comparing historical losses per the originator's internal rating classes vs. rating agency loss experience per rating category
- Comparing default occurrence per the originator's internal rating classes vs. rating agency loss experience per rating category
- Establishing the originator's rating dispersion compared with rating agency ratings
- Comparing the originator's ratings of non-publicly rated companies prior to obtaining public ratings
- Comparing the originator's rating transition experience to rating agency transition matrices
- Qualitative assessment of the originator's internal rating system (e.g., consistency, back testing, auditing).

Once completed and assuming that the bank's internal rating does not change or has been recalibrated, the agency may be able to reuse the derived mapping table as part of any further issuance for this particular originator or bank and any of its subsidiaries that use a similar internal rating table. In practice, this may be reflected in a quicker rating process for repeat issuance by the same originator and may reduce overall costs for assigning the credit ratings.

Although there are several ways in which originators can map the external credit ratings (Fitch, Moody's, and S&P) to its internally used ratings, it is recommended to use a similar or easily recognizable scale and classification for internal ratings.

	Fitch Ratings		Moody's		Standard & Poors		Mapped internal rating
	Long-term rating	Short-term rating	Long-term rating	Short-term rating	Long-term rating	Short-term rating	
Investment Grade	AAA	F1+	Aaa	P1	AAA	A-1+	iAAA
	AA+		Aa1		AA+		iAA+
	AA		Aa2		AA		iAA
	AA-	F1+ or F1	Aa3		AA-		iAA-
	A+		A1		A+	A-1	iA+
	A	F1	A2	P-1 or P-2	A	A-1 or A-2	iA
	A-	F1 or F2	A3	P-2	A-	A-2	iA-
	BBB+	F2	Baa1		BBB+		iBBB+
	BBB	F2 or F3	Baa2	P-2 or P-3	BBB	A-2 or A-3	iBBB
	BBB-	F3	Baa3	P-3	BBB-	A-3	iBBB-
Speculative Grade	BB+	B	Ba1	Not Prime	BB+	B Ranges within B-1, B-2 and B-3	iBB+
	BB		Ba2		BB		iBB
	BB-		Ba3		BB-		iBB-
	B+	C	B1		B+		iB+
	B		B2		B		iB
	B-		B3		B-		iB-
	CCC+		Caa1		CCC+	C	iCCC+
	CCC		Caa2		CCC		iCCC
	CCC-		Caa3		CCC-		iCCC-
	CC		Ca		CC		iCC
	C		C		C		iC
	DDD, DD, D	D			D	D	iD

Figure 5.1. Rating agency rating table and an internal rating scale.

This could easily be achieved by adding a simple prefix prior to the actual internal rating (e.g., an "i"). An external AAA rating could then be directly translated and mapped to an internal rating of "iAAA" which is more intuitive than, for instance, an "SP22" rating (given that there are 22 steps on the S&P long-term credit rating scale.)

Furthermore, someone who is not fully familiar with or who does not understand the meaning of such an internal rating will not require the tedious use of a ratings mapping table. As an added benefit, staff who are not using internal ratings frequently, and external parties such as auditors, regulators, rating agencies themselves, etc. will find a rating table which mirrors external long-term credit ratings much more intuitive.

Another important determinant when mapping the rating is finding a sensible level of granularity. Underlying risks can be more accurately represented by having a sufficiently granular breakdown of the internal rating scale. This holds particularly true for loans with lower ratings and, therefore, higher risk. The availability of granular-enough internal ratings can potentially make or break a securitization transaction. It is not unheard of for a bank to have refined its internal rating scale following an asset readiness study in order to allow future securitization for these particular assets and to support adequate treatment and pricing of riskier assets.

5.11 RATINGS MODELS

5.11.1 What is a "model" and what is it not?

A couple of things to keep in mind here are the following:

- A rating model will always be a "model" and never a true reflection of reality. The more you are relying on the model in your analysis the greater is your exposure to "model risk", meaning that the model did not do what it was meant to do (also, it is likely that it did work, but the assumptions may have been wrong or something else was a limiting factor).
- It is also important to trust your "common sense" and your "gut feeling" in the analysis you are undertaking. If something feels intuitively wrong (or smells "fishy") then it does not really matter if it's quantifiable how wrong it is (or how much it smells)—you shouldn't touch it. This is particularly important if it is other people's money that is involved and not your own. So, please *always* apply the necessary caution when using models or outputs that have been generated by models (such as credit scores, ratings, etc.).

5.11.2 Model risk

The ratings for any structured finance transaction are normally arrived at by using at least one statistical model, typically by combining several different models: for instance, synthetic CDOs are usually modeled by using a Monte Carlo model (MCM) that simulates random defaults for the selected pool of assets over a given period. The outcome of this model is then used as input for a cash flow model (CFM) that simulates the distribution of available revenue streams (i.e., interest and/ or principal) through the payment waterfall of the transaction's structure.

Typically, most of these models are based on an Excel file with some or all of the scenario simulations working on plug-ins in the background. Although the input values are usually clear and reconcilable, these values are used to undertake the Monte Carlo simulation which works via these Excel plug-ins. These plug-ins accommodate the large number of simulations necessary to get statistically meaningful results. However, they also have the disadvantage that some of these simulations are not easily reconcilable and, therefore, place some reliance on the proper functioning of these models.

Although rating agencies are trying to simulate as many factors as technically possible with these models, such modeled environments will never be fully able to mirror reality and, therefore, are naturally limited. That, in itself, represents the risk of overreliance on such models.

The rating agencies are aware of these limitations and are frequently trying to identify mitigants by adjusting the model assumptions as part of the qualitative deal analysis they undertake. Such adjustments are often reflected in the results of the rating models either by using additional

- *Stress factors*. These are multipliers for better rated tranches: for instance, five times (5×) for AAA rating stress, four times (4×) for AA rating stress, three times (3×) for A rating stress, etc.
- *Haircuts*. These are reductions of values that are used to determine, for example, assumed property values: 30% haircut at AAA rating scenarios, 20% haircut at AA rating scenarios, 10% haircut at BBB rating scenarios, etc.
- *Caps*. These are limitations applied, for instance, to recovery rates, assuming that the maximum recovery on a defaulted property that goes into foreclosure would be 60% of the last valuation for a AAA rating scenario, 70% for a A rating scenario, and 80% for a B rating scenario. Alternatively, we could say that there has been a 40% haircut on triple-A, 30% on single-A, and 20% on single-B rating scenarios.

5.11.3 Model selection risk

In addition to the model risk explained above, there is another model-related risk: the risk of selecting the "right" model. This applies where rating agencies are using different types of models for rating the same asset classes. Originators as well as investors are therefore somewhat reliant on the agency's selection of the appropriate model in order to assign the ratings to such a transaction.

5.11.4 Expected vs. unexpected (extreme) events

Most models are built to cater for expected events, such as expected defaults and expected recoveries leading to expected losses. By definition, however, this also means that unexpected events are usually not intrinsically reflected in these models. Some events of a more extreme nature may be addressed as part of the assumptions that were used to model such transactions; however, in many cases they have not always been clearly articulated.

5.11.5 Modeling method

Different modeling methods (and assumptions) will have a direct impact on the ratings output. For instance, a so-called Monte Carlo approach (named after the famous race track) is used for modeling the risk inherent in a corporate loan portfolio. This technique involves the random sampling of each probability distribution within the model to produce thousands of scenarios. Therefore, the distribution of the values calculated for the model outcome reflects the probability of the values that could occur. In modeling, for example, a CLO portfolio, up to 100,000 simulations will be used.

5.11.6 Model overview, by asset class and by rating agency

Table 5.6 shows what models are currently available by asset class and by rating agency. The information has been compiled based on information available on the agencies' websites.

Whilst the models and the methodology do not tend to change often, the assumptions used in these models can and do change frequently. Since the advent of the credit crisis, assumptions for the structured finance models by all three agencies have changed in some cases more than once within 6 months. I believe that the high frequency of changes to model assumptions not only reflects changed economic trends in the relevant models, such as decreasing house price index, market value declines of residential properties, and changed borrower attitudes particularly in the U.S., but is also due to the credit rating agencies tightening their models up in order to address some of the criticism they received during the credit crisis. In theory, ratings and the models used to assign these ratings follow a "through-the-cycle" approach, which means they should be relatively resilient to "market noise" and, therefore, unaffected by short-term volatility. However, as recent downgrades and agency research justifying these rating actions would suggest, ratings generally do not reflect extreme risks and, therefore, in many cases would not withstand extreme economic cycle movements as seen from 2007 to 2010. We could now also argue that lessons will have to be learned, not only by the agencies themselves, but also by the users of the agencies' rating models which may help to avoid overreliance on these models for future analysis.

Rating agency model overview

As already mentioned, Table 5.6 provides an overview of the publicly available rating agency models at the time of writing this book. It only lists the latest version of each available model, and the reader

Table 5.6. Rating models by asset class and agency

Rating agency	*Model*	*Description*	*Publication/ Release date*	*Comments*
		Asset-backed securities (ABS)		
S&P	"Auto model"?	Auto loan level analytics	April 24, 2007	
Fitch	ASB European VECTOR model	Multi-risk factor Monte Carlo simulation model	October 11 2006	
		Mortgage-backed securities (RMBS)		
S&P	LEVELS 6.4.3	U.S. RMBS loss severity scoring model	July 15, 2008	Revised assumption
S&P	SPIRE 3.1	U.S. residential mortgage cash flow model	April 7, 2008	More flexibility and revised assumptions
S&P	DACSS	Document and collateral scoring system	August 28, 2002	
Moody	MILAN		May 4, 2007	
Fitch	INTEX Dealmaker and OC Sizer	RMBS INTEX-based cash flow model	September 5, 2006	Assumptions published on Fitch's website
		Commercial mortgage-backed securities (CMBS)		
Moody		Market-based loan model	July 27, 2006	
		Collateralized debt obligations		
Fitch	VECTOR model V3.2	Multi-risk factor Monte Carlo simulation model	November 15, 2007	Updated model
Moody	CDOROMTM Japan	Synthetic CDO simulation model	March 3, 2008	New model
Moody	CDOROM	Synthetic CDO simulation model	January 9, 2008	Updated model
S&P	SPB Evaluator	U.S. small business portfolio model	November 6, 2007	Revised assumption
		Collateralized loan obligations, collateralized bond obligations, and CLNs		
Fitch	Portfolio Credit Model V.1.1.10	Multi-period Monte Carlo simulation model and structural form methodology	July 15, 2008	For CDO of corporate and asset-backed securities
S&P	CLO/CBO model	Default model applying to CLO/CBO and CLNs	February 24, 1999	New model
		Small-and-medium-enterprise CDO (SME CDO)		
Fitch	VECTOR SME Model V1.0	Multi-risk factor Monte Carlo simulation model (Build VECTOR V3.1)	March 1, 2007	New model
		Counterparty-related models		
S&P		Capital adequacy models for mortgage insurers and financial guarantors	May 7, 2007	Model adaptations

Source: Fitch Ratings, Moody's Investor Services, Standard & Poor's.

may find that some of these do change considerably over time. This holds particularly true for the 2-year period after August 2007. When the liquidity crisis and the subsequent credit crisis started, all three agencies became the subject of considerable pressure by the market and revisited their models in order to reflect the changed economic environment in the agencies' model assumptions.

As rating models should apply a through-the-cycle approach, this would further imply that the agencies need to be supplied with full historical information on the performance of the assets including both upward and downward cyclical movements. However, in practice, many innovative structured products have underlyings that themselves have only been in existence for a limited period of years and would not cover a whole cycle. One of these assets would be buy-to-let mortgages in the U.K. Based on the limited history of these types of loans—which crucially does not go back to 1992/1993, the last recession in the U.K.—it is difficult to see how these products could have been appropriately modeled by the agencies. Of course, the agencies would rightly acknowledge this fact and make adjustments to their assumptions (e.g., by applying harsher stresses or higher haircuts). However, applying such stresses does not necessarily mean that they are appropriate.

For more seasoned products where sufficient data could be available to cover a whole economic cycle, it is questionable whether the originator can actually supply such information—both for the period concerned and on the detailed level required by the agencies. Again, in practice it is likely that an originator has only been originating particular products for a limited number of years, or the originator's account systems may not have been built with a view to originate to distribute (i.e., securitize), and many general ledger systems of banks that hold the relevant customer and loan records were built 20+ years ago and, therefore, are outdated and in need of modernization.

In addition, an originator may simply have not stored a long history of data and chose to keep only the customer and loan information that is legally required by document retention rules.

Important: Table 5.6 should only be considered an overview to illustrate which models are currently publicly available from the rating agencies and by asset class. It has been compiled by searching the agencies' individual websites for the term "model" and then by further filtering for "structured finance". Such a search, however, relies on the proper "tagging" of information, and anecdotal evidence suggests that this is not always working correctly, meaning that although a model is available on the website, it may not be easily identifiable. I recommend for any originator planning to issue a new deal as well as to any investor looking at analyzing an existing transaction by using these models, to actively seek a dialogue with the relevant analyst at the rating agency in question. This is, first, to ensure that the correct model is selected for the right analytical task and, second, to confirm that an up-to-date model version is used.

From an originator's perspective, it is even more important to select the correct models at a very early stage of a transaction: the chosen model will have an impact on the fields required in order to fill it with the relevant information and be able to run it. In other words, the discussion and selection of the right model with the rating agencies involved should be led as part of the "asset readiness and feasibility study" phase. It may even help to provide more color on the anticipated deal from a rating agency perspective (e.g., any similar deals that are currently structured by other institutions and that may have an impact on pricing the originator's own deal).

The following section provides a brief overview of some of the methodologies used by CRAs in order to model these deals. It is by no means exhaustive and many of them are likely to have changed as a direct consequence of the credit crisis. Hence, it is of utmost importance that originators/structurers consult with the CRAs to understand which rating criteria are currently in use for a particular asset class.

5.12 RATING METHODOLOGIES

5.12.1 Overview

This chapter provides more details on the rating agency methodologies used to structure transactions. Structured by asset class and then further divided by rating agency, Appendix B lists the latest known rating methodologies (at the time of writing this book), refer to the latest model and model version used, look at typical assumptions used to analyze such structures, and look at rating agency typical stresses, such as rating multipliers for various rating levels, haircuts, length of historical data required—to name a few.

We will further take a closer look at the crucial assumptions made by the agencies to model these transactions and assign the ratings. Depending on the asset class and the agency model, typical model parameters are default assumptions (probability of default and expected default), loss assumptions (loss-given default, expected loss, unexpected loss), recovery assumptions (recovery rates), and correlation.

This information may be of particular use for originators who are familiar and have previously structured assets belonging to a particular asset class and would now like to extend their structuring activities.

Furthermore, readers coming from an investor background wishing to analyze a particular asset class and with a need to understand rating agency methodologies as well as models in greater depth may also find the information contained in Appendix B useful.

5.12.2 Initial deal analysis

A crucial component of completing any securitization transaction is securing ratings from the credit rating agencies. All three of the major agencies (i.e., Fitch Rating, Moody's, and Standard & Poor's) have been active in the structured finance market by covering the major asset classes. Whilst some deals are rated by all three agencies, there are quite a few transactions which carry only two ratings—the majority of these are rated by Moody's and Standard & Poor's. Far fewer transactions are rated by only one agency.

An originator needs to balance carefully between the cost of his transaction (as ratings can be expensive) and the core investor's attitude with regard to the number of ratings available for such a deal. Some investors have a preference for at least two different agencies rating the transaction they invest in. Other investors may be reluctant to purchase any bond that has not been rated by their preferred agency and so on.

5.12.3 Private vs. public rating

Another factor for the type of rating is the originator's future strategy for placing the particular deal in the markets. If it is a one-off placement with a small syndicate of sophisticated investors, then private ratings may be fully sufficient for the purpose of this transaction and in order to place the bond. Private ratings—sometimes also called "private credit assessments"—usually have specific caveats and exclusions in the rating analysis and explicitly state these areas are not part of the analytical process in the normal rating letter. Due to this fact and that, for instance, legal opinions may not be required, private ratings are usually considerably cheaper than public ratings.

However, in order to support secondary-market trading for a new issue, public ratings are a must, but no guarantee of any subsequent secondary-market trading activity.

Transactions that are not rated or have unfavorable ratings from the agencies may be penalized by investors. In that sense, it is a crucial part of the securitization process and of great importance to satisfy rating agency requirements regarding the transaction structure, modeling, loan origination and servicing, loan and structural legal documentation, and last but not least data collection.

From an originator's perspective, it is important to acknowledge that each of the agencies uses slightly different rating methodologies, all of which are published as "rating criteria" on their websites. However, each transaction's rating is to some extent also subject to unpublished qualitative judgments that can have an impact on the transaction's structure, the level of credit enhancement required, and the ultimate rating of the transaction.

5.12.4 Split rating

Whilst the models used by the agencies can be quite similar for certain asset classes, we would expect a transaction to get comparable ratings assigned by any agency. However, subtle differences in rating methodology, modeling assumptions, and qualitative analytical judgments together with the typical rating committee view decision may lead to differences in the final ratings—sometimes also referred to as "split ratings".

An originator or an arranging bank which is co-ordinating a bond issue would typically become aware of such rating agency differences at a late stage of a transaction and could then respond either by changing the capital structure, required credit enhancement levels, or by adding further structural safeguards, but any of these features would make a transaction more expensive. Alternatively, and this has happened frequently, originators that are facing a split-rating decision and are not willing to make amendments to the deal may ask the agency with the more stringent rating requirements not to assign a rating to the deal in question, a practice also known as "rating shopping". Of course, this action can have negative repercussions in the market. Investors who become aware of such circumstances may seek an active dialogue with the agency that has been asked to withdraw from the rating process in order to understand why it did not rate this particular deal and what the particular concerns were that could not be overcome. If this agency was the investor's risk management department's preferred agency for a particular asset class and would not provide a rating in such instance, investors may choose not to purchase such bonds due to the missing agency rating.

5.12.5 Due diligence

Analysis and desktop-based modeling may form the largest part of rating agency activities, but in order to understand the originator, its assets, and the operational setup, rating agencies will usually also undertake a so-called "due diligence" or "servicer review" visit. Such a due diligence review typically lasts a day, but can be longer, for instance, for pan-European CMBS deals where the assets that are to be securitized are geographically diversified.

Many topics that may have already been discussed at an earlier kickoff presentation of the anticipated deal can form part of such due diligence. The areas for discussion can vary greatly for different asset classes and originators; however, generic areas that are usually covered include

- Company overview
  - background
  - organizational structure
  - financial history and projections—ideally, a 5+-year history and a 5+-year forecast
  - finance operations and funding activities

- Overview of relevant line of business (e.g., mortgage origination)
  - background
  - organizational structure
  - competitive positioning
- Origination and underwriting of assets
  - sources of origination
  - marketing (geographic region, pricing, products and new business plans, customer base)
  - underwriting/lending criteria
    - loan characteristics, max/min loan size, average loan size, interest rates, maturity profile, payment dates, payment method
    - insurance, if required, including coverage, amount, provider, method or premium payment
    - borrower information, such as income verification, employment history, credit bureau checks, setting of borrower credit limits
  - lending process
  - credit scoring (score used in loan approval, system/scoring methodology, score review frequency)
  - approval process and credit review
    - organization/experience of staff
    - lending authority
    - quality controls and audit
    - fraudulent claims
    - file maintenance and retention
  - valuations
    - in-house/external
    - qualifications, training, and accreditation
    - servicing and collection of assets
  - collection procedures
  - writeoff, foreclosure, and impairment procedures
    - foreclosure stages
    - specific foreclosure stages
    - recovery timing
  - arrears management
    - organization and number of staff
    - in-house or external collection
    - seasonality of arrears/defaults
    - primary causes for arrears
    - legal costs for foreclosure proceedings
    - penalty interest policy
    - arrears/default definition and reporting
  - prepayments (procedures, reasons, penalities)
  - extension/rewrite policies
  - file storage and business continuity planning
  - size of organization and staff experience
- Technology and computer systems
  - software
    - software packages
    - backup procedures and facilities
    - disaster recovery plan
    - system "flagging" or identification of securitized loan

- ○ hardware
  - ▪ hardware configuration
  - ▪ backup procedures and facilities
  - ▪ disaster recovery plan.

5.12.6 Rating agency methodologies, models, and analytical assumptions

Appendix B provides an overview per asset class and rating agency of the current methodologies—sometimes referred to as rating criteria—that are applied in order to assign ratings to these transactions. In my view, describing the methodology is not an isolated view of the published rating criteria. It goes far beyond this level and should include the following aspects:

- Type of rating agency model and model version
- Modeling assumptions such as probability of default (PD), expected and unexpected losses (EL and UL), loss-given default (LGD) and various correlations (industry, region, etc.)
- Multipliers and haircuts applied for various rating levels
- Minimum data requirements, typically at least 3 years of historical data, better 5 years, and ideally 10+ years of data history that cover a full economic cycle.

Some of these rating parameters are more deal independent and should therefore apply to any given transaction in this particular asset class. These would be mainly quantitative factors that are part of the asset class methodology and model rather than parameters of the individual deal. However, as the agency analysis will always be a combination of quantitative and qualitative analysis, some parameters—such as haircuts, rating multipliers, and even correlations—will be more of a qualitative nature. Any analyst looking at the results of the ratings agency analysis should apply a cautious approach to understanding whether a particular parameter is more quantitative or qualitative in nature and the impact on and its contribution to the overall ratings. Ratings are, ultimately, nothing more than an expression of an opinion—and we can then decide whether it is an opinion worth agreeing with or whether there is room for disagreement.

Appendix B lists the currently published criteria from Fitch Ratings, Moody's, and Standard & Poor's by asset class in reverse chronological order and indicates whether the relevant criteria apply globally or to a certain region. The list per agency commences with the overarching criteria that apply to all structured finance bonds and are hence asset class generic; it then refers to counterparty-related criteria which are also asset class generic but may differ functionally (e.g., servicers, swap counterparties, facility providers, and financial guarantors). Each list then looks at asset class–specific criteria for: namely, asset-backed securitizations (ABS), collateralized debt obligations (CDOs) and related products, covered bonds, commercial mortgage-backed securitizations, real estate investment trusts (REITs), hybrid instruments, and residential mortgage-backed securitizations. Only this high-level categorization has been used in order to enable the reader to compare these criteria across different agencies. If, for instance, you are looking for "subprime"-related criteria, then you should look first under the heading "Residential mortgage-backed securitization" and then at the U.S. entries.

All this information has been sourced from the agencies' websites. You can find an Excel document on the book's companion website (*www.structuredfinanceguide.com*) which contains these lists and hyperlinks so that you can conveniently click and go straight to the agencies' websites for these reports. When doing so, please note that you may be required to set yourself up as a user. Once you've created a user profile for yourself (in fact, you will need three: one for Moody's, one for Standard & Poor's, and one for Fitch Ratings), you should in theory be able to access the relevant criteria information without having to subscribe (i.e., pay) for the agencies' services—unless you require additional information such as performance reports, etc. Unfortunately, I cannot, however, guarantee that you will always be able to get this information. Furthermore, note that the information in Appendix B is a reflection of the agencies' information at the time of writing this book and relies to some extent on the electronic tags applied to these reports by the agencies. Websites can change quickly and the agencies have recently been very active in improving their websites—some of this was of course due to political pressure and the European rating agency regulation that was finalized in the middle of 2010. Whilst Appendix B can give you a good overview of published criteria as well as an idea of how many of these ultimately underwent change during the credit crisis, please refer to the agencies directly in order to ensure that you are using the most up-to-date criteria.

Finally, looking at the sheer volume of published criteria, it is important that you ensure your firm has sufficient analytical staff to digest the relevant information in order to understand how certain deals are rated and the quantitative and qualitative differences that occur when analyzing them. If your firm is sitting, for instance, on a structured finance portfolio of say 750 bonds evenly spread across different asset classes and geographies, then you will probably need a small team of analysts who specialize in these asset classes so that you can stay on top of your portfolio's performance.

6

Pre close

6.1 TYPICAL EXECUTION TIMING

An ABS offering could be typically completed in approximately 3 months (see Table 6.1).

Table 6.1. An ABS offering

Preliminary events and rating agencies (Month 1)	*Documentation* (Month 2)	*Marketing and pricing* (Month 3)
All hands organizational meeting	Receive preliminary rating indications	Receive preliminary ratings
Discuss structure of documentation	Legal due diligence	Print and distribute "red herrings"
Due diligence	Preparation of offering circular	Roadshow
Finalize term sheet	Preparation of transaction documents	One-on-one meetings/calls with institutional investors
Initial meetings with rating agencies	Begin pre marketing	Price transaction
On-site rating agency due diligence	Continue rating agency discussions	Finalize all documentation
		Close transaction

6.2 EXECUTION RESOURCES

This section lists the key resources required by an originator to successfully execute a securitization transaction by outlining the typical personnel and department that would provide such a resource. In addition, we will take a closer look at the typical role such staff play as part of executing a transaction and give an indication of the required time (depending on the nature of the transaction).

In practice, this may vary to some extent, depending on the individual circumstances, such as nature and the jurisdiction of the originator's business, whether this is a tactical deal or forms part of a strategic securitization platform, and the asset class considered for securitization.

6.2.1 Board level

As outlined earlier, it is advisable to decide an organisation's securitization strategy at group board level to ensure these activities fit into the overall business model and finance strategy.

6.2.2 Senior management

Senior management should be involved at an early stage in the overall discussion and workshops, ideally from the asset readiness phase onwards. This enables the execution project team to gauge opinion and high-level insight at an early stage.

At a later stage, senior management will likely be involved in presenting the company's overall corporate strategy in rating agency and investor presentations. The required senior management time for both funded transactions as well as synthetic deals is moderate, but nevertheless crucial for a successful deal.

6.2.3 Deal manager or program director

A deal can be considered a large-scale project with various phases or key milestones. Hence, it is logical to set up an execution management that is closely aligned to a typical project management structure and governance structure where the deal manager coordinates the day-to-day activities between the various other internal and external execution counterparties involved. The key responsibilities among others here are to monitor, control, and liaise with execution personnel, legal counsel, accountants, rating agencies, and an arranger bank. The time required is usually lengthy for funded transactions and would in most cases justify a full-time program manager. Synthetic transactions, in contrast, require less of the program manager's time.

6.2.4 Chief legal counsel or legal department

The involvement of these internal departments is usually moderate for both funded and synthetic transactions as external law firms normally undertake the majority of the legal work. That said, the legal department's task is to review the transaction's necessary documentation as well as legal opinions provided by external lawyers. In addition, legal counsel can also coordinate communication with the regulatory authorities such as the FSA and credit rating agencies.

6.2.5 Systems and technology departments

Depending on how the overall structure is set up (i.e., tactical vs. strategic platform) and how closely the IT function is aligned with the relevant business areas, the systems or technology department can play either a greater or lesser role as part of any deal execution. That said, most of the static and to a larger extent dynamic data on securitized assets is typically derived from the originator's source systems, such as general ledger accounts, etc.

The key involvement of IT in funded transactions is the provision of portfolio data as well as ongoing performance data to the arranging/structuring bank as well as to the transaction's accountants, trustee, and the credit rating agencies.

The time it takes these technology areas and subject matter areas to carry out their tasks depends on the deal structure, and is considerably longer for funded transactions.

Given that the risk transfer for synthetic deals is on a "synthetic" basis, meaning that the securitized assets remain on the originator's balance sheet and are not physically removed, there's usually only a moderate requirement for IT department involvement in synthetic deal structures.

Technology departments can become involved at a very early stage of any transaction. The feasibility and asset readiness study requires detailed knowledge about asset data (i.e., information on loan data) and how this is processed in the originator's general ledger system, relationship management system, and risk management system. Systems experts usually become involved once it has become clear which assets are under consideration for securitization and it is clear what kind of data are required as part of this particular deal type, either by the market (i.e., investors) or by the rating agencies (i.e., pre-issuance, closing, and post-issuance data requirements).

These data requirements drive this discussion, which usually starts at a fairly senior level, and their fulfillment depends on answering the following questions:

- What asset-specific data are required, by whom, and in which format?
- Which systems are likely to hold this information? (It helps if the originator has a centralized data catalog for any kind of data field detailing the system in which this information is stored and who is responsible within the organization for these particular systems.)

Following this initial system identification, it is important to conduct a detailed discussion with the relevant systems owners in order to assess whether the particular system and the asset data held is suitable for securitization.

In addition, systems and technology departments play a crucial role in any completed securitization transaction: both the asset as well as the liability side require effective processing of transaction-related data. This could either be detailed information on the underlying assets on a loan-by-loan basis or cash management–related information on cash flows through the various transaction ledger accounts. Furthermore, most transactions have a given set of transactional triggers (i.e., early amortization triggers), thresholds and limits (i.e., borrower concentration limits), and "slicing and dicing" mechanisms (i.e., presenting portfolio delinquency, default, and loss data) in various "default buckets".

Overall, systems departments' responsibilities as part of any securitization will be to provide assistance in the development of the relevant transaction servicing and reporting capabilities, building the software that is necessary to support these activities, and to manage procedures as part of this process.

6.2.6 Loan operations unit or "asset" processing unit

These business units may need to provide some information or details of how the loans are currently processed and on the overall servicing procedures as part of rating agency due diligence. This may include information on systems solutions used to process the information, general high-level statistics of serviced pools, and potentially some information on the loan documentation and terms and conditions (T&Cs); for instance, the loan documentation that is currently used, particularly for the types of loan products that are to be included in the securitization transaction. Depending on the organizational setup of the originator (i.e., centralized loan origination/processing unit vs. specialized regional lending teams), it may be necessary for these teams to participate in the provision of a random sample of actual loan documentation.

In addition, it may be necessary to get these teams involved in the so-called "flagging" of loans which have been transferred to a special purpose vehicle and, therefore, need to be identified in the originator's loan administration system. Overall, the level of involvement from these business units for both funded as well as synthetic transactions is expected to be moderate to low.

6.2.7 Credit department and/or credit policy units

Whilst the actual involvement of these business units in the pre-close phase is moderate for both funded as well as synthetic transactions, involvement in the feasibility and asset readiness phases can be considerably higher.

Key tasks are the provision of details on underwriting and the overall credit review process. This will not only cover how (and based on which criteria) credit is currently underwritten and how the resulting risk is managed, but also potentially the historical evolution of terms and conditions and of the originator's underwriting process(es).

6.2.8 Accounting and/or tax management

It is useful to get the originator's accounting and/or tax management department involved at an early stage of the transaction. The key objective is to develop a robust strategy and procedures to account for assets securitized as part of any securitization transaction. Tax specialists are also required to evaluate the transaction structure and see whether and how this ties into the company's overall tax planning. One major benefit of using special purpose vehicles for securitization transactions is the optimization of tax efficiencies by selecting jurisdictions with beneficial tax regimes for these types of transactions, usually the British Isles, Ireland, Cayman Islands, etc. The company's tax department can help in developing and assessing the accounting and tax strategy for individual deals.

6.2.9 Relationship managers

Sampling of loan files and relevant obligor information by assessing electronic and paper files is one area that will most likely involve the assistance of relationship managers. The level of their involvement depends on whether there is a centralized loan operations function including file storage or if the information is stored locally (i.e., in the Main Street branch or regional processing units). A funded transaction would require a higher level of involvement as part of the loan sampling and documentation review.

Subject to type and size of the individual transaction structure and the number and granularity of loans involved, relationship managers can play an important part in securitization; however, they may not always be aware of the particular transaction and of the fact that some or all loans within their responsibility (i.e., the risk they have originally underwritten) may be or have been securitized. Random sampling and loan selection for the purpose of the securitization helps avoid "cherry-picking" and instances where relationship management passed their lower quality loans on to the securitization department and kept the higher quality and better performing loans on their own books.

6.2.10 Transaction support staff/business analysts

Depending on whether the deal scope is tactical or more strategic in nature, an originator can either identify and select a pool of staff within the departments listed as part of this section or, alternatively, assign this role to a team of business analysts and subject matter experts. The main support tasks are the location of physical and electronic client documentation and loan files for the random sample review. This review can have various requesters, such as the arranging bank, legal deal counsel, and likely the rating agencies. Th review can happen in various stages either in the asset readiness and feasibility phase or the pre-close phase.

In addition to documentation review, support staff may also be involved in further data collection, either from physical files or electronic entry of data (i.e., "hard" system flags—for loans that actually form part of the pool that will be securitized).

6.3 TRANSACTION COUNTERPARTIES

This section provides an overview of the typical counterparties involved in structured finance transactions, discusses the typical types of entities and their involvement in the deal, and the transaction document(s) that are normally entered into by the relevant parties. Section 6.4 explores these documents further. But, first, let us take a closer look at the counterparties and start with one of the most important ones.

6.3.1 Originator

The *originator* (also referred to as the "seller") of the assets is usually made up either by large financial institutions or large corporates or commercial entities that specialize in originating "assets". Being the driving force behind the securitization, the originator has usually generated the assets or receivables which are then sold to the SPV. Typically, the originator and seller of assets also acts as the servicer and provides further support to the SPV in the form of liquidity, subordinated loans, or by supplementing yield. The agreements entered into are the sale agreement, service agreement, as well as the credit enhancement and liquidity support agreement.

6.3.2 Investors

The other side in the equation of a structured finance transaction is taken, of course, by the *investors* (or buyers, bondholders, noteholders). Typically, they cover the spectrum of institutional investors meaning banks, financial institutions, insurance companies, asset managers, pension funds, hedge funds, companies, and in some instances high-net-worth individuals. Although there are no minimum amounts for such investments—depending on the seniority of the tranche, its rating, and other general market conditions—the realistic amounts you could see (i.e., in a functioning market) are between \$5m (for lowest rated equity or near equity tranches) up to \$150m (for highly rated senior tranches). Some institutions have considerably larger investments of super senior tranches up to \$500m and greater and would then typically have divested the credit risk by entering into credit default swaps, something that is known as "negative basis trade". The investors' relationship with the special purpose vehicle from which they are purchasing the notes and, in addition, the principal and interest payments by the SPV to the noteholders are governed by the securities purchase agreement.

Whilst the previous two counterparties are poles apart representing the "supply" (originator) and "demand" (investor) spectrum, the following counterparties sit somewhat in between them and facilitate the transaction in one way or another by passing on funds (cash managers, paying agents, trustees), providing the means to trading these deals (arrangers, managers), providing the reporting (seller, servicer, trustee, accountants), securing and representing counterparty interest (trustee, security trustee), looking after the collateral (investment or collateral manager, collateral administrator), providing structural safeguards (credit enhancement, liquidity facility, swap provider, and other financial guarantors), providing deal-related analysis (lawyers and credit rating agencies), providing settlement services (clearing systems), providing confirmation and verification of financial information (accountants), and last but not least ensuring proper listing and admission into trading (listing agent and stock exchange). Let us now take an in-depth look at these counterparties to understand their roles, types of entities, involvement in the transaction, and documents that govern these relationships.

6.3.3 Special purpose vehicle (SPV)

A key function in many structures is provided by the *special purpose vehicle* (SPV, sometimes referred to as the special purpose entity or SPE). The SPV is the "vehicle" to conduct the transaction and, therefore, is usually erected by the originator or the arranger. It issues debt securities to the investors to fund in turn the acquisition rights for the purchase of assets from the originator, and its major purpose is to isolate the assets or receivables that will serve to redeem the securities from the assets or receivables pool of the originator by "ring-fencing" and making them "bankruptcy remote" from the credit risk of the originator.

Whilst an SPV's precise legal status varies very widely with the jurisdiction in which it is established, the common denominator is that it is normally a separate legal entity and not legally related to any other participants in the securitization transaction. It is usually established solely for the purpose of the structured finance deal, will likely have no employees, and is not going to conduct any other business than that set out in the transaction documents. Furthermore, as SPVs are intended to be virtually cost neutral, they will often be incorporated in a low-tax or no-tax jurisdiction and, hence, there are countries and jurisdictions that are particularly SPV friendly. These include:

- British Virgin Islands
- Cayman Islands
- Guernsey
- Ireland
- Jersey
- Luxembourg

6.3.4 Services

For non-CDO transactions, another key part is played by the *servicer* of the transaction, which, in essence, is often (at least initially) the originator or a company within the originator's group of companies. In some cases, following its appointment by the originator, a third-party provider may be used to service the assets or receivables. Acting as an agent to the SPV, the servicer is typically appointed by the SPV, and their relationship is governed by the servicing agreement. The key responsibilities include ensuring that the underlying collateral is properly administered ("serviced") and monies due on the underlying assets or receivables are duly received, collected, and overdue payments properly enforced. The servicer is typically remunerated by the SPV for the duties is provides as part of the servicing agreement with the SPV.

6.3.5 Arranger

Another key role is played by the *arranger*, which is normally a financial institution that is appointed by the originator. The arranger is tasked with structuring the transaction by creating different tranches, arranging credit arbitrage, credit and liquidity support, developing methods to extract profit from the structure, and to find counterparties that are willing to collaborate by catering for some of the risks. Whilst the arranger is there to ensure the transaction progresses through each stage of the structuring lifecycle, he also agrees to initially buy the securities. There are various documents that are entered into by the arranger—namely, the subscription agreement, offering circulars, and agreements amongst other managers.

6.3.6 Managers

Managers (as counterparties to the transaction) are typically other financial institutions that agree, together with the arranger, to initially purchase the issued notes. Subsequently, managers are then tasked with finding appropriate investors that are willing to purchase the issued bonds from them.

6.3.7 Trustee and security trustee

Key to the transaction are the trustees—namely, the trustee and the security trustee. The trustee can also act as *security trustee*. Whilst this may be slightly confusing, one way to determine the different types of trustees is by looking at the deeds: the trust deed (for the trustee) and security trust deed (for the security trustee). Whilst both trustees are usually represented by a professional corporate trustee and are appointed by the SPV, the trustee holds benefits of covenants and rights in the securities on behalf of the investors, whereas the security trustee secures the interest of the investors and other parties.

6.3.8 Investment or collateral manager

For CDO-type transactions, another key counterparty that is appointed by the SPV is the *investment or collateral manager*, which is an independent party and usually has expertise and specialist knowledge in the investments held by the SPV. The relationship between both parties is governed by the investment management agreement. This applies typically to portfolios that are actively managed by such an investment manager due to the dynamic nature of the underlying receivables (e.g., in a managed CDO). The collateral manager's contractual duties include the following:

- Determination of the underlying portfolio
- Provide reporting and audit of the receivables
- Undertake asset valuations
- Manage the receivables purchase and disposal process
- May be required to hold a junior tranche of the transaction to ensure there is sufficient incentive to hold and manage these underlying assets.

Furthermore, the management fee that is typically paid to the investment manager can be based on a percentage of the average balance of the receivables portfolio or a fee incentive that represents a proportion of receipts that exceed certain minimum thresholds, which would indicate the portfolio has been successfully managed.

6.3.9 Collateral administrator

A *collateral administrator*, who will administer the collateral for the underlying securities, may also be appointed and, if so, will enter into a collateral administration agreement with the SPV. The key tasks of the collateral administrator are

- Provision and maintenance of an inventory or database containing the contents of the underlying asset portfolio
- Executing performance tests
- Report provision and managing asset valuations for the pool of underlying receivables
- Calculation of payment and other receivable requirements
- Administration of bank accounts and execution of payments subject to transaction documentation.

6.3.10 Swap counterparties

Most structured finance transactions make active use of one or more *swap counterparties* who enter a contract via swap documents and thereby take on certain transactional risks such as interest rate risk, exchange rate risk, basis risks, timing risks, and cash flow–based risks. The swap counterparty in turn will usually receive a fee for providing coverage for those risks.

6.3.11 Liquidity provider

The *liquidity provider* provides a liquidity facility which is meant to be a supporting source of cash that can be used to make timely payments of interest and principal for bond tranches that are experiencing a temporary shortfall in the cash flow that is generated by the underlying assets. Any amounts drawn under such a liquidity facility arrangement become a senior obligation of the issuer in the waterfall (unlike credit enhancement draws) and will then rank at least *pari passu* with the securities they support and relate to. For asset-backed commercial paper programs, the rating agencies require that such a liquidity facility is sufficiently sized so that it could support not only temporary cash flow problems on a transaction basis but also that the risk arising from disruption to the commercial paper market is covered. Furthermore, in case there is a currency mismatch between the issued ABCP and the underlying assets, the rating agencies will also ask for the liquidity facility to be sized in a way that could cover disrupted currency swap markets.

6.3.12 Rating agencies

The role played by *rating agencies* such as Moody's Investor Services, Standard & Poor's, and Fitch Ratings is far-reaching throughout the deal lifecycle: they get involved at relatively early stages when a transaction is structured, then undertake their initial analysis in order to rate a transaction, either publicly or privately, and play an integral part through their surveillance and performance analytics role that will accompany the deal throughout its life.

6.3.13 Lawyers

Independently of a transaction's nature, you will require the assistance of transaction *lawyers*, which are usually appointed by originators, arranger bank, trustees, investment managers, paying agents, and other parties via a retainer contract. Some law firms have specialist structured finance teams that will focus almost exclusively on securitization-related issues and within these teams there are lawyers that specialize in certain asset classes and transaction structures. Transaction lawyers ensure the legal efficacy of the transaction and their responsibilities include

- Provision of legal advice on legal, regulatory, and taxation aspects of the proposed transaction structure
- Managing documentation-related legal aspects and provision of guidance through the early life of the transaction from initial idea via term sheet to close.
- Drafting, negotiating the legal documents, and identifying any issues concerning the legal enforceability of the transaction documents
- Establishment of the legal entities involved in the transaction
- Undertaking due diligence of the underlying assets and aspects of the offering circular
- The law firm appointed by the arranger is typically tasked with drafting the transaction's principal documents and with coordinating, discussing, and liaising with the rating agencies in order to discuss new complex transactional features and understand their implications in legal terms.

6.3.14 Accountants

Accountants are also contracted by the originator and the SPV—typically on a retainer basis. Some of the information they produce is, with the accountancy firm's consent, included in the offering circular and is the result of the various activities and transactional responsibilities they get involved with:

- Execution of the transaction's cash flow modeling and financial analysis of the underlying collateral
- Confirmation of SPV-related and guarantor-related financial information, financial audit of the SPV, and provision of the SPV's financial statements
- Frequent due diligence of the SPV's financial position and statements.

6.3.15 Listing agent

A so-called *listing agent* will usually be appointed prior to the close of a transaction by either the arranger or the lawyers acting on behalf of the arranger. Typically, listing agents are specialized units of a law firm or corporate administration entity that is based within the jurisdictional reach of the stock exchanges where the issued notes will be listed. Subject to the relevant stock exchange's listing requirements, the individual forms that need to be prepared and submitted by the listing agent will differ; however, normally, the documents required for listing will include a draft offering circular in order to request the exchange's comments, feedback, and subsequent approval.

6.3.16 Stock exchange

The chosen *stock exchange* reviews, comments, and approves the submitted offering circular and will permit trading of and admit the notes onto its official list of trade securities. For structured finance transactions the stock exchanges involved are usually either those of Ireland, Luxembourg, or the U.K.

6.3.17 Clearing systems

Finally, *clearing systems* such as Euroclear and Clearstream in Europe and DTC in the U.S. provide the clearing and settlement services once the securities have been issued to the market.

6.3.18 Monoline insurers

Monolines are included for completeness, since some of the legacy structured finance transactions (i.e., the ones that were issued before 2008) are equipped with guarantees by so-called *monoline insurers* (also referred to as "monolines" or "wraps"), all of which were very adversely affected by the credit crunch. Monolines provide one sole line of specialist insurance which is for financial obligations in contrast to a multi-line insurance business that provides a range of insurance cover. Monoline wraps were used in some legacy structured finance deals to prep up the rating of the underlying bond tranche and, as the insurance companies that used to provide this cover were all rated AAA, the wrapped bond tranche in these cases would also achieve a higher rating, in many cases the same as the monoline itself. In contrast, the actual rating of an "unwrapped" bond (i.e., without cover by the financial guarantor—also referred to as "shadow rating" of the underlying) can be considerably lower. Once the market collapsed and the ratings of (most) monolines were lowered from AAA down to BBB– and below, then the rating of the underlying bonds would equally be downgraded to a point where it was level with the underlying rating. For reference and in case you come across some of those monolines, the names of these financial guarantors are: AMBAC, Assured Guaranty, CIFG, FIGC, FSA, Syncora (formerly XL). Furthermore, there is also Radian which provides secondary "wraps" to some bond instruments (i.e., after other monolines have provided primary "wraps"). From an investor's perspective, regardless of the status of the monoline industry, if you were to consider purchasing a monoline-wrapped structured finance bond instrument, I would recommend you check whether or not the bond is currently "drawing" under the wrap (i.e., utilizing some of this cover to pay interest and/or principal in line with the original payment schedule of the bond)—if so, then this would be a pretty clear indication that the underlying transaction is not performing well and substitute payments by the monolines may cover up the bond's underlying weakness. Unfortunately, this is not always reported very well, hence you would need to look very closely at the relevant investor reports—or ask the issuer, the monoline involved, or even the rating agencies.

6.4 TRANSACTION DOCUMENTS

Deal documentation can be a legal minefield if you are not familiar with the various documents and the legal implications of them. Even if there are common themes for documents, law firms drafting the majority of these documents will not always follow a set pattern when preparing them—hence, even someone quite familiar with them may have to search through them to find what they are after. In addition, some of the language used is quite formalized and not always easy to read, which can in some cases add an additional layer of complexity—this may or may not be deliberate. Personally, I think life is difficult and complex enough, why making it harder for people who have to read these papers to understand?

One of the interesting aspects of legal documentation is that most of it is not really "tested", and when I say "tested" I mean actually used as part of an actual court case to see whether it does what it is expected to do. Legal documents, particularly legal opinions, are—as the name itself suggests—an "opinion". By being an opinion, it further means that the lawyers' viewpoint is not necessarily based on fact or knowledge—according to the definition of "opinion" in the *Oxford English Dictionary* (as mentioned earlier). Hence, there will always remain a risk that if a document is actually being tested in court, it may turn out that the legal opinion on which a transaction was built and understood to be working does not actually hold up.

That's the risk you take when entering into a structured finance transaction which, looking at it from a legal perspective, is a construct of many individual contracts between some or all of the counterparties that were referred to in Section 6.3. The following sections look closer at the typical deal documents used in the structured finance area and discusses the purpose of the documents, areas that are covered, and parties that would usually work on or enter into these documents.

6.4.1 Offering circular

Sometimes, this is also referred to as a prospectus, offering memorandum, or short OC. The OC represents one of the key selling documents of a structured finance transaction and, in the European Union, legally constitutes a "prospectus" if the securities are listed. Generally speaking, the OC is the main disclosure document that is used by the arranger of the transaction explaining to investors how the proposed transaction will work. The offering circular

- Explains the bond's terms and conditions (T&Cs)
- Contains an executive summary of the relevant transaction
- Outlines and identifies major risks for the noteholders
- Lists all major counterparties involved in the transaction and identifies their roles and responsibilities
- Provides further information about the special purpose vehicle (SPV) that issues the notes
- Discloses cursory information on the underlying pool of assets
- Provides additional details on areas such as listing, bond clearing, and tax issues, etc.

The typical arrangement is that the OC complies with the legal requirements of two jurisdictions: the jurisdiction where the securities are listed and the jurisdiction of the SPV's incorporation.

The main counterparties to the OC are the SPV itself, the arrangers (typically an investment bank), and the managers of the assets (usually the originator).

6.4.2 Terms and conditions

The *terms and conditions (T&Cs)* of the issued notes are disclosed in the OC and govern the eventualities of bond liabilities and are also attached to the trust deed; amongst the areas that are typically covered by T&Cs are

- Definition of "notes outstanding" and in which circumstances outstanding notes can be cancelled or redeemed, as well as the restriction of particular noteholders' voting rights.
- Noteholders' votes and whether or not and how votes can be overturned by investors at different levels within the structure (e.g., senior noteholders may be able to overturn junior noteholders' votes, but does this also apply *vice versa*?).
- If there is a conflict between senior and junior noteholders will the trustee act on behalf of the senior noteholders? Usually, that would be the case.
- Ordinary as well as extraordinary resolutions and the percentage majority required to achieve effective noteholder approval (i.e., percentage of quorum required and then percentage of votes cast).
- Principal and interest allocation to noteholders (i.e., whether there is a predefined repayment schedule, passthrough structure or a soft/hard-bullet structure, etc.). Furthermore, this clarifies the distribution of both interest and principal cash flows between senior, mezzanine, and junior tranches and the order in which the notes are expected to mature (i.e., sequential or *pro rata*).
- Priority of payments including senior third-party expenses and relevant taxes such as VAT, backup servicing fees (if there is a backup servicer in place), payments to the liquidity facility provider if any. Excess cash (or plain profit for the originator) should ideally come last in the priority of payments.
- Note redemption conditions, particularly the timing of such redemptions (i.e., on the note redemption date), redemption price (typically, par value plus accrued interest), whether redemption is mandatory or optional (either due to tax reasons affecting the assets, notes, swap agreement, sometimes affecting the issuer, or due to a "clean-up call", when the notes, for instance, have paid down to 10% of the original outstanding note balance). Deposit bank conditions for the redemption fund deposit bank and advance or other notifications to noteholders.
- Payment dates and frequency, identifying possible timing mismatches between asset interest payment and notes interest payment dates (the rating agencies are quite keen on this point since they rate the "timeliness of interest payments" and hence there should be no payment delay other than for genuine credit reasons) and how reinvestment risks are structurally addressed (i.e., either by "authorized investments" or "guaranteed investment contracts" or GICs to bridge the timing difference between receipt and payment of funds). Facilitation of the actual payments via the payment agent, and how "commingling risks" are addressed in the management of these payments.
- Currency (or currencies) which should ensure that all assets as well as the supporting documentation are denominated in the same currency as the notes—or otherwise suitable swap arrangements have been put in place to address the risk of currency mismatch due to foreign exchange rate differences.
- Interest rates on the underlying notes as well as the issued notes and how mismatches, for instance, between fixed rate (i.e., on the notes) and floating rate (i.e., on the assets) are structurally addressed, typically by a suitable swap arrangement that also covers all expenses which rank prior to the notes. Or if there are floating interest rates applying to both notes as well as assets, which index is used to determine the differences, if any.

- Maturity date of the notes and how mismatches of this with the maturity dates of the assets are addressed in the structure (i.e., reinvestment risk when the asset maturity date < notes maturity date or funding mismatch when the asset maturity date > notes maturity date).
- Withholding tax that may apply to the structure in question (i.e., on the assets, notes, and maybe also on some or all of the support agreements). If notes are subjected to withholding tax, are there any suitable support arrangements in place that can effectively remove this obligation from the investors to other parties?
- Events of default and applicable grace periods, monetary vs. non-monetary defaults, suitable remedies, trustee's rights in relation to defaults (e.g., have they got the right to waive an event of default if it's not materially prejudicial to the noteholders), who can enforce the security of the notes (typically, only the trustee)?
- Notifications to noteholders and the rating agencies, applicable modifications to the structure, if any, and treatment of replacement and further issuance/taps.

6.4.3 Trust deed

The *trust deed* is another important document which serves as a legal instrument that constitutes the securities that are offered and outlines the relationship between the SPV and the trustee. A trustee's responsibilities in structured finance transactions can vary considerably between different countries and jurisdictions and to some extent also depend on the regulatory framework, commercial practices, and local custom. Although the trust deed is extremely important to structured finance deals, they do not tend to differ too much between different types of transactions and, moreover, they are easier to get to grips with than some of the other documents.

Some of the trustee duties for structured finance transactions may involve protection of the noteholders' security, which can include the day-to-day administration and, if necessary, also the enforcement of these securities, and the trustee has an overarching duty to act on behalf of all noteholders. The areas outlined in the trust deed typically cover the following:

- Schedule of the T&Cs set out in the OC
- Determines how the securities are represented and the form of the certificates
- Details of the SPV's promise to pay in the certificates as well as the payment covenant to which the SPV has to adhere
- The trustee's fiduciary responsibilities such as preservation of the estate which he has been entrusted with, best representation of noteholders' interest, exercising its duties with appropriate care and prudence, protection of noteholders' security and enforcement of it if necessary, security registration, appointment of receiver or administrator if necessary, monitoring of the transaction as well as the movement of loan documents and title deeds, conduct noteholder meetings
- Furthermore, it is the trustee's duty to report full redemption of note tranches, breaches of agreements as well as default events, changes or termination of any party, termination of any party or agreements
- Segregation/Custody requires that the issuer's assets, documents, funds, and accounts must be segregated from others held by the same trustee. Furthermore, these items also need to be immune against the trustee's insolvency and the trustee cannot dispose of assets unless this conforms to the transaction's documentation
- Retirement/Resignation of the trustee is not possible without a suitable successor in place and noteholders need to be given adequate notice of the trustee's wish to retire or terminate the agreement. In such a case, any unearned "trustee fee" needs to be returned.

6.4.4 Security trust deed

A *security trust deed* (sometimes referred to as a "deed of charge") sets out the relationship between the special purpose vehicle and the security trustee. The deed of charge tends to follow a standard format and parties agreeing to it are typically bound by limited recourse as well as non-petition language. In addition, it legally creates security over the SPV's assets which form the security package favoring the investors. The parties entering into the deed of charge are typically the special purpose vehicle and the security trustee on behalf of and representing all secured parties including the noteholders. The security trust deed provides rights, legally empowers the trustee, and usually covers areas such as

- Legal powers of the trustee
- Deals with assets that make up the security package in favor of investors
- Creates security over assets and determines whether the security is of a fixed or floating nature
- Beneficiaries of the security
- Suitable enforcers of the security and payment priorities in case of enforcement
- Legal protection offered to third parties, potential receivers, and the trustee
- Additional covenants, warranties, and other conditions that may apply to the seller, third parties, or the SPV
- Subordinated noteholders' claims on assets and revenues pre and post issuer default.

6.4.5 Paying agent agreement

The *paying agent agreement*—which is more mechanical in nature than legal—sets out the paying agent's powers, rights, duties, and responsibilities. It is agreed between the special purpose vehicle and the paying agent(s). Processes and mechanics typically described in the paying agency agreement are

- Presentation of the investors' securities in exchange for payment
- Treatment of exchange of damaged or replacement of lost certificates
- Exercise of investors' rights under the securities
- Particulars of how and where investors can obtain security information.

6.4.6 Subscription agreement

The *subscription agreement* is entered into by the SPV, the arranger bank, and the transaction's managers whereby they agree to purchase the issued securities. The following points are usually covered in such an agreement:

- Purchase of the issued securities at the issued date at an agreed initial purchase price by the arranger subject to the listing and rating of the securities and the SPV's legal status
- Provision for material adverse events between entering the subscription agreement and close of the deal in which case the investors can pull out from the purchase.

6.4.7 Servicing agreement(s)

The servicing agreement (and sometimes the backup servicing agreement which can be in the same document or separate) defines the terms on which the assets or receivables will be administered on a going concern basis by the servicer. Usually, this is entered into by the servicer (and initially also by the originator of these assets or receivables). The servicing agreement (sometimes also referred to as the administration agreement) constitutes an important transaction document and can cover a wide range of activities:

- Servicing
  - servicing arrangements including collection of principal receipts, interest payments, insurance receipts, and taxes
  - monitoring and pursuing of arrears as well as foreclosure procedures
  - discharging of loans and related security documents upon redemption
  - ongoing treatment of records and loans or receivables documentation
- Management of further advances, conversions, and substitutions as well as retention of securitized loans or receivables
- Reporting to the trustee and rating agencies as well as investor reporting
- Provision of appropriate servicing framework including compatible information technology; data storage, maintenance, and protection; secure loans or receivables document storage; asset segregation (securitized vs. non-securitized); data quality, audit, and assurance
- Retirement and termination provisions prohibit resignation of the servicer without any suitable successor; refund of any unearned servicer fees and notification of the trustee and the credit rating agencies
- Equally, the trustee is empowered to terminate the servicer upon the occurrence of predetermined servicer termination events. Any replacement servicer will need to fulfill the same requirements as the predecessor and termination by the trustee should only be permitted with a suitable successor in place.
- Backup servicer coordination (depending to some extent on the type of backup servicing arrangement that has been put in place). Generally speaking, backup servicer requirements are the same as for the servicer.

6.4.8 Sale agreement

The *sale agreement* between the seller/originator and the special purpose vehicle plays an integral part in true sale securitization as it governs the clean transfer of the transaction's receivables. Sale agreements are fairly standard documents and need to

- Be sufficient to effect a clean and proper receivables or assets transfer
- Contain a repurchase obligation for the originator to buy non-eligible receivables back from the SPV at the initial asset transfer price or other appropriate remedial actions
- Provide recourse rights to the SPV which can be claimed against the originator in case of representations and warranties breaches
- Detailed representations and warranties criteria and other receivables criteria that must be satisfied prior to an asset transfer to the SPV.

6.4.9 Agreement among managers

The *agreement among managers* is a contractual arrangement between the special purpose vehicle, the lead manager (which is usually the arranger), and furthermore the co-managers (if any) whereby the parties involved agree amongst themselves the number of securities from the issuance they will buy and then document the specifics of such agreement. The agreement will include and cover the following areas:

- Security tranche and number of issued bonds that are purchased by each party
- Remuneration and distribution of each party's commission—this is usually agreed on and governed by a standard form supplied by the International Professional Managers Association (IPMA)

- Delegation of powers to the lead manager which can then act on behalf of the co-managers if and when required.

6.4.10 Investment or collateral management agreement

An *investment or collateral management agreement* may be entered into by the investment or collateral manager and the SPV if the underlying assets require active management (e.g., for a managed collateralized debt obligation or CDO). Such an agreement contains strict eligibility guidelines for the inclusion of assets in the managed pool and the collateral manager will carry the burden of contractual obligations to comply with those requirements.

6.4.11 Liquidity agreement

The purpose of the *liquidity agreement* is to describe the details of the liquidity facility and the agreement is entered into by the SPV and the liquidity facility provider. Since the actual facility itself is usually provided by means of a loan, the governing document will detail the standard loan terms and conditions, the total amount of such loan, and the instance when the liquidity facility can be drawn upon. From a tax perspective it is quite important to ensure that this facility is not considered as credit enhancement.

6.4.12 Credit enhancement agreements

Credit enhancement agreements depend largely on which type and provider of credit enhancement is chosen to improve the overall bond structure and to provide sufficient credit enhancement. The form of agreement depends largely on the underlying assets as well as which particular credit enhancement method has been selected to support the transaction. For instance, whether or not there is monoline insurance involved or another financial counterparty is going to provide credit support.

6.4.13 Swap document(s)

The provision of swap(s)—and, yes, there can be more than one swap with different counterparties acting as swap providers—is governed by the *swap document(s)* setting out the risks taken by the relevant swap counterparty and the fee it receives for providing such risk cover. In a true sale transaction, depending on the transaction structure (i.e., are notes issued in a single currency or more than one denomination?), the nature of the underlying collateral (i.e., fixed and floating interest rate mortgages), timing mismatches (i.e., short-term trade receivables vs. long-term notes), basis risk (i.e., underlying collateral spread based on the Bank of England base rate vs. floating rate interest on the notes based on the EURIBOR), different swap documents may be required that detail these risks and the coverage provided by the various swap arrangements that are put in place.

Furthermore, for synthetic transaction structures, swap documents cover the credit default swaps that are typical for these types of deals and will be used to define credit default events and reference assets. Regardless of the nature of the transactions, swap documentation normally uses ISDA's (International Swap and Derivatives Association) templates—the so-called ISDA master agreement. It is important to understand such ISDA agreements since the devil is usually in the detail and you do not want to find out that a certain credit event is not covered when you thought you could rely on the swap.

6.4.14 Guaranteed investment contract (GIC)

A *guaranteed investment contract* (also known as deposit agreements) can be agreed by the issuer and a financial institution that is appropriately rated (whereby the "appropriateness" is usually determined by the credit rating agencies' criteria for counterparties in structured finance transactions). The purpose of such an agreed guaranteed investment contract is to cover any reinvestment risks that may occur because prepaid deposited assets may or may not earn as much interest as they did when they were on the balance sheet of the originator.

6.4.15 Subordinated loan agreement

A *subordinated loan agreement* ("startup loan") is often arranged between the originator and issuer. The originator will provide a structurally subordinated loan to the issuer in order to prefund the initial setup costs of the transaction as well as the minimum required initial layer of credit enhancement (often in the form of a prepaid cash reserve account).

6.4.16 Declaration of trusts

Bank agreements or *declaration of trusts* deal with all the issuer's bank accounts and are particularly important in terms of flow of funds. By declaring the trust over these accounts, the issuer takes legal security over so-called "commingled" accounts (i.e., accounts in which another party may retain an interest—and in doing so reduces the commingling risk of these funds). Areas covered include

- The flow of funds throughout the transaction and the traceability of cash flows from borrowers via servicer and issuer to the noteholders
- Ability and appropriateness of the servicer identifying funds that belong to the issuer
- Maintenance of information and documents necessary in order to have robust legal evidence of rightful ownership of these funds in case of insolvency of the servicer
- Coverage and safeguards to remedy potential shortfalls and/or losses
- Finding answers to questions like: Are changes to the servicer permitted?; What time frame would be necessary to do so?; and How much would such a servicer change cost?

6.4.17 Legal opinion(s)

Legal opinions prepared by law firms are required by various parties for different reasons and for different aspects of a deal: arrangers, trustees, rating agencies, credit enhancement, and liquidity providers are amongst them. Among the transaction details that will be covered in such legal opinion are

- Counterparties' legal capacity and the basis on which they are authorized to enter the transaction
- Availability, receipt, and registration of valid requisite consents and authorities
- Compliance will all transaction-related formalities
- Effectiveness of the security interests in the various transaction documents.

Whether or not a transaction is actually doable and legally feasible often comes down to legal opinion. Interestingly enough, even rating agencies put their faith in legal opinions assuming to some extent that whatever is presumed by the lawyers will actually work. However, please bear in mind that—similarly to rating opinions—a legal opinion would according to the definition given by the *Oxford English Dictionary* be a view or standpoint that is not necessarily based on facts or knowledge. There is a degree of uncertainty around legal opinions and whether or not one is valid and can withstand legal challenge in the courts. Consequently, most if not all legal opinions have not been tested and I suggest you keep this in mind when you review one of them. Furthermore, I have previously worked on transactions where I got to see two legal opinions by two different law firms on the same issue with two views that completely differed. In case you wonder which one of those we went with—well, we literally "played" the various situations through in our minds and then tried to identify the one that—at least from a common sense perspective—would seem most sensible.

6.4.18 Comfort letters

Comfort letters are issued by the special purpose vehicle's auditors in order to confirm that unaudited information in the offering document is correct. These letters are supposed to reassure managers prior to purchasing the securities and whilst they are binding for the auditors, the accountants who write the letters often try to limit their legal liability. More than one of these letters can be issued at different stages of the transaction.

6.5 DEAL CONFIGURATION

It is crucial to define high-level parameters of the forthcoming transaction and to configure the anticipated deal characteristics prior to starting any actual structuring work on the provisional pool. Parameters to be specified are

- Nature of deal (i.e., synthetic or true sale)
- Type of deal structure (master trust, standalone)
- Deal name
- Deal brand
- Underlying assets/asset class
- Jurisdiction of assets and any implications on structure
- Currency or currencies.

Furthermore, some of the more operational features of the deal would need to be determined. They would cover areas such as

- Cash management methodology
- Applicable criteria for representations and warranties
- Trigger tests.

For example, the type of deal must be specified (master trust, standalone static securitization, covered bond, etc.), together with parameters to determine the way in which the deal will operate (cash management methodology, applicable R&W criteria, and trigger tests). Some of these parameters will remain fixed for the life of the deal, others can be altered right up until just before issuance (e.g., configure representations and warranties criteria).

6.5.1 Provisional pool

The "provisional" pool represents a selection of underlying assets targeted for securitization. This will be carried out by applying all the asset selection criteria, representations and warranties tests, etc. for the targeted transaction: for instance, an originator would select a pool of residential mortgages in order to structure a residential mortgage-backed securitization. This initial pool in essence simulates the anticipated pool without executing the true sale of the assets to the SPV—which typically happens at close of the transaction.

The following section covers activities that are usually included in getting the desired pool cut for the "provisional pool" such as identification of the assets and subsequent "flagging" in the originator's source system, data quality review, representations and warranties test, asset selection, deselection if necessary (e.g., if an asset is not necessary in order to achieve the desired pool cut) . The result of all this analysis and checking is the eligible (but still provisional) pool.

6.5.2 Asset identification and flagging

Asset identification and flagging in essence requires the originator to go through their books of, say, mortgages and then identify which of these loans are eligible for inclusion in the provisional pool. Once they have been identified, such assets for inclusion would typically receive a "hard" flag (i.e., some kind of marker or system flag that identifies the asset as belonging to the new transaction and *not* to the originator).

This is pretty important, because if the deal actually closes and the transaction has been included in the transaction and the ownership has been transferred by means of an actual sale to the SPV (i.e., a true sale), then subsequently the originator will have no formal ownership of the asset.

6.5.3 Data quality review

Before each securitization issuance or topup, the quality of available assets must be analyzed to identify assets (e.g., loans, mortgages, etc.) which are eligible for entry to the securitization pool. Assets are analyzed by subjecting them to data population, data quality and assurance, and representations and warranties (R&W) tests.

Once an underlying asset has been selected for inclusion in the provisional pool it will be flagged as part of the firm's securitization to ensure that such assets are properly identified in the firm's book of records. Typically, assets that will eventually be removed from the bank's balance sheet since they will be sold as part of the true sale will be "hard-flagged" in the relevant source firms effectively identifying that they no longer belong to the firm. Furthermore, the underlying assets will carry various system flags in the firm's securitization system in order to determine which test (i.e., the R&W test, etc.) they have passed. At each of these stages they will receive an additional system flag that allows the firm to trace the states of assets in the securitization system—best described as the "flagging state".

For deal types with multiple flagging states, a different series of tests will be run for each flagging state. For example, a hybrid covered bond deal type has three flagging states: namely, non-mortgage bond collateral, additional covered bond collateral portfolio, and RMBS/covered bond eligible portfolio. In this case, three series of tests will be run to determine which assets are eligible for each flagging state and, ultimately, suitable for different types of transactions.

Assets which pass the data population tests for a particular flagging state for a pre-deal topup are considered eligible for the data quality tests for that same flagging state.

The data quality test ensures that assets without the desired quality for a particular flagging state are removed from the securitization pool during the selection process. Assets that successfully pass all data quality tests qualify for the next screening test which is the representations and warranties test.

6.5.4 Representations and warranties

As part of establishing the provisional pool, an originator needs to configure the representations and warranties test (R&W test) criteria for analysis of the assets that are to be securitized. These R&W test criteria need to be defined for each of the flagging states applicable to the particular pre-deal.

Assets that pass the data population and data quality tests for a particular flagging state for a pre-deal are considered eligible for the R&W test for that same flagging state. R&W tests ensure that the assets entering into the securitization pool satisfy all legal and asset performance requirements for the particular deal and will be different depending on the deal type, the transaction structure, and underlying pool (master trust, static pool, covered bond hybrid etc). Assets that successfully pass all R&W tests qualify for the next selection process which is the random selection of assets.

Post issuance, R&W tests are run for each flagging state periodically (i.e., daily) to ensure that the underlying pools for each flagging state still conform to the flag-specific R&W criteria. The test is needed because the source data (e.g., the pool of underlying mortgages) can undergo continuous change.

R&W criteria against which the assets are tested post issuance are different from pre-deal R&W criteria. This function also allows the user to configure post-deal R&W criteria. Note that post-deal R&W criteria should also be configured at the pre-deal stage, although R&W criteria can change once the deal has closed provided such pool changes are permissible within the terms of the transaction documents.

A topup to an existing deal would typically use the same R&W criteria as the original issuance prior to the topup (as these will be defined in the legal documents).

Thus, there will be two sets of R&W criteria for each flagging state of a deal, one for pre-deal provisional pool stages ("forward-flagging") and one for post-issuance final pools ("backward-deflagging").

6.5.5 Asset selection, deselection, and eligible pools

Assets must pass the data quality test and satisfy the representations and warranties criteria for a flagging state to be eligible for inclusion for that particular flagging state. By applying these various tests the original pool of assets will become smaller by passing through each flagging state and non-eligible assets will be deselected (or "deflagged") from the potential deal. Consequently, assets that remain flagged will make up the pool of assets eligible for inclusion to the transaction's provisional pool. The eligible asset pool will be larger than the number of assets actually needed to back the subpool represented by the particular flagging state. For instance, the deal type represented by a hybrid covered bond has three flagging states: namely, non-mortgage bond collateral pool (serving as collateral for the covered bond), additional covered bond mortgage collateral pool, covered bond/ RMBS eligible pool.

Random selection

Subsequently, once flags have been assigned to the various collateral pools, a random selection process will be applied in order to determine eligible asset pools to identify and earmark assets for the provisional pool. The guiding principle behind randomly selecting and earmarking these assets is to prevent so-called "cherry-picking"—in other words, preventing the originator from keeping assets deemed to be better risk for himself and passing the higher risk of weaker quality assets on to investors.

Once an asset has been selected for a particular flagging state of a deal, it is earmarked for the deal and cannot be selected for any other deal. In essence, this means that if an originator has selected and earmarked certain mortgages for one particular issuance, they cannot be reused for another issuance—

unless they are randomly deselected. (Note that covered bond structures, however, are an exception to this rule as an originator's whole pool of mortgages will typically serve as collateral for the entire covered bond instruments issued by this particular originator.)

Random deselection

If, after running the random selection process, too many assets have been selected for the provisional pool and the value of the earmarked assets exceeds the minimum required assets, some of these assets can also be randomly deselected.

Based on the new reduced value of the flagging state entered by the user, assets will be selected randomly from the provisional pool and earmarking will be removed. The deselected assets will continue to be a part of the lower level flagging state of the deal even after random deselection because they have already passed all the tests of the said flagging state of the deal. For example, for a hybrid cover bond deal, if a mortgage has been randomly deselected from the RMBS portfolio, it will become a part of the non-mortgage bond collateral portfolio. Additionally, this mortgage will also remain eligible for random selection for the covered bond mortgage pool because it had already passed all tests applicable for this particular flagging state.

6.5.6 Rating agency pool submission

Pre-deal pool (provisional pool) analysis

Prior to each issuance or pool topup (replenishment and/or substitution), the originator needs to analyze the loan data to identify assets which qualify for entry to the pool to support the issuance. Hence, provisional pool activities at this stage are focused on assembling a pool of assets to the required standard and quality to execute and issue the transaction.

The loan data and pool parameters for this pre-deal pool must be passed to the ratings agencies for assessment. The agencies will then run either this provisional pool or, in case of replenishment/substitutions, the resulting changed pool through the relevant models to determine whether the pool is in line with the agency's requirements according to their rating criteria and pool requirements.

The following steps are required before the data can be sent to the rating agencies:

1. The mortgage or loan data are subjected to data population and data quality tests. Mortgages/loans that do not have correctly populated data for critical fields will be eliminated from the provisional or topup pool
2. Mortgages/loans that pass this first hurdle are tested against the representations and warranties (R&W) criteria according to the particular deal documentation. R&W criteria for each deal will not be available until the deal's transaction legal documents have been produced
3. The originator will then further analyze the mortgages/loans that have passed the R&W tests and may eliminate additional mortgages if they fail this test or are not necessary to be added as the target size of the to-be-securitized pool has been achieved
4. Mortgages/loans that remain after passing the originator's initial selection procedures are subsequently put through a random selection process to reduce the number of loans to the required value of the deal. The random selection procedure as part of this step is crucial to avoid cherry-picking, preventing the originator from keeping higher quality assets on his book whilst securitizing lower quality assets.
5. Once the provisional pool has reached this stage, asset trigger tests are performed and, if they fail, further representations and warranties (R&W) tests may need to be introduced.

6. Once the originator feels comfortable with the provisional pool, the loan-by-loan data are sent to the rating agencies in the format specified by them.

This first initial data submission to the agencies happens typically around 3 months prior to close of the transaction, although this time varies and depends on factors such as asset class, complexity of the deal structure, resources and responsiveness at both the rating agencies' analytical department and the originator's structuring department.

Similarly, depending on these parameters, the agencies will spend 2-to-3 weeks for the initial analysis of the provisional pool and will subsequently resolve any analytical questions with the originator and/or the arranging bank. The format of agency data submission templates may change at this stage to reflect features of the deal and/or pool-specific features for which the agencies will expect to see updated reports within a few days.

The actual review of the deal's legal transaction documents starts usually around 2 months before issuance and this may result in a change to the representations and warranties criteria. The documents can initially be reviewed by the originator's in-house legal counsel; however, it is also advisable in some cases to request legal opinion from a law firm specializing in securitization and, ideally, in the particular asset class in question. Legal opinions can further be required by the rating agencies, which would be a law firm different from the originator's to avoid conflict of interest. Some CRAs use their in-house legal counsel for more standardized asset classes whereas complex transactions and new structures may be given to an external law firm. Depending on the work undertaken by these law firms, legal opinion can become an important cost factor. These costs are usually factored into the pricing of the relevant transaction.

Investor presentations—so-called "marketing phase" or "roadshows"—take place around 6 weeks prior to deal issuance and originators need to be able to answer queries based on the entire mortgage book, not just the characteristics of the provisional pool. Three-month agency data are used for the offering circular and, therefore, need to be retained for investor queries following the marketing phase.

A final release of the agency reports is required 1 month before the deal date. The representations and warranties test needs to be run at this time to update the pool.

On the day before issuance, mortgages in the pre-deal pool will be flagged with the deal ID and mortgages will be effectively securitized at this stage. For a master trust deal the agency reports must be run again on the day of issuance.

6.5.7 Due diligence

Due diligence reporting

10b-5

Under U.S. law, any securities sold in the U.S. are subject to Rule 10b-5 of the Securities Exchange Act. Under this rule, it is "unlawful for any person, directly or indirectly, to

- Employ any device, scheme, or artifice to defraud,
- Make any untrue statement of a material fact or to omit to state a material fact necessary in order to make the statements made, in the light of the circumstances under which they were made, not misleading, or
- Engage in any act, practice, or course of business which operates or would operate as a fraud or deceit upon any person, in connection with the purchase or sale of any security."

The main requirement from this is to disclose, via reports to the Securities Exchange Commission (SEC), the details of the assets and their credit history underpinning the securitization. The 10b-5 reporting is done at the pre-deal stage.

Reg AB

The U.S. Securities and Exchange Commission (SEC) has approved new rules (Regulation 'Reg' AB) that provide for a comprehensive securities regulatory framework for publicly issued mortgage and asset-backed securities (collectively referred to as "ABS"). They are expected to bring increased transparency and consistency of practice to the ABS markets. The new rules primarily address four areas of securities regulation:

- Registration requirements under the Securities Act of 1933
- Disclosure rules
- Communications during the offering process
- Ongoing reporting requirements under the Securities Exchange Act of 1934.

The main requirement from this is disclosure of asset details via a report to the Securities Exchange Commission (SEC). Up to 5 years' worth of delinquency, loss, and prepayment data are required, some of it for prior securitizations. The SEC allows these data to be published via a website provided there is unrestricted access that is free of charge and that the data are retained for at least 5 years.

The Reg AB report is done at the pre-deal stage, but will also be a regular requirement post deal (e.g., when topups to the deal are done).

6.5.8 Credit ratings and regulatory approval

Credit rating approval letter

Once the credit ratings agencies have assigned the respective ratings, they will either issue a ratings/credit assessment letter (for private bond issues) or issue pre-sale/new issuance reports for public bond issuance.

U.K. statutory and regulatory reporting

There is a requirement under U.K. law to provide statutory reports to the regulator (The Financial Services Authority, Basel II) and the Bank of England; similar requirements exist in other jurisdictions.

7

At close

7.1 DEAL DOCUMENTS, MARKETING, AND ROADSHOW

7.1.1 Deal documents

Key documents that are produced and used during the marketing phase and roadshow are given in the following subsections.

Term sheet

The term sheet is often one of the first documents related to a new bond issuance that becomes available. Generally, it is a non-binding agreement or, simply, a document that expresses the basic terms and conditions for a new security.

Term sheets are not much different from "letters of intent" in that they are usually non-binding documents which simply express preliminary terms, and in structured finance markets these are usually more in the form of a non-agreed proposal. Term sheets are usually fairly brief and outline some (not all) of a deal's specifics in bullet-point-style narrative or very brief descriptions.

"Red" or "red herring"

The "red herring" or, in short, just "Red" is a preliminary filing and gets its name from the warning—printed in red on the title page—stating that the document is currently being reviewed by the SEC (or other relevant regulators) and, hence, can be subject to change.

Red herrings usually represent a summary of a forthcoming formal prospectus and may often not contain certain offering details, such as the price of the security, total value of the offering, and the number of shares that will be sold, for instance.

"Black" or black-lined version

Each prospectus typically goes through various stages of a drafting process and each resulting prospectus should be "black-lined", meaning that the changes are marked up in the actual document. Typically, additions to the previous version are identified by black underlining and removals of text by striking the removed parts through—in black (you guessed it).

7.1.2 Marketing

One of the key instruments that are used in order to market a transaction and handed out during the investors' roadshow is the so-called "pitch book".

A typical pitch book contains the following sections which may differ from firm to firm and also depending on the underlying asset class. Most of these pitch books are by nature marketing presentations and as such the formats typically take the form of a Power Point presentation (i.e., slides in landscape orientation). The following sections are from an actual public U.K. RMBS master trust deal that was issued during the credit crunch in September 2009:

- *Front page*. Name of transaction, name/logos of originators, arranger(s), joint lead manager(s), and bookrunners, confidentiality level, and territorial restrictions (if any)
- *Disclaimer*. The legal small print including restrictions on distribution of this document, purpose, reproduction rules, information only—and clarification/statement that this document represents no investment advice, no solicitation to sell, representations, declaration of interest in the securities of parties involved, distribution restrictions, restrictions on forward-looking statements, etc.
- *Table of contents*. Broken down into content headers and appendices
- *Executive summary*. Deal highlights, *n*th issue of master trust program, prime collateral quality, transaction parties, expected timeline (for pricing and closing), indicative capital structure (including expected ratings, currency, note size, GBP equivalent, coupon and repayment type, expected maturity date, stepdown date, percentage of series, expected average life, legal maturity, credit enhancement), main features of the notes
- *Overview of the originator*. Organizational structure (org chart), description of business division as part of the group, interim financial results of the retail division (as originator of the underlying mortgages)
- *Description of the originator's mortgage business*. Competitive landscape (U.K.), breakdown of mortgage origination by brand (%), brand strategies (breakdown into origination channels, e.g., branches, telephone, intermediary, mainstream, specialist lending such as buy-to-let), mortgage funding platforms (i.e., conduits, covered bonds, and other funding vehicles), credit overview (credit policy framework, credit scoring and assessment, affordability model), collections strategy (customer payment department, litigation process and repossession, in-house asset managers and outsource capacity, recoveries), collections and recoveries overview (flow diagram)
- *U.K. mortgage market overview*. U.K. mortgage lending (gross vs. net lending); U.K. house prices and affordability; arrears, repossessions and unemployment; inflation, base rates, credit scoring, housing supply; negative equity
- *Transaction overview*. Indicative capital structure and features; legal structure of the trust program (structure diagram); capital structure (comparison with previous issuance); credit enhancement (excess spread, reserve fund, subordination); yield enhancement and extension risk; maturity purchase agreement (timeline and individual steps); asset and non-asset triggers (pre- and post-trigger events); key risks with structural mitigants (rating agency stress levels vs. market and appropriate structural mitigation)
- *Appendices*. Portfolio stratifications (collateral pool, payments and arrears, substitution effects, original and current loan-to-value cohorts, geographical diversification, breakdown by origination channel, use of proceeds and repayment type).

Of course, this is only a sample structure and content for a pitch book as a **marketing device** used by investment banks, because that's exactly what it is. However, it can give you a fair level of information at the outset of a transaction, when other information on the transactions (apart maybe from the term sheet) is relatively hard to come by.

7.1.3 Roadshow

The pitch book itself together with the preliminary prospectus are used as key marketing instruments during the so-called "roadshow", which is essentially a series of 1-to-2-hour meetings which feature oral presentations of the transaction that is marketed. These presentations are well-structured verbal walkthroughs of the pitch book and typically conducted by senior management staff from the originator together with the lead arranger or underwriting team.

Primarily designed to stimulate interest in prospective investors, roadshows are usually carefully orchestrated and attendees typically receive no other information than the preliminary prospectus—even notetaking is typically not permitted (this is to avoid selective disclosure and ensuring everyone attending has the same level of information—which otherwise may constitute a breach of securities laws).

If you are an active issuer, then it may be useful to consult your in-house legal team when preparing for your roadshow, simply because there are so many potential legal pitfalls and to ensure your roadshow is successful and does not turn into a disaster before the deal even goes to market.

7.2 PRE-SALE REPORT

At close of a public transaction, rating agencies typically provide two types of documents that describe the analysis that has been done in order to assign new ratings to the transaction in question: the so-called "pre-sale report"' (pre sale) and the "new issuance report" (new issue, see Section 7.4). The structure of these documents is usually very similar, but the content may slightly differ.

The pre-sale report is a summary of the rating agency's analysis which has likely been based to some extent on incomplete information from the originator and/or issuer. Whilst this may be sufficient to undertake the rating analysis on the basis of the information that has been supplied, it is usually not sufficient to make a final rating decision. However, the agency will publish its analytical narrative together with "expected"/"provisional" (i.e., "exp") or "preliminary" (i.e., "P") ratings. The ratings' designation for such expected ratings differ by CRA and are currently (i.e., as of writing this book, 2010) as follows (using the example of a AAA/Aaa rating assigned by all three agencies):

- Moody's (P) Aaa
- Standard & Poor's (P) AAA
- Fitch AAA (exp)

You can find out more about the relevant rating definitions either by visiting the rating agencies' websites or by using the RATD function on Bloomberg.

A good pre-sale report should state the date on which the information provided in the pre-sale report is based and also make clear that the ratings are of a preliminary nature and, hence, still subject to change. In practice, however, it is likely that the final ratings are very close to, if not the same as, the ones stated in the pre-sale report.

7.3 DEAL PRICING AND CLOSE

Provisional pool activities are focused on assembling a pool of assets to the required standard and quality to execute and issue the transaction. Once the portfolio of assets for the securitization has been compiled and internally agreed, the last activities relate to the marking or "flagging" of the assets to identify that they belong to this particular transaction. It is particularly important to have a flag or asset identifier that allows identifying which bond issuance any flagged loan or mortgage belongs to.

This activity is normally done the day before the actual issuance by the originator. Once the securitized assets have had their final flag assigned and, therefore, been essentially earmarked as assets which no longer belong to the originator, they become irreversible. This can, of course, change at later stages in the deal for individual assets which fail certain asset triggers or are in breach of representations and warranties, etc.

For a static pool structure, flagging is a one-off process for each issuance whereas revolving pools will require the ability to flag dynamically (i.e., select and deselect assets that are part of or excluded from a certain securitization).

For a master trust, at deal launch, assets up to the overall total value of the deal will be flagged. However, the actual bonds may be issued in several tranches, of smaller values, at different times during the life of the master trust, up to the overall total value of the deal. The tranches of notes are still part of the same overall master trust deal. The value of bonds issued to investors belongs to the "investors'" part of the master trust. The income from the remaining flagged mortgages for the deal belongs to the "seller" part of the master trust. This is known as the "seller/investor split".

The value of the investor part of the master trust remains constant (as the bonds have been issued); however, the value of the seller part of the pool varies with the total movement in value of the pool.

The seller/investor split will be configured at the pre-deal stage but will also vary at different stages within the life of the master trust. The seller is always considered to be a single entity (e.g., XYZ Banking Group) even though assets in the master trust's seller portion may belong to different brands of the same banking group (i.e., the seller is one portion when splitting the cash receipts into investor and seller portions).

As an example, the master trust deal may be launched with mortgages flagged up to a total value of £10bn. The first tranche of notes may be issued for £3bn. The income (cash received) from the £3bn share of the master trust belongs to the investors. The income from the rest of the master trust's £7bn is the seller's share (until further tranches of notes are issued, when it will decrease accordingly).

The investor/seller split is very important to master trust cash management and will need to be reflected in the processing of cash receipts. Cash receipts will be split between the investors and sellers on a monthly basis.

For a master trust, as the value of the assets flagged for the deal fall below the overall total value of the deal at issuance, so-called "topups" (new assets coming into the pool) can take place frequently. The total value of the pool of mortgages flagged for the master trust can also be increased (topped up) beyond the value set for the deal at issuance.

7.4 NEW-ISSUANCE REPORTS

The so-called "new issue" report is the final report by the credit rating agency, confirming the previously expected credit ratings (and in some rare cases also amending them). Often, this is almost 100% identical to the "pre-sale" reports; however, it may provide additional information that has come to light or, simply, fills in some of the data gaps in the pre-sale report.

8
Post close

8.1 SERVICING AND REPORTING

The activity of the underlying securitized assets must be tracked separately from the rest of the on-balance-sheet portfolio on a monthly or quarterly basis and, in certain circumstances, on a daily basis. Ongoing transaction reporting is a crucial part of any securitization, not only for the deal originators themselves, but more so for the investors, rating agencies, trustees, and other interested parties.

Transaction reporting has become increasingly important over the past 5 years, particularly for the development of any secondary market in these products. This was further accelerated by the credit crisis, resulting in investors placing much less reliance on the rating agencies as part of their analytical process. The times have gone when portfolio managers were able to write a single A4-page deal analysis accompanied by the rating agencies' pre-sale reports in order to get a signoff for a USD50m structured finance bond with a view to hold this for the next 14 years. Structured finance bond analysis has become increasingly sophisticated, which in turn has raised the levels of demand for deal-related information and performance data.

Following the credit crisis, investors have—for the first time in the past decade—been able to demand very detailed asset information, depending on the relevant asset class sometimes down to the loan-by-loan level; and the originators of such papers which have grown accustomed to these demands are happily fulfilling requests from investors where, previously, similar requests had been turned down.

In addition, key players in the structured finance markets recognized and acknowledged that there was a clear need to provide additional information to enable investors to undertake their own analysis. Subsequent industry initiatives such as that by the European Securitization Forum (AFME/ESF) and SIFMA (the American Securitization Forum) to name a couple have helped to detail these requirements and, ultimately, to revive the market.

Other players, such as the rating agencies, have previously published—at least to some extent—the data they would typically like to see as part of normal investor reporting. With this in mind, Fitch published so-called "post-issuance requirements" for various asset classes on their website back in 2004 and also introduced the Fitch "issuer report grades" in which rating agencies grade the quality of the investor reporting that accompanies individual transactions in Europe.

Subsequent updates to these statistics showed a considerable improvement for European structured finance transactions in terms of transactional reporting.

Servicer reporting requirements

This section provides an overview of the typical information that will need to be provided as part of the transaction's ongoing servicer reporting:

- Remaining balance
- Amount of collections attributed to the payment of principal (including prepayments), interest, other fees, etc.
- Delinquency status

- Repossessions/buyouts/chargeoffs
- Recoveries, when and if received
- Portfolio concentrations and analysis.

It will also be important to track payaheads, servicer advances, and actuarial balances. Historical portfolio information will be needed for rating agency presentations and prospectus disclosure; rating agency information can be very extensive or minimal depending on the objectives of the issuer.

Monthly/Quarterly servicer and investor reports

Each month/quarter the servicer/cash manager will be required to calculate

- The application of funds allocated to the investors
- Other payments in the waterfall, and
- Reserve requirements.

Monthly/Quarterly certificates

Each month/quarter the servicer will be required to provide two certificates to the trustee, the paying agent (typically, the trustee). and the rating agencies. These certificates are

- "Monthly Payment Instructions and Notification to the Trustee" certificate, which describes the application of funds allocated to the investor
- "Monthly Certificate Holders' Statement", which describes the amount of money to be paid to investors and how the trust has performed.

The servicer's accountant will be required to review these standards and confirm their accuracy on an annual basis.

SPV or trust management and transaction maintenance

The trust or the SPV itself will require limited active management:

- For purposes of servicing and collecting, the loans will be serviced identically to other on-balance-sheet loans and their inclusion in the trust/SPV should be transparent to the originator's employees—typically, by a so-called "hard flag" in the originator's loan book systems
- Additionally, the trust/SPV should be monitored closely for WAC, delinquency, and loss levels to provide warning of potential problems (i.e., triggers or early payout) and provide ample opportunity to take corrective actions.

8.1.1 Requirements

A key post-close requirement is the timely provision of deal-related performance information to Bloomberg, the relevant listing authorities, and last but not least the credit rating agencies.

8.1.2 Resources and components

Table 8.1 provides a brief overview of the required business resources and components that provide the relevant framework and reporting environment. It also takes a closer look at the level of involvement of these resources and how this differs for funded vs. synthetic transactions.

Table 8.1. Business resources and components providing the relevant framework and reporting environment.

Personnel/Department	*Role*	*Funded time requirement*	*Synthetic time requirement*
Program director	Responsible for overseeing all ongoing aspects of the transaction(s), may also function as transaction deal manager	High	High
Transaction administrator	Ensures that the transaction is serviced according to the relevant legal documentation (eligibility criteria, etc.), coordinates with a financial institution's personnel, rating agencies, trustees, and other parties on an ongoing basis	Moderate	Moderate
Systems function	Maintains systems and reporting integrity to ensure monthly loan data are reported accurately	Moderate	Low
Loan operations	Updates loan maturity schedules, principal and interest collections, "flags" new loans that are added to the transaction	Moderate	Moderate
Credit department	Provides ongoing credit review according to a financial institution's established methodology	Moderate	Moderate
Collections/Workout department	Performs necessary collections and workout of all delinquent/defaulted loans, transaction procedures/process may be different from a financial institution's	Low	NA
Accounting	Performs gain-on-sale analysis of loans added to a transaction during the revolving period for a master owner trust structure	Moderate	NA

8.1.3 Agency and investor reporting

Agency reporting

Once the provisional pool has been "flagged" as part of a particular securitization transaction, or after identifying the mortgages for replenishment of an existing transaction, detailed pool-specific information will need to be reported to the rating agencies.

Rating agencies require both pre-deal and post-deal information on the characteristics of the underlying pool in order to analyze a particular transaction throughout the deal lifecycle. Whilst the level of detail needed for most deals is the same, each agency usually has their own template for what is relevant. Although originators are not necessarily required to comply with these formats, it is advisable to provide the information in the requested formats and layout. This will help in bringing about a speedier upload and process of this information into the agencies' rating models and, ultimately, can help to speed up the analytical process.

In addition, it is advisable to provide as much historical performance, portfolio, and loan-level data as possible to support the agencies' rating analyses. Agencies tend to apply haircuts or conservative assumptions if presented with few datapoints. This in turn will have a direct impact on the capital structure suggested by the agencies' rating models and, ultimately, the determination of required credit enhancement levels.

Requirements for these reports can, depending on asset class and the relevant agency, change frequently and such changes can impact the reporting format. Although the agencies give normally an advance notice allowing for implementation of these amendments for a short period (such as the next reporting or interest payment date), it is advisable to respond to the changes quickly. It is therefore important for an originator to be able to reconfigure the data content as well as the format.

For instance, in the case of an RMBS transaction, the rating agency may require the following information as part of the agency reporting:

Liabilities: Principal distribution

- Class
- Original face value of notes
- Beginning principal balance of notes
- Principal distribution
- Ending notes balance
- Factor
- Beginning principal shortfall
- Current principal shortfall
- Payments of principal shortfall.

Liabilities: Interest distribution

- Class
- Beginning notes balance
- Current interest rate
- Current accrued interest
- Total interest distribution
- Beginning interest shortfall
- Current interest shortfall
- Payments of interest shortfall
- Ending cumulative interest shortfall.

Liabilities: Principal shortfall and deficiency ledgers

- Class
- Beginning principal shortfall
- Current principal shortfall
- Payments of principal shortfall
- Ending principal shortfall
- Beginning principal deficiency ledger
- Current principal shortfall
- Payments of principal deficiency
- Ending principal deficiency.

Ratios and triggers

- Trigger/Covenant descrition
- Nominator
- Denominator
- Ratio
- Trigger level
- Pass/Fail.

Bond information

- ISIN
- CUSIP
- Ticker
- Currency
- Current balance in currency of issued covered bond
- Current balance (in default currency)
- Expected maturity date (dd/mm/yyyy)
- Legal final (or "extended" maturity date, dd/mm/yyyy)
- Next interest payment date (dd/mm/yyyy)
- Next principal payment date (dd/mm/yyyy)
- Interest payment frequency
- Principal payment frequency
- Principal redemption type

- Interest rate type
- Interest margin where floating rate
- Date of issuance
- Interest rate where fixed rate
- Basis over which interest margin is calculated
- Series number.

Default currency

- Date
- Exchange rate.
- Foreign currency

Overcollateralization (OC)

- OC required by covered bond framework
- OC required by terms and conditions of the bonds
- Target OC agreed with Moody's
- In terms of basic OC
- Form of basic OC 1: Nominal OC or NPV OC
- Form of basic OC 2: Eligible only
- In terms of additional OC for specific legal risks
- In terms of additional OC for reinvestment risk
- Form of additional OC
- Total OC
- Nominal OC currently in cover pool based on eligible only
- Nominal OC currently in cover pool based on all assets (i.e., with ineligible included)
- Swap indicator
- In terms of basic OC
- In terms of additional OC for specific legal risks
- Additional OC for reinvestment risk
- Total OC.

Investor reporting

All investors in a securitization must be provided with monthly reports in PDF format, which is done by publishing them on Bloomberg, the U.K. Listing Authority (UKLA), and Luxembourg (depending on the listing of the program).

The data required for investor reports is a combination of the data required for agencies together with additional calculations plus balances extracted from the accounting systems and business-managed fields.

8.1.4 Pool management

Topups and replenishment

Post issuance, owing to redemption, further advances, product switches, and representations and warranties failures, the value of the underlying asset pool supporting an outstanding deal will diminish over time. To maintain the deal value and the required underlying collateral at desired levels and continue servicing the deal, more assets may need to be added to the pool. The process of adding new assets to a pool of already securitized assets is called "topup".

Run topup refers to all the functions that need to be performed in order to top up a given deal. This function encompasses a number of other pre-deal functions. Topups are done using a random selection process, from the available set of assets, provided that they pass the data quality and representations and warranties tests for the flagging states defined for the deal.

There are two scenarios for topup and, therefore, the execution of such a topup process will also depend on the applicable scenario.

Top up the deal using new assets

This applies when new "fresh" assets (i.e., not part of any deal yet) are subjected to the deal-specific data quality and representations and warranties tests and then added to the deal.

Top up a particular flagging state in the deal from the existing pool

This occurs when a particular flagging state needs a topup. The topup could be achieved by moving assets from a previous flagging state to the flagging state which requires a topup. For instance, in a hybrid covered bond pool, there are three different flagging states: non-mortgage bond collateral portfolio, additional covered bond portfolio, and covered bond/RMBS eligible portfolio. If the covered bond/RMBS eligible portfolio's pool value is going down and needs a topup, eligible assets from the additional covered bond portfolio can be moved to the covered bond/RMBS portfolio resulting in a topup for the covered bond/RMBS portfolio. To achieve this topup, data quality and representations and warranties tests, which enforce the rules of the covered bond/RMBS portfolio, would be run on all assets of the additional covered bond portfolio. Those assets that pass the tests would again be subjected to a random selection process to facilitate selection of assets worth the topup value. These selected assets would then be moved to the RMBS portfolio.

If there is a topup involving multiple flagging states (but not using new assets), then data quality and representations and warranties tests as well as random selection should be executed for each flagging state until the assets reach the flagging state that requires a topup.

R&W tests after issuance

After the deal has been launched and issued, there are a number of activities that need to take place on a regular basis. These activities ensure that the pool performs in the expected way and that none of the mortgages falls below the quality requirements for the pool as stated in the legal documents published to support the deal.

The representations and warranties tests will be run on a daily basis for the pool as a whole, using the latest configured version of the tests for the pool. This process is similar to that performed at the provisional pool stage, the major difference being that mortgages that fail the R&W tests post deal will be automatically removed (deflagged) from the pool. The value of any deflagged mortgages will reduce the value of the current pool supporting the deal.

Asset trigger tests to determine the performance of the pool as a whole will also be run daily, using the latest configured version of the tests for the pool. This process is the same as that done at the provisional pool stage (although the tests may be different post deal).

Post deal, there is also a need to be able to change the treatment of further advances and product switches by borrowers coming into the pool, because a borrower with an existing (flagged) mortgage has been granted a further loan or may have switched products. It may be necessary, for instance, to "exclude" all subaccounts for further advances from the flagged mortgage pool for a period of time, because they affect the overall balance of the pool (as determined by asset trigger tests). During this time, the cash flows from these subaccounts and any new advances coming into the pool for a "flagged" mortgage will form part of the seller's share (sometimes referred to as "seller's interest") of the pool, rather than the investor's share.

After a period of time of "exclusion" it may be necessary to "reinclude" all existing further advance subaccounts for flagged mortgages together with any new ones coming into the pool for existing flagged mortgages. During the period of exclusion, subaccounts are not available for inclusion in any other deals. Any subaccount movements in and out of the deal pool will increase or decrease the total value of mortgages supporting the deal accordingly.

As mortgages are redeemed over time, the value of the mortgage pool supporting the deal will decrease. For a master trust structure, the deal pool can be topped back up to the original value for the deal and, in addition, it can be topped up to a value exceeding the value of the deal at issuance (maximum and minimum thresholds will need to be adhered to).

8.1.5 Cash management

The cash received on securitized mortgages must be held in separate bank accounts for each deal. On a daily basis the cash must be split into interest and principal components according to the rules defined by the business. The cash is booked daily in the firm's ledgers and swept daily.

Various reports are produced on a daily and monthly basis to show cash movements. Originators need to be able to view the cash transaction data on any day for any specified period (not just normal calendar periods).

8.1.6 Hedging

There are three types of hedging or swap agreements entered into by the SPV when issuing a securitization to protect it against variations in interest rates and currency fluctuations.

Interest rate hedging

Payments received by the SPV (the issuer of the notes for a securitization) from the mortgages included in the pool will be subject to variable and fixed rates of interest. To hedge the potential variance between these rates and the 3-month sterling LIBOR (London Interbank Offering Rate)—the interest rate on some of the notes issued—the SPV will enter into an interest rate swap with the interest rate swap provider and the security trustee under an interest rate swap agreement.

Basis risk hedging

Net payments received by the SPV from the mortgages in the pool and the interest rate swap agreement will be linked to the 3-month sterling LIBOR. To hedge the potential variance between the 3-month sterling LIBOR and the 1-month sterling LIBOR, and to ensure the SPV has sufficient funds to pay interest on the notes, the SPV will enter into a basis rate swap with the basis rate swap provider and the security trustee under a basis rate swap agreement.

Currency risk hedging

Payments received by the SPV from the mortgages in the pool and the interest rate swap agreement will be in sterling. To enable the issuer to make payments on the interest payment dates in respect of dollar or euro notes (if notes are going to be issued in the U.S. or Europe), the SPV will enter into a currency swap for each of the currencies in which the notes are issued.

8.1.7 Accounting and controling

Originators need to be able to prepare monthly management and yearly statutory accounts for the SPV on a standalone basis, while also reporting the results from the retail division ("retails") as if it were business as usual (BAU).

Daily reconciliation of flagged and unflagged mortgage balances is required between the source system(s) and the securitization system and between the bank's general ledger and statutory reporting and the securitization system. A number of accounting reports are also required.

8.2 DEAL PERFORMANCE MEASUREMENT

There are of course many ways to describe and define "reporting". In the context of this book, however, *reporting* means presenting data to internal users such as front office, risk management, credit risk controling, and last but not least senior management up to board level. Furthermore, various external bodies are also users of some and, increasingly more, reported information. They include shareholders, regulators, rating agencies, the general public, and specific stakeholder groups.

Existing management information systems (MIS) serve to compile the relevant information—typically, from more than one source system—and to produce the reports which are simply means of presenting data.

8.2.1 Surveillance

Surveillance can be defined as systematic and ongoing collection, collation, and analysis of data. Data collection for surveillance purposes is typically dynamic in nature and may change at any time. Theoretically, this data-gathering process should therefore be real time. However, in practice, some of these data will only be updated at predetermined points in time. For instance, the dissemination of monthly trustee reports would need only updating of performance-related data from this particular source in line with the respective 4-week reporting frequency of this trustee report.

A key objective of surveillance is an ongoing monitoring process in order to enable real-time detection of changes in the trend or distribution of transaction data that are under surveillance. Predetermined trigger levels (e.g., pool concentration levels), thresholds (e.g., percentage of outstanding notes), changes (e.g., deltas, such as rating changes) of individual values, and plausibility checks (e.g., total number of columns vs. total number of rows) are all straightforward methods that can be applied fairly easily. Whilst such methods may not be completely accurate, they are clearly distinguished by their practicability, uniformity, and rapidity and as such are deemed fit for purpose for deal surveillance.

Once a trend or distribution of changes has been identified, surveillance initiates further investigative measures to verify these observations. Subsequently, following such surveillance analysis, adequate control measures can be activated. This could be, for instance, changes of internal ratings or placement of an underperforming transaction on the company's internal watch list.

Surveillance, by definition, has a retrospective view which spans from the past (e.g., historical vintage data) to the present (e.g., rating changes or news flow). The limitation of the surveillance time horizon, at least in this sense, represents in practice a clear limitation when—from an analytical point of view—future performance trends would need to be identified.

8.2.2 Performance analytics

In order to paint a complete analytical picture, structured finance analysis requires a holistic view, not only of the past and present, but more importantly also the future. This can be achieved by moving away from a reactive surveillance function towards proactive *performance analysis*. Automatic processing of large data volumes (e.g., loan-level data) combined with the use of forecasting methods (e.g., base case expectations and scenario analysis, such as best case, worst case, most likely, and extreme scenarios) can efficiently support forward-oriented trend analysis. In an ideal world, purpose-built performance analysis systems may enable system-driven detection and prediction of performance trends before other market participants, competitors (at least the ones with largely manual data processing), and the rating agencies' surveillance teams manage to identify these changes in underlying performance. Ultimately, such timelier identification may translate into real relative value, if banks were confident enough of the analytical conclusion and acted purely on such information *before* the underlying performance can manifest itself in price deterioration.

8.3 THE PERFORMANCE ANALYTICS PROCESS

The following sections will focus on the components that can make up a robust performance analytics function.

8.3.1 Performance data: Dynamic information

One of the key requirements to undertake efficient and effective performance analysis is the possession of deal-related performance data with which to conduct the analysis. Five years ago most of this information was predominantly available both to a selected audience (i.e., password-protected web-sites) and in a format that would not easily permit automatic feeding and processing of an investor's portfolio management systems (i.e., printed hardcopies, faxes, PDF files, etc.). This changed when specialist data providers such as Lewtan Technologies, Trepp, Intex—to name a few—discovered how they could translate bulk data from investor reports into more digestible and usable data formats such as comma-separated files (CSV) or extensible markup language (XML).

Automatic processing has many major advantages compared with manual entry of performance data. It is typically quicker and timelier and also avoids data errors caused by simple typographical errors. In addition, automatic document-processing methods combined with intelligent character recognition (ICR) allow bulk processing of reports in various file formats as soon as they become available. Subsequent automatic data validation (e.g., automatic checks of data formats, types, ranges, etc.) can further increase the overall data quality of such automated processing.

After receipt from the data provider, "scrubbed" or cleansed data can easily be loaded into the investor's internal portfolio management and performance analytics platform for further analysis.

8.3.2 Key performance indicators (KPIs)

Performance data in isolation are not automatically useful. They need to be interpreted and should undergo a careful thought process to identify which items out of the available data universe of deal-specific information allow meaningful analysis. For instance, 90+-day delinquencies as a predictor for expected losses (EL) or typical recovery rate (RR) as an estimator for loss-given defaults (LGDs) are such performance data items that, if used and interpreted appropriately, can serve as early warning for deteriorating performance.

When using KPIs supplied by data providers acting as intermediaries, particular care should be taken to understand which of these performance items are directly taken from the transaction's performance report or whether they are calculated values. For instance, if you are investing in a portfolio of 25 U.S. RMBS bonds and you were to compare KPIs for these individual deals, the calculation of some of them could follow different formulas for different bonds. However, the actual performance parameter name (i.e., CPR) may be called the same for each of these bonds. There is no shortcut to identifying which KPIs are calculated and subsequently used to analyze the relevant formulas. You may then conclude that the discrepancies in calculating these KPIs are far too great to justify usage of the data provided to you and you might eventually end up calculating them yourself.

8.3.3 Credit ratings

Rating actions

Long-term vs. short-term ratings

Most structured finance transactions carry long-term ratings, although short-term or financial strength ratings are used for vehicles with a short-term funding nature: for instance, asset-backed commercial paper conduits (ABCPs)—which essentially roll over and renew every 364 days—and some short/medium-term notes.

Rating actions

Rating actions are any changes to the transaction's rating. They include actual changes in the rating itself. These changes can be "affirmation"/"confirmation", "upgrade", and "downgrade". Some agencies differ between affirmation and confirmation, whereby the first action is an agency-initiated action and the latter a reiteration of an agency's rating following a request from a relevant party, such as the originator or trustee.

Furthermore, ratings can also be withdrawn (WDR) for a variety of reasons. Formal withdrawal of ratings are usually either requested by the issuer or because the agency chose to withdraw the ratings. CRAs will remove a bond rating and flag this on their websites as paid in full (PIF) when a bond has been redeemed as expected and there are no remaining outstanding balances for the particular bond tranche left.

Rating watch

In addition to the rating itself, rating modifiers may be assigned to ratings which typically either indicate some uncertainty ("evolving", with a 50% rating upward probability and a 50% rating downward probability) or some uncertainty about the likelihood of an upgrade ("rating watch positive") or of a downgrade ("rating watch negative"). The definition of rating watch states differs by agency in terms of likelihood and timeframe: The agency that placed a particular bond on rating watch will be undertaking further analysis to clarify the uncertainty around the affected ratings. Once the agency has concluded its analysis, it will then action the rating itself and usually remove the watch status.

Outlook

Rating watch status covers a short-term period of time, typically between 1 month and 6 months. Rating agencies also indicate their medium-term view on transactions they rate. This medium-term view is called "rating outlook" and covers a period between 12 months to 18 months. Similar to the rating watch, this can either be "outlook positive", "outlook negative", or "evolving".

Intra-agency rating nuances

As if these scales were not enough, I am aware of cases where an agency used rating modifiers (i.e., watches and outlooks) differently, depending on which regional office was undertaking the analysis. This particular CRA had rating outlooks available for the EMEA region for some time, but outlooks did not exist for structured finance transactions in the U.S. and were only introduced in mid-2008. Until the introduction of the outlook rating modifier to the U.S., rating watches were used in some instances instead of the outlook.

New developments for additional rating qualifiers

The credit crisis put rating agencies in the limelight, questioning the transparency, clarity, and meaning of what a rating should and should not express. Subsequent calls for more regulation of CRAs and introduction of additional measures to increase the transparency of agencies' ratings triggered a major revisit of the currently used rating classifications. The agencies' own initiatives proposed various changes and amendments to their commonly used structured finance ratings, which included suggestions to include additional information on liquidity, volatility, etc.

Different ways to report rating actions

There are different ways of looking at rating changes over a given period of time and this can lead to different ways of reporting them. This became particularly apparent during the first half of 2008 when literally thousands of structured finance ratings suddenly became subjected to—in many cases—multiple rating changes by all three agencies. The way in which such rating changes can be measured depends on the particular dimension we would like to report on:

(1) Deal dimension
(2) Tranche dimension
(3) Rating action dimension
(4) Time dimension.

Although it was quite unusual to see changes in transaction ratings more than once by the same CRA in a short period of time (i.e., a month) in the pre-2007 market, this changed completely with the onset of the credit crisis and liquidity crisis. There were periods in late 2007 and the first two quarters of 2008 when the ratings of many deals were changed more than once within a month by the same agency (and by the other agencies at the same time). Most of these actions were driven by the downgrade of the monoline insurers AMBAC, CIFG, FIGC, MBIA, RADIAN, and XLCA. In addition, as part of the vicious circle of downgrades, complex instruments such as CDO of ABS and CDO^2s became subject to blanket rating watches and downgrades in short succession by multiple agencies. Consequently, investors holding large portfolios of these instruments were challenged as to how to report the impact of these changes to their portfolios. In most cases, such actions require reporting not only to senior management, but also to external third parties such as the investor's external auditors, the regulator, rating agencies, and external investors/shareholders.

These actions on their own posed a major challenge for some institutions regarding their reporting capabilities and management information systems. In addition, there was the more generic question of how to report these changes. Whilst there is no right or wrong answer, it clearly depends on the audience and the message that is to be conveyed when reporting a portfolio's rating migration. The remainder of this section explains differences in the identification and presentation of rating migration over a given period of time (e.g., the second quarter of 2008).

The *deal dimension* means simply reporting on the number and type of rating actions impacting direct holdings (i.e., the tranche which a particular investor holds on her book) and related tranches within the capital structure of this particular deal, which could either be senior or subordinated tranches relative to the tranche held by the investor. The different questions that could be asked are

(Q1)	*How many deals have seen rating actions in the selected period (i.e., 2Q08)?*

or

(Q2)	*How many rating actions have happened in the reporting period for the selected deal(s)?*

On a tranche level, it could well be that, whilst our holding has not directly been impacted by any rating action, subordinated tranches below ours may have experienced changes to their ratings.

(Q3)	*How many subordinated tranches have been impacted by any changes to their ratings?*

This could mean that the credit enhancement provided by subordination, overcollateralization, and excess spread could slowly be eroding over time and, if so, our holding may become more susceptible to changes of the rating in the near future. Alternatively, we could also ask

(Q4)	*How many tranches of direct holdings have seen rating actions in the selected period?*

From a *rating actions dimension* viewpoint, an investor could be interested in any kind of rating change (upgrade, downgrade, affirmation, withdrawal, rating watch, outlook) or any subset of these iterations. If an investor is capable of querying this information for his portfolio to understand, for instance, the rating differential between his internal rating and the respective external ratings, then he could take a conservative stance from a risk management perspective. Such analysis can, for instance, help in identifying bonds where the internal rating is currently higher than the external rating(s) and the internal rating could subsequently be adjusted to the lower external rating—unless there is a concrete reason or the internal rating is considered to be more adequate than the external rating.

Furthermore, rating watches (positive, negative, and evolving) can give an investor a good indication as to whether he may experience potential changes to the rating in the near term. Rating watches would typically cover a period of uncertainty from 1 month to 6 months, in some cases longer—but the agency would normally try to specify this period of uncertainty. If an investor can foresee and pre-empt future rating changes, he may be placed to realize relative value from such instruments on rating watch, either by disposing of them or buying them. This does, of course, require a liquid secondary market. Although the secondary market for structured finance instruments had virtually diminished at the time of writing this chapter, I would hope to see some market activity returning by mid-2011.

The analysis of rating changes for a given portfolio over a *different time dimension* is probably one of the most interesting questions concerning the subject of rating changes. The two fundamental questions that can be asked are

(Q5) *What were the rating changes over the selected observation period?*

or

(Q6) *How have the ratings moved relatively over a given period?*

The answer to the first question is usually simpler. In essence, it involves listing all rating actions for the observed period by any agency.

Tracking rating changes

Ideally, performance analytics for structured finance transactions should be able to measure deal performance in near real time and support the identification of performance outliers compared with initial base case expectations for the individual deal and compared with peers in the same asset class. Subsequently, such analysis can support pre-emption of forthcoming rating changes once the rating agencies run the performance through their own internal surveillance function and performance analysis models, which takes time. We could now argue that tools to identify and track rating changes if and when they are published by the relevant agency are not necessary if there is a robust enough system in place to support internal analysis.

In reality, however, banks and financial institution are well advised to build and maintain sufficient systems and procedures in order to track rating changes by the larger rating agencies. The key reasons for such a requirement are as follows.

Basel II risk weights

In order to calculate Basel II risk weights, investors in structured finance instruments are required to calculate the capital charges for the bonds they hold and need the rating attributes of these instruments as parameter and key driver of such calculation. Hence, unless the bond's portfolio size is small (i.e., 25 to 250 bonds), it is advisable to have some automated procedure in place that allows real-time or near-real-time tracking of rating changes.

Investment guidelines for conduits

Conduit managers are bound by the investment guidelines of the structured vehicles they run. These guidelines usually involve calculation rules to determine the credit enhancement levels required for the conduit, which are based on ratings and other factors like various concentration levels for asset classes, countries, and industry. As conduits can contain a larger number of bonds—in some cases more than 1,000—an automated mechanism to monitor rating migration which in turn drives the credit enhancement calculation is pivotal. Whilst the market has seen massive downward migration of ratings, there have been occasional upgrades in the same period.

Downgrades—particularly those that involve 10 or more notches (i.e., from AAA to speculative-grade ratings in one single action)—can have a considerable impact on credit enhancement calculation. In turn, upgrades can reduce the level of credit enhancement required. Any rating migration should be identified in near real time which helps to optimize a conduit's efficiency.

Central banks' repurchase agreement guidelines

All central banks—particularly the Federal Reserve Bank in the U.S., the European Central Bank, and the Bank of England in the U.K.—reacted promptly during the credit crisis by establishing new liquidity schemes to enable banks and financial institutions to pledge to a large extent a variety of structured finance instruments and to use them as part of repo agreements. The rules allow highly rated bonds to be pledged in return for cash or government bonds. These repurchase (repo) agreements are subject to strict rules and it is the banks' or financial institutions' responsibility to manage the collateral that has been pledged appropriately. This includes notification of the relevant central bank of any change to ratings of assets that are pledged as and when they occur. If there are rating changes rendering pledge collateral ineligible for the relevant central bank repo scheme, then there is a limited window within which the bank has to either replace ineligible collateral with another suitably rated bond or, alternatively, remove the asset from the pledged pool altogether.

Regulatory reporting

In light of the credit crisis, financial regulators have become considerably more aware of banks' and financial institutions' structured finance portfolios and their particulars. Some of my clients, for instance, who have large portfolios (>1,000 bonds) have been inundated with questions from the regulators and related authorities with a particular focus on the following aspects of their structured portfolios:

- Bond breakdown by asset class, region, internal rating (if applicable), weighted average life, negative basis trade counterparties, and monoline exposure
- Seniority of the assets
- Suitability of assets for inclusion (or exclusion) of the various government asset protection schemes
- Usage of central bank repo facilities
- Tracking of rating changes, etc.

Consequently, even with the best in-house performance analytics function, banks need to have efficient ways and means built into their processes to identify any rating changes in an efficient and timely manner. The following section discusses the advantages and disadvantages of a variety of readily available tools in order to track such rating changes effectively.

CRA client portfolio alerts

A simple way of tracking rating changes is by using the agencies' own "portfolio" functions. This permits the setup of one or more portfolios based on the ISIN, CUSIP, or bond ticker, which will trigger a specific email notification: any deal-specific or sector-specific rating action would trigger the transmission of an automated email notification for the impacted bonds to a predefined email address.

Advantages:

- Easy to set up and comes as part of the subscription to agency websites at no additional cost
- You can use a group's or department's inbox so that several people will be alerted at the same time.

Disadvantages:

- Client portfolios regularly require maintenance to reflect changes to the bank's structured credit portfolio (i.e., bond purchase and asset disposal)
- Client portfolios need to be set up with each CRA individually—some may permit bulk upload of a list of deals, others don't have this capability yet

- Overwhelming number of emails at peak times of rating changes (I consulted an institution with a portfolio of approximately 1,100 deals which received up to 1,000 emails per week during the credit crisis in 2007—even a dedicated surveillance team of three analysts would find it difficult and time-consuming to work its way through so many emails)
- The email is generic and not tailored to a financial institution's individual needs as it contains no holding information, etc.

CRA rating data delivery feed

The three main CRAs (and some smaller ones) offer a rating action data delivery feed whereby they provide frequent information on any rating action they have taken for the sector or portfolio that has been subscribed for. Subscribers to this service usually receive the whole data universe of ratings (of the subscribed sector) in electronic file format. Subsequent changes to this rating information are then distributed as "deltas" and subscribers to this service will therefore always have updated rating information available. This can then be further fed into the investor's proprietary systems.

One of the advantages of using the rating agency delivery feed is that the information comes directly from the source (i.e., the rating agencies themselves). This helps to eliminate the potential for errors in the transmission of this information, which can be due to third parties that are sitting in between the rating agencies and the end-user—such as Bloomberg and Reuters. Although Bloomberg is pretty good, there have been instances where they have gotten the rating wrong on the Bloomberg terminal. Such errors can and will get rectified by Bloomberg very quickly, but once the information has been corrected, there is no trace on its terminal that would indicate that the information had been wrong.

The rating agencies offer this as a "real-time" service meaning you can get delta updates of such rating changes every 15 minutes or so if you really wanted, but at an additional cost.

Consequently, one of the disadvantages of having a direct rating agency feed is the cost. This is, however, further exacerbated by the fact that if you want to subscribe to such a service from all three rating agencies, you will need to enter into three individual subscription agreements. Some of my clients are paying in excess of $200,000 per year for having such a "service" and it makes me wonder whether or not it is really worth having. I guess to some extent it comes down to the level of information that is provided as part of this service. If you feel that you require, for instance, detailed information on rating outlooks as well as additional rating-related parameters that some of the agencies started developing in order to address some of the rating shortfalls experienced during the credit crisis, then I would say, yes, take a close look at these products. Contact the agencies' product specialists for such data feeds and request a sample file to give you an impression of what the actual file you would receive as part of this service looks like. Furthermore, having the actual file helps you to look through and understand whether or not the specific datapoints you are after are actually contained in the file. Furthermore, when you talk to agencies, enquire about the data-licencing arrangement for this product and what internal uses of this information are permitted or not. In addition, you may find that other divisions in your area may be interested in a similar feed of rating data (e.g., business areas that would use corporate rating information rather than structured finance rating information). You may discover that agencies can offer you considerable benefits if you increase the sectors covered by such a subscription.

The agencies usually refer to the "added value" of passing (already publicly available) rating information on, but the only value I think they are referring to is the electronic availability of the data—which means data can be fed directly into your proprietary system. If you go down that route, however, you can expect some system-tweaking to be necessary as there is no standard format for these rating extracts: the files you will be receiving from the different agencies all have a slightly different file format; and it will require some development skills and implementation time to build an interface that can be used to load this information into your firm's proprietary system.

Suitable alternatives: Market-implied ratings

If you are considering investing in rating agencies' data feeds then you may wish to consider looking at their offering in terms of so-called "market-implied ratings", which are ratings based on market data/information and movements thereof (e.g., CDS prices).

Bloomberg portfolio uploader

If you have access to a Bloomberg terminal (either a dedicated one on your desk or a terminal with shared access for all your team-members) then some of the disadvantages related to the rating agency data feed can easily be overcome by using the "Bloomberg portfolio uploader". This is essentially an Excel spreadsheet-based Bloomberg tool that enables the user to bulk-upload a list of bond identifiers (Ticker, ISIN, CUSIP, WKN, etc.) into the user's Bloomberg terminal environment. Such a so-called "client portfolio" can then subsequently be analyzed (e.g., for rating changes, etc.). It can also be shared with your colleagues.

Once you have uploaded such a portfolio into the Bloomberg terminal, you will find two particular functions very useful at enabling the tracking of such rating changes: MTGE RATC and CORP RATC. As their names suggest, the first function relates to mortgage (MTGE) tickers whereas the latter can be used to identify rating changes for corporate (CORP) tickers. The majority of structured finance tickers used for the more generic asset classes (i.e., ABS/MBS) are MTGE tickers. CORP tickers are typically assigned by Bloomberg to vehicles such as single-name CDO/CLOs and some whole business securitization structures. Whilst it is possible to search for a particular structured finance transaction on Bloomberg by entering its MTGE ticker, using the CORP ticker instead does not work: Bloomberg requires the ISIN or CUSIP to be entered in order to get deal information.

Assuming a client portfolio has been uploaded into Bloomberg by means of the Bloomberg uploader, the reader will be able to query a selected date range, relevant CRAs, select the direction of rating movements (i.e., upgrades and/or downgrades). The results of this analysis can then be conveniently exported as comma-separated value files (CSV) into Excel for further data interrogation. Once this portfolio has been set up, such a Bloomberg terminal-based analysis of rating changes is fast and can be undertaken by any end-user who has a valid Bloomberg license.

One of the great advantages of using Bloomberg is that you are using a single data "source" that provides you with rating change information for four rating agencies (in addition to Moody's, Standard & Poors', and Fitch's ratings this feed also includes rating changes by Dominion Bond Rating Service) rather than having to subscribe to four individual data feeds.

There's virtually no interface development time or any implementation costs involved since the Bloomberg data uploader is a simple Excel sheet (with Bloomberg proprietary macros) and as such an off-the-shelf product that easily integrates into your firm's IT environment and analytical platform. Furthermore, as far as cost is concerned, when comparing it with the pricey rating agency data feeds, this solution only requires a Bloomberg license which you are likely to have anyway (unless you are using Reuters, but I would imagine they may offer something similar).

One of the downsides to using this approach is that you may have to split the portfolio (as well as the data query for this information) into two parts: one for the MTGE part of the portfolio and one for the CORP part. This is due to the fact that Bloomberg's rating functions for mortgage tickers and corporate tickers are slightly different as a result of the way Bloomberg treats such bonds in its systems and the underlying data structure. If you are lucky and your portfolio is made up purely of MTGE tickers, then all you need do is run the RATC function against your client portfolio. This will return rating changes for the relevant list of tickers that make up your deal list.

Chances are, however, that your portfolio contains at least a few CORP tickers and, in that instance, you will need to use a separate Bloomberg data uploader in order to maintain this portfolio in like manner with the mortgage portfolio. Once you manage to upload the relevant information, you will need to run the CORP RATC function against this portfolio and Bloomberg will identify all relevant rating changes. Note that the simple RATC function will not work for CORP tickers.

This method is probably sufficient if you just need to be aware of and see rating changes for a certain portfolio on a frequent (normally daily) basis. But if you want to use this information for further analysis or additional data interrogation then you will need to export the results of your RATC queries into Excel first which can become a little tedious after a while—and you may be well advised to consider using the Bloomberg API (see the next section), instead.

Another disadvantage of this particular method is that frequently changing portfolios require regular updating to reflect any changes, such as additions or removal of bonds. This, of course, carries the potential for human error should the bonds not be reflected properly and, therefore, rating changes may not be detected and hence missed.

Bloomberg desktop or server APIs

Bloomberg offers two application programming interfaces (APIs): the desktop and server APIs. As their names suggest, these interfaces plug seamlessly either as add-ons to the user's desktop-based Excel or Access or, as is the case for the server API, they reside on the user's centralized internal server.

Both APIs allow the dynamic sending and receiving of data to and from Bloomberg and offer a more flexible approach for bespoke solutions. For instance, it is possible to build a database tool that allows you to send Bloomberg—via the API—a list of tickers (MTGE and CORP, if required) and get rating actions for these tickers returned to your own database environment. To reiterate, the major advantage here is that you need only subscribe to one third party in order to receive information from all rating agencies rather than having to enter individual rating agency data delivery feed agreements with all three agencies individually. Hence, this route is likely to be a considerably cheaper solution.

Furthermore, instead of having to rely on three different sources (i.e., the three agencies), you will be getting the required data from a single source and in a single data format. Consequently, you will only need one data interface (your Bloomberg API). This tool is well documented via the WAPI function and a well-versed Excel or Access rapid applications developer can work real wonders using the API.

One of the major advantages of the API is that it is highly dynamic and flexible. If you combine an investor's exposure tool (or limit management tool) which can provide proprietary holding information in real time or at least near real time (i.e., any time when bonds are purchased or disposed of by the investor), with the Bloomberg API, then you can use these data to get relevant information for your changed portfolio at any time and without any manual intervention. A limitation is that you may require the assistance of a systems developer or analyst who is familiar with the Bloomberg API. If you want to build a long-term solution that can execute powerful performance analytics for a large portfolio of structured finance assets (i.e., more than 1,000), then this is a feasible way to do so.

Deploying the Bloomberg API tool requires some knowledge of how Bloomberg structures the data in their systems, which can sometimes show some weird quirks that need getting used to. Help is at hand here with Bloomberg's own product specialists (there are a few in Europe and a handful in the U.S.). These specialists are extremely valuable, so if you happen to know one make sure you keep in touch. (In case you are wondering, I do not get paid by Bloomberg for praising them, but I have been working closely with some of their guys for the past 5 years and was pleasantly impressed by their level of professionalism and knowledge.)

8.4 DEAL REDEMPTION

If everything goes to plan with the transaction and the cash flows are sufficient to support regular and timely payments of interest and equally frequent and timely payments of principal, then investors will likely be able to see an ordinary redemption of the notes.

Expected maturity

The "expected maturity" (sometimes referred to as the "scheduled maturity date") is the point in time (or date) when the issued notes are scheduled or expected to repay.

Early redemption date

However, in more flexible structures, the originator may also be permitted to redeem an outstanding bond earlier, typically upon the occurrence of an "early redemption event". Such events can include the following:

- A call option due to tax changes
- Following a so-called "cleanup call" one of the remaining outstanding principal balances is less than a certain percentage (typically 10%) of the initial principal balance
- Call option on certain or all note classes due to regulatory change
- Breach of replenishment conditions.

In the case of an early redemption event or if the scheduled redemption date is reached, the outstanding notes will be repaid in full with the cash that has been accumulated so far and, hence, is available in the bond's structure but this will typically exclude the principal on those notes which corresponds to principal on defaulted underlyings. Payment on these notes will be deferred until such losses have been settled.

Part III
Toolbox

9
Understanding complex transactions

Whilst the previous two parts of this book focused on the general underlying principles for a deal as well as the different life stages of a transaction, the following part focuses more on the different tools that are available at these stages and which you may wish to use in order to understand different areas of transactions and different deal-related processes throughout the life of such deals. Although these tools may address different needs there's at least one commonality: they are all designed to make your life—regardless of whether you are an investor, issuer, analyst, regulator, lawyer, portfolio manager, etc.—easier. All of these tools have been used by me and have been functioning properly at the time of writing. However, due to the very dynamic nature of this particular capital market arena, you need to ensure that you keep abreast of any developments, be it regulatory or market-driven changes, because just doing that may give you a competitive edge.

I'm particularly excited about Part III of this book because it's where I am hoping to be able to add value to what you do and on a larger scale to the market. Whilst some of the tools are free and do not need any other prerequisites in order to use them, the majority will require that you have access to certain portals or data providers such as Bloomberg or subscription access to the rating agencies' websites. Both of these requirements do not come cheap, but, equally, if your firm is looking at investing hundreds of millions if not billions in this market, then I guess the annual cost of subscribing to these services is probably easily justified. It's not good enough, though, just having access—you need to actively use the tools.

The guiding principle in using some or all of these tools is simple and applies now more than ever: understanding complex transactions. Only when you fully appreciate and understand the risks in these deals will you be able to reap the rewards. If you find some of what is to follow useful and apply it to increase your understanding of deals, which in turn may help to inject a little more confidence, then I feel I've done "my bit" to help the market revive. Now, read on, enjoy, and try the tools out.

9.1 STRUCTURE DIAGRAMS

Throughout this book I refer to "structured" finance and, as illustrated in many of the previous chapters, this usually involves several counterparties to a transaction who are interconnected via various legal arrangements that govern the flow of funds throughout the transaction.

Some structures are fairly simply, but equally—often depending on the relevant jurisdiction—you can find some transactions that have highly complex structures with many counterparties, including sometimes more than one special purpose vehicle. Theoretically, that is fine, but in practice the more counterparties involved, the more legal agreements there are in place between them and the greater the interconnectedness of these structures—leading ultimately, like it or not, to considerably increased risks of one or more counterparties falling away or becoming bankrupt which in turn can trigger the collapse of the entire structure or at least to considerable interruption of the cash flows for a prolonged period of time.

There are several ways of tackling these problems: from an issuer's perspective I suggest adopting KISS (keep it simple) as one of the guiding principles when structuring these transactions. This will make investors' lives easier and help saving setup and running costs when originating such deals. Prior to the credit crisis there was often a desire to artificially increase the opaqueness of transactions in order to discourage price transparency. Such behavior is not appropriate for the new market where standardization and transparency and the removal of information asymmetries will be key to the engagement of investors.

From an investor's perspective—or indeed from the perspective of anyone wishing to understand how deals actually work (or not)—it does help to draw up a structure diagram when reading deal-related documentation and then comparing it against the deal structure diagram in the offering circular. When I used to look at many of these bonds as an investor, I always found it helpful to draw a picture of the structure whilst reading the rating agencies' new issue reports. Whilst I was reading these reports, I transferred my understanding of the structure's narrative into the picture of the transaction's structure. After I completed my drawing, I compared this against the structure diagrams in the rating agencies' analysis as well as the offering circular. Occasionally, as a result of this kind of visual analysis, I noticed issues that things did not stack up and, hence, identified either errors in the rating reports or the deal documentation where things appeared a little odd.

Of course, you need not only time to do this, but also the analytical capabilities—both combined are a worthwhile investment on their own.

9.2 ANALYTICAL CAPABILITIES

9.2.1 People, tools such as models, rating agency subscriptions, Bloomberg

As already alluded to in previous chapters, depending on the size of the portfolio—by and large this means the number of structured finance bonds you chose to invest in rather than the notional value of the portfolio—and depending on the level of seniority of these investments (super senior, senior, mezzanine, junior, or equity tranches), you need to build team(s) with different analytical capabilities. Post credit crisis this has become even more important since it is no longer recommended to "outsource" your analysis to the credit rating agencies and in return just worry about the rating itself and ignore the fact that you should be doing your homework (i.e., undertake a thorough analysis which will help you form your own opinion as to whether or not the risk/reward profile of the potential investment you are looking at can justify the purchase).

Equally, if you already have a large portfolio (say, 1,500 bonds) as well as surveillance and performance analytics systems that are capable of managing such a sizable portfolio in a semi-automatic or even fully automated fashion, then the last thing you want to do is decommission such tools. But this is exactly what one of my previous clients did:

> Following a forced takeover, my client decommissioned the takeover candidate's system and moved to a more or less manual process and, whilst claiming a dynamic monitoring system was in place, actually moved towards doing most of their analysis "manually".
>
> As a consequence, the remaining analysts at this firm were completely overwhelmed—perversely, as it happens, they were from the entity that took over the other one. They were used to doing this manual work for the relatively small portfolio they had previously, but unfortunately this was not a scalable solution to manage 1,500 bonds efficiently.
>
> So, first, the systems were put to sleep and then the analysts came in and, subsequently, much of the analytical capability (which was a combination of robust working technology and highly qualified analysts many of whom were ex-rating agency staff and specialists in many of the asset classes) of the other firm disappeared.

I recommend you consider very carefully whether you have the analytical capabilities in terms of staff and systems—otherwise, the regulators may undertake this analysis for you and you may not like the outcome when your regulator discovers that you are lacking the analytical firepower.

9.3 THE RISK OF OVERRELIANCE ON RATINGS

Yes, I know, throughout this book I keep referring to rating agencies but, like it or not, they are an integral part of this market. Rightly or wrongly, throughout the credit crisis they were heavily criticized for failing to see the problems looming and their reputation was severely dented and I fear they may never be able to restore this back to pre-crisis levels.

However, they are by no means the only culprits: investment banks pressurized the agencies to churn out ratings and, prior to the crisis, I kept saying to people that the agencies had to some extent turned into "conveyor belt analysts"—meaning they sit there, get the information (and the pressure) from investment bankers, digest the information quickly, convene hastily arranged rating committees, assign the "desired" ratings, publish the new-issue report, and move on to the next deal, only to do it all over again.

And then, at the other end of the spectrum, there were investors that were also under pressure from arrangers who "invited" them to participate in "heavily oversubscribed" deals, which putting it bluntly meant "you had better be quick in coming back to us to let us know whether or not you would like to invest in such bonds, but we need your feedback pretty much pronto, almost kind of now."

What would investors do in such a pressurized scenario? Well, they would have a look at the rating agencies' presale reports, quickly identify the bond's strengths and weaknesses (mainly based on the agencies' rating designator), ensure the pricing looks appropriate for such a bond, and then make a quick decision—based to a large extent on the rating agencies' analyses.

9.3.1 What the "users" of ratings think . . .

Although this appeared all very well pre credit crunch, it was certainly not good enough and many investors were gutted when they discovered during the credit crisis that sole reliance on AAA ratings was actually a dangerous approach that should have been avoided in the first place.

Throughout the credit crisis I gave a series of talks and seminars on the topic of "rating agencies and overreliance on ratings" and was surprised how many myths were out there with regard to ratings, sometimes leading to a dangerous level of overreliance by the various users of ratings. The questions I asked during this series were:

Question *Do you use and, if so, what is the frequency of your use of rating agencies?*

The respective responses were as follows: a total of 24% answered that they do not use them, 16% use them once a day or more, 16% use them once a week or more, and 44% said they use them but only infrequently. This means that 76% of respondents use rating agencies and, hence, should be familiar with credit ratings. But the following answers would indicate they do not necessarily understand the meaning of ratings.

In the survey, 32% believed that a Fitch AAA rating is the same as a AAA from Standard & Poor's and a Aaa from Moody's. They were not aware that Fitch's and S&P's ultimate default risk view, which uses the probability of default (PD)—in other words, the first dollar of loss—differs from

Moody's expected loss (EL) methodology, which focuses on the amount of net loss suffered (i.e., by multiplying the PD by the loss-given default (LGD).

Even more revealing, a stark 47% thought that all the agencies mark a defaulted instrument with a D rating and that the D is the same for all three agencies. A close look at the lowest rating category, however, reveals that Moody's lowest rating category is the C rating (it does not have a D rating). An easy way to remember that "Fitch" and "S&P" have D ratings is that there is no letter "D" in their names in contrast to Moody's who has no D ratings but does have a "D" in its name.[1]

A considerably more confident 87% concluded that two different structured finance bonds that are both rated AAA by all three agencies cannot directly be compared against each other because of both ratings being on the same level. However, the respondents had no explanation as to why that was so and were largely unaware of the AAA rating cap that exists in structures that have so-called "super senior" bond tranches.

9.3.2 Rating agency failures

Clearly, rating agencies have occasionally failed in the past and the list of failures for particular names as well as asset classes is long: AIG, Alt-A bonds, Bear Stearns, Bradford & Bingley, CDO of ABS, CDO^2, CDO^3, Enron, Icelandic banks, Lehman Brothers, monolines, Northern Rock, subprime bonds, Parmalat, etc.

The agencies publicly admitted their failures in front of various official committees such as the Treasury Select Committee (U.K.) and the U.S. Government Oversight and Reform Committee. In their own words, they said the following about the credit crisis:

- Moody's admitted it "... did not ... anticipate the magnitude and speed of the deterioration in mortgage quality or the suddenness of the transition to restrictive lending."
- S&P admitted "... it is now clear that a number of assumptions used in preparing ratings on mortgage-backed securities issued between 2005 and mid-2007 did not work."
- Fitch admitted it "... did not foresee the magnitude of the decline... or the dramatic shift in borrower behavior ..."

In the meantime, there have been more "public" commissions, enquiries, and unsettling admissions and discoveries. However, the purpose of this particular chapter is not to point the finger of blame, but to ensure that when you use credit ratings you are fully aware of the limitations that come hand in hand with ratings as analytical tools.

9.3.3 Ratings scope

Credit ratings, as the name already suggests, have limited scope and normally only capture "credit risk". Ratings do not capture market risk, liquidity risk, operational risk, and basis risk. Nevertheless, credit ratings do play an important role since they have been "hard-wired" by Basel II into banks' credit-rating models and are also an obligatory requirement in many investment guidelines and asset management mandates. By the way, this is where the distinction between investment grade (i.e., ratings good enough to undertake investments) and non-investment grade or speculative grade (i.e., ratings not permitted for investments) comes from.

[1] Yes, I know "Standard & Poor" has a letter "D", but "S&P" does not. The key is to remember the difference.

9.3.4 Use of credit ratings

Ratings are used by banks, other financial institutions, originators and issuers, investors, financial regulators, other rating agencies, and many other market participants. They are used by such market participants to "outsource analysis" (which can be dangerous and will be costly under the Basel III regime), determine required economic and regulatory capital charges, manage individual credit risks as well as portfolio-related risks, and occasionally have featured as input into various structured finance models. By the way, this is one of the reasons for the failure of some instruments (such as CDO of ABS, CDO^2, and CDO^3, etc.) that used other rated instruments and in doing so placed too much reliance on the ratings of the underlying instruments.

9.3.5 Common criticism

Rating agencies are often criticized for a variety of reasons. They are too slow to react in their analysis of business models. Example 9.1 illustrates what lies behind this complaint. Although fictitious very similar cases happened in the runup to the credit crisis.

Example 9.1. How "timely" are "timely rating actions"?

This example concerns a monthly reporting U.S. residential mortgage-backed transaction where the underlyings are subprime mortgages. It illustrates the "timeliness of rating actions" and clearly shows very practical limitations to timely rating decisions.

July 31. This the *reporting cutoff date for the pool of underlying subprime mortgages.* Any loan that defaults on, say, July 28 makes it into the report. If a loan defaults on August 3, it'll make it into the next report.

August 15. Distribution date for the investor report. The 15th of each month (if it falls on a weekend, then usually the next working day) is what is agreed in the transaction's documents. This is the day when the investor report is formally "distributed" by the trustee—either sent out or provided on the trustee's website for download. We assume here it's been sent to all relevant parties.

August 20. This is when the responsible *analyst at the rating agency "receives" the investor report.* He may have had the report for a couple of days sitting in his inbox. The rating agency has a collective email alias for receipt of these reports and the relevant analyst will pick "his" report up from these. Don't forget they receive an awful lot of reports each day because they rate many thousand different transactions. This can be bit of an administrative nightmare and it can take time for the report to reach the responsible analyst's desk.

August 27th. Our analyst now has a chance to enter all the key performance indicators into the rating agencies' proprietary model and has the *result of the first performance analysis* on his desk. The results look odd: suddenly there seem to be a high level of delinquencies and defaults and our analyst is concerned about the overall performance of this transaction. The names involved are pretty good. Well-known originator and robust servicer, well-diversified subprime mortgage loan portfolio, the previous months showed little tendencies for rising delinquencies but overall it didn't look too bad. Maybe it requires looking into a bit further. Anyway, it looks as if it may be an adequate move to place the transaction on rating watch negative (RWN) in order to further investigate. RWN signals to investors that the rating agencies are currently undertaking further analysis and may or may not need to amend the ratings after this analysis has been completed. This can take up to 6 months, so an RWN does not signal an immediate imminent rating change but is thought more of as a thumbs up (or down?). Good compomise thinks our analyst and finishes the committee paper in order to put this deal on RWN.

August 31st. The paper is finished and *submitted to the rating committee with a view of placing the underperforming bond on RWN.* It's a rather awkward situation right now because as a result of the market being so buoyant over the past 2 years or so, quite a few senior directors and managing directors have decided to move on and are now working for banks that pay a lot more. There seems to be an underlying pattern where investment banks are frequently snapping up staff from rating agencies. They suppose analysts from agencies have well-groomed analytical skills, know the rating agency business, and can add considerable value to them—investment banks are usually able and willing to pay them considerably more, particularly in a market that is doing so well. Back to our transaction: The committee papers to place the transaction on RWN have been submitted, but our analyst finds it quite difficult to achieve the required quorum at this time of the year: the main summer holiday season combined with the recent departure of senior agency staff do not mix very well.

September 15. More than 3 weeks have now passed since the analyst submitted the committee papers and today is the *first time the committee has considered the performance* of the underlying collateral and whether or not the instrument should be placed on RWN. Normally, the quorum would have agreed with the analyst's proposal, but the most experienced and senior quorum member is deeply concerned about some of the performance trends. Delinquencies and defaults appear to have jumped to an uncomfortable level and, if they continue increasing at the same pace, there really will not be sufficient credit enhancement in the next quarter. The committee feels that the observed underperformance is more severe than previously thought and refrains from placing the deal on RWN. Instead, they brief the analyst to have a chat with the originator, check the report from August that should have become available today, and then consider a couple of additional stress scenarios to see the likely impact on the erosion of credit enhancement.

October 9. Our analyst has returned from his holidays; fortunately, he was only away for a couple of weeks on vacation. He knows he had better *get stuck into the further analysis* he was briefly dealing with before he went away. So, off he goes to have a chat with the originator/servicer, and it looks like the performance is worsening. Looks like falling house prices are one of the reasons so many of these mortgages are now becoming delinquent. With falling house prices many borrowers seem to be realizing that all they have in their property now is negative equity. With that in mind, what's the incentive for them to pay off their debt? Well, there isn't any, hence the analyst will prepare more serious steps.

October 12. The results of the *second analysis and model run* are reflected in an updated rating agency's committee paper.

October 16. In addition to this particular deal, our analyst has also had a chat with the in-house economist and they both looked at the latest economic data only to realize that U.S. house prices in decline appear to be on a much larger scale than originally anticipated. Looking at the data, you could almost say this is a problem of national scale rather than just regional pockets. As a result the *analyst decides to recommend a downgrade (DG)* for many of this particular deal's bond tranches—including some of the currently AAA-rated mezzanine notes—and expects a somewhat controversial rating committee meeting.

October 23. Second committee meeting. This goes smoother than originally thought, but the analyst brought the agency's in-house economist with him to support his view that national house prices are in decline. The committee is not particularly happy that it has to downgrade some AAA-rated tranches to A+ and takes a view that AA− looks better than such a steep downgrade and opts for the AA− rating. But, this is really the least of their worries: declining house price issues seem to be a bigger problem as there had been similar committees like this one over the past week or so.

October 23. Some of the *senior committee members raise their concern* to their internal credit policy department as well as legal counsel about declining house prices and the wider implications for the thousands of similar transactions they rate.

October 25. Our analyst wonders why this has become such an internal hot topic? Literally, everybody in the rating agency is now talking about the impact the downgrades of "his" bond seem to have had. The rating agency is now considering placing all subprime deals they rate which total several hundred million USD on rating watch negative and reviewing all the ratings for this particular asset class. The market seems to be aware of the underlying issues, at least that's what some of the investors were telling him on the phone after *he published the press release for the downgrade of those bonds*. They were asking why it took the rating agency so long to do anything about this transaction and that downgrades like this should be much timelier. Little do they know what's coming their way . . .

Whilst there is no indication in Example 9.1 of the year this fictitious sequence of events happened, given the circumstances, it's probably pretty clear to you by now that the supposed year was 2007. However, it can also happen again with different asset classes but, hopefully, not on such a large scale.

The lessons that need to be learned are—even if rating agencies claim to be timely with their decisions—many impracticalities are there that really do detract from this objective. Furthermore, rating agencies are corporate entities comprising human beings. People make errors, such as getting analyses wrong, overlooking important facts, procrastinating actions that can delay rating decisions, having internal arguments over who can do what and who has most "power", politics as a result of either internal or external pressures, and being driven by market share, profit, and sometimes plain greed.

Where rating agencies as companies are different is that the impact of their rating decisions can have far-reaching impacts on the entities that are affected: this can be corporates with a few hundred or many thousands of employees or sovereigns where literally millions may be affected (such as when the AAA rating of a country is downgraded, as seen with several European countries in late 2010 and early 2011).

It is of utmost importance that rating agencies apply the necessary professional due diligence and care that comes with such a powerful position and do whatever is necessary to ensure that ratings decisions are conveyed in a timely fashion.

Further criticisms

One major critique is the rating agency business model (this applies to all four large rating agencies—Moody's, Standard & Poor's, Fitch Ratings, and Dominion Bond Rating Service—but not necessarily to the smaller of the 75 or so rating agencies that exist globally), also known as the "issuer pays" model. Key here is the common perception that a credit rating for an issuer that is being paid for by the issuer will never come across as unbiased and impartial. There are many examples to illustrate this, but my favorite is where a film company prior to the release of its new blockbuster asks a professional film reviewer to review the film and, of course, pays the reviewer for his work. The film reviewer, happy to have another paying client, reviews the film—which transpires to be "average" but he manages to spice his review up a little hoping that he may get repeat business with this producer—and gives the film company his "independent review" to use as they please. Of course, there are differences, but the underlying principle is the same—there is a perceived conflict of interest and even with regulation and the IOSCO's code of conduct, it naturally taints the perceived impartiality of the rating agencies.

Another major critique is that credit ratings can only capture credit risk, but not market risk, operational risk, basis risk, and liquidity risk. This means that the risk captured and expressed by ratings is limited. Whilst this may be sufficient for a credit officer, it certainly is not sufficient for someone looking at risk from a more holistic angle. Furthermore, some of these risks are interconnected and whilst they may initially manifest themselves in one form (e.g., liquidity risk during the first months of the credit crisis), they cannot always be clearly separated and of course can contaminate other risk categories (such as credit risk which manifested itself in later months of the credit crisis). Having a limited view on credit risk via a credit rating is still only a "limited view".

Using more than one external rating is fine as long as you are looking at just one agency. In practice, most banks and other financial institutions, however, use three external ratings. Typically, at inception of a structure you would find external ratings to be the same—if they are not, look closely at them to understand why. However, throughout the life of the deal, credit rating agencies will undertake their analysis independently and, hence, may or may not change the ratings that were originally assigned. You can then end up holding a bond tranche that is rated AAA by one agency, AA− by another, and A3 by the third, essentially resulting in so-called split ratings. In the case of split ratings the question is which agency's analysis do you trust most and, hence, which rating do you use as "the" rating for capital charge calculation, internal risk analysis, as well as internal and external portfolio analysis. This depends largely on the institution you are working for and whether or not they have internal ratings that can be used instead of external ratings.

Prior to the credit crunch, one other practice led to considerable criticism of the agencies—the practice of so-called "notching". Standard & Poor's and Moody's used to be very active in this area. Notching describes the practice in which one rating agency revises another agency's rating downward prior to using it in their model—just because it is from one of their competitors.

Rating agency models are nothing more than that: models. The fuel that powers these models is rating criteria, methodologies, and assumptions which is only a reflection of how the agency conveys that an instrument works.

More recently, there has been another interesting development in the rating agency space: *increasing internal "competition"* where some agencies ramp up their analytics and consultancy business—which is also owned by the relevant agency's holding company—but conduct analysis that may differ from traditional rating agency work. Moody's Analytics and Fitch Solutions are two such companies. These companies are usually independent of the core ratings business and fire-walled or have Chinese Wall policies in place which separate them from the ratings business. However, these consultant companies do use traditional credit ratings to compare their products against. These analytics companies offer a wide range of products including implied ratings (market, CDS, or equity implied) and integrated tools that use models and cash flow engines providing users with the ability to replicate some of the work that agency staff would use in order to rate transactions. Equally, they make the same underlying data available that are used by the rating agencies' own analytical staff who are rating the original deals.

Companies such as Moody's Analytics claim that their product would be capable of forecasting rating changes before the agency actually changes the ratings and support their claims with various samples. I leave it to you to determine whether or not the products can add value to your business, but they certainly do not come cheap. However, the point I am making is that these companies are now in an internal competition with their own sister companies by offering fairly similar products—I wonder if this is a good way forward but the agencies' parent companies seem to think there is certainly business to be made and there is also considerable interest in the market.

9.4 ANALYTICAL ROADMAP

Figure 9.1 is an analytical roadmap mainly from a credit portfolio and risk management perspective. It was developed over the years and sits on my desktop. I like having simple desktop references without having to reread a whole book on certain topics. In that sense, I hope you find it worth having on your

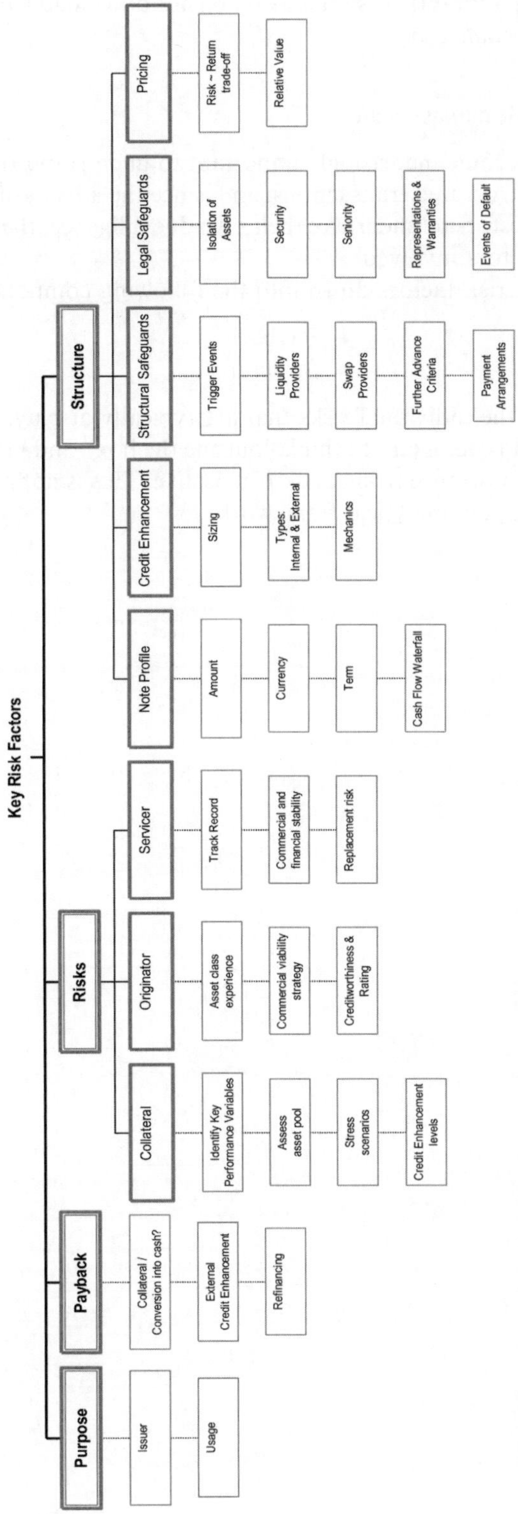

Figure 9.1. Credit portfolio and risk management roadmap.

desk too and, if so, note that a printable version is available for download from the book's companion website *www.structuredfinanceguide.com.*

9.4.1 Credit portfolio and risk management

Since the credit crisis, it has become increasingly important to understand the real risks investors are faced with when investing in structured transactions; and, since the advent of Basel III and additional stringent requirements for investors to undertake their own due diligence, there is an even greater need to understand the key risk factors involved.

Figure 9.1 breaks these key risk factors down into the following components of deals:

- Purpose
- Risk
- Payback
- Structure.

It then takes a closer look at the individual risks that are typically at play.

When using this, however, it is necessary to think "outside the box" and take potential other factors into account that may be of importance from a risk perspective. This is not meant to be an exhaustive list of risk factors, but more of an analytical framework.

10

Data

As mentioned throughout this book, securitization and structured finance is to a large extent about data and dissecting information. However, not only is it important to have the relevant information at hand and to be suitably equipped to publish this information, there should also be a certain amount of data quality checks and data checks by the issuer himself and then maybe followed by the trustees prior to publishing investor reports.

During the time I spent working at a rating agency I remember looking at one particular transaction that initially had dreadful reporting. The reports were distributed by a very large financial institution acting as a trustee who clearly either had no interest or at best a remote understanding of what these investor reports contained. Once we transposed the information into Excel it transpired that the "sums" of rows and columns did not add up and there also appeared to be €158m of collections "missing".

To cut things short, it turned out there were certain problems in the transaction too, which led to it, first, being placed on rating watch negative and, second, some of the lower rated tranches being downgraded. Longer term, we worked closely with the issuer to ensure that the investor reporting did align with the actual underlying performance of the assets, nothing was missing in the report, and the issuer also implemented simple but effective data quality and assurance checks to its report prior to publishing it via the trustee and on the issuer's website.

10.1 THE "MEANING" OF DATA

So there you have it. Providing the correct data is one issue—usually one of utmost importance for the originators, issuer, trustee, servicer, and cash managers. Another issue that is equally as important is that investors interpret information correctly—Example 10.1 illustrates this.

Example 10.1. One question—many (potential) answers

One of my clients underwent a major government-initiated takeover during the credit crisis and the combined entity had subsequently to draw on massive government support and various asset protection schemes in order to avert bankruptcy and another bank run.

As part of this arrangement with the government, the client had to give firm assurance to increase lending over time—one of the measures intended to stabilize the national economy in which this bank was now a major player. Furthermore, my client had to establish special reporting to the government which would indicate on a month-by-month basis how the bank's lending commitments were developing. The chosen measure was simple: just looking at the number of credit applications that were received each month on a group level and then further breaking this down into the number of lending applications received and the number thereof that were approved and declined. We also received from some areas the notional values of applications received/approved/declined, but this was not across the group and, hence, not easily compared.

Anyway, these figures were reported to the responsible government on a monthly basis as agreed, but in November 2009 there was a considerable decrease in these figures and the report was not sent until the reason for such a decline had been investigated. Interestingly enough, the message from the client relationship managers on the ground suggested that they had never been busier processing applications and could not understand where the discrepancies came from. So, the question was simple: Why was there an apparent decrease in lending commitments? Finding the answer was much more complex. What was the meaning of these simple data points (i.e., number of loans received/approved/declined) and what were the reasons for the observed reduction? Well, let's take a look at the various possibilities that could pass as plausible answers.

(1) The data were wrong—suggesting that lending commitments had not decreased but remained either stable or may even have increased. Let's take a closer look at the underlying reason this could have been the case and explore the "meaning" of these data.
(2) The data were correct—suggesting that lending commitments had in fact declined.

- *Lending commitments had actually declined.* This could have been the case, but, further investigation may find that one or a combination of the following reasons (which can be difficult to quantify unless you have conclusive data available at the micro-level) might be the driver behind this decline:
  - *Change in underwriting criteria.* A change of underwriting procedures—for instance, by using more conservative credit-scoring models for private borrowers or a new balance sheet analysis tool for corporate banking clients—may influence the outcome of an originator's lending decisions on a deal-by-deal basis which means an overall reduced number of approved loans. Typically, if that's the case, such changes to underwriting procedures should be clearly communicated and hence well documented, but this is not always so. In our particular case, where two organizations were going through the motions of a takeover and a subsequent harmonization of policies including lending criteria as well as the introduction of loan management systems from one organization to the other, these changes may also impact lending volumes. In such instances, however, a change in lending criteria would not always be communicated and documented as such and hence may be more difficult to detect. From a sound practice perspective, it pays if the originating institution maintains appropriate records and documentation that provides a historic trail of when and how such lending standards where changed. You may find that your organization is keeping this information without really being aware of it. One starting point where you may be able to find this is at the company's internal legal counsel.

    Typically, when a company's terms and conditions (T&Cs) need to change, the company's in-house counsel (as well as in some cases external law firms) may investigate the legal implications of such a change. If that's the case then you can expect to find the results of such legal analysis as well as the history of these changes documented.

    Furthermore, from an originator's perspective, it is well worth properly documenting and maintaining this information since this is one of the areas credit rating agencies will look at closely as part of their due diligence exercises for any new publicly rated transaction.
  - *Change in customer behavior.* At the other end of the borrower/lender spectrum is, of course, the borrower. There may have been a change in the behavior of borrowers across the board if a notable decline from one period to the next has been identified. This could be due to a change in macroeconomic factors, such as a country's economy going into or coming out of recession. Rather than relying on external funding sources by requesting further lending from banks, borrowers (retail as well as wholesale) may adopt a more prudent approach whereby they reduce the amount of money they owe rather than borrowing more. Or, some of the

clients may have become disgruntled with the new organization (after such a takeover) because some of the customer relationship managers they have become used to have left (or were made to leave). Or, the borrower as well as the lender may be looking at consolidating some debt or loan requests by consolidating several loan applications into one. This, of course, would mean a decrease in the number of loan applications but, usually, in return one could also observe an increase in lending commitments by notionals—depending on which kinds of data are looked at.

 ○ *Change in competitive environment.* Competitors fit in between the lender and borrower. There may be an external push by competitors to leverage off a benign (or malign) economic environment where funding is sparse and lending activities are government supported in order to increase lending figures. Customers may find themselves more attracted to a variety of lenders and, hence, may be inundated with loan offers. If so, they may simply decide to go to a better placed (or appearing to be better placed) lending institution that is able to offer cheaper loans with better terms. These days it's quite easy to go to your local bank branch (or the internet) to get a loan quote and run this information via a price comparison website to get the cheapest loan that matches and fulfills most of your individual circumstances.

- *Submission by the customer relationship managers may have somehow changed.* Assuming that the actual lending commitment on a going concern basis has not changed, maybe there are some factors as to how this information is gathered and then accumulated—first, on a divisional and, then, group level. Again, only further investigation into the sources as well as the process of transmitting this information may provide further answers. Some of the reasons this information is now transmitted differently could be:
  - ○ *Internal restructuring activities* could simply lead to changes in the organizational structure—instances where staff are leaving without any proper handover and, hence, those who remain may be either unaware or completely overwhelmed and quite simply overlook providing this important piece of information.
  - ○ *Establishment and implementation of new management information systems* that are theoretically capable of capturing this information but in practice require training of all customer relationship managers in order to use these systems and, hence, may be again either unable or overwhelmed by the task of entering and processing this information in a timely fashion.
- *Changes to the internal treatment of certain loan or product types or the accounting of them* may also influence how these instruments are reflected in overall lending commitment statistics:
  - ○ For instance, if some of these loans are transferred to a "bad bank" division, they may be treated as sanctioned new transactions (of the "bad bank") and count towards the overall numbers of new applications—so from a pure number count perspective this would probably be fine. However, if the notional amount or the actual exposures of these instruments are included, it may look as if the notional lending volume has decreased. The reason for what on the surface appears to be a reduced lending volume is that the transfers of loans or mortgages to the "bad bank" business would usually trigger an impairment or writeoff of some of the products impacted. Such impairments can represent a considerable portion of the outstanding loan amount—sometimes 75% or more.

    Consequently, the actual net exposures of such impaired loans, which are still treated as new "lending commitments" may be much smaller than the original gross outstanding loan amount and will blur the actual picture of the "bad bank's" loan book.
  - ○ Equally, it is important to understand how different types of loan applications are treated as part of the organization's operational model and that such treatment needs to be consistently applied throughout the firm. For instance, the treatment of "annual reviews" of already

outstanding loans needs to be clarified and communicated to the relevant customer relationship managers that report this information. It certainly will make a difference if a relationship manager has already got, for instance, 250 existing loan exposures that undergo an "annual review". Assume these are fairly evenly spread over the year, then he would cover around 25 loans each month as part of the annual review. If these cases are considered as "lending commitments" for the purpose of the government's statistical disclosure, that is fine because an annual review applied to outstanding exposures is quite similar to re-underwriting an existing or even a new transaction. However, the key is that such a message is robustly conveyed throughout the group's divisions that gather this information at a granular level and then accumulate this information upwards.

- ○ Terms of reference for "lending commitments". Lastly, but maybe most importantly, it needs to be clearly defined what the firm (or the government) considers "lending commitments" to be and such a definition needs to be clearly expressed and articulated to the business that is required to categorize their transactions and feed this information back. For instance, personal overdrafts may not count toward lending commitments, whereas personal loans do.

- *Seasonal factors (such as a holiday period) as well as macroeconomic factors may also play a role* in explaining why borrowers either refrain from applying for new funds or customer relationship managers appear not to be feeding the necessary information back to the centralized area that is tasked with collating it.

This simple example illustrates that, rather than just observing the data, it is much more important to understand the meaning of it as well as the sources of observed anomalies.

10.2 STATIC INFORMATION

"Data" in its widest sense is information which can have two opposite natures: it can either be dynamic (see Section 10.3) meaning always changing (or potentially fairly frequently) or static which means it tends to stay the same, at least for a long time. Note that static data can also change (e.g., the servicer in a transaction is meant to be the same throughout the life of a deal but may go bankrupt and hence requires replacing).

The concept of static data vs. dynamic data is widely used in structured finance: deal-related static data would for instance be the legal name of the deal, ticker, ISIN, CUSIP, counterparties that are involved in the transaction, the relevant contact details for them, the currency of the issued notes, the original issued notional of the notes, the final legal maturity.

Treatment of this information in origination platforms is likely to differ from dynamic information as it would not be expected to change too much over time. Furthermore, it seems to lend itself to be used in performance analytics templates across asset classes since the generic information is typically more of an asset class–unrelated nature.

10.3 DYNAMIC DATA POINTS

In stark contrast to static information are dynamic data points. As the name suggests, dynamic information usually never stays the same for long and changes frequently. The frequency, however, can be driven by many factors. For instance, take the delinquency figures in an investor report. The delinquencies of an underlying loan portfolio are driven by borrowers missing their contractual payments. These borrowers have predetermined payment schedules and frequencies for their interest and/or principal payments. If they miss such payments they are immediately in arrears. However, it will depend on the originator's loan and cash flow management system to identify such arrears as "delinquency" by comparing expected payments with actual receipts. This is typically done on a daily basis. Once this information has been gathered and affected loans are earmarked as "delinquent", loan-level data will typically be accumulated on a transaction level and gathered together right up until the relevant investor reporting cutoff date.

For a typical residential mortgage-backed transaction this would mean the data throughout one reporting period—usually a month—are gathered and distributed via the investor report. At the time this report is published to the market and disseminated to investors, however, these data will already be outdated due to the dynamic nature of the underlying information.

The resulting timelag between cutoff date for the report and receipt by the investors may not be a concern to many but, clearly, if you manage to receive such data in a timely fashion and in an easily digestible format, then you are certainly on top of your portfolio and possibly ahead of the competition and the majority of the market.

Taken a step further, if you manage to predetermine, for instance, forthcoming rating actions for a certain asset class based on the information that is available to you in near real time or, even better, on a real time basis, then you are well equipped to master the current market (or lack of liquidity) and dynamic data should give you the confidence you need in order to make robust investment decisions (or, where applicable, divestment decisions).

Assume you hold a legacy portfolio of CDO of ABS and are concerned about the level of serious rating downgrades experienced by the underlying individual bond instruments that form each of these CDO of ABS bonds. The conventional way to understand the rating distribution and rating migration of the underlying instruments would be to wait until you receive the monthly investor reports and manage to understand what has happened to the portfolio since you looked last month.

Alternatively and much more elegant, you may rebuild the underlying portfolio, for instance, in Excel by downloading the latest bond list from Intex. Once you have this information, you can further map this portfolio by using bond identifiers (ticker, ISIN, CUSIP) and combine this with Bloomberg's desktop API (application programming interface) which will enable you to download the ratings distribution at any time. Once you have got this far, you can use the information that has been derived in such a way by applying a simple algorithm (e.g., an "IF" statement in Excel) that allows you to compare the current ratings for the underlying instrument with the rating data you sourced previously in exactly the same fashion. Once you get there, you will be able to literally see which rating migration is shown in the investor or collateral management report, up to 4 weeks prior to the release of the official investor reports. That gives you up to a month to proactively initiate, for instance, a sale of assets where you can realize potential relative value.

So, having the data, being able to distinguish the nature of the information or data points you are looking at, and the ability to understand the limitations of the timeliness of this information are key factors. On the back of this insight you can certainly develop a more robust approach that will enable confident decision making; and your firm may also be well positioned to make some profit.

Profit potential is something vendors have realized, too. There are few select names in the structured finance space that provide granular deal information (sometimes referred to as "deal libraries") on a very granular (i.e., loan-by-loan level) basis and via electronic means. These used to be just Intex and ABSNet, but since the credit crunch they have been joined by Bloomberg, ABSXchange, Moody's Analytics and a few niche firms that focus on specialist tools (e.g., valuation tools that focus on particular asset classes). Chapter 11 takes a closer look at these vendors and discovers whether and how they enrich the raw data before they pass it on to end-users.

10.4 DATA PROVIDERS

As said earlier, in order to understand and manage financial products, you will require data. This holds even more true for complex financial instruments such as structured finance transactions, where both sides of the equation need to be considered: assets (loan-by-loan information on the underlying collateral pool) and liabilities (information on distribution of cash flow to the individual notes).

From an investor's perspective, there has been a clear need to receive the information that is contained in the usual documents that make up what's more generically known as "investor reporting". This need was exacerbated during the credit crisis when internal and external attention shifted towards financial institutions' structured finance portfolios and where rating agencies were not providing the necessary information on bond performance in a sufficiently timely manner.

Such a need would be further amplified if an investor holds more than, say, 250 bonds. Economies of scale suggest that when investing in a large number of bonds you should also have as automated a performance analytics system as possible in place to handle them. Ideally, it makes sense having an interface to a data provider so that investor reporting–related information can be sourced and processed automatically.

If you have no capability to source these data and feed them via an interface into your proprietary system, then the only other alternative will be employing a sufficiently large number of staff just to deal with getting investor reports and then plugging the data manually into whatever "system" there is. Typically, you will find that if your firm is unable to invest in a properly functioning and robust system (such as an Access database, Oracle, or the like) chances are that the "system" managing bond-related performance information is likely to be a combination of various Excel workbooks.

I am not suggesting that Excel cannot work. It can and also is very flexible, meaning it functions well in a rapidly changing environment such as this particular part of the capital markets. What I can see, however, is that you will need more than just Excel plus human resources to effectively manage a large bond portfolio as the following graphical example (Example 10.2) will illustrate.

Example 10.2. Why use power tools when we can do it "by hand"?

One of my larger clients, holding around 1,450 bonds totaling in excess of $100bn, had a stable, robust, functioning, bespoke surveillance and performance analytics platform including various interfaces to the bank's proprietary limit and exposure management system as well as APIs to ABSnet, Bloomberg, and Intex. It's worked fine for the past 5 years or so and a particular effort was made during the credit crisis to satisfy internal and external requirements. By no means was this perfect, but it provided a fit-for-purpose solution, tested and proven to work.

Following a takeover, the platform that had been there for 5+ years—which had worked well, saved untold man-hours during the credit crisis, and used to satisfy the regulator that everything is under control—was binned. Although scrapped for political reasons only, the new owners argued that everything the new bank needed was in place. Shortly after this decision, a hiring frenzy started to fill the gaps left by the decommissioned system with human bodies to do all this "by hand".

The opportunity costs for human resource is what data providers operating in this space turn into profit. The likes of ABSNet, ABSXchange, Bloomberg, Intex have all developed complex solutions in order to handle large volumes of data. Bloomberg, for instance, receives around 45 million data points each month and most of this information is processed in fully automated fashion.

This information is processed by a clever combination of optical character recognition, data scrubbing, automated comparison, algorithms that know what kind of data to expect and how to treat them, and, lastly but only if needed, human intervention. All of which enables vendors to operate with a fairly small number of specialized employees covering a large number of deals. Intex, for instance, provides deal libraries for more than 22,000 transactions, but only has around 100 staff.

Part IV
Analytical tools

11

Vendors

Similar to the provision of data, some third parties have recognized the commercial value of providing modeling tools. In fact, it is, of course, easier if you already have most of the data (i.e., the input into those models) which means you can then run models (i.e., the computation and procession of the data) with these data and provide the relevant results (i.e., the model output).

If you were to model certain asset classes, then you will need data—loads of it. Not just current data but also historical data points—most providers will charge you for the provision of historical deal data to compensate them for storing the data in deal libraries or repositories; and the large volume of data means you need to build powerful systems or data repositories to store and process all this information—something that is taken care of if you use commercial providers to handle, store, and supply this information if and when required.

Furthermore, if you were to subscribe to this information in an electronic downloadable format, then you would also typically need them to compensate for the fact that you are downloading some or all of their information—which enables you store this bulk data locally.

Finally, if you wish to run this information through various scenario models and/or cash flow models, then you will need to purchase or subscribe to the use of these models for which these firms will also charge. All in all, paid for subscriptions to data plus historical information plus the capability to model this information will accumulate to a considerable amount of money.

This part of the book covers a wide range of third-party vendors representing some of the key players in the market. The narrative has been reviewed (and in some cases was actually provided) by these companies thereby ensuring a high level of accuracy and factual representation of their products. Equally, where screenshots have been provided to me, I have included them in the book (some companies were not prepared to provide any since they felt they contained proprietary information, but I prefer having something written in this book rather than nothing).

I would like to thank everybody at those firms for their efforts in compiling and providing this information for the purpose of the book and my gratitude goes to those who worked on this in the background.

Finally, please note that these providers are listed in alphabetical order and no preference is given to any of them.

12
ABSXchange

12.1 INTRODUCTION

Standard & Poor's Fixed Income Risk Management Services (S&P FIRMS) delivers a portfolio of products and services to investors that serve the global financial markets by providing market intelligence and analytic insight for risk-driven investment analysis, including for debt, structured finance, derivative, and credit markets. Standard & Poor's Fixed Income Risk Management Services are performed separately from any other analytic activity of Standard & Poor's.

ABSXchange is a core offering of S&P FIRMS. It is an advanced structured finance analytic resource that combines performance data, a deal model library, and cash flow analytics for a wide range of deal types, including RMBS, CMBS, ABS, and cash CDOs. The functionality at the core of ABSXchange is a cash flow generation engine. The engine was originally designed in 1991 as a bond administration application widely used in the U.S. by CMO issuers. Over time, the application evolved into a market-facing resource for ABS analytics with a strong focus on European content.

ABSXchange combines offering circulars, investor reports, collateral and deal performance data, cash flow models, portfolio monitoring tools, and cash flow analytics. The goal of this service is to provide end-users with similar or an improved level of disclosure throughout the life of a transaction as existed at its initial offering. Importantly, the service addresses three major challenges that investors have typically faced in the secondary market:

- Gathering essential documentation
- Tracking deal performance including deal triggers; and
- Developing an appropriate cash flow model for deal projections.

The ABSXchange database and cash flow library are extensive. The database allows access to the most widely used data fields in investor reports. Users can receive automated updates of relevant information to monitor a deal's performance. Users can also look at historical performance on other transactions to create benchmarks. Moreover, each cash flow model includes the relevant triggers and structural features; these features are accurately modeled and will include loss allocations, prepayment penalty allocations, and interest-rate and f/x hedges. End-users can clearly track how deal triggers will perform over the course of a projection. Where possible, deals are updated with loan-level collateral.

ABSXchange covers a wide range of over 10,000 structured finance transactions including RMBS, CMBS, consumer ABS, leasing ABS, and CLOs. The application includes 100% coverage of all European public market transactions rated by any of the three major agencies as well as 100% of Australian RMBS transactions. ABSX also offers around 4,000 U.S. RMBS transactions.

The performance data are sourced and managed by S&P FIRM's data operations team. This team supports multiple S&P business units; the data that feed ABSXchange, for example, are also used by the ratings teams. S&P's data team provides a robust service that includes content acquisition, stewardship, data quality, and customer service. The customer service function is an important component of S&P data operations and focuses on three areas: quality metrics, audits, and process improvement programs that target the areas of data quality that matter most to end-users.

ABSXchange's deal models consist of a combination of required and optional components. Deal information, bond information, bond rules and collateral information are required; optional features are collateral rules, schedules including prepayment and reference, permanent variables and reporting templates. Users can perform various analytical computations in order to fully analyze a deal or a portfolio of deals. Different economic assumptions can be stressed to generate average life, yield, collateral cash flows, bond cash flows, and aggregate portfolio cash flows. Users can also specify assumptions according to standard conventions, such as CPR or CDR, for prepayments, defaults, and other analytical inputs.

Certain ABSXchange features are deal specific; these features will only appear for those deals where the given feature is applicable. For example, the ability to run cash flows using loan-level data would be available where that information is in the database.

This chapter is designed to provide users with an overview of how to perform key analytical functions effectively. The functions covered include tracking a deal's performance, performing surveillance on a portfolio of deals, and running cash flow projections. In addition, certain advanced features, such as creating a benchmark index, are included.

12.2 PERFORMANCE DATA

Two important elements of ABS analysis are understanding (1) the financial structure of the transaction and (2) the fundamental credit quality of the collateral pool. The first few modules of ABSXchange enable users to undertake this analysis. The ABSXchange database captures current and historical descriptive information as well as static performance data. This information is extensive and can be approached either on a deal-by-deal basis or on a portfolio approach. This section will review the relevant features that enable end-users to access descriptive information, to better understand a deal's structure, collateral performance, and the credit quality of the deals.

12.2.1 Deal-by-deal analysis

The starting point for deal-by-deal analysis is the `Overview` module. The `Overview` screen (Figure 12.1) gives a general summary of the assets and liabilities as well as providing information on special features of the deal, such as the current balance of the reserve fund, liquidity facility, or excess funds. Availability of this information is dependent on the information reported by the issuer.

Basic descriptive information is presented at the top of the `Overview` page. Specifically, the original issuance amount, issue date, the underwriter, and the type of collateral will be listed. This information will remain static throughout the life of the transaction. Below the basic descriptive information is an overview of the entire capital structure. This will include both rated and unrated tranches, including equity and/or residual classes. In addition, principal deficiency ledgers are presented for cash flow–modeling purposes.

For each class, a combination of descriptive and performance data is presented. For example, the end-user is able to find multiple reference identifiers, the currency in which the class was issued, interest and principal payment frequencies, the current and next coupon, the original and current rating, the current balance and factor, the original and current credit enhancement level as well as any swap exchange rates, stepup dates, and stepup margins for the coupon. By clicking on an individual class, the end-user can drill down and view current and historical data specific to the class. This includes all principal and interest payments; the current class balance, and the level of credit enhancement for the class.

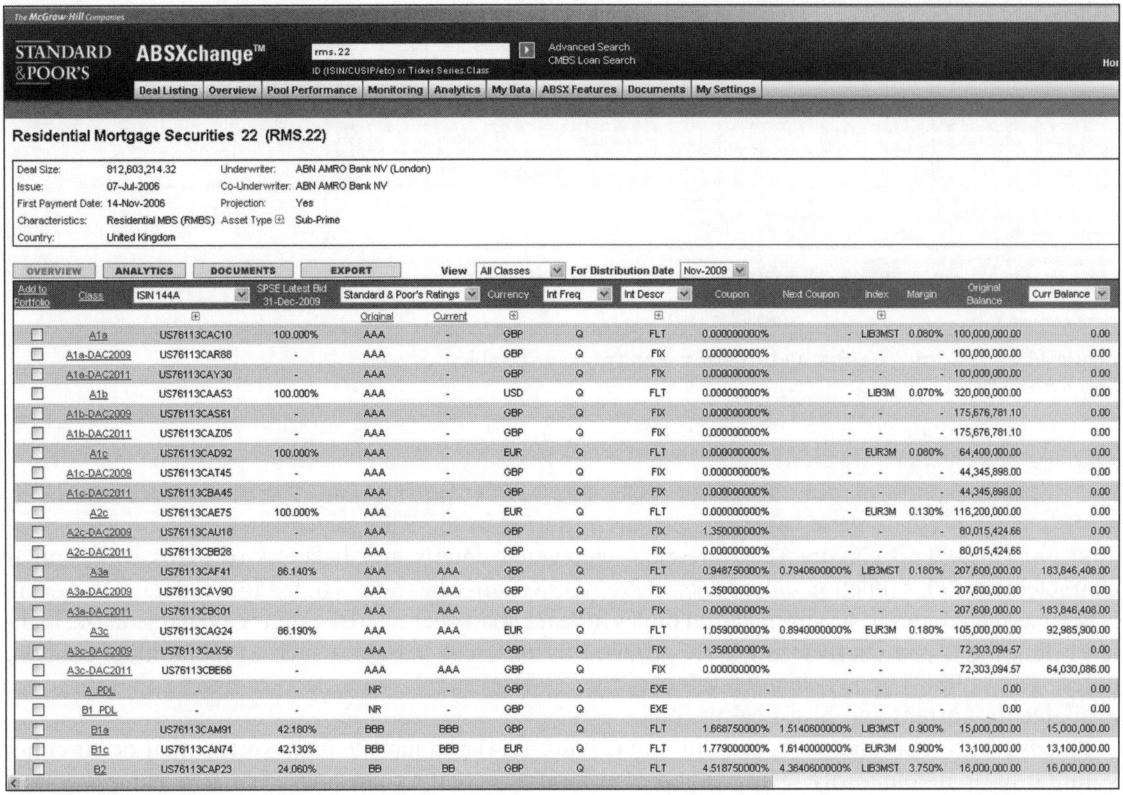

Figure 12.1. `Overview` screen.
Source: ABSXchange.

The bottom half of the `Overview` module presents a summary of the collateral with the latest statistics showing the original and current collateral balance, average age of the collateral, cumulative principal losses, and various prepayment categories.

Finally, users are provided with a summary of deal and class triggers or tests. A description of the relevant trigger will appear when a user clicks on the name of the trigger/test. This information is taken directly from the offering circular. The `Test/Trigger Table` (Figure 12.2) shows the current performance of the individual trigger as well as the threshold at which point it would breach. On the right-hand side, a summary of `Credit Enhancement` features such as reserve funds and/or liquidity facilities are presented. The `Credit Enhancement` amounts will feed into the class-specific credit enhancement, as appropriate, on the `Class Overview` page, where subordinated classes will be added. From the `Overview` page, the user can then drill down into the collateral performance by navigating to the `Pool Performance` module.

12.3 POOL PERFORMANCE

The `Pool Performance` module on ABSXchange allows the end-user to drill down into the collateral performance. For RMBS transactions, this module will present `Collateral Stratification`, `Prepayments`, `Delinquencies`, and general `Deal Performance`. In addition, current

Add for Analysis	Pool	Distribution	Char	Type	Original	Current	Net	Gross	Spread	Age (Mos)	Term (Mos)	Cum Prin Loss	Cum Prin Loss %	CPR1M	CPR3M	CPR6M	CPR1Y	CPRCUM
⊞	1	Nov-2009	SUBPRIME	ARM	800,054,525.93	367,988,551.00	6.2572479327%	6.2572479327%	3.82630%	35.88000	225.00000	18,042,824.00	2.26000%	13.90%	14.20%	16.40%	19.78%	19.90%

All collateral data reported in GBP. Green: Reported values; Blue: Calculated / Assumed values; Black: Source not indicated.

Test	Current	Trigger	Result
Class B1a Liquidity Facility Funds Available	0	20	PASS
Class B1c Liquidity Facility Funds Available	0	20	PASS
Class B2a Liquidity Facility Funds Available	0	20	PASS
Class M1a Liquidity Facility Funds Available	0	20	PASS
Class M1c Liquidity Facility Funds Available	0	20	PASS
Class M2a Liquidity Facility Funds Available	0	20	PASS
Class M2c Liquidity Facility Funds Available	0	20	PASS
Principal Loss Ratio for Reserve Stepdown	2.26%	1.25%	FAIL
Liquidity Drawn Amount	0.00	0.00	PASS
Pro-Rata Test	-	-	FAIL
Aggregate Balance of the Principal Deficiency Sub-Ledgers	0	0	PASS
Delinquency Ratio for Reserve Stepdown and Prorata Principal Payment	29.55%	22.50%	FAIL
Foreclosure Ratio for Reserve Stepdown	10.11%	2.25%	FAIL
Trigger Ratio	2.19%	2.83%	PASS
Reserve Drawn Amount	2.94%	2.70%	PASS

Feature	Value	Deal Percentage
Excess Spread	1,110,675.00	1.16%
Liquidity Facility Draw	0.00	0.00%
Liquidity Facility	55,192,619.00	15.00%
Reserve Fund	10,800,000.00	2.93%
Targeted Balance of Reserve Fund	10,800,000.00	2.93%

Excess Spread % is calculated using: Excess Spread Current * Number of Payment Periods * 100 / Collateral Balance Beginning Period

Figure 12.2. `Trigger tests` and `credit enhancement` table.
Source: ABSXchange.

and historical performance tables for deal `Tests/Triggers` and `Features` are available. ABSXchange presents these values as they are reported in servicing statements.

`Stratification` (Figure 12.3) presents aggregated counts and balances of loans with similar characteristics. This function only works where ABSXchange has access to loan-level data. The system is flexible and creates basic stratification tables for each loan characteristic that is available in the loan-level data file. Loan characteristics are grouped by different variables such as loan value, coupon, dates, geographic regions, loan-to-value ratios, and property type. `Stratification` tables are available for current and historical periods.

Prepayments are found under the `CPR` tab (Figure 12.4) and include prepayments that occur either voluntarily or involuntarily. This section also reports actual values and calculated values, with a distinction made in the font color. Prepayment values are annualized and available in 1-month, 3-month, 6-month, 1-year, and `Cumulative` categories for each distribution date. Users can choose whether to view reported values, calculated values, or a hybrid of the two. All values are presented in both tabular as well as graphical formats. The formulas for calculated values are presented at the bottom of the screen.

The `Delinquency` tab (Figure 12.5) shows current and historical information displayed in 30-day, 60-day, and 90-day buckets, corresponding to 30–59 days, 60–89 days, and 90–119 days, respectively. Additional buckets are presented where available, including 90+ days including repossession, 120 days, 150 days, 180+ days, foreclosures, and real estate owned (REO). Foreclosure represents the current outstanding amount of loans in foreclosure. REO represents the current outstanding amount of repossessions that have taken place but for which the issuer has not disposed of the property. Users can view the information as `Current Balance` (the value of the loans), `Current Balance %` (the value of the loans in the category as a percentage of all outstanding collateral), `Count` (the number of loans), and `Count %` (the number of loans in the category as a percentage of all outstanding loans in the collateral pool).

ABSXchange presents an `Asset Detail` tab (Figure 12.6) to report loan-level data for CMBS and CLO transactions. The `Asset Detail` screen displays a number of different fields populated with information relating to each loan in the deal. For a CMBS transaction, these fields might include debt service coverage ratio (DSCR); loan-to-value (LTV), and loan-to-value covenant. For a CLO transaction, these fields include the issuer name, the country in which the issuer has the greatest business risk, the S&P industry code, and currency and coupon information. In some instances, additional fields are available by clicking on the `Advanced View` box. Historical information can be viewed by selecting the corresponding period from the drop down list.

DELINQUENCY | STRATIFICATION | CPR | TRIGGER | FEATURES | PERFORMANCE | STATEMENT

View Current Balance For Pool All Pools For Sep-2009 EXPORT

Current Balance Distribution - All Pools

Range	Current Balance	Count	Current Balance %
0K - 50K	22,274,711.89	584	2.75%
50K - 100K	220,927,144.68	2,946	27.23%
100K - 150K	239,906,462.75	1,970	29.57%
150K - 200K	141,429,964.26	826	17.43%
200K - 250K	85,909,301.45	392	10.59%
250K - 300K	42,459,631.81	157	5.23%
300K - 350K	25,848,847.70	80	3.19%
350K - 400K	12,628,836.94	34	1.56%
400K - 450K	9,734,021.45	23	1.20%
450K - 500K	5,600,412.70	12	0.69%
> 500K	4,506,662.21	9	0.56%

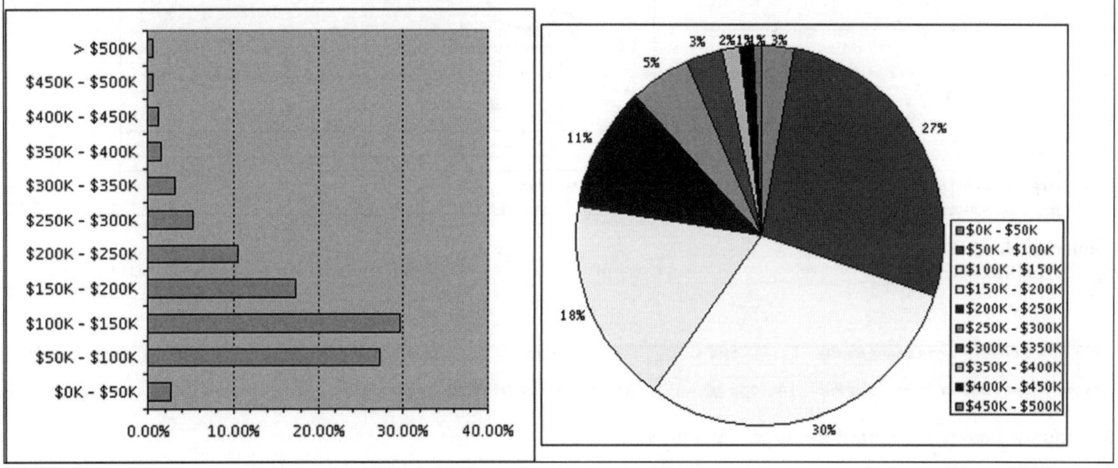

Figure 12.3. `Stratification.`
Source: ABSXchange.

12.4 PORTFOLIO MONITORING

Portfolio managers are interested in tracking the performance of their entire portfolio and will drill down into a specific deal when making an investment decision or when requiring detailed information. The `Portfolio Monitoring` module (Figure 12.7) enables portfolio managers and investment analysts to create reporting templates that are updated automatically when each new performance report is published. This module extracts information from the ABSXchange database for a user-defined set of transactions and displays the information either onto the webpage or directly into an MS Excel spreadsheet via the add-in functionality.

The `Manage Columns` function allows users to design and customize the reports. End-users can select from more than 1,500 fields related to the deal, class, collateral, tests, and/or features; once the field is selected all current and historical performance data associated with that field will be extracted from the ABSXchange database and populated in the table. Fields can be filtered down by asset class and sorted alphabetically. Additional types of fields can be created as well, including calculation fields that will calculate a value based on data in other fields or text columns. Users can also assign custom tests or triggers to performance variables; the user will be informed visually on the website or via an email alert when the test is breached. Once the column headers are selected, the user can save the table

DELINQUENCY | STRATIFICATION | CPR | TRIGGER | FEATURES | PERFORMANCE | STATEMENT

View: Hybrid — For Pool: All Pools — EXPORT — Hide Blank Columns ☑

Hybrid - All Pools

Distribution	CPR1M	CPR3M	CPR6M	CPR1Y	CPRCUM
Dec-2009	5.11%	7.05%	6.11%	9.47%	12.40%
Sep-2009	7.10%	7.76%	7.52%	17.97%	12.86%
Jun-2009	7.93%	8.39%	12.71%	21.35%	13.34%
Mar-2009	17.25%	17.90%	27.24%	21.68%	13.85%
Dec-2008	36.03%	36.46%	29.13%	19.43%	13.36%
Sep-2008	21.48%	22.12%	15.68%	11.81%	9.72%
Jun-2008	9.46%	10.62%	8.42%	8.33%	7.62%
Mar-2008	7.36%	8.75%	7.76%	6.93%	7.05%
Dec-2007	8.16%	9.92%	8.25%	5.58%	6.66%
Sep-2007	8.34%	10.18%	6.09%	-	5.66%
Jun-2007	3.78%	5.49%	2.83%	-	3.66%
Mar-2007	1.88%	2.70%	-	-	2.27%
Dec-2006	0.00%	-	-	-	-

Graph

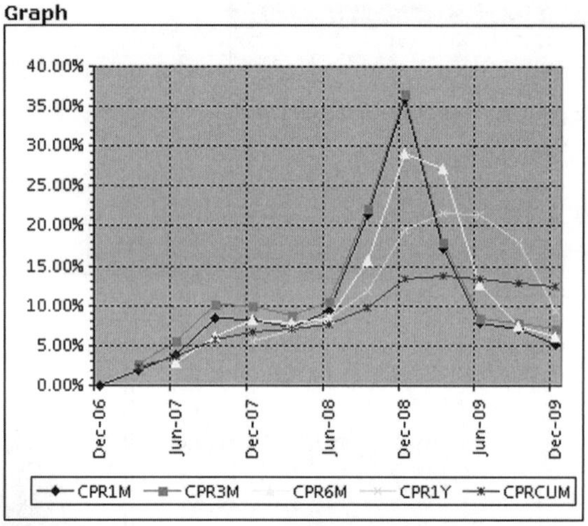

Green: Reported values; Blue: Calculated / Assumed values; Black: Source not indicated.

CPR1M is calculated using (1 - (Ending Collateral Balance / (Beginning Collateral Balance - Scheduled Principal))^{12}) * 100

Figure 12.4. CPR.
Source: ABSXchange.

DELINQUENCY | STRATIFICATION | CPR | TRIGGER | FEATURES | PERFORMANCE | STATEMENT

View: Current Balance % — For Pool: All Pools — EXPORT — Hide Blank Columns ☑

Delinquency as % of Current Balance - All Pools

Distribution	30 Days	60 Days	90 Days	90+ Days	120 Days	150 Days	180+ Days	REO	Total
Dec-2009	4.25%	3.03%	2.85%	22.94%	2.08%	2.02%	15.99%	0.71%	30.93%
Sep-2009	4.55%	3.34%	3.15%	21.95%	2.22%	2.04%	14.54%	0.99%	30.83%
Jun-2009	4.85%	3.94%	3.08%	21.41%	2.67%	2.26%	13.40%	1.47%	31.67%
Mar-2009	5.28%	4.57%	3.60%	18.99%	2.68%	2.45%	10.25%	1.99%	30.83%
Dec-2008	6.81%	3.97%	2.45%	10.20%	2.08%	1.33%	4.34%	2.23%	23.21%
Sep-2008	4.82%	3.01%	2.09%	7.20%	1.55%	0.98%	2.58%	1.77%	16.81%
Jun-2008	4.40%	2.75%	1.66%	6.23%	1.28%	0.95%	2.34%	1.37%	14.75%
Mar-2008	4.33%	2.29%	1.86%	6.20%	1.24%	0.76%	2.33%	1.12%	13.94%
Dec-2007	3.95%	2.46%	1.86%	5.36%	1.18%	0.68%	1.65%	0.82%	12.59%
Sep-2007	3.84%	2.05%	1.51%	4.62%	0.99%	0.65%	1.48%	0.30%	10.82%
Jun-2007	3.87%	2.20%	1.35%	3.31%	0.89%	0.69%	0.38%	0.07%	9.44%
Mar-2007	3.27%	1.89%	0.91%	1.22%	0.25%	0.06%	0.01%	0.00%	6.38%
Dec-2006	-	-	-	-	-	-	-	-	-

Figure 12.5. Delinquency.
Source: ABSXchange.

as a template. The template can be applied to any portfolio or can be appended or merged with another template.

There are multiple ways of creating and populating a portfolio: Users can either create a new portfolio on screen and add deals one by one via the web interface or, alternatively, users can upload a list of reference identifiers such as ISINs or tickers via an MS Excel spreadsheet. Worksheets can be either in XLS or CSV format, but the worksheet should include the word ISIN or security in Cell A1. Finally, users can add securities to an existing portfolio from the deal Overview page. Once a

ID	Issuer Name	Country	S&P Ind	Loan Name	Security Level	Security Name	Security Type	Currency	Original	Current	Factor	Gross	Net	Spread
57	JUPITER ASSET MANAGEMENT	GBR	20	-	SUB	TERM B - EURO/SWAP	L	EUR	20,045,318.37	20,045,318.37	-	3.0000000000%	3.0000000000%	1.77500%
80	ISTA INTERNATIONAL GMBH	DEU	8	-	SS	FACILITY B2	L	EUR	18,599,568.08	18,599,568.08	-	3.3350000000%	3.3350000000%	2.00000%
2	POMPES FUNEBRES GENERALES (OGF HOLDING SAS) [KA FINANCE SARL]	FRA	25	-	UNS	MEZZANINE	L	EUR	18,076,663.05	18,076,663.05	-	4.3070000000%	4.3070000000%	3.87500%
42	FORMULA 1 GROUP	GBR	30	-	SS	TERM B - EURO/SWAP	L	EUR	17,647,755.99	17,647,755.99	-	3.2690000000%	3.2690000000%	1.94680%
81	ISTA INTERNATIONAL GMBH	DEU	8	-	MEZZ	FACILITY C2	L	EUR	17,500,000.00	17,500,000.00	-	5.0850000000%	5.0850000000%	3.75000%
185	EUROPEAN DIRECTORIES, SA	NLD	33	-	SS	TRANCHE C	L	EUR	17,000,000.00	17,000,000.00	-	4.4271000000%	4.4271000000%	3.00000%
249	PARQUES REUNIDOS S.A.	ESP	30	-	MEZZ	2ND LIEN FACILITY	L	EUR	17,000,000.00	17,000,000.00	-	4.4280000000%	4.4280000000%	4.00000%

Figure 12.6. Asset Detail.
Source: ABSXchange.

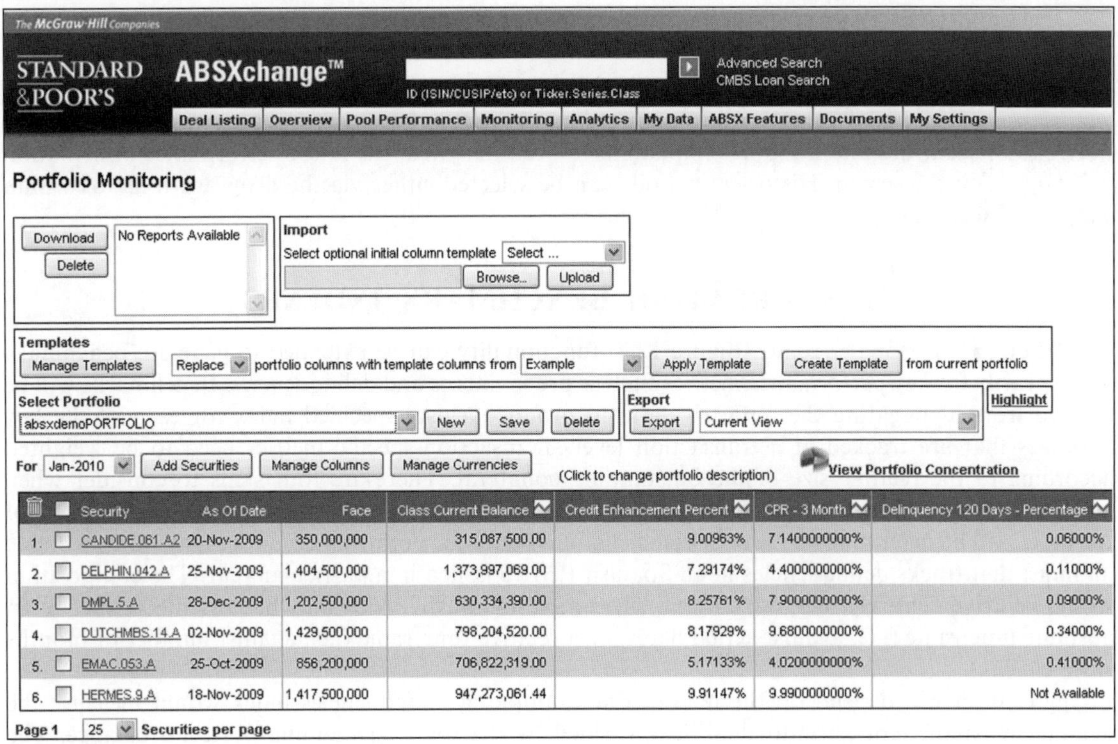

	Security	As Of Date	Face	Class Current Balance	Credit Enhancement Percent	CPR - 3 Month	Delinquency 120 Days - Percentage
1.	CANDIDE.061.A2	20-Nov-2009	350,000,000	315,087,500.00	9.00963%	7.1400000000%	0.06000%
2.	DELPHIN.042.A	25-Nov-2009	1,404,500,000	1,373,997,069.00	7.29174%	4.4000000000%	0.11000%
3.	DMPL.5.A	28-Dec-2009	1,202,500,000	630,334,390.00	8.25761%	7.9000000000%	0.09000%
4.	DUTCHMBS.14.A	02-Nov-2009	1,429,500,000	798,204,520.00	8.17929%	9.6800000000%	0.34000%
5.	EMAC.053.A	25-Oct-2009	856,200,000	706,822,319.00	5.17133%	4.0200000000%	0.41000%
6.	HERMES.9.A	18-Nov-2009	1,417,500,000	947,273,061.44	9.91147%	9.9900000000%	Not Available

Figure 12.7. Portfolio Monitoring.
Source: ABSXchange.

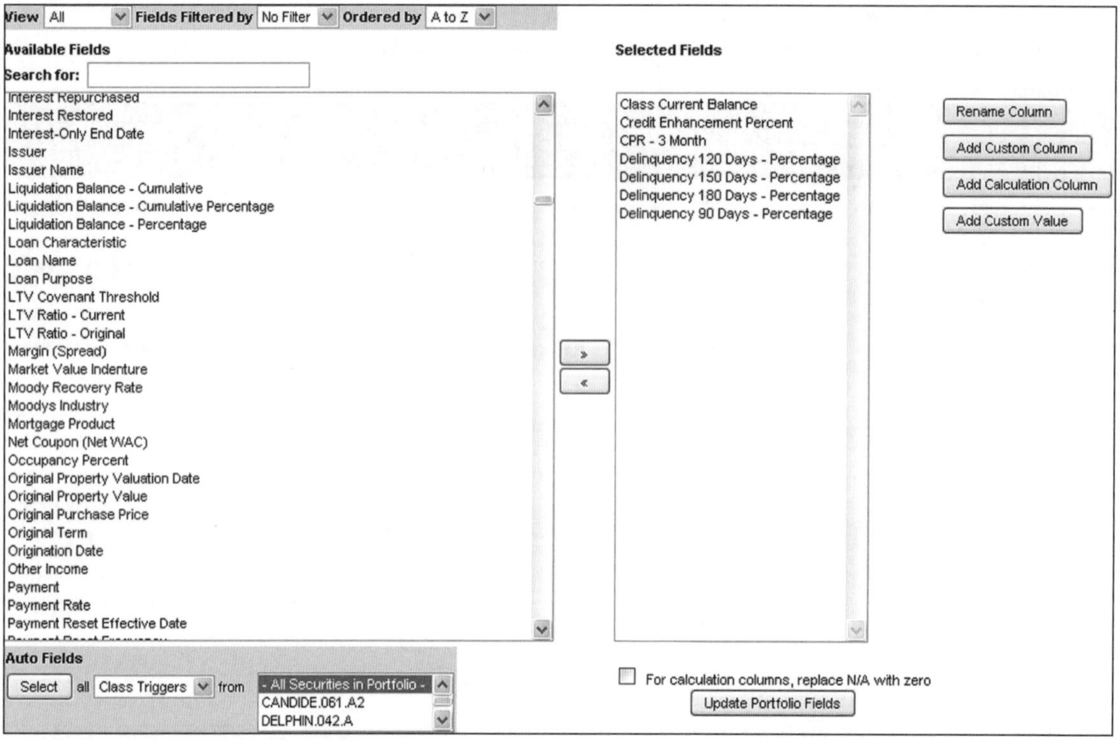

Figure 12.8. `Manage Columns` function.
Source: ABSXchange.

portfolio of securities and a report template have been matched, the latest performance information will appear on the screen. Historical periods can be selected either via the drop down list or within exported Excel reports.

12.5 CREATING BENCHMARK INDEXES

The `Portfolio Monitoring` (Figure 12.7) functionality can be extended to generate benchmark indices easily for key performance metrics such as prepayments and delinquencies. Benchmarks will be derived from aggregating the reported data, to produce a user-specified index for each of the key variables that are tracked at a transaction level. Transaction-specific metrics need to be weighted according to the relative size of the outstanding collateral. There are four steps to consider when creating an index: composition criteria, timeframe, aggregation, and interpolation. The composition of the index will be determined by user-selected eligibility criteria. For instance, a user may want to create an index that tracks delinquencies in all Spanish RMBS issued in a particular year. The composition would be driven entirely by these criteria. The timeframe of the index may be presented either in an absolute timeframe (i.e., against actual dates) or a relative timeframe (i.e., against number of months since closing).

Aggregation will depend on the metric. For example, a delinquencies index would measure the delinquent balance for an individual deal, divided by the total outstanding portfolio balance. The delinquency index is defined as the mean of delinquency rates across transactions, weighted by each transaction's current portfolio size. In some instances, datasets may be incomplete or inconsistent from one transaction to the next. In circumstances where a data period is unavailable, a straight-line interpolation can be used to arrive at interim periodic values.

Within the `Portfolio Monitoring` module or with ABSXchange's MS Excel `Add-In` function, users can add the members of the index and extract the relevant data points (e.g., 30-day delinquency and collateral balance) for the current and all historical periods. This information can be exported to Excel where the values can be aggregated and tracked.

12.6 CASH FLOW ANALYTICS

The standard method for understanding the value of a security is to calculate the present value of its expected future cash flows. In addition to valuations, cash flow sensitivity analysis is important to understand whether the credit enhancement is adequate to support any possible losses of principal or interest within a class. ABSXchange enables users to perform this analysis by combining the current performance of a transaction, a deal-specific cash flow model, and an advanced cash flow analytics engine. The cash flow model accurately covers all structural features of a transaction including the priority of payments, triggers, prepayment penalty allocations, and interest-rate or f/x hedges.

The analytics engine allows users to stress multiple components of a deal including economic variables and structural features. Users can create multiple scenarios to determine how sensitive a class is to a change in assumptions. The application will produce a price/yield table as well as a series of projection reports that illustrate the expected performance of the transaction, the collateral, and the waterfall. Sections 12.7 to 12.9 will provide an overview of single-bond analytics and portfolio-level analytics.

12.7 SINGLE-BOND CASH FLOW ANALYSIS

The `Analytics` (Figure 12.9) module allows users to run cash flow projections on a selected deal. The projection is performed using a unique cash flow model for each transaction based on information available in the offering circular and is updated when new information is made available. The collateral is projected to create asset cash flows and produces results for each set of assumptions. After selecting the class for which the user would like to run the cash flow analysis, a summary of current deal statistics are presented on the top of the page. The `Deal Notes` link presents a summary of assumptions made to build the deal model. Five scenarios are available by default; additional scenarios can be added and scenarios can be removed. Scenarios can also be enabled/disabled.

Via a drop down list, the user can select and input a value for the objective of their calculation such as price, yield, or discount margin. The model will generate a range of outputs above and below this first input. For instance, if the user selects a price of par, the model will display a corresponding range of outputs below, at, and above par. The user can vary the distance between each step in the range; by default the range will have 10 steps above and below par and each step will differ by 0.01. Next, the user can choose the `Settlement Distribution` date. By default, the system will either choose $T + 3$ or to the latest record date. In the box, `Orig Face`, the user should enter the notional value of their holdings.

After selecting the generic run options for the analysis, this user can then introduce economic assumptions. Economic assumptions will vary somewhat depending on the asset class. For a typical RMBS transaction, users will stress prepayments, delinquencies, defaults, and losses. ABSXchange offers multiple formats through which these variables can be stressed. For most of these variables, users can enter constant monthly or annualized rates or custom user-defined vectors.

The user can enter a constant prepayment speed or click on the symbol to the right of the window and choose a vector. The prepayment percentage is the rate at which the collateral is repaid over and

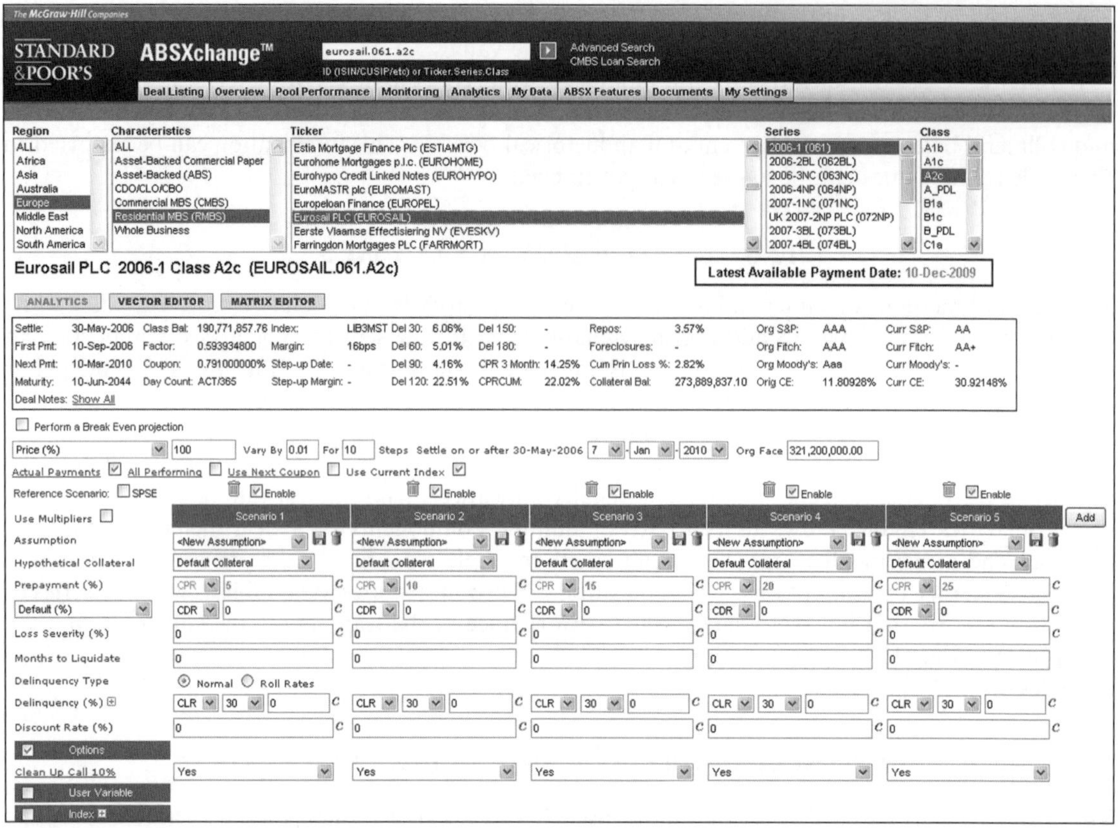

Figure 12.9. `Analytics` module.
Source: ABSXchange.

above the scheduled principal payments. For defaults/losses, a drop down menu offers three options: `Defaults %`, `Gross Loss %`, and `Net Loss %`. Defaults on the underlying collateral can be stressed as a constant rate for the duration of the projection, as a targeted gross default amount, or as a targeted net loss amount. The constant rate can either be an annual rate (CDR) or a monthly rate (MDR).

`Gross Loss %` is the total expected defaults within the collateral pool and is equally spread out over a specified period of months. `Net Loss %` is the total expected net losses within the collateral pool and is equally spread out over a specified period of months.

Loss severity is the percentage of the default balance that will ultimately be realized as a loss once the defaulted assets are liquidated. For example, a loss severity of 30% results in 70% of defaults being recovered after the liquidation period. When using `Net Loss %`, the system will automatically default to 100% loss severity. For example, if the user enters a `Net Loss %` of 10%, the system will assume realized losses of 10%. If the user were to enter a value for loss severity of, say, 50%, ABSXchange will gross up the collateral defaults so that the realized losses are 10%. Months to liquidate will account for the lag between a default and recovery of the loan. All defaulted assets will be liquidated after the number of months entered.

ABSXchange is very flexible for modeling delinquencies. Two types of delinquencies that can be modeled are (1) "normal", where a delinquency occurs in one period and cures in the following period;

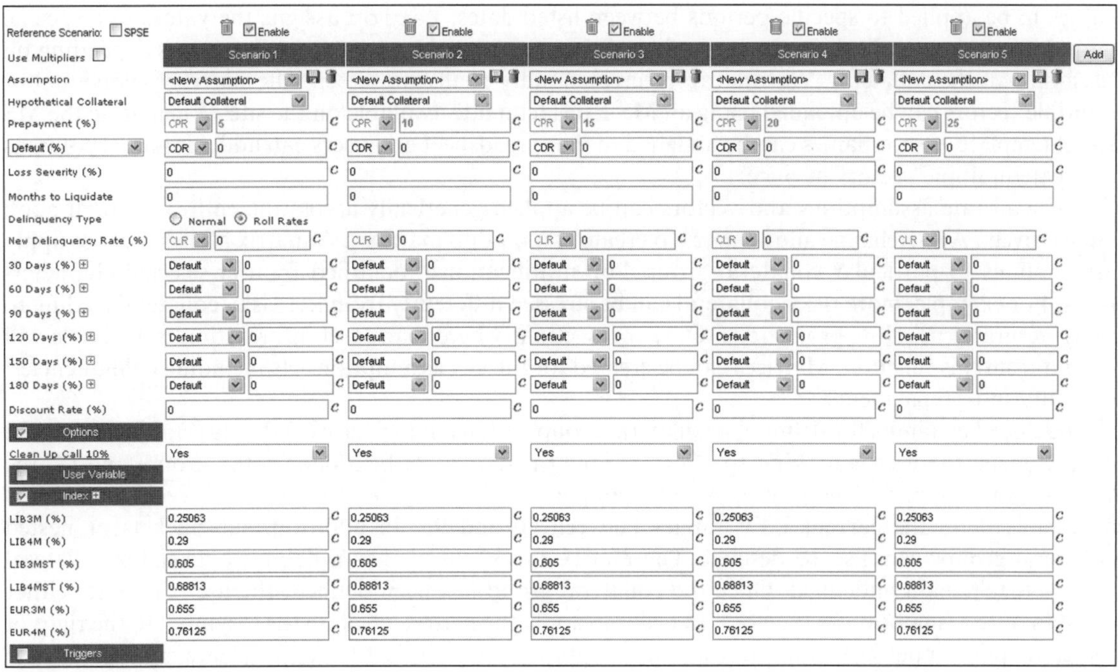

Figure 12.10. Scenario selection.
Source: ABSXchange.

and (2) "roll rates", where delinquencies will occur in one period and then either roll forward into another period, cure to an earlier period, prepay, or default. Users can select the delinquency type, the amount, and the delinquency bucket. Delinquency rates can be monthly (MLR) or annual (CLR).

For example, choosing `Normal/MLR/90 day/5%` would result in 5% of the performing balance falling delinquent every month, remaining delinquent for 90 days, and then curing. With the "roll rate" simulation, the `New Delinquency Rate` determines the percentage of new delinquencies that occur either annually or monthly. The percentage amounts entered for the roll options (e.g., cure, roll, default, prepay) will equate to the percentage of new delinquencies that will move into the selected buckets.

In addition to the economic variables, the user also has the flexibility to stress the structural components of a transaction. Users can decide whether to apply an option or not. In addition, users can stress underlying indices, model assumptions (also known as "user variables"), and triggers. Certain structural information is not publicly available during the modeling process. In order to build the cash flow model, ABSX modelers make assumptions, based on experience with previously modeled transactions. These structural assumptions are known as "user variables" and include items such as swap rates or servicing fees. The `Analytics` module exposes these assumptions and allows users to adjust these values based on their own assumptions. In addition, users can now stress individual deal triggers that influence cash flow projections. For instance, if a certain trigger is breached it might change the deal from paying sequentially to *pro rata*. Users can toggle a trigger to pass or fail in order to breach it.

Assumptions can be entered as constant rates or as custom curves, also known as vectors. Vectors are created and/or edited using the `Vector Editor`. Three types of vectors can be created for all categories of economic variables and for indexes: `Date`, `Period`, and `Deal Age`. `Date` allows the values to be applied to specific periods between listed dates; `Period` assigns the values to a specific period based on months from the beginning of the projection; `Deal Age` applies values depending on seasoning of the collateral. Vectors can be created individually on screen; alternatively, individual or multiple vectors can be uploaded using an MS Excel template available on the site. When using the MS Excel template, vector names can be assigned in the spreadsheet and users can add additional columns to create multiple vectors at once.

Constant rate assumptions and vectors can be applied generically across the entire collateral pool; alternatively, ABSXchange allows users to create assumption matrices. A matrix allows users to apply assumptions to particular collateral groups, or stratifications, identified by user-selected characteristics. For example, more risky collateral can be stressed differently from less risky collateral leading to more accurate cash flow projections. Only transactions where loan-level information is available will benefit from this function. Matrices can be created for the key assumption sets including delinquencies, defaults, and prepayments.

The three key inputs for defining a collateral group within a matrix are (1) the `Header`, which is the characteristic the user is looking to stress; (2) the `Operator`, which defines the group; and (3) the `Value`, which specifies the group. As an example, `CLTV/Range/[80:95]` will create a group of collateral where the current LTV ranges between 80 and 95. In addition, sub-buckets or nested collateral groups can also be defined. The matrix editor always has a default bucket for collateral groups that remain undefined. Once the collateral group has been defined, the user can enter either constant rate assumptions or vectors. In order to apply the matrix, click on the `C` symbol to the right of the assumption input box until the `[m]` symbol appears. Then select the appropriate matrix from the drop down options.

12.8 SINGLE CASH FLOW PROJECTION RESULTS

ABSXchange's cash flow projections will produce five types of results: (1) a price/yield table, (2) individual class-level cash flows, (3) collateral-level cash flows, (4) detailed projections for all classes (Figure 12.11), and (5) a waterfall report. The price/yield table is a quick summary of a cash flow projection. It shows a set of spreads/yields that will correspond to a series of prices. The user can customize this view. In addition, a summary of weighted average life, modified duration, collateral defaults, and collateral losses is displayed.

Class-level cash flow output will appear in a popup window displaying the coupon, principal paid, shortfalls, losses, and balances estimated based on the selected assumptions. Separately, collateral-level cash flow output will appear in another popup window and will display aggregated collateral for the deal including the coupon as well as principal and interest collections. In the collateral-level cash flow display window, the user is also able to see the progression of delinquencies, defaults, and losses.

For more detailed results, ABSXchange produces two MS Excel spreadsheets. The *deal projection report* presents class-level cash flow output as well as collateral-level cash flow output in a single report. In addition, the cash flows for all other classes and flows between structural features or accounts within the structure are presented; moreover, the impact of the projection on deal triggers is available. Finally, the *waterfall report* provides a detailed account of the sources and allocation of funds within the entire capital structure. The waterfall report is a transparent analysis that presents the priority of payments for the transaction and provides a clearer understanding of how ABSXchange originally modeled the transaction.

PROJECTION

Projection using Portfolio level information,
Servicer not advancing, and Actual Payments on

Price (%)	Discount Margin (bps) / Yield (%)				
99.90000%	18.416 / 0.79089%	19.474 / 0.80169%	20.633 / 0.81347%	21.863 / 0.82602%	23.155 / 0.83915%
99.91000%	18.174 / 0.78846%	19.127 / 0.79820%	20.169 / 0.80882%	21.277 / 0.82013%	22.439 / 0.83196%
99.92000%	17.932 / 0.78604%	18.779 / 0.79471%	19.706 / 0.80417%	20.690 / 0.81425%	21.723 / 0.82478%
99.93000%	17.691 / 0.78361%	18.432 / 0.79122%	19.243 / 0.79951%	20.104 / 0.80836%	21.008 / 0.81759%
99.94000%	17.449 / 0.78119%	18.084 / 0.78774%	18.779 / 0.79487%	19.517 / 0.80247%	20.292 / 0.81041%
99.95000%	17.208 / 0.77877%	17.737 / 0.78425%	18.316 / 0.79022%	18.931 / 0.79659%	19.577 / 0.80322%
99.96000%	16.966 / 0.77635%	17.390 / 0.78077%	17.853 / 0.78557%	18.345 / 0.79071%	18.862 / 0.79604%
99.97000%	16.725 / 0.77392%	17.043 / 0.77728%	17.390 / 0.78092%	17.759 / 0.78482%	18.147 / 0.78886%
99.98000%	16.483 / 0.77150%	16.695 / 0.77380%	16.927 / 0.77627%	17.173 / 0.77894%	17.432 / 0.78168%
99.99000%	16.242 / 0.76908%	16.348 / 0.77032%	16.464 / 0.77163%	16.588 / 0.77306%	16.717 / 0.77451%
100.00000%	16.001 / 0.76666%	16.001 / 0.76683%	16.001 / 0.76698%	16.002 / 0.76718%	16.002 / 0.76733%
100.01000%	15.759 / 0.76424%	15.654 / 0.76335%	15.539 / 0.76234%	15.416 / 0.76130%	15.288 / 0.76016%
100.02000%	15.518 / 0.76182%	15.307 / 0.75987%	15.076 / 0.75770%	14.831 / 0.75543%	14.573 / 0.75298%
100.03000%	15.277 / 0.75940%	14.960 / 0.75639%	14.613 / 0.75306%	14.245 / 0.74955%	13.859 / 0.74581%
100.04000%	15.036 / 0.75698%	14.613 / 0.75291%	14.151 / 0.74841%	13.660 / 0.74367%	13.145 / 0.73864%
100.05000%	14.795 / 0.75456%	14.266 / 0.74943%	13.688 / 0.74377%	13.075 / 0.73780%	12.430 / 0.73147%
100.06000%	14.553 / 0.75214%	13.920 / 0.74595%	13.226 / 0.73913%	12.490 / 0.73193%	11.716 / 0.72430%
100.07000%	14.312 / 0.74972%	13.573 / 0.74247%	12.764 / 0.73449%	11.905 / 0.72605%	11.003 / 0.71714%
100.08000%	14.071 / 0.74731%	13.226 / 0.73899%	12.302 / 0.72986%	11.320 / 0.72018%	10.289 / 0.70997%
100.09000%	13.830 / 0.74489%	12.880 / 0.73552%	11.839 / 0.72522%	10.735 / 0.71431%	9.575 / 0.70281%
100.10000%	13.589 / 0.74247%	12.533 / 0.73204%	11.377 / 0.72058%	10.150 / 0.70844%	8.862 / 0.69565%
Avg Life (Yrs)	4.24196	2.92844	2.18658	1.72271	1.4089
Class Principal Loss	0.00000% / 0.00	0.00000% / 0.00	0.00000% / 0.00	0.00000% / 0.00	0.00000% / 0.0
Modified Duration	4.12850	2.86996	2.15191	1.69997	1.3928
Present Value	197,082,135.80	195,163,860.85	194,080,271.83	193,402,845.19	192,944,419.6
Principal Window	10-Mar-2010 10-Dec-2019	10-Mar-2010 10-Mar-2017	10-Mar-2010 10-Jun-2015	10-Mar-2010 10-Jun-2014	10-Mar-201 10-Jun-201
Collateral Cumulative Defaults	0.000% / 0.00	0.000% / 0.00	0.000% / 0.00	0.000% / 0.00	0.000% / 0.0
Collateral Cumulative Losses	0.000% / 0.00	0.000% / 0.00	0.000% / 0.00	0.000% / 0.00	0.000% / 0.0
	View Report:	View Report:	View Report:	View Report:	View Report

EXPORT

Figure 12.11. Projected cash flows.
Source: ABSXchange.

12.9 ADVANCED FUNCTIONALITY

ABSXchange offers a series of advanced analytics functionality, including additional run options, single-bond breakeven analysis; portfolio analytics, and collateral editing.

Breakeven analysis enables users to determine the highest level of collateral defaults and losses before a tranche's interest and principal is impacted; users can solve for three variables and three outcomes (i.e., nine options). The three variables solved for are (1) `Cumulative Default %`, which is the cumulative level of defaults in the collateral from the beginning to the end of the projection as a percentage of the original balance; (2) `Cumulative Net Loss`, which is the cumulative level of losses in the collateral from the beginning to the end of the projection as a percentage of the original balance; and (3) `Constant Default Rate` or CDR, which is the average level of defaults in the portfolio over the life of the projections; the CDR will be a lower number than the cumulative default percent.

For all three variables, users need to enter a `Loss Severity` assumption otherwise the result will report as an `Error`. The three outcomes solved for are (1) `Projected Cash Short`, which is the first instance of an interest or principal payment shortfall; (2) `Projected Period Interest Shortfall`, which is the first instance of an interest payment shortfall; and (3) `Remaining Balance`, which is the lowest level of defaults or losses that will result in an unpaid principal balance at the end of the projection. The results should theoretically be related closely to the credit enhancements of the structure.

`Portfolio Analytics` is a modified, multi-deal version of the `Single Bond Analytics` module. This module enables users to project similar outputs for a portfolio of bonds such as spreads, yields, and price. The same set of inputs and run options are available in the `Portfolio Analytics` module as well as in the `Single Bond Analytics` module, with the exception of the breakeven analysis. In addition to single-bond results, `Portfolio Analytics` also calculates aggregated statistics such as aggregated weighted average life; proceeds, losses, etc. Finally, the `Collateral Editor` function allows users to modify the collateral used in cash flow projections. This feature can be used to create multiple rep lines or upload loan-level data, if available.

13
Bloomberg

One firm amongst those listed in Part IV of the book is running a slightly different business model and, hence, stands out from the crowd: Bloomberg.

If you are a Bloomberg user then you will, as part of the package you are subscribing to, already have access to *all* Bloomberg tools that come as part of the package. There's no tiered subscription model where you would have to pay extra for certain add-ons or historical data or the need to subscribe to additional deal libraries—which can be very expensive if you have a global portfolio with exposure in many different asset classes, or a large number of bonds.

Everything you need is there as part of the Bloomberg package. To me that's already a major advantage. If you sign up to their service then you will get access to masses of data, both current and historic, and you can use Bloomberg's cash flow tools including predefined scenario analysis as well as tools that also enable the user to customize and crucially save stress scenarios. Furthermore, these stress scenarios can also be shared and sent to other Bloomberg users.

However, this was not always the case: 4 years ago there was no real alternative to other specialist data providers and vendors. Hence, if you held a sizable structured finance portfolio and you wanted to do proper surveillance and performance analytics you would have had no option—you would have had to go to one or more of the specialist service providers in order to get the information or data you needed.

However, this changed drastically during the credit crunch and, at the time of writing this book (2008 to early 2011), Bloomberg was running a massive improvement project for its structured finance product suite. The firm realized that the structured finance market had completely changed during the credit crunch and was fully aware that many investors had become, whether they liked it or not, buy-and-hold investors, at least until market activity returned and the illiquidity of some structured finance products disappeared and could be replaced by secondary-market trading.

Furthermore, for the first time, probably since the establishment of the global structured finance market, decisive power moved from issuers to investors. Following the crisis, there was a notable change in attitude where—for the first time—investors were able to put pressure on issuers in terms of requesting information. Naturally, if you are investing considerable amounts of money (say, \$10m to \$50m) you would like to know what you are actually investing in. However, prior to the credit crisis investors usually had to use whatever information was given to them as part of the roadshow, pitch presentations, and, of course, the rating agency material. Pre crisis, only the largest (i.e., more powerful) investors were able to request more information from originating institutions or issuers and get it.

But now, within the changed market regime, investors (no matter how small or big) are in a well-placed position to demand deal-specific information, such as loan-level information. The often heard argument of issuers that this information is not available is economic with the truth: loan-by-loan level data are typically readily available as part of data submission to the rating agencies. Granted, bank secrecy laws and data protection rules may prohibit the provision of information but, generally, this information should be provided if regulations permit.

Bloomberg is in the convenient position of receiving investor reports of all sorts and has recognized the need to make this information widely available to investors and the market at large. The firm addressed this need by investing large amounts in developing innovative and clever technology that, combined with human interfaces and intervention, manages to source all information available from investor reporting into its datawarehouse. Consequently, Bloomberg is now able to provide this information via its terminal in an easily digestible and flexible electronic format. The icing on the cake of all these recent developments is so-called "clickthrough" transparency, which enables Bloomberg users to click on a reported value for a specific key performance indicator (KPI) and, subsequently, an electronic version of the relevant investor report opens at the appropriate page with the key performance indicator value highlighted in the report—giving investors, for the first time, the ability to drill down into the underlying data source as part of their analysis.

Furthermore, it enables usage of cash flow–modeling tools and scenario analysis tools and makes these functions available to investors via its terminals without the need to purchase individual "deal libraries" or other bespoke packages—everything is included as part of the subscription.

One of the big advantages of using Bloomberg is when you discover a function you need that's currently not available. Bloomberg gives you the option to raise a formal "change request". Bloomberg will subsequently look into your request, assess whether your proposed amendment is commercially viable (i.e., if the development costs that will be incurred are justified by the value the new tool would offer), and if there are other customers who have shown interest in having such a functionality available to them. If that's the case and the request is actually feasible, then the firm will pass your request to its developers and implement your suggestion—at no extra cost to you. Several times I had the pleasure of working with Bloomberg structured finance experts in Europe and the U.S. They are a bunch of highly knowledgeable specialists who were always more than happy to take my suggestions on board and transform them into new functions (some of which are referred to in Chapter 22: Bloomberg's structured finance tools).

14

CapitalTrack

14.1 CHANGING THE DATA MODEL USED FOR STRUCTURED FINANCE INSTRUMENT ADMINISTRATION

"25 years ago it was comparatively easy to acquire a sound knowledge of the general investment field—[but now] the different types of securities have multiplied in number to an almost unlimited extent ..."

John Moody, 1910

The hybrid (structured) instrument market started as far back as the 1850s with bonds containing equity-based variations. Today, the same industry has exploded into a wide range of instruments that make the above quote still look very contemporary.

The international structured finance instrument market is indeed vast, boasting a "footprint" that now exceeds U.S.$8tn and is *still* growing in terms of volume and product innovation. At one end of the market, hordes of rate-hungry investors continue to bet on instruments of all shapes and sizes and, at the other, issuers run a formidable global factory producing all manner of instruments on a seemingly endless conveyor belt. In between the two (the "middle ground"), the sector administrators make their money offering a range of services to keep the whole "machine" ticking over. They are typically banks, their affiliates (lawyers, accountants, and administrators), stock exchanges, and regulators who are charged collectively with all aspects of safekeeping, accounting, income gathering, funds transfer, jurisdiction rules, full disclosure, and, ultimately, for providing a formal marketplace where buyer and seller can conduct their business on a secure, accurate, and timely basis.

The explosion in instrument volume and complexity in recent years, however, has left the "middle ground" struggling under the pressures of an administration model that needs urgent modernization to ensure robust future growth. A combination of outdated and incohesive industry procedures—made all the worse by years of underinvestment—has rendered the "machine" an inefficient bloated mass of activity that is now costing the sector countless millions of pounds a year in downtime, duplication, confusion and compensation. The middle ground needs a radical change in the key areas of its methodology and operational models if it is to stay on track for expansion.

14.1.1 The chain

The administration of a structured finance instrument for its entire lifecycle of possibly 30 years or more can be quite convoluted and labor intensive. Instrument complexity plays a big role in determining the work required (and, of course, the cost), but this is compounded further by how the markets behave, how often the instrument changes hands, and by how many people take part in the process.

The current market structure entails the involvement of up to seven different administration entities known generally as servicing agents. Each performs specific roles at different stages of a process "chain" that is in essence responsible for paying interest to investors (whenever due) and, eventually, for returning the original sum invested. The first links in the chain disseminate instrument data (i.e., the

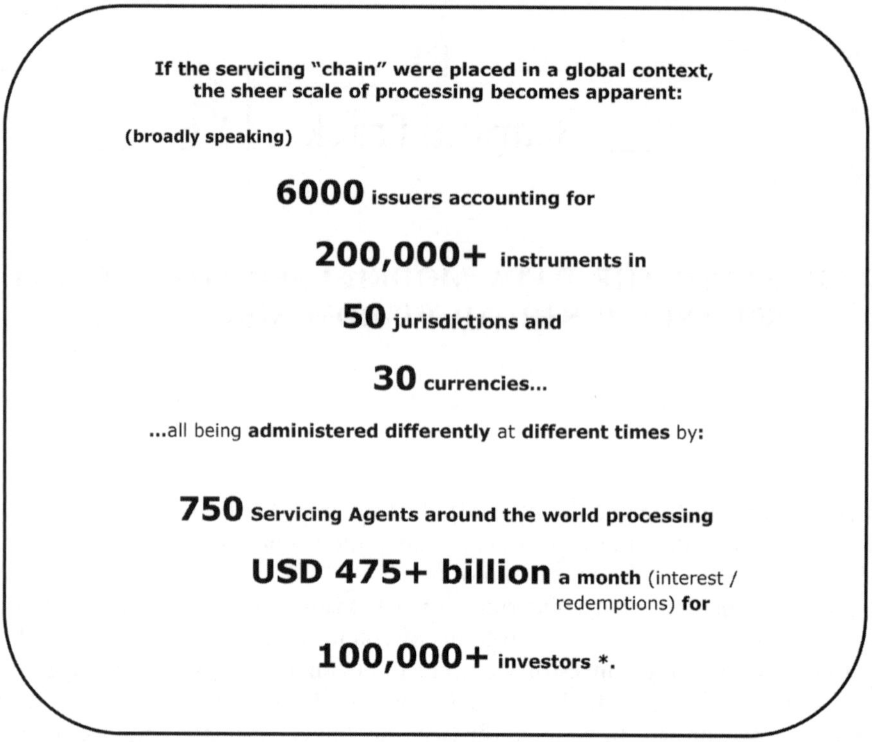

Figure 14.1. The servicing chain.
*A guesstimate as private client numbers are invisible.
Source: CapitalTrack.

new-deal specifics compiled by the issuer) to the links that then calculate the interest when due; some links move money to those who credit or debit investor accounts and others post data on stock exchanges. The "chain" element is the fact that they all fundamentally rely on each other for data to carry out their particular task successfully and at the right time.

14.1.2 The calculation

When an instrument is due for processing (i.e., monies are expected by investors) the agent responsible has to be aware of the timing so it can assemble the various bits of information needed to get the calculation done. This means an accurate diary "reminder" is required to begin the process and then the calculation is generally synthesized from two elements:

(i) a *basic set of mechanical data* (18–20 fields of "must have" particulars such as the start/end of an interest period, the formula, the currency, the payment date, and so on) taken from the prospectus ("Terms") and
(ii) an *interpretation* or confirmation of term stipulations (e.g., the use of a market figure observed at a particular point—like an index or a currency exchange rate) so as to ensure that the right mix of facts and figures is applied to the calculation process.

Clearly, there is a great deal of reliance on system setup, access to correct accurate data, and a level of expertise to get the job done. Nevertheless, be it early or late, right or wrong, the calculated rate has to be communicated to different parts of the chain (according to contractual relationships) so that each entity can get on with the job at hand. The end of the processing cycle happens only when all disclosures are made, monies are transferred, and investors finally receive a statement to confirm an account transaction and new position.

14.2 THE BIG FLY IN THE OINTMENT

Every instrument typically has

- A *different administration cycle*. Each cycle randomly starts when an instrument is issued.
- A *different construction and set of terms*. These can range from "vanilla" (e.g., base rate + 50 basis points every 3 months) right through to mathematically complex, subjective, retrospective, and even "only if it suits us" calculations and payment dates.
- A *different combination of servicing agents*. Competition and client relationships have spread the work far and wide around the globe. Technology enables servicing agents to conduct work in-house ("multi-location") or outsource to foreign or "factory" specialist administrators who conduct the work and pass it back to the agent on completion.
- A *different set of jurisdiction (and stock exchange) requirements*. These are chosen to suit investor tax/investment profiles which could mean, in effect, assets being held in numerous places depending on the stage of the tax year, accumulated gains/losses, and so on—and, of course, a local agent for each jurisdiction will be required.

The net result of all this is an almost intangible array of permutations of "who is doing what for whom then sending it where and when" nonstop 24 hours a day around the globe. Consider Figure 14.1.

Taking the numbers in Figure 14.1 and assuming an average (vanilla) process cycle of four times a year and a minimum of 18 data fields needed to accompany each rate calculation notice (for the 200,000 odd instruments), the sheer scale of processing becomes apparent: *millions upon millions of datasets* need to criss-cross the global middle ground every year to ensure that the right people process what is required—at the right time—in order to meet all manner of obligations and deadlines.

14.2.1 The middle ground

Over the years, the middle ground has grown to become quite an industry in its own right. In fact, expansion has been such that it is now a sprawling global fraternity involving thousands of people all chipping away at processing different parts of the issuer/investor relationship. They have all developed the tools they need to maintain their business (by hook or by crook) and, in general, they have all made a pretty good living out of it. The exchanges have had a constant flow of new-issue registrations, regulatory fees have poured in, and, at the "global player" end of the sector, gross incomes exceed £100m a year.

But *unchecked growth* invariably comes at a price: an industry that has expanded voraciously in every direction, to keep up with the issuance of all manner of instruments, at some point is bound to develop weaknesses where parts start to falter and become inefficient. In this case, the industry as a whole is being forced "to come up for air" because it is struggling to meet many long-standing key challenges across the processing spectrum. Accuracy and timeliness are the two largest parts that permanently falter but the overall problem is being made far worse now by global regulation (which has stepped up its demands), the investor (who is seeking far better service), and costs that have built over time (which are starting to hurt quite badly). The global machine would appear to be choking, unable to roll out the urgent changes it needs to make because there is no central effort, no collective solution or initiative for adoption across the board.

14.2.2 Data islands—and "reverse" chains

The cost of administration is directly related to the investment made in skills and systems. The cost of getting it wrong can be an expensive headache and a major competitive disadvantage. League tables are very quick to point out who is lagging behind, investors shriek with threats of taking business away and then industry bodies meet to take a collective aspirin whilst proposing remedial measures. The problem, however, at its sharpest point, is the fact that the middle ground has become a group of many unconnected "islands", each with its own ecosystem of machinery, priorities, contractual routes, politics, and budgets. Each one does its own thing (according to its own systems, records, and setup) and, as long as a task is carried out and is communicated to someone, the job is deemed done. The reality, though, is far from that. The sheer volume of data passing through an unstructured and unconnected environment, coupled with all the possibilities of error, disparity, or delay, makes it extremely difficult to stop the machine, identify and rectify the problem, and then carry on. For this reason just about every established operation that is involved with client monies bears the cost of having staff on permanent "chase" to avoid client backlash for delay or incorrect sums of money being moved in or out of accounts.

14.2.3 Chain reversal

In an attempt to anticipate calculations and dates (and avoid sliding down the league table), the chain has actually developed a reverse process across the sector. This entails groups sending each other expectation lists (i.e., what they think they are due from one party or another in an attempt to reconcile their databases or instrument setups before the event). Some lists are more formal than others, some groups are better set up than others to participate, but the net result is a massive secondary layer of administration that utilizes a lot of people/system hours as huge data files wash in and out of each operation in the hope that errors, mismatches, and inconsistencies will be picked up and washed out. Not always so.

14.2.4 Witness the U.S. Depository Trust and Clearing Corporation (DTCC)

> "Thousands of transactions *fail to be processed* in an accurate and timely manner each year . . .";
>
> ". . . more than *14%* of payable rates were unknown to the DTCC at the close of business the day prior to payable date . . .";
>
> "revisions that require adjustments in the actual payments made to participants remain virtually unchanged since 2002."

DTCC White Paper, June 2006

In fact, the DTCC alludes to the island syndrome as "structural discontinuity" in the servicing chain and tables it as being a major contributor to the sector's woes. It goes on to call for a "concerted industry effort" to turn things around—with suggestions like "simplification of terms" as being one possible place to start (though that might remove a lot of investor appetite for the asset class impacted). This calling, however, is far from straightforward as the discontinuity is so deeply entrenched right along the chain that it would be impossible for things to change organically. One agent would have little or no influence over another (competitor) so there would have to be a central push or edict with "sharp teeth" to rally everyone into change. To do this on a global basis, with everyone agreeing to implement standards, formats, etc. would simply be a very tough nut to crack for all kinds of cultural, jurisdictional, and political reasons.

So, the islands remain unconnected; each one tackling its own fires behind closed doors, with the intensity that reflects their position in league tables or the size of margin being eroded or lost from this particular part of their business.

It is therefore erratic sector development, a lack of international processing standards and any type of formal communication infrastructure that has ensured continued widespread sector fragmentation, massive duplication of work, frustratingly slow communication, "patchwork" systems, poor access to processing ownership and a wide array of very expensive, disjointed efforts ... the most costly and time-consuming of which are the "payment reversals" where the whole chain has to be stopped, the mistake found, amendments released, all systems updated, and the investor paid correctly (with possible compensation).

14.3 CAPITALTRACK—THE NEW MODEL

CapitalTrack Ltd. (CT) is an independent, financial data management company established in the spring of 2000. For nearly 10 years, CT has developed specialized services to unite the structured finance instrument industry into a common disciplined initiative in order to streamline the whole process of administration—covering the full product lifecycle from data creation, its management and storage, through to its effective communication from issuer to investor.

CT recognized early on that the initiative would require a decisive overhaul of core data activities across the board so as to "break" the reliance on the chain currently in operation. CT also recognized the need to get all participants involved, all playing on the same field, playing the same game, and speaking a common language.

Altering the course of a "tanker", however, was not going to be easy, but could be achievable with the right components: an independent catalyst that offered a win/win incentive for all; one that made good business sense, had no competitive implications whatsoever, treated everyone equally—and had the credentials to assist with sector-wide change.

14.3.1 Changing the data model

The solution was, is, and remains to establish a new link in the processing chain—a central information agent to polarize the sector and methodically facilitate the data changes required with minimal change or spend requirement.

Objectives:

To re-align data flow, quality, and availability by setting up:

(1) A *central repository* for the sole, definitive, standardized "golden source" data record per instrument
(2) A central hub offering robust *communication infrastructure* to link all the islands to one another *and* the golden source repository
(3) A data bridge from *issuer* to *investor*, removing all the data barriers between buyer and seller.

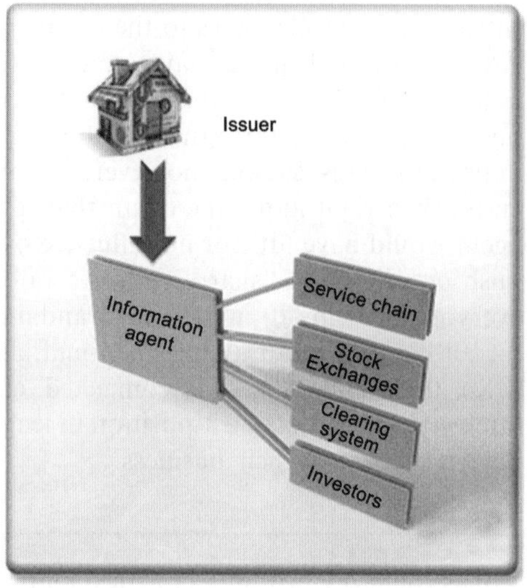

Figure 14.2. New link in the processing chain.
Source: CapitalTrack.

14.3.2 Back to the golden source

CT and a growing number of leading servicing agents recognize the importance of one standardized, accurate data source as being imperative to sector overhaul. Getting the data correctly set up from "square one" would have dramatic effects on all downstream work as there would be full inescapable transparency.

The problem, however, comes back to the current model of data transfer, transcription, and setup—and the island syndrome with all the differences, disconnects. and confusion it creates.

14.3.3 Data problems

Every instrument starts life with a prospectus from which a term sheet or pricing supplement is derived. In essence, this is a summary document setting out the deal's bare bones—the terms and conditions, promises and caveats. These are typically compiled by the issuer (or the issuer's agent/lawyer) and then disseminated to the chain so that each "link" is ready to carry out its particular role. It is here that problems start within the current administration model.

The crucial data required to administer an instrument (periods, dates, formulas, etc.) are stored via manual transcription. Every servicing agent (and stock exchange) typically conducts its own transcription and instrument setup (populating data fields in a processing machine) to ensure it has the data captured in the format its own system requires. There are differing methods of transcription (in-house/outsource/temp staff), differing levels of expertise, and differing levels of data capture (which can range from 8 to 40 data fields depending on the system being used). The result of all this work is the potential for one instrument to end up in a wide range of formats in a variety of storage systems in the chain. *If any error or omission* slips through, it is usually detected only once it is too late (i.e., when a delayed payment is questioned or a dispute is tabled). This forces costly downtime whilst all concerned try to establish *who* has the right data and thus who is liable. The net result of these breaks in processing is potentially all manner of compliance, regulatory, and client relationship/compensation issues.

14.3.4 Changing the data model

Changing the data model entails every issuer (or its agents) feeding new-issue data (in document form initially and then in electronic form when possible) straight to the central information agent for creation of a golden source record.

The transcription process is carried out once, centrally, applying the skill required for instruments of all complexities and the interpretation or calibration necessary for accurate timing (e.g., date setting to account for holidays/weekends, etc.). Once the transcribed data have been "signed off" by the issuer (i.e., confirmed as being an accurate extraction/calibration), the base document is then tagged, scanned, and stored with the instrument's golden source entry.

This establishes the definitive record that should be produced only once in a (software) language that all parties in the chain can assimilate and store in order to carry out their particular role. It is the one record that all processing should be based on, driven by, and concluded with. There should be no alternative data transcription/system alteration anywhere else in the chain.

14.3.5 The golden source—process & presentation

Up to *60 fields* are extracted from base documents and presented back to the party in question in MS Excel for approval. If "clean", the transcribed data are then converted to golden source format for online presentation and *read-only* access via the internet. The data are also simultaneously forwarded (in Excel) to all mandatory or interested parties—which the issuer can nominate—for them to populate their own storage points.

With all base data properly set up, the original document is scanned and attached to the record of each instrument, enabling immediate recall. Any other subsequent or linked documents (e.g., modifications like currency change or re-engineering) are added so that a full lifecycle of data is maintained.

All event-based announcements (corporate actions) pertinent to the instrument (issuer news, early or partial return of invested monies) are captured going forwards and appended for immediate access. This way, the golden source encapsulates the full quota of static, event-based, and operational data for all parties concerned in the chain. Figure 14.3 is a screenshot example of the golden source with an appended base document.

14.3.6 Communication infrastructure—linking the islands

Establishing a golden source database provides the starting point for the administration lifecycle of each instrument. The next piece of the equation is keeping the data up to date and linking all required parties to it—providing them with various tools to access and manipulate the data. This keeps everyone current, accurate, and in a position to know when a processing duty is required.

In 2003 CapitalTrack launched the FRS System to provide the first step on the road to linking the islands via an independent solution. Using a combination of web-based infrastructure and role-specific portals to access the golden source data, the system set out to link all participants into a common, disciplined initiative that would drive standardization and networking—with the aim of nurturing (or forcing) accuracy and timeliness.

Today this system has evolved into a formal standardized platform with *350* core market participants now interacting on a variety of levels (from daily uploads to bespoke data-processing work) and using a common language to link industry participants to a central data source *and* all their servicing agents, clients, and investors, respectively. Each link in the chain is given access to a secure

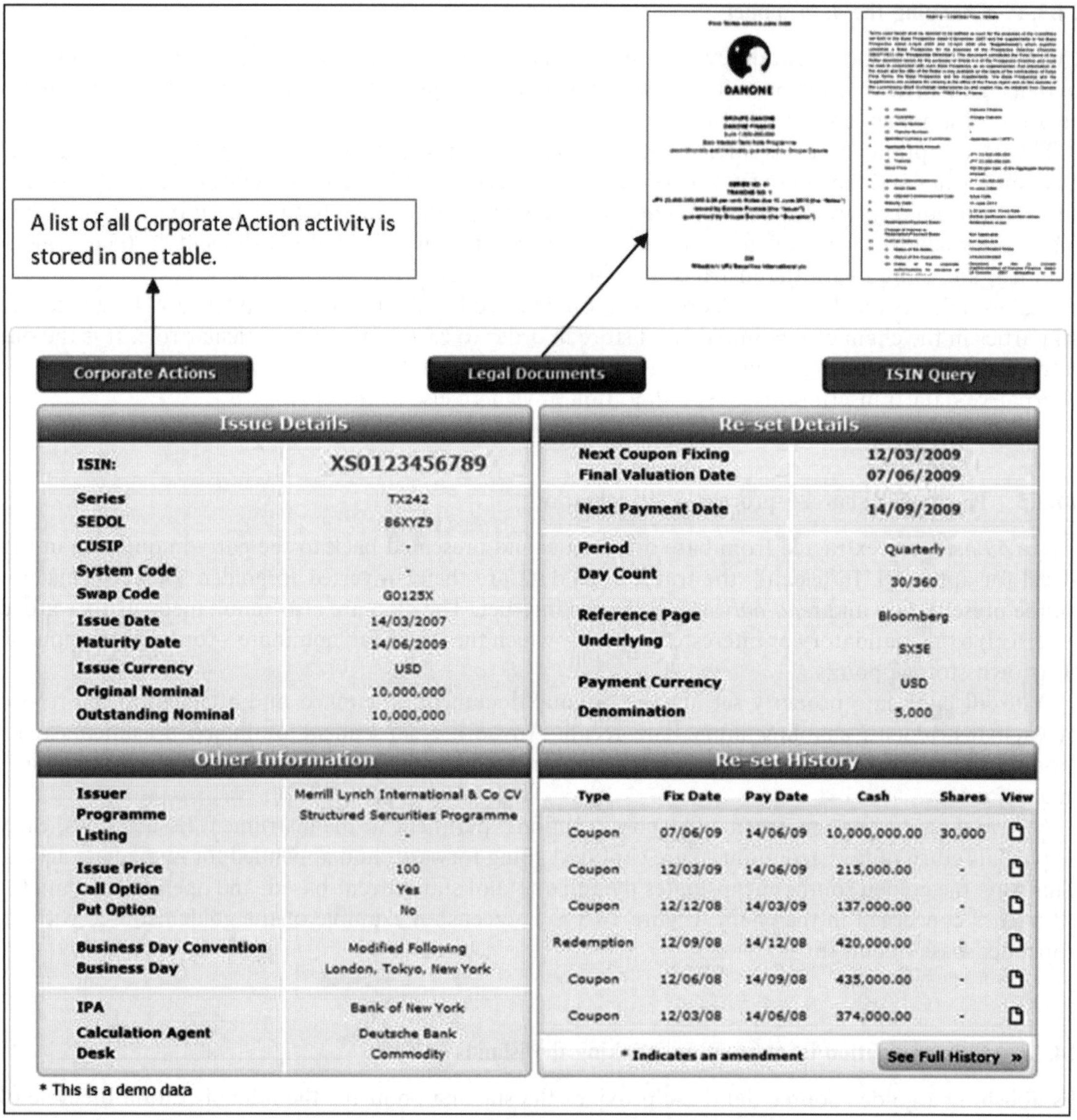

Figure 14.3. Golden source example.
Source: CapitalTrack.

portal created for their particular role in the market and this is linked directly to the instruments they require sight of, using instrument identifiers as the key searchable lowest denominator. The tools and infrastructure provided by the platform enable operational efficiency and accuracy, with constructive byproducts including STP, material cost benefits, instrument transparency, and automation of disclosure to all regulatory or investor bodies.

CT maintains the largest independent database of static, event-based, and operational data in the floating and variable rate space, processing and supplying an average of *29,700 coupon resets/corporate actions a month* for interest and redemption payments worth in excess of *£340bn*.

Using these definitive golden source data, tools have been developed to assist with every step of the administration process and are made available as an off-the-shelf solution. At the production end of the chain, issuers and calculation agents have tools to manage events (e.g., diaries for date-driven duties), the automated delivery or receipt of data notices (e.g., interest calculations), and a valuable built-in "window for resolution" before any breaks (errors) are permitted to slip through. At the end of the chain, the investor is provided with all manner of filtered automation—that is, on declaration (upload) of portfolio instrument holdings, all updates are pushed through when they occur, meaning the end to a life of waiting, not knowing who to chase for an update, and, then more importantly, who to contact in the event of a query or dispute. Figures 14.4–14.6 summarize the core functionality offered by CapitalTrack's FRS System.

The issuer portal

Linkage to all parties ensures full transparency including the ability to direct important data at investors/noteholders, who are, at the end of the day, the main players.

The calculation agent portal

The key areas to note are

1. Internal database cleanse (maintenance)—keeping all instruments set up true.
2. The XLS reconciliation with the main upstream/downstream relationships. This ensures that the calculation agent is always in line with external parties.
3. *Event management*. Golden source data are used to set up diaries so that all activity is clearly defined by timeframe—and remains on the system (in red) until cleared. All calculation parameters are

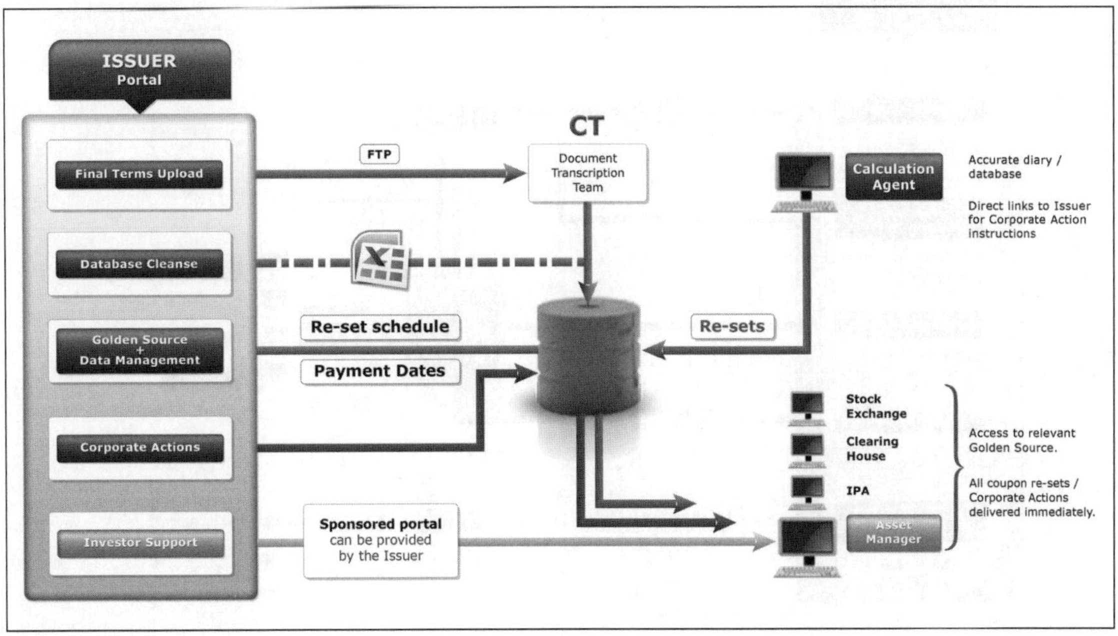

Figure 14.4. Issuer portal.
Source: CapitalTrack.

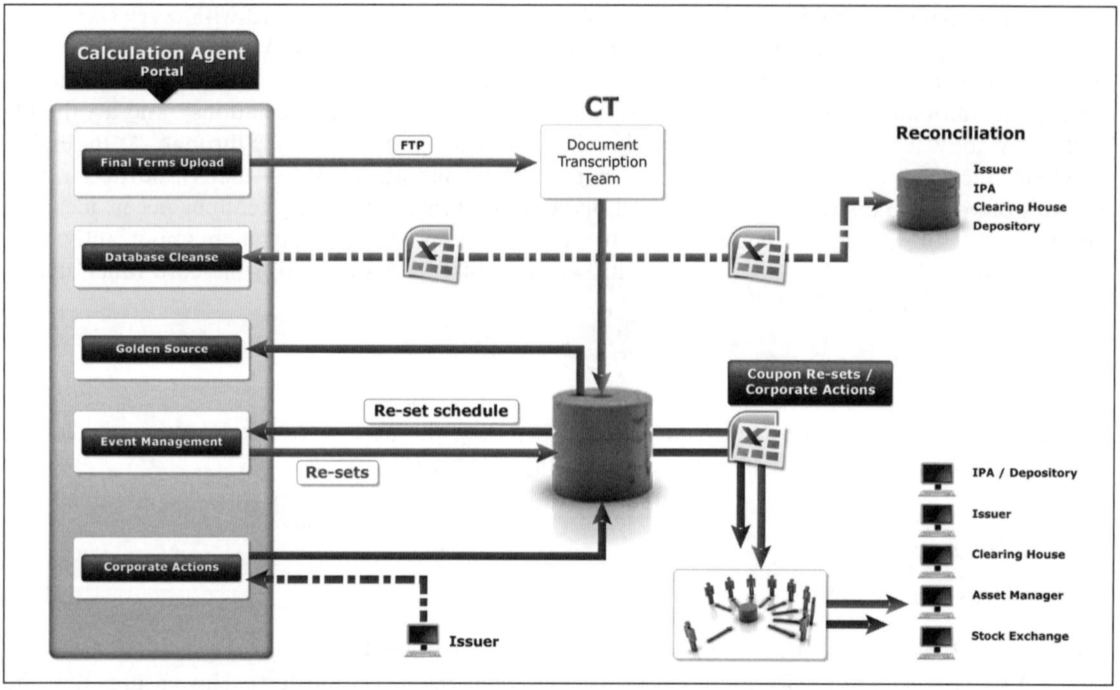

Figure 14.5. Calculation agent portal.
Source: CapitalTrack.

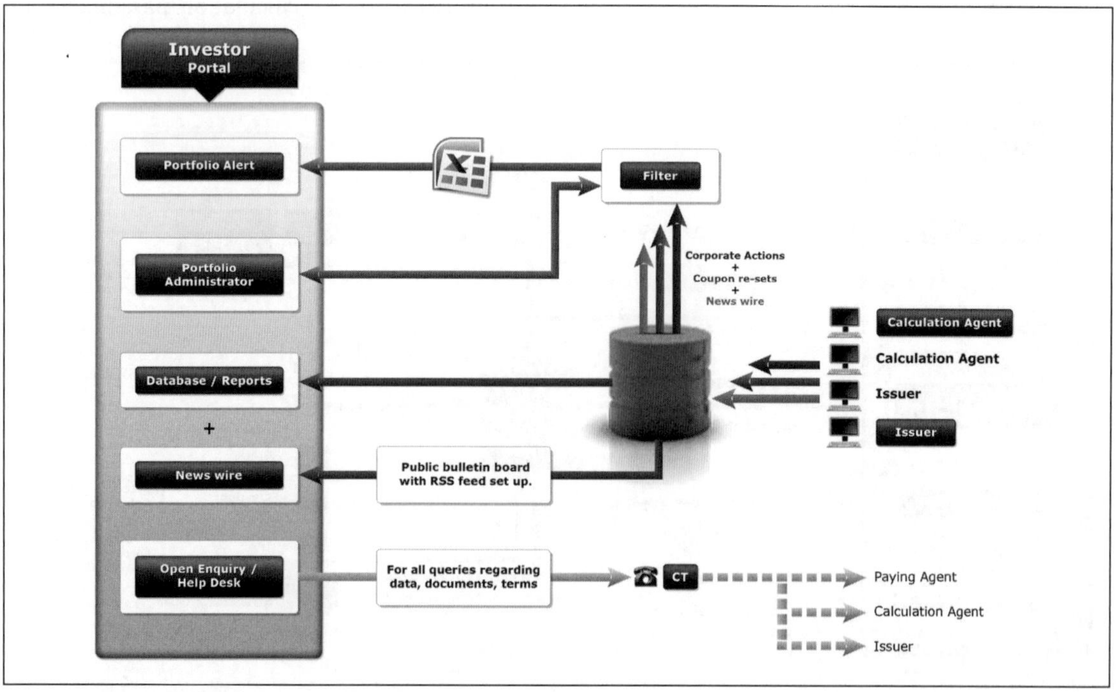

Figure 14.6. Investor portal.
Source: CapitalTrack.

presented in an easy format and then all data calculated are passed through a variety of checks (validated/formated) before release to the market.

4. *Distribution*. All mandatory recipients are preloaded with the relevant instrument signifiers and, on release of the data, a rapid "push" notification is achieved for full and timely disclosure (within 10 minutes of calculation).

The investor portal

The investor/noteholder (or indeed those acting on his behalf in an administration role) has typically always had to wait for statements, account updates, and any other notice to materialize. The path to querying something, disputing an amount, or simply confirming a timeline had always been quite a struggle, if not frustrating to the point of annoyance.

The concept of having a "data bridge" right through to the source has turned the old dynamics upside down and the FRS System now offers a window for data viewing, access, and an automated supply mechanism.

By loading all instruments into a simple (Excel), self-administered filter, the FRS System codes the investors' interest and when an update is received from any part of the chain, the data are automatically grabbed, formated, and delivered!

Access to the golden source also ensures access to all parties required for queries, disputes, and confirmations.

This level of transparency places the middle ground in a very strong proactive light and, in turn, drives investor confidence in the whole process.

15
Fitch Solutions

Fitch Solutions offers a range of comprehensive data, analytical tools, and related services to fixed income investors and other market participants. The firm also distributes Fitch Ratings' proprietary credit ratings, research, and data through a variety of platforms. Product offerings cover research services, risk and performance analytics, structured finance solutions, pricing and valuation services, quantitative analytics, and a specialist training firm for financial professionals.

Fitch Solutions' products and services provide market participants with greater insight into the growing complexity of the credit markets to enable more timely and informed business decisions.

15.1 PRODUCTS AND SERVICES

15.1.1 Research services

Fitch Research

This online subscription service provides access to Fitch Ratings' proprietary research and credit ratings, as well as analytical tools and ongoing market surveillance. Fitch Research includes market insights, objective credit opinions, and ratings alerts that can be customized for individual portfolios and delivered in a variety of formats. Additionally, clients gain access to experienced Fitch Ratings' analysts in over 50 offices around the world to help them monitor up-to-the-minute rating changes, understand credit trends, and make informed investment decisions.

`Peer Analysis Tool`, available via Fitch Research, provides access to key credit data on over 15,000 private and public banks, 900 corporate entities, and 100 sovereigns to facilitate cross-border analysis and reduce the time required to perform peer analyses.

15.1.2 Structured finance solutions

Surveillance offerings

Available with a Fitch Research subscription, Fitch Solutions' surveillance services covers the structured finance, covered bonds, and fund and asset management markets. By combining surveillance, benchmarking metrics, and market research with enhanced portfolio analytics, these surveillance offerings provide market participants with greater insight into the risks present in a transaction. For ongoing portfolio monitoring and management, Fitch Research also delivers email alerts about the latest research, rating actions, press releases, and performance data on transactions in these markets.

Residential mortgage models

Fitch Solutions offers a pair of quantitative modeling tools used to assess the credit risk of residential mortgage loans at both the individual loan and pool level:

- `ResiLogic` covers U.S. RMBS loans and incorporates loan characteristics, regional performance adjustment factors, primary mortgage insurance, and servicer ratings into one application.
- `ResiEMEA (enhanced)` helps determine the expected default probability, loss severity, and recovery on a loan-by-loan basis for EMEA RMBS transactions. In addition, the model enables users to enter their own house price index information.

15.1.3 Risk and performance analytics

Fitch risk and performance platform

This analytical platform provides a single source for credit-default-swap (CDS) pricing data, market-implied ratings, liquidity scores, probabilities of default, and portfolio-monitoring tools. Tailored for middle-office portfolio functions, the risk and performance platform gives market participants a framework to measure and monitor credit risk and price performance.

Integrated Data Service

Using common identifiers to link disparate data formats, Integrated Data Service brings together comprehensive market intelligence and delivers it via a single data feed. This service enables market participants to choose only the data they need from a cross-section of proprietary Fitch Ratings and Fitch Solutions content. Data are delivered in a standardized format that can easily integrate with a client's internal legacy applications. All file formats, data feeds, and delivery schedules are customizable to meet your institution's specific credit needs.

The following datasets are available via Integrated Data Service or as standalone data feeds:

- *Ratings Delivery Service*. A direct data feed providing timely updates of Fitch Ratings' proprietary ratings, watches, and outlooks, as well as up to 35 years of historical ratings data including data on defaulted entities.
- *Company financials*. This data feed covers 10,000 U.S. banks, 15,000 international banks, and 7,100 insurers.
- *Pricing data*. CDS and ABCDS pricing feeds from credit derivative market-makers. Liquidity scores at an entity and contract level are also included to measure and identify liquidity risk across the global CDS universe.

15.1.4 Pricing and valuation services

Fitch Pricing Services

This bundled pricing data service includes CDS pricing, ABCDS pricing, loan CDS pricing, and CDS benchmarking (CDS and ABCDS pricing data are also available via Integrated Data Service). Together they set the standard for providing premium quality pricing data at the most granular level from credit derivative market-makers. Additionally, Fitch Pricing Services also provides access to Fitch's market-leading liquidity scores on the most widely traded CDS assets.

Fitch Valuation Services

As a fully hosted tool, Fitch Valuation Services offers an objective valuation and comprehensive market risk–reporting facility for synthetic CDOs to enable market participants to evaluate the key drivers of price volatility.

15.1.5 Training

Fitch Training is a specialist training firm focused on the provision of credit and corporate finance workshops for experienced professionals. Courses are offered across three areas: financial institutions, corporate credit, and structured finance/securitization. Taught by industry experts, Fitch Training courses are practical, interactive, and market focused.

15.1.6 Quantitative Analytics

The Quantitative Analytics team conducts academic quality research on a broad range of quantitative finance modeling, including credit risk, liquidity risk, interest rate risk, and market risk. In an effort to add transparency and insight into the broader credit marketplace, the Quantitative Analytics team publishes formal research reports, presentations, and announcements available via Fitch Research.

Key benefits of products and services

- Offers access to industry-leading research, analysis, data, ratings, and methodologies for informed business decisions
- Provides comprehensive, customizable data feeds in a variety of standardized formats for accurate credit risk analysis
- Access to experienced Fitch Ratings' analysts in 50 offices around the world for increased market insight
- Distributes world-leading company financial information to facilitate regulatory compliance and risk management
- Enables timely decision making with cost-effective and operationally efficient platforms
- Reduces costs by eliminating the need to manually track, input, and maintain ratings, research, and financial data.

As mentioned above, whilst Section 15.1 provides an overview and introduction to Fitch Solutions' products and services, Section 15.2 will only focus and describe structured finance–related products.

15.2 RESEARCH SERVICES

15.2.1 Fitch Research

Fitch Research is an online subscription service that provides ratings and research as well as leading analytical tools and ongoing surveillance. Fitch Research covers a broad range of sectors, issuers, and securities in over 100 countries. It includes timely market insights, objective credit opinions, and ratings alerts that can be customized for individual portfolios and delivered in a variety of user-friendly formats.

Additionally, Fitch Research clients gain access to experienced Fitch Ratings' analysts in over 50 offices to help them monitor up-to-the-minute rating changes, understand credit trends, and make informed investment decisions. The ratings and research content available on Fitch Research is also offered as a data feed for importing into existing systems and applications.

Subscription benefits include, amongst others, direct access to

- Real-time research and information
- Customizable portfolios
- Email notification of critical changes in ratings or other news

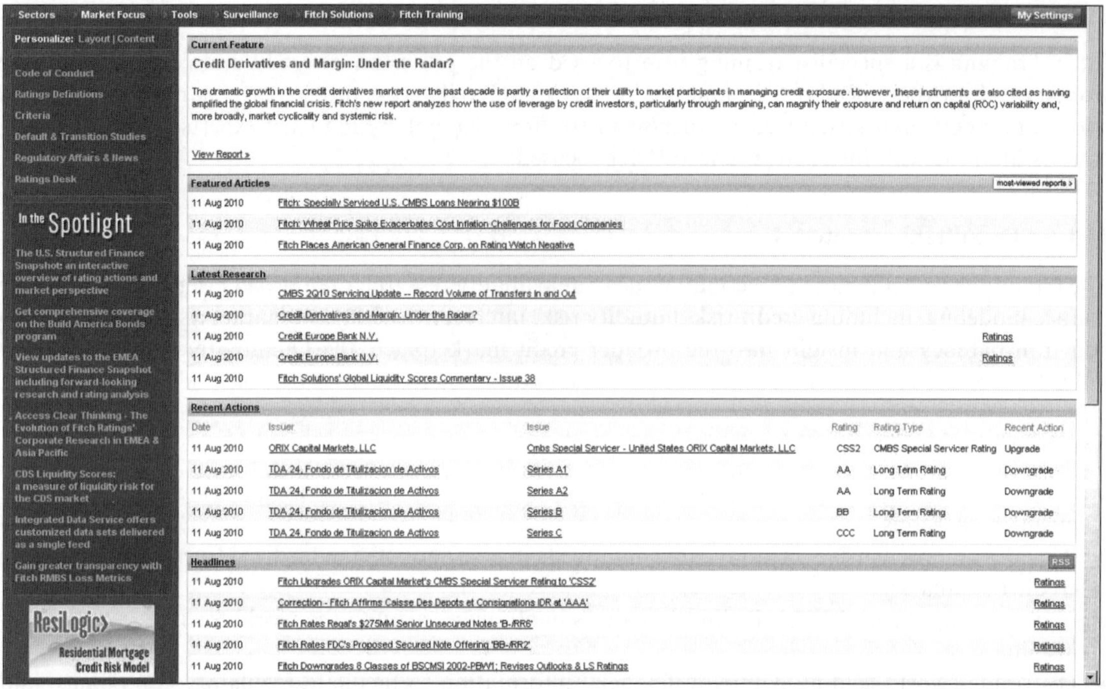

Figure 15.1. Fitch Research home screen. The Fitch Research home page provides access to reports, recent actions, and personalized portfolios. Subscribers can customize the layout and content of the home page to best meet their needs.
Source: Fitch Solutions.

- Criteria and methodology reports
- Interactive financial databases
- Detailed bond surveillance
- In-depth company reports
- Research feeds.

15.3 STRUCTURED FINANCE SOLUTIONS

Market-leading surveillance offerings

Fitch Solutions' surveillance offerings provide ongoing market surveillance for Fitch Ratings' entire structured finance–rated universe. By combining deal-specific surveillance, benchmarking metrics, and market research with enhanced portfolio analytics, these surveillance tools provide unique insight into the risks present within a securitized transaction.

Asset class coverage as of September 2010

Asset-backed securities

—Auto related: 112 deals, $59.7bn
—Credit card receivables: 105 deals, $257.1bn

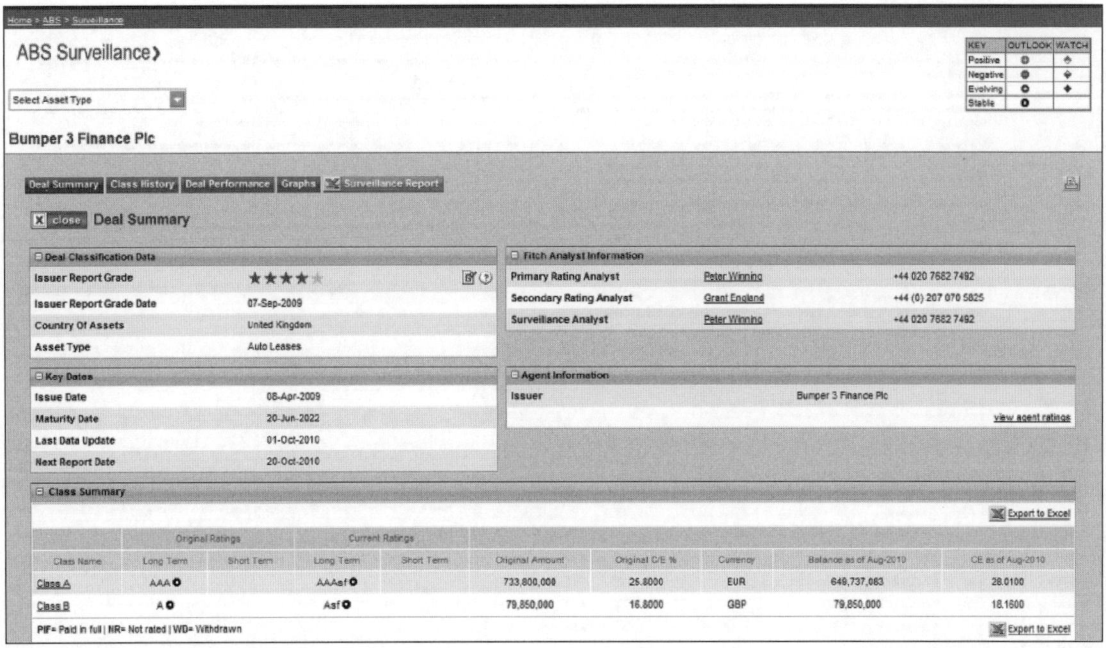

Figure 15.2. Surveillance summary screen. The surveillance summary screen for this sample deal shows the original ratings, current ratings, issuer report grades, credit enhancement, outlook, agent information, and analyst contact detail.
Source: Fitch Solutions.

— Tobacco: 50 deals, $22bn
— Student loans (FFELP): 599 deals, $279.6bn
— Aircraft: 34 deals, $13.4bn.

Commercial mortgage-backed securities

— 478 deals, $452bn.

Residential mortgage-backed securities

— Prime and Alt-A: 2,005 transactions, $505.6bn
— Subprime: 1,273 transactions, $226.3bn.

Additional tools and features of Fitch Solutions' surveillance offerings

Deal Review

`Deal Review` is a portfolio-monitoring feature that classifies a Fitch-rated structured finance transaction with a date indicating the transactions have been reviewed by Fitch Ratings' analysts and, therefore, do not warrant additional review. `Deal Review` provides investors with peace of mind and confidence knowing that their transactions are being evaluated on a timely and thorough basis by the agency's analysts.

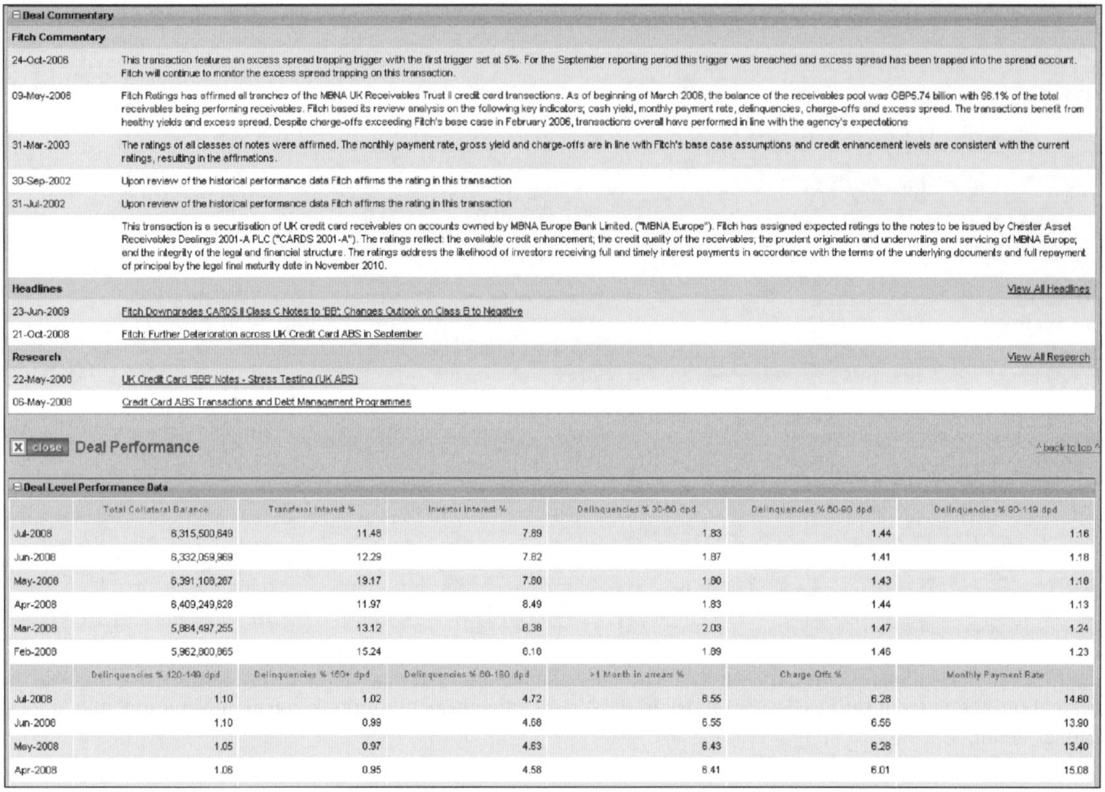

Deal Commentary

Fitch Commentary

24-Oct-2006	This transaction features an excess spread trapping trigger with the first trigger set at 5%. For the September reporting period this trigger was breached and excess spread has been trapped into the spread account. Fitch will continue to monitor the excess spread trapping on this transaction.
09-May-2006	Fitch Ratings has affirmed all tranches of the MBNA UK Receivables Trust II credit card transactions. As of beginning of March 2006, the balance of the receivables pool was GBP5.74 billion with 96.1% of the total receivables being performing receivables. Fitch based its review analysis on the following key indicators; cash yield, monthly payment rate, delinquencies, charge-offs and excess spread. The transactions benefit from healthy yields and excess spread. Despite charge-offs exceeding Fitch's base case in February 2006, transactions overall have performed in line with the agency's expectations
31-Mar-2003	The ratings of all classes of notes were affirmed. The monthly payment rate, gross yield and charge-offs are in line with Fitch's base case assumptions and credit enhancement levels are consistent with the current ratings, resulting in the affirmations.
30-Sep-2002	Upon review of the historical performance data Fitch affirms the rating in this transaction
31-Jul-2002	Upon review of the historical performance data Fitch affirms the rating in this transaction
	This transaction is a securitisation of UK credit card receivables on accounts owned by MBNA Europe Bank Limited. ("MBNA Europe"). Fitch has assigned expected ratings to the notes to be issued by Chester Asset Receivables Dealings 2001-A PLC ("CARDS 2001-A"). The ratings reflect: the available credit enhancement; the credit quality of the receivables; the prudent origination and underwriting and servicing of MBNA Europe; and the integrity of the legal and financial structure. The ratings address the likelihood of investors receiving full and timely interest payments in accordance with the terms of the underlying documents and full repayment of principal by the legal final maturity date in November 2010.

Headlines View All Headlines

23-Jun-2009	Fitch Downgrades CARDS II Class C Notes to 'BB'; Changes Outlook on Class B to Negative
21-Oct-2008	Fitch: Further Deterioration across UK Credit Card ABS in September

Research View All Research

22-May-2008	UK Credit Card 'BBB' Notes - Stress Testing (UK ABS)
06-May-2008	Credit Card ABS Transactions and Debt Management Programmes

X close Deal Performance ^back to top ^

Deal Level Performance Data

	Total Collateral Balance	Transferor Interest %	Investor Interest %	Delinquencies % 30-60 dpd	Delinquencies % 60-90 dpd	Delinquencies % 90-119 dpd
Jul-2008	6,315,500,649	11.48	7.89	1.83	1.44	1.16
Jun-2008	6,332,059,969	12.29	7.82	1.87	1.41	1.18
May-2008	6,391,108,287	19.17	7.80	1.80	1.43	1.18
Apr-2008	6,409,249,628	11.97	8.49	1.83	1.44	1.13
Mar-2008	5,884,497,255	13.12	8.38	2.03	1.47	1.24
Feb-2008	5,962,800,865	15.24	6.16	1.89	1.46	1.23

	Delinquencies % 120-149 dpd	Delinquencies % 150+ dpd	Delinquencies % 60-180 dpd	>1 Month in arrears %	Charge Offs %	Monthly Payment Rate
Jul-2008	1.10	1.02	4.72	6.55	6.28	14.60
Jun-2008	1.10	0.99	4.68	6.55	6.56	13.90
May-2008	1.05	0.97	4.63	6.43	6.28	13.40
Apr-2008	1.06	0.95	4.58	6.41	6.01	15.08

Figure 15.3. Surveillance commentary and deal performance data. Surveillance commentary provides an overview of relevant press releases and rating actions for the selected transactions and provides deal performance data (which can also be exported into Excel).
Source: Fitch Solutions.

Portfolio Update

With `Portfolio Update`, Fitch Research subscribers can build a customized portfolio tailored to specified market sectors, geographic areas, and/or specific issuers/bonds. Once a portfolio is created, users can set up email alerts filtered by report type, sector, geography, issuer, and issue to be delivered directly to the user's email inbox. Users can also generate customizable tables of data that are exportable to MS Excel, share content with other users in their company, and view all research specific to their portfolio.

15.4 RESIDENTIAL MORTGAGE MODELS

15.4.1 ResiEMEA (enhanced)

In response to growing demand in the European residential loan market for increased transparency and more accurate and predictive credit default assessment, Fitch Solutions offers an enhanced version of `ResiEMEA`, an analytical model that helps arrangers, originators, and investors with the risk assessment of residential mortgage loans in accordance with Fitch Ratings' RMBS criteria.

Available for the U.K., The Netherlands, Ireland, Italy, Spain, and Portugal, this residential model is used as the first stage in the quantitative analysis of an EMEA RMBS transaction and helps

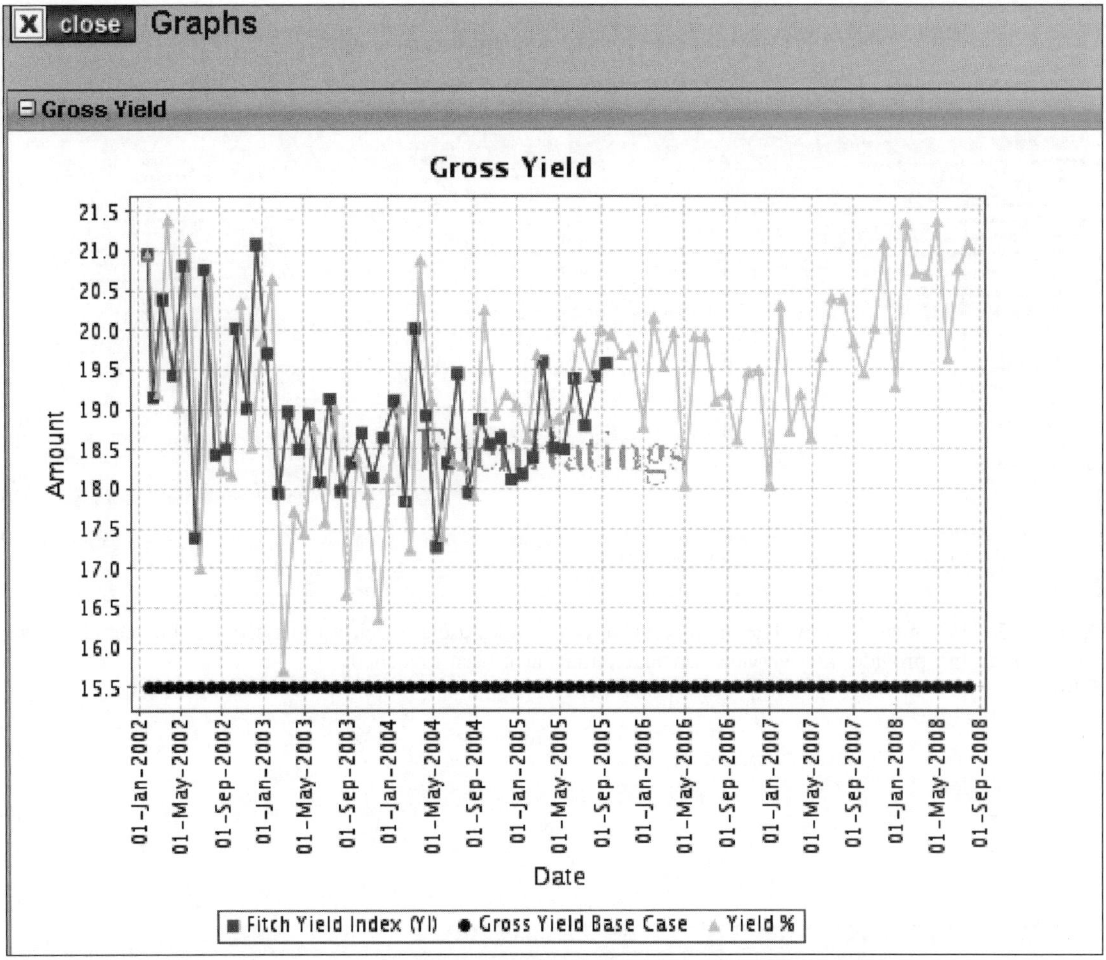

Figure 15.4. Performance analytics chart. The deal data are complemented by graphical representation of relevant key performance indicators, in this case benchmarked against the agency's index.
Source: Fitch Solutions.

determine the expected default probability, loss severity, and recovery on a loan-by-loan basis for transactions. The output from the model can then be utilized as inputs for RMBS cash flow modeling. In addition, investors are able to input post-closing pool cuts into `ResiEMEA (enhanced)` for surveillance purposes.

Key features

- A wizard and comprehensive help system to promote ease of use
- Fast engine–driven performance
- Country-specific validation checks prepare data for model runs
- Statistical analysis of underlying pool data available in Excel stratification reports
- Ability to enter user's own house price index information directly into the model
- Upon request, users can modify assumptions other than the house price index.

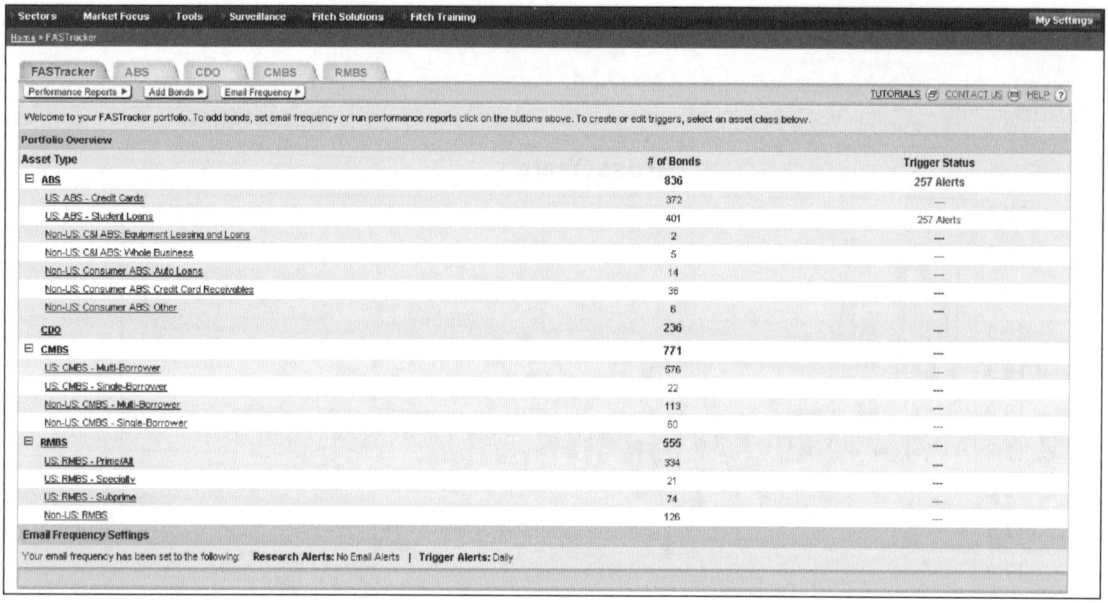

Figure 15.5. Main menu screen. The main menu screen enables users to select the asset and subasset classes for their analysis and provides an overview of triggers that have been breached.
Source: Fitch Solutions.

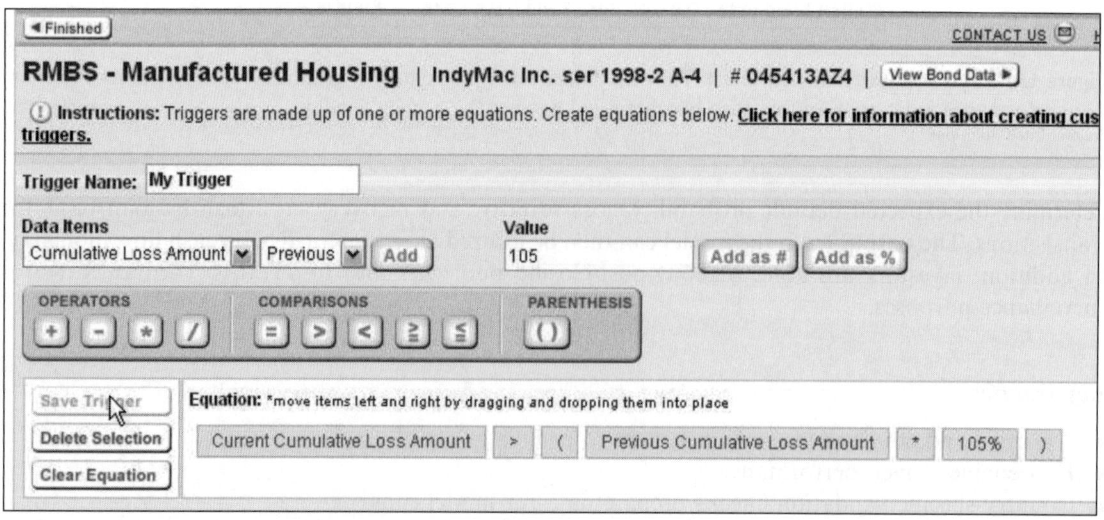

Figure 15.6. Specifying triggers. Users can specify customized performance triggers and will receive email alerts when such triggers have been breached.
Source: Fitch Solutions.

Key ResiEMEA (enhanced) benefits

- More quickly assess credit risk across residential mortgage-backed loans for the U.K., The Netherlands, Ireland, Italy, Spain, and Portugal
- Identify and evaluate individual loans enabling the user to fine-tune portfolio profiles
- Increase the efficiency and handling of large portfolios of master trust magnitude in minutes
- Easily export data to Excel for facilitated credit research and analysis
- Assist in evaluating RMBS securitization transactions backed by different risk types of mortgage collateral
- Evaluate post-closing pool cut data for surveillance purposes.

Flexible functionality and applications enable

- Uploading residential loan data into a template for quick processing and validation. Once validated, loan-level data are transferred back into the model
- Assessing weighted average default frequency, loss severity, and recoveries at different rating levels employing the user's own deal assumptions such as probability of default hits and market value hits amongst others
- Adjusting the agency's criteria assumptions and stressing the loan, borrower, and property-specific factors that most influence default probability and loss severity
- Storing and reusing deal-specific configurations.

15.4.2 ResiLogic

Used to evaluate U.S. RMBS, `ResiLogic` incorporates loan characteristics, regional performance adjustment factors, insurance coverage, and servicer ratings into one easy-to-use application. As an advanced risk–pricing tool, `ResiLogic` can also be used to estimate Fitch Ratings' credit ratings; thus enabling market participants to confidently perform critical credit risk analysis at the individual loan and pool level for all types of mortgage loans. `ResiLogic` is based on the same performance analytics used by Fitch Ratings' own RMBS analysts. Highlights of `ResiLogic` include

- *National and MSA risk multipliers.* `ResiLogic` expands beyond state-level risk multipliers to include 25 metropolitan statistical area (MSA) multipliers incorporating personal income and distribution, employment growth, housing construction, housing permits, and other economic metric indicators. Additionally, a national risk index (NRI) is included to reflect stressful national macroeconomic conditions such as GDP growth, inflation, and interest rate growth.
- *Seasoning component.* Based on a comprehensive statistical analysis of the effects of aging and delinquency patterns over time on default risk, `ResiLogic` includes frequency of foreclosure and loss severity dimensions, taking into account loan age, delinquency status, and home price movements between the time of origination and current age. It also provides a strong foundation for analyzing pools of highly seasoned loans, which may include resecuritized loans and so-called "scratch-and-dent" loans.
- *Risk layering.* Additional frequency of foreclosure penalty factors are included to reflect risk related to underwritten vintage loans where income or assets have not been verified and for loans that are originated with a simultaneous second lien.
- *Primary mortgage insurance.* This model can reduce loss severity credit given to loans that have borrower-paid and lender-paid primary mortgage insurance.

Key benefits

- Strengthens decision making and risk management with detailed stratifications of risk components including probability of default, frequency of foreclosure, and loss severity, as well as historical analysis of over 1.6 million loans over a 14-year observation period.
- Captures changing market conditions between loan origination and current age with the seasoning component.
- Increases efficiency by conducting best execution analysis, allocating risk-based capital, and ascertaining loan loss coverage reserve levels directly from the user's desktop.
- Estimates the ratings of a transaction based on Fitch Ratings' loan pool analysis empowering market participants to determine risk-based pricing.
- Obtains greater risk transparency by using the same model Fitch Ratings' analysts use for performance analytics and in the credit-rating process.

Key features

- Intuitive and easy-to-use model that resides on the user's desktop or integrates into corporate loan underwriting and pricing software.
- Analyzes prime, Alt-A, and subprime for first-lien and second-lien loans at the pool and loan level.
- Incorporates regional performance adjustment factors including state-level risk multipliers and 25 metropolitan statistical multipliers.
- Output reports include loss coverage detail, deal and pool loss coverage summary, and loan-level loss coverage detail.
- Expanded frequency of foreclosure and loss severity dimensions account for the age of the loan.

16
Intex

Intex Solutions, Inc. is a leading provider of structured fixed income cash flow models and related analytical software. The firm's clients include many hundreds of the world's best known financial institutions including most major investment banks, regional broker dealers, issuers, and investment managers. The company was founded in 1985, and remains an independent, privately held company with headquarters near Boston, Massachusetts. Intex also supports its many international clients with two foreign offices in London and Tokyo.

It is a provider of a comprehensive deal library of RMBS, ABS, CMBS, and CDO deal models, created and maintained for the generation of accurate cash flow projections and price/yield analytics. Intex supports deals issued in North America, Europe, Australia, Japan, and other regions of the globe. Since 1990, Intex has modeled over 20,000 individual deals and creates ongoing updates for each deal each month or quarter using investor reports and, when available, loan-level or asset-level information obtained directly from trustees, servicers, and issuers.

Intex's software solutions include `INTEXnet` for convenient web-based analysis, `INTEXdesktop` for those desiring a PC-based solution, `INTEX Subroutines API` for developers seeking to build proprietary applications, and `INTEX DealMaker` for investment banks and others who need to structure new deals. All Intex software applications have at their core the ability to calculate future principal and interest cash flows based on user-specified stress scenarios applied to interest, prepayment, default, recovery, and delinquency rates. Intex's cash flow projection tools have also been integrated into many specialized third-party applications targeted to specific vertical markets and industry segments. One of these third-party tools is Principia Partners' `Structured Finance Platform` which integrates seamlessly with Intex and is also introduced in this section.

16.1 COMPANY HISTORY

Intex has been a successful, independent financial software products company for over 20 years. The key milestones in the firm's history are

1985 Intex was founded and established as a developer of spreadsheet add-in products for Lotus 1-2-3 and later MS Excel.

1987 The company launches a novel bond calculator, both as a spreadsheet add-in and as a C-callable subroutine library.

1988 Introduction of the first MBS calculator add-in and subroutines library.

1990 Intex develops its proprietary "CDI" deal modeling language and the subroutines for PC and Unix platforms, along with initial release of its agency-backed CMO/REMIC deal model library. The firm gains recognition as the first independent software company to accurately model complex Re-REMIC deals.

1992 Expansion of the deal model universe to include non-agency residential whole loan-backed CMO/REMIC deals. Makes significant improvements to the deal-modeling language and subroutines in order to properly handle loss/severity stress scenarios characteristic of non-agency deals.

1994 Intex forges its first relationship with a third-party application provider. Today, clients can access and use Intex's deal model libraries within over two dozen specialized, third-party software products for applications ranging from trading and portfolio management to risk management and asset/liability management.

1995 The deal model library expands to include ABS deals, including home equity, manufactured housing, credit card, automobile, equipment, and other related ABS asset sectors. The firm's CMO and ABS deal model library surpasses 5,000 deals.

1996 Initial introduction of the Intex CMBS deal model library.

1997 The `INTEXdesktop` is introduced, a Windows-based end-user application, for use of the company's deal model libraries through a point-and-click interface.

1998 `INTEXnet` is launched, which provides a web-enabled alternative to `INTEXdesktop` that can be accessed from any location without the need for client-resident software or data downloads.

2000 Intex models its 10,000th deal.

2000 `Intex DealMaker` is released, which is a Windows structuring application that has become an industry standard for structuring RMBS, CMBS, and CDO deals.

2001 Introduction of the CDO deal model library. Intex becomes the first and only company to offer robust, accurate support for CDOs backed by structured assets, leveraging the firm's now comprehensive RMBS, ABS, and CMBS deal model libraries.

2003 Intex models its first European deal. Today, the European RMBS, ABS, CMBS, and CDO deal model libraries are used by major arranging banks and investors throughout Europe and around the world.

2004 Intex models its 15,000th deal and begins to expand its support for deals issued in other regions of the world, including Japan and other parts of Asia.

2006 The European office in London opens and the firm models its 1,000th European deal, each one capable of generating cash flow projections under user-specified prepayment and loss scenarios.

2007 Intex introduces a student loan ABS deal model library.

2008 Intex introduces a reverse mortgage deal model library and the company now covers over 20,000 deals, including a complete collection of European deals, each modeled for accurate cash flow and price/yield analysis under user-defined prepayment and loss scenarios.

16.2 OVERVIEW

Intex provides a variety of advanced software applications and tools for monitoring, analyzing, and structuring a wide range of structured fixed income securities from many global markets.

Intex supports four major global asset classes: RMBS, ABS, CMBS, and CDO. Within each sector are certain subasset classes; for example, RMBS includes agency-backed and whole loan-backed CMO/REMICs, ABS includes home equity, manufactured housing, credit card receivables, automobile, equipment, student loans, and other related sectors, and CDO includes cash and synthetic CLOs, CDO of ABS, CDOs-squared, CRE CDOs, trust-preferred CDOs, and other types.

Intex has modeled over 20,000 deals in these asset classes, far and away one of the most comprehensive deal library of its kind.

16.3 CASH FLOW MODELS AND DATA

The asset classes covered and modeled by Intex fall into the following four main categories.

RMBS

Intex's agency CMO deal model library offers complete coverage of CMOs administered by Fannie Mae, Freddie Mac, and Ginnie Mae.

The U.S. RMBS deal model library covers substantially all prime and Alt-A RMBS. All structural features are accurately modeled, including loss allocations, triggers, prepayment penalty allocations, and interest rate hedges. Whenever possible, deals are updated with loan-level data.

The European RMBS deal model library includes virtually all U.K. RMBS (prime and non-conforming), as well as substantial coverage for Dutch and southern European RMBS. Many Australian RMBS deals having euro-denominated tranches are also available. A growing number of European RMBS deals are now being updated with loan-level data.

The Japanese RMBS deal model library includes all GHLC/JHFA transactions, as well as CMOs backed by GHLC/JHFA deals. Selected coverage of other RMBS deals is available.

ABS

The home equity deal model library includes virtually all home equity deals, including deals backed by subprime loans and HELOC (Home Equity Line of Credits)s. All structural features are modeled, including loss allocations, triggers, prepayment penalty allocations, and interest rate hedges. Whenever possible, deals are updated with loan-level data.

Intex also provides deal model libraries for deals backed by manufactured housing loans, credit card receivables, auto loans and leases, equipment leases, student loans, dealer floorplans and business loans (including small-balance commercial mortgage loans and middle-market loans).

In Europe and Japan, the ABS deal model library includes coverage of deals backed by auto loans, consumer loans, leases and bank loans, with expanding coverage of uniquely European sectors such as pub-backed transactions.

CMBS

The U.S. CMBS deal model library includes substantially all active CMBS deals. Deals are modeled with loan-level data, and updated monthly with the latest performance information. All structural features are handled, including split loan structures and complicated prepayment penalty allocations.

Intex also maintains an extensive deal model library of European CMBS transactions, also updated on a timely basis with the most recent loan and property information.

U.S. and European CMBS deals are modeled while still at a pre-close stage, enabling analysis before the deal goes into pricing and closes.

CDO

The CDO deal model library is recognized as the industry standard for analyzing all types of CDOs. The library includes CLOs, CDO of ABS, CDOs squared, CRE CDOs, trust-preferred CDOs, and other types. CDOs backed by other structured finance instruments will always reference the Intex model for the underlying deals, when available, to allow for the most precise cash flow forecasting. Each deal's structural features are modeled, and the models are updated with trustee information, including asset-by-asset detail, as it becomes available.

Intex applications include the firm's implementation of the various rating agency methodologies to assist in post-issuance ratings analysis.

16.3.1 Deal performance data

Intex offers a variety of data solutions that complement the use of the Intex deal model libraries. These solutions are designed to augment surveillance and performance analysis, monitor credit events for CDS, and to provide critical input for client prepayment and default models.

INTEX Remitdata is designed for clients who require immediate access to standardized investor report data. Unlike the firm's other data products that derive their data from Intex deal model and update files, the Remitdata product contains deal, tranche, and collateral performance data sourced directly from the current investor report.

INTEX Historical Performance Data is a time series of monthly or quarterly collateral performance data for all Intex-modeled deals. Performance Data includes such items as prepayment speeds, delinquency, and loss rates. Performance Data is available either for viewing historical deal, collateral, and tranche-level data within INTEXdesktop, or as a text file for standalone use with a client-provided database application.

INTEXdesktop Data Analysis Module, which was introduced in 2008, allows INTEXdesktop users to quickly find information about deals, portfolios, asset classes, etc. by making internet calls to comprehensive databases maintained at Intex. Features include a robust graphing functionality that allows users to plot data by deal, issuer, vintage, issuer vintage, etc.; a deal/bond finder feature that enables users to search the Intex deal model libraries for deals or bonds that match specific user-defined criteria; an asset finder feature that allows users to search through the Intex CDO, CMBS, and Franchise library for exposure to specific assets; and stratification tools for individual deals or portfolios. INTEXnet users can also enjoy many of these same capabilities though INTEXnet's powerful research menus.

16.3.2 Tool suite

Intex's end-user applications for single-security and portfolio analysis include INTEXdesktop for Windows users, and INTEXnet for those preferring a web browser–based application. Both applications share many similarities and enable users to generate accurate cash flow projections for modeled deals under user-defined interest rate, prepayment, and default/recovery stress scenarios.

INTEXdesktop

INTEXdesktop is a Windows-based solution that provides access to single-security and portfolio analytics on any of the 20,000+ modeled deals. All data and results are stored in memory on the user's computer, making for efficient retrieval/display of results, and users have the ability to query an Intex relational database of static data over the web. This tool also allows users to

- Run scenario analysis for Intex modeled deals at both the deal and portfolio level
- Control interest rates, prepayments, defaults, triggers, deal-specific variables, etc.
- Set up custom assumption curves, group collateral into user-defined buckets
- Solve for various outcomes
- View and export cash flows, price/yields, etc.
- Operate an optional batch mode feature to enable INTEXdesktop to run on an automated basis.

INTEXnet

INTEXnet is an internet-based system providing single-security and portfolio analytics on any of the 20,000+ modeled deals through a web browser interface. All data are stored and all calculations are performed on Intex's servers. Results are delivered to the user in the form of a webpage. `INTEXnet` enables users to

- Run scenario analysis for Intex-modeled deals at both the deal and portfolio level
- Control interest rates, prepayments, defaults, triggers, deal-specific variables, etc.
- Set up custom assumption curves, group collateral into user-defined buckets
- Solve for various outcomes
- View and export cash flows, price/yields, etc.

The INTEX Subroutine and the INTEX Wrapper

`INTEX Subroutine` and `INTEX Wrapper` offer two alternative ways of accessing Intex's industry-standard structured securities cash flow engine in a programmatic fashion. These programming libraries are used by over 100 major financial institutional and third-party software providers for the purpose of building proprietary trading, portfolio management, risk management, and other fixed income systems. Both products

- Produce cash flows, analytics, and terms and conditions on the entire library of Intex-modeled deals
- Support all deal structures and tranche types within a single API (application programming interface)
- Are available as PC, Unix, and Linux libraries, and DLLs for Windows platforms
- Are useful for both interactive and batch applications.

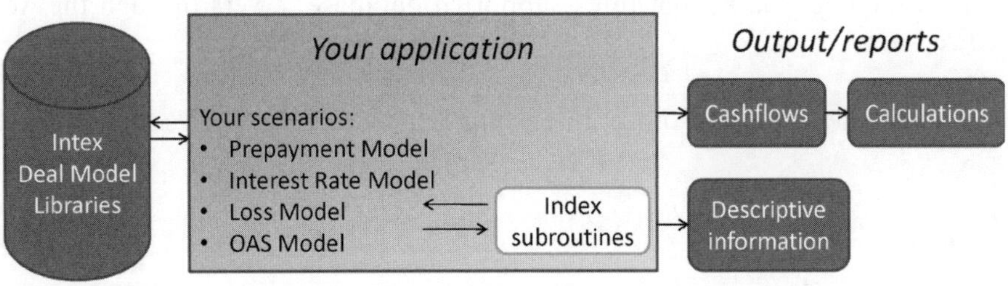

Figure 16.1. Intex's programming libraries.
Source: *www.intex.com*

`INTEX Subroutine` enables users to

- Access the library, which represents C-callable subroutines that integrate seamlessly into existing C-based applications
- Use any prepayment/credit model and/or interest rate process.

`INTEX Wrapper` provides the following functionality:

- Most commonly used in conjunction with Visual Basic, VBA in Excel, .NET, C#, or PERL. May also be used with C.
- Integrated with popular third-party prepay/default models.
- Contains various built-in business logics useful for application development.

INTEX DealMaker

`INTEX DealMaker` is a highly specialized and powerful Windows application created specially for those who need to structure new deals in the primary market.

`DealMaker` is designed for and used by structuring departments within major investment banks, issuers, monoline insurers, ratings agencies, and other institutions involved in the deal-structuring process. `DealMaker` provides a robust and commercially supported "point-and-click" interface that enables users to specify or import collateral, create the cash flow waterfall and priority of payments, and generate reports under rigorous prepayment and default stress scenarios; and, since `DealMaker` generates a standard Intex "CDI" file as output, users can provide their investor clients with "pre-price" deal model files, thereby enabling their investor clients to conduct their own analysis using the Intex software of their choice at an early stage prior to deal pricing.

Intex currently supports `DealMaker` for most asset sectors, including U.S., European, and Japanese RMBS, U.S. home equity ABS, U.S. autos, U.S. CMBS, and U.S. and European CDOs.

INTEXlink

`INTEXlink` is an Excel add-in developed to easily pull deal, bond, and asset pool performance data from any of the 20,000+ modeled deals directly into spreadsheets. The `INTEXlink` add-in is easy to install and use, giving you the power to

- Create customized spreadsheets to view deal-specific information
- Set up portfolio-monitoring spreadsheets where users define the content and format
- Instantly insert the latest data from Intex-supported database servers through the web into your customized reports.

`INTEXlink` is available as an add-on to an existing `INTEXdesktop` or `INTEXnet` subscription.

Third-party solutions

In addition to the Intex software applications described above, many clients with very specific needs—such as trading/portfolio management, enterprise risk management, or bank or insurance asset/liability management—may wish to look at a third-party provider application. Over two dozen different software applications offer the Intex cash flow functionality as a fully integrated component of their application. Conversely, certain third-party models, such as prepayment or credit models, may be used seamlessly with Intex's applications.

Coverage

Intex's roots are clearly in the U.S. and the firm's coverage of U.S.-issued deals in the supported asset sectors is close to 100%. However, the vendor also offers a substantial coverage of RMBS, ABS, CMBS, and CDO deals issued in other regions of the world including Canada, Europe, Japan, and Australia.

Intex continues to expand its coverage to include deals issued elsewhere around the globe including other parts of Asia and Latin America, and the firm has extended its support hours and office locations in order to better serve international clients.

North America

Intex's RMBS database includes residential CMOs (both agency and private label), while its ABS database covers subprime mortgages, manufactured housing, and other consumer types such as auto, credit card, student loan, and equipment.

CMBS deals are also modeled and available shortly after both the introductory "red" and final "black" prospectuses are issued, sometimes even sooner.

The firm's CDO database includes cash flow and synthetic CLOs, asset-backed CDOs, CDOs-squared, CRE CDOs, trust-preferred CDOs, and other types.

Europe

In support of the fast-growing and strategically important European securitization market, Intex now models vast collections of European RMBS, ABS, CMBS, and CDO deals and the firm's coverage in Europe is now, like the U.S., close to 100% across all asset classes.

Every model reflects the waterfall characteristics of the deal for rigorous and accurate cash flow stress-testing.

Prime and non-conforming RMBS deals from the U.K., Spanish SME CLOs, and Dutch RMBS transactions are among the types of deals that are covered. Best available information is used to model and update deals, which is obtained directly from the various arrangers and issuers. The models are able to handle and reflect the distinct characteristics of European transactions including liquidity facilities, reserve accounts, interest rate and currency hedges, and complex collateral coupon and amortization features.

Intex's U.K.-based office in London offers expanded support hours to Europe-based clients.

Japan/Asia

Intex models a growing number of RMBS, ABS, and CMBS deals from Japan and other Asian countries including Singapore, Korea, China, and elsewhere in the region. These deals utilize the best available information and incorporate structuring features unique to these markets.

The firm continues with the rapid expansion of its coverage for deals issued in Japan and Asia.

Other

As other regions have begun to emerge in the global securitization market, Intex has expanded to meet the demand. Today, the vendor has modeled a variety of deals issued in Australia, Russia, Latin America, and South Africa, and it is prepared to expand the coverage subject to market and client needs.

16.4 NEW DEVELOPMENTS/RELEASES

- *Reverse mortgage deals.* Intex now offers a library of reverse mortgage deals, ready for cash flow projection analysis.
- *Student loan ABS.* Intex now offers an extensive library of student loan ABS deal models, ready for cash flow projection analysis.
- *INTEXlink.* Licensable by registered users of `INTEXnet` or `INTEXdesktop`, the new Intex add-in enables you to pull the latest data from Intex servers through the web directly into Excel. Thus you can format reported deal and performance data content to your specifications.

- *TALF financing model.* More recently, Intex has launched an optional module for both its Windows-based end-user application (`INTEXdesktop`) as well as the web-based analysis tool (`INTEXnet`) that features a financing model of the Federal Reserve's Term Asset-Backed Securities Loan Facility (TALF) program.

  Implementation of the TALF-financing model generates TALF-adjusted analytics based on user-specified loan characteristics across multiple scenarios and allows for TALF-financing analysis on legacy and newly issued securities contained in Intex's comprehensive deal model libraries. This optional module contains a new TALF analysis report which allows for easy comparison of cash flows and analytics based on user-specified TALF-financing terms and Intex's standard suite of prepayment, default, and interest rate stress-test parameters. Moreover, users can review analytics on the target security, the loan made by the Federal Reserve to finance the purchase of the target security, and the target security net of the TALF loan.

16.5 PARTNERS

While Intex's own software applications offer many powerful and advanced capabilities for single-security and portfolio analysis, many market participants also want to take advantage of the vendor's capabilities within a more specialized third-party application designed for a specific function or market segment.

For this reason, Intex has teamed up with a wide variety of leading software providers offering turnkey systems or more specialized and customized solutions for applications such as trade capture/order entry, portfolio management, risk management, asset/liability management, and more.

The following vendors have integrated Intex structured fixed income data and analytical functionality directly into their respective systems and services:

- Algorithmics
- Andrew Davidson & Co.
- Aurora
- BlackRock Solutions
- Calypso Technology
- FactSet
- FT Interactive Data Corp.
- HubData
- IFS, a State Street company
- IPS Sendero
- Kamakura
- MBSRISK
- Milliman
- Misys—Summit
- MSCI Barra
- Murex
- Numerix
- OpenLink Financial
- PolyPaths
- Principia Partners
- Quantitative Risk Management
- Realpoint
- RiskSpan
- SS&C Technologies—BancMall
- SS&C Technologies—PTS
- SunGard—Bancware
- SunGard iWORKS Prophet
- SunGard Securities Processing
- Tillinghast-Towers Perrin
- ZM Financial Systems.

In addition, Intex offers clients ready access to various third-party data and models via interfaces in order to enhance Intex's own applications. These third-party offerings include industry-standard prepayment models, credit models, and more. A partial list of partners supplying Intex with data and models includes

- Andrew Davidson & Co.
- LPS Applied Analytics

Finally, users seeking systems integration assistance involving Intex products may find the following consultancies and organizations useful:

- Computech Corporation
- MBSRISK
- Michael Blum Consulting
- Vichara Technologies, Inc.

17

Lewtan Technologies

When Lewtan was founded in 1986 few technology solutions existed to support the securitization industry. The firm's founder Stuart Lewtan started developing customized and off-the-shelf software solutions for companies involved in securitization and structured finance activities.

These pioneering efforts would lead to the development of the firm's first product, the creation of a securitization-servicing platform designed specifically to handle the asset and liability nuances only months after the first ABS securitization took place in the U.S.

The securitization industry has changed a great deal since then, but Lewtan's mission of providing full service securitization solutions and being the premier technology provider remain unchanged.

17.1 PIONEERS IN A FAST-GROWING INDUSTRY

From inception, Lewtan's mission was to provide solutions to both investors and issuers in the securitization industry. With a deep expertise in these types of transactions, as well as knowledge of software development, Lewtan entered the market with a product called `ABS System`. This early product, which is still core to Lewtan's product portfolio, automated the administration and reporting needs of a securitization transaction. It is a customized solution that integrates pool selection, loan and trust accounting, reconciliation, bond administration, and analytics.

Automation of processes such as calculations, reporting, accounting, and reconciliation proved invaluable as the industry continued expanding and more and more regulatory scrutiny has been applied. This early system provided the answer as a fully auditable application which eliminated human errors that plagued some of the original transactions. `ABS System` incorporated a flexible reporting engine that enabled clients to keep transactions in compliance with deal covenants that are embedded within the deal to protect investors, while being able to quickly respond to regulatory changes in the market.

17.2 BROADENING THE HORIZON

From 1986 to 1998, the asset-backed industry worldwide grew at an extraordinary pace. In addition to the tremendous growth of the securitization industry, the advent of the internet was starting to change the way that people access information and communicate with one another. Both of these factors drove Lewtan's development of its first web portal where securitization participants could come together to access exclusive and industry-specific information.

Accurate information is required to make sound financial decisions. However, in the asset-backed securities industry getting high-quality data has historically proven difficult. The industry suffered from a lack of consistent guidelines (and to some extent still does) on reporting metrics and key performance indicators. Furthermore, the various parties who tracked deal-related information each had their own methods of distributing these data—some of this was disseminated in hard copy, some of it was faxed, and some has been internet based. These issues combined with the sheer number of

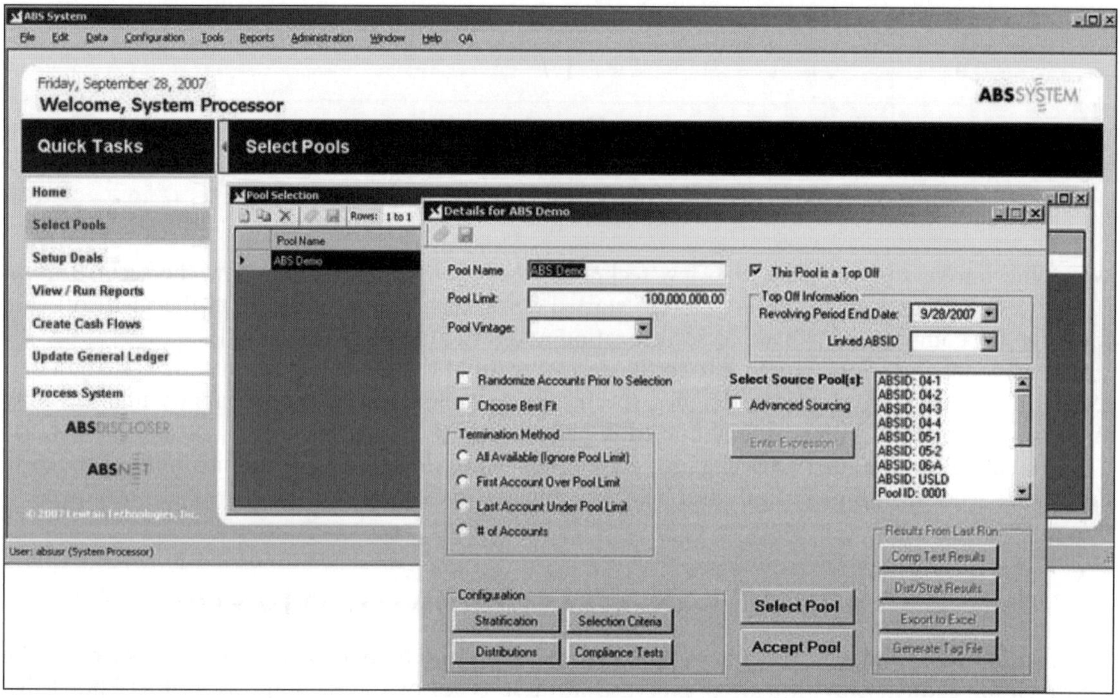

Figure 17.1. ABS System welcome screen.
Source: Lewtan Technologies.

structured finance transactions made keeping up with the disparate data sources and their respective reporting methodologies a monumental task. To address this problem, Lewtan developed a centralized data repository containing information on asset-backed securities. Leveraging its technological expertise, Lewtan's existing system evolved and the firm created ABSNet, a web-based service offering access to structured finance securities performance data and other related industry information.

ABSNet is still one of the structured finance industry's leading sources for asset-backed securities surveillance data, performance analytics, and business intelligence. Combining detailed performance data, powerful analytics, and a wealth of related information on asset-backed securities, the firm's product offers a valuable research, analysis, and decision support tool for buy-side and sell-side investors in asset-backed and mortgage-backed securities, as well as those who facilitate and support these transactions.

ABSNet provides users an advanced screening tool that combines static deal data (asset class, collateral type, underwriter, vintage, etc.) with current performance data (pool delinquencies, bond ratings, bond prices, etc.) helping to identify performance outliers in a portfolio or the entire ABS universe (such as bonds with prices not aligned with current ratings, or *vice versa*).

The company managed to establish one of the industry's most comprehensive databases of deal performance data. Rating agencies also rely on the company's tool to support their surveillance process along with thousands of investors, issuers, and other market participants with a need to monitor their portfolios.

The tool allows users to customize a collection of deals and/or bonds based upon advanced search utilities and compare key metrics for these deals in a single view for any single reporting period. Additional functionality includes:

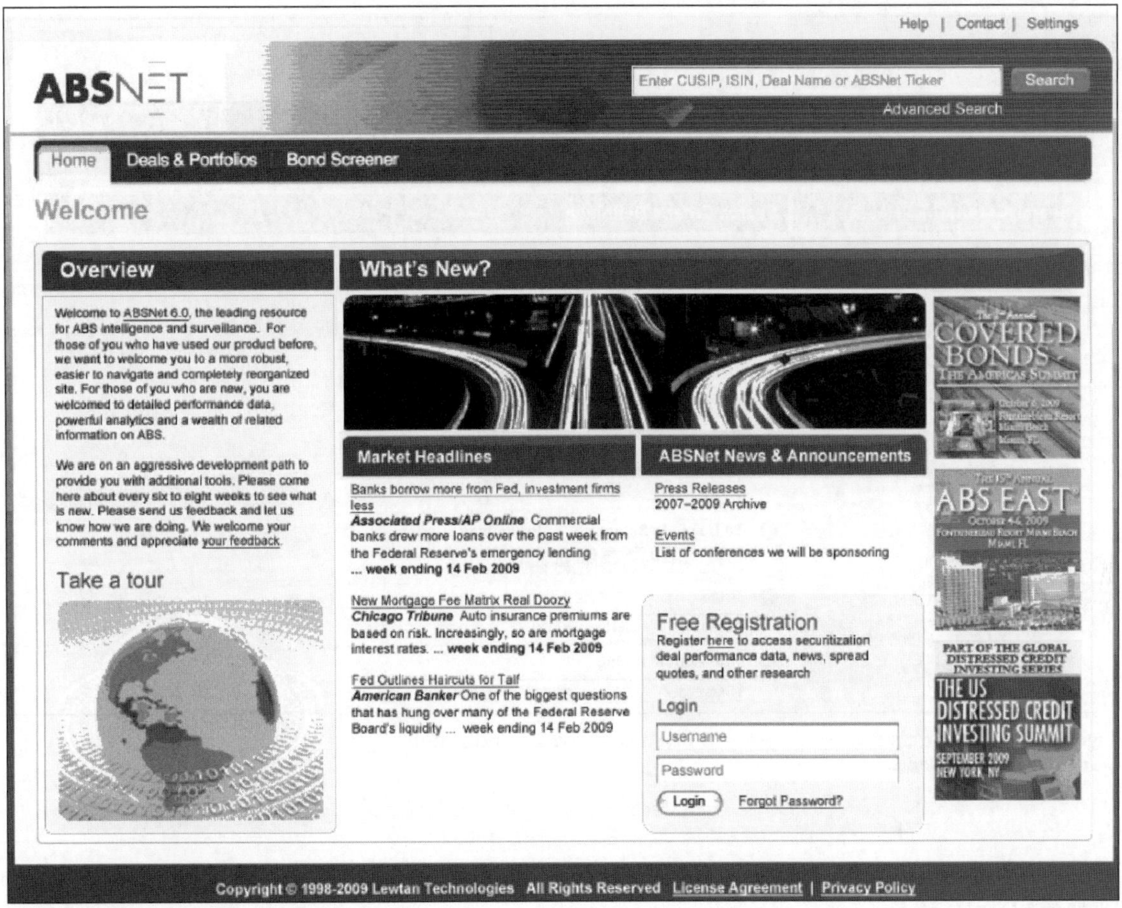

Figure 17.2. `ABSNet` home page.
Source: Lewtan Technologies.

- One of the industry's largest ABS performance databases containing thousands of issuers, 18,000+ deals, and 200,000+ bond tranches worldwide.
- This database also provides a very comprehensive coverage of current and historical performance statistics, tracking over 150 performance variables per deal. This includes years of historical data, often from deal inception to date, as well as deal notes, prospectuses, and servicer reports and other deal-related documentation.
- This is complemented by a library of 150,000+ servicer reports online which allows the user to go back to the actual data source that formed the basis for the firm's database.
- Furthermore, the tool also provides information on the underlying collateral pool as well as available credit support facilities.

The `Deal Snapshot` (as shown in Figure 17.5) provides an overview of all critical components of a transaction such as collateral pools, credit supports, triggers/covenants, and capital structure. Users can retrieve data on the most recent reporting period and immediately assess the relative health of a deal based upon the level of credit support and the status of the deal in relation to the triggers governing the distribution of principal and interest through the transaction's waterfall.

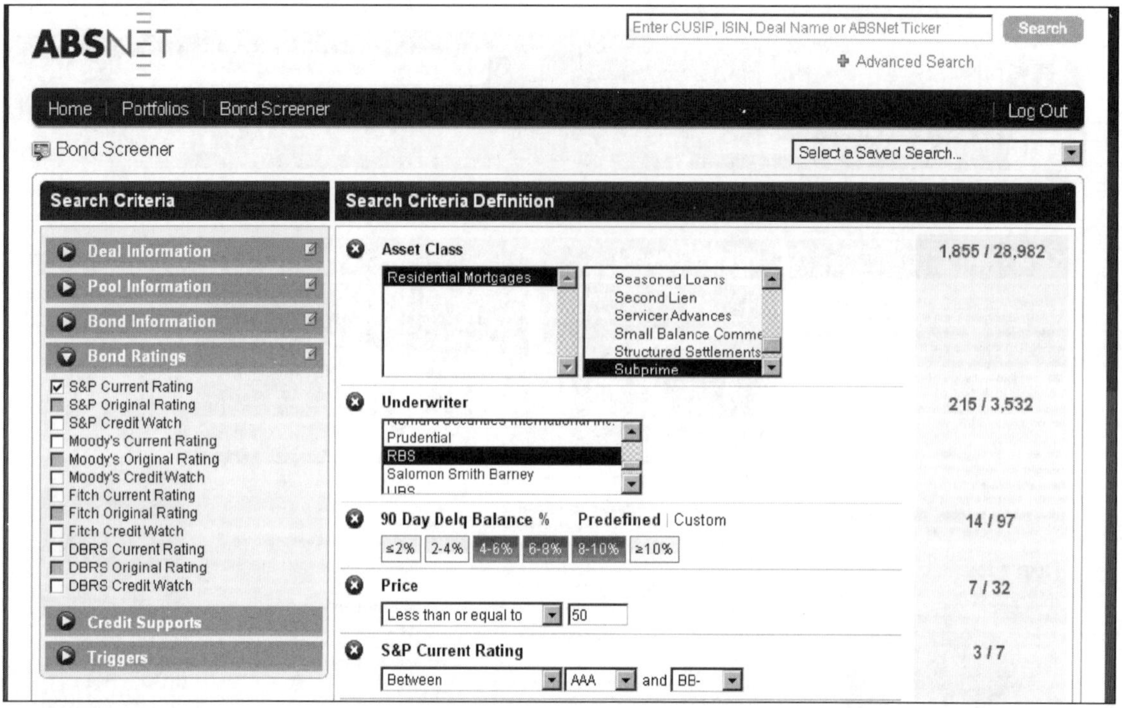

Figure 17.3. ABSNet's Bond Screener/Parametric Search tool
Source: Lewtan Technologies.

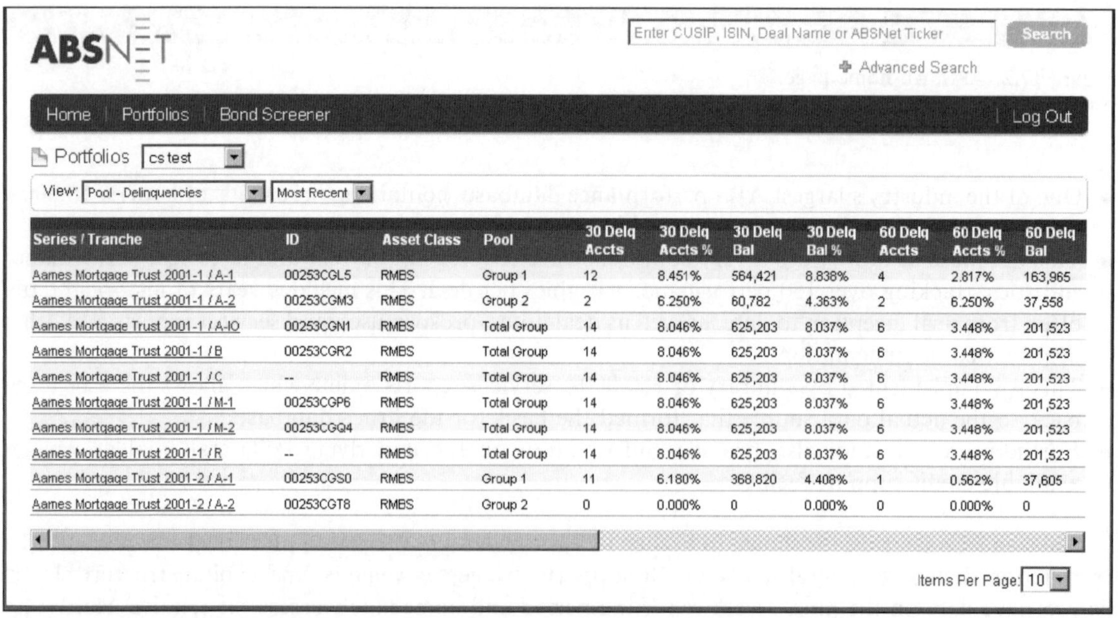

Series / Tranche	ID	Asset Class	Pool	30 Delq Accts	30 Delq Accts %	30 Delq Bal	30 Delq Bal %	60 Delq Accts	60 Delq Accts %	60 Delq Bal
Aames Mortgage Trust 2001-1 / A-1	00253CGL5	RMBS	Group 1	12	8.451%	564,421	8.838%	4	2.817%	163,965
Aames Mortgage Trust 2001-1 / A-2	00253CGM3	RMBS	Group 2	2	6.250%	60,782	4.363%	2	6.250%	37,558
Aames Mortgage Trust 2001-1 / A-IO	00253CGN1	RMBS	Total Group	14	8.046%	625,203	8.037%	6	3.448%	201,523
Aames Mortgage Trust 2001-1 / B	00253CGR2	RMBS	Total Group	14	8.046%	625,203	8.037%	6	3.448%	201,523
Aames Mortgage Trust 2001-1 / C	--	RMBS	Total Group	14	8.046%	625,203	8.037%	6	3.448%	201,523
Aames Mortgage Trust 2001-1 / M-1	00253CGP6	RMBS	Total Group	14	8.046%	625,203	8.037%	6	3.448%	201,523
Aames Mortgage Trust 2001-1 / M-2	00253CGQ4	RMBS	Total Group	14	8.046%	625,203	8.037%	6	3.448%	201,523
Aames Mortgage Trust 2001-1 / R	--	RMBS	Total Group	14	8.046%	625,203	8.037%	6	3.448%	201,523
Aames Mortgage Trust 2001-2 / A-1	00253CGS0	RMBS	Group 1	11	6.180%	368,820	4.408%	1	0.562%	37,605
Aames Mortgage Trust 2001-2 / A-2	00253CGT8	RMBS	Group 2	0	0.000%	0	0.000%	0	0.000%	0

Figure 17.4. ABSNet portfolios.
Source: Lewtan Technologies.

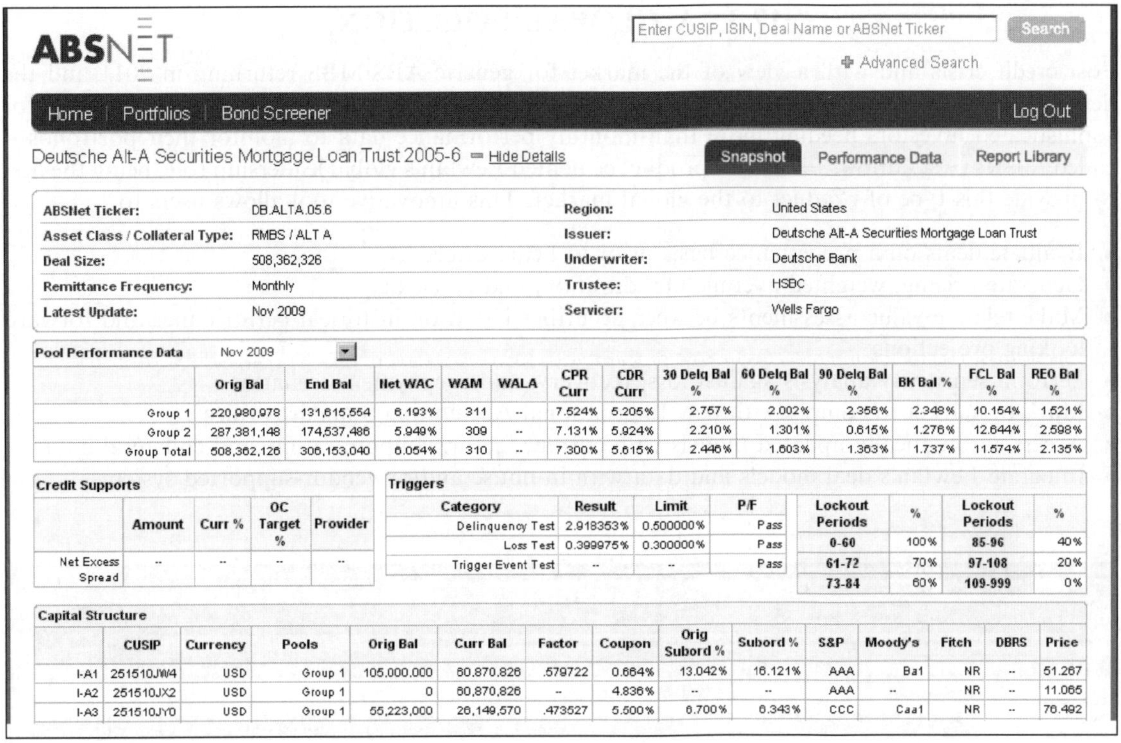
ABSNET

Enter CUSIP, ISIN, Deal Name or ABSNet Ticker | Search

Advanced Search

Home | Portfolios | Bond Screener | Log Out

Deutsche Alt-A Securities Mortgage Loan Trust 2005-6 — Hide Details | Snapshot | Performance Data | Report Library

ABSNet Ticker:	DB.ALTA.05.6	**Region:**	United States
Asset Class / Collateral Type:	RMBS / ALT A	**Issuer:**	Deutsche Alt-A Securities Mortgage Loan Trust
Deal Size:	508,362,326	**Underwriter:**	Deutsche Bank
Remittance Frequency:	Monthly	**Trustee:**	HSBC
Latest Update:	Nov 2009	**Servicer:**	Wells Fargo

Pool Performance Data Nov 2009

	Orig Bal	End Bal	Net WAC	WAM	WALA	CPR Curr	CDR Curr	30 Delq Bal %	60 Delq Bal %	90 Delq Bal %	BK Bal %	FCL Bal %	REO Bal %
Group 1	220,980,978	131,615,554	6.193%	311	--	7.524%	5.205%	2.757%	2.002%	2.356%	2.348%	10.154%	1.521%
Group 2	287,381,148	174,537,486	5.949%	309	--	7.131%	5.924%	2.210%	1.301%	0.615%	1.276%	12.644%	2.598%
Group Total	508,362,126	306,153,040	6.054%	310	--	7.300%	5.615%	2.446%	1.603%	1.363%	1.737%	11.574%	2.135%

Credit Supports

	Amount	Curr %	OC Target %	Provider
Net Excess Spread	--	--	--	--

Triggers

Category	Result	Limit	P/F
Delinquency Test	2.918353%	0.500000%	Pass
Loss Test	0.399975%	0.300000%	Pass
Trigger Event Test	--	--	Pass

Lockout Periods	%	Lockout Periods	%
0-60	100%	**85-96**	40%
61-72	70%	**97-108**	20%
73-84	60%	**109-999**	0%

Capital Structure

	CUSIP	Currency	Pools	Orig Bal	Curr Bal	Factor	Coupon	Orig Subord %	Subord %	S&P	Moody's	Fitch	DBRS	Price
I-A1	251510JW4	USD	Group 1	105,000,000	60,870,826	.579722	0.664%	13.042%	16.121%	AAA	Ba1	NR	--	51.267
I-A2	251510JX2	USD	Group 1	0	60,870,826	--	4.836%	--	--	AAA	--	NR	--	11.065
I-A3	251510JY0	USD	Group 1	55,223,000	26,149,570	.473527	5.500%	6.700%	6.343%	CCC	Caa1	NR	--	76.492

Figure 17.5. ABSNet's Deal Snapshot.
Source: Lewtan Technologies.

ABSNet took on the challenge of collecting, organizing, and validating performance data on thousands of asset-backed securities, creating a comprehensive database of performance statistics that ABS professionals could access via the internet. The firm further added software productivity tools enabling users to manipulate the data and to conduct "on-the-fly" analyses directly within the service.

In addition, Lewtan Technologies established an extensive library of structured finance information, consolidating news and research from leading trade journals, news services, rating agencies, and corporate research departments to make their product a "one-stop shop" for securitization and structured finance–related information.

Since its release, ABSNet has had, according to the company, over 6 million pages views and attracted more than 35,000 industry professionals to the site, many of whom visit frequently to obtain information to support their securitization activities. Nowadays, typical users represent a cross-section of industry participants, including issuers, investors, credit enhancers, sell-side analysts, traders, investment bankers, and rating agencies.

In addition, the company has forged partnerships with more than a dozen leading organizations within the securitization industry. These relationships, combined with ongoing enhancements to the service, enable the firm to deliver high-quality data and up-to-date information to securitization industry professionals.

The deployment of ABSNet can save time and money by consolidating comprehensive and accurate performance data, industry content, and surveillance tools in one convenient location.

17.3 A GLOBAL SOLUTION

Post credit crisis and with a view of the market for generic ABS/MBS returning in 2011 and the demand for analytical tools increasing, `ABSNet` is now providing advanced cash flow models for sophisticated investors needing more than monthly performance data to monitor their portfolios—called `ABSNet Cashflows`. This new product cemented Lewtan's global leadership role, being the first to provide this type of product to the global market. This innovative tool allows users to

- Evaluate deals on a pre-issuance basis prior to being priced
- Generate pricing, weighted average life, duration, and convexity
- Make relative value assessments between securities based on historical performance and forward looking projections
- Perform sensitivity analysis against loss, recovery, and prepayment scenarios
- Mark-to-market to comply with new International Accounting Standards rules
- Access automatically updated models with current factor, coupon, rating, and collateral data
- Integrate Lewtan's deal models and data with in-house and/or vendor-supported systems.

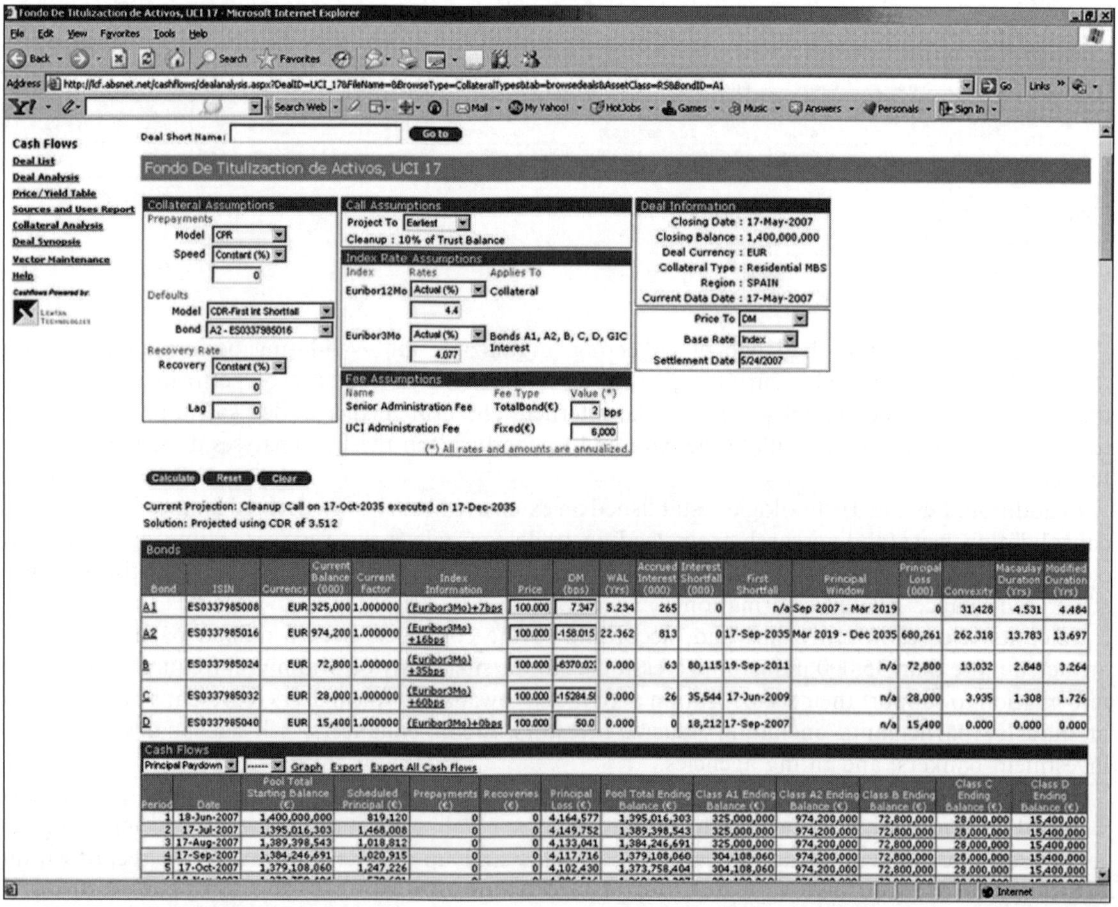

Figure 17.6. `ABSNet Cashflows`.
Source: Lewtan Technologies.

ABSNet Cashflows is focused primarily on transactions issued outside of the U.S. and is fully integrated with the company's European performance database; these models simulate the paydown of collateral and bonds in European ABS deals based on user-defined economic assumptions.

17.4 RESPONDING TO REGULATORY REQUIREMENTS

Working with industry leaders to develop a solution to increase transparency for publicly issued asset-backed and mortgage-backed securities (a requirement of the SEC's Reg AB, mandating a set of amended rules to address the disclosure and reporting requirements for new ABS issuances), Lewtan developed ABS Discloser to provide both best practice investor relations websites and Reg AB websites. ABS Discloser illuminates deal performance while leveraging the latest in web-based technology. These custom-developed and hosted websites provide greater insight to existing investors regarding an issuer's securitization while broadening transparency to potential investors.

ABS Discloser components include Deal Reporter, which provides aggregate-level performance data including

- *Deal performance statistics*. The same variables contained on ABSNet for each asset class. Each variable is available for users to create customized views and graphs.
- *Aggregate deal summary information*. Information held electronically, such as tranche balances, deal participants, and other aggregate-level information to provide a high-level snapshot of each deal.
- *Alerts*. A powerful tool for monitoring deal performance. Users can set and save criteria or trigger parameters so that the system notifies them via email whenever deals change to meet those criteria or triggers that have been pulled.
- *Comparisons*. Enabling peer analysis of deals in both tabular and graphical formats.
- *Investor reports*. Physical downloadable copies of remittance reports.
- *Portfolios*. Investors can create and save a customized set of data containing only the deals and data elements in their portfolios.
- *Deal search*. Search deals based on deal characteristics like deal name, CUSIP, seller, lead manager, etc..

Static Pool Reporter, which features loan-level analytics, including

- *Collateral analysis*. Dynamic capability to examine different aggregations of loan-level data. This provides issuers and investors the ability to aggregate deals and filter information by deal or by a specific group of assets.
- *Static pool analysis*. Data are organized by prior securitized pools to analyze asset performance over time.
- *Vintage analysis*. Data are organized by origination data to display asset performance over time.

Static Pool Filter, which was specifically developed to address Reg AB 1105 requirements, offers an easy-to-use Reg AB data extraction tool to create Reg AB–compliant static pool reports as needed.

17.5 STREAMLINING WORKFLOWS WITH AUTOMATION TOOLS AND DATA FEEDS

Over the years, several tools have been added to ABSNet to facilitate the export of the information available on the site and integration into internal applications and workflow. One of these tools integrates available data directly into Excel spreadsheets. ABSNet Excel Add In provides seamless

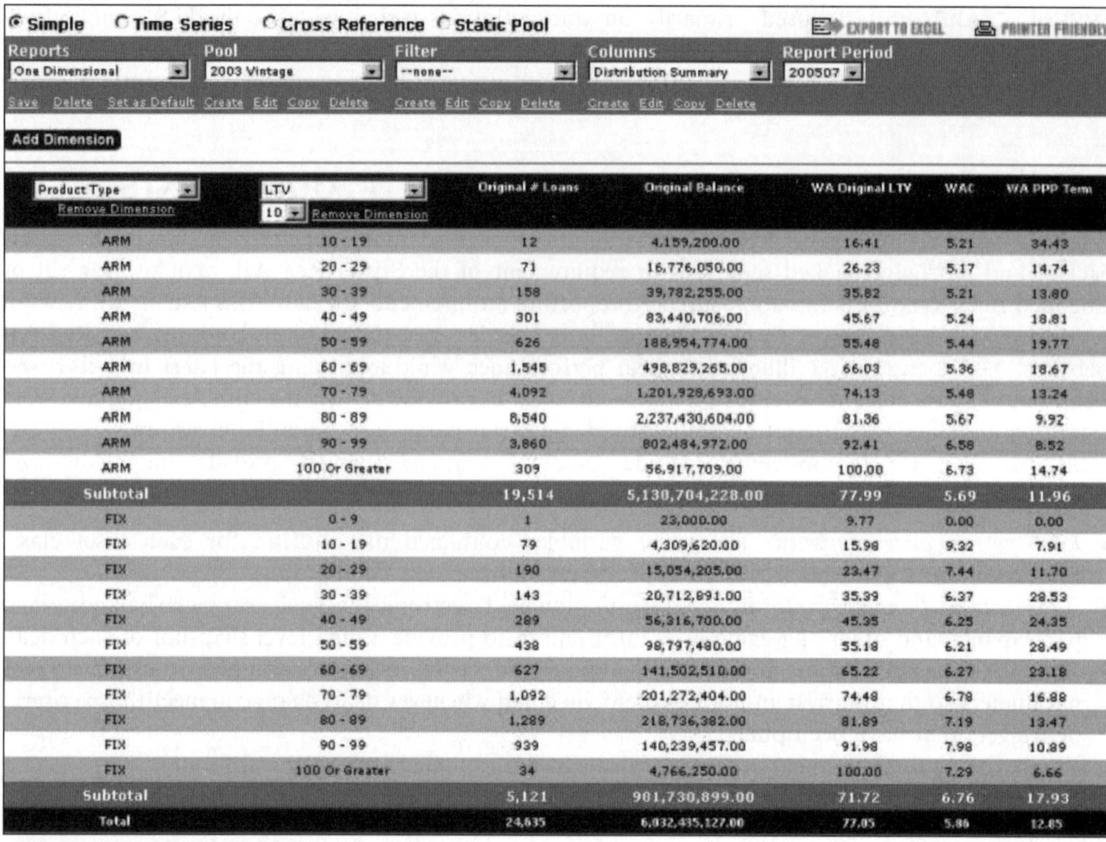

Product Type	LTV	Original # Loans	Original Balance	WA Original LTV	WAC	WA PPP Term
ARM	10 - 19	12	4,159,200.00	16.41	5.21	34.43
ARM	20 - 29	71	16,776,050.00	26.23	5.17	14.74
ARM	30 - 39	158	39,782,255.00	35.82	5.21	13.80
ARM	40 - 49	301	83,440,706.00	45.67	5.24	18.81
ARM	50 - 59	626	188,954,774.00	55.48	5.44	19.77
ARM	60 - 69	1,545	498,829,265.00	66.03	5.36	18.67
ARM	70 - 79	4,092	1,201,928,693.00	74.13	5.48	13.24
ARM	80 - 89	8,540	2,237,430,604.00	81.36	5.67	9.92
ARM	90 - 99	3,860	802,484,972.00	92.41	6.58	8.52
ARM	100 Or Greater	309	56,917,709.00	100.00	6.73	14.74
Subtotal		19,514	5,130,704,228.00	77.99	5.69	11.96
FIX	0 - 9	1	23,000.00	9.77	0.00	0.00
FIX	10 - 19	79	4,309,620.00	15.98	9.32	7.91
FIX	20 - 29	190	15,054,205.00	23.47	7.44	11.70
FIX	30 - 39	143	20,712,891.00	35.39	6.37	28.53
FIX	40 - 49	289	56,316,700.00	45.35	6.25	24.35
FIX	50 - 59	438	98,797,480.00	55.18	6.21	28.49
FIX	60 - 69	627	141,502,510.00	65.22	6.27	23.18
FIX	70 - 79	1,092	201,272,404.00	74.48	6.78	16.88
FIX	80 - 89	1,289	218,736,382.00	81.89	7.19	13.47
FIX	90 - 99	939	140,239,457.00	91.98	7.98	10.89
FIX	100 Or Greater	34	4,766,250.00	100.00	7.29	6.66
Subtotal		5,121	901,730,899.00	71.72	6.76	17.93
Total		24,635	6,032,435,127.00	77.05	5.86	12.85

Figure 17.7. `ABS Discloser`.
Source: Lewtan Technologies.

and automatic integration of ABS/MBS performance data into Excel spreadsheets providing a reduction of manual processes and simplification when generating portfolio performance reports.

With a simple graphical user interface, users can quickly select the deals, bonds, dates, and performance field needed to populate their customized spreadsheets with historical data, while easily updating these spreadsheets with current data, most importantly, with no need of rekeying the information.

17.6 ABSNet SCHEDULED EXPORT

Given the status of the markets following the credit crisis, timely access to critical information that impacts credit-sensitive investments has become more important than ever.

In addition, increased regulatory scrutiny requires the ability to demonstrate better risk management controls and reduce operational risk associated with structured finance investment activities.

Time-consuming labor-intensive data collection activities can now be streamlined and monthly performance data can be efficiently integrated into relational databases and systems via Lewtan's `ABSNet Scheduled Export` feed.

Users of this tool receive a daily file which includes collateral and bond performance information,

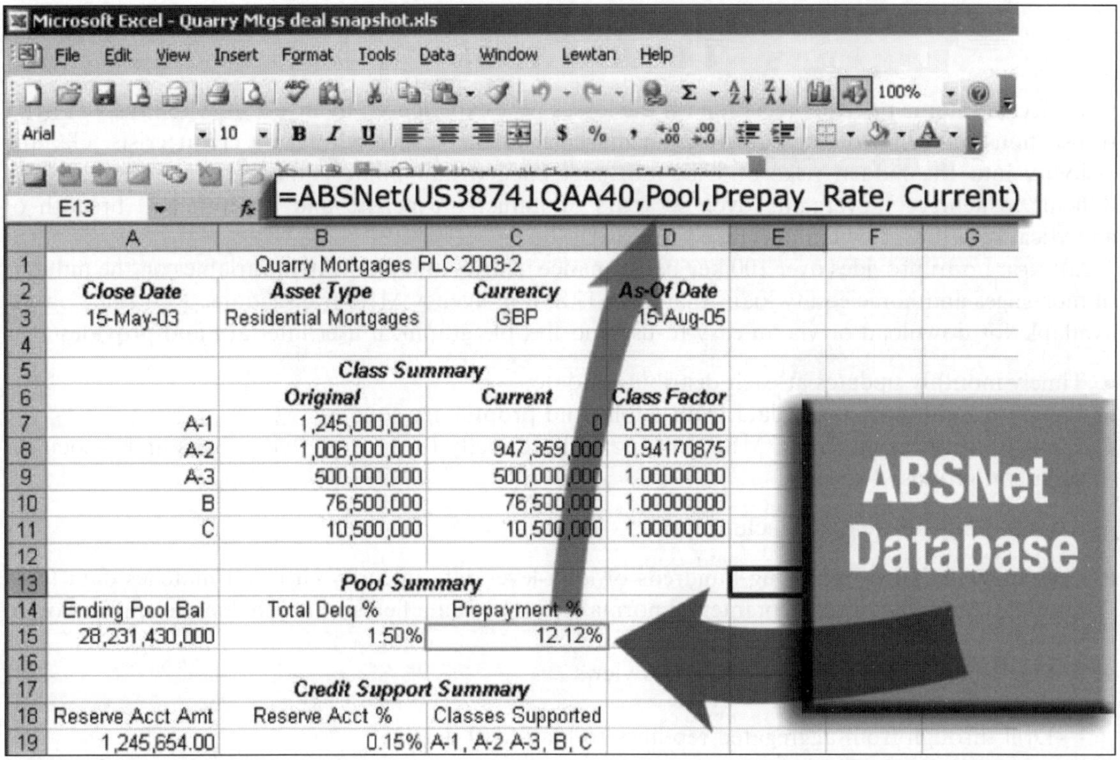

Figure 17.8. ABSNet Excel Add In.
Source: Lewtan Technologies.

original terms and conditions, and credit support information. The deal information is updated within 48 hours of remittance report availability, has an XML file structure, and provides complete documentation. If needed, full historical performance data are available and customized portfolio files are also provided by the firm.

The benefits of ABSNet Scheduled Export include

- Limit risk of damage to organizational reputation through investment in risk management data and systems
- Reduction of risk associated with errors resulting from manual data collection processing
- Elimination of operational rework and costs
- Reduction of data redundancy (data stored in multiple storage facilities, manufacturing using inconsistent/disparate sources)
- A source of independent data to reduce any risk of fraudulent information.

With the development of ABSNet Scheduled Export, Lewtan also formed a *dedicated Credit Surveillance Group* committed to coupling one of the most comprehensive asset-backed and mortgage-backed databases available with deep industry expertise. This team of dedicated support specialists is available to offer support and expertise in the integration of these complex data into an organization as well as offering timely responses to ongoing inquiries.

Significant opaqueness in the global securitization markets remains. The demand for credit surveillance data by investors is very high and the need for additional data and controls by both investors and issuers prevail for those firms that have survived the credit crisis.

17.7 HOME PRICE DEPRECIATION AND THE NEED FOR BETTER TOOLS

The effects of home price depreciation on the losses now experienced by investors who invest in MBS transactions have stifled the securitization markets, further exacerbating the credit crisis. Gaining visibility into the hidden risks of U.S. mortgage-backed and home equity transactions has been difficult to achieve. Leveraging over 20 years of industry expertise and a depth and breadth of analytical solutions, Lewtan developed `ABSNet Loan`.

`ABSNet Loan` provides over 100 key performance metrics and predicative variables on the millions of mortgages and home equity loans that back U.S. non-agency MBS transactions. `ABSNet Loan` is available for download or via an easy-to-use and flexible graphical user interface and provides

- Timely monthly updates at each distribution date
- Integrated and normalized data from public and proprietary sources
- Links from the bonds in an MBS/ABS portfolio directly to the underlying loans and associated collateral groups.

`ABSNet Loan`'s key features include

- *Collateral analysis*. Employing hundreds of loan-level data integrity checks it matches data from multiple sources to provide an integral normalized set of data fields which enable the application to provide
  - Single-period or historical time series views
  - Static pool analysis
  - Drill through from aggregated rep lines to loan-level detail.
- *Benchmark analysis*. The identification of loans and loan pools that share similar characteristics and save each loan cohort within or across deals to
  - Identify outliers of credit risk
  - Create rep lines with "like" loans that share similar original static and dynamic performance characteristics.
- *Flexible data delivery*. Provides monthly updates of each item of distribution data, which are offered through a variety of delivery options. In addition, the data are exportable into Excel or PDF for offline analysis.
- *Deal universe*. `ABSNet Loan` augments available data with proprietary datasets to provide a more comprehensive picture of the potential exposure on each loan. In addition, it provides an expanded set of original loan characteristics and deals that are not otherwise available in the market.

17.8 THE DEMAND FOR GREATER GRANULARITY

Prior to the onset of the credit crisis , home price analyses in non-agency mortgage-backed security and home equity securitizations (MBS) were either non-existent or relied on a broad-based (and incorrect) assumption that real estate is a homogeneous asset. Investors primarily relied on Case–Shiller or OFHEO/FHFA indices[1] to track the performance of property values.

[2] The S&P/Case–Shiller home price index measures the residential housing market, tracking changes in the value of the residential real estate market in 20 metropolitan regions across the U.S. (*http://www.standardandpoors.com/*). OFHEO/FHFA stands for Office of Federal Housing Enterprise Oversight/Federal Housing Finance Authority. The HPI is a weighted repeat sales index, meaning that it measures average price changes in repeat sales or refinancing on the same properties. This information is obtained by reviewing repeat mortgage transactions on single-family properties whose mortgages have been purchased or securitized by Fannie Mae or Freddie Mac since January 1975 (*http://www.fhfa.gov*).

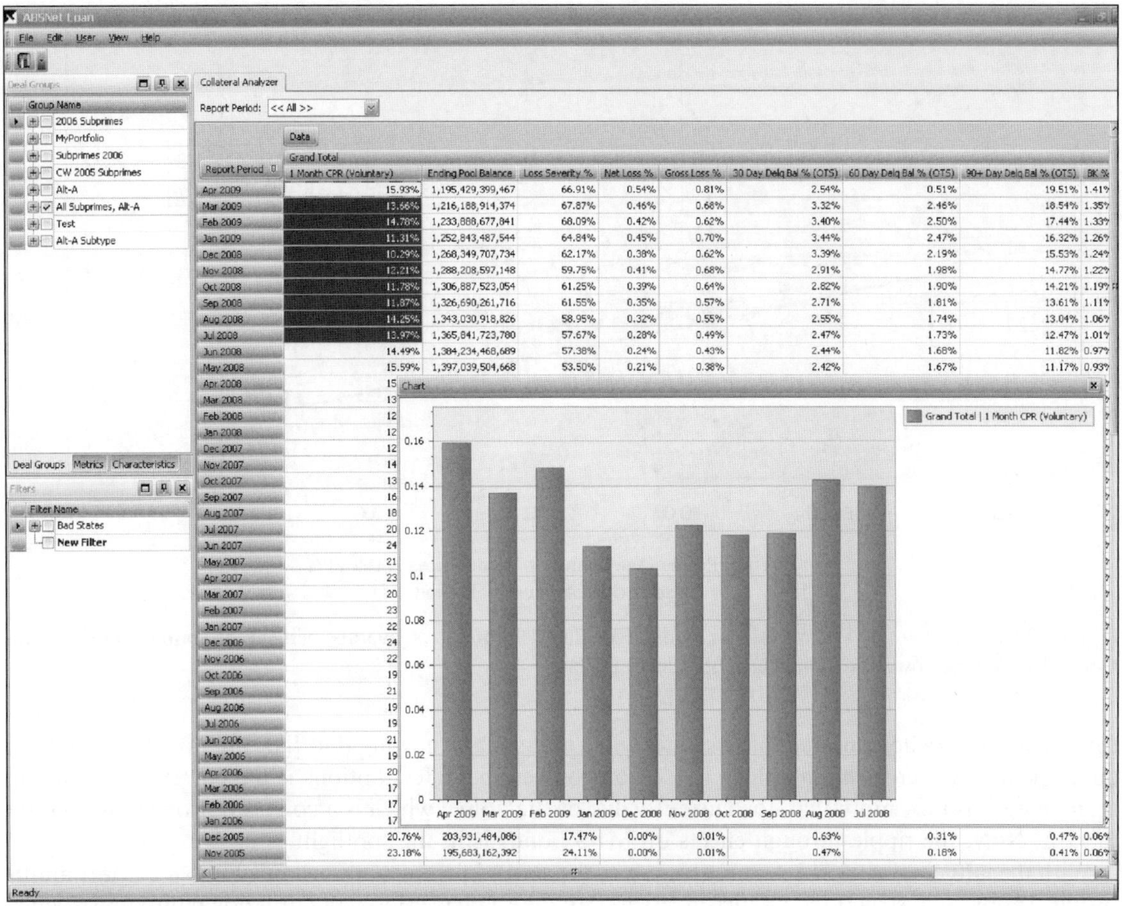

Figure 17.9. ABSNet Loan.
Source: Lewtan Technologies.

Most real estate submarkets were experiencing rapid appreciation from a combination of the trickle down effects of the stock market rallying in the middle of the decade, general real estate speculation, and unqualified borrowers' ability to receive financing at unreasonably low borrowing rates.

It was common in the securitization and non-securitization real estate segment to hear people discuss HPA, or home price appreciation. However, it was very rare to hear people talking about the other half of this equation—HPD, or home price depreciation. Figure 17.10 represents how a typical investor uses CBSA-level indices like Case–Shiller or OFHEO/FHFA and the lack of correlation between 150+-day delinquencies and home price changes.

In the pre–credit crisis real estate markets, most analysts presumed there would be steady home price appreciation and the homeowner's loan-to-value (LTV) ratio would steadily decrease as the borrower made principal and interest payments. Under these conditions, the impact of a mortgage default is significantly less than it is in the current market because a new owner would be purchasing an asset that sees its value appreciating over time.

From the second half of 2007 to the present (2011), there has been HPD exceeding 50% in some markets, causing the LTV ratios to increase rather than decrease. This created problematic situations

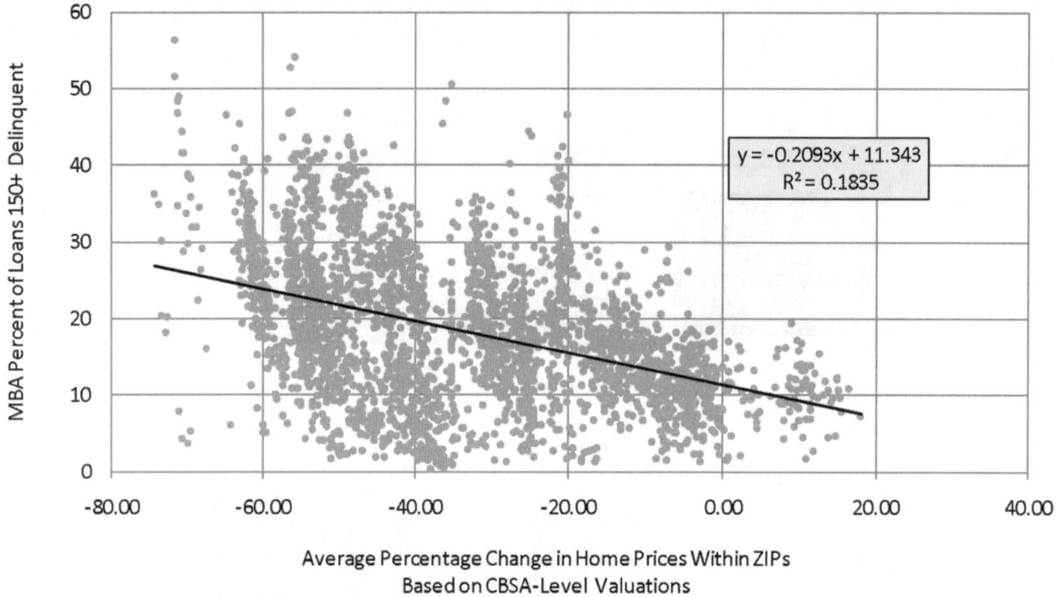

Figure 17.10. October 2009 percentage of loans 150+-day delinquent vs. average percentage change in price from original LTV price by zip code using CBSA-level HPIs.

for homeowners who continue to make mortgage payments, knowing that they are investing equity in an asset that is decreasing in value. These homeowners have few options if the current outstanding loan amount is now more than the current value of the home, which is a common problem in today's market. Now, the ripple-through effects on MBS bonds is in the spotlight.

With the launch of `ABSNet Loan HomeVal`, the second product in Lewtan's `ABSNet Loan` multi-pronged approach, structured finance investors can take a deeper look and drill down into non-agency MBS pools both at the loans themselves and at the specific property values for the loans that support an individual bondholding.

This created a new paradigm shift, for the first time ever interested parties can match the securitized loans in an MBS pool to actual homes. Data from over 150,000 micro-markets in the U.S. (there are roughly 40,000 zipcodes, so these micro-data are focused on neighborhood-level drivers of home price) are utilized to generate the most timely and accurate home price forecasts which in turn provide the most accurate picture of how much principal is at risk in a given mortgage pool.

Compared with using the CBSA-level indices as shown in Figure 17.11, when using zipcode-level data with AVM technology, there is a clear negative correlation between 150+-day delinquency and home price depreciation as illustrated by Figure 17.10.

This matching is accomplished by receiving updated loan information and monthly home valuations. The loans are valued by using automated valuation models (AVMs) developed by *Collateral Analytics, LLC (CA)*, ranked as one of the best of its kind in the industry. Matching loan-level data to specific properties and current home valuations enables `ABSNet Loan HomeVal` to determine the quality of the assets behind these loans.

Over the last 30 years, AVMs were developed to value properties based on different inputs such as the selling price on comparable properties. The advantages of AVMs are (1) they are relatively inexpensive compared with appraisals and BPOs, since they do not require an onsite visit, and (2) they are very fast to generate. The only shortcoming of AVMs with respect to their use in securitization is

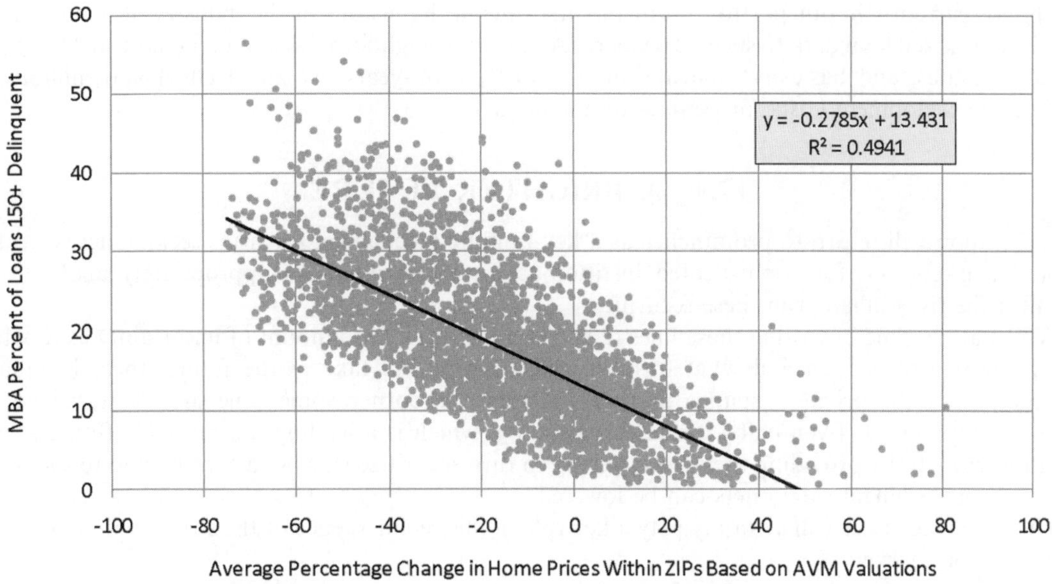

Figure 17.11. October 2009 percentage of loans 150+ days delinquent vs. average percentage change in price from original LTV price by zipcode using AVMs.
Source: Lewtan Technologies.

they require the investor to know the street address of the property to generate a current estimated home price.

Many investment banks have been using AVMs for years to value whole loan pools when they initially purchase them for the purpose of securitizing assets. This technology could not be utilized in existing MBS transactions because it was impossible to link the loans that were stripped of borrower name and address for privacy reasons to actual properties.

`ABSNet Loan HomeVal` has changed this impossible notion. Using a combination of public records information, loan-level information, and current sales listings information, true property analysis can be achieved for securitized mortgages. Users of this tool benefit from

- Home valuations for the loans in each securitized pool on a property-by-property basis
- Hedonic AVM models to matched properties
- A time-adjusted value and best comps value similar to an automated broker price opinion
- Hedonic characteristics about the property
- A "retro" AVM to determine what the actual value of the home was at loan closing
- Market analysis at the zipcode level
- Distressed indexes at the zipcode level that are automatically applied to loans in FC (foreclosure) or REO (real estate owned) status and which can be used to further stress various delinquency buckets in a pool.

Assessing the true value of properties that support the loans in mortgage-backed securities is critical to understanding a potential principal loss on the bonds. Responsibility for understanding credit risk inherent in the securities must be assumed by investors directly. Utilizing broad-based HPI indices is insufficient to gauge the specific risk embedded in individual loans supporting these transactions.

Only by viewing loan-by-loan and property-by-property data can we truly understand the negative equity that exists in today's markets and develop an appropriate view on the future creditworthiness of the bonds currently in our portfolio. For the first time in the history of the industry, it is possible to match securitized loan data to specific property AVMs and neighborhood-level time-adjusted property value estimates, and basically replicate hundreds of person-years' worth of effort and millions of dollars in development costs for pennies on the dollar.

17.9 A BRIGHTER FUTURE

Securitization will return to prominence as a key funding mechanism for firms seeking access to the capital markets and for sophisticated institutional investors who can appropriately analyze and monitor the risks inherent in these securities.

Whilst at the time of writing these lines (2009) there is still a fair amount of uncertainty as to when the recovery will happen and what form(s) securitization will take in the future, there is equally optimism that the private issuance market will turn the corner some time in 2011/12 aided by government support. Eventually, consumer spending, which is a leading indicator for future securitization growth (by providing the assets that are in turn securitized), will have recovered to the point where the government safety nets can be lowered.

The following issues will certainly play a key role in this re-emergence of the structured finance and securitization market:

- The split between government-sponsored securitization programs to increase Fannie Mae and Freddie Mac's purview or stimulate new issuance (e.g., GSE regulation, TALF, Treasury's Public Private Partnership Investment Program) and private securitization
- New rules governing compliance and regulatory oversight (e.g., Basel II, European Union's Capital Requirements Directive, IOSCO, and SEC rating agency reform)
- Expanded transparency initiatives (e.g., SEC transition to XBRL data filings, European covered bond initiatives), the European Union's Capital Requirements Directive, the possibility of legislation that changes the rules for structured finance investors ("cram down" legislation, loan modifications, U.S. House Financial Services Bill re: Credit Rating Agency Transparency and Disclosure Act) such that the fear of governmental intervention to overrule governing transaction documents permanently diminishes access to the capital markets.

Governments around the world are rewriting the rules that will define the capital markets for years to come. Combined with the depth of the current recession, 2010 will continue to be an extremely challenging year for all securitization market participants, including technology and data vendors such as Lewtan Technologies.

18

Moody's Wall Street Analytics

Moody's Wall Street Analytics (MWSA) is a wholly owned subsidiary of Moody's Corporation and a member of its analytics business. Founded in 1987, MWSA (*www.wsainc.com*) has been around for more than 20 years producing customized software and specialist data tools for the structured finance markets. These tools have been used for deal structuring, transaction analysis and management, and the servicing of structured finance instruments. The company's clients include many issuers, investment banks, and both buy-side and sell-side investors.

Wall Street Analytics was acquired by Moody's in December 2006 with Moody's intention to broaden its capabilities in the analysis and monitoring of complex structured debt securities. The acquisition extended Moody's CDO product suite and enhanced the firms ABS and MBS analytical capabilities. In return, synergies for Wall Street Analytics meant access to Moody's extensive deal libraries, its analytical staff, and the corporation's global reach and marketing capabilities.

MWSA's data products and software solutions can support detailed analysis of sophisticated structured finance deals spanning across ABS, MBS, CMBS, RMBS, CDOs, and CLOs.

This chapter provides an overview of MWSA products with a focus on different players in the structured finance arena, namely

- Investors
- Asset managers
- Issuers
- Structurers.

18.1 ABS/MBS INVESTORS TOOLS: STRUCTURED FINANCE WORKSTATION

MWSA offers a key tool for investors in ABS/MBS bonds—its `Structured Finance Workstation (SFW)` which allows investors to monitor, stress-test, and value ABS as well as MBS (RMBS and CMBS) portfolios.

Depending on the investor's needs `SFW` can be subscribed to in various ways:

- As a standalone *desktop installation.*
- *Online* at *sfw.moodys.com* which enables web-based access to portfolio, model, cash flow, and valuation analysis.
- *Web services API* (application programming interface), which supports automation of routine tasks and integrates the `SFW` desktop functionality into the investor's internal systems and contains custom macros for MS Excel.
- *Valuation services* which essentially enable investors to outsource the running of SFW to MWSA who in turn delivers the results of the analysis.

Both the desktop and online version of `SFW` provide investors with functionality to monitor, value, and stress-test their ABS, RMBS, and CMBS investments, which eliminates the need to gather performance data as well as validating transaction waterfalls—as this information is readily available to MWSA.

This deal-related information integrates in SFW seamlessly with Moody's macroeconomic forecasts from *Economy.com* and utilises access to Moody's Investor Services' credit risk models.

18.2 CDO INVESTORS' TOOLS

MWSA offers three key tools to investors in collateralized debt obligations (CDOs): CDOnet Investor, CDOcalc, and CDO Enhanced Monitoring Services (EMS).

18.2.1 CDOnet Investor

CDOnet Investor is an adaptive software platform that supports cash flow analytics either on a single-deal level or portfolio level by accessing the firm's comprehensive global deal library which includes CLOs, CDO of ABS, TRUPS, and other types of CDOs. Bespoke CDOs or deals that are not yet included in the library are modeled by MWSA and added on request of the investor.

The tool enables users to review cross-deal exposure, identifies risk concentration, and monitors cash flow performance across CDO portfolios. Furthermore, it reports on eligibility criteria, performs cash flow scenario runs with different projected interest rates, prepayment, and default rates, and allows Monte Carlo stress-testing based on the various selected stress scenarios.

Furthermore, CDOnet users that also subscribe to Moody's Investor Services can download Moody's ratings and related deal information directly into the selected portfolios. The tool links also to third-party data vendors such as Markit in order to source pricing information or other relevant syndicated loan data.

CDOnet's API interface and macro-language enables powerful automation of standard procedures and enables investors to create their own scripting, code, or macros in order to initiate a large variety of functions which can be run frequently or as periodic batch jobs.

18.2.2 CDOcalc

CDOcalc (*www.CDOcalc.com*) is a web-based interface enabling investors to access MWSA's comprehensive deal library and accommodating user-friendly analyses via the internet.

The tool enables the analysis of both individual tranches as well as whole portfolios and can be used to compare past, current, and future performance of investor CDOs.

CDOcalc can calculate defaults on either a global or issuer level, first losses, and can solve for yield. Default analysis can be either based on decreasing/defaulting asset ratings or systemic risk such as whole sectors going into default. This is complemented by scenario analysis for customized interest rate or prepayment scenarios and allows setting of simple recovery assumptions. Price/Yield and analysis of average life are also possible.

The tool's reporting function includes coverage tests (current and projected), compliance reporting, cash flows for underlying collateral, hedges, and liabilities. Current asset-level data can be downloaded and results from default runs for cash flow comparisons can be saved. This is complemented by an export function (PDF and MS Excel).

CDOcalc's portfolio-tracking features enable investors to set up custom portfolios by adding tranches from different transactions, accommodate running aggregate cash flow analysis, and produce transaction exposure reports based on industry, rating, issuer, and other common parameters.

18.2.3 CDO Enhanced Monitoring Service (EMS)

`EMS` enables a concise and standardized view of over 1,000 cash flow CDOs that are rated by Moody's Investor Services.

Detailed CDO collateral information is enriched in `EMS` by portfolio risk analysis, market comparisons, and default risk information that is based on the same data source that is used by the corporation's analysts when these transactions are rated and put under surveillance.

`EMS` lists and provides details on the underlying collateral such as market prices, bond identifiers, and up-to-date Moody's ratings. Current vs. trigger levels for various collateral characteristics such as overcollateralization (O/C), weighted average rating factor (WARF), diversity factor, and ratings buckets are also available in EMS.

18.3 ABS/MBS ISSUER TOOLS

MWSA suite of ABS issuer tools can help issuers to manage ABS and MBS through the entire deal lifecycle starting with warehousing of the loans to transaction modeling and through to bond administration and post-issuance reporting.

18.3.1 Structured Finance Workstation for Issuers (`SFW Issuer`)

`SFW Issuer` offers similar deal modeling and analytics functionality that can be found on typical structured finance underwriting and trading desks and the tool itself can either be used for deal origination or to reverse-engineer structured finance deals.

Issuers can also model their own transactions to understand the modeling that was done by the investment bank and underwriters of the deal, which can be used to verify third-party analysis.

In addition, issuers are able to run their own scenario analysis, both at transaction close and throughout the deal's lifecycle, enabling them to price their own bondholdings including residuals and servicing fees.

`SFW Issuer`'s integrated toolkit supports the following analytics: price/yield tables, sensitivities, total rate of return horizon, bivariate grids, scalar and vector prepayment/default rates, loan-specific assumptions, property-level analysis, user-defined profitability, fee and strip valuations, residual cash flow, and bond pricing.

`SFW Issuer` offers a one-stop-shop solution and covers the following asset classes: whole loans, subprime, home equity/HELOC, manufactured housing, CMBS, auto loans/leases, student loans, equipment leases, credit cards, resecuritization, and agency pools.

The tool's collateral features permit viewing of collateral cash flows either on a loan or pool level and include more than 300 asset-related data fields further enhanced by user-definable fields and complemented by loan as well as pool pricing and comprehensive loan selection tools.

The structuring features include collateral stratification, loan bucketing, targeting and solving for average life, price, yield, and bond coupon, split by floater and inverse floater, zero-coupon bond creation, breakeven loan pricing, calculation of first–loss structuring templates, and a powerful scripting language.

Finally, `SFW Issuer`'s comprehensive reporting package features hundreds of customized reporting templates, presentation of quality 3D graphics, copy and paste into Windows-based applications, deal summaries and reports on the transaction's profitability, graphical presentation of asset and liability cash flows, post-issuance investor and servicer reports, and static pool information.

18.3.2 Bond Administration Workstation for Issuers (`BAW Issuer`)

`BAW Issuer` integrates bond administration and investor-reporting functionalities for ABS and MBS (which covers CMBS and RMBS) and, combined with the `SFW Issuer`, provides a comprehensive package for transaction administration and analysis.

The tool's deal-modeling functionalities include a flexible and simple-to-use script module for customized cash flow waterfall modeling, ability to run forward cash flow projections prior to as well as after close, execution of complex default and prepayment scenarios that are used to generate decrement tables and price yield tables, and ongoing deal cash flow analytics and valuation including fees and capital structures.

`BAW Issuer`'s bond administration and validation modules enable the user to run batch processes for any number of deals at the same time, import asset-level or pool-level information, customize loan-level data feeds, use data-scrubbing and validation mechanisms, calculate complex bond and fee payments, issue level compliance testing, store monthly payment information at asset level, and receive full issuer and investor reporting.

The reporting functionality of this tool enables production of customizable servicing and bondholder reports including historical and static pool information complemented by advanced stratification and graphical presentation capabilities. The resulting reports are printable and can be exported to Excel (either at the loan, pool, or bond level) or posted on the issuer's website. File formats are compatible with DTC, Bloomberg, EDGAR, and other websites.

18.3.3 ABScalc

`ABScalc` (*www.ABScalc.com*) is a web-based tool aimed at facilitating transparency in the ABS market enabling ABS issuers to easily distribute pool-level performance information. Being compliant with the SEC's Reg AB, issuers can provide information on their securitizations to investors and other deal-related counterparties via a custom-built hosted website.

These client-branded customized websites are hosted by MWSA on its own server eliminating the need for website maintenance by the issuer. Functionalities include data normalization features across various services and loan products, reporting functions for material performance information, accommodating customizable cross-deal reporting, provision of reports in graphical as well as table format and stratification across pools, exporting capability into Excel, and seamless integration with MWSA's other issuer and bond administration tools.

18.4 CDO TOOLS FOR ASSET MANAGERS

`CDOnet Asset Manager (CDOnet AM)` is capable of managing all types of cash and synthetic CDOs and enables users to perform compliance testing, and run cash flow analysis and hypothetical trades.

The tool's collateral history module has an interface to the custom-reporting facility enabling accurate performance reporting either individually or at a pool group level.

Since `CDOnet AM` uses the same waterfall and analytics tools used by investors and underwriters, managers are enabled to run pre-close and post-close analysis similar to that run by originators and investors.

As the tool is also linked into MWSA's global CDO deal library, users are enabled to compare the past and current performance of their deals as well as comparing forecasts for future expected performance.

Asset types that CDOnet AM handles are corporate bonds, bank loans, ABS/MBS, short/long CDSs, caps, floors, and collars; and multiple currencies are also supported.

CDOnet's collateral administration comprises an asset database that contains historic information and that can be centrally administered and updated (Asset master). It provides an interface into clients' proprietary back-office systems and produces daily exception reports for cash reconciliation purposes.

The product's robust tools enable transparent modeling so that users can see and drill down into all components of a transaction. This is complemented by templates for the generation of cash and synthetic CDOs whereas more complex transactions can be structured with the help of its powerful scripting language. The tool permits and supports features such as incentive management fees, customizable reinvestment assumptions, multiple currency transactions, tie-out of equity return pre close and the easy import and export of data. CDOnet uses the CDOcalc tool to produce relevant investor reporting.

Like other MWSA tools, it contains an API and macro language enabling users to call a large objects-and-routines library. Multiple languages exist for C++, Visual Basis, and VBA users to support such function calls that can be used to manipulate CDOnet's data, cash flows, and analytics and, hence, supports integration in users' existing proprietary applications or other vendors' systems.

The integrated Monte Carlo engine for cash flow, synthetic, and hybrid structures can be used to imply risk-neutral probabilities of default from CDS spreads. It supports the handling of stochastic recovery rates via beta distribution, calculates tranche details, and runs T-copulas for default dependencies. Through this model engine users can obtain tranche prices, loss-given defaults (LGDs), and hedging ratios.

Since asset managers typically want to be able to manage multiple deals simultaneously, the tool's multi-deal asset management functionality with its ability to execute batch updates, manage bank loans, and batch trading facilities enables users to do just that. Deal data maintenance is easier and more efficient via the tool's SQL server functionality which facilitates a single centralized relational database file structure and depository.

The underlying CDO deal library allows running comparisons as well as linking the underlying CDOs in a CDO-squared deal to the firm's comprehensive CDO deal library which provides dynamic cash flows.

18.5 CDOEdge FOR STRUCTURERS

CDOEdge provides CDO structurers access to the same tool that Moody's analysts use to rate and monitor cash CDOs.

The tool's structure and waterfall engine enable users to create, view, and edit structure files. The engine's design means that cash flows can be run through the structure more than 100× faster than in Excel and waterfalls are displayed in a concise and intuitive graphical format.

Structurers using CDOEdge can either use prepackaged CDOEdge models to structure their transactions or, alternatively, integrate their own proprietary models. Users can also use Moody's Binominal which is the model of choice for the agency's analysts to analyze the impact of collateral and structural changes and to estimate ratings.

The data library provides subscription access to Moody's comprehensive CDO deal library which contains deal structures that are maintained by the agency's team of analysts resulting in one of the most accurate structure templates available. Alternatively, structurers can create, save, and maintain their own structure files.

18.6 CDOnet UNDERWRITER

`CDOnet Underwriter` can be used to structure any type of deal for any asset class and for the whole deal lifecycle. It links to third-party vendors and incorporates rating agency methodologies, allows users to import and export their deal-specific data, and, via running cash flow projections, can be used to optimize the target deal structure.

Underwriters can create their own scripts supported by a sophisticated macro language giving them the ability to control and execute a multitude of functions—significantly reducing the time that's normally needed to run periodic batch jobs or other routine tasks.

The robust structuring tool provides a transparent modeling interface allowing users to see and visualize all components of a transaction. Cash deals as well as synthetic CDOs can easily be set up with the help of templates supplemented by the tool's powerful scripting language, which can be used for more complex transactions. Similar to other products in the MWSA suite, the tool permits and supports features such as incentive management fees, customizable reinvestment assumptions, multiple currency transactions, tie-out of equity return pre close, and easy import and export of data.

One of the leading cash flow analytics systems, the tool's capabilities include default analysis; Monte Carlo simulations; running various interest rate, prepayment, and currency scenarios; calculation of current and historic returns; first-loss and breakeven analysis; rating agency–style testing of tranche sizing and relevant capital structures; multiple scenario and deal analysis; and cross-deal analytics.

The `S&P Credit Solver` simplifies the process of satisfying S&P ratings criteria for CDO underwriters:

- When structuring a deal, underwriters are limited by S&P's minimum requirements for first-loss levels under a variety of interest rate scenarios, loss timings, and loss distributions; and tranches must pass all these scenarios in order to satisfy the requirements necessary to achieve a particular rating.
- By creating most of the scenarios based on a few inputs, this process can be greatly automated using this tool and structurers can subsequently run and test these scenarios for all tranches in a batch job. Consequently, this reduces the time and effort necessary to meet and test S&P's criteria in `CDOnet` significantly.

19

Principia Partners: The Principia Structured Finance Platform

Recent industry reforms aim to ensure that any investor with an interest in structured finance has the operational backbone and information to support the necessary level of risk oversight and understanding of their investments. Since 1995, Principia Partners has been dedicated to the innovation, development, and support of software that addresses the ever changing requirements of structured finance market participants.

The founding partners—Theresa Adams, Brian Donnally, and Woodward Hoffman—bring over three decades of structured finance and capital markets experience to the company, having held senior management positions in institutions such as Drexel Burnham Lambert, Republic National Bank of New York, Salomon Brothers, and Mercadian Capital.

The `Principia Structured Finance Platform (Principia SFP)` is an end-to-end software solution used by financial institutions and independent investment managers. It provides an operational platform to help them understand and manage their structured credit and fixed income instruments from front to back office. Principia aims to provide the most comprehensive solution available for the consolidated management of the specific deal analysis, risk surveillance, compliance reporting, and accounting activities unique to ABS, MBS, CDO, and structured fixed income portfolios.

It unifies the unique data, analysis, reporting, and operational requirements of these portfolios on a dedicated platform. The ability to drill down and monitor underlying collateral helps portfolio managers to evaluate and optimize investments while risk managers can quickly identify and manage sensitivities and exposures across the entire business.

Principia SFP provides the operational backbone to overcome the proliferation of, and limitations caused by, the use of multiple ancillary systems and resource-intensive spreadsheets. By integrating activities across the deal lifecycle it helps to increase transparency, accuracy, and workflow control—from portfolio management, through risk oversight, and into accounting.

The platform supports the full range of assets, liabilities, and hedging instruments. It includes core modules for market-ready investment and risk analysis, standardized risk, performance, accounting and operational reports and out-of-the-box workflows for rapid implementation. Additionally, it is built within a fully customizable framework so business-specific workflows, reports, and processes can be created. The solution is available on a hosted subscription-based software-as-a-service basis, or can be fully deployed onsite under license, depending on individual clients' requirements.

Following consultation with users and industry participants, Principia was awarded *Credit* magazine's annual Technology Innovation Award in 2008, 2009, and 2010. This recognizes continued innovation in the creation of new products that provide a clear benefit to participants in the credit and structured finance markets.

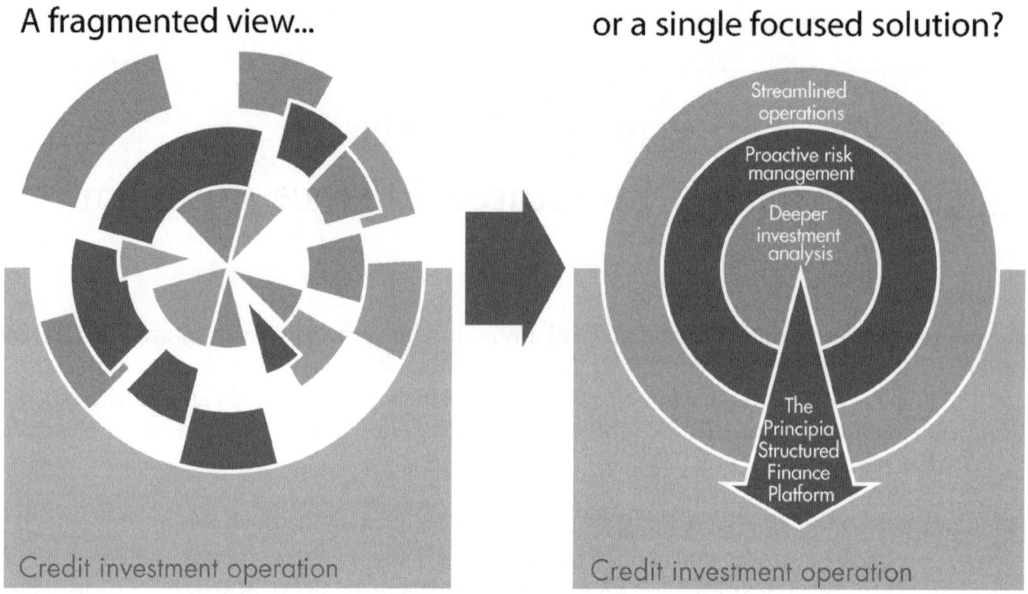

Figure 19.1. Benefits of `Principia SFP`—know your investments.
Source: Principia Partners LLC.

Table 19.1. Benefits of `Principia SFP`—know your investments

Deeper investment analysis	• Unify performance and deal data from any source for on-demand portfolio analysis • Insight into future performance with advanced cash flow analytics and forecasting • Slice and dice by any combination of collateral, deal, or portfolio characteristics • Assets, liabilities, and hedges in one place to analyze across deals and portfolios
Proactive risk management	• Define, analyze, track, and report on collateral performance to highlight sensitivities • Stress interest, default, delinquency, and prepay rates to better forecast behavior • Process and disseminate risk reports for any stratification of the business • Maintain accurate and timely internal, investor, and regulatory compliance
Streamlined operations	• Centrally manage all deals and portfolios to increase efficiency and transparency • Operational backbone from deal analysis, through risk control and into accounting • Eliminate inconsistencies and maintain audit control from front to back office • Establish rules-based workflows to ensure operational compliance and efficiency

Source: Principia Partners LLC.

19.1 PORTFOLIO MANAGEMENT

Following the market events of late 2007, 2008, and 2009, structured finance investors have been made aware in the most dramatic way possible that it is not enough to rely on credit ratings or apply standard fixed income analytics (e.g., duration or convexity) to a structured investment portfolio. The complex nature of the investments and the unique support provided by the securities' underlying collateral mean that changes in the market (e.g., interest rates, house prices, prepayment rates) have a very different effect on a structured finance investment compared with a standard fixed income instrument.

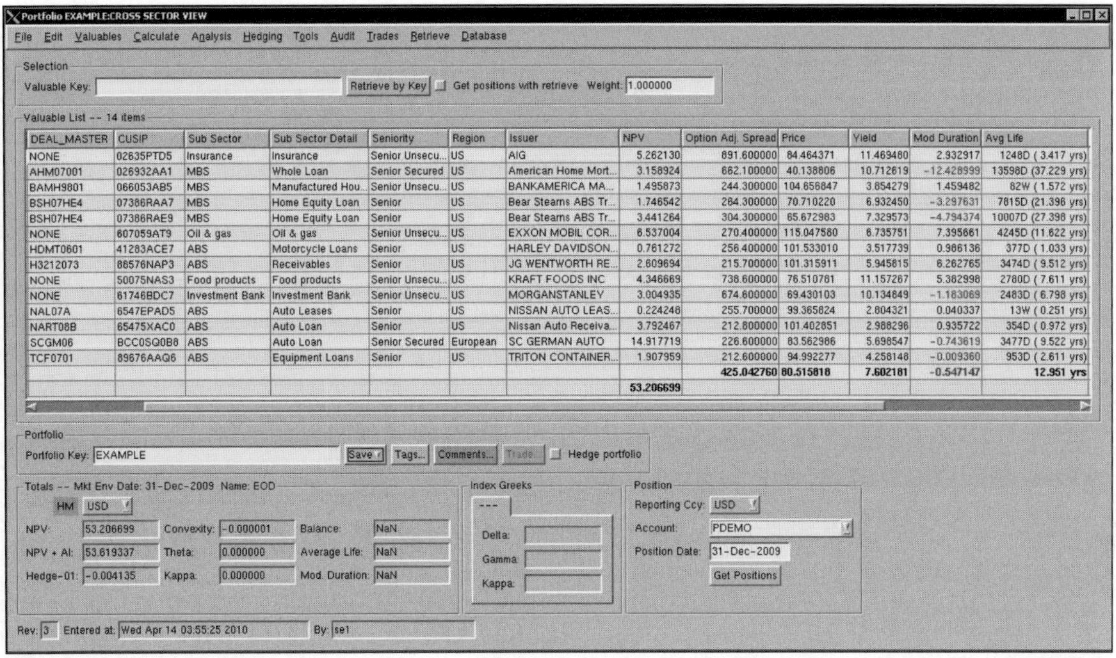

Figure 19.2. Consolidated portfolio view of ABS and MBS positions, associated calculations and sector descriptions.
Source: Principia Partners LLC.

To fully understand an investment, investors need to perform the necessary drill-down analysis, value and project cash flows, or run scenario analysis under stressed collateral prepayment and delinquency assumptions. The misunderstanding of a deal or portfolio can lead to serious material losses, major breaches of compliance, and reputational damage.

`Principia SFP`'s portfolio management capabilities provide an intuitive framework for front-office functions including asset structuring, deal capture, funding, liability management, and hedging activities.

The portfolio management component of `Principia SFP` provides powerful transaction analysis and user-configurable views of asset positions, outstanding issues, and hedges. Importantly though, the portfolio management interface can be used for the valuation of anything from a plain vanilla swap, to a complex and full-blown hedge or the scenario analysis of a portfolio consisting of many transactions.

The portfolio management interface can be user-defined to serve the specific requirements of multiple users. It is a portfolio "scratchpad", an asset-structuring tool and a risk manager's analytical environment. Information can be manipulated by any combination whether at the business line, portfolio, deal, tranche, or collateral level.

19.1.1 Investment analysis and deal structuring

It is now critical to be able to continually monitor bond issuance data and underlying collateral performance information. With disparate data sources and portfolio management systems used to meet the varying requirements of different asset classes, consolidating data and dynamic collateral

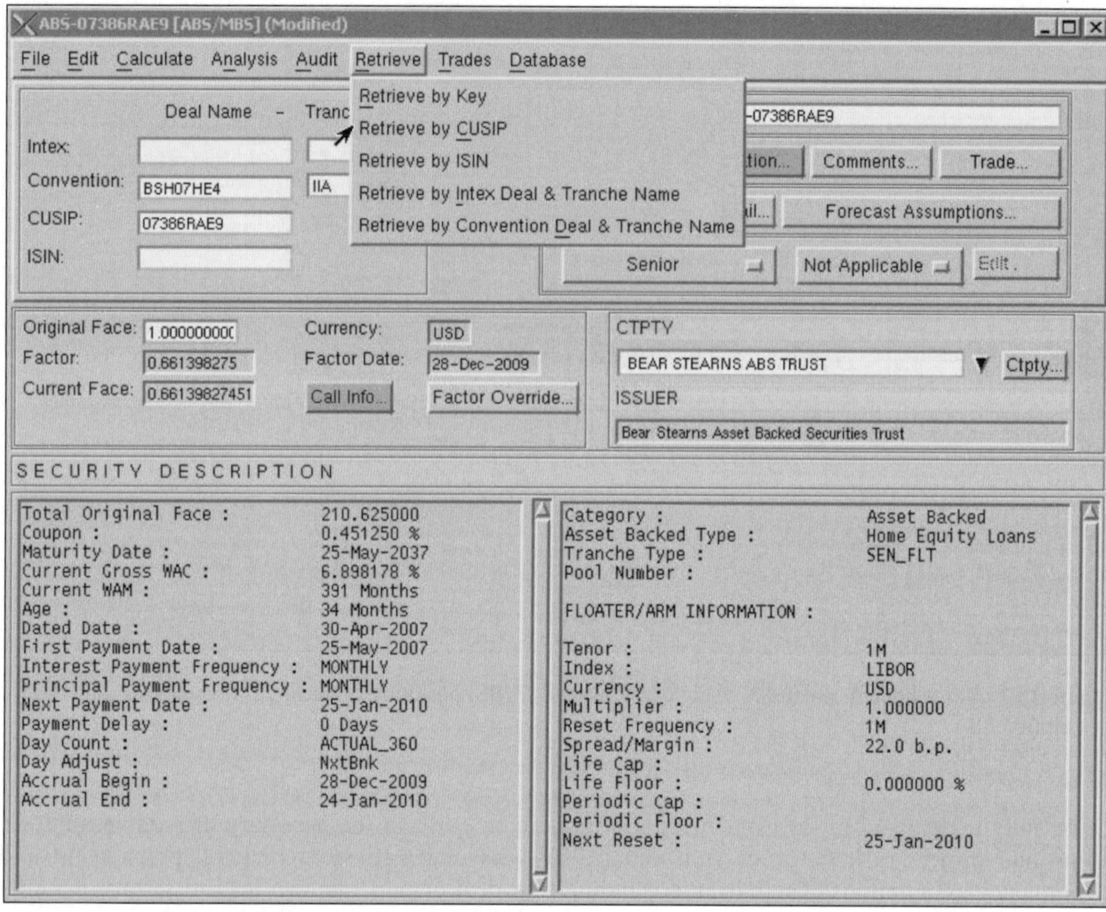

Figure 19.3. Asset interface.
Source: Principia Partners LLC.

information is no easy task. Principia SFP has been developed to provide support for all levels of the deal structure (underlying collateral, tranche, and deal master) to perform in-depth deal analysis, cash flow analysis, and forecasting (including prepayment, default, and delinquency).

This is supplemented with the ability to integrate and normalize deal structure information, issuance data, and performance data for multiple assets from multiple issuers and industry data providers (such as Intex™ and Lewtan™, see Chapters 16 and 17, respectively) alongside internal research.

Principia SFP's investment analytics integrate industry-standard structuring capabilities, with issuance and performance data, to give clients the sophisticated portfolio management and risk assessment tools they need to thoroughly understand their investments.

19.1.2 Product support: assets, liabilities, and hedges in one place

From vanilla to highly structured products, Principia SFP provides a flexible interface for creating and managing the wide array of assets and financial instruments used in the management of structured finance portfolios. These range from loans with simple cash flows to more complicated structured

Table 19.2. `Principia SFP` coverage

Assets	*Funding instruments*	*Derivatives*
Receivables ABS/MBS/CDO Municipals Corporates Sovereign bonds High-yield bonds FRNs Loans	Debt issuance Repos MTN programs Commercial paper	Interest rate derivatives Credit derivatives FX derivatives Equity index derivatives *Vanilla and highly structured*

Source: Principia Partners LLC.

products, hedges, and complex derivatives. Users can access, monitor, and manage all asset positions, liabilities, and associated hedging products from a single platform. The changing relationships between these instruments can be called upon, analyzed, audited, and managed throughout the portfolio lifecycle and into accounting.

From a securities perspective, the coverage includes asset-backed securities (ABS), mortgage-backed securities (MBS), collateralized debt obligations (CDOs), corporate, sovereign, and financial bonds and loans. Additionally, `Principia SFP` offers dedicated interfaces to both Intex and Lewtan. This allows users to structure and monitor cash flow projections based on specified prepayments (including prepayment models from Andrew Davidson & Co.) and define and drill into collateral performance.

Product support also encompasses asset receivables (including trade, credit card, auto loans, and equipment leases) as well as credit derivative products (including credit default swaps and single-tranche CDOs).

In addition, the asset management interface captures and calculates the fees associated with the management of individual or multiple business units. These include credit support, liquidity support, and administrative fees, which flow downstream into accounting and operations.

19.1.3 Capture the entire deal structure

Investors need to capture all the static deal information and dynamic tranche issuance data when structuring and monitoring their deals. Within `Principia SFP`, tranches can be evaluated in the context of the original securitization or across all the deals being managed in a portfolio. It allows these data to be analyzed alongside collateral pool performance data from any specified internal or external source.

Bond-level trustee data (e.g., static data such as names of swap providers, the servicer, and the original balance; or dynamic data such as the percentage of fixed rate loans, principal paid, and credit enhancement applied) can be processed on receipt of updated trustee and servicer reports through a dedicated external XML interface. Investors can then monitor deal performance at a glance (e.g., percentage of loans outstanding by geography) and supplement this information with proprietary internal analysis to make informed decisions about the investment.

19.1.4 Forecasting assumptions

`Principia SFP` allows you to forecast prepayments, defaults, loss severity, and delinquencies for ABS and MBS assets. This functionality allows portfolio and risk managers to have the flexibility to

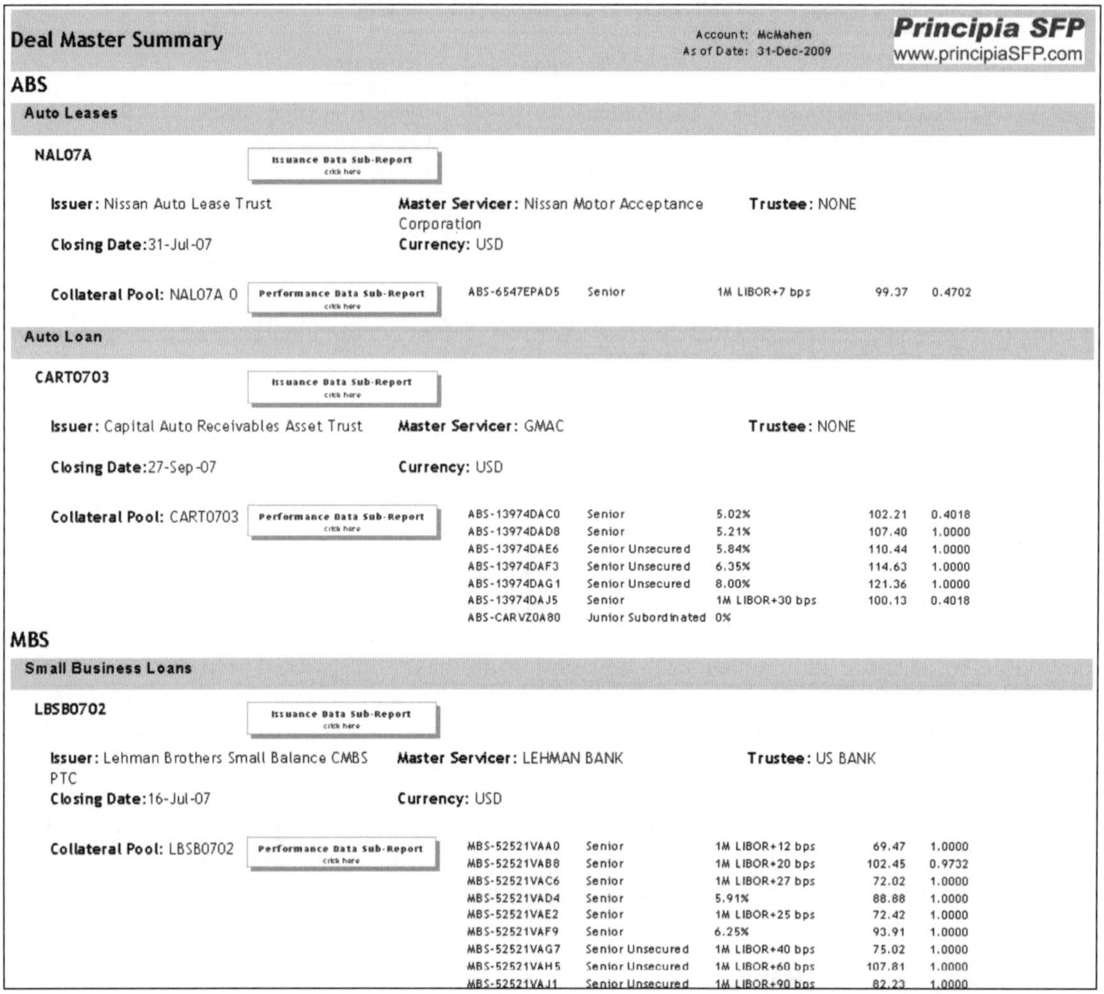

Figure 19.4. Deal structure view. `Principia SFP` holds the entire deal structure from deal description to critical collateral, tranche, and credit enhancement details.
Source: Principia Partners LLC.

stress-test individual deals or to apply assumptions across multiple tranches. With the platform's dedicated interface to Intex, for example, users can upload Intex deal data into the database and perform forecast calculations directly from the platform.

Integrating all the necessary issuance and performance data and with the ability to monitor the changing performance of underlying collateral, forecasting assumptions in `Principia SFP` allow users to apply hypothetical stresses to performance measures and identify how these scenarios may affect future cash flows.

Forecasting can be applied on an *ad hoc* basis or saved for ongoing reporting. With increasing scrutiny on the nature of the assumptions made throughout the term of a deal and the need for disclosure of these assumptions throughout the lifecycle, this functionality adds value to third-party performance data by automating the adjusted cash flow projections so they flow through to risk reporting, compliance, and accounting.

Such stress-testing can also be automated within `Principia SFP`'s risk scripting framework to provide on-demand or automated end-of-day risk analysis reports.

19.1.5 Interrogate portfolios: "Slicing and dicing"

Portfolio managers are presented with many barriers when trying to accurately pool and summarize portfolio or deal information for analysis. Often, integration problems between spreadsheets and systems, a need for additional processing scripts, or a lack of consistent data can lead to time-consuming or insufficient analysis. `Principia SFP`'s `Portfolio Query` allows users to define, save, and execute dynamic portfolio queries based on existing or potential trades. It provides a way to filter trades based on attributes like trade status and product type, combined with performance or bond issuance data attributes. These queries can be saved and modified and any changes to the underlying portfolio data will be reflected upon execution of a query.

The query criteria consist of a wide range of valuable and trade-based fields, including all asset classification fields, product types, sector and subsector definitions. Up to 15 different query criteria can be entered at once and then combined using advanced specifications.

Once saved, a query can be stored in the system for direct execution within portfolio management and for use in the Principia application interface, `Principia XTP`.

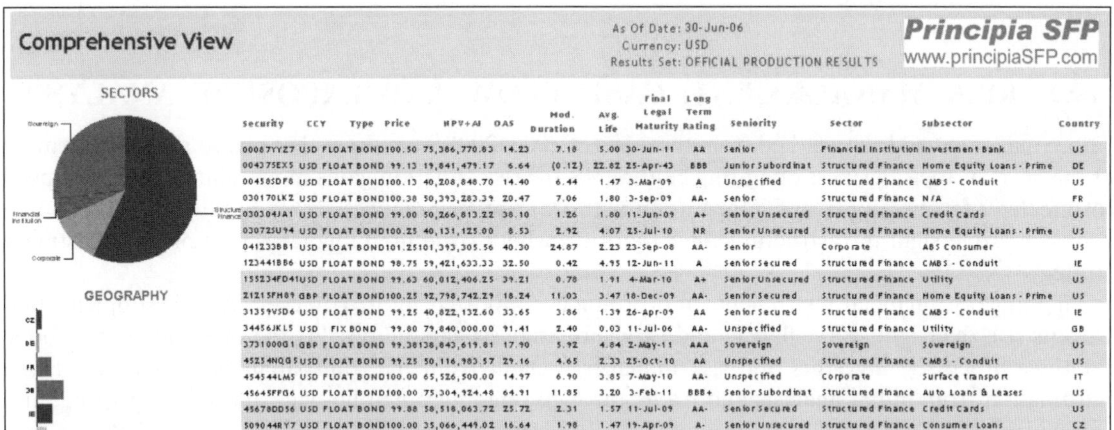

Figure 19.5. Portfolio composition report: "Slice and dice" to see tranches or portfolios by cash flows, sectors, ratings, or any other performance-level or bond-level attribute.
Source: Principia Partners LLC.

19.1.6 Managing funding and hedging requirements

Users can manage funding strategies across one or several business entities or operating units. The funding strategy represents the liability inventory to finance the asset position in need of funding. It then allocates the daily accrued funding interest to each asset assigned to the funding group—based on the allocation amount.

For many credit investment managers, maintaining a market-neutral position remains an important aspect of satisfying operating guidelines and prudent risk management. Within `Principia SFP`, users can easily apply default system recommendations for hedges and hedging strategies, built on proven capital market formulations. Hedging may be applied by instrument, portfolio, or business unit or even by groups of instrument types.

19.1.7 Mark-to-market valuations

The accurate valuation of derivatives is a fundamental aspect of an investment manager's activities. Portfolios may contain a wide range of securities and associated derivative instruments which require more sophisticated analytics. `Principia SFP` provides the valuation capabilities at both the portfolio level and the individual instrument level.

Principia is unique in the marketplace in collecting and distributing daily closing data, further reducing clients' operational efforts. These data allow clients to obtain end-of-day market valuations for their derivatives and funding instruments.

19.2 RISK MANAGEMENT: CASH FLOW AND EXPOSURE ANALYSIS

Those that emerged least scathed from the crisis of 2007–2009 were those that placed risk management at the heart of their business operating culture. As the risk function gains more influence and the need for greater interoperability and cooperation with front-office practices grows, organizations require a robust risk oversight infrastructure. This is critical where structured finance is part of the investment strategy.

The range of financial instruments and products supported by `Principia SFP` is supplemented with its risk oversight, surveillance, and exposure analysis capabilities. As the operational backbone for these processes, investors and risk managers benefit from the transparent flow and use of risk information from initial analysis and trade, through ongoing portfolio-wide analysis, reporting, and compliance.

Investing in structured finance is different from investing in more traditional vanilla instruments. The risks call for a tailored due diligence process. IOSCO's findings in 2009 highlighted that investment managers should analyze the underlying assets of structured finance instruments, including the availability, reliability, and relevance of information available, both on the market and on the underlying assets. In addition, IOSCO suggested that analyzing the structure itself—both in "normal" and in "stress" scenarios along with analysis of other structural features—and questioning whether the price is right for the risks taken on behalf of investors should form an integral part of investment managers' due diligence best practices.

When conducting that analysis, investment managers must ensure that all the relevant risks are identified and assessed. Although the focus often tends to be on market risk (including risks linked to market parameters such as interest rates), other types of risks must not be disregarded. In particular, recent market events have shown that structured finance instruments often embed a liquidity risk and counterparty or issuer risk that should be carefully assessed.

19.2.1 Exposure analysis: Securities portfolio reporting and compliance

Gaining a complete understanding of overall portfolio composition is fundamental to understanding the exposures and sensitivities affecting a portfolio of assets and its associated instruments. This is influenced by whether an organization can gain a consolidated and detailed summary of any given portfolio on request. In organizations that use multiple systems, databases, and spreadsheets, achieving this level of portfolio transparency can be a major operational challenge.

`Principia SFP` provides the flexibility to summarize the details of a portfolio(s) and supplement this view with all the granular information about the asset characteristics therein. Risk managers are able to get a snapshot of potential exposures, with a clear view on factors such as asset diversification, concentrations (e.g., ratings), and geographical or sector distribution.

Beyond cash flow analysis, structured finance operations may be subject to additional tests on asset portfolios that are mandated by the managers and risk surveillance teams of the organization. For structures that depend on the characteristics of assets to meet certain ratings or performance criteria more intensive portfolio compliance and monitoring techniques are required.

It was well documented during the crisis that many financial institutions and structured finance operations failed to effectively monitor the triggers and limits established as part of their investment and compliance guidelines. Performing daily and periodic exposure analysis to meet a broad range of compliance and surveillance tests is a core activity for `Principia SFP` users. Integrated compliance limit features are driven by a dedicated compliance engine. This exposure information flows into a wide variety of standard compliance reports.

Portfolio Report

Account: MCMAHEN
As Of Date: 31-Dec-09
Currency: USD
Results Set: 1PRODUCTION RESULTS

Principia SFP
www.principiaSFP.com

Asset	Market Value	Average Life (Days)	CCY	Sector	Sub-Sector	Sub-Sector Detail	Country	Final Legal Maturity	Long Term Rating
ABS-XS0266760700	14,940,292.44	9.52	EUR	Structured Finance	ABS	Auto Loan	DE	10-Jul-19	AA+
CORP-607059AT9	6,722,142.02	11.62	USD	Corporate	Oil & gas	Oil & gas	US	15-Aug-21	AAA
MBS-52521VAH5	5,761,996.36	27.48	USD	Structured Finance	MBS	Small Business Loans	US	25-Jun-37	NR
FIN-02635PTD5	5,292,501.54	3.42	USD	Financial Institution	Insurance	Insurance	US	1-Jun-13	B-
CORP-50075NAS3	4,490,275.36	7.61	USD	Corporate	Food products	Food products	US	11-Aug-17	BB-
MBS-XS0370504820	3,983,692.80	42.15	GBP	Structured Finance	MBS	Whole Loan	GB	17-Feb-52	AAA
ABS-65475XAC0	3,799,880.14	0.97	USD	Structured Finance	ABS	Auto Loan	US	15-Apr-12	AA+
MBS-07386RAE9	3,441,527.02	27.40	USD	Structured Finance	MBS	Home Equity Loan	US	25-May-37	NR
MBS-026932AA1	3,159,266.18	37.23	USD	Structured Finance	MBS	Whole Loan	US	25-Mar-47	NR
FIN-61746BDC7	3,013,700.60	6.80	USD	Financial Institution	Investment Bank	Investment Bank	US	18-Oct-16	A+
ABS-36159EAA0	2,943,093.01	9.17	USD	Structured Finance	ABS	Small Business Loans	US	16-Nov-34	AA+
ABS-88576NAP3	2,620,998.24	9.10	USD	Structured Finance	ABS	Receivables	US	15-Aug-35	AA+
MBS-65537FAA9	2,620,419.26	16.82	USD	Structured Finance	MBS	Home Equity Loan	US	25-Jul-36	CCC
MBS-88522UAP2	2,454,674.49	28.38	USD	Structured Finance	MBS	Whole Loan	US	25-Apr-38	NR
MBS-55660AAD4	2,439,664.73	22.23	USD	Structured Finance	MBS	Manufactured Housing Loan	US	25-Mar-32	NR
MBS-33736XFT1	2,433,921.86	2.06	USD	Structured Finance	MBS	CMBS - Conduit	US	12-Jan-12	NR
MBS-52521VAB8	1,947,336.87	27.48	USD	Structured Finance	MBS	Small Business Loans	US	25-Jun-37	NR
ABS-89676AAQ6	1,908,083.74	2.61	USD	Structured Finance	ABS	Equipment Loans	US	26-Feb-15	AA+
ABS-15132CAJ1	1,842,193.75	1.01	USD	Structured Finance	ABS	Floorplan	US	21-Mar-12	AA+
MBS-07386RAA7	1,746,638.83	21.40	USD	Structured Finance	MBS	Home Equity Loan	US	25-May-31	NR
ABS-25151NAA1	1,592,116.34	17.95	USD	Structured Finance	ABS	Whole Loan	US	1-Sep-37	AA+
MBS-066053AB5	1,501,658.91	1.57	USD	Structured Finance	MBS	Manufactured Housing Loan	US	10-Apr-23	NR
MBS-60935LAC1	1,407,030.61	18.12	USD	Structured Finance	MBS	Small Business Loans	US	15-Feb-28	NR
ABS-05377RAA2	1,356,780.51	2.43	USD	Structured Finance	ABS	Floorplan	US	20-Aug-12	AA+
ABS-250854AD8	1,276,364.74	0.68	USD	Structured Finance	ABS	Receivables	US	1-Mar-13	AA+
MBS-33736XFV6	924,748.93	2.15	USD	Structured Finance	MBS	CMBS - Conduit	US	12-Feb-12	NR
ABS-41283ACE7	762,951.32	1.03	USD	Structured Finance	ABS	Motorcycle Loans	US	15-Oct-12	AA+
MBS-38373M4M9	450,715.85	17.66	USD	Structured Finance	MBS	Commercial Mortgage	US	16-Aug-27	NR
MBS-55660AAC6	325,293.72	22.23	USD	Structured Finance	MBS	Manufactured Housing Loan	US	25-Mar-32	NR
ABS-6547EPAD5	224,280.34	0.25	USD	Structured Finance	ABS	Auto Leases	US	15-Feb-13	AAA
US_TRESASURY4375NOV39	16,406.25	29.87	USD	Sovereign	Sovereign	Sovereign	US	15-Nov-39	AAA
US_TREASURY325DEC16	135.42	7.00	USD	Sovereign	Sovereign	Sovereign	US	31-Dec-16	AAA

Figure 19.6. Portfolio summary report sample.
Source: Principia Partners LLC.

Table 19.3. Standard compliance and other summary reports

Diversification/Composition	*Portfolio*
ABS composition Financial composition Corporate composition Sovereign composition Portfolio composition Rating composition Geographical composition	Portfolio distribution Weighted average life Collateral performance Portfolio deal master Tranche performance Guarantor/Wrapped exposure
Market sensitivity	*Liquidity risk/capital adequacy*
Parallel yield curve shift Point-to-point yield curve shift Foreign exchange rate shift	Net cumulative outflow Eligible liquidity Liquidity coverage Capital leverage and adequacy

Source: Principia Partners LLC.

The compliance engine calculates and then pushes the data to be used for securities compliance reporting to a relational database. It performs the calculations and data processing according to rules specified by runtime parameters.

Diversification may be an essential component of the investment mandate. The asset manager needs to ensure that the portfolio complies with pre-established limits on an ongoing basis. These may include concentration limits with respect to geography, industry, ratings, or counterparties. For example, investment policy may dictate that a given business unit must have at least 90% of its credit portfolio invested in securities rated A or above. `Principia SFP`'s rules library allows clients to fully customize their compliance policies within the system. The results of compliance tests are then displayed on reports with a `PASS` or `FAIL` tag.

Maintaining a market-neutral portfolio may be mission critical. In this situation, daily market sensitivity reporting is key to demonstrating that any exposure to interest rate or currency movements has been effectively managed.

Organizations can gain a complete understanding of exposures to structured finance investments across business lines (whether on balance sheet or off balance sheet) and apply surveillance and compliance controls for individual business units as well as for the organization as a whole.

In the past, creating new reports has been regarded as a slow and painful process. In `Principia SFP` it is possible to create customized intuitive reports, without having to use code or develop script. This drag-and-drop functionality opens up the use and creation of reports to more sophisticated business users and frees up time for investors to focus on their core activities.

19.2.2 Stress-testing

For more advanced assets and hedging instruments, the system provides robust capital market sensitivity analysis functionality. These include

- Yield curve shifts and tilts
- Credit curve shifts
- FX rate and volatility shifts
- Cross-product basis shifts
- Prepayment, default, and recovery stress-testing.

ABS Composition Test By Category

Account: MCMAHEN
As Of Date: 31-Dec-09
Currency: USD
Results Set: 1PRODUCTION_RESULTS

Principia SFP
www.principiaSFP.com

Sub-Sector	Market Value	% of Portfolio	Limit	Test Result
Auto Leases	224,280.34	0.26%	12.50%	PASS
Auto Loans & Leases	18,740,172.59	21.44%	10.00%	FAIL
CMBS - Conduit	3,358,670.79	3.84%	25.00%	PASS
Commercial Mortgage	450,715.85	0.52%	12.50%	PASS
Equipment Loans	1,908,083.74	2.18%	10.00%	PASS
Floorplan	3,198,974.26	3.66%	25.00%	PASS
Home Equity Loan	7,808,585.10	8.93%	25.00%	PASS
Manufactured Housing Loan	4,266,617.37	4.88%	5.00%	PASS
Motorcycle Loans	762,951.32	0.87%	25.00%	PASS
Receivables	3,897,362.98	4.46%	15.00%	PASS
Small Business Loans	12,059,456.84	13.80%	25.00%	PASS
Whole Loan	11,189,749.81	12.80%	10.00%	FAIL
Total Finance Assets	67,865,620.98	77.65%	100.00%	PASS

Ratings Composition Test

Account: MCMAHEN
As Of Date: 31-Dec-09
Currency: USD
Results Set: EXAMPLE

Principia SFP
www.principiaSFP.com

Rating	Market Value	Limit (m)	Test Result	% of Portfolio	Limit	Test Result
AAA/Aaa	10,946,656.83	60	PASS	18.49%	100%	PASS
AA/Aa	34,990,091.10	36	PASS	59.10%	60%	PASS
A/A	3,013,700.60	6	PASS	5.09%	10%	PASS
BB/Ba	10,252,271.72	3	FAIL	17.32%	5%	FAIL

Figure 19.7. Compliance test sample reports.
Source: Principia Partners LLC.

These analyses can be run in any combination on an individual transaction or on a portfolio of transactions, across the entire range of products (financial assets, funding instruments, and derivatives) using consistent methodologies on a common platform.

`Principia SFP` can calculate a full range of Greeks and sensitivities—ranging from term structures of DV01, convexity, theta and vega to index duration, effective convexity, average life, and option-adjusted spread (OAS).

Clients can specify their market environment and understand how the application of standard or client-specific scenarios would affect cash flow and valuations for both individual securities and the portfolio as a whole. Such stress-testing can be applied across any of the factors that affect valuations and cash flows (such as interest rates, basis and spread curves, exchange rates, prepayments, credit curves, delinquencies, recoveries, and option volatilities).

Risk managers need to regularly perform scenario analysis and measure portfolio performance. For this reason, Principia introduced `Principia XTP`—a scripting language that allows clients to save any scenario they devise and run it at any defined time. `Principia XTP` automates the stress-testing process and allows the same scenarios, with the same assumptions and forecasts, to be run at regular intervals.

19.2.3 Deal monitoring and performance analytics

In today's environment the ability to track, monitor, analyze, and report on collateral pool performance and bond issuance information is fundamental. `Principia SFP` allows users to

Table 19.4. Stress-testing

		Prepayment			
Default	*Data*	*0% PSA*	*50% PSA*	*100% PSA*	*150% PSA*
0% CDR	NPV WAL (years)	5.73 5.0	5.72 4.7	5.71 4.4	5.70 4.1
4% CDR	NPV WAL (years)	5.72 4.6	5.71 4.3	5.70 4.1	5.69 3.9
8% CDR	NPV WAL (years)	5.71 4.2	5.70 4.0	5.69 3.8	5.69 3.7
12% CDR	NPV WAL (years)	5.70 3.9	5.69 3.8	5.68 3.6	5.68 3.5
16% CDR	NPV WAL (years)	5.69 3.7	5.68 3.6	5.68 3.5	5.67 3.4
20% CDR	NPV WAL (years)	5.69 3.9	5.68 3.8	5.67 3.6	5.67 3.3

Source: Principia Partners LLC.

consistently and efficiently manage ongoing collateral performance data, regardless of the asset class or data source. Portfolio managers, risk analysts, and compliance staff can choose from a comprehensive set of over 300 predefined performance measures to "slice and dice" portfolios.

This includes the ability to monitor, analyze, and report on LTV (loan-to-value) ratios and cumulative loss at the deal level; to stress-test default, recovery, and prepayment rates; and the ability to view the 30, 60, or 90-day delinquency rate of the collateral pool or any stratification of that pool. Managers and administrators can define key attributes of the performance measures they wish to track. Different measures may be tracked at different levels within the deal hierarchy as follows:

- Deal (e.g., cumulative loss)
- Tranche (e.g., average life, principal payment, or excess spread)
- Collateral (e.g., foreclosure or delinquency rates)
- Credit enhancement (e.g., fund names, type, and level).

Clients can also add their own performance measures, as demanded by the requirements of their business. `Principia SFP` brings in performance data via a general XML interface, as well as through native adaptors to industry providers like Lewtan and Intex. These dedicated interfaces allow the performance metrics specified by these vendors to be tracked and used as standard throughout the deal lifecycle.

Fully integrated ongoing performance measurement and the centralized management of all the deals in a portfolio provide the basis from which to perform rigorous stress-testing. User-defined performance metrics that can be monitored at the collateral level of a deal help to deliver the sound oversight, risk management, risk surveillance, and analytics practices that many structured finance market participants lacked before the financial crisis.

Performance surveillance reports can be created on demand with the definition and straight-through processing of collateral pool performance metrics. In Figures 19.8 and 19.9 you can see how collateral

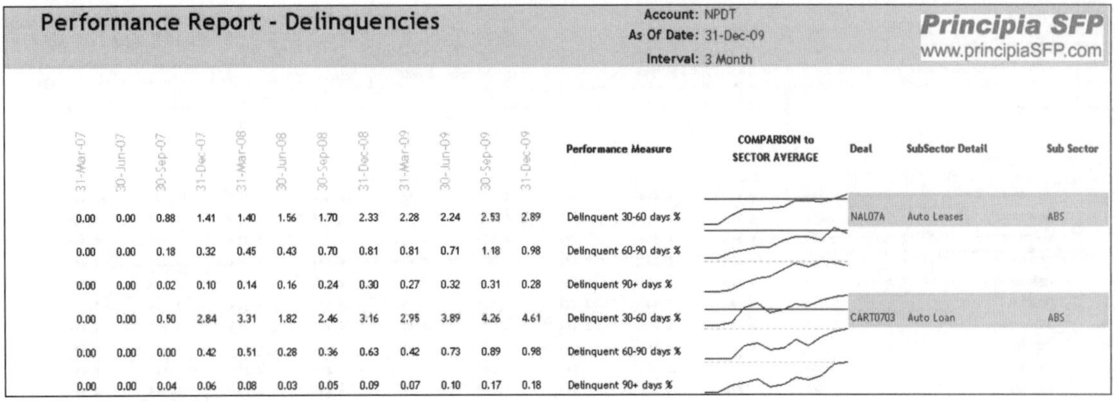

Performance Report - Delinquencies

Account: NPDT
As Of Date: 31-Dec-09
Interval: 3 Month

Principia SFP
www.principiaSFP.com

31-Mar-07	30-Jun-07	30-Sep-07	31-Dec-07	31-Mar-08	30-Jun-08	30-Sep-08	31-Dec-08	31-Mar-09	30-Jun-09	30-Sep-09	31-Dec-09	Performance Measure	COMPARISON to SECTOR AVERAGE	Deal	SubSector Detail	Sub Sector
0.00	0.00	0.88	1.41	1.40	1.56	1.70	2.33	2.28	2.24	2.53	2.89	Delinquent 30-60 days %		NAL07A	Auto Leases	ABS
0.00	0.00	0.18	0.32	0.45	0.43	0.70	0.81	0.81	0.71	1.18	0.98	Delinquent 60-90 days %				
0.00	0.00	0.02	0.10	0.14	0.16	0.24	0.30	0.27	0.32	0.31	0.28	Delinquent 90+ days %				
0.00	0.00	0.50	2.84	3.31	1.82	2.46	3.16	2.95	3.89	4.26	4.61	Delinquent 30-60 days %		CART0703	Auto Loan	ABS
0.00	0.00	0.00	0.42	0.51	0.28	0.36	0.63	0.42	0.73	0.89	0.98	Delinquent 60-90 days %				
0.00	0.00	0.04	0.06	0.08	0.03	0.05	0.09	0.07	0.10	0.17	0.18	Delinquent 90+ days %				

Figure 19.8. Delinquencies snapshot across multiple deals.
Source: Principia Partners LLC.

performance data can be compared over time and across multiple deals. The example shows the different delinquency durations (30–60 days, 60–90 days, or 90 days+) for the selected deals compared with the average delinquency rates across the portfolio. Delinquency rates above the portfolio average are highlighted in gray.

Once uploaded, performance data may be accessed through `Principia SFP`'s compliance engine and portfolio reporting to generate a range of powerful reports. Integration into the compliance engine allows clients to monitor performance deterioration across a large number of performance indicators and asset types.

19.2.4 Derivative counterparty credit exposure

Derivative counterparty credit exposure analysis is available by counterparty (netted and gross), by issuer and reference credit entity, by transaction, by portfolio, by product, or any combination thereof.

Principia has developed a statistical model that calculates potential future loan-equivalent exposures based on statistically derived market scenarios. These potential exposures are calculated with a user-defined standard deviation stressing of interest rates, FX rates, and/or equity indices.

19.2.5 Cash flow analysis

A key characteristic of structured finance portfolios is the dynamic nature of their interest and principal cash flows. `Principia SFP`'s managed scheduling capability helps users manage (and import from any external data source) specific types of flows and schedules. The managed schedule can be modified to reflect actual activity such as drawdowns, paydowns, and amortizations and can be used in conjunction with the system's risk management and cash flow projection tools. Throughout, `Principia SFP` maintains a historical time series record and projects schedules.

Cash flow management and effective liquidity and capital management go hand in hand. The new world demands that financial institutions demonstrate they can accurately manage cash flow exposures for structured finance investments. This control is integral to addressing internal operating guidelines, investor demands for transparency, and compliance with regulatory mandates.

As part of this liquidity monitoring, a manager will often look to daily net cash flows of the operation on a rolling period basis. They may be required to commit liquidity facilities to cover peak

Performance Report

Account: MCMAHEN
As Of Date: 31-Dec-09
Interval: 3 Month

Principia SFP
www.principiaSFP.com

Delinquency	Deal Master	09/30/2007	12/31/2007	03/31/2008	06/30/2008	09/30/2008	12/31/2008	03/31/2009	06/30/2009	09/30/2009	12/31/2009
30-60 Days	AHM07001	0.00%	0.00%	0.00%	5.58%	5.74%	8.21%	11.42%	11.50%	12.32%	11.11%
	BAMH9801	1.17%	1.35%	0.82%	0.88%	1.11%	1.82%	1.04%	1.09%	1.20%	1.31%
	BSH07HE4	4.86%	6.92%	6.65%	7.47%	8.58%	8.63%	6.91%	7.81%	7.49%	8.46%
	CATF07A	N/A	2.97%	4.34%	5.18%	4.70%	5.62%	8.57%	7.80%	7.16%	5.60%
	GEBL0602	0.00%	0.00%	0.00%	0.00%	0.00%	0.19%	0.52%	0.07%	0.00%	0.00%
	HDMT0601	3.32%	3.60%	3.44%	3.56%	4.62%	4.51%	4.10%	4.73%	5.12%	5.45%
	MAMH020A	1.46%	1.67%	1.09%	1.38%	1.33%	1.62%	0.92%	1.01%	1.25%	1.34%
	MSBL9901	0.53%	1.03%	0.76%	0.66%	0.00%	0.00%	1.32%	0.73%	0.81%	8.48%
	NAL07A	0.89%	1.40%	1.39%	1.56%	1.69%	2.32%	2.27%	2.23%	2.52%	2.88%
	NART08B	N/A	N/A	N/A	N/A	0.57%	0.99%	0.95%	1.29%	1.47%	1.40%
	NMHE06F2	5.23%	6.30%	5.64%	4.92%	5.55%	7.31%	5.16%	4.90%	5.04%	4.52%
	THR08001	N/A	N/A	0.69%	0.55%	0.19%	0.97%	1.55%	1.86%	2.03%	1.62%
	Average	1.94%	2.52%	2.26%	2.89%	2.84%	3.52%	3.73%	3.75%	3.87%	4.35%
60-90 Days	AHM07001	0.02%	0.14%	0.16%	2.30%	1.18%	1.77%	2.75%	1.93%	2.02%	2.26%
	BAMH9801	0.43%	0.47%	0.30%	0.20%	0.21%	0.46%	0.26%	0.38%	0.42%	0.57%
	BSH07HE4	3.30%	4.15%	4.03%	3.31%	3.39%	3.82%	4.15%	4.30%	4.69%	4.34%
	CATF07A	N/A	0.71%	1.14%	1.24%	1.79%	1.92%	2.37%	2.53%	2.99%	3.17%
	GEBL0602	0.00%	0.00%	0.00%	0.00%	0.15%	0.80%	0.39%	0.22%	0.28%	0.28%
	HDMT0601	1.32%	1.56%	1.32%	1.13%	1.79%	1.80%	1.35%	1.23%	1.59%	2.16%
	MAMH020A	0.34%	0.43%	0.34%	0.39%	0.46%	0.46%	0.45%	0.45%	0.44%	0.48%
	MSBL9901	1.11%	0.00%	0.00%	0.00%	0.00%	0.00%	0.00%	1.21%	0.18%	1.03%
	NAL07A	0.17%	0.31%	0.44%	0.42%	0.67%	0.80%	0.80%	0.70%	1.19%	0.99%
	NART08B	N/A	N/A	N/A	N/A	0.10%	0.21%	0.20%	0.28%	0.33%	0.33%
	NMHE06F2	3.07%	3.19%	3.00%	3.47%	4.31%	3.46%	4.31%	3.77%	3.80%	4.39%
	THR08001	N/A	N/A	0.06%	1.51%	1.48%	0.50%	1.93%	0.68%	0.36%	1.80%
	Average	1.08%	1.10%	0.98%	1.27%	1.29%	1.33%	1.58%	1.47%	1.53%	1.82%
90+ Days	AHM07001	0.00%	0.11%	0.35%	0.27%	1.77%	2.83%	4.56%	5.82%	7.11%	5.54%
	BAMH9801	0.71%	0.84%	0.46%	0.61%	0.69%	0.59%	0.68%	0.63%	0.83%	0.70%
	BSH07HE4	2.64%	2.30%	8.71%	10.78%	7.02%	7.08%	8.25%	5.68%	13.60%	14.39%
	CATF07A	N/A	0.29%	0.98%	1.82%	2.42%	4.74%	4.79%	8.03%	9.82%	13.70%
	GEBL0602	0.00%	0.00%	0.22%	0.28%	0.40%	0.56%	0.94%	2.22%	3.64%	4.48%
	HDMT0601	0.87%	1.06%	1.24%	0.83%	1.04%	1.68%	1.34%	0.99%	1.24%	1.79%
	MAMH020A	0.93%	0.96%	0.79%	0.65%	0.75%	1.02%	0.99%	1.00%	1.04%	1.08%
	MSBL9901	0.00%	1.16%	0.00%	0.00%	0.00%	0.00%	0.00%	0.00%	1.93%	2.62%
	NAL07A	0.01%	0.09%	0.12%	0.16%	0.23%	0.29%	0.26%	0.33%	0.33%	0.31%
	NART08B	N/A	N/A	N/A	N/A	0.00%	0.05%	0.08%	0.07%	0.07%	0.07%
	NMHE06F2	3.23%	3.80%	4.41%	2.97%	2.18%	6.72%	11.20%	13.64%	14.96%	19.33%
	THR08001	N/A	N/A	0.00%	0.00%	0.66%	0.65%	1.32%	1.74%	2.62%	1.66%
	Average	0.93%	1.06%	1.57%	1.67%	1.43%	2.18%	2.87%	3.35%	4.77%	5.47%

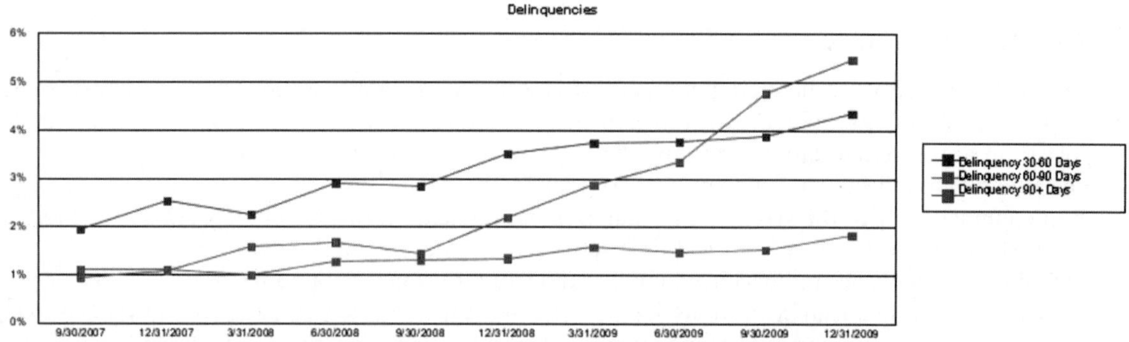

Figure 19.9. Another delinquencies snapshot across multiple deals.
Source: Principia Partners LLC.

Full Cash Movements

Start Date: 31-Dec-09
End Date: 31-Jan-10
Position Date: 31-Dec-09
Cash Postings: No

Principia SFP
www.principiaSFP.com

Counterparty	Position Name	Product / Flow	Pmt Type	Amount
Settlement Date: 31-Dec-09 Currency: USD				
BARCLAYS	US_TREASURY325DEC16	FIXED BOND	TRD	-1,487,550.00
BARCLAYS	US_TRESASURY4375NOV39	FIXED BOND	TRD	-2,891,717.25
			31-Dec-09 USD Subtotal:	-4,379,267.25
Settlement Date: 11-Jan-10 Currency: EUR				
SC GERMAN AUTO	ABS-XS0266760700	ABS	INT	17,700.81
			11-Jan-10 EUR Subtotal:	17,700.81
Settlement Date: 11-Jan-10 Currency: USD				
BANKAMERICA MANU HOUSE SE	MBS-066053AB5	MBS-FIXED	INT	8,266.19
BANKAMERICA MANU HOUSE SE	MBS-066053AB5	MBS-FIXED	PRI	33,969.69
			11-Jan-10 USD Subtotal:	42,235.88
Settlement Date: 12-Jan-10 Currency: USD				
FIRST UNION COMMERCIAL MOR	MBS-33736XFT1	MBS-FIXED	INT	11,821.43
FIRST UNION COMMERCIAL MOR	MBS-33736XFV6	MBS-FIXED	INT	4,746.15
			12-Jan-10 USD Subtotal:	16,567.57
Settlement Date: 15-Jan-10 Currency: USD				
GE BUSINESS LOAN TRUST	ABS-36159EAA0	ABS-INTEX	INT	1,248.60
GE BUSINESS LOAN TRUST	ABS-36159EAA0	ABS-INTEX	PRI	8,734.34
HARLEY DAVIDSON EAGLEMARK	ABS-41283ACE7	ABS-INTEX	INT	3,149.07
HARLEY DAVIDSON EAGLEMARK	ABS-41283ACE7	ABS-INTEX	PRI	28,984.72
JG WENTWORTH RECEIVABLES	ABS-88576NAP3	ABS-INTEX	INT	13,200.97
JG WENTWORTH RECEIVABLES	ABS-88576NAP3	ABS-INTEX	PRI	19,235.25
NISSAN AUTO LEASE TRUST	ABS-6547EPAD5	ABS-INTEX	INT	58.91
NISSAN AUTO LEASE TRUST	ABS-6547EPAD5	ABS-INTEX	PRI	23,959.39
Nissan Auto Receivables Owner	ABS-65475XAC0	ABS-INTEX	INT	13,900.33
THE Money Store Business LBC	MBS-60935LAC1	MBS	INT	5,833.33
			15-Jan-10 USD Subtotal:	118,304.90

Figure 19.10. Cash movement and balance sheet report sample.
Source: Principia Partners LLC.

exposure over a specified time horizon. The ability to prevent duration mismatches between the flows of underlying assets and those of issuances is an ongoing operational process.

19.2.6 Risk control and customization

The nuances of risk analysis and modeling are often particular to an organization or portfolio strategy, or outside the realms of an existing system's standard provisions. This is particularly true within the area of structured finance where risk control and capital calculations are usually specific to the nature of the operation and are often proprietary. `Principia SFP`'s risk scripting framework allows managers to easily address and implement any specific requirements with minimal resources. The framework provides the ability to modify instruments, portfolios, market environments, and calculation attributes using a simple business scripting language.

The framework exposes core data, algorithms, and analytical functions of the system, which can then be manipulated and applied to any level or aggregation of trades/instruments to perform complex market scenario analysis. Without any modifications to the data model or addition of application-programming objects, it enables business users to effectively generate their specific deal and portfolio analyses. The results can be viewed on demand and saved to the database for future reference or sent to the system's standard reporting.

All risk scenario analysis functionalities can be flexibly and dramatically enhanced through the use of risk scripts. A number of the firm's clients are using customized risk scripts to

- Incorporate proprietary capital adequacy models
- Incorporate rating agency–negotiated criteria into standard compliance reporting
- Stress yield curves and volatilities according to any user-defined scenario
- Change prepayment, delinquency, and default probability assumptions in risk analysis
- Add user-defined algorithms for drawdown exposure analysis
- Modify (stress-test) rating information for concentration limit testing, actual, and what if.

This powerful functionality is increasingly being used in helping firms to rapidly implement proprietary risk analytics to meet internal business analysis and regulatory reporting requirements.

19.3 OPERATIONS AND ADMINISTRATION

19.3.1 Central management of multiple businesses

In the past, the treatment of structured credit assets within bank treasuries and investment management firms has often been characterized by an inefficient combination of siloed processes. Often portfolio management, risk management, and accounting functions are performed using disparate bespoke systems, across different business units, managing different portfolios. These weaknesses have often prevented them from being able to effectively integrate the management, oversight, and disclosure of the activities carried out by these operations, particularly as portfolios and off-balance-sheet asset exposures are consolidated onto the balance sheet.

The establishment, maintenance, and monitoring of documented risk management, compliance, and internal control policies and procedures by credit investment operations has become a priority. An integrated approach to risk management, surveillance, performance analytics, and operational processing is key to delivering the requirements of these new internal control policies and procedures.

`Principia SFP` provides a platform to manage any number of separate business operations or portfolios. This helps reduces disparities in the application of pricing, risk analysis, and end-to-end processing across portfolios so organizations can achieve greater operational efficiency and enforce risk policy.

Each business can be established as a separate entity on the platform, with the application of different operational controls, compliance mandates, and accounting treatments. Consolidated risk and exposure analysis can then be performed across business units in an integrated manner for on-balance-sheet disclosure of the entire credit investment operation.

19.3.2 Operational control and end-to-end reporting

`Principia SFP` provides numerous off-the-shelf reports supporting administration, risk management, portfolio management, securities compliance, operations, and accounting. These reports may be run manually or scheduled to run automatically. This supports users automating end-of-day processes and reporting needs overnight for review the following morning.

Reports can be filtered by a variety of criteria and produced in standard PDF format. The report data are also made available in a number of alternative formats for further manipulation or analysis within other third-party tools like MS Excel and database reporting tools like `Crystal Reports`. A list of some typical reports is provided below:

- Mark-to-market
- Counterparty credit exposure
- Hedge analysis
- Option expiration

- Portfolio analytics
- Trial balance
- Trade tickets
- Payment/Reset
- Regulatory reporting
- Liability tracking
- Funding gap
- Asset-funding projection
- Audit
- Deal master report
- Cost of funds report.

19.3.3 Accounting

`Principia SFP`, through its subledger, provides full general ledger (GL) support for assets, liabilities, administrative fees, and hedges, allowing users to maintain a complete balance sheet on a single platform. A comprehensive interface to external GLs or other accounting systems is included. Since 1999, the system has delivered full regulatory compliance with derivatives and hedge accounting based on standards set by the Financial Accounting Standards Board (FAS133, FAS138, FAS 157, FAS166/167) and International Accounting Standards Board (IAS39). Complicated accounting processes such as adjustments to amortized premiums/discounts on ABS instruments can be fully automated.

`Principia SFP` supports hedge, mark-to-market, accrual, multi-currency, and multi-entity accounting. The subledger provides users with a means to structure charts of accounts that incorporate user-defined rules, enabling extensive customization for client-specific accounting needs. Companies can elect to use various methods of hedge accounting to eliminate or reduce income statement volatility arising from reporting changes in a derivative's fair value. Specific subledger capabilities include

- Marking derivatives to market
- Linking specific assets and liabilities with specific hedge instruments
- Designating hedge strategies as "fair value", "cash flow", or "foreign currency net investment" and driving hedge-accounting effectiveness-testing and measurement methodologies from these designations
- Documenting hedge relationships
- Effectiveness-testing, prospective as well as retrospective
- Ability to assign strategies and allocations dynamically to every transaction that requires compliance tracking.

19.3.4 Workflow control: Consistency, efficiency, and compliance

`Principia SFP` provides a fully configurable workflow management tool for controlling the operation's management. This can be implemented to match any specific operating manual. Furthermore, the state control and workflow can be defined on an entity-by-entity basis. It permits a formal workflow process to be specified by each client for any given set of functions in accordance with pre-established criteria. The entire set of core functions is protected within an access control framework.

It is safe to assume that most organizations have some degree of "four-eyes principle" process in place over the different data entry points from front to back office. However, the degree to which it is enforced varies. In many cases, there are four eyes on the actions performed, but without visibility or consideration of the state of the trade they were performed in.

State control functionality in `Principia SFP` allows you to tailor permissions, not just for the actions performed on a given data object, but for the actions performed on a data object in a specific

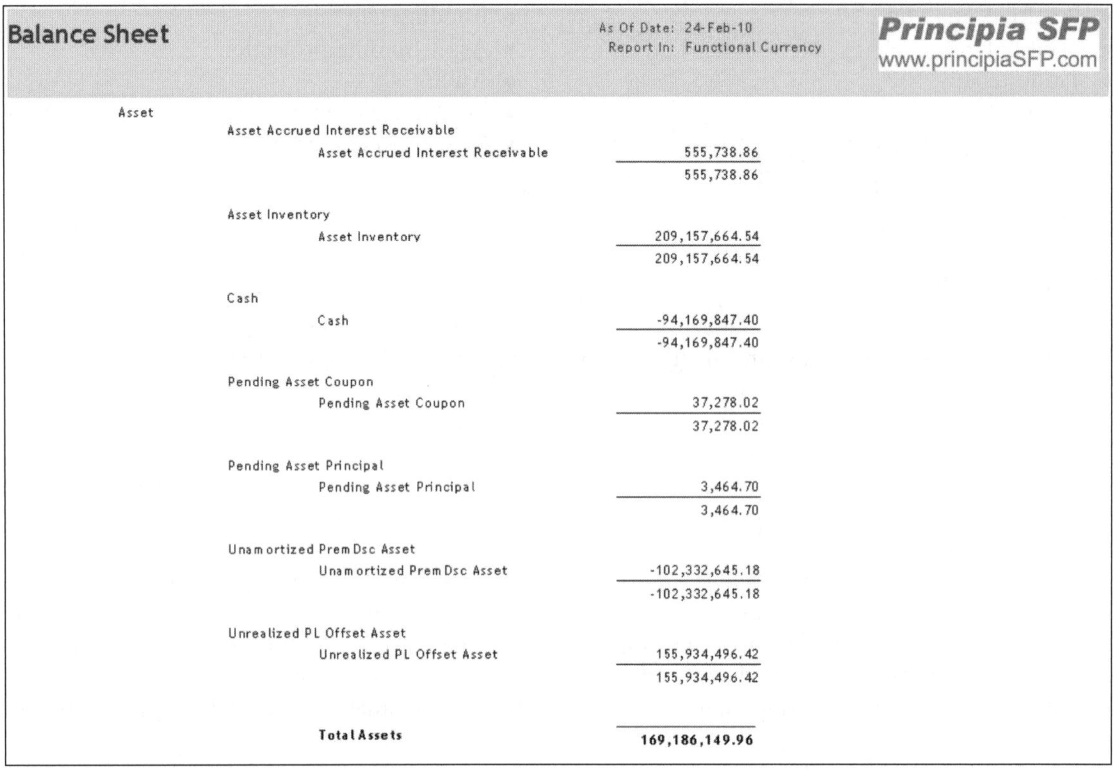

Balance Sheet

As Of Date: 24-Feb-10
Report In: Functional Currency

Principia SFP
www.principiaSFP.com

Asset			
	Asset Accrued Interest Receivable		
		Asset Accrued Interest Receivable	555,738.86
			555,738.86
	Asset Inventory		
		Asset Inventory	209,157,664.54
			209,157,664.54
	Cash		
		Cash	-94,169,847.40
			-94,169,847.40
	Pending Asset Coupon		
		Pending Asset Coupon	37,278.02
			37,278.02
	Pending Asset Principal		
		Pending Asset Principal	3,464.70
			3,464.70
	Unamortized PremDsc Asset		
		Unamortized PremDsc Asset	-102,332,645.18
			-102,332,645.18
	Unrealized PL Offset Asset		
		Unrealized PL Offset Asset	155,934,496.42
			155,934,496.42
		Total Assets	**169,186,149.96**

Figure 19.11. Balance sheet reports.
Source: Principia Partners LLC.

state (e.g., a trade that is either "approved" or "hypothetical", etc.). In this way, operational staff can place different permissions and conditions on items. It can also be used to create a consolidated log and record of the entire process to aid diagnostics and day-to-day management.

As a rules-driven engine, it can be used in any number of ways to ensure that specific operating guidelines are enforced. For example, it could be used to

- Prevent changes to matured deals unless there is special approval
- Make sure that required descriptor tag values are filled in (and that they require different values according to the asset type)
- Ring alarm bells to the right people when certain kinds of changes are made—like coupon or factor overrides
- Impose a specific naming convention on valuables, counterparties, strategies, users, etc.
- Guide users through their next steps by providing informative customized workflow messages
- Modifications to data are recorded in audit tables and auditing reports show the history of changes. This detailed process control framework helps to mitigate operational risk throughout the lifecycle of a deal.

Changes made in the system are fully audited. Audit reports are available to identify specific changes made over a period of time, as defined and required by the user.

Example 19.1. Override stale interest factors

According to a Depository Trust & Clearing Corporation (DTCC) white paper entitled *Structured Securities Processing Challenges*, "Thousands of transactions fail to be processed in an accurate and timely manner each year. The most common reason involves the servicer updating the underlying collateral data, which may be the actual collection data or involve delinquent payments after initial reporting to the agent."

ABS/MBS structuring in any system can involve managing lots of complex deal information, but, for many, one of the most inefficient and laborious jobs is the accurate management of factors and interest payments. `Principia SFP`, the uniquely developed asset interface, greatly simplifies the modeling of future cash flows and the ability to control and manage current factor and interest payments. With just a single entry of an ISIN or CUSIP, users have the flexibility to deal with late or incorrect factors.

For example, when factors and interest amounts are late (e.g., 0-day delay securities paying on the 25th), users may upload data received from their paying agent in order to complete month-end closings on time.

- *Complete data management and control.* Factors and interest amounts are stored in a database table so users can correct mistakes in the historical factors and/or interest amounts, ensuring accurate data for FAS91 reporting.
- *Automated alerts.* Informs users of new factors downloaded from Intex that will affect their portfolio.
- *Flexible factor management.* Users may choose to accept Intex data downloads or maintain new factors in suspense, pending review.
- *Automated data reconciliation.* The system automatically reconciles manually added factors or interest with equivalent Intex-downloaded information.
- *Firm-wide straight-through processing.* All users of the system (trading, risk management, operations, and accounting) have access to the same historical and projected cash flows.

19.4 SUMMARY

Governments, policymakers, and industry working groups are in the process of redesigning and reregulating the global financial system. The business of securitization sits at the heart of this change and is seen as vital to the future stability of the global economy. The motivations, economics, and fundamental factors driving structured finance have changed. Regulatory momentum is increasing.

Organizations with long-term strategies that involve structured finance are facing pressure from rules being introduced by Basel II, the European Capital Requirements Directive, the Securities and Exchange Commission, and IOSCO, to name but a few.

Policymakers are making sure that organizations with long-term investment goals involving securitized assets have a robust operational framework in place to really understand their investments on an ongoing basis. As independent credit analysis and a focus on managing ongoing collateral performance become prerequisites, spreadsheets and undedicated ancillary systems that are not developed to adapt to these dynamic requirements will struggle to cope with the additional processes and functionality required.

`Principia SFP` is designed with these evolving needs in mind. It provides financial institutions and independent managers with the most comprehensive software solution for the management of structured finance investments. Organizations can perform thorough investment analysis, transpar-

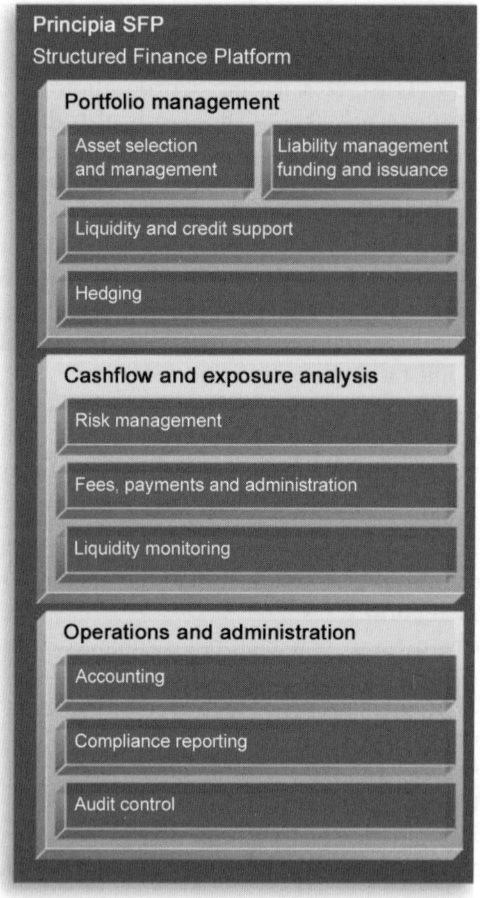

Figure 19.12. Principia's `Structured Finance Platform`.

ently manage and report ongoing risk exposures, and achieve seamless operational control, all the way through to accounting. It unifies data from external vendors and internal sources in a dedicated investment management environment so portfolio managers, risk staff, and operations staff can more consistently evaluate and manage transactions and portfolios across the enterprise.

20
Trepp

20.1 COMPANY HISTORY

Trepp has been a pioneer in the structured finance community since it was founded in 1980. As the CMBS industry has evolved, the firm has remained at the forefront of the market and continues to be the leading provider of CMBS and commercial mortgage information, analytics, and technology to the global securities and investment management industries. Trepp is a wholly owned subsidiary of DMG Information, which is a part of the Daily Mail Group, a large media corporation in the U.K.

Trepp's contributions to the CMBS market go far beyond the role of a traditional service provider and have become an integral part of the industry's framework since its inception. From modeling the first CMBS and CRE CDO deals and being a founding member of the Commercial Mortgage Securities Association (CMSA) to the creation of unique solutions that support complicated instruments such as CRE derivatives and CDS—the company is a provider of CMBS cash flows to Bloomberg LP and cash flow power behind Markit's CMBX indexes—Trepp's reputation for excellence and accuracy is highly recognized by the industry. The company further cemented their market leader status when they were selected by the Federal Reserve Bank of New York as the collateral monitor for the TALF Lending Program in June 2009.

The firm provides both primary-market and secondary-market participants with the tools to increase their market intelligence, operational efficiencies, and information transparency. The Trepp CMBS Deal Library is the largest commercially available database of CMBS and the industry's standard model dataset that drives CMBS secondary trading worldwide. The deal library contains comprehensive information and history on the deals, loans, and properties within the global securitized commercial market with billions of dollars of CMBS modeled by using the firm's product suite.

20.2 PRODUCT SUITE

Trepp has a comprehensive range of products and delivery methods that are utilized throughout a transaction's lifecycle:

- *Structuring.* Trepp's structuring tools aid issuers' structuring processes and scenario modeling. In addition, these tools are often used during the marketing phase of the deal, and structurers regularly ask the firm to model the issuances early in order to validate their waterfall calculations.
- *Marketing.* Investors are normally provided with access to the firm's model during the marketing of deals to help investors make their decisions and, equally, issuers will commonly include or refer to model results within their investor packs.
- *Surveillance and asset identification.* After the deal close, Trepp provides updated deal information, models to support investors' ongoing surveillance, and reporting on the deals. Over the last few years, there has also been a growing need to satisfy ever stricter internal governance as well as external reporting requirements, and Trepp is regularly used by teams in areas such as compliance, portfolio pricing, and throughout the external auditing process. In addition, investors and broker dealers regularly use the company's products to identify attractive assets for trading purposes.

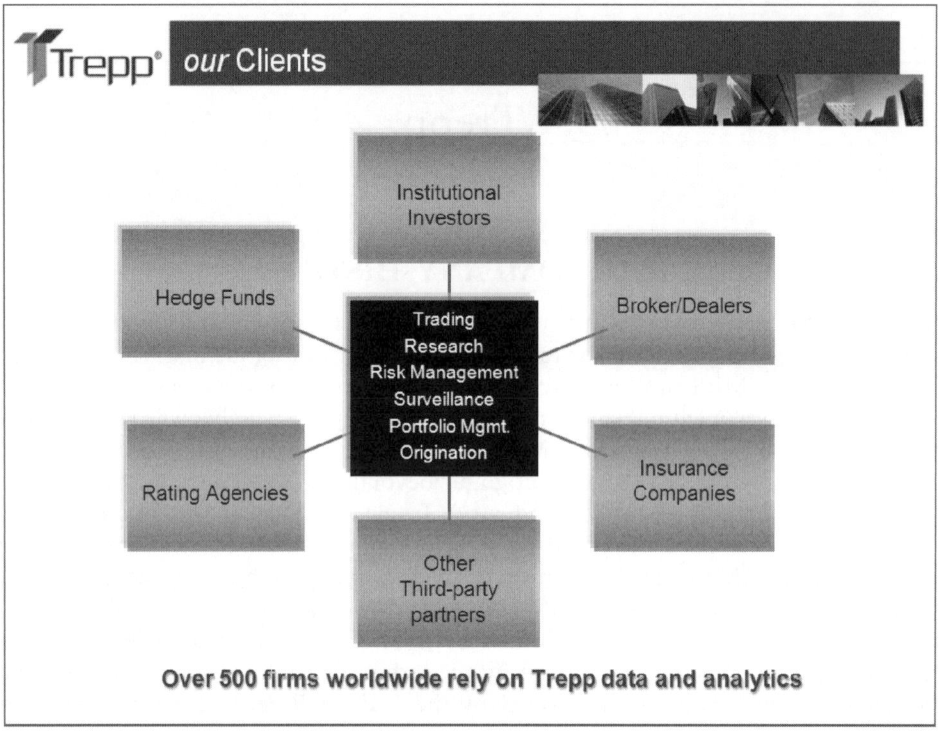

Figure 20.1. Key users and supported roles.
Source: Trepp, LLC.

- *Trading*. Secondary traders and investors regularly use these tools for the pricing of trades, etc.
- *Research*. Whether users are researching defined markets for refinancing risk or for transactions with certain loan characteristics, Trepp provides the most comprehensive coverage commercially available.

Trepp has a reputation for the quality of its models, which is based upon comprehensive processes and tests to ensure that the firm's models provided to external clients also satisfy its internal standards.

Every deal that is modeled undergoes an extensive "tying-out" process before releasing the deal-related information. For every posted tranche, the prices, yields, average life, and cash flows produced by the firm's own models is compared with those of the lead underwriter, under a number of scenarios designed to identify differences in all relevant money terms. Examples of the scenarios can be found below:

- No prepayments, no defaults (the "0/0" case)
- Prepayments after lockout with yield maintenance and premiums passing through ("CPR")
- Prepayments after yield maintenance with premiums passing through ("CPY")
- Prepayments after all prepayment restrictions are over ("CPP")
- Prepayments after lockout with yield maintenance and premiums passing through combined with defaults, losses, and months to recover ("Prepay/Default").
- No prepayments, no defaults with cleanup call exercised ("Cleanup Call")
- No prepayments, no defaults with balloons extended ("Balloon Extension").

Based on this so-called "tying-out" process, Trepp assigns every deal a "modeling status" describing the degree to which Trepp's cash flows are in agreement with the underwriter's, and the pricing status of the deal. Every CMBS analytic screen indicates the modeling status by using the following designations:

- *Black Trading Quality*. This indicates that the deal has tied out with the underwriter's final pricing runs for the following scenarios: 0/0, CPR, CPY, CPP, and a default scenario, as well as any scenarios particular to the transaction. Deals do not need to have been tied out to clean up call or extension scenarios in order to be considered Trading Quality.
- *Black Limited Trading Quality*. This indicates that the 0/0 and CPR scenarios have been tied out with the underwriter's final runs.
- *Black Prospectus Quality*. This indicates that the model reflects pricing tranche balances and coupons but has not been tied out with the underwriter's final pricing runs.
- *Red Trading Quality*. This indicates that the transaction has tied out with the underwriter's initial prepricing runs for the following scenarios: 0/0, CPR, CPY, CPP, and a default scenario, as well as any scenarios particular to the transaction. Deals do not need to have been tied out to clean up call or extension scenarios in order to be considered Trading Quality.
- *Red Limited Trading Quality*. This indicates that the 0/0 and CPR scenarios have been tied out with the underwriter's initial prefinal runs.
- *Red Prospectus Quality*. This indicates that the model has not been tied out with the underwriter.

After tying out with the lead manager, the collateral for each deal is updated on each payment date with specific trustee data. Frequently, as part of its validation process, differences between the underwriter's data and the trustee's data are identified. In such cases, the model uses the underwriter's assumptions until receiving confirmation that the trustee's data are correct at which time the data will be updated. The exceptions to this rule are payment, payment basis (or daycount basis), and rate changes. In the case of these variables, if an issue is new, the firm's analysts will pursue verification with the trustee. If the issue is seasoned and has been serviced with the same payment and payment basis for a number of months, it is assumed that the loan will continue to be serviced in that manner and the underwriter's assumption will be replaced with trustee data. Issues with data modifications will include a note under "Deal Notes". The firm maintains a full database of changes to underwriter data to identify changes to the model in the event this becomes necessary. A number of unit and benchmarking tests designed to provide the level of comfort are also run to confirm the results.

The company also employs similar processes in order to update the key surveillance data available. As can be seen from Figure 20.2, information is obtained from a variety of sources. The information is made available to Trepp in a variety of formats, from a daily data feed, to a monthly or even quarterly set of IRP/E–IRP files. A significant effort is made to update the deals accurately and in a timely fashion.

Much of the data received is processed automatically and populates a proprietary database only after passing several data integrity checks. Some deals, particularly in Europe where E-IRP does not enjoy the same levels of use as IRP does in the U.S., require manual updates.

20.3 TREPP FOR CMBS

`Trepp for CMBS`, which is the firm's central product, comprises a number of different modules and delivery mechanisms.

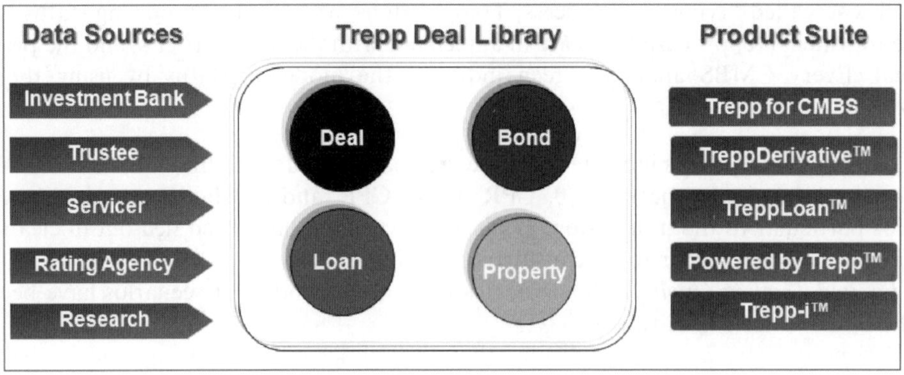

Figure 20.2. Overview—deal library and product suite.
Source: Trepp, LLC.

20.3.1 TreppWatch and Analytics

Whilst, according to Trepp, the vast majority of its clients now use access to the website, Trepp's very first CMBS offering was in fact delivered via Bloomberg Professional terminals. Although the firm continues to maintain and update its Bloomberg-based service, there has been a strong demand recently from users to migrate to its web-based service. The significant change in appetite is due in part to the additional reports and corresponding levels of detail, together with significantly enhanced portfolio functionality made possible by the more flexible web-based medium.

With the backing of issuers, this allowed users to gain an independent view of CMBS transactions for the first time. Recognized throughout the CMBS industry for providing trading quality accuracy achieved through its high modeling standards, the company's well-regarded financial analysts work closely with lead managers to model and "tie out" every nuance of a transaction before it is released to the market. Furthermore, as deals pay each month in the U.S. and quarterly in Europe, rigorous quality control procedures ensure continued accuracy of the data and bond models.

The service continues to offer extensive surveillance information across the most comprehensive publicly available library of CMBS and CRE CDO transactions (including updated delinquency data, collateral stratifications, and loan and property detail), as well as the ability to tag pools of loans, groups of loans, and even individual loans to default, extend, or prepay, and see the effect on the price/yield and cash flows of the corresponding bonds.

The `Analytics` module provides an intuitive user interface and simple scenario definition functions, enabling investors to spend more time analyzing bonds and less time trying to gather information from multiple sources. This is complemented by the ability to generate real-time cash flows, yield tables, and bond-level total return analysis over a range of user-defined default, prepay, and extension assumptions. The product provides a flexible and robust set of credit-based analytic tools geared towards portfolio and asset managers. Integration with the `Trepp CMBS Pricing Service` and powerful processing capabilities for batch calculations across its proprietary trading quality CMBS database has ensured that this tool is widely recognised as the market standard for CMBS trading, research, pricing, and portfolio analysis.

Powerful analytics reports, such as the `Price/Yield Table` (Figure 20.3), not only allow users to specify simple prepayment and/or default speeds, and extension periods, but also give full control of other factors such as interest rates. Users can assign speeds to the collateral pool as a whole, or have the system automatically identify loans by characteristic (e.g., all loans on the servicer's watchlist), or even assign individual speeds to individual loans.

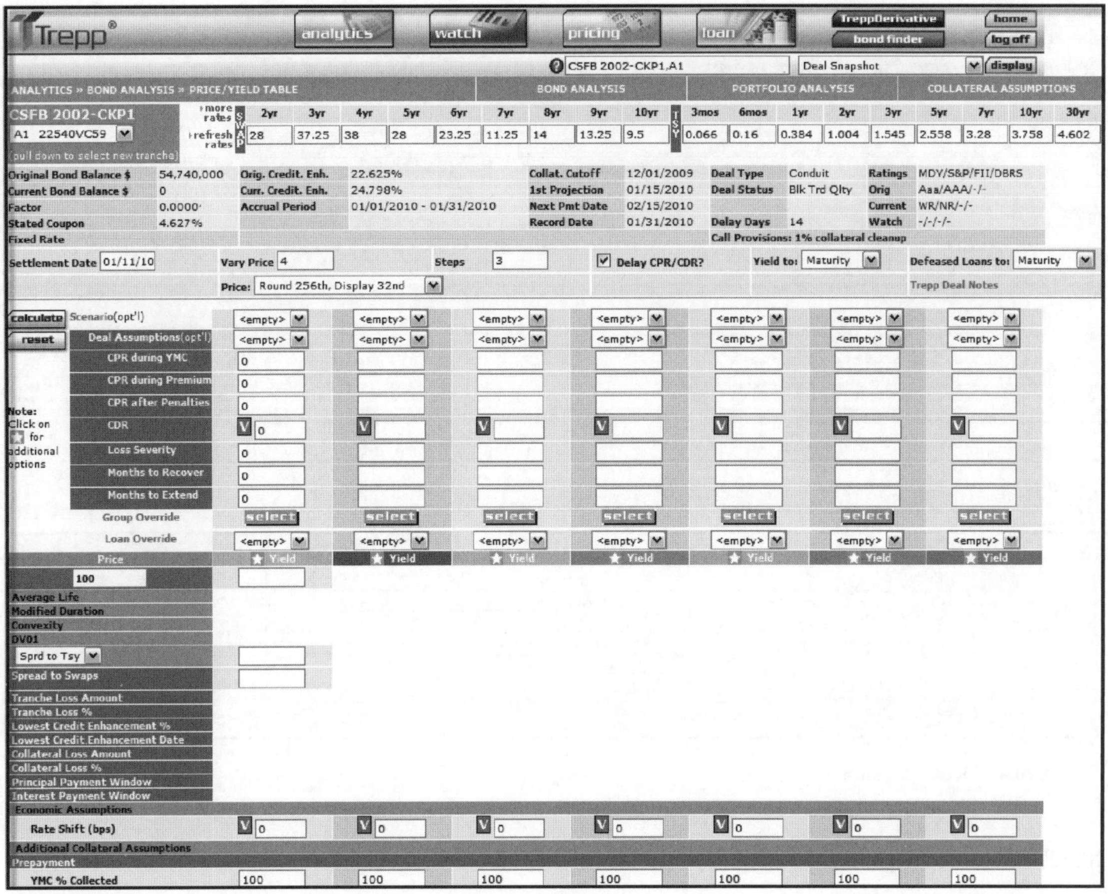

Figure 20.3. `Bond Analytics—Price/Yield Table.`
Source: Trepp, LLC.

This is enhanced by `TreppWatch`, a research and surveillance tool for CMBS market participants which provides detailed information and powerful reporting on the deal, loan, and property levels. Examples of the data provided can be found below:

- In-depth CMBS market information at the deal, bond, collateral, and property levels
- Instant online access to Annex As, servicer watchlists, remittance reports, and prospectuses
- Robust search capabilities on market, portfolio, tenant, and deal levels
- Extensive ability to monitor geographic exposure and drill down into loan detail
- Flexible and customized stratification reporting
- Powerful portfolio tools and reporting capabilities
- Simple downloading and printing of information and reports (Excel and PDFs).

Summary reports, such as the deal snapshot (Figure 20.4), display deal data in a simple easy-to-understand format allowing users to quickly identify key data, and facilitating drill-down into more detailed reports, which can be exported into Excel and PDF files.

Together, `TreppWatch` and `Analytics` provide one of the most complete CMBS monitoring and evaluation tools currently available.

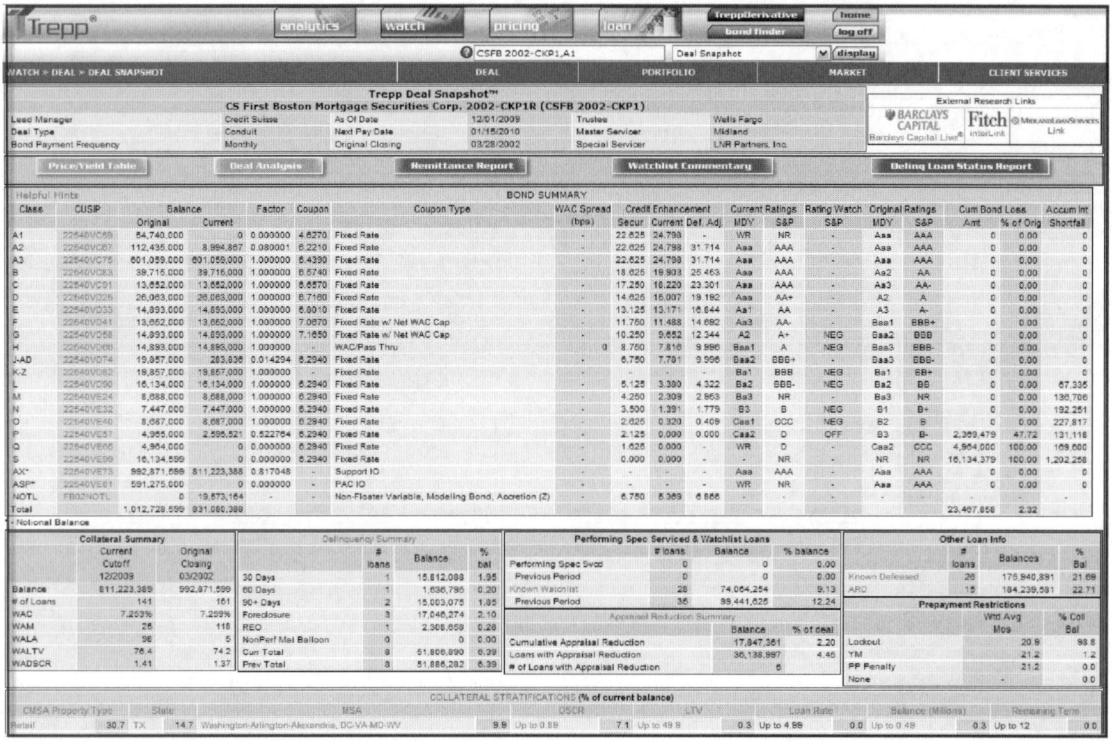

Figure 20.4. Deal snapshot.
Source: Trepp, LLC.

20.3.2 Morning Update/Morning Update Loan Edition

Both, the `Trepp Morning Update` and `Trepp Morning Update Loan Edition` are daily email services highlighting potentially important collateral changes that have taken place in the CMBS market within the last 24 hours. The update is an early warning device and risk management tool that provides a distinct trading advantage to investors. It is designed to be used as a starting point in determining potential problems within CMBS deals as well as commercial real estate loans.

After the daily update process finishes, an automatic process generates a file that is distributed via email to help subscribers identify trends in the market as they unfold, map collateral events against individual portfolios, prioritize and rationalize surveillance efforts, and spot potential problem loans before they become especially serviced or delinquent. Both editions of this service look for and highlight collateral changes such as:

- New appraisal or reductions/bankruptcy flag status/defeasances
- Loans with deteriorating or improving delinquency status codes
- Loans with a new NOI DSCR or NCF DSCR less than 1
- Loans newly extended/liquidated/prepaid/in REO/in special servicing/ with new workout codes.

20.3.3 Pricing Service

`Trepp's CMBS Pricing Service` provides daily valuations for U.S. investment-grade CMBS assets. Trepp has a CUSIP-by-CUSIP and generic spread history dating back nearly a decade, which is vital for month-end valuations as well as volatility and trend analysis.

While CMBS is categorized as a mortgage-backed security, the process of establishing prices for CMBS bonds is quite different from pricing residential MBS. In the RMBS universe, credit concerns are dwarfed by interest rate risk considerations. In the CMBS universe, however, the opposite is true. Credit risk dominates the analytical process in CMBS as interest rate sensitivity, while still relevant, is of secondary concern.

Due to the unique sensitivity to credit risk, proper valuation of CMBS requires in-depth understanding of the collateral backing CMBS. In order to properly value CMBS debt, a number of elements are taken into consideration including

- Property type diversity
- Ongoing financial performance of collateral
- Exposure to troubled tenants
- Unique geographical risk
- Delinquency statistics
- Appraisal reductions
- Loan modifications
- Loan defeasances.

Pricing requires the ability to quickly reflect changes in collateral performance; therefore, timely analysis of collateral data and access to multiple sources of information are imperative. The firm's valuations for CMBS bonds are delivered every business day based on the 3 : 00 PM EST treasury curve and are rolled out to the market by approximately 4 : 20 PM EST.

Trepp's data are recognized industry wide as the highest quality CMBS information available. In addition to being the exclusive source of CMBS cash flows to Bloomberg LP worldwide Trepp is a Standard & Poor–approved CMBS pricing provider for investment-grade structured transactions. Its pricing, deal models, and cash flows are scrutinized daily by leading investors and other market participants, enabling the ultimate quality control.

The pricing service collates a number of external factors such as CMBS spreads to treasury (Figure 20.5) and treasury yields, and users can quickly access the data regardless of the delivery mechanism selected for the service.

20.4 TREPP DERIVATIVE

`TreppDerivative` (Figure 20.6) is a powerful tool for navigating the complex world of CMBS credit default swaps (CMBS CDS). With the explosive growth in the global CDS market and the recent concern with underwriting standards, the need for surveillance has never been greater. Underwriters, traders, investors, hedge funds, and CDO managers reduce operational risk, increase workflow efficiency, and deal intelligence by leveraging this tool's flexible interface to manage CDS exposure.

`TreppDerivative` supports the creation, surveillance, and valuation of CMBS CDS (whether single-name CDS, Bespoke baskets, CMBX indexes, or synthetic CDOs). From its easy-to-use interface, it also allows users to create and manage contracts (manual or automated options exist), share information internally, and, with counterparties, create and send ISDA confirmation forms, and perform valuation and analytics calculations.

The product allows investors to value CDS contracts and evaluate price sensitivity using either a contingent claim or net present value approach. Clients may also run stress tests on the collateral of underlying reference obligations, such as defaulting individual loans or groups of loans at specific loss severities and dates, in order to project contract payouts and/or view the overall carry and cash flow projections across a book of holdings. Using breakeven analysis, investors can see at what default rate the credit enhancement on the underlying reference obligation would erode and floating payments would occur.

Subscribers can export contract terms and conditions compiled within this tool for submission to `Markit` for valuation. This single interface for analytics, cash flows, and valuations helps streamlining

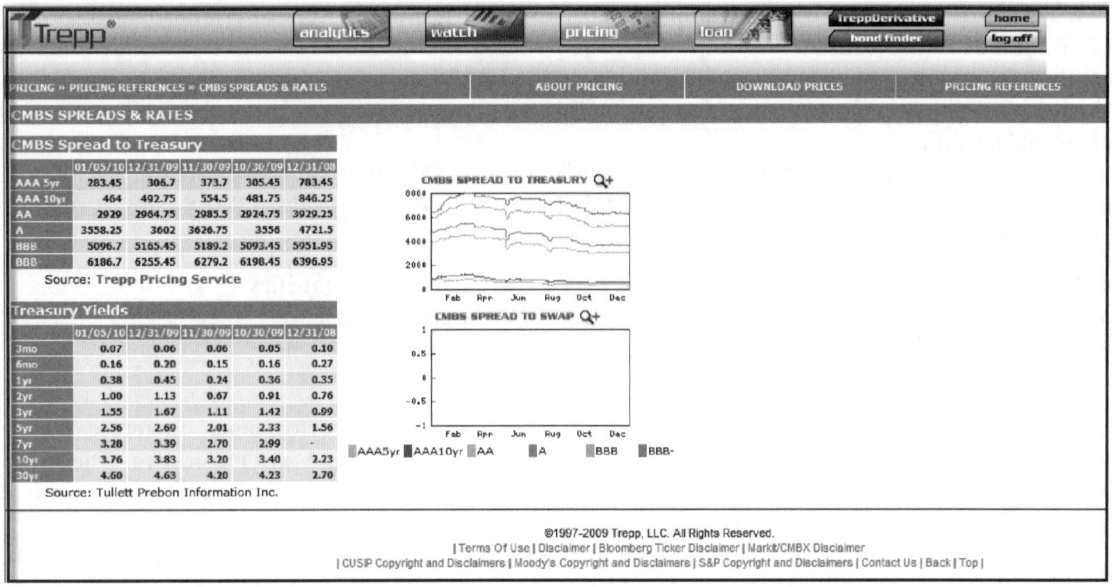

Figure 20.5. CMBS spreads and rates.
Source: Trepp, LLC.

the process for the end-user significantly and, hence, results in greater efficiency and accuracy of trade input.

Deal updates are consistently processed and distributed as soon as they become available; depending on the deal, this can be several days prior to the actual CDS payment date. Investors can monitor recent CDS credit events, track material changes in the collateral backing the reference obligations, and create customized email alerts to receive notices as soon as the CMBS deals are updated. In addition to this functionality, additional features allow users to

- View loan detail and stratification reports for the underlying reference obligations, including delinquency data and servicer watchlist commentary
- Review deal documents such as prospectuses and remittance reports
- Access CMBS deal snapshots for all related reference obligations.

As the exclusive cash flow provider to `Markit` (*www.markit.com*)—the CMBX index administrator—Trepp's CMBS cash flows represent not only the industry standard for the cash CMBS market, but also for the emerging derivative market.

The monitoring capability of `TreppDerivative` allows users to quickly identify the underlying CMBS deals with the largest improvements and deteriorations in the performance of the underlying collateral, and users can then quickly drill down for more detailed reports.

20.5 TREPP LOAN

Leveraging the firm's capital market quality CMBS database, `TreppLoan` provides a unique perspective for monitoring and analyzing both securitized and non-securitized American commercial mortgages and properties, whole loan portfolios, and nationwide commercial mortgage finance statistics.

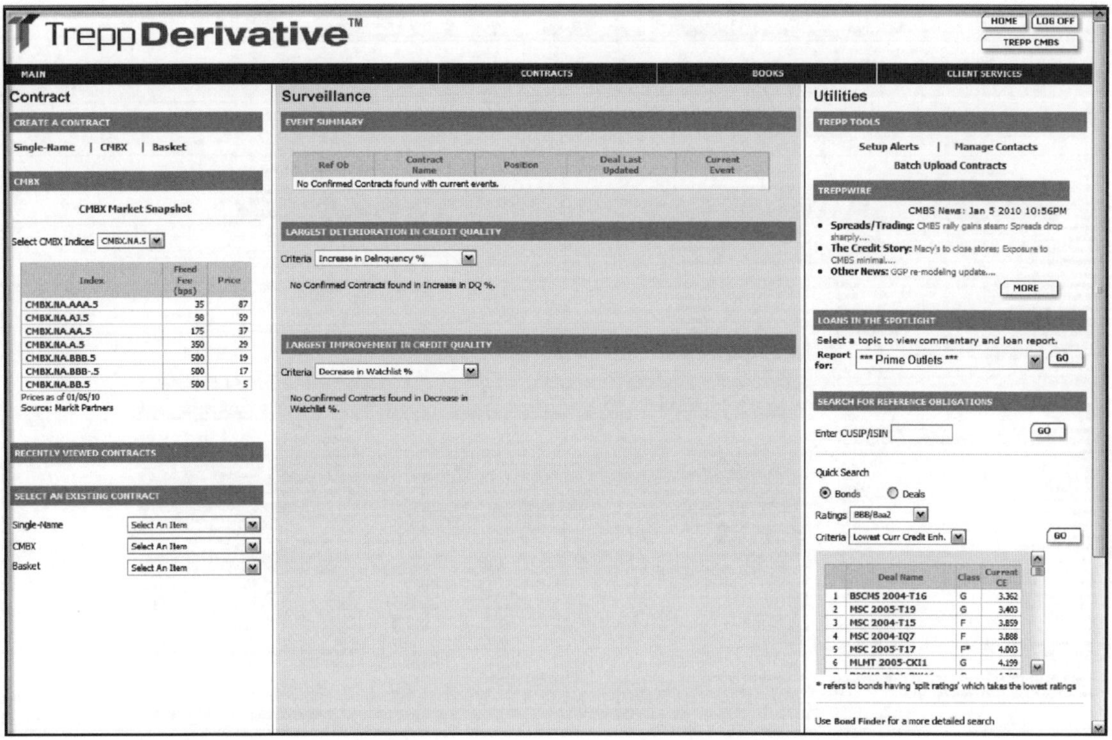

Figure 20.6. `TreppDerivative`'s dashboard.
Source: Trepp, LLC.

The product is comprised of three powerful modules that form a comprehensive web-based information and analytics platform for originators, underwriters, mortgage brokers, and commercial real estate investors.

Users can quickly drill down from summary reports or search results to in-depth reports that not only identify loan characteristics, but also property details. Full commentary on A/B splits and CMBS deals which include portions of the loans is also available.

20.5.1 Portfolio

The `TreppLoan Portfolio` module provides a standardized platform for commercial real estate risk management, reporting, and pricing. This product allows balance sheet lenders to perform stress tests and analyze the credit risk within commercial loan holdings. The module provides a consistent, consolidated approach to commercial real estate risk management and reporting. The module also offers the ability to create pricing runs on individual loans and portfolios. Using user-defined spread tables, the product provides a three-dimensional spread matrix based on LTV, DSCR, and property type. Key features include

- Simple upload of whole loan portfolios
- Running of extensive stratification reports to quantify concentration risk and portfolio diversity
- Benchmarking portfolio concentrations vs. the CMBS universe
- Accessing in-depth market-level statistics such as spreads and delinquencies

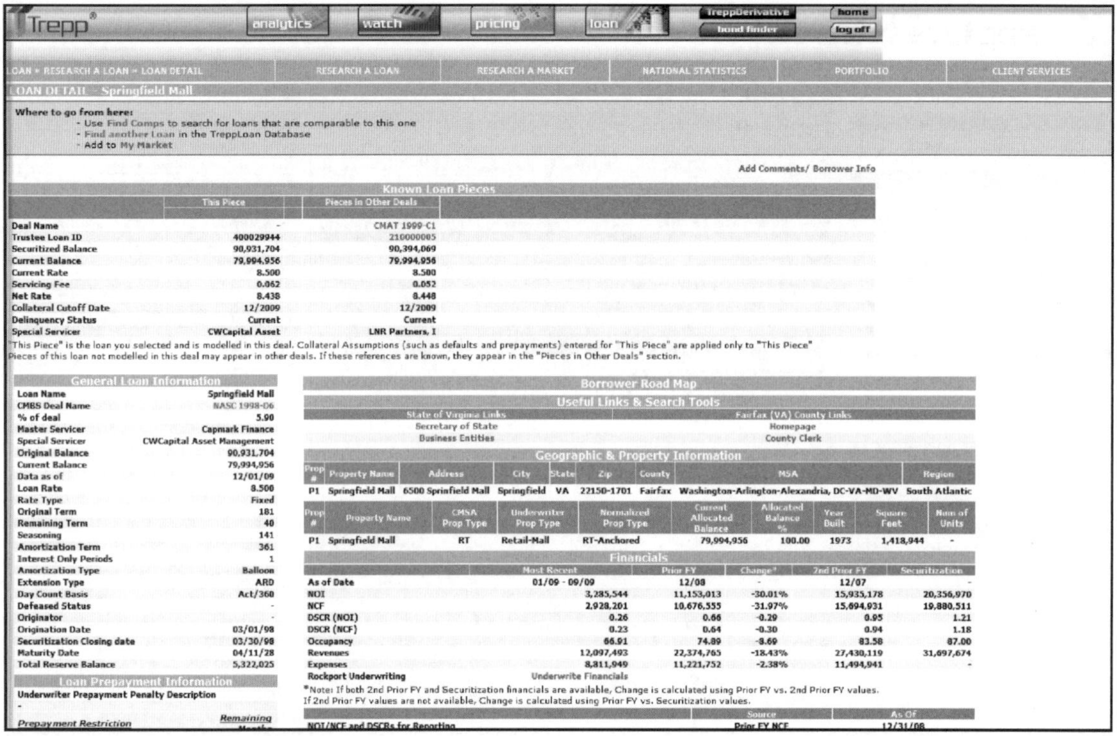

Figure 20.7. `TreppLoan` details.
Source: Trepp, LLC.

- Incorporating third-party probability of default (PD) models
- Invoking pricing runs on individual loans and portfolios
- Uploading pricing inputs using variable assumptions
- Viewing of maps for all properties within the portfolio
- Integrating seamlessly with the `Research` and `Lead Finder` modules of `TreppLoan`.

20.5.2 Lead Finder

The `TreppLoan Lead Finder` module identifies refinance and workout opportunities within the multi-billion dollar U.S. securitized commercial mortgage market. By leveraging its database of nearly all U.S. commercial real estate (CRE) transactions, commercial real estate professionals can access the largest available database of securitized commercial real estate loans. The flexible design supports customized searches for more targeted prospecting and lead generation. Key features include

- Sourcing of refinance and workout opportunities from the largest publicly available commercial mortgage database
- Identification of borrower details
- Quantification of prepayment amounts, yield maintenance charges, and fixed prepayment premiums
- Evaluation of detailed property and financial information
- Search for defeasance opportunities

- Performing trend analysis in select markets and property types
- Tracking of competitor activity.

20.5.3 Research

The `TreppLoan Research` (Figure 20.7) module provides a unique perspective for monitoring and analyzing commercial real estate, individual loan, property, and overall market performance. The module provides direct lenders, underwriters, brokers, advisors, opportunity funds, REITS, and equity investors with access to capital market quality data. The proprietary CRE database leverages billions of dollars in outstanding loans and powers this research tool to create a platform for examining and evaluating market trends. Key features include

- Analyzing loan performance statistics across all property types
- Tracking nationwide commercial mortgage-lending activity
- Analyzing current underwriting trends by property type and originator
- Evaluation of detailed property and financial information
- Improving loan pricing and underwriting by comparative analysis
- Searching the database for comparable properties, ranking prospective deals vs. peers
- Monitoring competitor activity and performance
- Download of data to generate powerful reports for analysis.

20.6 POWERED BY TREPP

The `Powered by Trepp` suite provides "industrial" strength access to its proprietary data and technology for added flexibility. `Powered by Trepp` applications have been utilized throughout the CMBS market by institutions requiring the added freedom to develop more powerful scalable solutions.

20.6.1 Data Feed

`Trepp Data Feed` integrates the best of various information sources to provide sophisticated CMBS and commercial real estate analysts with a single consistent source of high quality easy-to-use data. These standardized files—delivered nightly via file transfer protocol (ftp)—combine data from servicers, special servicers, trustees, and prospectuses. With a complete history available dating back to 1998, the data feed is ideal for research and surveillance. Benefits of this tool include

- *Cost reductions/greater efficiency*. Providing a consistent format by offering information on all deals in a standardized layout.
- *Value-added data*. Including dozens of additional calculations to facilitate internal development efforts in addition to the standard loan, property, and bond information.
- *Clean data*. Using multiple data sources ensures the information in the data feed is of the highest quality. Easily integrated, these files are available historically from 1998 and are ideal for
    - risk management departments
    - research groups
    - surveillance teams
    - commercial real estate databases.

The standard data feed is comprised of a deal file, a bond file, a loan file, and a property file. In addition to the standard feed components, Trepp offers the following supplemental data files:

- Performance history
  - deal level
  - loan level
  - prepayments
  - losses
  - bond payments
  - delinquencies
- CMBS pricing
  - daily CMBS prices
  - CMBS spread history
  - CMBS price history
- Additional information
  - `TreppDeal` snapshot PDFs (which are ideal for integrating into portfolio summaries)
  - normalized servicer watchlist commentary.

20.6.2 Engine

The backbone of the firm's entire collection of products, `TreppEngine` is a set of C-function library subroutines. Embedded into proprietary environments throughout the capital markets and real estate finance community, this solution is critical for many leading buy-side institutions, broker/dealers, and third-party fixed income providers for risk management and cash flow projections.

`TreppEngine` can be used to access all deals within Trepp's CMBS deal library. These subroutines offer the versatility to allow the calculative engine to be called by client-developed or third-party systems and can run in any LAN, Intranet, or standalone environment. Due to Trepp's compliance with industry-standard architecture, the subroutines can be easily integrated into systems used for trading, bond administration, risk management, portfolio management, and pricing.

`Trepp C-Function Library` subroutines are flexible enough to accommodate the unique nuances of commercial real estate analysis and stress-testing. The design allows for a range of vector or logic-based scenario assumptions at the individual loan, group, and pool levels for CMBS transactions with callback capabilities to use proprietary default and prepayment models.

The open architecture system offers unlimited flexibility for UNIX, Windows, or Linux environments. Since there are no global variables used by the Trepp API, multi-processing and multi-threading can be easily accomplished. The API also allows for recursive calls, thereby allowing it to handle multi-level CDOs of any depth.

20.6.3 Structuring

`TreppStructuring` is an intuitive and powerful "best of breed" system to structure, reverse-engineer, and analyze CMBS. Designed to handle virtually every type of CMBS deal structure, the system is a comprehensive source for verifying and analyzing tranche cash flows, solving for bond sizes and coupons, calculating deal profitability, and performing a wide range of bond and collateral analytics. Major issuers utilize this tool to hedge their loan pipeline, analyze deal profitability, and support loan pricing. It is also used by many of the largest dealers, bond insurers, and "B" piece buyers. Features of the system include

- Flexible collateral Screens
- Accepts "cut and paste" functionality from Excel or other Microsoft applications
- Free-form input does not require rigid column ordering
- Extensive field potential of 200 possibilities with only the "balance" and "term" fields required
- Complex capital structures

- Any combination of fixed rate, floating rate, and WAC bonds
- Multiple payment terms can also be accommodated in the deal structure
- Scenario analysis
- Set performance assumptions at the deal, group, or loan level
- Loan-level performance includes full sorting and filtering capabilities
- Global assumption sets available
- Reporting
- Stratifications
- Price/Yield analysis
- Cash flows
- Deal pricing.

`TreppStructuring` is widely considered to be one of the best CMBS structuring and reverse-engineering tools and has been "battle-tested" by major issuers to hedge their loan pipeline, analyze deal profitability, and support loan pricing. A flexible building block approach and wizards enhance ease of use.

20.7 RECENT DEVELOPMENTS

In addition to the core modules mentioned above, Trepp continues to innovate and has recently launched two new services, while others are slated for future release.

20.7.1 TreppWire

In August 2009, Trepp, LLC expanded its commercial real estate platform to include a daily commentary and market observations under the banner of `TreppWire`.

Each business morning, `TreppWire` identifies potential credit events and trading ideas which may impact investors' CMBS and CRE positions; the product has quickly become a "must read" for portfolio managers, traders, risk managers, distressed asset buyers, and commercial real estate professionals.

In addition to market-level trends, the service covers loan, property, borrower, and tenant-specific credit changes and daily pricing movements. In its short existence, numerous stories were exposed that did not make their way into the national press until days later. The data capitalize on the company's state-of-the-industry commercial mortgage database which is used by over 600 institutions worldwide.

20.7.2 TREPP-i

In response to the extended period during which market upheavals have led to reduced certainty in pricing, Trepp, LLC launched the `Trepp Real Estate Portfolio Pricing Index (TREPP-i)` as a new source of information for the pricing and valuation of commercial real estate loans in February 2009.

The index is calculated based on a weekly survey of active lenders who form a cross-section of participants in the commercial real estate arena. The spreads are "indicative"—based on fixed rate loans for good-quality borrowers—and cover five property types.

This provides an alternative source of data on indicative spread levels for commercial real estate loans and is targeted to lenders who retain their commercial real estate loans as a portfolio or balance sheet investment. The index provides a timely consistent source of information that is less influenced by the conditions of a particular loan.

20.8 TREPP'S MARKET AFFILIATIONS

Trepp is a proud and active member of several leading trade associations that foster dialogue, organize decision making, and ensure market transparency and progress. The leading trade associations and organizations which the firm supports financially through its membership and through its personal involvement include the Commercial Mortgage Securities Association (CMSA), Mortgage Bankers Association (MBA), American Securitization Forum (ASF), and Risk Management Association (RMA).

In particular, the growth of the CMBS market prior to the credit crisis has been synonymous with the creation and growth of the CMSA, and the company has remained committed to the CMSA since its inception. As well as being active on committees, Trepp's CEO, Annemarie DiCola, has held a number of varied roles including President of the CMSA.

One of the key developments made by the CMSA has been the creation of a standardized reporting format for CMBS deals, which includes loan-level and property-level information (a feature that is much requested/desired by the ABS classes).

As the markets have grown, and become global, so too have Trepp and the CMSA. Europe has developed differently from the U.S., however, and has specific issues that have necessitated that the market and product therefore develop along divergent paths from its U.S. counterparts. Examples of the differences can be found below:

- *Structural differences*. For example, fixed vs. floating, interest rate swaps vs. interest rate caps, large lumpy loans vs. smaller loans, often one loan per property.
- *Regulatory and legal differences*. U.S. deals regulated by one body and subject to one law, whereas European deals are potentially subject to multiple jurisdictions with inherent cross-border issues, disclosure requirements, etc.
- *Mature vs. developing market*. U.S. market is developed and often has a dedicated CRE desk compared with a developing market in Europe which is broadly characterized by CMBS being a small part of a larger ABS portfolio, and a comparative lack of specialist CRE knowledge within teams.
- *Differences in disclosure*. Perhaps one of the starkest differences between U.S. and European deals is the level of information that is reported. European deals are often characterized by a lack of information being reported when compared with U.S. deals (due to borrowers being unable or unwilling to report/divulge certain data) and cash managers/servicers reporting in a proprietary format (e.g., providing headline stratifications without tying the data back to individual loans or properties).

Trepp has taken a leading role throughout the development of the European market, and CMSA European issuers and investors have been using the firm since the inception of the European market to help facilitate the sales process as well as the ongoing surveillance and analytics of transactions. Through participation on the E-IRP committee, Trepp has brought its experience of the U.S. market, and involvement in the development of IRP, to assist the creation and adoption of E-IRP. Trepp's commitment to the European market is demonstrated by its representation on CMSA Europe's Board of Governors and its role as chair of the Membership Committee.

In Asia, CMSA-Japan plays a key role in supporting the growth and viability of commercial mortgage-backed securities (CMBS). As the market continues to expand in Japan, which is currently the second largest real estate market in the world, CMSA-Japan is engaged in discussions with several regulatory bodies concerning the benefits of CMBS to the Japanese economy. The chapter is also engaged in educational initiatives to bring additional interest and knowledge to the market.

Trepp has a small number of Asian deals available and has staff based in Asia to ensure that the service reflects any developments in the market. To date, the majority of issuances in Asia has been done out of Japan, and the participation, documentation, and ongoing reporting for most of these deals is based upon the Japanese language which obviously raises concerns about interpretation during the translation process.

20.9 THE FUTURE

Given the recent economic turmoil and following the credit crisis, the firm continues to work with clients and market participants to improve the product offering and their use of the products. As the markets recover, Trepp remains committed to accommodating client requests, not only by improving existing products or launching new services, but also by active participation in the CMSA.

A key aspect of the company's development through the years has been the neutrality of the product. Whilst information is gathered from numerous external sources such as the credit rating agencies, it is clearly displayed as being their information, without any interpretation by Trepp. This stance allows the user to pool the broadest level of data in one place to make their key decisions. Trepp's evolution as a "data hub" with links to third-party websites and services remains central to the organization.

A good example of the principle mentioned above is the ability to update servicers' property valuations and rental income figures using the firm's `Credit Based Analytics` module. As different organizations have different approaches to economic forecasting, basing Trepp's capabilities on a single methodology would obviously be unhelpful to many users. The fact that it allows users to update these numbers based upon their chosen methodology, or external data provider, will continue to ensure that this remains a key tool for market participants as it will continue to easily fit into the individual philosophies of each and every player.

Following the credit crisis and as a consequence of more stringent regulation in the structured finance arena, there is a growing need for business intelligence tools and information and the firm is committed to support the commercial real estate capital markets by delivering timely and relevant information during this period of economic recovery, and beyond.

21
Author's toolbox

21.1 OVERVIEW

The following section provides you with an insight into my own toolbox—whereby "tools" can be either a simple list, a collection of information, a graphical representation of areas that would require otherwise lengthy narrative to describe, useful spreadsheets, further mention and discussion of third-party vendor tools, website references to trade bodies and free information portals, and other "tricks of the trade".

Many of these tools require Bloomberg access and some basic Excel skills—something most banks and other financial institutions are readily using or supplying to their employees. Depending on which business area someone is working in, there may already be access to either a shared Bloomberg terminal or, even better, a standalone one. Because Bloomberg has become such a useful tool for the structured finance market and after having undergone a major function evolution during the credit crisis, I have included a comprehensive section on Bloomberg tools.

Granted, there may be additional requisites to turn these tools into "powertools", as you may need, for instance, access to rating agency websites or need to be a subscriber to third-party services such as Bloomberg and ABSnet. However, such subscriptions are not at all unusual and their relative costs could be considered affordable when compared with the large sums of money that are traded in the structured finance marketplace.

A good way of trying out some of these products and tools is, well, by means of a "trial". Most third-party vendors including the rating agencies will happily provide you with a trial in order to give you a better understanding and appreciation of their offerings and, eventually, turn you into a paying customer or subscriber of their services. Some of these trials can last for several months and, depending on how much or little you use those trials, this tip on its own could be worth several thousand dollars.

The book's companion website *www.structuredfinanceguide.com* is where you can find some of the tools described in this chapter for download.

21.2 RATINGS TOOLS

21.2.1 Rating table

The following rating mapping table (Table 21.1) enables you to look at the rating agencies—Moody's, Standard & Poor's, and Fitch's—and compare and contrast them on the following levels: investment grade vs. speculative grade, short term vs. long term, and intra-agency vs. inter-agency.

When using this table we need to be cautious and at the same time aware that this is not thought to be a "mapping" table whereby you can map the different agencies' ratings with each other, and, although you may be tempted to do so, it would certainly be incorrect. The mathematical reason that these ratings do not map in a one-to-one relationship is that the underlying probability of defaults (PD) are different, because the agencies slightly differ. They are closely related, but still differ, and a closer look at the underlying probability of default curves confirms this view. If we were to undertake

Table 21.1. Mapping table

	Fitch Ratings		*Moody's*		*Standard & Poor's*		*Mapped internal rating*
	Long-term rating	*Short-term rating*	*Long-term rating*	*Short-term rating*	*Long-term rating*	*Short-term rating*	
Investment grade	AAA		Aaa		AAA		AAA
	AA+	F1+	Aa1		AA+	A-1+	AA+
	AA		Aa2	P1	AA		AA
	AA−	F1+ or F1	Aa2		AA−		AA−
	A+		A1		A+	A-1	A+
	A	F1	A2	P-1 or P-2	A	A-1 or A-2	A
	A−	F1 or F2	A3	P-2	A−	A-2	A−
	BBB+	F2	Baa1		BBB+		BBB+
	BBB	F2 or F3	Baa2	P-2 or P-3	BBB	A-2 or A-3	BBB
	BBB−	F3	Baa1	P-3	BBB−	A-3	BBB−
Speculative grade	BB+		Ba1		BB+		BB+
	BB	B	Ba2		BB	B	BB
	BB−		Ba3		BB−	Ranges within B-1, B-2, and B-3	BB−
	B+		B1		B+		B+
	B		B2		B		B
	B−		B3	Not prime	B−		B−
	CCC+	C	Caa1		CCC+		CCC+
	CCC		Caa2		CCC	CCC	
	CCC−		Caa3		CCC−		CCC−
	CC		Ca		CC		CC
	C		C		C		C
	DDD DD D	D			D	D	D

such a PD curve analysis, we would find that, whilst the PD curves for Moody's, S&P, and Fitch are fairly close to each other on a short-term observation horizon (i.e., one year), the differences will become more noticeable when we increase the horizon to 5 or 10 years or even beyond.

The reason I have still named this a "mapping" table is simply because it can indeed be used as a mapping tool to map a bank's internal ratings to external ratings. This will still enable us to map an internal rating across to the different external ratings without having to know the internal probability of default (PD) and loss-given default (LGD) parameters for the particular bond or counterparty in question.

21.2.2 Rating notching table

The following rating notching table (Table 21.2) is closely related to the rating mapping table (Table 21.1). The difference is that it measures the distance of each rating to AAA (i.e., from the top rating) to the lower rating in so-called "notches" by **counting the gaps** in between AAA and the rating in question. So, for instance, if a AAA rating has been downgraded by nine notches it will be a ...?

The correct answer is BBB–. You can see that on the previous rating table if you count the lines between AAA and BBB– (which equals nine notches). Although the BBB– rating is still just about investment grade, it's on the "cusp" of speculative grade.

The same logic applies to the short-term ratings scale (Table 21.3); however, since the short-term ratings categories are not as clearcut as the long-term ratings categories it makes identifying the notch difference a little bit more tricky: Short-term ratings have some weird "or" categories whereby some of the rating identifiers can overlap. For instance S&P has "F1+ [or] F1", "F1 [or] F2", and a "F2 [or] F3" category. Similar ones apply to Moody's and Fitch—take a look at the rating table (Table 21.1).

Assume you are an investor who holds a structured finance portfolio with around 1,500 bonds and, whilst the other bank you just took over had internal ratings which were used to classify the bonds you hold and prioritize the deal workflow, etc., your new entity decided to decommission the internal ratings. Although your new firm wants to classify the bonds and manage the increased workflow with reduced resources, how can this be achieved?

Well, you could base your analysis almost entirely on external rating information and use this to rank your bond instruments. In order to do so, you will need to translate the letter-based rating information into some other parameters that are comparable on an intra-agency as well as inter-agency basis. You should then be able to do certain statistical calculations and I guess it would help if this can work automatically in order to handle the large number of bonds in your portfolio.

21.2.3 Notching tables

One way of doing all such analysis is by using the following two notching tables (Tables 21.2 and 21.3). Both notching tables translate the rating as well as any information in terms of rating watch status into a numeric value. Of course, if you are not particularly concerned with rating watch information, then you would end up with a slightly shorter table. However, since the rating watch status is easily available from Bloomberg you can easily factor in an additional layer of information (i.e., in the case of rating watches and early warning indicators of potentially looming problems) and, hence, I recommend you look closely and consider carefully any additional information that may be available on top of the actual rating.

You only need to do this exercise once—or you can save yourself time and download these notching tables from the companion website (*www.structuredfinanceguide.com*). Either way, the beauty of it is the simplicity with which you can translate a combination of rating letters that are not easy to process into numerical values, which you can then subject to all sorts of mathematical operations. For instance, one way of looking at the resulting set of data points per bond is by finding the lowest external rating and then using it as your worst case scenario to estimate the direction in which the overall rating tendency of such bonds is moving. During the height of the credit crisis the market witnessed literally hundreds of thousands of rating actions, mainly rating watches and downgrades by all three agencies. Some originally AAA-rated bonds experienced several downgrades in short periods

Table 21.2. Long-term ratings notching table

Notches	*S&P's*	*Moody's*	*Fitch*	*Internal rating*
1	AAA/*+ (*)	Aaa/*+ (*)	AAA/*+ (*)	iAAA/*+ (*)
2	AAA	Aaa	AAA	iAAA
3	AAA/*– (**)	Aaa/*–	AAA/*–	iAAA/*–
4	AA+/*+ (**)	Aa1/*+	AA+/*+	iAA+/*+
5	AA+	Aa1	AA+	iAA+
6	AA+/*–	Aa1/*–	AA+/*–	iAA+/*–
7	AA/*+	Aa2/*+	AA/*+	iAA/*+
8	AA	Aa2	AA	iAA
9	AA/*–	Aa2/*–	AA/*–	iAA/*–
10	AA–/*+	Aa3/*+	AA–/*+	iAA–/*+
11	AA–	Aa3	AA–	iAA–
12	AA–/*–	Aa3/*–	AA–/*–	iAA–/*–
13	A+/*+	A1/*+	A+/*+	iA+/*+
14	A+	A1	A+	iA+
15	A+/*–	A1/*–	A+/*–	iA+/*–
16	A/*+	A2/*+	A/*+	iA/*+
17	A	A2	A	iA
18	A/*–	A2/*–	A/*–	iA/*–
19	A–/*+	A3/*+	A–/*+	iA–/*+
20	A–	A3	A–	iA–
21	A–/*–	A3/*–	A–/*–	iA–/*–
22	BBB+/*+	Baa1/*+	BBB+/*+	iBBB+/*+
23	BBB+	Baa1	BBB+	iBBB+
24	BBB+/*–	Baa1/*–	BBB+/*–	iBBB+/*–
25	BBB/*+	Baa2/*+	BBB/*+	iBBB/*+
26	BBB	Baa2	BBB	iBBB
27	BBB/*–	Baa2/*–	BBB/*–	iBBB/*–
28	BBB–/*+	Baa3/*+	BBB–/*+	iBBB–/*+
29	BBB–	Baa3	BBB–	iBBB–
30	BBB–/*–	Baa3/*–	BBB–/*–	iBBB–/*–
31	BB+/*+	Ba1/*+	BB+/*+	iBB+/*+

Notches	*S&P's*	*Moody's*	*Fitch*	*Internal rating*
32	BB+	Ba1	BB+	iBB+
33	BB+/*−	Ba1/*−	BB+/*−	iBB+/*−
34	BB/*+	Ba2/*+	BB/*+	iBB/*+
35	BB	Ba2	BB	iBB
36	BB/*−	Ba2/*−	BB/*−	iBB/*−
37	BB−/*+	Ba3/*+	BB−/*+	iBB−/*+
38	BB−	Ba3	BB−	iBB−
39	BB−/*−	Ba3/*−	BB−/*−	iBB−/*−
40	B+/*+	B1/*+	B+/*+	iB+/*+
41	B+	B1	B+	iB+
42	B+/*−	B1/*−	B+/*−	iB+/*−
43	B/*+	B2/*+	B/*+	iB/*+
44	B	B2	B	iB
45	B/*−	B2/*−	B/*−	iB/*−
46	B−/*+	B3/*+	B−/*+	iB−/*+
47	B−	B3	B−	iB−
48	B−/*−	B3/*−	B−/*−	iB−/*−
49	CCC+/*+	Caa1/*+	CCC+/*+	iCCC+/*+
50	CCC+	Caa1	CCC+	iCCC+
51	CCC+/*−	Caa1/*−	CCC+/*−	iCCC+/*−
52	CCC/*+	Caa2/*+	CCC/*+	iCCC/*+
53	CCC	Caa2	CCC	iCCC
54	CCC/*−	Caa2/*−	CCC/*−	iCCC/*−
55	CCC−/*+	Caa3/*+	CCC−/*+	iCCC−/*+
56	CCC−	Caa3	CCC−	iCCC−
57	CCC−/*−	Caa3/*−	CCC−/*−	iCCC−/*−
58	CC	Ca	CC	iCC
59	C	C	C	iC
60	D	—	D	iD

* Although AAA is the highest external rating category available, some banks internally use AAA+ either to identify super senior bond tranches or liquidity facilities that sit "above" AAA-ranked tranches and, from a risk perspective, rank senior.

** /*+ denotes "rating match positive" and /*− denotes "rating match negative".

Table 21.3. Short-term ratings notching table

Notches	*S&P's*	*Moody's*	*Fitch Ratings*
1	A-1+	P1	F1+
2	A-1	P-1	F1
3	A-2	P-2	F2
4	A-3	P-3	F3
5	B-1	Not prime	B
6	B-2		C
7	B-3		D
8	C		
9	D		

of time and some of my clients' AAA-rated CDO of ABS eventually ended up—at least, rating-wise—in the lower speculative-grade rating areas (i.e., CCC and below) and, I guess by now, some of these are probably classed as "D"efaulted—or what is now referred to as "toxic" assets.

Another useful comparison is to use the simple average of all external ratings that are available for one particular bond. By doing so, you may be looking at a more balanced rating for the bond selected.

From a regulatory and capital charge calculation perspective, you may also be able to use the notching table to run your firm's capital charge calculation, etc.

Another useful application of these notching tables is that you can compare current ratings by translating them into a numerical value with an expected numerical value for anticipated rating changes. By doing so, you can measure current ratings against rating triggers in certain bonds or minimum required rating levels for counterparties and credit enhancement providers—typically known as "hard triggers". Furthermore, you could set so-called "soft triggers" for certain ratings (i.e., a higher rating level than the hard rating trigger level) and, by doing so, could have an early warning indicator when counterparties for some of your bond instruments are experiencing downgrades.

22

Bloomberg's structured finance tools: Tricks and tips

This chapter provides you with an in-depth look at Bloomberg's suite of analytical tools specifically focused on structured finance. There are many more non-structured finance–specific functions that can be useful to support your analysis; however, this also depends to a large extent on the focus of your particular area.

For the generic function please use Bloomberg's online resources such as:

- Help.
- 24/7 Live chat.
- Cheat sheets.
- Bloomberg university, etc.

The functions that follow can all be accessed via the main menu for mortgages—`<MTGE><Go>`.

22.1 STRUCTURE PAYDOWN FUNCTION (SPA)

The `Structure Paydown` (`SPA`) function is useful to chart projected cash flow patterns for all tranches within Bloomberg's selected CMO/ABS/CMBS mortgage deal credit group allowing users to display and visualize the waterfall for the selected deal.

Once you enter the Bloomberg ticker `<MTGE>SPA<Go>`, the structure paydown screen (see Figure 22.1) appears, where users are presented with the following options:

- *Change*. To change the data that appear, the user can enter/choose the appropriate information in/from the highlighted fields that appear followed by pressing `<Go>`.
- *Display*. To display the corresponding historical information for a specific data item that appears at the top of the screen, the user can select and click on the appropriate data item.
- *Create a new vector or curve*. To create a new vector or curve to be used within the analysis assumptions, choose `Create Vector` from the highlighted `Prepay`, `Default`, `Svrty/Lag`, or `Delinquency` field dropdown menu.
- *Create custom cash flow assumptions*. To create a custom cash flow assumption, the user can enter/choose the appropriate information in the highlighted fields, then click on the `9)` button.
- *Apply/use saved cash flow assumptions*. To apply a saved set of cash flow assumptions, the user can click on the `9)` button.
- *Display/Hide parameters*. To display/hide the current balance, bond type, or a WAL indictor for each tranche that appears in the graph, the user can click on the appropriate checkbox so that a checkmark appears/disappears.
- *Display additional information*. To display additional information for a specific data item, if applicable, the user can move her cursor over the appropriate data item. The complete information appears highlighted in blue.
- *Display corresponding tranche data*. To display the corresponding data for a specific tranche name/bar in the chart/WAL indicator, the user can move her cursor over the appropriate name/bar/indicator.

- *Display additional data.* To display additional data, if applicable, the users can click on the Page (X)/(Y) link that appears at the top of the screen—*or* press <PAGE FWD>/<PAGE BACK>.

22.1.1 Vector/Curve creation with SPA

You can use either static or dynamic assumptions for various components of the analysis. For dynamic analysis, you can create customized vectors or curves for prepayments, defaults, severity, and delinquency, as applicable. To create a vector/curve with SPA, complete the following steps:

1. From the Structure Paydown screen, choose Create Vector from the appropriate highlighted CPR, CDR, PSA, Default, Svrty/Lag, or Delinquency field dropdown menu. The corresponding Vector Editor window appears.
2. Enter the appropriate information in the highlighted Type, Start, Rate, Months, and S/R fields, then press <Go>—or drag and drop the vector information from an Excel spreadsheet to the vector table on the left-hand side of the window.
3. Enter a name for the vector in the highlighted Name field.
4. Click the Save button.

22.1.2 Create/Save cash flow assumptions

Once you enter the ticker symbol <MTGE>SPA<Go>, the Structured Paydown screen appears where you can enter and save prepayment, default, severity, lag and trigger assumptions. The cash flow assumptions you enter apply to the entire collateral group. To create and save a set of assumptions, complete the following steps:

Tips

The assumptions you save can be imported to the Cash Flows (CFT), Credit Support (MTCS), and Super Yield Table (SYT) functions. The corresponding <HELP> for each function displays further information. You can use standard prepayment and default speeds or incorporate custom vectors.

1. Enter/choose the appropriate information in/from the highlighted fields that appear directly above the graph, then press <Go>.
2. Click on the Assumptions Editor button—identified by the label "9)" that appears to the left of the Prepay field. The My Assumptions window appears.
3. Enter a name for the assumption set in the highlighted Current Assumptions field, then click on the Save Current Assumptions button.

22.1.3 Apply saved assumptions

Once you enter the Bloomberg ticker symbol <MTGE>SPA<Go>, the Structured Paydown screen appears where you can apply saved prepayment, default, severity, lag, and trigger assumptions by completing the following steps:

Tip

The saved assumptions that appear could have been created in the `Cash Flows (CFT)`, `Credit Support (MTCS)`, and `Super Yield Table (SYT)` functions. The corresponding `<HELP>` for each function displays further information.

1. Click on the `Assumptions Editor` button—identified by the label `9)`. The `My Assumptions` window appears.
2. Click on the appropriate saved assumption `Name` from the list that appears. The corresponding row highlights in white.
3. Click on the `Apply Saved Assumption` button.

22.1.4 Credit-driven scenarios

CMBS assets are generally non-recourse loans secured by income-producing property. These loans exhibit substantial credit risk and the likelihood that each loan may prepay or default depends upon changes in the credit quality of the underlying property(ies). Furthermore, the performance of these loans is driven by the combination of interest rates and credit quality.

Credit-driven analysis is a set of rules that retain the underlying mechanics of traditional prepayment and default analyses, but extend these analyses to take full account of the credit risk of commercial mortgage loans. It is based on the premise that prepayment and default assumptions should be applied to each loan individually, depending on the loan's projected credit quality.

CMBS financial reporting typically includes quarterly or annual disclosure of each underlying property's income statement. `Credit Driven` analytics offer a direct mechanism to incorporate this information into bond pricing.

`Credit Driven Scenarios` allow you to model different prepayment, default, and recovery scenarios and you can also specify net operating income (NOI) growth, future cap rate trends, and refinancing terms. Specifically, `Credit Driven Scenarios` allow you to grow and shrink projected NOI and to forecast property value by specifying a capitalization rate. In addition, you can model the terms under which a borrower can refinance or extend their loan.

`Credit Driven Scenario` analysis is available in the following functions: `MTCS (Credit Support)`, `CFT (Cash Flow Table)`, `SYT (Super Yield Table)`, `SPA (Structured Paydown Analysis)`, `SCEN (Scenario Manager)`, and `LM (Loan Manager)`.

To create a `Credit Driven Scenario` in the `SPA` function, complete the following steps:

My Scenario window

1. From the toolbar, click `Scenario > Credit Driven Scenario`. The `My Credit Driven Scenarios` window appears.

Scenario assumptions

2. The top of the `My Credit Driven Scenario` window displays the name, description, and last update date for any credit-driven scenarios you have previously saved.

The bottom of the window is broken down into six assumption sections defined by the six checkboxes that appear: `Property`, `Refinancing Terms`, `Recovery`, `Prepay`, `Default`, and `Extend`. Each section allows you to enter parameters for the scenario.

From the `My Credit Driven Scenarios` window you can either modify a previously saved credit-driven scenario or create a new credit-driven scenario.

If you are modifying an existing scenario, click the appropriate scenario `Name` from the top of the screen so that it is highlighted. The bottom half of the screen updates with information from the selected scenario.

If you are creating a new assumption set, most of the assumption parameter fields at the bottom of the screen appear blank.

To enter the assumptions for the credit-driven scenario, toggle the checkbox to the left of the appropriate section. A checkmark activates the related assumption parameters. Enter the appropriate information in the highlighted fields.

The assumption sections and associated assumption parameters are as follows:

- `Property` allows you to enter property performance information such as the capitalization rate and NOI growth rate assumptions.
- `CapRate` is the capitalization rate. It measures a property's ability to generate cash before taxes and debt service. The value you enter is used to calculate a projected value for each period. If a cap rate is not entered, the projected appraisal value uses an implied cap rate calculated by projected NOI and cutoff value. You can enter a vector for the capitalization rate value by clicking on the `CapRate` field label.
- `Growth%` is net operating income growth. You may grow or shrink projected NOI by entering a growth rate in this field. For each asset, the latest full year financial data that are available are used as a starting point to project-reported NOI. You can enter a vector for the growth rate value by clicking on the `Growth%` field label.
- `Refinancing Terms` allows you to calculate the refinancing proceeds (the gross proceeds from refinancing an existing loan) using the spread, amortization, and the debt service coverage ratio, or the loan-to-value ratio.
- `Sprd` is the refinance spread. The spread over a 10-year treasury is used to determine the fixed rate coupon on the new loan in basis points. The field defaults to zero basis points.
- `LTV` allows you to calculate refinancing proceeds (the gross proceeds from refinancing an existing loan) using a loan-to-value ratio requirement (the LTV method). An LTV requirement for the new loan is optional. An LTV test is not imposed on the refinance calculation.
- `DSCR` allows you to enter a debt service coverage ratio (DSCR) requirement for the new loan. The DSCR is the ratio of the annualized scheduled payments of principal and/or interest on the mortgage loan to the net operating income or net cash flow for the property. The field defaults to the DSCR from the original cutoff date. It is assumed that a lender would underwrite a new loan using the DSCR established by the original lender at cutoff.
- `Amort` is the amortization term requirement for the new loan. It defaults to the information from the loan cutoff. It is assumed that a lender would underwrite a new loan using the existing loan's original amortization term. You can specify a different amortization term by entering the number of months of amortization. Enter a zero for interest-only loans.
- `Recovery` allows you to enter information for the recovery amount assumption.
- `Mode` allows you to choose the mode used to calculate the amount of principal recovered in conjunction with the `Default` or `Extend` assumptions. The highlighted dropdown menu displays the following options:
  - `Loss Severity` allows you to enter the loss severity percentage (similar to a constant default rate or CDR assumption) in the `Svrty` field from the `Default` section of the window.
  - `Refinance` allows you to refinance proceeds (the gross proceeds from refinancing an existing loan), calculated based on the `Refinance` terms you enter. The refinance terms are then used as

recovery against the defaulted balance. If the difference between the refinancing proceeds and the loan balance is net-positive, there is no loss to the loan. If the difference between the refinancing proceeds and the loan balance is net-negative, the difference is the loss.

  - `Dispose`. The sale proceeds from a projected value of the property (based on the capitalization rate, or `CapRate`) are used as recovery against the defaulted balance. If the property value is greater than the loan balance, there is no loss. If the property value is less than the loan balance, the difference between the loan balance and value of the property is the loss. This is used in conjunction with the `Property` assumptions.
  - `Loss Amount`. Generally applied to a single loan once the loan has been isolated into a group. It is assumed that the loan loss has been predetermined but has not been factored into the trust, as of yet. Choosing this mode allows you to enter the loss amount in the `Loss` or `Loss Amt` field within the `Recovery` assumptions.

- `Fee` allows you to enter the transaction fee, if applicable.
- `Loss Amt` or `Loss` applies to `Loss Amount Mode` and allows you to enter the loss amount in the corresponding currency.
- `Prepay` allows you to enter loan prepayment assumptions. Property owners have an incentive to prepay a loan when they can refinance and take out cash.
- `If Excess>` allows you to enter the percentage of excess proceeds that will trigger a (refinance) prepayment. Excess proceeds are calculated as the refinancing proceeds minus the sum of the scheduled outstanding loan balance and any required prepayment premium.
- `Prepay Rate` and `Type` (context-sensitive—i.e., label may not appear). The two leftmost highlighted fields in the `Prepay` section allow you to enter prepayment speed and type assumptions. The prepay type dropdown menu displays a list of choices, including creating a vector. The `BPN (Bloomberg Prepayment Notation)` function displays further information on the available prepayment speed types.
- `YM` allows you to enter a trigger value that determines when prepayments are applied. You can enter `LOCK` to apply prepayments after the yield maintenance period—or you can enter a numeric value to apply prepayments if the projected yield maintenance penalty rate for the loan falls below the value you enter in the `YM` field. The value you enter is the minimum yield maintenance premium (a prepayment penalty) rate.

Tips

When using a `CPR` prepayment assumption, if the `YM` field is blank, prepayments occur immediately, or after any hard lockout or defeasance periods, with a corresponding projected prepayment penalty fee.

When using a `CPR` prepayment assumption, if the `YM` field's value is greater than zero, prepayments are allowed if the projected prepayment penalty rate for the loan falls below the value in the `YM` field. For example, if you enter `100 CPR` in the `Prepay` field and `10` in the `YM` field, then the `100 CPR` prepayment speed applies if the projected prepayment penalty rate for the loan falls below 10%.

When using a `CPY` prepayment assumption, the `YM` field automatically defaults to `LOCK` which prevents prepayments from occurring during the yield maintenance period. Prepayments will occur after the yield maintenance period ends.

When using a `CPP` prepayment scenario, the `YM` field automatically defaults to `LOCK`.

- `FP` allows you to enter a trigger value that determines when prepayments are applied. You can enter `LOCK` to apply prepayments after the fixed penalty period—or you can enter a numeric value to apply prepayments if the projected fixed penalty rate for the loan falls below the value you enter in the `FP` field. The value you enter is the minimum fixed penalty (a prepayment penalty) rate.

Tips

If you use a `CPR` prepayment scenario where the `FP` field is blank, then prepayments occur immediately, or after any hard lockout or defeasance periods, with a corresponding projected prepayment penalty fee.

If you use a `CPR` prepayment scenario where the `FP` field's value is greater than zero, then prepayments are allowed if the projected prepayment penalty rate for the loan falls below the value in the `FP` field. For example, if you enter `100 CPR` in the `Prepay` field and `3` in the `FP` field, then the `100 CPR` prepayment speed applies if the projected prepayment penalty rate for the loan falls below 3%.

- `ToOp` applies to `CPR` prepayment rate scenarios. If `ToOp` is set to `Yes`, then the outstanding principal balance prepays at 100% at the first freely prepayable (open) period. If the `ToOp` field is set to `No`, the outstanding principal balance of the loan does not prepay at 100% at the first open period.
- `Default` allows you to enter loan default assumptions. A default occurs when a property owner cannot meet their debt service obligations (scheduled loan payments). For instance, when the property's debt service coverage ratio (DSCR) falls below 1.0 × NOI generated by the property, it is insufficient to cover loan payments. In `Credit Driven` analysis, you can specify the DSCR that triggers a default. Following a specified delay, the severity of the default is calculated to reflect the underlying property's performance and eligibility for financing by selecting the `Recovery` option.
- `If DSRC <` allows you to enter the debt service coverage ratio that will trigger loans to default. If the projected DSCR falls below the value you enter, the default assumption is applied.
- `Default Rate` and `Type` (context-sensitive—i.e., label may not appear). The two leftmost highlighted fields in the `Default` section allow you to enter default speed and type assumptions. The default type dropdown menu displays a list of choices, including creating a vector. The `BPN (Bloomberg Prepayment Notation)` function displays further information on the available default speed types.
- `(Default) Svrty` is the loss severity, which is the percentage of the principal loan balance at the time of default, which determines the loss amount. You must choose `Loss Severity` mode from the `Recovery` section of the assumptions to activate this field.
- `(Default) Lag` is the number of months between the time of default and the recovery. If a loss is incurred, it is applied to the principal balance at recovery.
- `RcvMat` is the recovery to maturity. If you use a `CDR` default assumption with a `Lag` greater than zero, then a `Yes` in the `RcvMat` field indicates that the last period principal is recovered and losses are applied on the loan's maturity date. A `No` in the `RcvMat` field indicates a delay between when the last period of principal is recovered and losses are applied. The delay is equal to the number of lag periods *after* the maturity date. This applies if the `CDR` speed is less than 100.

- Extend allows you to enter information for the loan extension assumptions. For any loans that have a balloon payment on the maturity date, the Extend assumptions allows you to push out the final balloon payment past the loan's maturity date to simulate a loan extension, or a balloon default scenario. When a property owner cannot refinance a balloon repayment because the property's debt service is less than the balloon repayment amount, the asset is likely to extend.
- Extend Rate (context-sensitive—i.e., label may not appear) is the extension rate percentage. The percent of the balloon amount to default.
- If Shrtfall > allows you to specify the percentage shortfall that triggers the balloon extend assumptions. A shortfall occurs when the amount of a property's debt service is less than its balloon repayment amount.
- (Extend) Svrty is the percentage of the loan balance to default. Applies only if you choose Loss Severity from the Recovery mode.
- (Extend) Lag is the number of months between the time of default and the recovery. If a loss is incurred, it is applied to the principal balance at recovery.
- Opt Ext is the optional extension, a provision permitting extension of the original term of the mortgage under terms agreed upon at origination. The dropdown menu displays the following choices:
  - None means no extension scenario is applied.
  - 1st represents a scenario that exercises the first optional extension for CMBS deals.
  - 2nd represents a scenario that exercises the second optional extension for CMBS deals.
  - All represents a scenario that exercises *all* optional extensions for CMBS deals.
- Advn. A Yes indicates that the servicer is advancing principal and interest payments. A No indicates that the servicer is not advancing principal and interest payments.

User options

3. Choose from the following options:

   - To save the new credit-driven scenario assumption set you created, enter a name for the scenario in the highlighted Name field. Then, click the Save & Apply button. The Structure Paydown screen appears updated with calculations based on the assumption set you created and saved.
   - To save the changes you made to a previously saved scenario, click the Save & Apply button. The Structure Paydown screen appears updated with calculations based on the assumption set you modified and saved.
   - To apply the credit-driven scenario to SPA analysis without saving the scenario for future use, click the Apply button. The Structure Paydown screen appears with calculations based on the credit-driven scenario you entered.
   - To close the My Credit Driven Scenarios window without saving or applying any information you entered, click the Close button. The Structure Paydown screen appears without any updates.

Use vectors in credit-driven scenarios

Within the My Credit Driven Scenarios window, you can enter either static or dynamic vector assumptions for certain types of loan assumptions. A vectored assumption means that the rate applied to the assumption characteristic changes at user-determined points in time, instead of assuming one constant rate for the duration of the loan(s).

For `Prepay` and `Default` assumptions you can apply a vector you have previously created or choose `Create Vector` from the corresponding rate-type dropdown menus. The `Prepay Vector Editor` or `Default Vector Editor` window appears. The "How to create a vector/curve" section of this chapter displays further information on creating prepayment and default vectors.

For capitalization rate (`CapRate`) and NOI growth (`%Growth`) assumptions, you can create and apply vectors by completing the following steps:

1. Click the `CapRate and/or Growth% field label`. The `Vector Description Entry` window appears.
2. Enter the vector information in the highlighted field using the following syntax:

```
(rate1)(#periods)(S/R)(rate2) ...
```

The non-static rates within a vector can either assume a sudden transition, a step (S), or a gradual transition, a ramp (R). A step applies a flat rate over the specified number of periods. A ramp applies incremental rates to attain the target rate at the end of the specified number of periods.

Examples

(1) Entering a `Growth%` vector "5.5 12S 7.5 24S 10" indicates the growth applied in the first 12 projected periods is 5.5%. In Period 13, it increases (steps up) to 7.5% for the next 24 periods. In Month 25, it steps up to 10% and applies 10% to the remaining life of the loan.
(2) Vector "0 12R 5 24R" applies 0% in the first projected period and increases the rate incrementally to the target of 5% at the end of Period 12. From Period 12 to Period 36, the rate will grow incrementally from 5% to 10%. In Month 37, it applies a flat rate of 10% for the life of the loan.

In addition to determining step and ramp rate transitions for a vector, you can also anchor a vector on a certain date. The anchor date is the date upon which the vector becomes effective. If you leave an anchor date unspecified, the vector is anchored on the next payment date.

To anchor a vector, you must enter "A" and the date in mm/dd/yyyy format followed by the vector rate information.

Example

For example, to anchor vector "5.5 12S 7.5 24S 10" to January 1, 2010, enter: "A 01/01/2010 5.5 12S 7.5 24S 10".

3. Once you enter the vector information, click the `Done` button. The `Vector Description Entry` window closes and a "V" appears to the right of the field for which you entered a vector.

To **edit the vector**, click on the appropriate `Cap(V)` or `Grw(V)` field, make the change(s) in the `Vector Description Entry` window, then click `Done`.

Example

Assume there is a balloon loan with a 7-year term, 81 months of yield maintenance periods, and 3 months of freely prepayable periods. The borrower can prepay anytime within the 81 months, but the borrower will also have to pay a yield maintenance premium (prepayment penalty fee). If the borrower does not prepay during the yield maintenance period, then the borrower also has the option to prepay for 3 months without incurring a prepayment penalty. In a scenario with a `25 CPR` and the `ToOp` field set to `Yes`, the loan prepays at `25 CPR` *during* the yield maintenance period. Also, when the loan enters the first freely prepayable (open) period, the loan automatically prepays the outstanding principal balance at `100 CPR`.

Parameter description

`Trig`. The initial state of the delinquency trigger within the selected deal. The dropdown menu displays a list of choices.

`Type`. The assumption type. The dropdown menu displays the appropriate choices.

`VPR`. The historical voluntary prepayment rate.

`WAL Indicator`. A checkmark indicates that the weighted average life appears as a white diamond for each tranche bar in the graph.

`YM`. Applies to commercial mortgage-backed securities only. The `YM` field allows you to enter a trigger value that determines when prepayments are applied. The following are valid inputs:

- `LOCK` applies prepayments after the yield maintenance period.
- `(Numeric value)` applies prepayments *if* the projected yield maintenance penalty rate for the loan falls below the value you enter in the `YM` field. The value you enter is the minimum yield maintenance premium (a prepayment penalty) rate.
- The following **rules apply**:
  - When using a `CPR` prepayment scenario, if the `YM` field is blank, prepayments occur immediately, or after any hard lockout or defeasance periods, with a corresponding projected prepayment penalty fee.
  - When using a `CPR` prepayment scenario, if the `YM` field's value is greater than zero, prepayments are allowed if the projected prepayment penalty rate for the loan falls below the value in the `YM` field. For example, if you enter `100 CPR` in the `Prepay` field and `10` in the `YM` field, then the `100 CPR` prepayment speed applies if the projected prepayment penalty rate for the loan falls below 10%.
  - When you use a `CPY` prepayment scenario, the `YM` field automatically defaults to `LOCK` which prevents prepayments from occurring during the yield maintenance period. Prepayments will occur after the yield maintenance period ends.
  - When you use a `CPP` prepayment scenario, the `YM` field automatically defaults to `LOCK`.

Once you enter (ticker symbol) `<MTGE>SPA<Go>`, the `Structure Paydown` screen appears with a chart of projected cash flow patterns for all tranches within the selected CMO/ABS/CMBS mortgage deal's credit group.

The graph that appears displays a chart of the projected cash flow patterns for all tranches within the selected CMO/ABS/CMBS mortgage deal's credit group. Time appears on the horizontal x-axis; the name of the tranche that corresponds to each bar on the chart appears on the vertical y-axis.

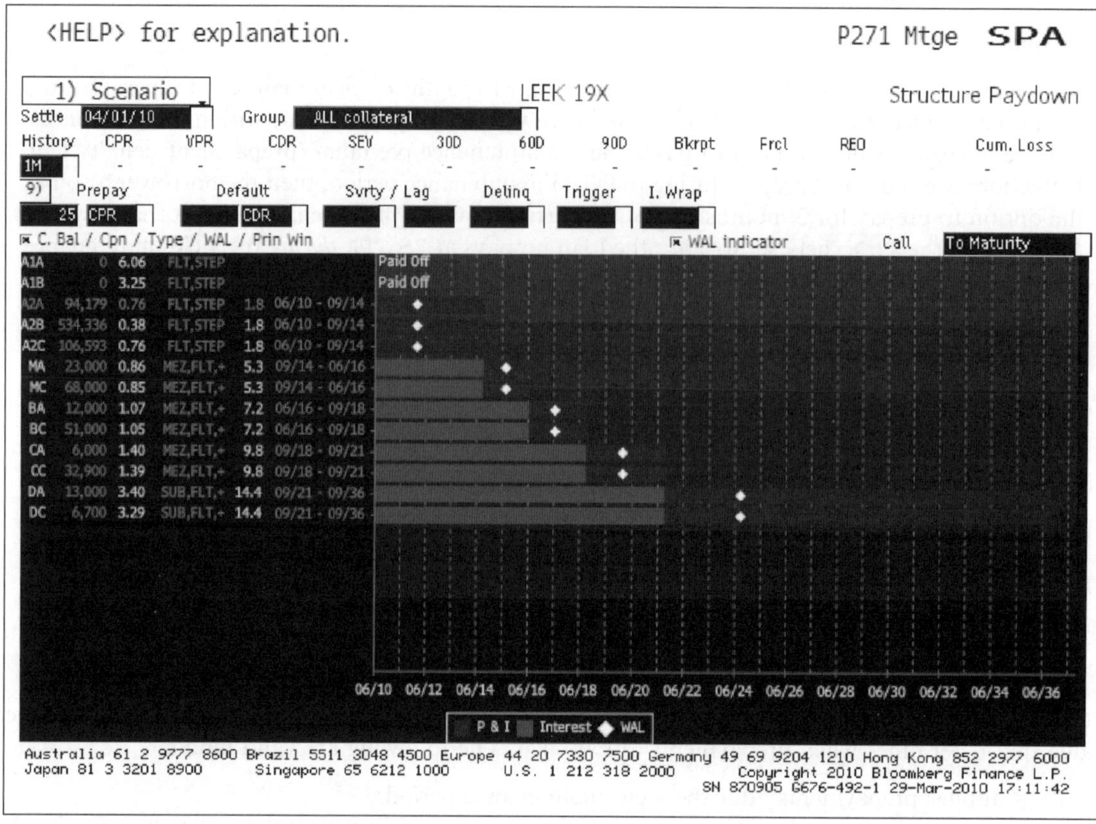

Figure 22.1. The SPA screen.

Depending on the security and view that you choose, some of the following fields may appear, listed here in alphabetical order:

- `9)`. The `Assumptions Editor` button allows you to apply/create saved cash flow assumptions using the `My Assumptions` window.
- `30D`. The total number of loans that are 30 days delinquent, expressed as a percentage.
- `60D`. The total number of loans that are 60 days delinquent, expressed as a percentage.
- `90D`. The total number of loans that are 90 days delinquent, expressed as a percentage.
- `Apply Saved Assumptions` allows you to apply the set of assumptions you select from the `My Assumption` window.
- `Bkrpt`. The total number of mortgage holders in the selected collateral group that have reported bankruptcy, expressed as a percentage.
- `C. Bal(000)/Bond Type`. A checkmark indicates that the current balance, expressed in thousands, and bond type information for the tranches appears to the left of the graph.
- `Call`. The manner in which the cash flows are run. The dropdown menu displays the appropriate choices.
- `CDR` is the 1-month historical conditional default rate.
- `CPR` is the 1-month historical conditional prepayment rate.

- Cum. Loss. The cumulative loss, which is the total amount of the collateral that is written down because of losses on the underlying loan, expressed as a percentage.
- Current Assumption allows you to enter/display the name for the set of assumptions you select from/save in the My Assumptions window.
- Default. The default speed and assumption used to calculate the cash flows for the selected deal. The dropdown menu displays a list of choices.

> **Tip**
>
> BPN4<Go> displays further information on default rate notations.

- Delay. The number of months after which the state of the deal trigger changes, if applicable.

> **Tip**
>
> If the Delay field is empty, the state of the deal trigger will not change.

- Delinquency allows you to enter either a static or dynamic (vectored) delinquency assumption that is used as an input to the shifting interest and trigger tests associated with a deal.

> **Tip**
>
> The Structured Finance Notes function (SFNS) displays further information.

- Description. A brief description of the assumption parameters.
- Extend applies to commercial mortgage-backed securities only. The percent of the balloon amount to default. For any loans that have a balloon payment on the maturity date, the Extend field allows you to push out the final balloon payment past the loan's maturity date to simulate a loan extension, or a balloon default scenario.
- FP applies to commercial mortgage-backed securities only. The FP field allows you to enter a trigger value that determines when prepayments are applied. The following are valid inputs:
  - LOCK applies prepayments after the fixed penalty period.
- Frcl. The total number of loans that resulted in the homeowner's property being seized by the mortgage holder, expressed as a percentage.
- Graph (label does not appear). This applies to the Vector Editor window. The graph of the vector. The number of months appears on the horizontal *x*-axis; the rate appears on the vertical *y*-axis.
- Group. The collateral group for which the data appear. The dropdown menu displays the appropriate choices.

> **Tip**
>
> The Group field defaults to the credit stack for the last security you loaded.

- `History`. The historical period for which the corresponding speeds appear. The dropdown menu displays a list of choices.
- `Lag`. The number of months between the date on which the loan defaults and the recovery.

> **Tip**
>
> If a loss is incurred, the lag is applied to the principal loan balance at the time of recovery.

- `Modified`. The date on which the corresponding vector was most recently updated.
- `Months`. The number of months over which the corresponding rate is applied to the vector.
- `Name`. The name of the corresponding vector/assumption.
- `Opt Ext` applies to commercial mortgage-backed securities only. The optional extension is a provision permitting extension of the original term of the mortgage under terms agreed upon at origination. The dropdown menu displays the following choices:
  - `None` means no extension scenario is applied.
  - `1st` represents a scenario that exercises the first optional extension for CMBS deals.
  - `2nd` represents a scenario that exercises the second optional extension for CMBS deals.
  - `All` represents a scenario that exercises *all* optional extensions for CMBS deals.

> **Worth knowing**
>
> When a loan has optional extension terms, "0(36), E1(12), E3(12)", the E1, E2, and E3 indicate that the loan has up to three optional extension terms that the borrower can exercise before defaulting on the balloon. The number in parentheses represents the length of the optional extension term. In this example, the borrower has three opportunities to pay off the loan. If the borrower is unable to repay the loan after exercising *all* optional extensions, the principal balloon goes into default. The CMBS `Loan Description` screen (`LDES`) displays optional extension term information in the `Rem. Protection` field. `LDES <HELP>` displays further information.
>
> You can simultaneously apply assumptions from the `Opt Ext` field and `Extend` fields. If the loan has optional extension terms and you select an option for the `Opt Ext` field, the cash flow projections will apply to the `Opt Ext` field's assumptions *first*, then to the `Extend` field's assumptions.

- `Prepay`. The speed and prepayment type that make up the prepayment speed assumption, which is used to calculate the cash flows for the selected deal. The dropdown menu displays a list of choices.

> **Tip**
>
> The `Prepayment Rate Notion function (BPN)` displays further information on valid prepayment types.

- `Rate`. The rate of the vector.
- `RcvMat` applies to commercial mortgage-backed securities only. The recovery to maturity. If you

use a CDR default assumption with a Lag greater than zero, then a Yes in the RcvMat field indicates that the last period principal is recovered and losses are applied on the loan's maturity's date. A No in the RcvMat field indicates a delay between when the last period of principal is recovered and losses are applied. The delay is equal to the number of lag periods *after* the maturity date. This applies if the CDR speed is less than 100.

Example

If Lag = 18 and RcvMat = YES, with a loan maturity date of June 2009, then the principal is recovered and losses are applied in June 2009.

If Lag = 18 and RcvMat = NO, with a loan maturity date of June 2009, then the principal is recovered and losses are applied in December 2010.

- REO. The total number of properties owned by the bank that were not taken as the result of defaulted loans, expressed as a percentage.
- S/R. The manner in which the corresponding data appear in the graph. The dropdown menu displays the appropriate choices.
- Save Current Assumption allows you to save the cash flow assumptions you entered.
- Settle. The settlement date used in the calculation. The button to the right of the highlighted field displays a calendar from which you can choose the appropriate date.
- SEV. The historical severity.
- Start. The first date for which the vector data appear. The dropdown menu displays the appropriate choices.
- Svrty. The percentage of the principal loan balance at the time of default which is used to calculate the loss amount.
- Svrty. The loss severity. When using a default scenario (CDR and Extend), it is the percentage of the defaulted principal cash flow that is unrecoverable.
- Lag. The months to recovery. The number of periods from the time of default until principal is recovered and losses are realized. When used with the Extend field, it is the number of months that the defaulted balloon payment is extended beyond the loan's maturity date. The following rules apply:
  - If the Lag field is blank or has a value of zero, then the principal recovery and/or loss is applied to the first projected period.
  - If the Lag field has a value greater than zero, then the principal recovery and/or loss is not applied until x number of periods from the first period cash flow is defaulted.

Example

If the Lag value is 18, and the date of the defaulted cash flow projection is January 2009, then the principal recovery/loss is applied in July 2010.

- Time/Date (label does not appear). The time and date on which the selected vector was most recently updated.

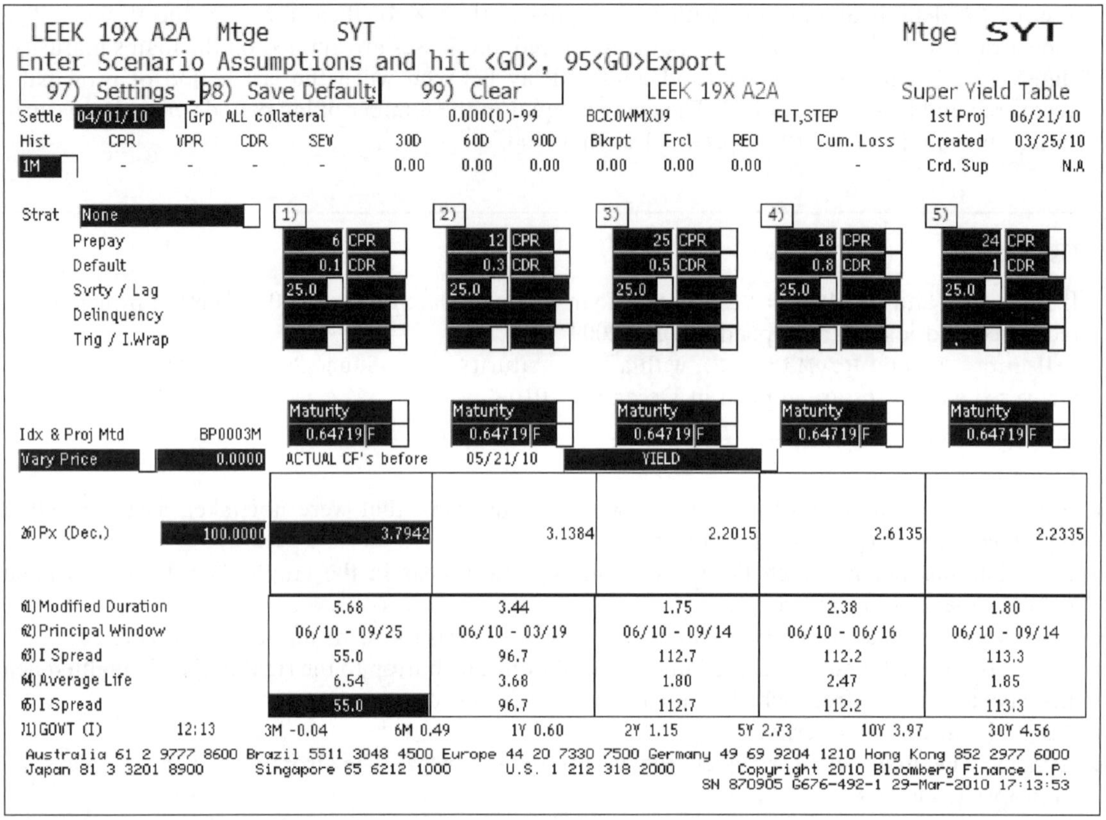

Figure 22.2. Super Yield Table (SYT) screen.

- ToOp applies to commercial mortgage-backed securities only. It applies to CPR prepayment rate scenarios. If ToOp is set to Yes, then the outstanding principal balance prepays at 100% at the first freely prepayable (open) period. If the ToOp field is set to No, the outstanding principal balance of the loan does not prepay at 100% at the first open period.

22.2 SUPER YIELD TABLE (SYT)

Bloomberg's Super Yield Table (SYT) function performs price, yield, and spread analysis for all non-agency RMBS, ABS, and CMBS products. You can stratify a deal's collateral in numerous ways and assign both prepayment and default assumptions to the stratified pieces of the collateral. Instead of assuming that all collateral is behaving the same, you can make various assumptions for different stratifications of the collateral.

SYT screen options

Once you enter the Bloomberg ticker symbol <MTGE>SYT<Go>, the Super Yield Table screen appears (Figure 22.2). Choose from the following options, if applicable:

> **Tip**
>
> The type of security you choose determines the fields/options that appear on the screen and there are additional functions available for CMBS deals. See further for more details.

- To save the information you enter/choose in/from the `Idx & Proj Mtd`, `Yield to` (label does not appear), `Vary Price`, `Discount Margin/Yield`, `Spread/Sensitivity Measurement` (label does not appear), and `Curve` fields, if applicable, click on `Settings > Save Current Settings` from the toolbar.
- To restore the original defaults, click on `Settings > Restore Initial Settings` from the toolbar.
- To save the assumption sets for the five scenarios that appear, click on `Settings > Sticky Assumptions/Scenarios` from the toolbar so that a checkmark appears.

> **Tip**
>
> The `Sticky Assumptions/Scenario` option distinguishes between assumption sets for residential mortgage backed securities and commercial mortgage backed securities.

- To send the data for a specific scenario to the `Mortgage Scenario Manager` function (`SCEN`), click on `Save Defaults > Save to SCEN` from the toolbar. The "How to send data to SCEN" section of this chapter displays further information.
- To send the data that appear to the `Stratified Yield Table Defaults` function (`SYTD`), click on `Save Defaults > Save to SYTD` from the toolbar.

> **Tip**
>
> The `Save to SYTD` option does not appear active if you select `None` from the `Strat` field dropdown menu.

- To clear the data that appear, click on the `Clear All` toolbar button.
- To display additional information for a specific data item/column heading, if applicable, move your cursor over the appropriate data item/column heading. The complete information appears highlighted in blue.
- To display additional historical prepayment/default speeds, click on the corresponding data in the `CPR/VPR/CDR/SEV` field. The `Class/Deal Pay History` screen appears.
- To display historical collateral delinquency details, click on the corresponding data in the `30D/60D/90D/Bkrpt/Frcl/REO/Cum. Loss` field. The `Collateral Performance` screen appears.
- To display the selected bond's credit support, click on the corresponding data in the `Crd. Sup` field. The `Credit Support` screen (`MTCS`) appears.
- To assign delinquent loan assumptions and stratification of the collateral (60 day + 90 day + REO + Foreclosure), click on the checkbox to the left of the `Delinq 60Day+` field so that a checkmark appears.

Tip

The Delinq 60Day+ field does not appear when you choose None from the Strat field dropdown menu.

- To value the selected mortgage bond/deal, enter/choose the appropriate information in/from the highlighted fields that appear, then press <Go>.
- To create a new vector or curve to be used within the analysis assumptions, choose Create Vector from the highlighted Prepay, Default, Svtry/Lag, or Delinquency field dropdown menu.
- To create/save custom cash flow assumptions, enter/choose the appropriate information in the highlighted fields, then click on the white menu number to the left of the appropriate scenario.
- To apply a saved set of cash flow assumptions, click on the white menu number to the left of the appropriate scenario.
- To enter credit assumptions for a structured finance deal, choose the appropriate criterion from the highlighted Strat dropdown menu, then click on the white number to the left of the appropriate scenario.
- To display the Structured Finance Notes function (SFNS) for the data that appear in another Bloomberg Professional service window, click on Svrty/Lag or Trig/Dly. Applies only when you choose None from the Strat field dropdown menu. SFNS <HELP> displays further information.
- To display loan-level data, click on the appropriate menu item number beneath the highlighted Strat field. The SYT Loan Details screen appears.
- To change the price format, click on Px (Dec.)/Px (32nd).

Loan Details screen

Once you click on the appropriate menu item number beneath the highlighted Strat field, the Loan Details screen appears. Choose from the following options:

- To choose the criterion by which the data that appear are stratified, choose the appropriate option from the highlighted Statify By field dropdown menu.
- To display the data that appear in an Excel spreadsheet, click on the Export toolbar button.
- To display additional information for a specific data item/column heading, if applicable, move your cursor over the appropriate data item/column heading. The complete information appears highlighted in blue.
- To sort the data that appear by column, right-click and hold on the appropriate column heading, then choose the appropriate option from the menu that appears.
- To change the width of a column, click and hold on the dividing line to the right of the appropriate column heading so that a double-arrow appears, then drag the line to the appropriate location and release.
- To display additional information, if applicable, click on the up/down or right/left scrollbar.

Send data to the Bloomberg Scenario Manager (SCEN)

1. From the Super Yield Table screen, click on Save Defaults > Save to SCEN from the toolbar. The Save to SCEN <Go> window appears.
2. Enter the appropriate information in the highlighted fields, then press <Go>.

3. Click on the checkbox that appears to the left of the appropriate scenario so that a checkmark appears/disappears.

> **Tip**
>
> A checkmark indicates that you want the corresponding scenario to be saved in `SCEN`. You can select/deselect all scenarios by clicking on the checkbox to the left of `Scenario Name` so that a checkmark appears/disappears.

4. Click on the `Save to SCEN` button.

Analyze CMBS deals

To perform price, yield, and spread analysis for commercial mortgage-backed securities (CMBS), choose from the following CMBS-specific options in the `Super Yield Table` screen (`SYT`):

- To perform basic scenario analysis, choose `Basic` from the `Analysis Type` field (label does not appear) dropdown menu, enter/choose the appropriate information in/from the highlighted fields, then press `<Go>`.
- To perform stratified collateral analysis, click on the `Analysis Type` field (label does not appear) and choose `Filter Stratification` from the dropdown menu that appears. Enter/choose the appropriate stratification category(ies) and corresponding value(s) in the highlighted field(s) that appears on the far left of the screen.

> **Tips**
>
> The number that appears in the % column represents the percentage of the loan that fits within the corresponding stratification. If a loan does not meet any of the filter criteria, it remains in the `Main Group` category.

- To display the individual loans within a filter group, click on the corresponding number that appears to the left of the group name—or click on the number that appears to the right of the `Main Group` heading.
- To perform a highly customized level of collateral analysis, click on the `Analysis Type` field (label does not appear) dropdown menu, then choose `Advanced Scenario`. Choose `Edit Scenario` from one of the five `Edit Scenario` field dropdown menus that appear so that the `CMBS Scenario Editor Window` appears. The "How to use the CMBS Scenario Window for Advanced Scenario analysis" section of this chapter displays further information.

Perform CMBS Advanced Scenario analysis

To create, save, and apply custom prepayment and default assumptions for custom loan groups, complete the following steps:

1. Click on the `Analysis Type` field (label does not appear) from the left-hand side of the screen and choose `Advanced Scenario`.

2. Click on one of the highlighted `Edit Scenario` fields and choose `Edit Scenario` or a saved scenario. The `CMBS Scenario Editor` window appears.
3. To manage the loan group(s) for the advanced scenario analysis, choose from the following options:
   - To create a custom loan group to which you can apply your custom assumptions, click on the `Add Group` button. The "How to add a CMBS Loan Group" section of this chapter displays further information.
   - To delete a loan group from the `CMBS Scenario Editor` window, click on the corresponding red X button that appears to the right side of the screen, then click on `YES` from the `Confirmation` window.
   - To apply a saved scenario, click on the `My Scenarios` button so that the `My CMBS Scenario` window appears. Click on the name of the appropriate scenario, then click on the `Apply` button.
   - To export the grouping information to an Excel spreadsheet, click on the `Export` button.
4. To manage the assumptions for the advanced scenario analysis, choose from the following options:
   - To apply custom prepayment and default assumptions to a loan group, enter/choose the appropriate information in/from the corresponding highlighted fields that appear, then click on the `Apply` button.
   - To apply prepayment and/or default assumptions you previously saved to a loan group, click on the number that appears to the left of the `Prepay` field for the appropriate group. Click on the appropriate name from the `My Assumptions` window that appears, then click on the `Apply Saved Assumption` button.
   - To clear all the assumptions from the `CMBS Scenario Editor` window, click on the `Clear` button.
5. To save the entire scenario (loan groups and prepayment/default assumptions) you created, click on the `Save Scenario` button, enter a name in the highlighted `Scenario Name` field that appears, then click on the `Save` button.

Add a CMBS loan group

To create the loan group(s) to which your customized assumptions are applied, complete the following steps:

1. Click on the `Analysis Type` field (label does not appear) from the left-hand side of the screen and choose `Advanced Scenario`.
2. Click on one of the highlighted `Edit Scenario` fields and choose `Edit Scenario` or a saved scenario. The `CMBS Scenario Editor` window appears.
3. Click on the `Add Group` button.
4. Choose from the following options:
   - To create a custom loan group consisting of individual loans that you choose, click on the `Loan Select Grouping` radio button so that a dot appears. Click on the individual loans you want to include in the group so that they appear highlighted in blue in the bottom half of the screen.
   - To create a custom loan group based on custom rule criteria, click on the radio button to the left of the `Rule Based Loan Grouping` field so that a dot appears. Enter/choose the appropriate rule criteria in/from the highlighted fields that appear.
   - To choose a loan grouping that you have previously saved, click on the `My Groups` button so that the `My CMBS Groups` window appears. Click on the appropriate group name.
5. Click on the `Apply` button.
6. To save the loan group you have created, click on the `Save Group` button, enter the appropriate name in the `Group Name` window that appears, then click on the `Save` button.

SYT screen functions

Once you enter (ticker symbol) <MTGE>SYT <Go>, the `Super Yield Table` screen appears, where you can perform price, yield, and spread analysis for all non-agency RMBS, ABS, and CMBS products. Depending on the security and option(s) you choose, some of the following fields may appear, listed here in alphabetical order:

- `%` displays the percentage of the outstanding collateral balance that is included in the corresponding filter.
- `#`. The `Editor` button allows you to apply/create saved cash flow assumptions using the `My Assumptions` window, or apply/create saved scenarios using the `Scenario Editor/CMBS Scenario Editor` windows, as applicable.
- `X.XX(X)XXX`. The current gross weighted average coupon, weighted average months to maturity, and the pool age.
- `1st Proj`. The first projected cash flow date, based on the selected collateral assumptions.
- `30D/60D/90D`. The numer of loans that are 30/60/90 days delinquent, expressed as a percentage.

> **Tips**
>
> Loans in foreclosure and real estate–owned (REO) loans are excluded.

- `Analysis Type` (label does not appear) applies to commerical mortgage-backed securities only and allows you to choose the type of prepayment/default assumptions and scenarios you can apply. The dropdown menu displays the following choices:
  - `Basic` allows you to enter custom prepayment and default assumptions into the highlighted fields that appear.
  - `Credit Assumption` allows you to create or apply a credit-driven scenario.
  - `Filter Stratifications` allows you stratify the main loan group using criteria you choose and then apply custom prepayment and default assumptions to the individual groups by clicking on the number that appears at the top of each scenario column.
  - `Advanced Scenario` allows you to create/save/import custom loan groupings and corresponding prepayment and default assumptions in/from the `CMBS Scenario Editor` window.
- `Bkrpt`. The number of mortgage holders in the selected collateral group who have reported bankruptcy, expressed as a percentage.
- `CDR`. The speed for the default rate.
- `CPR`. The speed for the constant prepayment rate.
- `CPR/PSA`. The constant prepayment rate/prepayment standard assumption. The dropdown menu displays a list of choices.
- `Crd. Sup`. The current credit support for the selected security.
- `Created`. The date on which the cash flow `CDI` file was most recently updated.
- `Cum. Loss`. The cumulative amount of the collateral that was written down because of losses on the underlying loans, expressed as a percentage.
- `Current`. The current collateral balance as of the tape date.
- `Curve`. The time at which the data that appear were loaded, the curve type, and the curve value at the corresponding points. The dropdown menu displays a list of choices.
- `Cusip` (label does not appear). The CUSIP number for the corresponding security.

- `Cutoff`. The cutoff collateral balance as of the cutoff date.
- `Default`. The default speed and assumption used to calculate the cash flows for the selected deal. The dropdown menu displays a list of choices.

> **Tip**
>
> `BPN4<Go>` displays further information on default rate notations.

- `Defeased`. The percent of the outstanding pool balance that is in defeasance.
- `Delinq 60Day+`. A checkmark indicates that you can assign delinquent loan assumptions and stratification of the collateral.

> **Tip**
>
> The `Delinq 60Day+` field does not appear when you choose `None` from the `Strat` field dropdown menu.

- `Delinquency` allows you to enter either a static or dynamic (vectored) delinquency assumption that is used as input to the shifting interest and trigger tests associated with a deal. The `Structured Finance Notes` function (`SNFS`) displays further information.
- `Dfs Adj CS`. The defeased adjusted credit support. The current credit support adjusted for loans in defeasance.
- `Discount Margin/Yield`. The manner by which an adjustable rate security is valued. The dropdown menu displays the following choices:
  - `Discount Margin`. The margin relative to the base index rate, where the present value of cash flows equals the price plus accrued interest.
  - `Yield`. The rate of return, based on the coupon rate, the length of time to maturity, and the market price.
- `Edit Scenario` allows you to create/import an advanced scenario in/from the `CMBS Scenario Editor`. The dropdown menu displays a list of choices, as applicable.
- `Extend` applies to commercial mortgage-backed securities only. The percent of the balloon amount to default. For any loans that have a balloon payment on the maturity date, the `Extend` field allows you to push out the final balloon payment past the loan's maturity date to simulate a loan extension, or a balloon default scenario.
- `Filters`. The stratification filter(s) criteria you choose appear below this heading. The dropdown menu(s) displays the appropriate options.
- `FP` applies to commercial mortgage-backed securities only. The `FP` field allows you to enter a trigger value that determines when prepayments are applied. The following are valid inputs:
  - `LOCK` applies prepayments after the fixed penalty period.
  - `(Numeric Value)` applies prepayments *if* the projected fixed penalty rate for the loan falls below the value you enter in the `FP` field. The value you enter is the minimum fixed penalty (a prepayment penalty) rate. The following rules apply:
    - If you use a `CPR` prepayment scenario where the `FP` field is blank, then prepayments occur immediately, or after any hard lockout or defeasance periods, with a corresponding projected prepayment penalty fee.

- If you use a CPR prepayment scenario where the FP field's value is greater than zero, then prepayments are allowed if the projected prepayment penalty rate for the loan falls below the value in the FP field.

Example

If you enter 100 CPR in the Prepay field and 3 in the FP field, then the 100 CPR prepayment speed applies if the projected prepayment penalty rate for the loan falls below 3%.

- Frcl. The percentage of the outstanding pool balance that is in foreclosure.
- Grp. The collateral group for which the data appear.
- Hist. The historical period for which the corresponding speeds appear. The dropdown menu displays a list of choices.
- I.Wrap appears when a bond/deal has an insurance wrap. The following options appear:
  - ON. Apply insurance wrap.
  - OFF. Immediately turn off insurance wrap.
  - #. The number of months until the insurance wrap is turned off.

Tip

The Mortgage Settings (MDF) function allows you to choose the default setting for this field.

- Idx & Proj Mtd. The index rate of the underlying indexes that are used for cash flow projections and the projection method by which the underlying indexes are incorporated into your projected cash flows. The dropdown menu displays the following choices:
  - C allows you to utilize a constant (non-changing) level of the index for all projections.
  - F allows you to base projected cash flows on forward curve assumptions generated from the Swap Manager function (SWPM) for all of the underlying indexes associated with the deal.

Tip

The Mortgage Cashflow Forward Rates function (MCFR) displays further information on rates used for the underlying indexes.

- Lag. The months to recovery. The number of periods from the time of default until principal is recovered and losses are realized. When used with the Extend field, it is the number of months that the defaulted balloon payment is extended beyond the loan's maturity date. The following rules apply:
  - If the Lag field is blank or has a value of zero, then the principal recovery and/or loss is applied to the first projected period.
  - If the Lag field has a value greater than zero, then the principal recovery and/or loss is not applied until x number of periods from the first period cash flow have defaulted.

Example

If the `Lag` value is 18, and the date of the defaulted cash flow projection is January 2009, then the principal recovery/loss is applied in July 2010.

- `Main Group` displays the percentage of the collateral that is not included in the filter(s) you choose.
- `OptE` applies to commercial mortgage-backed securities only. The optional extension, which is a provision permitting extension of the original term of the mortgage under terms agreed upon at origination. The dropdown menu displays the following choices:
  - `None` means no extension scenario is applied.
  - `1st` represents a scenario that exercises the first optional extension for CMBS deals.
  - `2nd` represents a scenario that exercises the second optional extension for CMBS deals.
  - `All` represents a scenario that exercises *all* optional extensions for CMBS deals.

Example

If a loan has optional extension terms, "0(36), E1(12), E3(12)", the E1, E2, and E3 indicate that the loan has up to three optional extension terms that the borrower can exercise before defaulting on the balloon. The numbers in parentheses represent the length of the optional extension term. In this example, the borrower has three opportunities to pay off the loan. If the borrower is unable to repay the loan after exercising all optional extensions, the principal balloon goes into default. The `CMBS Loan Description` screen (`LDES`) displays optional extension term information in the `Rem. Protection` field. `LDES<HELP>` displays further information.

Tip

You can simultaneously apply assumptions from the `Opt Ext` field and `Extend` fields. If the loan has optional extension terms and you select an option for the `Opt Ext` field, the cash flow projections will apply to the `Opt Ext` field's assumptions *first*, then to the `Extend` field's assumptions.

- `Px (Dec.)/(32d)`. The current price, expressed in decimals/32nds.
- `REO`. The percentage of the outstanding pool balance that is real estate owned.
- `RcvM` applies to commercial mortgage-backed securities only. The recovery to maturity. The following options are available:
  - If you use a CDR default assumption with a `Lag` greater than zero, then a `Yes` in the `RcvMat` field indicates that the last period principal is recovered and losses are applied on the loan's maturity date.
  - A `No` in the `RcvMat` field indicates a delay between when the last period of principal is recovered and losses are applied. The delay is equal to the number of lag periods *after* the maturity date. This applies if the CDR speed is less than 100.

Example

If Lag = 18 and RcvMat = YES, with a loan maturity date of June 2009, then the principal is recovered and losses are applied in June 2009.

If Lag = 18 and RcvMat = NO, with a loan maturity date of June 2009, then the principal is recovered and losses are applied in December 2010.

- Settle Date. The settlement date used in the calculation. The button to the left of the highlighted field displays a calendar from which you can choose the appropriate date.

Tip

The settlement date defaults to the standard settlement convention for the bond under analysis ($T + 3$ days).

- SEV. The loss severity (applies to commercial mortgage-backed securities only). When using a default scenario (CDR and Extend), it is the percentage of the defaulted principal cash flow that is unrecoverable.
- Svrty/Lag allows you to enter either a static or dynamic (vectored) assumption for the severity and lag information. Severity is the percentage of the principal loan balance at the time of default, which determines the loss amount. Lag is the number of months between the time of default and the recovery.
- Sev/Lag/OptE applies to commercial mortgage-backed securities only. Allows you to enter Sev, Lag, and OptE assumptions in the corresponding highlighted fields that appear to the right.
- Sev/Lag/RcvM applies to commercial mortgage-backed securities only. Allows you to enter Sev, Lag, and RcvM assumptions in the corresponding highlighted fields that appear to the right. The individual Sev, Lag, and RcvM fields in this chapter display information on the respective fields.
- Spread/Sensitivity measurement (label does not appear): The spread/sensitivity measurement of the bond. The dropdown menu displays the following choices:
  - Mod Duration. The percentage price change of a bond for a given change in yield. The higher the modified duration of a bond, the higher its risk. Modified duration is calculated as:

    (100 * Value of .01) * 100/Full price.

  - Principal Window. The start and end date of the mortgage principal window.
  - First Loss. The forward first loss on the security.
  - Projected Bond Cum. Loss $. The projected cumulative loss on the bond, expressed in dollars.
  - Projected Bond Cum. Loss %. The projected cumulative loss on the bond, expressed as a percentage of the original face.
  - Projected Collateral Cum. Loss $. The projected cumulative loss on the collateral, expressed in dollars.
  - Projected Collateral Cum. Loss %. The projected cumulative loss on the collateral, expressed as a percentage of the original face.

- Projected Collateral Loss % (Curr Face). The projected cumulative loss on the collateral, expressed as a percentage of the current face.
- Current Collateral Liquidated %. The percentage of the current collateral which is liquidated based upon the user's severity assumption. It is calculated as:

$$\text{Calculation} = \frac{\text{Projected Collateral Loss \% (curr face)}}{\text{Severity Assumption}}.$$

- Total Collateral Cum. Loss $. The sum total of the historical and projected cumulative losses on the collateral, expressed in dollars.
- Total Collateral Cum. Loss %. The sum total of the historical and projected cumulative losses on the collateral, expressed as a percentage of original face.
- Average Life. The average number of years that each dollar of unpaid principal due remains outstanding, computed as the weighted average time to the receipt of all future principal payments due to be paid. The dollar amounts of each principal paydown are used as weights.
- I Spread. The conventional yield spread to the interpolated yield curve.
- J Spread. The conventional yield spread to the interpolated nominal yield curve.
- A Spread. The conventional yield spread to the nominal (actual) treasury benchmarks.
- Z Spread. The cash flow spread–implied spot curve.
- S Spread. The cashflow spread to the actual U.S. strip curve.
- D Spread. The conventional yield spread to the duration-matched U.S. strip benchmark.
- N Spread. The conventional yield spread to the swap curve.
- E Spread. The cash flow spread to the Eurodollar spot curve (IMM).

Tip

<MTGE>SPREAD<Go> provides further information and definitions on spread types.

- Strat. The manner by which the collateral behind the deal is stratified. Depending on the deal type and the data provided by the trustee within the monthly reporting files on the underlying mortgage loans, the dropdown menu displays some or all of the following choices:
  - Reset. Stratification by ARM-backed mortgage loan:
    - Vanilla. No reset.
    - 2/1. Initial 2-year reset and yearly thereafter.
    - 3/1. Initial 3-year reset and yearly thereafter.
    - 5/1. Initial 5-year reset and yearly thereafter.
    - 7/1. Initial 7-year reset and yearly thereafter.
    - >7/1 and fixed. Initial 7-year+ reset and yearly thereafter.
  - Fixed/ARM. Fixed rate loans and adjustable rate loans:
    - Fixed rate. Fixed rate loans.
    - ARM. Adjustable rate mortgage loans.
  - Loan Size. Stratification by original loan size:
    - <99K. Loans less than $99,000.
    - 99K-418K. Loans between $99,000 and $418,000.
    - 418K-999K. Loans between $418,000 and $999,000.
    - 999K, Loans greater than $999,000.
  - IO TERM. Stratification by interest-only terms:
    - None. No IO terms.

    - 1Year. 1-year IO terms (12 months).
    - 2Year. 2-year IO terms (24 months).
    - 3Year. 3-year IO terms (36 months).
    - 4+Year. 4-year+ IO terms (48 months plus).
  - Delinquency. Stratification by various delinquency buckets:
    - Current. No delinquencies.
    - 30Day. Delinquencies 30–59 days.
    - 60Day. Delinquencies 60–89 days.
    - 90Day. Delinquencies 90+ days.
    - Foreclosure. Bank-seized property loans.
    - REO. Real estate–owned loans.
  - Delinq. Pipeline. Stratification by severely delinquent loans:
    - Current. No delinquencies.
    - 30Day. Delinquencies 30–59 days.
    - 60Day+. Delinquencies 60+ days, foreclosure and REO.
  - Owner Occupied. Stratification by owner occupancy:
    - Owner Occ. Owner-occupied loan.
    - Invst/Vaca/Unkn. Investment, vacation, or unknown occupancy loan.
  - Credit Score (FICO). Stratification by FICO scores:
    - >720 (Prime). Loans with credit scores greater than 720.
    - 660-720 (Alt-A). Loans with credit scores betwen 660 and 720.
    - <660 (B/C) Loans with credit scores less than 660.
  - Lien Status. Stratification by first and second liens:
    - 1st Lien. First-lien mortgage loans.
    - 2nd Lien. Second-lien mortgage loans.
  - Penalty Terms. Stratification by prepayment penalty terms.
    - None. No prepayment penalty terms.
    - 1 Year. Prepayment penalty premium for the first year.
    - 2 Year. Prepayment penalty premium until the second year.
    - 3 Year. Prepayment penalty premium until the third year.
    - 4+ Year. Prepayment penalty premium for life of loan.
  - None.

Tip

The value that appears to the right of each stratification is the percentage of the underlying mortgage loans that exhibits the specific stratification type.

- Tape Date. The date on which the loan data was last updated.
- ToOp applies to commercial mortgage-backed securities only. Applies to CPR prepayment rate scenarios.
  - If the ToOp field is set to Yes, then the outstanding principal balance prepays at 100% at the first freely prepayable (open) period.
  - If the ToOp field is set to No, the outstanding principal balance of the loan does not prepay at 100% at the first open period.

Example

Assume there is a balloon loan with a 7-year term, 81 months of yield maintenance periods, and 3 months of freely prepayable periods. The borrower can prepay anytime within the 81 months, but the borrower will also have to pay a yield maintenance premium (prepayment penalty fee). If the borrower does not prepay during the yield maintenance period, then the borrower also has the option to prepay for 3 months without incurring a prepayment penalty. In a scenario with a `25 CPR` and the `ToOp` field set to `Yes`, the loan prepays at `25 CPR` during the yield maintenance period. Also, when the loan enters the first freely pre-payable (open) period, the loan automatically prepays the outstanding principal balance at `100 CPR`.

- `Trig/Dly`. The trigger and delay assumptions. The trigger controls the delinquency and/or shifting interest component of a deal's trigger. The cumulative loss component is controlled by the CDR and severity assumptions. The delay is the number of months to toggle the state of the trigger and is used to control the delinquency component of a deal's trigger.
- `Values` allows you to set a value or range of values for the corresponding filter criteria.
- `Vary Price`. The incremental price(s), which is used to calculate the various yields for the selected criteria settings.
- `VPR`. The speed for the voluntary prepayment rate.
- `Yield to` (label does not appear) allows you to choose the redemption date for the yield calculation. The dropdown menu displays a list of choices:
  - `YM` applies to commercial mortgage-backed securities only. The `YM` field allows you to enter a trigger value that determines when prepayments are applied. The following are valid inputs:
    - `LOCK` applies prepayments after the yield maintenance period.
    - `(Numeric value)` applies prepayments *if* the projected yield maintenance penalty rate for the loan falls below the value you enter in the `YM` field. The value you enter is the minimum yield maintenance premium (a prepayment penalty) rate. The following rules apply:
      - When using a `CPR` prepayment scenario, if the `YM` field is blank, prepayments occur immediately, or after any hard lockout or defeasance periods, with a corresponding projected prepayment penalty fee.
      - When using a `CPR` prepayment scenario, if the `YM` field's value is greater than zero, prepayments are allowed if the projected prepayment penalty rate for the loan falls below the value in the `YM` field. For example, if you enter `100 CPR` in the `Prepay` field and `10` in the `YM` field, then the `100 CPR` prepayment speed applies if the projected prepayment penalty rate for the loan falls below 10%.
      - When you use a `CPY` prepayment scenario, the `YM` field automatically defaults to `LOCK` which prevents prepayments from occurring during the yield maintenance period. Prepayments will occur after the yield maintenance period ends.
- `YM/FP/ToOp` apply to commercial mortgage-backed securities only. They allow you to enter `YM`, `FP`, and `ToOp` assumptions in the corresponding highlighted fields that appear to the right. The individual `YM`, `FP`, and `ToOp` fields in this chapter display information on the three individual fields.

Managing user-specific assumptions with the My Assumptions window

Once you click on the white number to the left of the appropriate scenario, the `My Assumptions` window appears, where you can save the prepayment and credit assumptions you entered for the corresponding scenario.

Tip

A total of five scenarios appear on the `Super Yield Table` screen. This option only applies to RMBS when `None` appears in the highlighted `Strat` field or for CMBS when `Basic` appears in the `Analysis Type` (label does not appear on screen) field.

Depending on the security you choose, the following fields may appear, listed here in alphabetical order:

- `Close` closes the `My Assumptions` window.
- `Current Assumption` allows you to enter a name under which to save your current assumptions.
- `Default`. The default assumption for the scenario. The dropdown menu displays a list of choices.
- `Description`. A brief description of the saved assumptions you saved under the corresponding name.
- `Dly`. The delay, which is the number of months until the trigger should switch from pass to fail/fail to pass.
- `Extend`. This option applies to commercial mortgage-backed securities only and impacts the percentage of the balloon amount to default. For any loans that have a balloon payment on the maturity date, the `Extend` field allows you to push out the final balloon payment past the loan's maturity date to simulate a loan extension, or a balloon default scenario.
- `FP` applies to commercial mortgage-backed securities only and allows you to enter a trigger value that determines when prepayments are applied.
- `Lag`. The number of months between the time of default and the recovery.

Tip

If a loss is incurred, it is applied to the principal balance at recovery.

- `Modified` displays the date on which the corresponding saved assumption set was modified and saved.
- `Name`. The name of a set of assumptions you have saved.
- `Opt Ext`. This field applies to commercial mortgage-backed securities only and shows the optional extension, which is a provision permitting extension of the original term of the mortgage under terms agreed upon at origination.
- `Prepay`. The prepayment assumption for the scenario.
- `Save Current Assumptions` allows you to save the current assumptions under the name you entered in the `Current Assumptions` field.
- `Svrty`. The percentage of the principal loan balance at the time of default, which determines the loss amount.
- `ToOp` applies to commercial mortgage-backed securities only and specifically only to `CPR` prepayment rate scenarios. If the `ToOp` field is set to `Yes`, then the outstanding principal balance prepays at 100% at the first freely prepayable (open) period. If the `ToOp` field is set to `No`, the outstanding principal balance of the loan does not prepay at 100% at the first open period.
- `Trig`. The initial state of the deal trigger.

Tip

The `Structure Finance Notes` function (SFNS) displays further information.

The dropdown menu displays the following choices:

- `Pass` indicates that the deal is currently passing the corresponding tests, which means that the trigger is not in effect.
- `Fail` indicates that the deal is currently failing the corresponding tests, which means that the trigger is in effect.

The Scenario window

Once you click on the white number to the left of the appropriate scenario, the `Scenario` window appears, where you can enter prepayment and credit assumptions for the corresponding scenario on the base assumption as well as specified sections of collateral.

Tip

A total of five scenarios appear on the `Super Yield Table` screen. This option does not apply if `None` appears in the highlighted `Strat` field.

The following fields appear:

- `Prepay`. The prepayment assumption for the scenario.
- `Default`. The default assumption for the scenario. The dropdown menu displays a list of choices.
- `Svrty`. The percentage of the principal loan balance at the time of default, which determines the loss amount.
- `Lag`. The number of months between the time of default and the recovery.

Tip

If a loss is incurred, it is applied to the principal balance at recovery.

- `Trig`. The initial state of the deal trigger.

Tip

The `Structure Finance Notes` function (`SFNS`) displays further information.

The dropdown menu displays the following choices:

- `Pass` indicates that the deal is currently passing the corresponding tests, which means that the trigger is not in effect.

- Fail indicates that the deal is currently failing the corresponding tests, which means that the trigger is in effect.
- Dly. The delay, which is the number of months until the trigger should switch from pass to fail/fail to pass.

The Vector Editor window

Once you click on Create Vector from the Prepay, Default, Svrty/Lag, or Delinquency field dropdown menu, the Prepay Vector Editor Window appears, where you can create a new vector. The following fields appear:

- Name. The name of the vector.
- Type. The type of vector. The dropdown menu displays the appropriate choices.
- Start allows you to choose when you want your vector to begin. The dropdown menu displays the following choices:
  - Projected. The first element of the vector is applied to the first projected cash flow.
  - Loan Origination. The first element of the vector is applied to the first projected payment after the loan origination.
- Rate. The prepayment speed.
- Months. The number of months applied to the prepayment rate.
- S/R. The vector behavior. The dropdown menu displays the following choices:
  - S-Step. The vector automatically steps up/down to the next prepayment speed.
  - R-Ramp. The vector automatically ramps to the next speed (e.g., 10S).

Tip

When a vector steps up/down to the next prepayment speed, it moves to the next rate entirely, all at once.

When a vector ramps to the next speed, it moves gradually, over time.

VECT<HELP> provides further information on creating vectors.

The Loan Details screen

Once you click on the appropriate menu item number beneath the highlighted Strat field on the Super Yield Table screen, the Loan Details screen appears with aggregated loan-level data that is grouped by specific criteria. The corresponding ticker symbol and series of the deal's collateral appears at the top of the screen. Depending on which option you choose from the Stratify By field dropdown menu, some of the following fields appear, listed here in alphabetical order:

Important

A maximum of 8,000 loans can be displayed at one time.

- %. The percentage of the total face value of the loan(s).
- 30D%/60D%/90D%. The percentage of the corresponding loans that are 30/60/90 days delinquent.
- 60D+%/90D+%. The percentage of the corresponding loans that are 60/90 or more days delinquent or that are specially serviced.

- `Age`. The age of the loan, in months.
- `All Loans`. The groupings that correspond to the loan count.
- `ARM%`. The number of adjustable rate mortgages (ARM) loans, expressed as a percentage.
- `As of`. The date on which the data that appear were most recently updated.
- `Bank%`. The weighted average of the corresponding loans that are in bankruptcy, expressed as a percentage.
- `Count`. The total number of corresponding loans.
- `Curr. Amt`. The current face value of the loan.
- `Delinq Days`. The number of days the loan is delinquent.
- `Fclr%`. The weighted average of the corresponding loans that are in foreclosure, expressed as a percentage.
- `GEO`. The state that corresponds to the loan.
- `Group`. The collateral group for which the data appear.
- `Index`. The index used to determine the rate for ARMS loans.
- `Loan No.` The identification number assigned to the corresponding loan.
- `LTV`. The loan-to-value ratio.
- `MTM`. The number of months until the corresponding loan matures.
- `MTR`. The number of months until the loan's initial reset.

> **Tip**
>
> A negative value indicates that the corresponding loan already passed its initial reset.

- `Orig. Amt`. The original face value of the loan.
- `Pay History`. The string of characters represents up to 24 months of historical payment status information for the corresponding loan. Each character represents the status for an individual month, chronologically, with the first character in the string representing the payment status for the current month. The following characters may appear:
  - `C`. Current.
  - `B`. Bankruptcy.
  - `F`. Foreclosure.
  - `R`. REO (real estate owned).
  - `3`. 30 days delinquent.
  - `6`. 60 days delinquent.
  - `9`. 90 days delinquent.
- `Rate`. The loan rate.
- `REO%`. The weighted average of the corresponding loans that are REO, expressed as a percentage.
- `Score`. The corresponding credit score.
- `Spcl Svc`. The specially serviced status of the loan.

> **Tip**
>
> The specially serviced status only appears for loans that are in bankruptcy or foreclosure.

- `Stratification Criterion` (label does not appear). The stratification criterion you selected.
- `Stratify By`. The manner in which the data that appear are stratified. The dropdown menu displays a list of choices.
- `Type`. The loan type.

- WAC. The weighted average coupon of the individual loans underlying the selected security, where the balances of each loan are used as the weights.
- WAM. The weighted average maturity of the individual loans underlying the selected security, where the balances of each loan are used as the weights.
- WALA. The average age of all the loans in a pool, where the balances of each loan are used as the weights.
- WALTV. The original dollar-weighted average amortized loan-to-original value of the loans underlying the collateral.
- Zip Code. The zipcode for the corresponding property.

The CMBS Scenario Editor window

Once you choose the option Advanced Scenario from the Analysis Type (label does not appear) dropdown menu, and click on Edit Scenario, the CMBS Scenario Editor Window appears, where you can enter/save custom prepayment and default assumptions for the loan groups you create in the CMBS Loan Groups Editor window. The following options are available:

- My Scenarios allows you to import saved scenarios from the CMBS Scenario Editor window.
- Save Scenario enables you to save the information you entered as a customized scenario.
- Clear allows you to clear all of the information from the highlighted fields.
- Export enables you to export the information that appears to an MS Excel spreadsheet.
- Assumptions (ticker). The loan group(s) you created appears beneath the Assumptions (ticker) heading with a corresponding pie chart, where the percentage of the underlying collateral balance included in each group appears.
- Add Group allows you to create loan groups with the CMBS Loan Groups Editor window.
- Prepay allows you to import saved prepayment assumptions from the My Assumptions window.
- Balance. The total outstanding loan balance for the loans in the corresponding group.
- #Lns. The number of loans in the corresponding group.
- WA LTV. The weighted average loan-to-value ratio for the loans in the corresponding group.
- WA CPN. The weighted average coupon for the loans in the corresponding group.
- WA DSCR. The weighted average debt service coverage ratio for the loans in the corresponding group.
- YM. The YM field allows you to enter a trigger value that determines when prepayments are applied. The following are valid inputs:
  - LOCK applies prepayments after the yield maintenance period.
  - (Numeric value) applies prepayments if the projected yield maintenance penalty rate for the loan falls below the value you enter in the YM field. The value you enter is the minimum yield maintenance premium (a prepayment penalty) rate.

Please note that the following rules apply:

- When using a CPR prepayment scenario, if the YM field is blank, prepayments occur immediately, or after any hard lockout or defeasable periods, with a corresponding projected prepayment penalty fee.
- When using a CPR prepayment scenario, if the YM field's value is greater than zero, prepayments are allowed if the projected prepayment penalty rate for the loan falls below the value in the YM field. For example, if you enter 100 CPR in the Prepay field and 10 in the YM field, then the 100 CPR prepayment speed applies if the projected prepayment penalty rate for the loan falls below 10%.
- When you use a CPY prepayment scenario, the YM field automatically defaults to LOCK which

prevents prepayments from occurring during the yield maintenance period. Prepayments will occur after the yield maintenance period ends.

- When you use a `CPP` prepayment scenario, the `YM` field automatically defaults to `LOCK`.
- `FP`. The `FP` field allows you to enter a trigger value that determines when prepayments are applied. The following are valid inputs:
  - `LOCK` applies prepayments after the fixed penalty period.
  - `(Numeric Value)` applies prepayments *if* the projected fixed penalty rate for the loan falls below the value you enter in the `FP` field. The value you enter is the minimum fixed penalty (a prepayment penalty) rate.

The following rules apply:

- If you use a `CPR` prepayment scenario where the `FP` field is blank, then prepayments occur immediately, or after any hard lockout or defeasable periods, with a corresponding projected prepayment penalty fee.
- If you use a `CPR` prepayment scenario where the `FP` field's value is greater than zero, then prepayments are allowed if the projected prepayment penalty rate for the loan falls below the value in the `FP` field. For example, if you enter `100 CPR` in the `Prepay` field and `3` in the `FP` field, then the `100 CPR` prepayment speed applies if the projected prepayment penalty rate for the loan falls below 3%.
- `ToOp`. This option applies to `CPR` prepayment rate scenarios only:
  - If the `ToOp` field is set to `Yes`, then the outstanding principal balance prepays at 100% at the first freely prepayable (open) period.
  - If the `ToOp` field is set to `No`, the outstanding principal balance of the loan does not prepay at 100% at the first open period.

For example, assume there is a balloon loan with a 7-year term, 81 months of yield maintenance periods, and 3 months of freely prepayable periods. The borrower can prepay anytime within the 81 months, but the borrower will also have to pay a yield maintenance premium (prepayment penalty fee). If the borrower does not prepay during the yield maintenance period, then the borrower also has the option to prepay for 3 months without incurring a prepayment penalty. In a scenario with a `25 CPR` and the `ToOp` field set to `Yes`, the loan prepays at `25 CPR` *during* the yield maintenance period. Also, when the loan enters the first freely prepayable (open) period, the loan automatically prepays the outstanding principal balance at `100 CPR`.

- `Default`. The default assumption for the scenario. The dropdown menu displays a list of choices.
- `RcvMat`. The recovery to maturity. If you use a `CDR` default assumption with a `Lag` greater than zero, then selecting `Yes` in the `RcvMat` field indicates that the last period principal is recovered and losses are applied on the loan's maturity date. Selecting `No` in the `RcvMat` field indicates a delay between when the last period of principal is recovered and losses are applied. The delay is equal to the number of lag periods *after* the maturity date. This applies if the `CDR` speed is less than 100.
- `Extend`. The percent of the balloon amount to default. For any loans that have a balloon payment on the maturity date, the `Extend` field allows you to push out the final balloon payment past the loan's maturity date to simulate a loan extension, or a balloon default scenario.
- `Svrty`. The loss severity. When using a default scenario (`CDR` and `Extend`), it is the percentage of the defaulted principal cash flow that is unrecoverable.
- `Lag`. The months to recovery. The number of periods from the time of default until the principal is recovered and losses are realized.

When used with the `Extend` field, it is the number of months that the defaulted balloon payment is extended beyond the loan's maturity date.

The following rules apply:

- If the `Lag` field is blank or has a value of zero, then the principal recovery and/or loss is applied to the first projected period.
- If the `Lag` field has a value greater than zero, then the principal recovery and/or loss is not applied until *x* number of periods from the first period cash flow have defaulted. For example, if the `Lag` value is 18, and the date of the defaulted cash flow projection is January 2009, then the principal recovery/loss is applied in July 2010.
- `Opt Ext`. This field only applies to commercial mortgage-backed securities. The optional extension is a provision permitting extension of the original term of the mortgage under terms agreed upon at origination—the dropdown menu displays the following choices:
  - `None` means no extension scenario is applied.
  - `1st` represents a scenario that exercises the first optional extension for CMBS deals.
  - `2nd` represents a scenario that exercises the second optional extension for CMBS deals.
  - `All` represents a scenario that exercises *all* optional extensions for CMBS deals.

Tip

For example, when a loan has optional extension terms, "0(36), E1(12), E3(12)", the E1, E2, and E3 indicate that the loan has up to three optional extension terms that the borrower can exercise before defaulting on the balloon. The numbers in parentheses represent the length of the optional extension term. In this example, the borrower has three opportunities to pay off the loan. If the borrower is unable to repay the loan after exercising *all* optional extensions, the principal balloon goes into default. The `CMBS Loan Description` screen (`LDES`) displays optional extension term information in the `Rem. Protection` field. `LDES<HELP>` displays further information.

You can simultaneously apply assumptions from the `Opt Ext` field and `Extend` fields. If the loan has optional extension terms and you select an option for the `Opt Ext` field, the cash flow projections will apply to the `Opt Ext` field's assumptions *first*, then to the `Extend` field's assumptions.

- `Apply` allows you to apply the information from the `CMBS Scenario Editor` to the `Super Yield Table` analysis.
- `Close` closes the `CMBS Scenario Editor` window without applying the assumptions to the `Super Yield Table` analysis.
- `Group(#)` appears once you have more than one group. Allows you to differentiate the loan groups.
- `Selected` appears once you have more than one group. The percentage of the total pool balance that belongs to the corresponding loan group.

The CMBS Loan Group Editor window

Once you click on the `Add Groups` button from the `CMBS Scenario Editor` window the `CMBS Loan Group Editor` window appears where you can create custom loan groups to which you can apply custom prepayment and default assumptions. The following fields appear:

- `My Groups` allows you to import saved loan groups.
- `Save Group` allows you to save the loan group you create.
- `Clear` allows you to clear all of the information you entered.
- `Loan Select Grouping`. A dot in the corresponding radio button allows you to choose the individual loans that comprise a group.
- `Rule Based Loan Grouping`. A dot in the corresponding radio button allows you to set criteria by which loans are grouped using the `Loan Rules` section of the window.
- `Loan Groups (pie chart)`. The chart displays a breakdown of the collateral groups as a percentage of the entire outstanding loan balance.
- `(Ticker)` (label does not appear on screen). The ticker for the security you have entered.
- `Balance`. The total outstanding loan balance(s) for the loan(s) in the corresponding category(ies).
- `Loans`. The number of loans included in the corresponding category(ies).
- `WA LTV`. The weighted average loan-to-value ratio for the loan(s) in the corresponding category(ies).
- `WA CPN`. The weighted average coupon for the loan(s) in the corresponding category(ies).
- `WA DSCR`. The weighted average debt service coverage ratio for the loan(s) in the corresponding category(ies).
- `Loan Rules` allows you to enter criteria for a loan grouping.
- `LTV` allows you to enter a loan-to-value range or value criteria for the loan group.
- `Coupon` allows you to enter a coupon range or value criteria for the loan group.
- `DSCR` allows you to enter a debt service coverage ratio range or value criteria for the loan group.
- `Balance` allows you to set an outstanding balance range or value criteria for the loan group.
- `Loan Status` allows you to choose loan status criteria for the loan group. The dropdown menu displays a list of choices.
- `Property` allows you to set a property-type criterion for the loan group. Click on the button that appears to the left of the highlighted field to display a list of choices.
- `Delinquency` allows you to choose a delinquency period as a criterion for the loan group. The dropdown menu displays a list of choices.
- `State` allows you to choose a state(s) as a criterion for the loan group. Click on the button that appears to the left of the highlighted field to display a list of choices.
- `Maturity Type` allows you to choose a maturity type as a criterion for the loan group. The dropdown menu displays a list of choices.
- `MSA` allows you to choose a `Metropolitan Statistical Area(s)` as a criterion for the loan group. Click on the button that appears to the left of the highlighted field to display a list of choices.
- `List View` allows you to choose which loans appear at the bottom of the screen. The dropdown menu displays a list of choices.
- `Loan Name`. The name of the property related to the loan.
- `Status`. The current status of the corresponding loan.
- `Curr Bal`. The current balance outstanding for the corresponding loan.
- `Coupon`. The gross coupon for the corresponding loan.
- `Mat. Date`. The maturity date for the corresponding loan.
- `LTV`. The loan-to-value ratio for the corresponding loan.
- `DSCR`. The debt service coverage ratio for the corresponding loan. It is the ratio of the annualized scheduled payments of principal and/or interest on the mortgage loan to the net operating income or net cash flow for the property.
- `Group` displays if/how the loan is part of a loan group. The following terms may appear:
  - `Rule`. The loan has been grouped based on rule-based grouping.
  - `Custom`. The loan has been grouped based on loan select grouping.
  - `Remaining`. The loan has not been grouped.

  ○ Selected appears for new groups only. The loan meets the current grouping criteria.
- Apply allows you to save and apply the loan group to the scenario you create in the CMBS Scenario Editor window.
- Close closes the CMBS Loan Groups Editor window without saving the information.

Using vectors "on the fly"

The Super Yield Table (SYT) function also enables you to enter vector information directly into the assumption fields on SYT (and also on CFT, SPA, and MTCS) "on the fly".

There are two ways in which you can achieve this:

(1) Use shorthand logic to create a vector. The syntax is (rate1)(periods)(S/R)(rate2), where S is a step and R is a ramp transition between rates. For example, you can enter 10 12R 20 into the Prepay field (with CPR selected from the adjacent dropdown menu) to indicate 10 CPR for 12 months, ramping up to 20 CPR for the remaining life of the bond.
(2) You can copy and paste a string of values in to the appropriate prepayment, default, or severity fields. For example, in MS Excel, right-click on the cell with the string of values, and select Copy. Then, right-click in the appropriate field on the SYT function and select Paste. Press <Go> to update SYT with the cash flows corresponding to the vector information you copied and pasted.

22.3 MORTGAGE CREDIT SUPPORT (MTCS)

The Mortgage Credit Support (MTCS) screen on Bloomberg displays credit support for an entire structured deal. MTCS allows you to display the amount of credit support of a specific tranche at origination. You can also display what your credit support is supposed to be, based on a horizon date, as well as display historical credit support on a monthly basis.

Note that the information that appears in the MTCS is security sensitive and, hence, changes depending on the Bloomberg ticker you enter.

Once you enter the Bloomberg ticker <MTGE>MTCS<Go>, the Credit Support screen appears. Choose from one of the following options:

- To change the view of the data that appear on screen in the Credit Support section, choose either Current/Horizon or Historical from the dropdown menu of the highlighted Credit Support Section View (title does not appear) field that appears at the top of the screen.
- To display additional information in the Historical view, click on the scroll bar that appears at the bottom of the screen to move right or left, if applicable.
- To generate a credit support horizon scenario, enter/choose the appropriate information in/from the highlighted fields that appear in the Analysis section of the screen, then press <Go>.

> **Tip**
>
> You can only generate a horizon scenario from the Current/Horizon view.

- To create a new or display/edit an existing scenario, click on the checkbox next to the Scenario label so that a checkmark appears, then choose the appropriate option from the highlighted Scenario field dropdown menu. SCEN<HELP> displays further information on creating/updating a scenario.

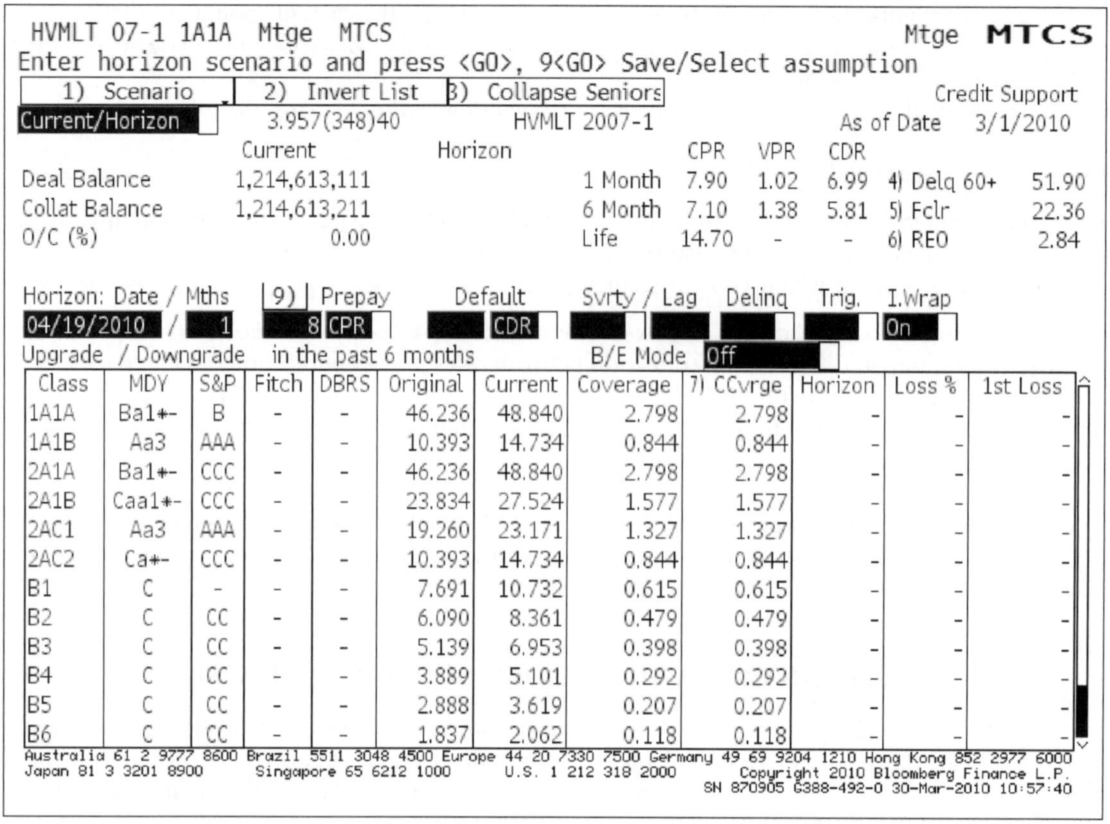

Figure 22.3. The `Mortgage Credit Support (MTCS)` screen.

- To sort the data that appear on screen in the Credit Support section into ascending/descending order, according to the class of bond, click on the `1) Invert List` toolbar button.

> **Tip**
>
> The default display lists senior bond classes first, followed by subordinate bond classes.

- To collapse/expand the senior bond class data that appear on screen in the `Credit Support` section, click on the `Collapse/Expand` toolbar button.

> **Tip**
>
> The default displays an expanded list of senior bond classes. `Collapse` consolidates this list into the single line item `Senior`.

- To apply or apply and save customized coverage ratios, click the CCvrge column header, enter the appropriate information in the highlighted fields on the Custom Coverage Formula window that appears, then click on the Apply/Apply & Save button.
- To create a custom cash flow assumptions, enter/choose the appropriate information in the highlighted fields, then click on the 9) button.
- To apply a saved set of cash flow assumptions, click on the 9) button. The "How to apply saved assumptions" section of this chapter displays further information.
- To display loan-level details for the corresponding mortgage, click on Delq 60+/Fclr/REO from the Credit Support screen. The Loan Details screen appears.
- To choose the criterion by which the data in the Loan Details screen are stratified, choose the appropriate option from the Stratify By field dropdown menu.
- To export the data that appear on the Loan Details screen, click on the Export toolbar button.
- To display a brief description of a column heading, highlighted in blue, move your cursor over the appropriate column heading.
- To display additional data, click on the up/down or left/right scroll bar.

Create/Save cash flow assumptions

Once you enter the Bloomberg ticker <MTGE>MTCS<Go>, the Credit Support screen appears where you can enter and save prepayment, default, severity, lag and trigger assumptions. The cash flow assumptions you enter apply to the entire collateral group. To create and save a set of assumptions, complete the following steps:

Tip

The assumptions you save can be imported to the Cash Flows (CFT), Structured Paydown (SPA), and Super Yield Table (SYT) functions. The corresponding <HELP> for each function displays further information.

1. Enter/choose the appropriate information in/from the highlighted fields that appear, then press <Go>.
2. Click on the Editor button—identified by the label 9)—that appears to the left of the Prepay field. The My Assumptions window appears.
3. Enter a name for the assumption set in the highlighted Current Assumption field, then click on the Save Current Assumptions button.

Depending on the option(s) you choose, some of the following toolbar buttons may appear:

- Collapse/Expand allows you to collapse/expand the senior bond class data that appear on screen in the Credit Support section.
- Export allows you to export the data to an MS Excel spreadsheet.
- Invert List allows you to sort the data that appear on screen in the Credit Support section into ascending/descending order according to the class of bond.

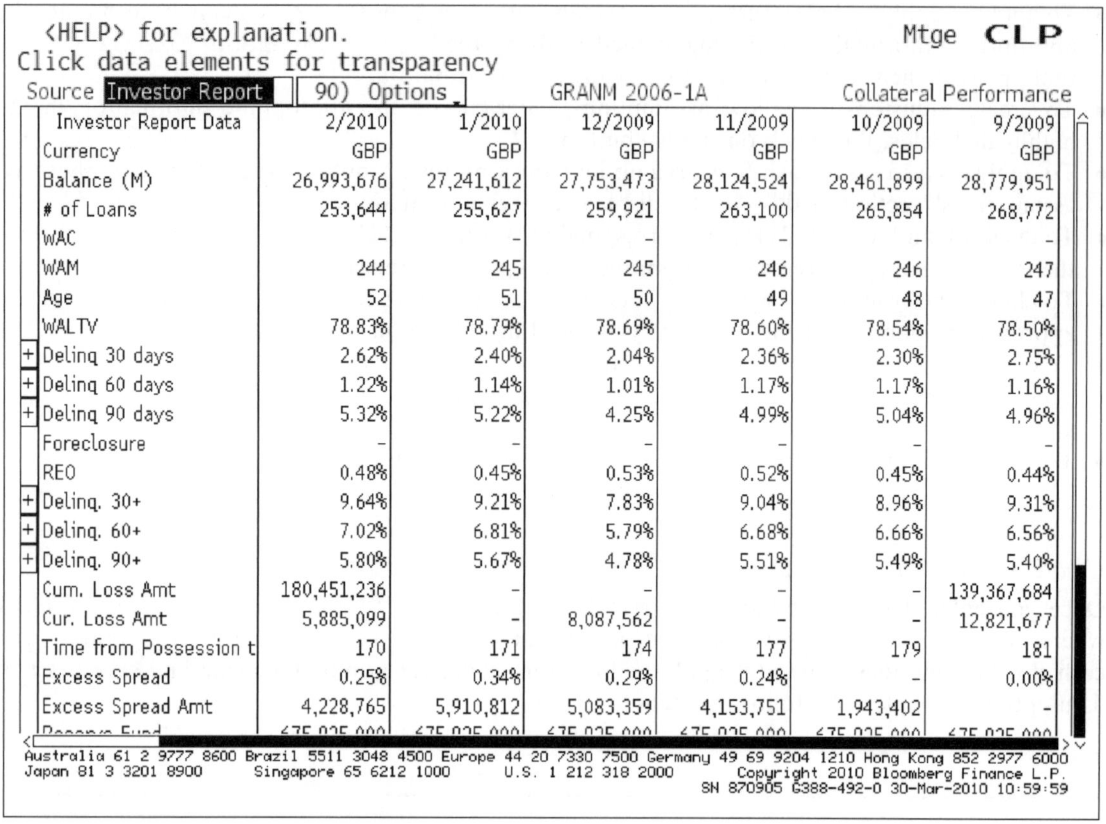
<HELP> for explanation. Mtge CLP
Click data elements for transparency
Source Investor Report 90) Options GRANM 2006-1A Collateral Performance

Investor Report Data	2/2010	1/2010	12/2009	11/2009	10/2009	9/2009
Currency	GBP	GBP	GBP	GBP	GBP	GBP
Balance (M)	26,993,676	27,241,612	27,753,473	28,124,524	28,461,899	28,779,951
# of Loans	253,644	255,627	259,921	263,100	265,854	268,772
WAC	-	-	-	-	-	-
WAM	244	245	245	246	246	247
Age	52	51	50	49	48	47
WALTV	78.83%	78.79%	78.69%	78.60%	78.54%	78.50%
+ Delinq 30 days	2.62%	2.40%	2.04%	2.36%	2.30%	2.75%
+ Delinq 60 days	1.22%	1.14%	1.01%	1.17%	1.17%	1.16%
+ Delinq 90 days	5.32%	5.22%	4.25%	4.99%	5.04%	4.96%
Foreclosure	-	-	-	-	-	-
REO	0.48%	0.45%	0.53%	0.52%	0.45%	0.44%
+ Delinq. 30+	9.64%	9.21%	7.83%	9.04%	8.96%	9.31%
+ Delinq. 60+	7.02%	6.81%	5.79%	6.68%	6.66%	6.56%
+ Delinq. 90+	5.80%	5.67%	4.78%	5.51%	5.49%	5.40%
Cum. Loss Amt	180,451,236	-	-	-	-	139,367,684
Cur. Loss Amt	5,885,099	-	8,087,562	-	-	12,821,677
Time from Possession t	170	171	174	177	179	181
Excess Spread	0.25%	0.34%	0.29%	0.24%	-	0.00%
Excess Spread Amt	4,228,765	5,910,812	5,083,359	4,153,751	1,943,402	-

Australia 61 2 9777 8600 Brazil 5511 3048 4500 Europe 44 20 7330 7500 Germany 49 69 9204 1210 Hong Kong 852 2977 6000
Japan 81 3 3201 8900 Singapore 65 6212 1000 U.S. 1 212 318 2000 Copyright 2010 Bloomberg Finance L.P.
SN 870905 G388-492-0 30-Mar-2010 10:59:59

Figure 22.4. `Collateral Performance (CLP)` screen.

22.4 COLLATERAL PERFORMANCE FUNCTION (CLP)

Use `CLP` to display current and historical collateral statistics for a residential mortgage-backed security (RMBS), asset-backed security (ABS), or commercial mortgage-backed security (CMBS).

There are up to four different ways to display the data, depending on the selected security:

- With `Loan Data View`, the statistics reflect analysis of detailed loan-level performance data that cooperating private issuers provide to Bloomberg on a monthly basis.
- With the `Contributed Data View`, the statistics reflect values contributed by a third-party on a monthly basis.
- With `Remit Data View` and `Investor Report View`, the statistics reflect values reported directly in monthly remittance trustee reports to provide greater transparency.

Collateral Performance (CLP) functionality

There are various ways to access `CLP`: enter (security identifier) `<MTGE>CLP<Go>`.

Examples

You could enter any one of the following:

—94985RAC6<MTGE>CLP<Go> (RMBS with Loan Data and Remit Data views)
—ALBA 2007-1 A2<MTGE>CLP><Go> (RMBS with Investor Report and Contributed Data views)
—SASC 2007-GEL1 M1<MTGE>CLP<Go> (ABS)
—92978NAA2<MTGE>CLP<Go> (CMBS)

Once you enter (security identifier) <MTGE>CLP <Go>, the Collateral Performance screen (Figure 22.4) appears. Choose from the following options:

- To change the data that appear on the screen, enter/choose the appropriate information in/from the highlighted fields at the top of the screen.
- To display additional information on the screen, use the scroll bars on the right-hand side and at the bottom of the screen.
- To expand or collapse the rows of data that appear, when applicable, click on the corresponding plus [+] or minus [-] sign.

Tip

To expand or collapse *all* of the rows of data, select Options > Expand/Collapse from the toolbar.

- To display a window with expanded statistics for a specific month within a collapsed [+] data row, click the appropriate cell.
- To display current loan-level data for a collateral statistic, when applicable, click on the number that appears to the left of the appropriate row to make the Loan Details screen appear.
- You can switch between the Remittance, Investor Report, or Contributed Data views. Depending on the security you choose, you may be able to specify the source of the collateral data on the CLP screen. To change the source of the data, click the highlighted Source field from the toolbar and then select the appropriate option from the menu that appears. The screen updates accordingly.

Depending on the security you choose and the screen that appears, some of the following toolbar buttons may appear, listed here in alphabetical order:

- Expand/Collapse allows you to display/hide additional data in the WALTV, Balance, and Historical Prepayment Speed sections.
- Export allows you to export the data that appear to an MS Excel spreadsheet. The result of such an export looks like Table 22.1.
- Grp allows you to select the collateral group within the deal for which data appear. The groups that appear in the dropdown menu correspond to those displayed on the Collateral Grouping Statistics (CGS) function.

Table 22.1. Sample of Bloomberg data extract into Excel

GRANM 06-1A A6 (Sample)					
Investor report data	2/2010	1/2010	12/2009	11/2009	10/2009
Currency	GBP	GBP	GBP	GBP	GBP
Balance (million)	26,993,676	27,241,612	27,753,473	28,124,524	28,461,899
# of loans	253,644	255,627	259,921	263,100	265,854
WAC	—	—	—	—	—
WAM	244	245	245	246	246
Age	52	51	50	49	48
WALTV	78.83%	78.79%	78.69%	78.60%	78.54%
Delinquent (30 days)	2.62%	2.40%	2.04%	2.36%	2.30%
Delinquent (60 days)	1.22%	1.14%	1.01%	1.17%	1.17%
Delinquent (90 days)	5.32%	5.22%	4.25%	4.99%	5.04%
Foreclosure	—	—	—	—	—
REO	0.48%	0.45%	0.53%	0.52%	0.45%
Delinquent (30+ days)	9.64%	9.21%	7.83%	9.04%	8.96%
Delinquent (60+ days)	7.02%	6.81%	5.79%	6.68%	6.66%
Delinquent (90+ days)	5.80%	5.67%	4.78%	5.51%	5.49%
Cumulative loss amount	180,451,236	—	—	—	—
Current loss amount	5,885,099	—	8,087,562	—	—
Time from possession to sale	170	171	174	177	179
Excess spread	0.25%	0.34%	0.29%	0.24%	—
Excess spread amount	4,228,765	5,910,812	5,083,359	4,153,751	1,943,402
Reserve fund	675,925,000	675,925,000	675,925,000	675,925,000	675,925,000
Liquidity draw	—	—	—	—	—
1-month CPR	10.48%	20.30%	14.68%	13.45%	12.61%
1-month SMM	0.92%	1.87%	1.33%	1.20%	1.12%
Seller share	13.80%	13.57%	12.24%	12.04%	11.86%
Seller share amount (million)	3,724,895	3,696,422	3,397,609	3,386,985	3,376,160
Min. seller share	9.10%	9.14%	9.14%	9.14%	9.12%
Min. seller share amount (million)	2,456,037	2,488,808	2,535,479	2,569,955	2,596,908

Source: Bloomberg LLP.

- Options allows you to expand or collapse all of the rows of data that have a [+] or [-] to their left, respectively. It also allows you to display a graph of the collateral data (Graph), or export the data to an MS Excel spreadsheet (Export).
- Source allows you to specify the source of the collateral data that appear. The dropdown menu displays the following options:
  - Loan Data. All the statistics are calculated from loan-level data obtained by Bloomberg (e.g., 94985RAC6 <MTGE>CLP<Go>).
  - Remit Data. The data presented on the page are taken directly from monthly remittance trustee reports. If you select this option you can double-click on a data item to display the Source Document window with the value you selected highlighted in the body of the remittance report (e.g., 94985RAC6 <MTGE>CLP<Go>).
  - Contributed Data. The statistics reflect values contributed by a third party on a monthly basis (e.g., ALBA 2007-1 A2 <MTGE>CLP<Go>).
  - Investor Report. The statistics reflect values reported directly in monthly remittance trustee reports to provide greater transparency (e.g., ALBA 2007-1 A2 <MTGE>CLP<Go>).

22.4.1 Collateral Performance screen fields

Once you load a security and enter CLP<Go>, the Collateral Performance screen appears and, depending on the type of security you choose and the view you choose from the Source dropdown menu, some of the following fields may appear, listed here in alphabetical order:

- # of Loans. The number of loans outstanding in the loan pool.
- 1/3/6/12 Mo/Life CPR. The historical 1/3/6/12 month/historical lifetime CPR (prepayment speed) for the deal or group.
- 1/3/6/12 Mo/Life SMM. The historical 1/3/6/12 month/historical lifetime Single Monthly Mortality (prepayment speed) for the deal or group.
- ARM Collat. %. The percentage of loans within the deal that are ARMs.
- Balance (M). The sum of the current outstanding loan balances for all of the loans underlying the security (in thousands).

Important—please note

Bloomberg uses the investor balance (not the obligor balance) and all dollar-weighted values. The investor balance represents the outstanding balance of the mortgage as passed through by the servicer. On the other hand, the obligor balance represents the remaining principal obligation from the borrower to the servicer. The obligor balance should be greater than or equal to the investor balance.

- Balance < 417. The percentage of loans with a current balance that is less than $417,000.
- Balance > 1MM. The percentage of loans with current balances over $1,000,000.
- Balance 417-1MM. The percentage of loans with a current balance between $417,000 and $1,000,000.
- Bankruptcy. The percentage of all bankruptcies reported among mortgage holders within a mortgage deal (collateral group). Applies to Remittance View. Percentage of loans which are in bankruptcy for a specified period.
- Bankruptcy (M). Amount of loans which are in bankruptcy for a specified period.

- Bankruptcy Period. Specified period within which mortgage loans are in bankruptcy.
- CDR (1m). The Conditional Default Rate for the current month or 1 month. Page 4 of the the Bloomberg Prepayment Notation (BPN) function displays further information.
- CDR (3m). The Conditional Default Rate for 3 months. Page 4 of the Bloomberg Prepayment Notation (BPN) function displays further information.
- CDR (6m). The Conditional Default Rate for 6 months. Page 4 of the Bloomberg Prepayment Notation (BPN) function displays further information.
- CDR (12m). The Conditional Default Rate for 12 months. Page 4 of the Bloomberg Prepayment Notation (BPN) function displays further information.
- CDR LIFE. The Conditional Default Rate for the life of the deal. Page 4 of the Bloomberg Prepayment Notation (BPN) function displays further information.
- Cum. Loss applies to commercial mortgage-backed securities only. The current percentage of cumulative loss on the underlying loans within the collateral group to which the security belongs. The cumulative loss is the amount that is not recovered and has been taken as a writeoff on the balance sheet.
- Cum. Loss applies to Remittance View. Current percentage of cumulative loss on the underlying loans comprising the collateral specific to the group to which the security belongs. Cumulative loss is loss that will not be recovered and has been taken as a writeoff on the balance sheet.
- Cum. Loss (M). The cumulative dollar amount of the collateral that has been written down due to the losses on the underlying loans. Applies to Remittance View. Current amount of cumulative loss on the underlying loans comprising the collateral specific to the group to which the security belongs. Cumulative loss is loss that will not be recovered and has been taken as a writeoff on the balance sheet.
- Cur. Loss Amt. Amount of principal that has been written off due to losses in the current period.
- Cum. Modif (M). The amount of loan modifications made over the life of the CMO deal.
- Cur Modif (M). The amount of loan modifications made during the current reporting period.
- Current Loss (M). Current amount of loss on the underlying loans comprising the collateral specific to the group to which the security belongs. Current loss is loss that will not be recovered and has been taken as a writeoff on the balance sheet for the current month.
- Current Prin Loss (M). Current principal amount of loss on the underlying loans comprising the collateral specific to the group to which the security belongs. Current principal loss is principal loss that will not be recovered and has been taken as a writeoff on the balance sheet for the current month.
- Current Int Loss (M). Current interest amount of loss on the underlying loans comprising the collateral specific to the group to which the security belongs. Current interest loss is interest loss that will not be recovered and has been taken as a writeoff on the balance sheet for the current month.
- Defeased applies to commercial mortgage-backed securities only. The current percentage of defeased loans in the collateral. Defeasance indicates the loan's cash flows have been replaced with those of U.S. Treasury obligations.
- Delinq. Percentage of loans that are delinquent for a specified period.
- Delinq. 60+. The sum of the percentage of loans that are grouped within the 60, 90 REO and foreclosure delinquency buckets.
- Delinq 90+. The sum of the percentage of loans that are grouped within the 90 REO and foreclosure delinquency buckets.
- Delinq (M). Amount of loans that are delinquent for a specified period.
- Delinq (XX) Days. The percentage of loans that are 30, 60, or 90 days delinquent. While the industry has designated the standard 30/60/90 labels, the breakdown is actually 30–59, 60–89, and

90+ days. Additionally, loans that are in foreclosure or are real estate owned (REO) are excluded from the calculations.

- `Delinq Wavg`. Rolling average of delinquent loans as an amount incorporated in the delinquency trigger test.
- `Delinq Wavg (M)`. Rolling average of delinquent loans as a percentage incorporated in the delinquency trigger test.
- `Excess Spread`. Amount of funds remaining after senior transaction fees and expenses and class certificate interest, expressed as an annualized percentage. Refer to relevant prospectus and transaction documents to confirm this information and for a more detailed description.
- `Excess Spread Amt`. Amount of funds remaining after senior transaction fees and expenses and class certificate interest for the current period. Refer to relevant prospectus and transaction documents to confirm this information and for a more detailed description.
- `Fixed Collat. %`. The percentage of loans within the deal that are fixed coupon loans.
- `Foreclosure`. The percentage of loans that force the mortgage holder to seize the property of a homeowner who is delinquent in mortgage and interest payments. These values are directly derived from values from the loan tapes, and some servicers do not provide the data necessary to compute these values. Applies to `Remittance View`. Percentage of loans which are in foreclosure for a specified period. Percentage of loans for property seized by mortgage holder due to delinquency.
- `Foreclosure (M)`. Amount of loans which are in foreclosure for a specified period. The amount of loans for property seized by the mortgage holder due to delinquency.
- `Foreclosure Period`. Specified period within which mortgage loans are in foreclosure.
- `Full Document`. The percentage of loans that have full borrower information associated with them. Bloomberg only distinguishes between full, limited, and unknown.
- `Full IO` applies to commercial mortgage-backed securities only. The current percentage of the loans comprising the collateral that are fully interest only.
- `Geo 1st/2nd/3rd/4th`. The four highest ranked property locations by percentage. Anomalies can occur over time as relative positions shift. For example, a 1% state becomes 100% if the loans in all other states are paid off. The `State Codes-States & Territories` function (`SCD`) displays further information.
- `Group`. The collateral group. The down arrow to the right of the highlighted field displays a list of choices.
- `Liquidity Draw`. Cash or liquid assets drawn to satisfy the issuer's obligations in the priority of payments, when there remain insufficient amounts available for distribution for the current period. Refer to the relevant prospectus and transaction documents to confirm this information and for a more detailed description.
- `Loss Severity`. Percentage of collateral principal in default that is deemed lost for the current period. Refer to the relevant prospectus and transaction documents to confirm this information and to further clarify periodicity.
- `LTV > 80% (Amort)` applies to CMOs/ABSs. The amortized loan dollar-weighted share of the whole loan pool that is attributable to loans whose original loan-to-value ratio was greater than 80%. The loan-to-value ratio is the ratio of a property's appraised value to the amount of the mortgage.
- `Min Seller Share`. Minimum amount of the seller share that is determined on a periodic basis and often figures in the calculation of various triggers. Applicable to master trust structures.
- `Overall Trig Evt`. Initial state of the deal triggers. Valid states are `PASS`, indicating the deal is currently passing the tests and the trigger is not in effect, and `FAIL`, indicating the deal is currently failing the tests and the trigger is in effect. The trigger tests are `Cumulative Loss Trigger`

Tests (AN133, CUM_LOSS_TRIGGER_TESTS) and Delinquency Trigger Tests (AN134, MTG_DELINQ_TRIGGER_TESTS).

- Partial IO applies to commercial mortgage-backed securities only. The current percentage of the loans comprising the collateral that is partially interest only.
- PDL. Ledger account established in order to record principal deficiencies as they occur. Principal deficiencies are generally losses or defaults, uncovered after application of revenue in the transaction priority of payments for the current period. Refer to the relevant prospectus and transaction documents to confirm this information and for a more detailed description.
- Pool Factor. The current collateral pool balance divided by the original pool balance. It can only be computed if the original pool balance is known.
- Prepaid applies to commercial mortgage-backed securities only. The current percentage of prepaid loans in the collateral.
- REO. The percentage of all bank-owned property, except that taken in consideration of a defaulted loan. These values are directly derived from values from the loan tapes, and some servicers do not provide the data necessary to compute these values. Applies to Remittance View. Percentage of loans which are REO (real estate–owned loans) for a specified period.
- REO (M). Amount of loans that are REO (real estate–owned loans) for a specified period.
- REO Period. Specified period within which mortgage loans are REO (real estate owned).
- Reserve Fund. Cash or a liquid asset created to provide limited coverage for shortfalls in amounts due under the priority of payments for the current period. Refer to the relevant prospectus and transaction documents to confirm this information.
- Seller Share. The share of the seller in the trust property, expressed as a percentage of the total mortgage pool. The total mortgage pool is typically composed of the seller share and the funding share. Applicable to master trust structures.
- Seller Share Amt (M). Cash balance of the seller share, expressed in thousands.
- Senior Prepayment %. Percentage of subordinate class balance to total deal balance adjusted for overcollateralization.
- SEV (1m). The severity of default for 1 month.
- SEV (3m). The severity of default for 3 months.
- SEV (6m). The severity of default for 6 months.
- SEV (12m). The severity of default for 12 months.
- SEV Life. The severity of default for life of the deal.
- SEV (M). The amount of severity of default for 1 month.
- Target OC. Target overcollateralization as a percentage for the deal.
- Target OC (M). Target overcollateralization as an amount for the deal.
- Table /Graph. The data display. The down arrow to the right of the highlighted field displays a menu of choices.
- Time from Possession to Sale:. Average number of days it takes to sell the property once it has been repossessed.
- Stepdown Date indicates if the stepdown date has occurred for the CMO collateral group. Stepdown is a provision put in place to protect senior bondholders by redirecting cash flows when excessive losses or other triggers have been met.
- WA DSCR applies to commercial mortgage-backed securities only. The weighted average DSCR within the specified deal. The debt service coverage ratio (DSCR) is the ratio of the annualized scheduled payments of principal and/or interest on the mortgage loan to the net operating income or the net cash flow of the mortgage property.
- WAC. The weighted average coupon of the individual loans underlying the security, using the balance of each loan as the weights.

- `WALTV (Amort)`. The dollar-weighted average amortized loan-to-original value of the underlying loans. The value reported is often the lesser of the appraisal amount and purchase amount.
- `WAM/Age`. The weighted average maturity of the individual loans underlying the security, using the balance of each loan as the weights. Age is the average age of all the loans in the pool as of the date, using the principal balance of each of the loans as the weights.

Graph View: Collateral Performance screen

Once you click `Options` > `Graph` from the toolbar of the `Collateral Performance` screen, the `Graph View` appears where you can graph two data series against one another. The highlighted fields in the upper right-hand corner and the upper left-hand corner of the graph, respectively, allow you to choose the data elements. The down arrow to the right of the highlighted field displays a menu of choices.

Loan Details screen: Stratified view

Once you click on the appropriate option from the `Collateral Performance` screen, the `Loan Details` screen's `Stratified` view appears, where you can display aggregated loan-level data grouped by specific criteria and export the data that appear to an Excel spreadsheet. The corresponding ticker symbol and series of the deal's collateral appears at the top of the screen. The following fields appear:

> **Tip**
>
> This view does not currently apply to commercial mortgage-backed securities.

- `Stratify By` allows you to choose the criterion by which the data that appear are stratified. The dropdown menu displays a list of options.
- `Group`. The collateral group that corresponds to the deal that appears.
- `(Selected Stratification)`. The stratification criterion that you selected.
- `As of`. The as of date of the collateral.
- `All Loans`. The groupings that correspond to the loan count.
- `Count`. The total number of loans in the category.
- `Curr. AMT (USD)`. The current face value of the loan.
- `%`. The percentage of the total face value of the loans in this category.
- `WALTV`. The original dollar-weighted average amortized loan-to-original value of the underlying loans comprising the collateral.
- `Score`. The corresponding credit score.
- `Orig. AMT (USD)`. The original face value of the loan.
- `WAC`. The weighted average coupon of the individual loans underlying the security, using the balance of each loan as the weights.
- `WAM`. The weighted average maturity of the individual loans underlying the security, using the balance of each loan as the weights.
- `WALA`. The average age of all the loans in a pool, using the balance of each loan as the weights.
- `ARM%`. The percentage of ARM loans in the category.
- `30D%`. The percentage of loans that are 30 days delinquent.
- `60D%`. The percentage of loans that are 60 days delinquent.

- 90D%. The percentage of loans that are 90 days delinquent.
- 60D+%. The percentage of loans that are ≥60 days delinquent or are specially serviced.
- 90D+%. The percentage of loans that are ≥90 days delinquent or are specially serviced.

Loan Details screen: Loan view

Once you choose None from the Stratify By field dropdown menu on the Loan Details screen, the Loan view appears, where you can display loan-level data grouped by specific criteria and export the data that appear to an Excel spreadsheet. The corresponding ticker symbol and series of the deal's collateral appears at the top of the screen.

> **Tip**
>
> A maximum of 5,000 loans can be displayed at a time. This view does not currently apply to commercial mortgage-backed securities.

The view is divided into the following sections:

- Weighted Average Characteristics Section (title does not appear on the screen).
- Individual Loan Details Section (title does not appear on the screen).

The following fields appear above the sections:

- Stratify By allows you to choose the criterion by which the data that appear are stratified. The dropdown menu displays a list of options.
- Group. The collateral group that corresponds to the deal that appears.
- (Selected Stratification). The stratification criterion that you selected.
- As of. The as of date of the collateral.

Weighted Average Characteristics section (title does not appear)

The Weighted Average Characteristics section displays the weighted average characteristics of all the loans that appear, based on the selected stratification. The following fields appear:

> **Tip**
>
> This view does not currently apply to commercial mortgage-backed securities.

- All Loans. The total number of loans that correspond to the Count field.
- Count. The total number of loans included in the summary information that appear to the right.
- Curr. AMT (USD). The current face value of the loans.
- %. The percentage of the total face value of the loans.
- WALTV. The original dollar-weighted average amortized loan-to-original value of the underlying loans comprising the collateral.
- Score. The weighted average credit score.
- Orig. AMT (USD). The original face value of the loans.
- WAC. The weighted average coupon of the individual loans underlying the security, using the balance of each loan as the weights.

- `WAM`. The weighted average maturity of the individual loans underlying the security, using the balance of each loan as the weights.
- `WALA`. The average age of all the loans in a pool, using the balance of each loan as the weights.

Individual Loan Details section (title does not appear)

The `Individual Loan Details` section displays the individual loan details by loan number. The following fields apppear:

> **Tip**
>
> This view does not currently apply to commercial mortgage-backed securities.

- `Loan No`. The number assigned to the individual loan.
- `Pay History`. The string of characters represents up to 24 months of historical payment status information for the corresponding loan. Each character represents the status for an individual month, chronologically, with the first character in the string representing the payment status for the current month. The following characters may appear:
  - `C`. Current.
  - `B`. Bankruptcy.
  - `F`. Foreclosure.
  - `R`. REO (real estate owned).
  - `3`. 30 days delinquent.
  - `6`. 60 days delinquent.
  - `9`. 90 days delinquent.
  - `Curr. AMT (USD)`. The current face value of the loan.
  - `Orig. AMT (USD)`. The original face value of the loan.
  - `Rate`. The loan rate.
  - `LTV`. The loan-to-value ratio.
  - `Score`. The credit score for the loan.
  - `Age`. The age of the loan in months.
  - `MTM`. The months to maturity (i.e., the number of months to maturity of the loan).
  - `Type`. The loan type.
  - `Index`. For ARMS, the index used to determine the rate.
  - `MTR`. The months to reset (i.e., the number of months to the intial reset of the loan).

> **Important**
>
> A negative value represents a loan that has already passed its intial reset.

  - `GEO`. The state that corresponds to the loan.
  - `Delinq Days`. The number of days the loan is delinquent.
  - `BFRL`. The specially serviced status of the loan. Shows if loan is in bankruptcy or foreclosure.
  - `PaidThru`. The date until which the loan is paid through.
  - `Zip Code`. The zip code for the property.

Calculation methodologies and reconciliation issues

Reconciling the values in CLP vs. alternative sources may be difficult because of varying reporting conventions. All values that Bloomberg displays on CLP are derived directly from the loan-level data as received from the issuer/servicer.

Moody's Investor Services weights values by obligor dollar balance. Bloomberg weights values by investor dollar balance (where indicated). Standard and Poor's weights values by loan count.

Discrepancies can occur when Bloomberg breaks a single deal into two entities to reflect the collateral segmentation as reflected in the prospectus. For example, SMART 93-1A and 93-1B are the same legally defined deal, but their respective collateral statistics on CLP reflect the analysis of only those loans that back the classes in the subdeal.

22.5 CMBS LOAN DETAIL SCREEN (LDES)

Use LDES to display loan-level information for the collateral that backs a specific commercial mortgage-backed security (CMBS).

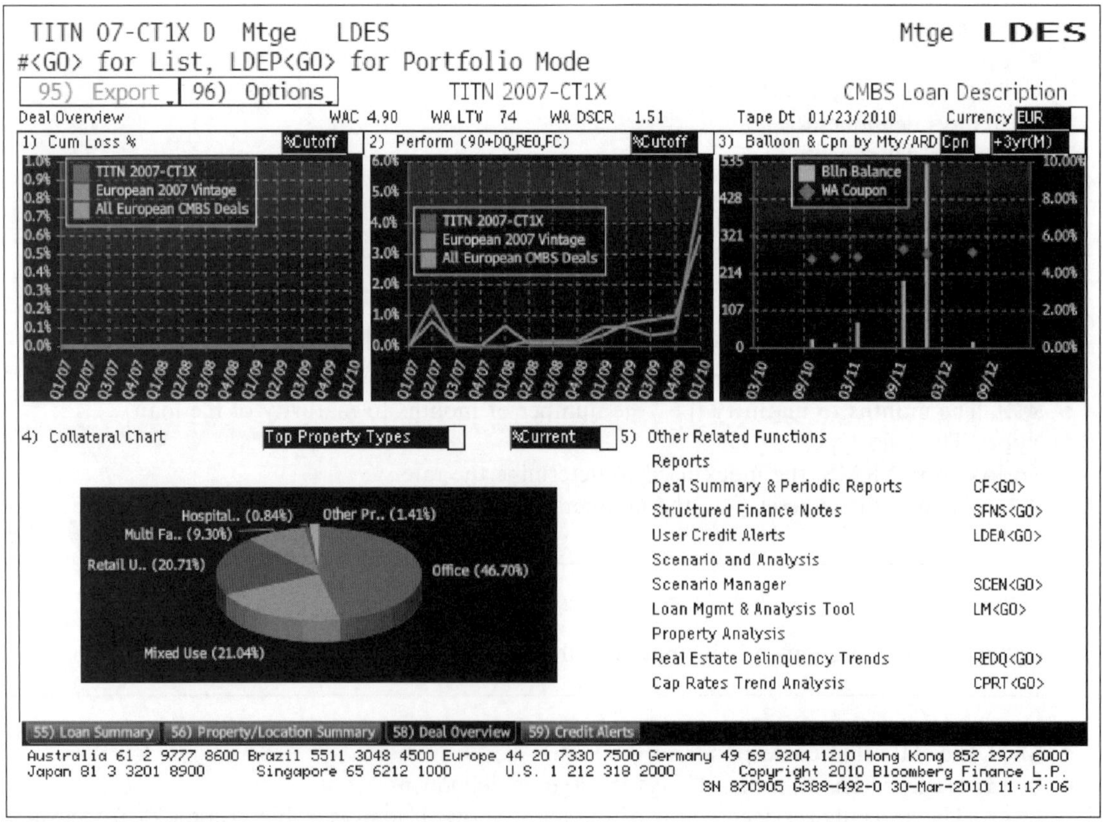

Figure 22.5. CMBS Loan Detail screen (LDES).

Analyze summarized loan Data

Once you enter (ticker symbol) `<MTGE>LDES<Go>` (e.g., `07388YAA <MTGE>LDES<Go>`), the `Loan Summary` view's `CMBS Loan Description` screen (Figure 22.5) appears. Choose from the following options:

- To export the data that appear to an MS Excel spreadsheet, click on the `Export` toolbar button.
- To save/reset default settings, click on `Options` from the toolbar and choose the appropriate option from the dropdown menu that appears or, alternatively, enter `96<Go>` and choose the appropriate option from the `Options` window that appears.
- The following functions apply to the `Deal Overview` view only:
  - To display the information in a table/graph, click on `Options > Show Data as Tables/ Charts` from the toolbar.
  - To show/hide information that corresponds to the security's deal/vintage/shelf/region on the graphs, click on `Options > Show/Hide Deal/Vintage/Shelf/Region Series` from the toolbar.
- To display additional views of summarized loan information, click on the appropriate tab at the bottom of the screen.
- To change the data that appear, enter/choose the appropriate information in/from the highlighted fields.
- To display complete information for a specific data item, if applicable, move your cursor over the appropriate data item. The complete information appears highlighted in blue.
- To display the loans/properties/leases comprising a specific subcategory, click on the appropriate subcategory so that the corresponding `Loan Detail` view's `CMBS Loan Description` screen appears.
- To sort the data that appear by column, if applicable, click on the appropriate column heading until the arrow that appears points in the appropriate direction. The arrow points up/down for descending/ascending order.

Once you display the `Loan Detail` view's `CMBS Loan Description` screen, choose from the following additional options:

- To display the loan/property/tenant list for the loan(s), click on the appropriate tab that appears at the bottom of the screen.
- The following options apply to the `Loan List` view only:
  - To display up to three periods of historical data, click on the checkbox to the left of the `Show History` field so that a checkmark appears.
  - To change the information that appears in the list, enter/choose the appropriate information in/ from the highlighted fields that appear.
  - To sort the data that appear by column, click on the appropriate column heading until the arrow that appears points in the appropriate direction. The arrow points up/down for descending/ ascending order.
  - To display the full name of an abbreviated column heading, move your cursor over the appropriate column heading.
- To display further details for a specific loan/property/lease, click on the appropriate loan/property/ lease name from the list. The corresponding `CMBS Loan Description` screen's `Loan Detail` view appears.

Analyze loan-level data

Once you click on a specific loan/property/lease from the `Loan/Property/Lease List` screen, the `CMBS Loan Description` screen's `Loan Detail` view appears with corresponding loan-level information. Choose from the following additional options:

- To display the cash flows for a specific loan, click on the `Cashflows` toolbar button. The `Cash Flows` screen appears. `CFT<HELP>` displays further information.
- To show/hide all properties collateralizing a loan, if applicable, click on the `Show Prop List/ Hide Prop List` toolbar button.
- To change the property for which data appear in the `Property` view, in cases where multiple properties collateralize the loan, click on the highlighted `Collateralizing Property` (label does not appear) field dropdown menu and choose the appropriate option, or, alternatively, click on the `Show Prop List` toolbar button, then click on the appropriate property from the list that appears at the top of the screen.
- To display additional information for the selected loan, click on the appropriate tab at the bottom of the screen.
- To display a list of loans that are cross-collateralized/cross-defaulted to a specific loan, if applicable, click on `Yes` to the right of the `Crossed Loans` field in the `Loan Details` view.

Tip

If `No` appears, there are no cross-collateralized/cross-defaulted loans.

- To display the full watchlist criteria and the threshold to remove the loan from the watchlist, if applicable, click on the `WList Commentary` tab.

Tip

The `WList Commentary` tab appears only when a loan is watchlisted.

- To enter and save your own notes for a loan, click on the `User Notes` tab, enter your text in the highlighted section of the screen, then click on the `Save` button. The notes you enter only appear in your login and cannot be viewed by other users.

Tip

You can click on the `Delete` button to delete a note you have previously saved.

Toolbar buttons

Depending on the security, view, and/or screen that you choose, some of the following toolbar buttons may appear, listed here in alphabetical order:

- `Cashflows` allows you to display the cash flows for the corresponding loan. `CFT<HELP>` displays further information.

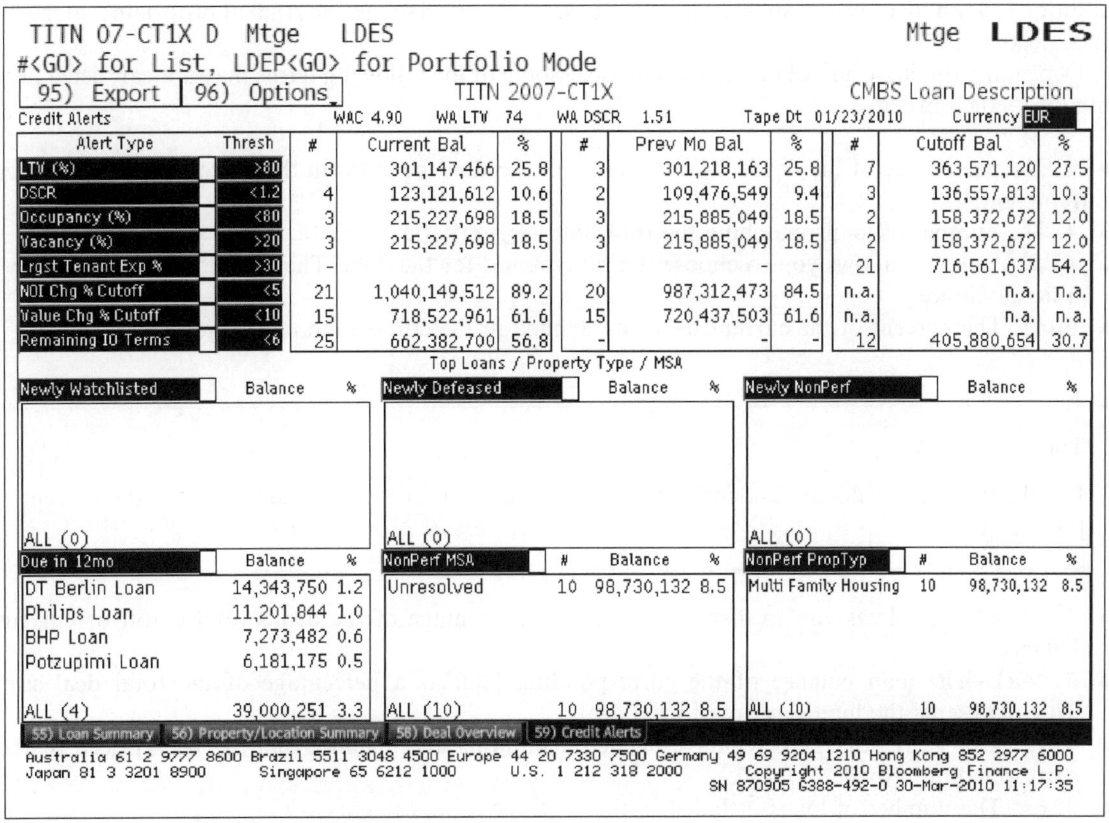

Figure 22.6. `LDES Credit Alerts` screen.

- `Export` allows you to export the information that appears to an MS Excel spreadsheet.
- `Options` enables you to set display defaults.

> **Tip**
>
> If you choose `Options > Save Current View as Default` from the `Credit Alerts` view (see sample screenshot in Figure 22.6), the information you entered in the highlighted fields is saved.

- `Show/Hide Prop List` allows you to show/hide a list of properties collateralizing the selected loan, if applicable.

Analysing specific loans with the CMBS Loan Description screen

The `Loan Summary` view's `CMBS Loan Description` screen displays aggregated information on the underlying loans in the selected `CMBS` deal. Tabs at the bottom of the screen allow you to display loan, property/location, and credit summaries along with a deal overview and credit alerts. You can display additional loan details on subsequent `List` screens by clicking on the appropriate category/subcategory.

Depending on the security and view you choose some of the following terms may appear, listed here in alphabetical order:

- `%`. The percentage of the deal's total current balance that the loans in the corresponding category represent.
- `#`. The number of loans matching the threshold alert criteria.
- `+(#)yr(M/Y)` allows you to choose the time period for the data. The dropdown menu displays a list of choices.
- `%Bal`. The percent of the current balance included in the corresponding category.

> **Tip**
>
> For the `Current` category under the `All Loans` heading, the `%Bal` is equivalent to the current pool factor.

- `Cuto/%Curr` allows you to display values as a percentage of the deal's total cutoff or current balance.
- `% Deal`. The loan balance of the corresponding loan as a percentage of the total deal size. This represents the loan exposure to the deal.
- `% of Deal Priced`. The percentage of the outstanding loan balance that has been priced by the corresponding provider.
- `#Lns`. The number of loans included in the corresponding category.
- `#Prop`. The number of properties included in the corresponding category.
- `(Month abbreviation) YY Bal`. The month and year for the corresponding `#`, `Bal`, and `%` fields. The `Bal` value is the total current balance for the loans included in the corresponding alert category.
- `Alert Type`. The criterion for the alert information.
- `All (#)`. Displays the total balance and the total balance as a percentage of deal balance for all loans included in the category you selected from the `Top Category` field (label does not appear).
- `All Loans`. The loans within the deal. The following categories appear:
  - `Cutoff`. The information as of the cutoff date.
  - `Current`. The information as of the tape date.
  - `Terminated`. The information for terminated loans. A loan can be terminated due to payoff at maturity, prepayment, or liquidation.
- `Amount`. The dollar amount of the entire deal that the category comprises.
- `ASER`. The appraisal reductions, which reduce the amount of a monthly special servicer advance on a delinquent loan in anticipation of an unrealized loss.
- `Bal (Mln)`. The balloon balance for the corresponding maturity date, expressed in millions.
- `Bal as %`. The loan balance for the corresponding category, expressed as a percentage of the deal's total current balance or cutoff balance.
- `Balance`. The current loan balance included in the corresponding category.
- `Balloon & (Cpn/GM) by Mty/ARD` displays a chart/table of information on the balloon balance and weighted average coupon/weighted average gross coupon for the loans by maturity/anticipated repayment date (ARD).

The following comment applies to the chart only: The horizontal x-axis displays the maturity/anticipated repayment date. The vertical y-axis on the left displays the balloon balance amounts, and the y-axis on the right displays the weighted average coupon/weighted average gross margin values.

> **Tip**
>
> If the underlying loans are adjustable rate loans, weighted average gross margin information appears instead of weighted average coupon information.
>
> If the underlying loans are adjustable rate and fixed rate loans, the `Cpn` field appears.
>
> You can hide/display data for the corresponding deal/vintage/shelf/region series by clicking on `Options > Hide/Show Deal/Vintage/Shelf/Region Series` from the toolbar.
>
> Once you click on the field, the `CMBS Balloon Risk Analysis` function (`BLNR`) appears in a fifth Bloomberg Professional service window. `BLNR<HELP>` displays further information.

- `Bankrupt Loan` displays information for loans where the borrower has filed for bankruptcy.
- `City`. The city where the property is located.
- `Collateral Chart` displays a chart/table of information on the collateral composition, as a percentage of the deal's total cutoff balance or current balance.

> **Tip**
>
> To display complete information for a specific data item, if applicable, move your cursor over the appropriate data item. The complete information appears highlighted in white.
>
> You can click on a pie piece to display the individual properties and loans that are represented.
>
> Once you click on the field, the `Collateral Composition Graph` function (`CLCG`) appears in a fifth Bloomberg Professional service window. `CLCG<HELP>` displays further information.

- `Count`. The number of loans in the category.
- `CPN`. The current coupon of the loan.
- `Cpn`. The weighted average coupon for the corresponding maturity date. Applies to the `Deal Overview` view only and allows you to display weighted average coupon information for the fixed rate or floating rate loans in the collateral. The dropdown menu displays the appropriate choices.
- `Ctry`. The country where the property is located.
- `Cum Loss %` displays a chart/table of information on the cumulative loss amounts, as a percentage of the deal's total current or cutoff balance. Applies to the chart only, where the horizontal x-axis displays the period and the vertical y-axis displays the collateral loss percentage values.

> **Tip**
>
> You can hide/display data for the corresponding deal/vintage/shelf/region series by clicking on the `Options > Hide/Show Deal/Vintage/Shelf/Region Series` from the toolbar.
>
> Once you click on the field, the `Collateral Performance function (CLP)` appears in a fifth Bloomberg Professional service window. `CLP<HELP>` displays further information.

- Curr Bal. The adjusted balance that reflects all scheduled and unscheduled principal payments as of the tape date.
- Currency allows you to choose the currency for the information. The dropdown menu displays a list of choices. The Country/Currency Codes section of this chapter displays further information.
- Current Balance. The adjusted balance that reflects all scheduled and unscheduled principal payments as of the corresponding date. Applies to Deal Overview view only, showing the deal's total current balance as of the tape date.
- Current WAvg Price (price provider). The weighted average price estimate from the corresponding provider for the loan using the current balance of the loans as the weights.

Tip

DXML<Go> displays further information on DebtX's pricing methodology.

- Cuto Balance. The deal's total cutoff balance.
- Date. The date for the corresponding data, in mm/yy format.
- Deal displays aggregated data for the deal.
- Defeased Loans displays information for the defeased loan(s) in the collateral. Defeasance indicates that the loan's cash flows have been replaced with those of U.S. Treasury obligations.
- Delinquent Loans (Excl Fore&REO) displays information for delinquent loans, excluding loans in foreclosure and real estate owned (REO). The following categories may appear:
  - Grace & <30. Loans that are delinquent, but within the grace period or fewer than 30 days delinquent. The grace period is defined in the prospectus.
  - 30. Loans that are 30–59 days delinquent.
  - 60. Loans that are 60–89 days delinquent.
  - 90+ (incl > 12m). Loans that are 90 days to 12 months delinquent.
  - >12m. Loans that are more than 12 months delinquent.
  - Total. The total from all of the other categories that appear.
- DSCR. The debt service coverage ratio, which is the ratio of the annualized scheduled payments of principal and/or interest on the mortgage loan to the net operating income or net cash flow of the property.
- Due. The maturity date or anticipated repayment date of the loan.
- Excluded Properties displays information on properties that were not included in the property and location statistics because of their defeased status.
- Expiration. The expiration date of the lease for the tenant holder.
- Exposure. The allocation of the loan amount based on tenant exposure percentage.
- Lease Name. The name of the tenant to which the loan applies.
- List. The description of the information that appears on the screen.
- Loan Concentration. The largest loans within the collateral. The following categories appear:
  - AB Loans. Loans that have A-note and B-note components.
  - Largest. The loan with the largest current balance.
  - Second Largest. The loan with the second largest current balance.

  - Third Largest. The loan with the third largest current balance.
  - Top 10. Summarized information from the 10 largest loans.
- LoanExp. The percentage of the space of the loan that the tenant occupies.
- Loan Name. The name of the loan.
- Loan Status. The status of the loan for the correspondng date. The following statuses apply:
  - Perform indicates the loan conforms to repayment structure.
  - Graced indicates the loan is in a grace period.
  - Hyper Amortizing indicates the loan is hyper-amortizing, which is the accelerated paydown of a loan achieved by allocating its scheduled principal and interest.
  - Watchlist indicates that the loan is currently being watched for possible defaults.
  - Del () indicates that the loan is currently delinquent. Appears as 30 day, 60 days, or 90 days. When the loan is more than 90 days delinquent, the lender usually has the right to begin foreclosure proceedings.
  - Foreclosed indicates the loan is foreclosed.
  - REO. Real estate owned. Indicates the loan is out of foreclosure and being managed by the special servicer.
  - Bankrupt indicates the loan's borrower is bankrupt.
  - Special indicates the loan has been transferred to the special servicer.
  - Defeased indicates the loan's cash flows have been replaced with those of U.S. Treasury obligations.
  - Prepaid indicates a prepayment has been made on the loan outside of scheduled repayments.
  - Matured indicates the loan has reached its due date.
- Loan Type displays a breakdown of the loans by coupon type.
- Lrgst Tenant Exp %. The largest tenant exposure percentage.
- LTV. The loan-to-value ratio, which is the ratio of the current mortgage balance to the property's appraised value.
- LTV (%). The current loan-to-value ratio.
- Matur. The maturity date for the data.
- Mo DQ. The number of months that the corresponding loan is delinquent.
- Name. The name/abbreviation of the collateral composition category. The State Codes - States & Territories function (SCD) displays further information, if applicable.
- NCF % Cutoff. The percentage change in the most recently reported full year's net cash flow (NCF) from the NCF at securitization.
- Net CPN. The loan gross coupon less administrative fees.
- NOI Chg % Cutoff. The percentage change in the net operating income (NOI) since cutoff.
- NOI/NCF. Net operating income/net cash flow are the revenues earned by a property's ongoing operations, less expenses.
- Occupancy (%). The property occupancy percentage.
- Other Related Functions displays a list of other CMBS analysis functions. The corresponding <HELP> for each function displays further information.
- Percent. The percentage of the entire deal that the category comprises.
- Perform (60+DQ,REO,FC) displays a chart/table of information on the cumulative non-performance status (aggregating 60+ days delinquent, REO, and foreclosure statuses) of loans as a percentage of the current or cutoff balance. Applies to the chart only, where the horizontal *x*-axis displays the period and the vertical *y*-axis displays the percentage values.

Tip

You can hide/display data for the corresponding deal/vintage/shelf/region series by clicking on the Options > Hide/Show Deal/Vintage/Shelf/Region Series from the toolbar.

Once you click on the field, the Delinquency Report function (DQRP) appears in a fifth Bloomberg Professional service window. DQRP<HELP> displays further information.

- Property Name. The name of the property to which the loan applies.
- Property Type displays information for loans within the deal by property type.
- Protection. The protection for the loan.

Tip

The protection is typically followed by a number in parentheses. This is the term of the protection (i.e., YM(14) indicates that the loan has a yield maintenance of 14 months). If no term in parentheses follows the protection type, 12 months is implied. If the term is followed by a [^], it means there is a minimum premium amount (i.e., YM^1(17) states that the greater of the yield maintenance penalty, or a fixed penalty, of 1% for 17 months applies if prepayments occur). The following protection codes apply:

- Due. The loan has reached its due date.
- L. The lockout period during which voluntary principal prepayments are prohibited.
- YM. Yield maintenance is the period in which prepayments are permitted, but are charged a yield maintenance penalty.
- #. Fixed penalty amount, where prepayments are charged a fixed penalty. For example, if the string starts with 5(7), the loan can be prepaid with a 5% penalty for the covered 7 months.
- D. The defeasance period, in which the loan's cash flows can be replaced with those of U.S. Treasury obligations.
- E. Optional extension, which is a provision permitting extension of the original term of the mortgage under terms agreed upon at origination.
- O. Open period, during which voluntary principal prepayments may be made freely without any prepayment premium.
- X. Exit fees that apply when a loan is paid off.

- Pricing Date. The date the information was last updated.
- Primary Data Filter (label does not appear) appears on the Loan/Property/Lease List screen. Allows you to display the loans/properties/leases within the category you choose. The dropdown menu displays a list of choices.
- Region displays aggregated data for deals of the same region as the selected deal.
- Secondary Data Filter (label does not appear) allows you to refine the display criteria you set with the Primary Data Filter (label does not appear) field. The dropdown menu displays a list of choices.
- Shelf displays aggregated data for deals of the same shelf as the selected deal.

- `Show History`. A checkmark in the checkbox displays 3 months of loan status and current balance history for the loans.
- `Special Serviced Loans` displays information for the specially serviced loans within the collateral. The following categories appear:
  - `Grace & <30`. Loans that are in a grace period or loans that are less than 30 days delinquent.
  - `Curr & Spl Srvcd`. Loans that are not delinquent and are specially serviced.
  - `Delnq & Spl Srvcd`. Loans that are delinquent and specially serviced.
  - `REO`. Real estate–owned loans.
  - `In Foreclosure`. Loans in foreclosure.
  - `Matured`. Loans that have matured.
  - `Total`. The total sum of the loans in the other categories.
- `St`. The state where the property is located. The `State Codes-States & Territories` screen (`SCD`) displays further information.
- `Status:`. The current status of the loan. The following states apply:
  - `Performing` indicates the loan conforms to the repayment structure.
  - `Graced` indicates the loan is in a grace period.
  - `Hyper Amortizing` indicates the loan is hyper-amortizing, which is the accelerated paydown of a loan *achieved* by allocating its scheduled principal and interest.
  - `Watchlist` indicates that the loan is currently being watched for possible defaults.
  - `Delinquency` indicates that the loan is currently delinquent. Appears as 1 month, 2 months, or 3 months. When the loan is more than 90 days delinquent, the lender usually has the right to begin foreclosure proceedings.
  - `Foreclosed` indicates the loan is foreclosed.
  - `REO` (real estate owned) indicates the loan is out of foreclosure and being managed by the special servicer.
  - `Bankrupt` indicates the loan's borrower is bankrupt.
  - `Special` indicates the loan has been transferred to the special servicer.
  - `Defeased` indicates the loan's cash flows have been replaced with those of U.S. Treasury obligations.
  - `Prepaid` indicates a prepayment has been made on the loan outside of scheduled repayments.
  - `Matured` indicates the loan has reached its due date.
- `Tape Dt`. The payment date through which the collateral has been updated.
- `Thresh` allows you to enter a threshold level for the corresponding alert-type criterion.

Tip

Greater than (>), less than (<), equal to (=), greater than or equal to (>=), and less than or equal to (<=) are acceptable notations when used in combination with a positive (+) or negative (-) numerical value. For example, to specify loans with a 10% or greater drop in net operating income since the cutoff, you can enter `>=-10` in the highlighted `Thres` field to the right of the `NOI Chg % Cutoff` field.

- `Top` allows you to choose a category for the collateral composition information. The dropdown menu displays a list of choices.
- `Top Category` (label does not appear) allows you to display the largest loans/property types/MSAs, by current balance, for the category you choose. The dropdown menu displays a list of choices.

- `Top Countries`. The countries in which the greatest number of properties within the collateral are located.
- `Top Loans/ Property Type/ MSA` allows you to display the top loans/property type(s)/MSAs, by current balance, for the criteria you choose. The six dropdown menus display a list of criteria choices.
- `Top Originators` The top-3 originators within the deal.
- `Top MSA`. The metropolitan statistical areas in which the greatest number of properties within the collateral are located.
- `Top States:`. The U.S. states in which the greatest number of properties within the collateral are located.
- `Trustee ID`. The trustee loan identifier.
- `Type`. The type of property for the corresponding loan.
- `Vacancy (%)`. The property vacancy percentage.
- `Value`. The appraised value of the property.
- `Value Chg % Cutoff`. The percentage change in the appraisal since cutoff.

Tip

The corresponding `Cutoff Bal` section of the screen displays n.a.

- `Vintage` displays aggregated data for all deals of the same deal vintage, within the same region as the selected deal.
- `WA DSCR`. The weighted average debt service coverage ratio for the deal.
- `WA LTV`. The weighted average loan to value for the deal.
- `WAC:`. The weighted average coupon for the deal.
- `Watchlist Loans`. The information for loans placed on the servicer's watchlist.

The CMBS Loan Description screen and the Loan Detail functionality

Once you click on a loan from the `CMBS Loan Description` screen's `List` view, the `Loan Detail` view appears, where you can display specific details about the loan. Tabs appear at the bottom of the screen which allow you to display information about the property to which the loan applies and financial and payment information pertinent to the loan.

Depending on the security and view you choose, some of the following fields may appear, listed here in alphabetical order:

Tip

In the cases where multiple properties collateralize the loan, the information on the `Financials` tab represents the aggregate property financials of all the underlying properties.

- `#Prop`. The number of properties included in the category.
- `2nd Prev Yr`. The value of the corresponding measure from 2 years prior.
- `Actual Bal` applies to the `Loan Details` view. The legal remaining outstanding principal balance related to the borrower's mortgage note. For partial defeasances, the balance should reflect

the appropriate allocation of the balance prior to the defeasance between the non-defeased and defeased loans, based on the provisions of the loan documents.

- `Added to Watchlist`. The date the loan was added to the watchlist.
- `Address`. The address of the property.
- `Admin Fees`. Also known as the servicing strip, the administration fees consist of the fees paid to the master servicer and trustee for their duties of servicing, administration, and reporting.
- `Amort`. The number of periods on which scheduled payment of principal and interest is based. If the loan is interest only, the `Amort` value is 0.
- `Amort Type`. The amortization type that describes the payment structure of the loan. The following amortization types apply:
  - `IO (Interest Only)`. The borrower is required to make interest payments on the loan.
  - `Partial IO (Partial Interest Only)`. The borrower initially makes interest payments, then begins paying principal towards the loan to reduce the outstanding principal balance.
  - `Balloon Amort`. The borrower makes interest and principal payments towards the loan, but requires a balloon payment at the loan's maturity date.
  - `Fully Amortizing`. The borrower makes interest and principal payments towards the loan and pays down the loan to zero (no balloon) at the loan's maturity date.
- `Amount`. The principal payment at the time the loan was terminated.
- `Appraisal Value` The appraised property value, as of the cutoff date.

> **Tip**
>
> If the loan was reappraised, it appears in the second row with the date the property was reappraised.

- `Annualized YTD`. The amount of the loan that has been annualized in the year to date.
- `ARA`. The appraisal reduction amount is the difference between the loan balance and the appraisal amount, plus advances to date, plus expenses. The appraisal reduction amount is used to determine recent `ASER`.

> **Tip**
>
> `ARA` is generally defined in the pooling and servicing agreement along with the corresponding calculation.

- `ARD`. The anticipated repayment date of the loan, which is the expected date the loan will pay off. If the loan does not pay on the anticipated repayment date, the loan enters into a hyper-amortization period, in which case loan terms may be unfavorable to the borrower.
- `As Of`. The date the property appraisal was completed.
- `As of Tape Date`. The tape date for the corresponding commentary.
- `ASER`. The cumulative ASER (appraisal subordinate entitlement reductions) amount from the prior reporting periods, plus the most recent ASER for the current reporting period.
- `Balance`. The outstanding balance of the loan for each corresponding tape date.
- `Balance Pct`. The loan exposure to the deal, expressed as a percentage where the numerator is the current trust balance and the denominator is the outstanding deal balance.

- `Borrower`. The person(s) or legal entity taking out the loan. In CMBS, the borrower is a single purpose entity (SPE).
- `Built`. The year the property was built.
- `Calendar`. The calendar of country or countries used to determine the number of days interest accrued for the purpose of calculating interest payments. The calendar is specifically used for loans that accrue interest based on actual business days. For example, if the loan accrues interest based on an actual business day count, business days and holidays are based on the calendar of the corresponding country, such as:
  - `USD`. United States.
  - `CAD`. Canada.
  - `IRL_GBR_FRA_DEU`. Ireland, Great Britain, France, and Germany.
- `Cap` applies to floating rate loans only. The highest coupon (index + gross margin) the loan pays, regardless of how high the base index may rise.
- `Cap Rate`. The capitalization rate for the corresponding property. The cap rate measures a property's ability to generate cash before taxes and debt service, and is often used to compare similar properties in a specific market. It is the annual net operating income (NOI) divided by the appraisal value of a property.
- `Capex`. The capital expenditures that are the expenses related to property improvements. Capital expenditures are not considered ongoing operating expenses.
- `City`. The city where the property is located.
- `Close` closes the `Watchlist Code Descriptions` window.
- `County`. The county in which the property is located.
- `Coupon`. The current gross coupon of the loan. For adjusting rate loans, the coupon is the index plus a specific gross margin.
- `Collateralizing Property` (label does not appear) allows you to choose a specific property for which to display property, tenant, and financial information in cases where the loan is collateralized by multiple properties. The dropdown menu displays a list of choices.
- `Crossed Loans`. Also referred to as cross-collateralized/cross-defaulted loans, crossed loans are where the collateral backing the loan is also pledged to support other loans within the same deal, and *vice versa*. Crossed loans have the same borrower and typically have the same loan terms. In a case where one of the crossed loans defaults, all associated loans are considered in default. `Yes` indicates that the loan is cross-collateralized/cross-defaulted with other loans in the deal; `No` indicates that the loan is not crossed.

Examples of crossed loans

—Enter `CSMC 2006-C4 A1 MTGE LDES<Go>`, then choose the Briarwood Apartments loan.
—Enter `BACM 2006-4 A1 MTGE LDES<Go>`, then choose the Mississippi MHP loan.

- `Ctry`. The country where the property is located.
- `Cum ASER`. The cumulative appraisal entitlement reduction.
- `Cutoff`. The value of the corresponding measure as of the loan cutoff date.
- `Cutoff Bal`. The loan balance as of the cutoff date of the deal, which reflects amortization since the origination date.
- `Cutoff NOI`. The cutoff net operating income, which is the revenue earned by the property's ongoing operations, less expenses.

- Cutoff Tenant. The three largest tenants as of the cutoff date.
- Curr Bal. The outstanding loan balance as of the tape date of the deal.
- Curr Collat Allocated Amount. The current collateral allocated amount. The amount of the loan exposed to the property. It is the outstanding loan balance multiplied by the current collateral allocated percentage.
- Curr Allocated Bal per Unit. The current allocated balance per unit. The current allocated amount per property unit (or square foot).
- Curr Collat Allocated Percent. The current collateral allocated percentage. The percentage of the loan exposed to the property. If the loan is secured by one loan, the allocated percentage is 100%. If the loan is secured by multiple properties, it is the percentage of the loan supported by the property.
- Curr Occupancy. The square footage of the property that is leased as of the Occupancy As of date, expressed as a percentage of the total property square footage.
- Current Tenant. The three largest tenants as of the lease rollover review date.
- Currency. The currency denomination of the loan. The "Country/Currency Codes" section of this chapter displays further information.
- Cutoff NCF. The cutoff net cash flow of the property.
- Date. The date of the latest change in loan status.
- DayCount. The daycount of the loan used for calculating interest. Daycount types are:
  - 30/360.
  - Actual/360.
  - Actual/365.
  - Actual/Business/360.
  - Actual/Business/365.
  - Actual/Actual.
  - Actual/Business/Misc (for European-issued deals with multiple countries).
- Debt Service. The amount of cash needed in a given timeframe to pay interest and principal on outstanding debt.
- Def Maintenance. Based on the last site inspection, the loan servicer determines if deferred maintenance has occurred. A Yes indicates that deferred maintenance occurred, but has not yet been addressed (cured). A No indicates that either deferred maintenance has been addressed (cured), or deferred maintenance existed.
- Delete allows you to delete the note entered for the loan.
- Delinquency Commentary displays information and commentary on the loan's watchlist status, if applicable.
- DSCR NCF. The debt service coverage ratio of the property's net cash flow.
- DSCR NOI. The debt service coverage ratio of the property's net operating income.
- Due. The maturity date of the loan.
- Dx Mark. The price estimate for the loan provided by DebtX. DXMK<Go> displays a white paper that describes the methodology used by DebtX to derive the corresponding prices.
- End Date. The end date of the loan.
- Ends. The end date of the payment term.
- Escrow. The account funded by the borrower and required by the lender for purposes of covering certain expenses, such as taxes and insurance.
- Expires. The expiration date of the tenant's lease.
- Expense. The expense to maintain the property during the corresponding time period.
- Exposure. The loan amount exposed to the tenant.
- ExtraPrin. The amount of extra principal paid.
- Fee. Also known as the admin fee or the servicing strip, the fee consists of the fees paid to the master servicer and trustee for their duties of servicing, administration, and reporting.

- `Floor` applies to floating rate loans only. The lowest coupon (index + gross margin) the loan pays, regardless of how low the base index may drop.
- `Ground Lease`. A `Yes` indicates that the borrower is leasing the land.
- `ICR`. The interest coverage ratio, which is the ratio used to determine how easily a company can pay interest on outstanding debt.
- `Initial Reserves`. The reserve amount established when the loan was funded to cover future expenses, including replacement costs, tenant improvements, and capital expenses.
- `Is Bankrupt` indicates if the borrower has declared bankruptcy.
- `Is CTL`. A `Yes/No` indicates that the loan is/is not a credit tenant lease.
- `Is Watchlist` indicates if the loan is placed on the servicer watchlist.

Tip

If a loan is watchlisted, a `Servicer Notes` tab appears that displays the full watchlist critieria and the threshold to remove the loan from the watchlist.

- `Last Inspected`. The date of the most recent site inspection.
- `Last SS Dt`. The date the loan was transferred to the special servicer.
- `Lease Rollover (Graph)`. The vertical *y*-axis displays the square footage of leases as a percentage of the total square footage of the property while the horizontal *x*-axis displays the lease expiration date ranges, expressed in a number of months.
- `Lien Position`. The legal claim on a property as security for a debt or other obligation.

Tip

A first-lien position takes a higher priority over subsequent liens (second liens, third liens, etc.).

- `Liq. Expense` applies to a liquidation event only. The total expenses incurred by the special servicer to sell the property or properties. This could include finding a buyer, lawsuits, administration fees, workout fees, etc.
- `Loan Age (mos)`. The age of the loan in months since the origination date. Loan age is also known as the "seasoning".
- `Loan Cpn Type` indicates whether or not the loan has a fixed or adjustable rate coupon.
- `LoanExp`. The percentage of the loan amount exposed to the corresponding tenant.
- `Loan ID`. The identification number of the current loan.
- `Loan Purpose`. The reason for obtaining a loan. The following loan types apply:
  - `Acquisition`. A loan made to acquire or purchase a property.
  - `Refinance` indicates a borrower has taken out a loan to replace an existing loan.
  - `Cash-out refinance loan`. A loan where the borrower takes out equity from the property by obtaining a loan that is larger than the existing loan.
- `Lockbox`. The bank account, controlled by the servicer, into which all income from the property is deposited. The following are different types of lockboxes:
  - `Hard`. Income from the subject property is paid directly into a lockbox account controlled by the servicer on behalf of the trust.

  - Soft. Income from the subject property is paid to the borrower or a property manager that is affiliated with the borrower, and then deposited into a lockbox account controlled by the servicer on behalf of the trust.
  - None at Closing-Springing Hard. Income from the subject property is paid to the borrower or a property manager that is affiliated with the borrower. Upon the occurrence of a trigger event, such as a loan default, all income from the subject property is paid directly into the lockbox account.
  - None at Closing-Springing Soft. A soft lockbox is established by the borrower upon the occurrence of a trigger event.
  - Soft at Closing-Springing Hard. A lockbox that was initially soft becomes hard upon the occurrence of a trigger event.
- Loss:. The principal loss, which occurs if the total proceeds from the sale of a property or several properties are insufficient to cover the outstanding mortgage and liquidation expenses. If a loss is greater than zero and the current balance is greater than zero, the loss represents unrecovered principal due to a partial liquidation/writedown.
- LTV. The loan to value, which is the ratio of the current mortgage balance to the property's appraised value.
- Months Late:. The number of months the borrower is late in making payments.
- Mstr Svcr. The master servicer, which is a firm engaged to service the mortgage loans collateralizing a CMBS deal on behalf of and for the benefit of the certificate holders. Responsibilities vary according to the pooling and servicing agreement. Common responsibilities include, but are not limited to, the following:
  - Collecting mortgage payments and passing the funds to the trustee.
  - Advancing any late payments to the trustee.
  - Providing mortgage performance reports to bondholders.
  - Passing all loans to the special servicer that are non-performing.
- MSA. The metropolitan statistical area in which the property is located.
- NCF. The net cash flow, which is a revenue earned by a property's ongoing operations, less expenses.
- Next Index applies to floating rate loans only. The index rate used to determine interest payment for the next payment period.
- NOI. The net operating income, which is a revenue earned by a property's ongoing operations, less expenses.
- Non-Recoverablity. A Yes indicates whether or not the master or special servicer has stopped advancing.
- Occupancy. The percentage of the property that is occupied.
- Occupancy As Of. The date the current occupancy (Curr Occupancy) information was last updated.
- Occupancy as of Date. The effective date of the current occupancy percentage.
- Orig Bal. The original loan balance at the time the loan was closed.
- Orig Date. The origination date, or closing date, of the loan.
- Originator. The name of the originator of the loan.
- Other Adv. The other expense advance outstanding, if applicable.
- Ownership Int:. The type of ownership interest held by the borrower.
- P&I Adv. The total P&I advance outstanding.
- Payment. The scheduled payment made towards the loan by the borrower. This is the principal and interest payment for an amortizing loan and interest payment for an interest-only loan. If the loan has a specified principal schedule that is not based on an amortization schedule, the payment value number is 0 and the Type = Periodic.

- PP/Liq'd indicates if a loan has been prepaid, liquidated, or disposed.
- PP/Liq'd Dt. The date of the prepayment, liquidation, or diposition event.
- Prev Yr. The previous year value of the corresponding measure.
- Previous Year. The previous year value of the corresponding value.
- Pricing Dt. The date when DebtX last updated the DxMark.
- Proceeds. The net proceeds received upon the sale of the properties.
- Propty/Collat Contrib Date. The property/collateral contribution date. The date the property was contributed to the deal. If the property is an original property, the date reflects the deal's closing date. If the property was defeased or substituted, then it is the effective date of the substitution or defeasance.
- Prop Condition. The assessed condition of the property.
- Prop Status. The status of the property: In Foreclosure, REO, Defeased, Partial Release, Substituted, or Same as Contributed may appear.
- Prop Type. The type of property.
- Property. The name of the property to which the loan applies.
- Property Details. The pertinent details about the property.
- Property Financials applies to Property view. Displays a summary of financial information for the property corresponding to the loan.

Tip

If the loan is collateralized by multiple properties, you can choose a specific property for which to display information using the Choose Property field dropdown menu. Once a property is selected, the screen displays the corresponding property, financials, and tenant information for the property.

In the cases where multiple properties collateralize the loan, the information represents the aggregate property financials of all the underlying properties.

- Property Value As of. The appraised value of the property, and the date the property appraisal was completed.
- Rem. Protection. The remaining call protection of the loan as of the tape date. For example, the remaining protection of L(6)-, YM(84), O(6) means the loan is locked out for the next six payment dates, then enters into a yield maintenance period for the next 84 payment dates, at which point it is freely prepayable for the next six payment dates. The following protection codes apply:
  - Due. The loan has reached or is past its maturity date.
  - L. The lockout period during which voluntary principal prepayments are prohibited.
  - YM. The yield maintenance period during which prepayments are permitted, but the borrower is charged a yield maintenance penalty. If YM is followed by [^], a minimum fixed rate penalty is required.
  - [#]. The fixed penalty period during which prepayments are permitted, but are charged a fixed rate penalty (e.g., 5(12) indicates a 5% fixed penalty rate for 12 months).
  - D. The defeasance period for which the borrower can substitute the property with non-callable U.S. Treasury obligations or, in certain cases, other government securities as collateral for the related mortgage loan.

  - E. The optional extension, which is a provision that permits extending the maturity date past the original maturity date without going into default. Optional extension terms are typical in floating rate deals.
  - O. The open period during which voluntary principal prepayments may be made freely without any prepayment penalty fee.
  - X. The exit fees that apply when a loan is paid off.
- Renovated. The year the property was most recently renovated.
- Reserve Bal. The remaining balance in the reserve account.
- Resolution/FC Date. The date the loan is expected to be resolved.
- Revenue. The current revenue (income) of the property.
- Review Date. The effective date when the rent rolls were reviewed to determine the square footage of the lease that is expiring.
- Save allows you to save the note you entered for the loan.
- Sched Pmt. The scheduled principal and interest payments made that correspond to each tape date.
- Sponsor. The sponsor of the loan.
- Sp Svcr. The special servicer, which is a firm that specializes in loan workouts. The special servicer is responsible for managing loans that go into default and conducting the workout process. There are various types of special servicers, such as:
  - Those that retain first-loss pieces.
  - Those that invest in B-pieces in return for special servicing rights.
  - Those that are appointed solely because of their specialized asset management expertise.

Tip

CMBS transactions have a separate special servicer, in addition to the master servicer.

- Spcl Srv Dt. The date the loan was transferred to the special servicer.
- Sq Feet. The total square footage of the property.
- Start Date. The start date of the loan.
- State. The U.S. state in which the property is located. The State Codes-States & Territories function (SCD) displays further information.
- Status. The current status of the loan. Loan types are as follows:
  - Perform/Perform (w). The borrower is up to date with its payments. The (w) indicates that the loan has been placed on the servicer's watchlist.
  - Late/Late (w). The borrower is less than 30 days delinquent with its loan payment. The (w) indicates that the loan has been placed on the servicer's watchlist.
  - In Foreclosure. A legal proceeding in which the special servicer is in the process of seizing the property.
  - REO (Real Estate Owned) indicates the loan is out of foreclosure and being managed by the special servicer.
  - Del 30/Del 30 ss. The borrower is 30 days delinquent with its loan payment. The ss indicates that the loan has also been transferred to special servicing.
  - Del 60/Del 60 ss. The borrower is 60 days delinquent with its loan payment. The ss indicates that the loan has also been transferred to special servicing.

  - Del 90+/Del 90+ ss. The borrower is 90 days or more delinquent with its loan payment. The ss indicates that the loan has also been transferred to special servicing.
  - Prepaid. The borrower has prepaid the loan.
  - Defeased. The loan has been 100% defeased.
  - Matured. The loan has paid off at maturity.
- T&I Adv. The total T&I advance outstanding.
- Tape Dt. The date the collateral was most recently updated. Applies to Payment Info view. The date the collateral was most recently updated for the corresponding payments and advances made toward the loan.
- Tenant. The name of the tenant to which the loan applies.
- Trust % of Deal. The loan exposure to the deal, expressed as a percentage where the numerator is the trust balance and the denominator is the outstanding deal balance.
- Trust Bal. The principal balance of the loan pooled into the trust. The trust balance is the amount of the loan that is securitized in the deal. In the case of AB loan structures or *pari passu* loans, the trust balance is generally different from the total current loan balance. Similarly, if the servicer is advancing, the trust balance could be lower than the amount owed by the borrower.
- Trustee ID. The identification number of the loan, provided by the trustee. The Trustee ID number is also used in the CMSA Periodic Loan file.
- Target Bond. The specific tranche of the deal that the loan's final principal, typically a balloon, is expected to pay off.
- Totl P&I Adv. The total principal and interest advances made by the servicer.
- Type. The payment description of the terms of the loan, if applicable. The type describes the interest-only term, the amortization term, and/or the optional extension term(s). If the loan has a specified principal schedule that is not based on an amortization schedule, then click on Type = Periodic.
- Underwritten. The amount of the loan that has been underwritten.
- Unpd Adv Int. The cumulative accrued unpaid advance interest.
- Watchlist Code. The watchlist code for the loan. The Watchlist Codes section of the screen displays further information.
- Watchlist Codes allow you to display guideline and threshold information for watchlist codes in the Watchlist Code Descriptions window.
- Watchlist Commentary displays information and commentary on the loan's watchlist status, if applicable.
- Workout indicates that the special servicer is trying to mitigate potential losses to the trust, which could result in different outcomes, including the start of foreclosure proceedings, short sales, or modifying the loan terms.

Tip

Workouts in CMBS are typically carried out by a special servicer.

- Year To Date. The year-to-date value of the corresponding measure.
- YTD. The year-to-date value of the corresponding measure.
- Zip. The zipcode for the corresponding property.

22.6 DELINQUENCY REPORT (DQRP)

Bloomberg's `Delinquency Report (DQRP)` displays a list of structured finance deals ranked by their collateral performance. The deals are sorted by the 60-day delinquency percentage. `DQRP` allows you to choose the sector and issuance year of the deal to be included in the report.

Functionality

Once you enter `DQRP<Go>`, the `Delinquency Report` screen (Figure 22.7) appears, where you can choose from the following options:

- To sort the data that appear in a specific column, choose from the following options, which depend on which column you choose to sort:
  - In the deal column, click on the appropriate column heading. An up or down arrow appears and indicates whether you have selected an ascending or descending sort order.
  - In other column headings, click on the appropriate column heading, then choose the appropriate sort option from the dropdown menu that appears. An up or down arrow appears and indicates whether you have selected an ascending or descending sort order. This sort option retrieves the top/bottom 2,000 deals that correspond to the selected column heading.

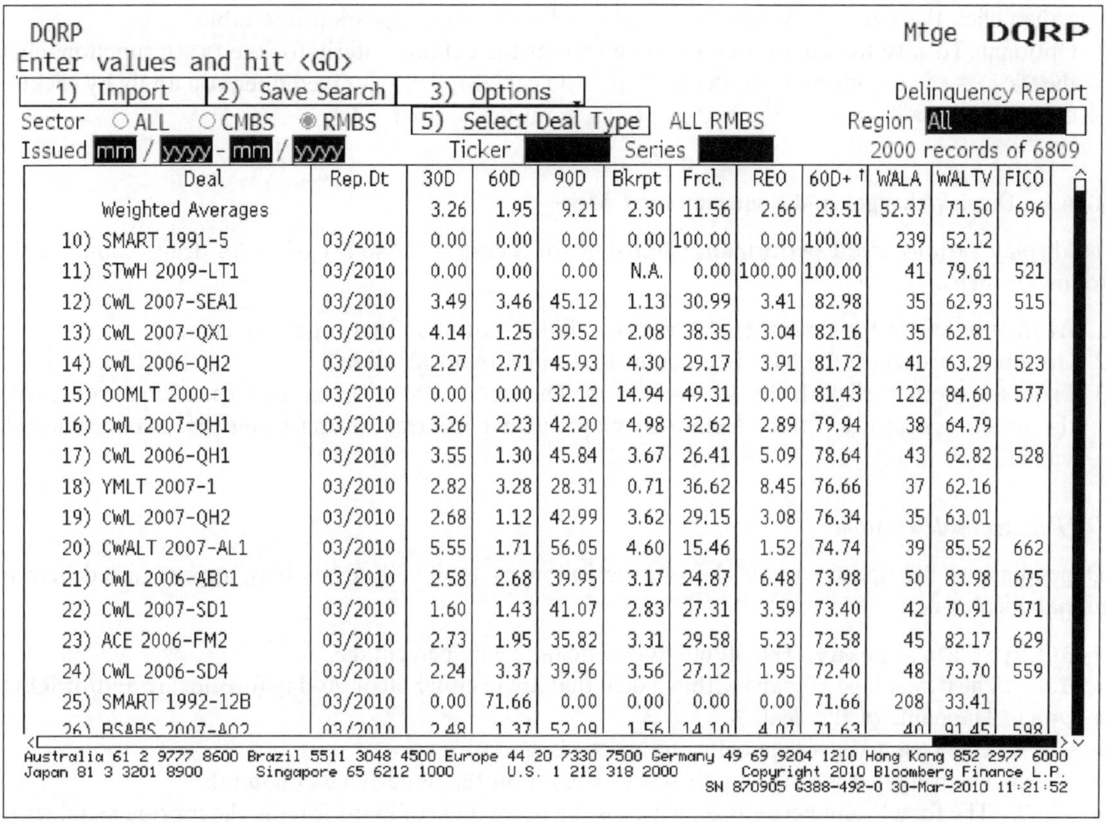

DQRP Mtge **DQRP**
Enter values and hit <GO>
1) Import | 2) Save Search | 3) Options | Delinquency Report
Sector ○ALL ○CMBS ◉RMBS | 5) Select Deal Type | ALL RMBS | Region All
Issued mm / yyyy - mm / yyyy | Ticker | Series | 2000 records of 6809

Deal	Rep.Dt	30D	60D	90D	Bkrpt	Frcl.	REO	60D+ ↑	WALA	WALTV	FICO
Weighted Averages		3.26	1.95	9.21	2.30	11.56	2.66	23.51	52.37	71.50	696
10) SMART 1991-5	03/2010	0.00	0.00	0.00	0.00	100.00	0.00	100.00	239	52.12	
11) STWH 2009-LT1	03/2010	0.00	0.00	0.00	N.A.	0.00	100.00	100.00	41	79.61	521
12) CWL 2007-SEA1	03/2010	3.49	3.46	45.12	1.13	30.99	3.41	82.98	35	62.93	515
13) CWL 2007-QX1	03/2010	4.14	1.25	39.52	2.08	38.35	3.04	82.16	35	62.81	
14) CWL 2006-QH2	03/2010	2.27	2.71	45.93	4.30	29.17	3.91	81.72	41	63.29	523
15) OOMLT 2000-1	03/2010	0.00	0.00	32.12	14.94	49.31	0.00	81.43	122	84.60	577
16) CWL 2007-QH1	03/2010	3.26	2.23	42.20	4.98	32.62	2.89	79.94	38	64.79	
17) CWL 2006-QH1	03/2010	3.55	1.30	45.84	3.67	26.41	5.09	78.64	43	62.82	528
18) YMLT 2007-1	03/2010	2.82	3.28	28.31	0.71	36.62	8.45	76.66	37	62.16	
19) CWL 2007-QH2	03/2010	2.68	1.12	42.99	3.62	29.15	3.08	76.34	35	63.01	
20) CWALT 2007-AL1	03/2010	5.55	1.71	56.05	4.60	15.46	1.52	74.74	39	85.52	662
21) CWL 2006-ABC1	03/2010	2.58	2.68	39.95	3.17	24.87	6.48	73.98	50	83.98	675
22) CWL 2007-SD1	03/2010	1.60	1.43	41.07	2.83	27.31	3.59	73.40	42	70.91	571
23) ACE 2006-FM2	03/2010	2.73	1.95	35.82	3.31	29.58	5.23	72.58	45	82.17	629
24) CWL 2006-SD4	03/2010	2.24	3.37	39.96	3.56	27.12	1.95	72.40	48	73.70	559
25) SMART 1992-12B	03/2010	0.00	71.66	0.00	0.00	0.00	0.00	71.66	208	33.41	
26) RSABS 2007-A02	03/2010	2.48	1.37	52.09	1.56	14.10	4.07	71.63	40	91.45	598

Australia 61 2 9777 8600 Brazil 5511 3048 4500 Europe 44 20 7330 7500 Germany 49 69 9204 1210 Hong Kong 852 2977 6000
Japan 81 3 3201 8900 Singapore 65 6212 1000 U.S. 1 212 318 2000 Copyright 2010 Bloomberg Finance L.P.
SN 870905 G388-492-0 30-Mar-2010 11:21:52

Figure 22.7. `Delinquency Report` screen (`DQRP`).

- To display the collateral performance of a structured deal in the CLP (Collateral Performance) function, which appears in another Bloomberg service window, click on the appropriate deal.

Customize the list of securities

You can customize the list of deals that appears in the table using various filter criteria, or by importing securities from a portfolio you have previously created.

1. To customize the list of securities that appear in the Delinquency Report screen, choose from the following options:
   - To filter the list by issue date range, shelf ticker, series ticker, or geographic region, enter the appropriate information in the highlighted Issued, Ticker, Series, and Region fields, respectively. Then, press <Go>. The updated list of deals appears in the table.
   - To filter the list by type of collateral backing the deal, click the Select Deal Type button. The Select Collateral Types window appears. Select the checkbox(es) that appears to the left of the appropriate option(s) so that a checkmark(s) appears, then click Update. The updated list of deals appears in the table.
   - To import a list of securities from a portfolio you created previously in the PRTU (My Portfolios) function, click the Import toolbar button. The Security List Import window appears. Select the appropriate portfolio name from the Select Name dropdown menu, then click the Import button. The updated list of deals appears in the table.
2. Optional: To save the filter criteria you entered as the default criteria for the DQRP function, click the Save Search button from the toolbar. You can also delete a saved filter you apply by clicking on Options > Reset Search Criteria from the toolbar.

22.6.1 Display changes in delinquency for CMBS

To display various credit performance statistics for a customizable list of CMBS deals, complete the following steps:

1. At the top left of the screen, click the CMBS radio button so that a dot appears.
2. Optional: Customize the list of securities that appears in the table.
3. From the toolbar, click the Updates button. The CMBU (CMBS Updates) function appears with the selected securities. CMBU<HELP> displays further information on using the CMBS Updates screen.

DQRP screen description

Depending on the option(s) you choose, the following toolbar buttons may appear, listed here in alphabetical order:

- 30Day/60Day/90Day. The 30/60/90-day delinquency percentage.
- 60D+. The percentage of loans within a deal that are in either 60 or 90-day foreclosure and/or REO.
- Deal. The name of the deal.
- DSCR. The weighted average debt service coverage ratio.
- FICO. The weighted average credit score (FICO) on the underlying collateral.
- Frcl. The foreclosure percentage, which is the percentage of loans forcing the mortgage holder to seize the property of a homeowner who is delinquent in mortgage and interest payments.
- Issued. The issuance range of the deals included in the report.

- `Loans`. The number of loans remaining in the deal, as of the most recent report date.
- `Losses`. The percentage of cumulative loss, expressed as a percentage of the original pool balance.
- `Region`. The geographical region for the deals.
- `REO`. The percentage of all bank-owned properties, except those taken in consideration of a defaulted loan.

> **Tip**
>
> These values are derived directly from values from the loan tapes.

- `Rep. Dt`. The reporting date for the collateral of the deal that appears.
- `Sector`. The market sector. The following options appear:
  - `All`. Both commercial mortgage-backed securities (CMBS) and residential mortgage-backed securities (RMBS) deals.
  - `CMBS`. Commercial mortgage-backed securities. Deals that have real estate as collateral, such as retail properties, office properties, industrial properties, multi-family housing, and hotels.
  - `RMBS`. Residential mortgage-backed securities. Loans backed by a residential property.
- `Select Deal Type` opens the `Select Collateral Type` window where you can select the types of deals that appear in the `Delinquency Report` table. The following deal types appear:
  - `Residential`. All loans of all residential collateral types.
  - `Res B/C`. Loans consisting of a majority of subprime or B-rated and C-rated loans. Subprime mortgages are characterized by loans under which one or more previous payments were 30 or more days delinquent. This option also includes deals with a classified collateral type of home equity. Bloomberg classifies the collateral based on the loan purpose, credit scores, and the name of the legal issuer.
  - `Alt A`. Loans made to borrowers whose qualifying mortgage characteristics do not meet the underwriting criteria established by the GSEs (government-sponsored enterprises). `Alt A` loans typically have a higher credit score than `Res B/C` loans but below `Whole Loans`. The `Alt A` designation is stated in the prospectus or identified by the lead manager.
  - `Whole Loans`. Loans backed by residential mortgage loans. Bloomberg classifies the collateral type as `Whole Loan` based on the loan purpose, credit scores, and the name of the legal issuer. `Whole Loans` have a higher credit score than `Res B/C` and `Alt A` loans.
  - `CMBS`. All loans of all CMBS collateral types.
  - `Agency`. A deal issued by Ginnie Mae, Fannie Mae, or Freddie Mac.
  - `Conduit`. A deal backed by loans that are typically fixed rate with loan sizes from \$5MM to \$20MM, and have diverse property types, property locations, and borrowers. Some deals include large loans (> \$20MM).
  - `Credit Tenant Lease`. Deals backed by properties rented to highly rated tenants on long-term net leases.
  - `European`. Deals backed by European collateral.
  - `Japanese`. Deals backed by Japanese collateral.
  - `LrgLoan/Other Floaters`. Deals backed by floating rate loans. Large-loan floating rate CMBS deals (large-loan floaters) are typically collateralized by shorter term loans with loan sizes greater than \$20MM.
  - `Portfolio`. A deal that includes seasoned loans (loans that have aged more than 6 months as of the deal closing date).

- ○ `Single Asset/Single Borrower`. A deal backed by a single asset or a single borrower. A single-asset deal is backed by one loan on one large property. A single-borrower deal is backed by one loan on multiple properties.
- ○ `CDO`. Collateralized Debt Obligation. Structured debt security backed by a portfolio of CMBS bonds and/or other commercial real estate debt.
- ○ `Other`. Deals that are outside the scope of other deal-type categories.
- `Series`. The additional descriptor of the deal, if applicable.
- `Ticker`. The ticker for which you want to display the corresponding structured finance deals.
- `WALA`. The weighted average loan age, which is the average age of all the loans within the deal.
- `WALTV`. The dollar-weighted average amortized based on the loan-to-original value of the underlying loans.
- `Weighted Averages`. The average of the list of data that appear in each column.
- `WList`. The percentage of the deal placed on watchlist.

22.7 COLLATERAL COMPOSITION GRAPH (CLCG)

The Collateral Composition Graph (CLCG) (Figure 22.8) is useful to display a graphical representation of the collateral backing of a structured finance security. The information that appears on the

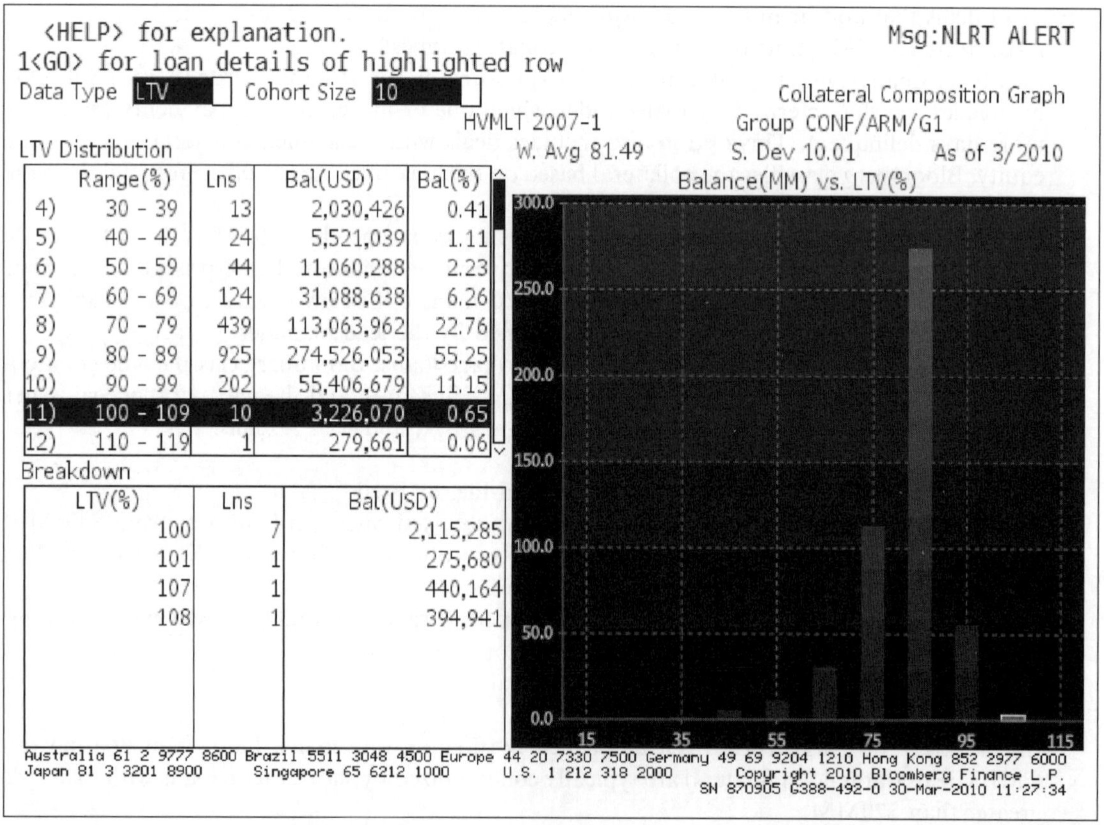

Figure 22.8. `Collateral Composition Graph` screen (`CLCG`).

CLCG screen is similar to that which appears on the Collateral Composition function (CLC), however, CLCG displays more granular breakouts on the collateral buckets.

22.7.1 Analyzing a deal's collateral composition with the CLCG function

Once you choose a mortgage-backed security, enter CLCG<Go> to display the Collateral Composition Graph screen. Choose from the following options:

- To change the data type, click on the down arrow in the Data Type highlighted field and choose another type from the list that appears.
- To display further information in the table, if applicable, move the scroll bar on the right-hand side of the table up or down.
- To highlight a specific range in the table, click on the corresponding bar in the histogram so that it appears highlighted in blue.

Collateral Composition Graph screen

Once you choose a mortgage-backed security and enter CLCG<Go>, the Collateral Composition Graph screen appears. The screen is composed of three sections:

- Data Type information.
- Data Table/Histogram.
- Data Type Information section.

The Data Type Information section of the screen displays the following information:

- Data Type. The data that appear in the table and on the graph. The down arrow in the highlighted field displays a list of choices. CLC<HELP> displays further information.
- Bucket Size. The increments used to group the data in the data table. The down arrow in the highlighted field displays a list of choices. It only appears when LTV, OSZE, CSZE, FICO, IO, CPN, MAT, or AGE appears in the Data Type field.
- W. Avg. The weighted average remaining maturity. The average remaining term of the mortgages underlying the security.
- Group appears depending on the product type of the deal. The collateral type for the class.

Please note

"All collateral" indicates that the class of bonds is backed by all of the collateral in the deal.

- S. Deviation. The standard deviation. A measure of the degree to which an individual probability value varies from the distribution mean. The higher the number, the greater the risk.
- As Of. The date from which the collateral data are reported.

22.7.2 Data Table/Histogram section

The Data Table/Histogram section of the screen displays a tabular representation of the data type, while the histogram section displays the same information in graph form. When appropriate, a tabular breakdown of the collateral from the highlighted range will appear with additional information.

Loan Details screen: Stratified view

Once you click on the appropriate option from the Collateral Performance screen, the Loan Details screen's Stratified view appears, where you can display aggregated loan-level data grouped by specific criteria and export the data that appears to an Excel spreadsheet. The corresponding ticker symbol and series of the deal's collateral appears at the top of the screen. The following fields appear:

- Stratify By allows you to choose the criterion by which the data that appear are stratified. The dropdown menu displays a list of options.
- Group. The collateral group that corresponds to the deal that appears.
- {Selected Stratification}. The stratification criterion that you selected.
- As of. The as of date of the collateral.
- All Loans. The groupings that correspond to the loan count.
- Count. The total number of loans in the category.
- Curr. AMT (USD). The current face value of the loan.
- %. The percentage of the total face value of the loans in this category.
- WALTV. The original dollar-weighted average amortized loan-to-original value of the underlying loans comprising the collateral.
- Score. The corresponding credit score.
- Orig. AMT (USD). The original face value of the loan.
- WAC. The weighted average coupon of the individual loans underlying the security, using the balance of each loan as the weights.
- WAM. The weighted average maturity of the individual loans underlying the security, using the balance of each loan as the weights.
- WALA. The average age of all the loans in a pool, using the balance of each loan as the weights.
- ARM%. The percentage of ARM loans in the category.
- 30D%. The percentage of loans that are 30 days delinquent.
- 60D%. The percentage of loans that are 60 days delinquent.
- 90D%. The percentage of loans that are 90 days delinquent.
- 60D+%. The percentage of loans that are $\geq$60 days delinquent or are specially serviced.
- 90D+%. The percentage of loans that are $\geq$90 days delinquent or are specially serviced.

Loan Details screen: Loan view

Once you choose None from the Stratify By field dropdown menu on the Loan Details screen, the Loan view appears, where you can display loan-level data grouped by specific criteria and export the data that appear to an MS Excel spreadsheet. The corresponding ticker symbol and series of the deal's collateral appears at the top of the screen.

Please note

A maximum of 8,000 loans can be displayed at a time.

The view is divided into the following two sections:

- Weighted Average Characteristics section (title does not appear on screen).
- Individual Loan Details section (title does not appear on screen).

The following fields appear above the sections:

- `Stratify By` allows you to choose the criterion by which the data that appear are stratified. The dropdown menu displays a list of options.
- `Group`. The collateral group that corresponds to the deal that appears.
- `{Selected Stratification}`. The stratification criterion that you selected.
- `As of`. The as of date of the collateral.

Weighted Average Characteristics section (title does not appear on screen)

The `Weighted Average Characteristics` section displays the weighted average characteristics of all the loans that appear, based on the selected stratification. The following fields appear:

- `All Loans`. The total number of loans that correspond to the `Count` field.
- `Count`. The total number of loans included in the summary information that appears to the right.
- `Curr. AMT (USD)`. The current face value of the loans.
- `%`. The percentage of the total face value of the loans.
- `WALTV`. The original dollar-weighted average amortized loan-to-original value of the underlying loans comprising the collateral.
- `Score`. The weighted average credit score.
- `Orig. AMT (USD)`. The original face value of the loans.
- `WAC`. The weighted average coupon of the individual loans underlying the security, using the balance of each loan as the weights.
- `WAM`. The weighted average maturity of the individual loans underlying the security, using the balance of each loan as the weights.
- `WALA`. The average age of all the loans in a pool, using the balance of each loan as the weights.

Individual Loan Details section (title does not appear on screen)

The `Individual Loan Details` section displays the individual loan details by loan number. The following fields apppear:

- `Loan No`. The number assigned to the individual loan.
- `Pay History`. The string of characters represents up to 24 months of historical payment status information for the corresponding loan. Each character represents the status for an individual month, chronologically, with the first character in the string representing the payment status for the current month. The following characters may appear:
  - `C`. Current.
  - `B`. Bankruptcy.
  - `F`. Foreclosure.
  - `R`. REO (real estate owned).
  - `3`. 30 days delinquent.
  - `6`. 60 days delinquent.
  - `9`. 90 days delinquent.
- `Curr. AMT (USD)`. The current face value of the loan.
- `Orig. AMT (USD)`. The original face value of the loan.
- `Rate`. The loan rate.
- `LTV`. The loan-to-value ratio.
- `Score`. The credit score for the loan.
- `Age`. The age of the loan in months.
- `MTM`. The months to maturity (i.e., the number of months to maturity of the loan).
- `Type`. The loan type.
- `Index`. For ARMS, the index used to determine the rate.

- MTR. The months to reset (i.e., the number of months to initial reset of the loan).

> **Tip**
>
> A negative value represents a loan that has already passed its initial reset.

- GEO. The state that corresponds to the loan.
- Delinq Days. The number of days the loan is delinquent.
- BFRL. The specially serviced status of the loan. Shows if loan is in bankruptcy or foreclosure.
- PaidThru. The date until which the loan is paid through.
- Zip Code. The zipcode for the property.

Shortcuts

The following shortcuts enable you to switch quickly from different views:

- {ticker symbol}<MTGE>CLCG LTV<Go> specifies the loan-to-value data type.
- {ticker symbol}<MTGE>CLCG GEO<Go> specifies the geographic data type.
- {ticker symbol}<MTGE>CLCG OSZE<Go> specifies the original loan size data type.
- {ticker symbol}<MTGE>CLCG CSZE<Go> specifies the current loan size data type.
- {ticker symbol}<MTGE>CLCG FICO<Go> specifies the FICO (financing corporation) data type.
- {ticker symbol}<MTGE>CLCG IO<Go> specifies the interest-only data type.
- {ticker symbol}<MTGE>CLCG PEN<Go> specifies the prepayment penalty data type.
- {ticker symbol}<MTGE>CLCG WAC<Go> specifies the weighted average coupon data type.
- {ticker symbol}<MTGE>CLCG WAM<Go> specifies the weighted average maturity data type.
- {ticker symbol}<MTGE>CLCG WALA<Go> specifies the weighted average loan age data type.

22.8 CASH FLOW TABLE (CFT)

Use the Cash Flow Table function to display a cashflow table for a selected pool, generic mortgage-backed security, collateralized mortgage obligation (CMO), asset-backed security (ABS), and commercial mortgage-backed security (CMBS).

CFT also allows you to display the collateral cash flows for a structured security (CMO/ABS/CMBS). Depending on the security you choose, the projected cash flows can be based upon prepayments (CPRs), defaults (CDRs), severities, and forward curve analysis, so you can better determine the cash flows a bond/deal may generate which match with any asset and liability concerns.

> **Tip**
>
> The information that appears in CFT differs depending on the selected security.

Cash Flow Table functionality

Once you enter (ticker symbol) <MTGE>CFT<Go>, the Cash Flows screen (Figure 22.9) appears. Choose from the following options:

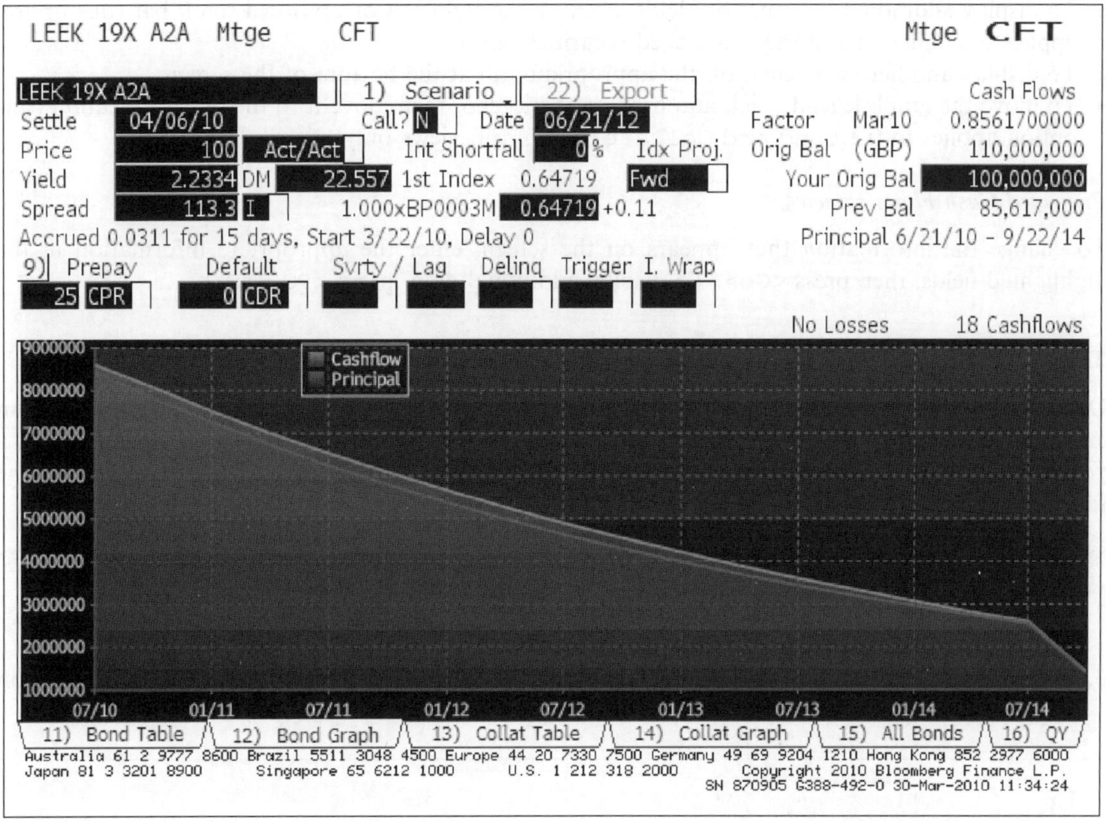

Figure 22.9. `Cash Flow Table` screen (`CFT`).

- To export the data that appear to an MS Excel spreadsheet, click on the `Export` toolbar button.
- To change the data that appear on the screen, enter/choose the appropriate options in/from the highlighted fields.
- To display the `Treasury Curve` window with a list of corresponding yield curves, click on `Yield Curve` directly beneath the highlighted `Prepay` field (this option applies to commercial mortgage-backed securities only).
- To display the full description of the `Yield Curve` option, highlighted in blue, move your cursor over `Yield Curve` directly beneath the `Prepay` field (this option applies to commercial mortgage-backed securities only).
- To create a new or display/edit an existing scenario, click on the `Scenario` toolbar button, then click on the menu number to the left of the `View/Edit Scenario` label, then enter/choose the appropriate option(s) from the highlighted fields from the `Scenario Editor/CMBS Scenario Editor` window. `SCEN<HELP>` displays further information on creating/updating a scenario.
- To create a custom cash flow assumptions, enter/choose the appropriate information in the highlighted fields, then click on the `9)` button. The "How to create and save custom assumptions" section of this chapter displays further information.
- To apply a saved set of cash flow assumptions, click on the `9)` button. The "How to apply saved assumptions" section of this chapter displays further information.

- To display additional information/fields, click on the right/left or up/down scroll bar (this option applies to commercial mortgage-backed securities only).
- To display another view, click on the appropriate tab at the bottom of the screen.
- To move the graph legend, click and hold on the legend, then move it to the desired location (this option applies to the `Bond and Collateral Graph` views only.)

Projected Cash Flows screen

To change the information that appears on the screen, enter the appropriate information in the highlighted fields, then press <Go>. To display additional data, press <PG FWD>.

22.8.1 Create/Save Cash Flow assumptions

Once you enter (ticker symbol) <MTGE>CFT<Go>, the `Cash Flows` screen appears where you can enter and save prepayment, default, severity, lag, and trigger assumptions. The cash flow assumptions you enter apply to the entire collateral group. To create and save a set of assumptions, complete the following steps:

1. Enter/choose the appropriate information in/from the highlighted fields that appear, then press <Go>.
2. Click on the `Editor` button—identified by the label `9)` that appears to the left of the `Prepay field`. The `My Assumptions` window appears.
3. Enter a name for the assumption set in the highlighted `Current Assumption` field, then click on the `Save Current Assumptions` button.

> **Tip**
>
> The assumptions you save can be imported to the `Structured Paydown (SPA)`, `Credit Support (MTCS)`, and `Super Yield Table (SYT)` functions. The corresponding <HELP> for each function displays further information.

22.8.2 Apply basic saved assumptions

Once you enter (ticker symbol) <MTGE>CFT<Go>, the `Cash Flows` screen appears where you can apply saved prepayment, default, severity, lag, and trigger assumptions by completing the following steps:

1. Click on the `Editor` button—identified by the label `9)`. The `My Assumptions` window appears.
2. Click on the appropriate saved assumption `Name` from the list that appears. The corresponding row highlights in white.
3. Click on the `Apply Saved Assumption` button.

> **Tip**
>
> The saved assumptions that appear could have been created in the `Structured Paydown (SPA)`, `Credit Support (MTCS)`, and `Super Yield Table (SYT)` functions. The corresponding <HELP> for each function displays further information.

22.8.3 Create a vector/curve

In CFT you can use either static or dynamic assumptions for various components of the analysis. For dynamic analysis, you can create customized vectors or curves for prepayments, defaults, severity, and delinquency. To create a vector/curve, complete the following steps:

1. From the Cash Flows screen, choose Create Vector from the appropriate highlighted CPR, CDR, PSA, Default, Svrty/Lag, or Delinquency field dropdown menu. The corresponding Vector Editor window appears.
2. Enter the appropriate information in the highlighted Type, Start, Rate, Months, and S/R fields, then press <Go>—*or* drag and drop the vector information from an MS Excel spreadsheet to the vector table on the left-hand side of the window.
3. Enter a name for the vector in the highlighted Name field.
4. Click the Save button.

Use Credit Driven Scenarios

CMBS assets are generally non-recourse loans secured by income-producing property. These loans exhibit substantial credit risk. The likelihood that each loan may prepay or default depends upon changes in the credit quality of the underlying property(ies). Loan performance is driven by the combination of interest rates and credit quality.

Credit-driven analysis is a set of rules that retain the underlying mechanics of traditional prepayment and default analyses, but extend these analyses to take full account of the credit risk of commercial mortgage loans. It is based on the premise that prepayment and default assumptions should be applied to each loan individually, depending on the loan's projected credit quality.

CMBS financial reporting typically includes quarterly or annual disclosure of each underlying property's income statement. Credit-driven analytics offer a direct mechanism to incorporate this information into bond pricing.

Credit Driven Scenarios allow you to model different prepayment, default, and recovery scenarios. You can specify net operating income (NOI) growth, future cap rate trends, and refinancing terms. Specifically, Credit Driven Scenarios allow you to grow and shrink projected NOI and to forecast property value by specifying a capitalization rate. You can also model the terms under which a borrower can refinance or extend their loan.

Credit Driven Scenario analysis is available in the following functions:

- MTCS (Credit Support).
- CFT (Cash Flow Table).
- SYT (Super Yield Table).
- SPA (Structured Paydown Analysis).
- SCEN (Scenario Manager).
- LM (Loan Manager).

22.8.4 How to create Credit Driven Scenarios

To create a Credit Driven Scenario in the CFT function, complete the following steps:

1. From the toolbar, click Scenario > Credit Driven Scenario. The My Credit Driven Scenarios window appears.
2. The top of the My Credit Driven Scenario window displays the name, description, and last update date for any credit-driven scenarios you have previously saved.

The bottom of the window is broken down into six assumption sections defined by the six checkboxes that appear: `Property`, `Refinancing Terms`, `Recovery`, `Prepay`, `Default`, and `Extend`. Each section allows you to enter parameters for the scenario.

From the `My Credit Driven Scenarios` window you can either modify a previously saved credit-driven scenario or create a new credit-driven scenario:

- If you are modifying an existing scenario, click the appropriate scenario `Name` from the top of the screen so that it is highlighted. The bottom half of the screen updates with information from the selected scenario.
- If you are creating a new assumption set, most of the assumption parameter fields at the bottom of the screen appear blank.

To enter the assumptions for the credit-driven scenario toggle the checkbox to the left of the appropriate section. A checkmark activates the related assumption parameters. Enter the appropriate information in the highlighted fields. The assumption sections and associated assumption parameters are as follows:

- `Property` allows you to enter property performance information such as the capitalization rate and NOI growth rate assumptions.
- `CapRate`. The capitalization rate measures a property's ability to generate cash before taxes and debt service. The value you enter is used to calculate a projected value for each period. If a cap rate is not entered, the projected appraisal value uses an implied cap rate calculated by projected NOI and cutoff value. You can enter a vector for the capitalization rate value by clicking on the `CapRate` field label. The "How to use vectors in Credit Driven Scenarios" section of this chapter displays further information.
- `Growth%`. Net operating income growth. You may grow or shrink projected NOI by entering a growth rate in this field. For each asset, the latest full year financial data that are available are used as a starting point to project reported NOI. You can enter a vector for the growth rate value by clicking on the `Growth%` field label. The "How to use vectors in Credit Driven Scenarios" section of this chapter displays further information.
- `Refinancing Terms` allows you to calculate the refinancing proceeds (the gross proceeds from refinancing an existing loan) using the spread, amortization, and the debt service coverage ratio, or the loan-to-value ratio.
- `Sprd`. The refinance spread. The spread over a 10-year Treasury is used to determine the fixed rate coupon on the new loan in basis points. The field defaults to 0 basis points.
- `LTV` allows you to calculate refinancing proceeds (the gross proceeds from refinancing an existing loan) using a loan-to-value ratio requirement (the LTV method). An LTV requirement for the new loan is optional. An LTV test is not imposed on the refinance calculation.
- `DSCR` allows you to enter a debt service coverage ratio (DSCR) requirement for the new loan. The DSCR is the ratio of the annualized scheduled payments of principal and/or interest on the mortgage loan to the net operating income or net cash flow for the property. The field defaults to the DSCR from the original cutoff date. It is assumed that a lender would underwrite a new loan using the DSCR established by the original lender at cutoff.
- `Amort`. The amortization term requirement for the new loan. It defaults to the information from the loan cutoff. It is assumed that a lender would underwrite a new loan using the existing loan's original amortization term. You can specify a different amortization term by entering the number of months of amortization. Enter a zero for interest-only loans.
- `Recovery` allows you to enter information for the recovery amount assumption.

- Mode. Allows you to choose the mode used to calculate the amount of principal recovered in conjunction with the Default or Extend assumptions. The highlighted dropdown menu displays the following options:
  - Loss Severity allows you to enter the loss severity percentage—similar to a constant default rate (CDR) assumption—in the Svrty field from the Default section of the window.
  - Refinance. Refinance proceeds (the gross proceeds from refinancing an existing loan) are calculated based on the Refinance terms you enter. The Refinance terms are then used as recovery against the defaulted balance. If the difference between the refinancing proceeds and the loan balance is net-positive, there is no loss to the loan. If the difference between the refinancing proceeds and the loan balance is net-negative, the difference is the loss.
  - Dispose. The sale proceeds from a projected value of the property (based on the capitalization rate, or CapRate) are used as recovery against the defaulted balance. If the property value is greater than the loan balance, there is no loss. If the property value is less than the loan balance, the difference between the loan balance and value of the property is the loss. This is used in conjunction with the Property assumptions.
  - Loss Amount. Generally applied to a single loan once the loan has been isolated into a group. It is assumed that the loan loss has been predetermined but has not been factored into the trust, as of yet. Choosing this mode allows you to enter the loss amount in the Loss or Loss Amt field within the Recovery assumptions.
- Fee allows you to enter the transaction fee, if applicable.
- Loss Amt or Loss applies to the Loss Amount mode, which allows you to enter the loss amount in the corresponding currency.
- Prepay enables you to enter loan prepayment assumptions. Property owners have an incentive to prepay a loan when they can refinance and take out cash.
- If Excess > allows you to enter the percentage of excess proceeds that will trigger a (refinance) prepayment. Excess proceeds are calculated as the refinancing proceeds minus the sum of the scheduled outstanding loan balance and any required prepayment premium.
- Prepay Rate and Type (label may not appear). The two leftmost highlighted fields in the Prepay section allow you to enter prepayment speed and type assumptions. The Prepay Type dropdown menu displays a list of choices, including creating a vector. The BPN (Bloomberg Prepayment Notation) function displays further information on the available prepayment speed types.
- YM allows you to enter a trigger value that determines when prepayments are applied. You can enter LOCK to apply prepayments after the yield maintenance period or, alternatively, you can enter a numeric value to apply prepayments if the projected yield maintenance penalty rate for the loan falls below the value you enter in the YM field. The value you enter is the minimum yield maintenance premium (a prepayment penalty) rate.

Tip

When using a CPR prepayment assumption, if the YM field is blank, prepayments occur immediately, or after any hard lockout or defeasable periods, with a corresponding projected prepayment penalty fee.

When using a CPR prepayment assumption, if the YM field's value is greater than zero, prepayments are allowed if the projected prepayment penalty rate for the loan falls below the value in the YM field. For example, if you enter 100 CPR in the Prepay field and 10 in the YM field, then the `100 CPR` prepayment speed applies if the projected prepayment penalty rate for the loan falls below 10%.

When using a `CPY` prepayment assumption, the `YM` field automatically defaults to `LOCK` which prevents prepayments from occurring during the yield maintenance period. Prepayments will occur after the yield maintenance period ends.

When using a `CPP` prepayment scenario, the `YM` field automatically defaults to `LOCK`.

- `FP` allows you to enter a trigger value that determines when prepayments are applied. You can enter `LOCK` to apply prepayments after the fixed penalty period, *or* you can enter a numeric value to apply prepayments *if* the projected fixed penalty rate for the loan falls below the value you enter in the `FP` field. The value you enter is the minimum fixed penalty (a prepayment penalty) rate.

Tip

If you use a `CPR` prepayment scenario where the FP field is blank, then prepayments occur immediately, or after any hard lockout or defeasable periods, with a corresponding projected prepayment penalty fee.

If you use a `CPR` prepayment scenario where the `FP` field's value is greater than zero, then prepayments are allowed if the projected prepayment penalty rate for the loan falls below the value in the `FP field`. For example, if you enter `100 CPR` in the `Prepay` field and `3` in the `FP` field, then the `100 CPR` prepayment speed applies if the projected prepayment penalty rate for the loan falls below 3%.

- `ToOp` applies to `CPR` prepayment rate scenarios. If the `ToOp` field is set to `Yes`, then the outstanding principal balance prepays at 100% at the first freely prepayable (open) period. If the `ToOp` field is set to `No`, the outstanding principal balance of the loan does not prepay at 100% at the first open period.
- `Default` allows you to enter loan default assumptions. A default occurs when a property owner cannot meet his debt service obligations (scheduled loan payments). For example, when the property's debt service coverage ratio (DSCR) falls below 1.0 × NOI generated by the property it is insufficient to cover loan payments. In `Credit Driven` analysis, you can specify the DSCR that triggers a default. Following a specified delay, the severity of the default is calculated to reflect the underlying property's performance and eligibility for financing by selecting the recovery option.
- `If DSCR` < allows you to enter the debt service coverage ratio that will trigger loans to default. If the projected DSCR falls below the value you enter, the default assumption is applied.
- `Default Rate and Type` (label may not appear). The two leftmost highlighted fields in the `Default` section allow you to enter default speed and type assumptions. The `Default Type` dropdown menu displays a list of choices, including creating a vector. The `BPN (Bloomberg Prepayment Notation)` function displays further information on available default speed types.
- `(Default) Svtry`. The loss severity. Severity is the percentage of the principal loan balance at the time of default that determines the loss amount. You must choose `Loss Severity` mode from the `Recovery` section of the assumptions to activate this field.
- `(Default) Lag`. The number of months between the time of default and the recovery. If a loss is incurred, it is applied to the principal balance at recovery.
- `RcvMat`. The recovery to maturity. If you use a `CDR` default assumption with a `Lag` greater than zero, then a `Yes` in the `RcvMat` field indicates that the last period principal is recovered and losses

are applied on the loan's maturity's date. A No in the RcvMat field indicates a delay between when the last period of principal is recovered and losses are applied. The delay is equal to the number of lag periods *after* the maturity date. This applies if the CDR speed is less than 100.

- Extend allows you to enter information for the loan extension assumptions. For any loans that have a balloon payment on the maturity date, the Extend assumption allows you to push out the final balloon payment past the loan's maturity date to simulate a loan extension, or a balloon default scenario. When a property owner cannot refinance a balloon repayment because the property's debt service is less than the balloon repayment amount, the asset is likely to extend.
- Extend Rate (label may not appear). The extension rate percentage. The percent of the balloon amount to default.
- If Shrtfall > allows you to specify the percentage shortfall that triggers the balloon extend assumptions. A shortfall occurs when the amount of a property's debt service is less than its balloon repayment amount.
- (Extend) Svrty. The percentage of the loan balance to default. Applies only if you choose Loss Severity from Recovery Mode.
- (Extend) Lag. The number of months between the time of default and the recovery. If a loss is incurred, it is applied to the principal balance at recovery.
- Opt Ext. The optional extensions are provisions permitting extension of the original term of the mortgage under terms agreed upon at origination. The dropdown menu displays the following choices:
  - None means no extension scenario is applied.
  - 1st represents a scenario that exercises the first optional extension for CMBS deals.
  - 2nd represents a scenario that exercises the second optional extension for CMBS deals.
  - All represents a scenario that exercises *all* optional extensions for CMBS deals.
  - Advn. A Yes indicates that the servicer is advancing principal and interest payments. A No indicates that the servicer is not advancing principal and interest payments.

3. Choose from the following options:
   - To save the new Credit Driven Scenario assumption set you created, enter a name for the scenario in the highlighted Name field. Then, click the Save & Apply button. The Cash Flows screen appears updated with calculations based on the assumption set you created and saved.
   - To save the changes you made to a previously saved scenario, click the Save & Apply button. The Cash Flows screen appears updated with calculation based on the assumption set you modified and saved.
   - To apply the Credit Driven Scenario to CFT analysis without saving the scenario for future use, click the Apply button. The Cash Flows screen appears with calculations based on the Credit Driven Scenario you entered.
   - To close the My Credit Driven Scenarios window without saving or applying any information you entered, click the Close button. The Cash Flows screen appears without any updates.

Use vectors in Credit Driven Scenarios

Within the My Credit Driven Scenarios window, you can enter either static or dynamic vector assumptions for certain types of loan assumptions. A vectored assumption means that the rate applied to the assumption characteristic changes at user-determined points in time, instead of assuming one constant rate for the duration of the loan(s).

For Prepay and Default assumptions you can apply a vector you have previously created or choose Create Vector from the corresponding rate-type dropdown menus. The Prepay Vector

`Editor` or `Default Vector Editor` window appears. The "How to create a vector/curve" section of this chapter displays further information on creating prepayment and default vectors.

For capitalization rate (`CapRate`) and NOI growth (`%Growth`) assumptions, you can create and apply vectors by completing the following steps:

1. Click the `CapRate` and/or `Growth%` field label. The `Vector Description Entry` window appears.
2. Enter the vector information in the highlighted field using the following syntax:

`(rate1)(#periods)(S/R)(rate2) ...`

22.8.5 Vector transitions

The non-static rates within a vector can either assume a sudden transition, a step (`S`), or a gradual transition, a ramp (`R`). A step applies a flat rate over the specified number of periods. A ramp applies incremental rates to attain the target rate at the end of the specified number of periods.

Example

Entering a `Growth%` vector "5.5 12S 7.5 24S 10" indicates the growth applied in the first 12 projected periods is 5.5%. In Period 13, it increases (steps up) to 7.5% for the next 24 periods. In Month 25, it steps up to 10% and applies 10% to the remaining life of the loan.

In another example, vector "0 12R 5 24R" applies 0% in the first projected period and increases the rate incrementally to the target of 5% at the end of Period 12. From Period 12 to Period 36, the rate will grow incrementally from 5% to 10%. In Month 37, it applies a flat rate of 10% for the life of the loan.

22.8.6 Anchoring a vector

In addition to determining step and ramp rate transitions for a vector, you can also anchor a vector on a certain date. The anchor date is the date upon which the vector becomes effective. If you leave an anchor date unspecified, the vector is anchored on the next payment date.

To anchor a vector, you must enter `A` and the date in mm/dd/yyyy format followed by the vector rate information.

For example, to anchor vector "5.5 12S 7.5 24S 10" to January 1, 2010, enter: `A 01/01/2010 5.5 12S 7.5 24S 10`.

3. Once you enter the vector information, click the `Done` button. The `Vector Description Entry` window closes and a `(V)` appears to right of the field for which you entered a vector.

To edit the vector, click on the appropriate `Cap(V)` or `Grw(V)` field, make the change(s) in the `Vector Description Entry` window, then click `Done`.

Once you enter (ticker symbol) <MTGE> `CFT` <Go>, the `Cash Flows` screen appears, where you can display projected cash flows for various types of structured, residential, asset-backed securities, and commercial mortgage-backed securities, specify assumptions (`CPR & CDR`), and display the actual cash flow projection results on both the bond and collateral level. The following tabs appear at the bottom of the screen:

- Bond Table displays the cash flows that correspond to the selected bond, based on the selected assumptions.
- Bond Graph displays a graph of the total and principal cash flows for the bond, based on the selected assumptions.
- Collat Table displays the monthly projected cash flows that correspond to the collateral, based on the selected assumptions.
- Collat Graph displays a graphical representation of the collateral's total cash flow and principal, based on the selected assumptions.
- All Bonds displays the cash flows for each bond within the deal and its corresponding projected principal/interest/losses payment for each month, based on the selected assumptions.
- QY displays the Quick Yield function (QY) within the Cash Flows screen.

Depending on the security and view you selected, some of the following fields appear, listed here in alphabetical order:

- 9). The Editor button allows you to apply/create saved cash flow assumptions using the My Assumptions window, or apply/create saved scenarios using the Scenario Editor/CMBS Scenario Editor windows, as applicable.
- 1st Index (applies to floating rate securities only). The index that was used at the time the cash flows were created.
- 1,000x{index}. The index coefficient, as well as the index, that is used to calculate the interest payment coupon for the security.
- {X} Cashflows. The total number of cash flows.
- {X} Losses. The date (mm/dd/yy) the first loss is realized, if applicable. If no loss is projected, then No Losses appears.
- Accrual applies to commercial mortgage-backed securities only. The interest cash flow that is added to the outstanding principal balance of the bond.
- Accrued. The accrued interest factor.
- Actual O/C(%). The overcollaterization of the deal, expressed as a percentage. The typical formula for O/C is

  1 - (Sum of the bonds / Sum of the collateral).

- Apply Saved Assumptions allows you to apply the set of assumptions you select from the My Assumption window.
- Balance. The amount of the original face value still outstanding as of the payment date.
- Call? The call feature of the security. The dropdown menu displays a list of choices.
- Cashflow. The total amount projected to be paid on the payment date.
- Coupon. The coupon rate as of the corresponding payment date.
- Cum Loss Test displays the projected results of the Cumulative Loss Test, which is used to test the trigger mechanism within the structure. The result of the Cumulative Loss Test is based on the assumptions you enter in the Prepay, Default, and Svrty fields. The Cum Lost Test column displays a Pass, Fail, or NA result for each cash flow period. The Trigger Details function (TRIG) displays further information.
- Current Assumptions allows you to enter/display the name for the set of assumptions you select from/save in the My Assumptions window.
- Date allows you to enter a call date for the security based on your assumptions.
- Default Speed. The rate of default on the loans.
- Default Type. The rate type. The dropdown menu displays the following choices:

  - SDA defaults as a factor of the standard default assumption curve.
  - CDR. The percentage of defaults per year.
  - MDR. The percentage of defaults per month.

Tip

BPN 4<Go> displays further information on default rate notations.

- Delay. The payment delay.
- Delinq Test displays the projected results of the delinquency test, which is used to test the trigger mechanism within the structure. The result of the delinquency test is based on the assumption you enter in the Delinq field. The Delinq Test column displays a Pass, Fail, or NA result for each cash flow period. The Trigger Details function (TRIG) displays further information.
- Delinquency allows you to enter either a static or dynamic (vectored) delinquency assumption that is used as an input to the shifting interest and trigger tests associated with a deal. The Structured Finance Notes function (SFNS) displays further information.
- Description, A brief description of the assumption parameters.
- DM. The discounted margin, which is the margin relative to the base index rate, such that the present value of cash flows equals the price plus accrued interest.
- Extend applies to commercial mortgage-backed securities only. The percentage of the balloon amount to default. For any loans that have a balloon payment on the maturity date, the Extend field allows you to push out the final balloon payment past the loan's maturity date to simulate a loan extension, or a balloon default scenario.

Please note

You can use the Extend field in combination with the Svrty/Lag field. For example, to extend a balloon for 5 years with a 35% principal loss, enter 100 in the Extend field, and 35 and 60 in the Svrty and Lag fields, respectively. If you enter a value in the Extend field and the Svrty and Lag fields are left blank, then the cash flow assumes zero for the Svrty and Lag fields.

- Factor {date}. The date of the most current factor available for the security.
- For. The number of days in the current accrual period, based on the settlement date.
- FP applies to commercial mortgage-backed securities only. The FP field allows you to enter a trigger value that determines when prepayments are applied. The following are valid inputs:
  - LOCK applies prepayments after the fixed penalty period.
  - (Numeric Value) applies prepayments *if* the projected fixed penalty rate for the loan falls below the value you enter in the FP field. The value you enter is the minimum fixed penalty (a prepayment penalty) rate.

The following rules apply:

- If you use a CPR prepayment scenario where the FP field is blank, then prepayments occur immediately, or after any hard lockout or defeasable periods, with a corresponding projected prepayment penalty fee.

- If you use a CPR prepayment scenario where the FP field's value is greater than zero, then prepayments are allowed if the projected prepayment penalty rate for the loan falls below the value in the FP field. For example, if you enter 100 CPR in the Prepay field and 3 in the FP field, then the 100 CPR prepayment speed applies if the projected prepayment penalty rate for the loan falls below 3%.
- If you use a CPP prepayment scenario, then the FP field automatically defaults to LOCK. Prepayments will occur after the fixed penalty period ends.

Tip

The projected fixed penalty rate appears in the Prem Rate (%) column on the Collat Table tab for the security.

- {frequency}. The frequency of payments that you want to display. The dropdown menu displays a list of choices.
- Interest. The amount of interest projected to be paid on the payment date.
- Int Shortfall allows you to enter a value which is a percentage of interest reduction applied to the projected interest paid to the bond.
- Losses. The loss amount projected to be incurred on the payment date.
- Modified displays the date on which the corresponding assumption set was last updated.
- O/C Deficiency. The difference between the actual O/C and the target O/C for each period.

Tip

The smaller the difference, the closer the deal is to meeting the expected performance when the deal was issued.

- Opt Ext applies to commercial mortgage-backed securities only. The optional extension is a provision permitting extension of the original term of the mortgage under terms agreed upon at origination. The dropdown menu displays the following choices:
  - None means no extension scenario is applied.
  - 1st represents a scenario that exercises the first optional extension for CMBS deals.
  - 2nd represents a scenario that exercises the second optional extension for CMBS deals.
  - All represents a scenario that exercises *all* optional extensions for CMBS deals

Please note

For example, when a loan has optional extension terms, "0(36), E1(12), E3(12)", the E1, E2, and E3 indicate that the loan has up to three optional extension terms that the borrower can exercise before defaulting on the balloon. The numbers in parentheses represent the length of the optional extension term. In this example, the borrower has three opportunities to pay off the loan. If the borrower is unable to repay the loan after exercising *all* optional extensions, the principal balloon goes into default. The CMBS Loan Description screen (LDES) displays optional extension term information in the Rem. Protection field. LDES<HELP> displays further information.

You can simultaneously apply assumptions from the Opt Ext field and Extend fields. If the loan has optional extension terms and you select an option for the Opt Ext field, the cash flow projections will apply to the Opt Ext field's assumptions *first*, then to the Extend field's assumptions.

- Orig Bal (currency). The original balance of the security and the currency denomination. "The Country/Currency Codes" section of this guide displays further information.
- Premium applies to commercial mortgage-backed securities only. When a prepayment scenario is applied, the premium is the projected prepayment penalty for loan(s) corresponding to the prepay amount for each period.

Tip

If the loan's prepayment penalty is based on the yield maintenance model, the premium value is based on the Treasury Curve window, which appears when you click on the Yield Curve field.

- Prepay. Prepay speed (i.e., the rate of prepayment of the loan).
- Prepay Type. The type of rate. The dropdown menu displays the appropriate choices. The fields allow you to enter your prepayment assumption for the cash flows. The dropdown menu that corresponds to the right-hand highlighted field displays a list of options. The Prepayment Rate Notion function (BPN) displays further information on valid prepayment types.
- Prepay (column heading). The unscheduled principal payment for the collateral based on the information you enter in the highlighted Prepay fields. Also called the voluntary prepayment of principal.
- Prev Bal. The balance of the security on the previous payment period. This balance updates if the settlement date is updated.
- Price. The current market price of the security or the price of the security based on a selected yield. The dropdown menu that corresponds to the right-hand highlighted field displays a list of discount basis options from which you can choose.
- Principal. The principal window.

Please note

The principal window is based on the assumption you selected.

- Principal (column heading). The amount of principal paid on the payment date.
- Recovery applies to non-agency deals when credit assumptions are used. The recovered principal based on the CDR and the Extend fields with severity and lag assumptions.
- RcvMat applies to commercial mortgage-backed securities only. The recovery to maturity. If you use a CDR default assumption with a Lag greater than zero, then a Yes in the RcvMat field

indicates that the last period principal is recovered and losses are applied on the loan's maturity date. A No in the RcvMat field indicates a delay between when the last period of principal is recovered and losses are applied. The delay is equal to the number of lag periods *after* the maturity date. This applies if the CDR speed is less than 100.

Example

- If Lag = 18 and RcvMat = YES, with a loan maturity date of June 2009, then the principal is recovered and losses are applied in June 2009.
- If Lag = 18 and RcvMat = NO, with a loan maturity date of June 2009, then the principal is recovered and losses are applied in December 2010.

- Save Current Assumptions allows you to save the cash flow assumptions you entered.
- Scenario allows you to display/edit a prepayment and/or loss scenario.
- Sched Prin. The scheduled principal payment for the bond/loan(s) based on standard amortization.
- Settle. The date securities must be delivered and paid for to complete a transaction.
- Spread. The spread of your security to the selected benchmark curve. The dropdown menu that corresponds to the right-hand highlighted field displays a list of choices.
- Start. The start date of the accrual period.
- Sub (%) applies to commercial mortgage-backed securities only. The credit support (subordination) level at each month, based on the corresponding assumptions.
- Support(%) applies to residential mortgage-backed securities only. The credit support (subordination) level at each month, based on the corresponding assumptions.
- Svrty/Lag:
  - Svrty. Loss severity. When using a default scenario (CDR and Extend), it is the percentage of the defaulted principal cash flow that is unrecoverable.
  - Lag. The months to recover. The number of periods from the time of default until the principal is recovered and losses are realized. When used with the Extend field, it is the number of months that the defaulted balloon payment is extended beyond the loan's maturity date. The following rules apply:
    - If the Lag field is blank or has a value of zero, then the principal recovery and/or loss is applied to the first projected period.
    - If the Lag field has a value greater than zero, then the principal recovery and/or loss is not applied until x number of periods from the first period cash flow have defaulted. For example, if the Lag value is 18, and the date of the defaulted cash flow projection is January 2009, then the principal recovery/loss is applied in July 2010.
- Target O/C(%). The target overcollaterization level set forth within the prospectus. This is generally respresented as a percentage of the original face of the deal. The Target O/C percentage is a target level for the deal to try to maintain.
- ToOp (applies to commercial mortgage-backed securities only). ToOp applies to CPR prepayment rate scenarios. If the ToOp field is set to Yes, then the outstanding principal balance prepays at 100% at the first freely prepayable (open) period. If the ToOp field is set to No, the outstanding principal balance of the loan does not prepay at 100% at the first open period.

Example

Assume there is a balloon loan with a 7-year term, 81 months of yield maintenance periods, and 3 months of freely prepayable periods. The borrower can prepay anytime within the 81 months, but the borrower also will have to pay a yield maintenance premium (prepayment penalty fee). If the borrower does not prepay during the yield maintenance period, then the borrower also has the option to prepay for 3 months without incurring a prepayment penalty. In a scenario with a `25 CPR` and the `ToOp` field set to `Yes`, the loan prepays at `25 CPR` *during* the yield maintenance period. Also, when the loan enters the first freely prepayable (open) period, the loan automatically prepays the outstanding principal balance at `100 CPR`.

- `Trig/Delay`:
  - `Trig`. The inital state of the deal trigger. The dropdown menu display the following choices:
    - `PASS` indicates that the deal is currently passing the tests and the trigger is not in effect.
    - `FAIL` indicates that the deal is currently failing the tests and the trigger is in effect.
  - `Delay` indicates whether and when to change the state of the deal (e.g., not to toggle at all or the number of months after which to toggle). For instance, if you choose `PASS` from the `Trig` field dropdown menu and enter `6` in the `Delay` field, the trigger is off (the deal passes the test) for 6 months and then on (the deal fails the test) until maturity.
- `Trigger`: displays the projected result for the trigger for each cash flow period. `Pass`, `Fail`, or `NA` are the possible results. The `Trigger` result is determined by the results of both the cumulative loss test (`Cum Loss Test`) and delinquency test (`Delinq Test`). If either of these tests are `Fail`, the `Trigger` is `Fail`. A trigger has the potential to change the priority of cash flows to specific bonds based on the underlying collateral performance. The highlighted `Trig` assumption field in the middle of the screen controls the overall trigger. Choose `Fail` from the `Trig` dropdown menu to specify that a deal pays with the trigger failing even though the inputs for the cumulative loss test and delinquency test do not cause the deal to fail.
- `Yield`. The current yield of the security or the yield of the security based on a selected price.
- `YM` applies to commercial mortgage-backed securities only. The `YM` field allows you to enter a trigger value that determines when prepayments are applied. The following are valid inputs:
  - `LOCK` applies prepayments after the yield maintenance period.
  - `(Numeric value)` applies prepayments *if* the projected yield maintenance penalty rate for the loan falls below the value you enter in the `YM` field. The value you enter is the minimum yield maintenance premium (a prepayment penalty) rate.

The following rules apply:

- When using a *CPR* prepayment scenario, if the `YM` field is blank, prepayments occur immediately or after any hard lockout or defeasable periods, with a corresponding projected prepayment penalty fee.
- When using a `CPR` prepayment scenario, if the `YM` field's value is greater than zero, prepayments are allowed if the projected prepayment penalty rate for the loan falls below the value in the `YM` field. For example, if you enter `100 CPR` in the `Prepay` field and `10` in the `YM` field, then the `100 CPR` prepayment speed applies if the projected prepayment penalty rate for the loan falls below 10%.
- When you use a `CPY` prepayment scenario, the `YM` field automatically defaults to `LOCK` which prevents prepayments from occurring during the yield maintenance period. Prepayments will occur after the yield maintenance period ends.

- When you use a CPP prepayment scenario, the YM field automatically defaults to LOCK.

> **Tip**
>
> The projected yield maintenance premium rate appears in the Prem Rate (%) column on the Collat Table tab for the security.

- Your Orig Bal. The original balance of the security.

Screen navigation

Projected Cashflows screen

Once you enter (mortgage pool) <MTGE>CFT<Go>, the Projected Cashflows screen appears, where you can display projected cash flows for the selected bond based on the yield, settlement date, prepayment assumption, and face amount.

Cash Flow Graph (CFG) view

Once you press <PG BACK> (once) from the initial Projected Cash Flows screen, the Cash Flow Graph view (Pools/Generics/TBAs) appears, where you can analyze how changing prepayment assumptions affect the security's cash flows. CFG<HELP> displays further information on the Projected Cash Flow screen's Cash Flow Graph view.

Quick Yield (QY) Analysis view

Once you press <PG BACK> (twice) from the initial Projected Cash Flows screen, the Quick Yield Analysis view appears, where you can measure risk, such as Macaulay's and modified duration, using both a static prepayment assumption and a dynamic prepayment model that allow you to change the prepayment rates and/or benchmark yield based on your market assumptions. QY<HELP> displays further information on the Projected Cash Flow screen's Quick Yield Analysis view.

Prepayment and default rate assumptions

The Prepayment Rate Notation function (BPN) displays further information on various prepayment rate and default rate notations. You can also use the following shortcuts:

- For PSA (portfolio scenario analysis/shock and horizon analysis) information, enter BPN3<Go> and choose the appropriate option.
- For CPR/CPY/CPP (prepayment rate analysis) information, enter BPN2<Go> and choose the appropriate option.
- For CPJ (prepayment rate notation including involuntary prepayments analysis) information, enter BPN1<Go> and choose the appropriate option.
- For SMM (single monthly mortality analysis) information, enter BPN3<Go> and choose the appropriate option.

22.9 CLASS PAY DOWN (CPD)

Use the Class Pay Down (CPD) function to display the historical amortization table for a specific asset-backed mortgage (ABS) or collateralized mortgage obligation (CMO) (Figure 22.10). CPD dis-

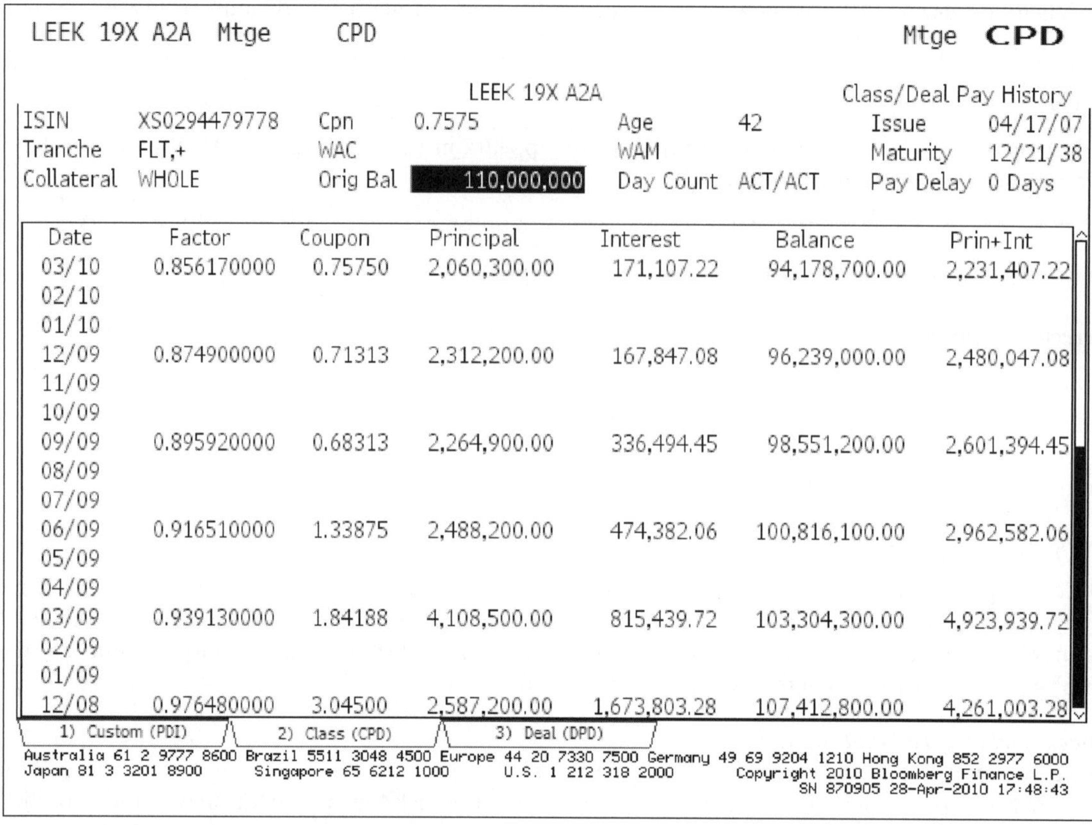

LEEK 19X A2A Mtge CPD Mtge **CPD**

LEEK 19X A2A Class/Deal Pay History

ISIN	XS0294479778	Cpn	0.7575	Age	42	Issue	04/17/07
Tranche	FLT,+	WAC		WAM		Maturity	12/21/38
Collateral	WHOLE	Orig Bal	110,000,000	Day Count	ACT/ACT	Pay Delay	0 Days

Date	Factor	Coupon	Principal	Interest	Balance	Prin+Int
03/10	0.856170000	0.75750	2,060,300.00	171,107.22	94,178,700.00	2,231,407.22
02/10						
01/10						
12/09	0.874900000	0.71313	2,312,200.00	167,847.08	96,239,000.00	2,480,047.08
11/09						
10/09						
09/09	0.895920000	0.68313	2,264,900.00	336,494.45	98,551,200.00	2,601,394.45
08/09						
07/09						
06/09	0.916510000	1.33875	2,488,200.00	474,382.06	100,816,100.00	2,962,582.06
05/09						
04/09						
03/09	0.939130000	1.84188	4,108,500.00	815,439.72	103,304,300.00	4,923,939.72
02/09						
01/09						
12/08	0.976480000	3.04500	2,587,200.00	1,673,803.28	107,412,800.00	4,261,003.28

1) Custom (PDI) 2) Class (CPD) 3) Deal (DPD)

Australia 61 2 9777 8600 Brazil 5511 3048 4500 Europe 44 20 7330 7500 Germany 49 69 9204 1210 Hong Kong 852 2977 6000
Japan 81 3 3201 8900 Singapore 65 6212 1000 U.S. 1 212 318 2000 Copyright 2010 Bloomberg Finance L.P.
SN 870905 28-Apr-2010 17:48:43

Figure 22.10. `Class Pay Down` screen (`CPD`).

plays the schedule based on the reported factor and coupon rather than the amount. The amount actually paid is based on events, including deferred interest and losses. To display the actual payment information for the month, enter `PAID<Go>` from the security. `PAID<HELP>` displays further information.

Tip

`CPD` displays the `Class/Collat History` function (`PDI`) for pools. `PDI<HELP>` displays further information.

Functionality

Once you enter `CPD<Go>`, the `Class/Deal Pay History` screen appears. Choose from the following options:

- To change the information that appears on the screen, enter the appropriate information in the highlighted field(s) that appear at the top of the screen.

- To display additional data, click on the up/down scrollbar on the right-hand side of the screen.
- To display a corresponding function, click on the appropriate tab at the bottom of the screen. The corresponding <HELP> for each function displays further information.

The Class/Deal Pay History Screen

Once you enter CPD<Go>, the Class/Deal Pay History screen appears with a historical amortization table for the selected asset-backed mortgage (ABS) or collateralized mortgage obligation (CMO). The group for the specific class and the ticker/series/class of the security appears at the top of the screen. The top section of the screen displays class-level and group-level, or deal-level, information. The bottom section of the screen displays the historical amortization table. The following fields appear:

- CUSIP. The CUSIP for the specific class that appears.
- Cpn. The current coupon of the specific class.
- Age. The current age of the underlying collateral group or deal (note that this value displays the most recently reported age).
- Issue. The date the security was issued.
- Tranche. The class descriptors. The CMO Class Types function (CLASS) displays further information on the corresponding definitions.
- WAC. The weighted average coupon (gross) for the underlying collateral group or deal (note that this value displays the most recently reported WAC).
- WAM. The current weighted average maturity of the underlying collateral group or deal (note that this value displays the most recently reported WAM).
- Maturity. The latest possible maturity date for the group or deal based on the underlying collateral.
- Collateral. The collateral type of the underlying collateral.
- Orig Bal. The original balance for the class.
- Day Count. The daycount for the specific class.
- Pay Delay. The number of days between the end of the accrual period and the payment date.
- Date. The monthly/quarterly/semi-annual/annual period, based on how the class pays.
- Factor. The percentage of the original principal balance still outstanding.
- Coupon. The accrual coupon for payment in the next period.
- Principal. The principal amount paid for the specific period.
- Losses. The reported bond writedowns for the current period.
- Interest. The interest amount paid for the specific period.
- Prin + Int. The combined principal and interest amount for the selected period.
- Balance. The ending balance for the selected period.

22.10 RATING CHANGES (RATT)

Bloomberg's tool to analyze credit rating changes (rating action tracking tool, or RATT) is one of those well-hidden but very powerful analytical gems that displays credit-rating migration trends and allows direct comparison and benchmarking of rating agency information, supporting either consolidated analysis or detailed drilldown into the following "views":

- By bond type:
  - Mortgage ratings.
  - Corporate ratings.

- By rating agency actions for
  - Moody's.
  - Fitch Ratings.
  - Standard & Poor's.
  - Dominion Bond Rating Service (DBRS).
- By collateral further broken down into
  - All.
  - ABS.
  - CDO.
  - CMO.
  - CMBS.
- By region enabling analysis of
  - All.
  - Europe.
  - Asia.
  - Other.
  - U.S.A.
  - Australia.
  - Canada.
- By rating-type capturing
  - All.
  - Short (-term rating).
  - Long (-term rating).
- By credit watch status changes
  - All.
  - Exclude watch.
  - Watch only.
- Also by rating criteria
  - All.
  - Non-investment grade.
  - Investment grade.

Furthermore, all these views can be run either for preset periods (year-to-date, month-to-date, quarter-to-date, mid-year-to-date) or for custom dates (watch out for the date notation: mm/dd vs. dd/mm). This is a particularly useful feature meaning that RATT saves you from having to wait for the rating agencies to release their credit-rating migration reports—which are usually in PDF format that does not support further analysis.

With RATT, however, you are provided with Bloomberg's analytical power to undertake your analysis at any time either to verify an instinct about the market or delve deeper into observed trends. The two rating action evolution charts in this book covering the period 1Q07 to 3Q10 and comparing agencies' downgrade activities have only been possible thanks to RATT.

The underlying data used in RATT come from issuer-level rating changes that Bloomberg tracks on the `Company Credit Rating Revision` function (RATC). The corresponding information appears in the `Credit Profile` function (CRPR). Please refer on your Bloomberg terminal to `RATC/CRPR<HELP>` for further information.

Using the Rating Changes (RATT) screen

Once you enter `RATT<Go>` on your Bloomberg terminal, the `Credit Ratings Trends` screen (Figure 22.11) appears. Choose from the following options:

- To change the information that appears on the screen, enter/choose the appropriate information from/in the highlighted fields.
- To move the graph legend, click and hold on the legend and drag it to the desired location on the graph.
- To display the total number of upgrades/downgrades, click on a green/red highlighted upgrade/downgrade value in the `Results for the Selected Period` section. The `Credit Ratings Trends Upgrade/Downgrade` screen appears.

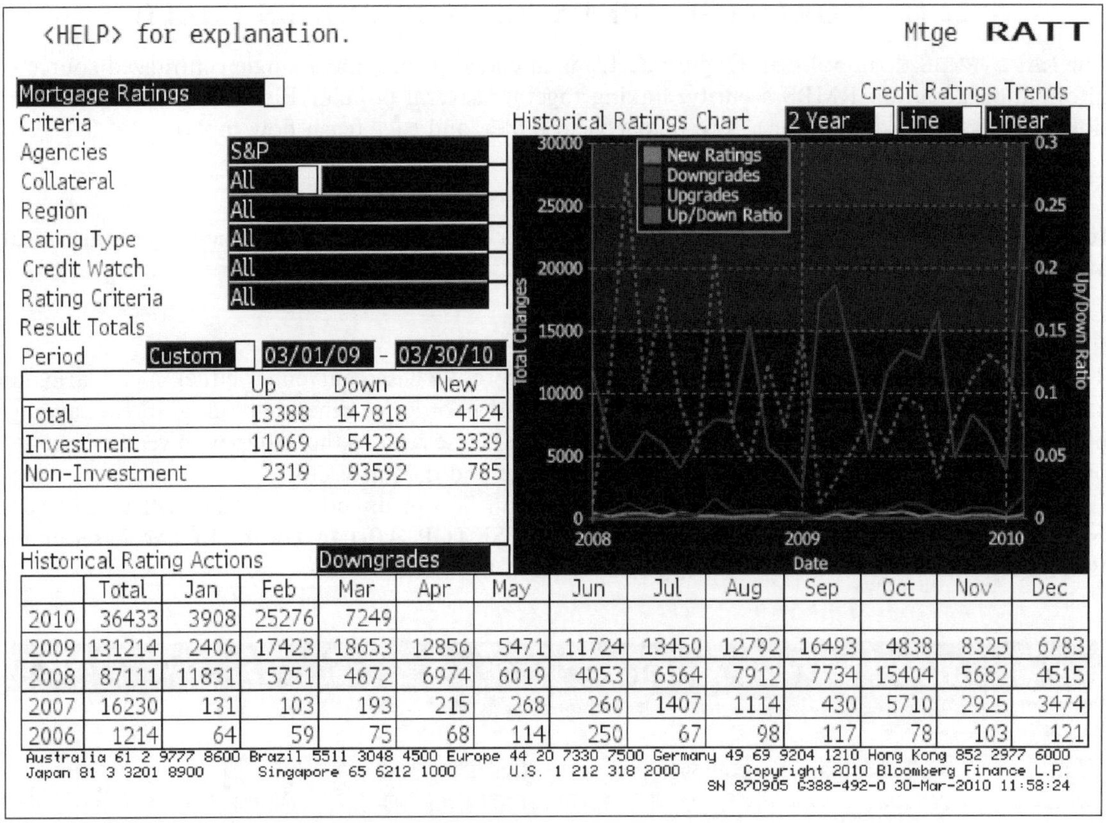

Figure 22.11. `Rating Changes (RATT)` screen.

- To display functions related to the issuers listed on the `Credit Ratings Trends Upgrade/Downgrade` screen, click on the row of the selected company. The `Related Functions` window appears, where you can choose from a list of related function options.

Related Functions window

Once you click on a specific company name from the `Credit Ratings Trends Upgrades/Downgrades` screen, the `Related Functions` window appears where you can choose to display a related function for the company you previously selected. The following fields appear:

- `CRPR Corporate Ratings` allows you to display the `Credit Profile` function for the selected company. `CRPR<HELP>` displays further information.
- `RELS Related Securities` allows you to display the `Related Securities` function for the selected company. `RELS<HELP>` displays further information.
- `ISSD Issuer Information` allows you to display the `Issuer Information` function for the selected company. `ISSD<HELP>` displays further information.
- `CN Security Related News` allows you to display the `All News/Research` function for the selected company. `CN<HELP>` displays further information.

22.11 MORTGAGE API EXCEL WORKBOOKS (MAPI)

The `MAPI-RMBS Combosheet` (Figure 22.12) is intended to provide a single centralized source of information about an RMBS security, linking together several popular Bloomberg mortgage functions, such as `DES` (description), `SYT` (super yield table), and `CFT` (cash flow table).

Tearsheet tab

Input a ticker or CUSIP into the salmon-colored ticker input cell (D6). All of the current, historical, and deal data will automatically fill in.

Analysis tab

This tab replicates the functionality of the Bloomberg `SYT` screen; enter either a scenario, an assumption, or specific inputs as requested in rows 22–41 in order to generate pricing, spread, average life, duration, and loss estimates for up to 10 scenarios. Please refer to the "Help with vectors" section of this chapter for more detail on creating prepayment and default vectors.

Prepayment, default, and severity curves/vectors can be run directly from the API spreadsheet. Note that you *must* have V3 (Version 3 of the DESKTOP API) to check. In Excel, select the Bloomberg dropdown menu `Live Support -> About`.

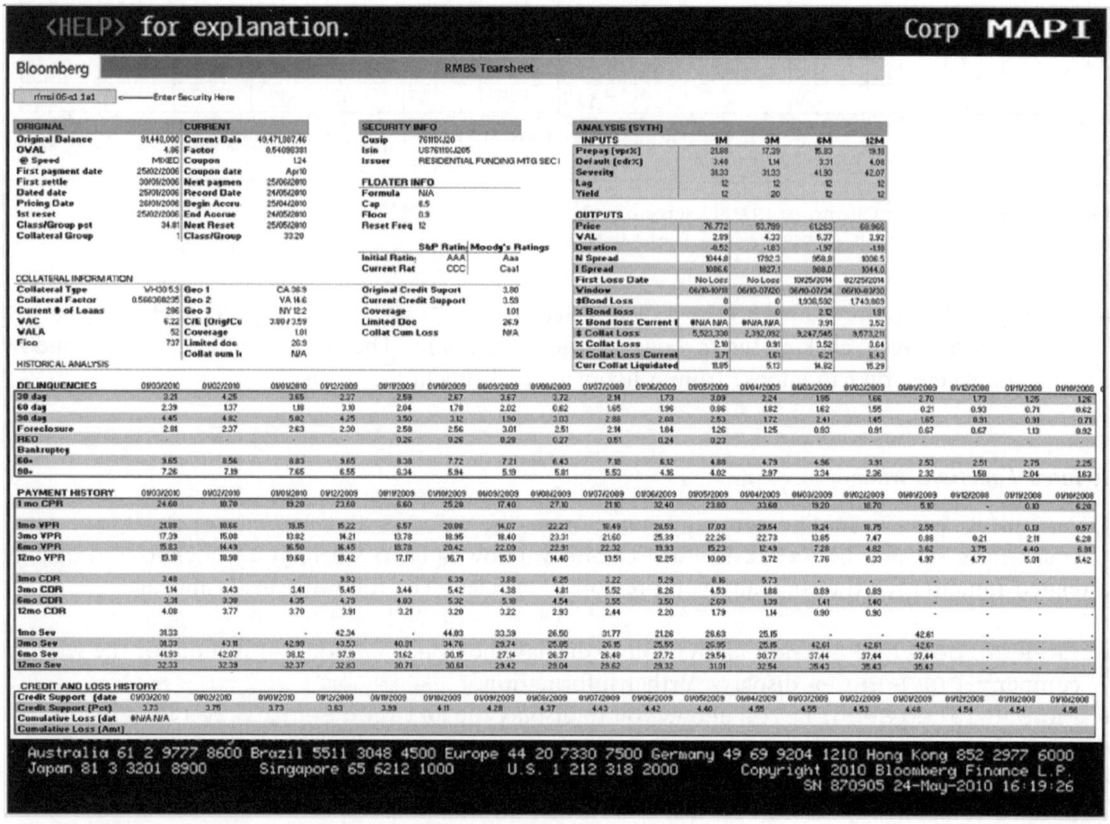

Figure 22.12. `MAPI-RMBS (SEV/CLP/SYTH Combosheet).`

There are two new fields that *must* be used to run the VECTORS: PREPAY_SPEED_VECTOR and DEFAULT SPEED VECTOR.

Note the new fields of PREPAY SPEED VECTOR and DEFAULT SPEED VECTOR have priority over the older fields of <MTGE>PREPAY SPEED and DEFAULT TYPE, However, <MTGE>PREPAY SPEED and DEFAULT TYPE can be used in conjunction with the new fields and will scale the percentage of the vector that is used. The following vector types can be entered into the vector fields.

Vector types

(1) 1 2 3 4 5 → Projected and 1-month intervals for the entered speeds.
(2) 2 12 R 20 → Projected 2 ramping over 12 months to 20 CDR.
(3) O 2 4 6 → O = Origination 2 4 6 (maps into WALA).
(4) O 2 12R 20 → O = Origination 2 CPR ramping over 12 to 20 CDR.

The input fields on this tab are as follows:

- MTG_PREPAY_SPEED (e.g., 100): Percentage of the prepayment vector that should be used that is defined in cell B26.
- MTG_PREPAY_TYP (e.g., CPR): Prepayment type can be CPR or PSA.
- PREPAY_SPEED_VECTOR (e.g., 5 12 R 2): Prepayment vector defined directly in the spreadsheet.
- ALLOW_DYNAMIC_CASHFLOW_CALCS (Y or N): Needs to be set to Y to allow credit assumptions to be run.
- DEFAULT PERCENT (e.g., 100): Percentage of the DEFAULT vector that should be used that is defined in cell B29.
- DEFAULT SPEED VECTOR (e.g., 20 12 R 36): DEFAULT vector defined directly within the spreadsheet.
- DEFAULT TYPE (e.g., CDR): DEFAULT type used can be CDR or SDA.
- LOSS SEVERITY (e.g., 85 12 R 40): The Loss Severity curve used to solve for the Price.
- YLD CONV ASK (e.g., 20): The Yield that is used along with the above-mentioned prepayment and default assumptions to solve for the Price in B39.
- MTG_FACE_AMT (e.g., 45,000).

Cashflows tab

This tab generates future cash flows for each of the scenarios/input sets created on the Analysis tab; it reads all of its inputs from the Analysis tab.

The MAPI–Non-agency RMBS Portfolio Pricing and Surveillance Sheet (Figure 22.13) enables you via BBG API to determine and solve for yield, *Z*-spread, WAL, duration, and loss percentage (of the original face value).

In addition, it also allows you to source/download key performance indicators such as credit support, delinquency stats, and additional collateral data such as the number of loans, WAC, WALA, FiCo Scores, geographical distribution, WALTVs, WACPNs. This is further enhanced by providing historical CPRs, VPRs, CDR and loss severities, each for 1 month, 3 months, 6 months, 12 months, and the whole transaction life.

Scenario and Assumption fields can be used to recall previously saved scenarios/assumptions:

- An Assumption refers to a specific prepay/default/severity/trigger combination, including any vectors used. A Scenario involves different assumptions being applied to different parts of the underlying collateral.
- The Scenario manager function (SCEN<Go>) stores all your MBS scenarios and assumptions.

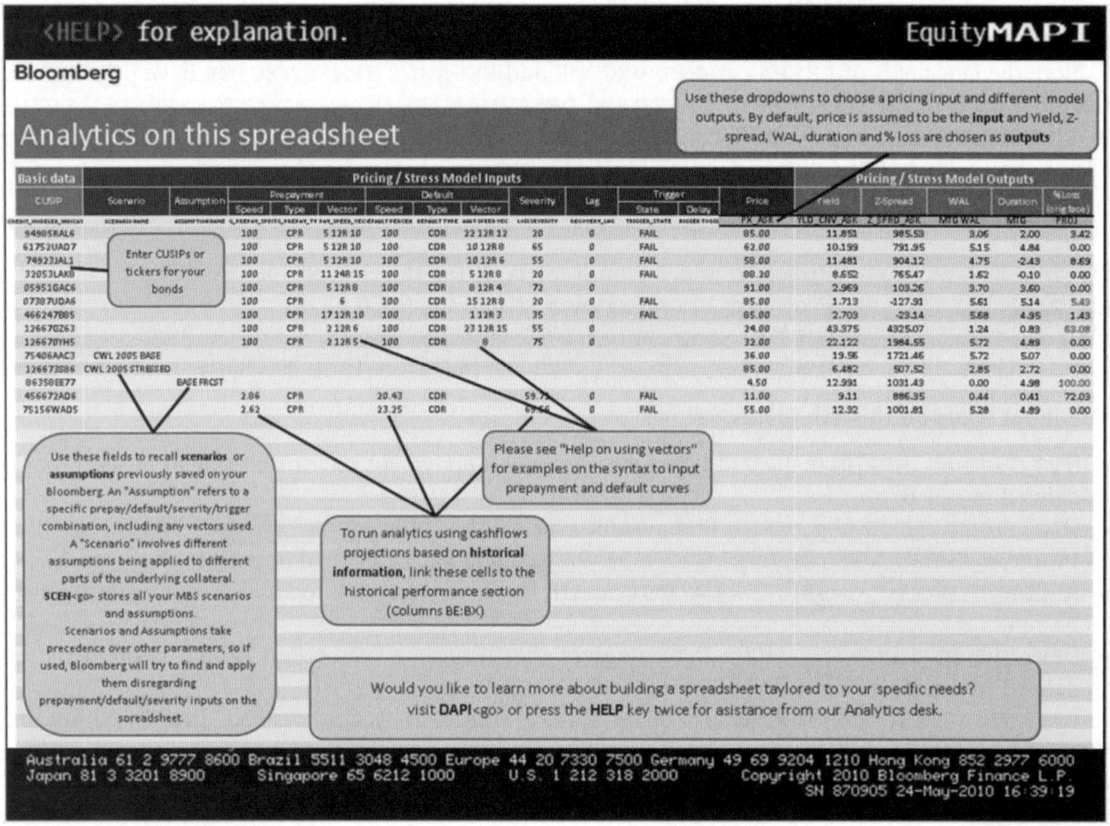

Figure 22.13. MAPI-RMBS Portfolio Surveillance & Analytics.

Scenarios and Assumptions take precedence over other parameters; so, if used, Bloomberg will try to find and apply them disregarding prepayment/default/severity inputs on the spreadsheet.

Prepayment and default vectors (i.e, prepayment/default assumptions that change over time) can be run directly from the API spreadsheet for Bloomberg-modeled cash flows (defaults are only applicable to credit-modeled bonds). When using a vector, two fields need to be taken into consideration:

- PREPAY/DEFAULT SPEED defines what percentage of the vector will be used. For example, 100 means using 100% of the vector, while 200 will linearly multiply the curve 2× on every point.
- PREPAY/DEFAULT SPEED VECTOR allows you to input the curve as per the definitions below.

By default, the vectors start on the first projected date. By specifying O at the beginning of the vector, users can set the vectors to start at origination (this will use the weighted average seasoning of the pool to compute the relevant speeds for future periods). The VECTOR fields have priority over the SPEED fields.

PREPAY/DEFAULT speeds can change over time gradually by linear interpolation of two different speeds ("ramping") or discretely ("stepping"). Note that Severity must be entered when running a default speed/vector.

Table 22.2 shows nine different examples of these rules.

Table 22.2. Examples of rules

Prepay speed	*Prepay speed vector*	*Means*
(1) 100	`10 11 12 13`	Specified values in monthly intervals: 10% first month, 11% second month, 12% third month, etc.
(2) 100	`2 12R 20`	2% first month, ramping up to 20% over a 12-month period
(3) 100	`O 2 4 6`	O = Starts at origination, 2%, 4%, 6% in monthly intervals
(4) 100	`O 2 12R 20`	O = Starts at Origination, 2% ramping over 12 months to 20 months
(5) 100	`30 15R 20 12S 5`	30% ramping down to 20% over 15 months, then stepping down to 5% after 12 months
(6) 100	`10`	Flat 10% CPR
(7) 200	`2 12R 20`	4% first month, ramping up to 40% over a 12-month period
(8) 150	`10`	Flat 15% CPR
(9) 10		Flat 10% CPR

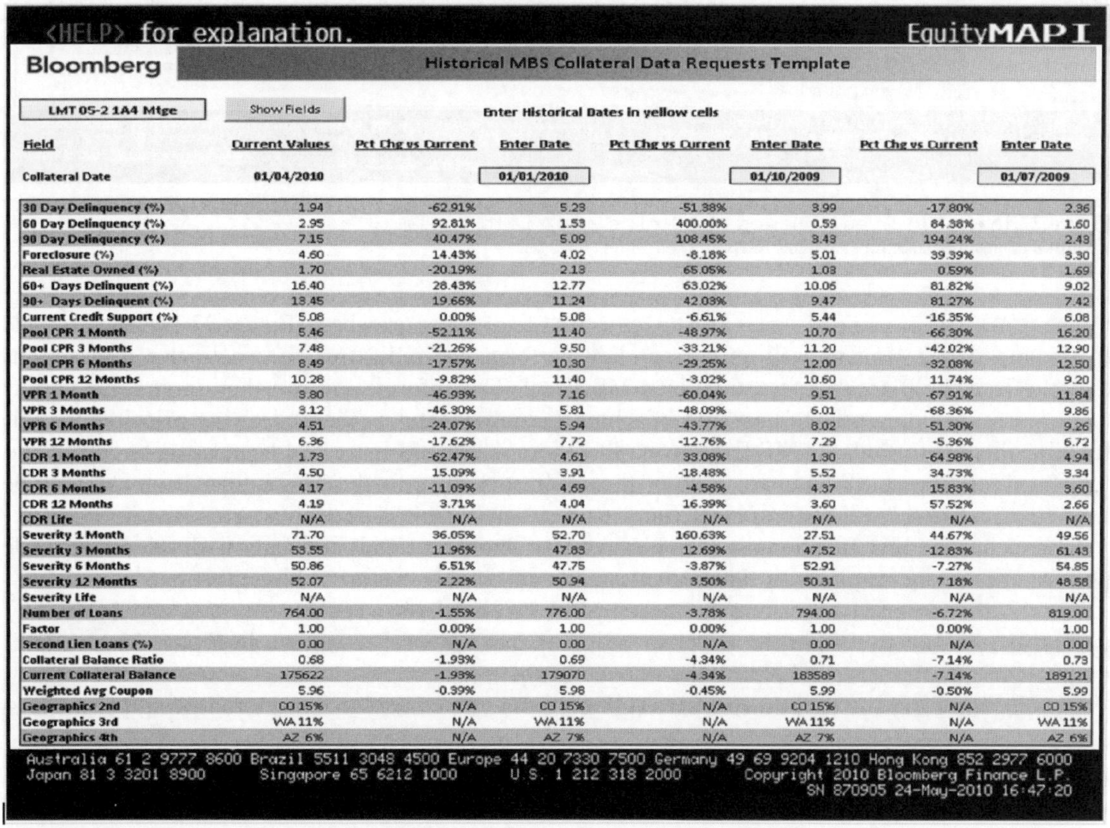

Field	Current Values	Pct Chg vs Current	Enter Date	Pct Chg vs Current	Enter Date	Pct Chg vs Current	Enter Date
Collateral Date	01/04/2010		01/01/2010		01/10/2009		01/07/2009
30 Day Delinquency (%)	1.94	-62.91%	5.23	-51.38%	3.99	-17.80%	2.36
60 Day Delinquency (%)	2.95	92.81%	1.53	400.00%	0.59	84.38%	1.60
90 Day Delinquency (%)	7.15	40.47%	5.09	108.45%	3.43	194.24%	2.43
Foreclosure (%)	4.60	14.43%	4.02	-8.18%	5.01	39.39%	3.30
Real Estate Owned (%)	1.70	-20.19%	2.13	65.05%	1.03	0.59%	1.69
60+ Days Delinquent (%)	16.40	28.43%	12.77	63.02%	10.06	81.82%	9.02
90+ Days Delinquent (%)	13.45	19.66%	11.24	42.03%	9.47	81.27%	7.42
Current Credit Support (%)	5.08	0.00%	5.08	-6.61%	5.44	-16.35%	6.08
Pool CPR 1 Month	5.46	-52.11%	11.40	-48.97%	10.70	-66.30%	16.20
Pool CPR 3 Months	7.48	-21.26%	9.50	-33.21%	11.20	-42.02%	12.90
Pool CPR 6 Months	8.49	-17.57%	10.30	-29.25%	12.00	-32.08%	12.50
Pool CPR 12 Months	10.28	-9.82%	11.40	-3.02%	10.60	11.74%	9.20
VPR 1 Month	3.80	-46.93%	7.16	-60.04%	9.51	-67.91%	11.84
VPR 3 Months	3.12	-46.30%	5.81	-48.09%	6.01	-68.36%	9.86
VPR 6 Months	4.51	-24.07%	5.94	-43.77%	8.02	-51.30%	9.26
VPR 12 Months	6.36	-17.62%	7.72	-12.76%	7.29	-5.36%	6.72
CDR 1 Month	1.73	-62.47%	4.61	33.08%	1.30	-64.98%	4.94
CDR 3 Months	4.50	15.09%	3.91	-18.48%	5.52	34.73%	3.34
CDR 6 Months	4.17	-11.09%	4.69	-4.58%	4.37	15.83%	3.60
CDR 12 Months	4.19	3.71%	4.04	16.39%	3.60	57.52%	2.66
CDR Life	N/A	N/A	N/A	N/A	N/A	N/A	N/A
Severity 1 Month	71.70	36.05%	52.70	160.63%	27.51	44.67%	49.56
Severity 3 Months	53.55	11.96%	47.83	12.69%	47.52	-12.83%	61.43
Severity 6 Months	50.86	6.51%	47.75	-3.87%	52.91	-7.27%	54.85
Severity 12 Months	52.07	2.22%	50.94	3.50%	50.31	7.18%	48.58
Severity Life	N/A	N/A	N/A	N/A	N/A	N/A	N/A
Number of Loans	764.00	-1.55%	776.00	-3.78%	794.00	-6.72%	819.00
Factor	1.00	0.00%	1.00	0.00%	1.00	0.00%	1.00
Second Lien Loans (%)	0.00	N/A	0.00	N/A	0.00	N/A	0.00
Collateral Balance Ratio	0.68	-1.93%	0.69	-4.34%	0.71	-7.14%	0.73
Current Collateral Balance	175622	-1.93%	179070	-4.34%	183589	-7.14%	189121
Weighted Avg Coupon	5.96	-0.39%	5.98	-0.45%	5.99	-0.50%	5.99
Geographics 2nd	CO 15%	N/A	CO 15%	N/A	CO 15%	N/A	CO 15%
Geographics 3rd	WA 11%	N/A	WA 11%	N/A	WA 11%	N/A	WA 11%
Geographics 4th	AZ 6%	N/A	AZ 7%	N/A	AZ 7%	N/A	AZ 6%

Figure 22.14. `MAPI: Historical Collateral Surveillance` (non-agency).

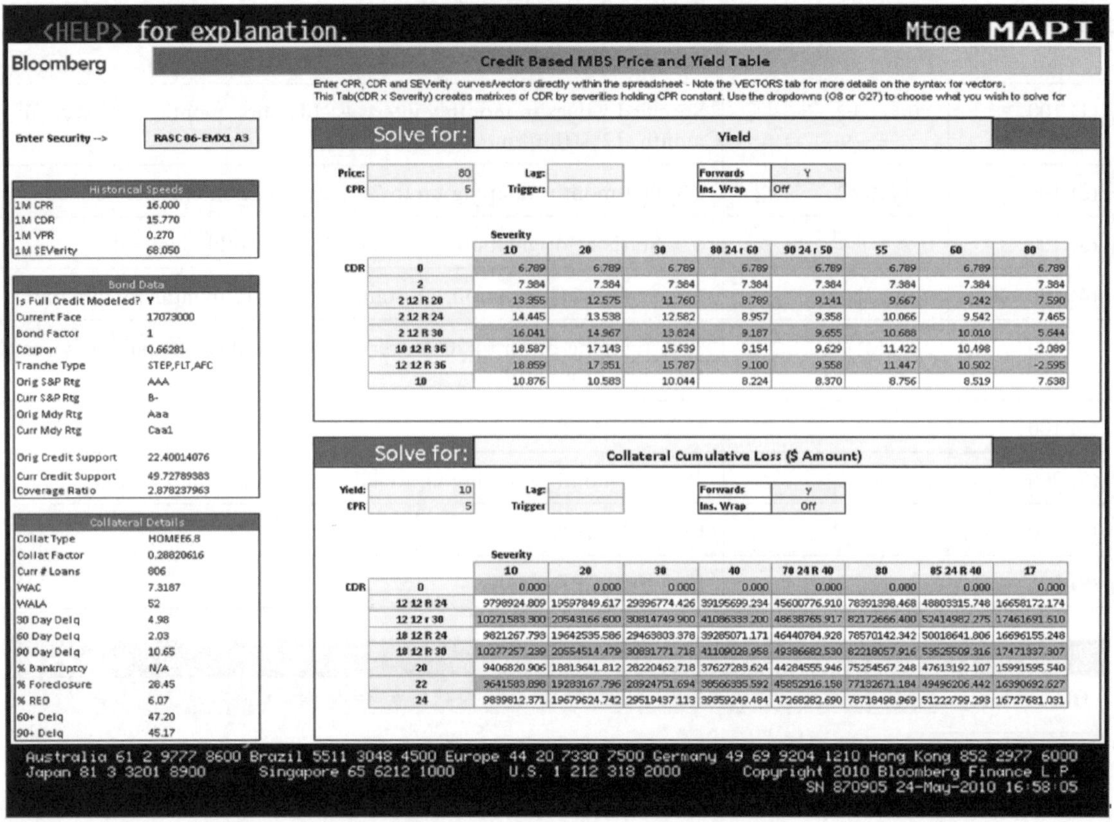

Figure 22.15. MAPI: Credit Based MBS Price and Yield Table.

The MAPI: Historical Collateral Surveillance spreadsheet (Figure 22.14) enables users to download historical as well as current key performance indicators for particular transactions directly from the Bloomberg terminal into MS Excel. This information can then serve for a variety of purposes including peer-to-peer and benchmark analysis; and as the underlying principle for this functionality are formulas in MS Excel, rows like those shown in Figure 22.14 can easily be copied and replicated, and historical dates for each of them adjusted accordingly. This information can then be used to visualize these KPIs graphically and particularly for large portfolios.

In conclusion, this functionality enables you to build a rapid application development–style performance analytics platform that provides agile and highly customizable reporting.

The Credit Based MBS Price and Yield Table allows you to enter CPR, CDR, and Severity curves/vectors directly within the Excel spreadsheet. The spreadsheet shown in Figure 22.15 creates matrixes of CDR by severity holding the CPR constant.

By selecting from the dropdown boxes (G8 or G27) you can solve for the following parameters:

- Price.
- Yield.
- Modified duration.
- J-spread.
- Weighted average life.
- Discount margin.
- I-spread.
- A-spread.

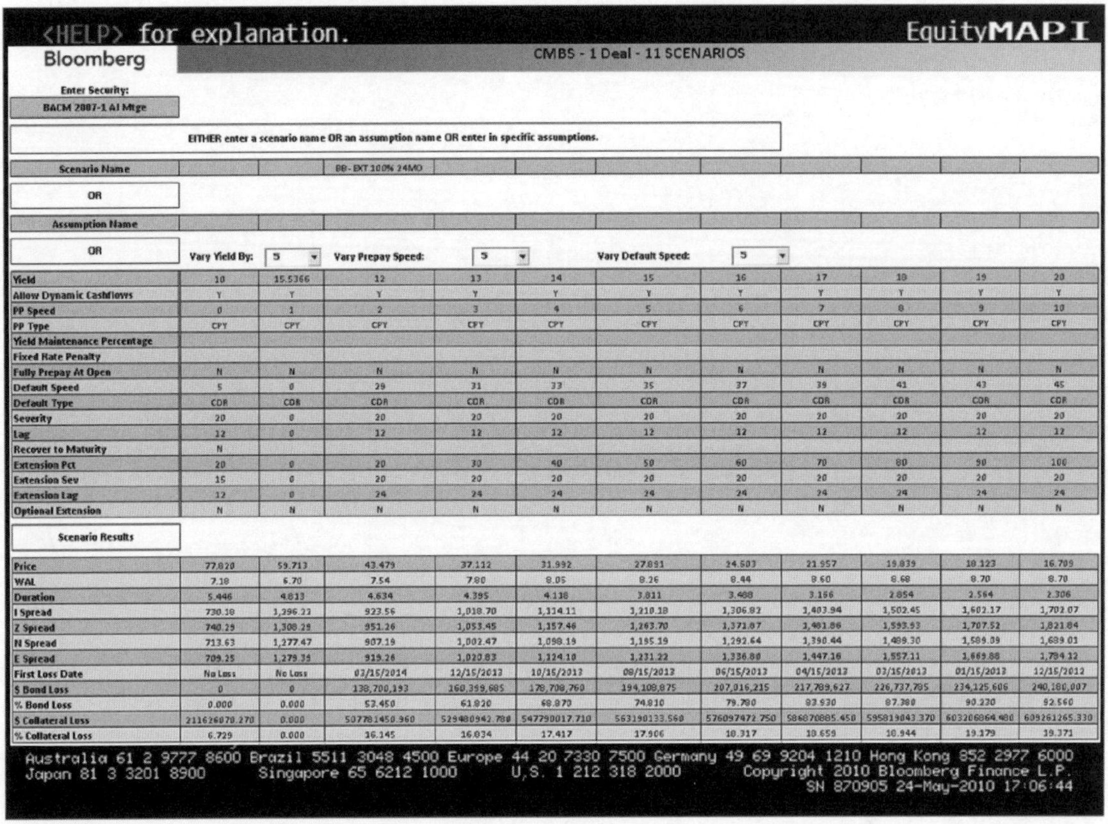

Scenario Name			BB-EXT 100% 24MO								
Assumption Name											
Yield	10	15.5366	12	13	14	15	16	17	18	19	20
Allow Dynamic Cashflows	Y	Y	Y	Y	Y	Y	Y	Y	Y	Y	Y
PP Speed	0	1	2	3	4	5	6	7	8	9	10
PP Type	CPY	CPY	CPY	CPY	CPY	CPY	CPY	CPY	CPY	CPY	CPY
Yield Maintenance Percentage											
Fixed Rate Penalty											
Fully Prepay At Open	N	N	N	N	N	N	N	N	N	N	N
Default Speed	5	0	29	31	33	35	37	39	41	43	45
Default Type	CDR	CDR	CDR	CDR	CDR	CDR	CDR	CDR	CDR	CDR	CDR
Severity	20	0	20	20	20	20	20	20	20	20	20
Lag	12	0	12	12	12	12	12	12	12	12	12
Recover to Maturity	N										
Extension Pct	20	0	20	30	40	50	60	70	80	90	100
Extension Sev	15	0	20	20	20	20	20	20	20	20	20
Extension Lag	12	0	24	24	24	24	24	24	24	24	24
Optional Extension	N	N	N	N	N	N	N	N	N	N	N

Scenario Results											
Price	77.820	59.713	43.479	37.112	31.992	27.891	24.503	21.957	19.839	18.123	16.709
WAL	7.18	6.70	7.54	7.80	8.05	8.26	8.44	8.60	8.68	8.70	8.70
Duration	5.446	4.813	4.634	4.395	4.138	3.811	3.488	3.166	2.854	2.564	2.306
I Spread	730.18	1,296.22	923.56	1,018.70	1,114.11	1,210.18	1,306.82	1,403.94	1,502.45	1,602.17	1,702.07
Z Spread	740.29	1,308.29	951.26	1,053.45	1,157.46	1,263.70	1,371.87	1,481.86	1,593.93	1,707.52	1,821.84
N Spread	713.63	1,277.47	907.19	1,002.47	1,098.19	1,195.19	1,292.64	1,390.44	1,489.30	1,589.39	1,689.01
E Spread	709.25	1,279.39	919.26	1,020.83	1,124.10	1,231.22	1,336.80	1,447.16	1,557.11	1,669.88	1,784.12
First Loss Date	No Loss	No Loss	03/15/2014	12/15/2013	10/15/2013	08/15/2013	06/15/2013	04/15/2013	03/15/2013	01/15/2013	12/15/2012
$ Bond Loss	0	0	138,700,193	160,399,685	178,708,760	194,108,875	207,016,215	217,789,627	226,737,785	234,125,606	240,180,007
% Bond Loss	0.000	0.000	53.450	61.820	68.870	74.810	79.780	83.930	87.380	90.230	92.560
$ Collateral Loss	211626070.270	0.000	507781450.960	529480942.780	547790017.710	563190133.560	576097472.750	586870885.450	595819043.370	603206864.480	609261265.330
% Collateral Loss	6.729	0.000	16.145	16.834	17.417	17.906	18.317	18.659	18.944	19.179	19.371

Figure 22.16. MAPI-CMBS Super Yield Table.

- E-spread.
- Principal window.
- Bond cumulative loss (% original face).
- Bond cumulative loss (% current face).
- Collateral cumulative loss ($ amount).
- Collateral cumulative loss (% original face).
- Collateral cumulative loss (% current face).
- First-loss date.
- Bond cumulative loss ($ amount).

Refer to the Vector tab in the Excel workbook for more details on the syntax for vectors.

The CMBS Super Yield Table (Figure 22.16) enables you to use Bloomberg's Cash Flow Engine directly in Excel for commercial mortgage-backed securities. To do this, enter a security identifier followed by <MTGE> in Cell C8. Complete the worksheet with your scenario assumptions in cells D22–N37 and the results will be displayed in D42–N52. If you have loan-level scenarios or assumptions that have been defined on Bloomberg's Scenario Manager SCEN<Go>, then you will be able to enter these specific scenarios in Row 12 or 17.

23

Websites and other resources

23.1 TRADE BODIES

- ***American Securitization Forum*** (ASF)
  www.americansecuritization.com
- ***Asia Securities Industry & Financial Markets Association*** (ASIFMA)
  www.asifma.org
- ***Association for Financial Markets in Europe*** (AFME)
  www.afme.eu
- ***British Bankers' Association*** (BBA)
  www.bba.org.uk
- ***European Securitization Forum*** (AFME/ESF)
  www.afme.eu/dynamic.aspx?id=2294
- ***Global Financial Markets Association*** (GFMA)
  www.gfma.org
- ***International Swaps and Derivatives Association*** (ISDA)
  www.isda.org

23.2 FREE DATA PORTALS

Global ABS Portal
www.globalabsportal.com

Lewtan Technologies is an experienced long-time provider of structured finance surveillance data, analytics, and software. In order to promote transparency in the markets, it has established the Global ABS Portal, which you can access via the above link by requesting a free user password and accepting a licensing agreement.

Once you have signed yourself up you will be able to access the most recent investors' reports and original offering circulars (OCs) for public European securitization transactions. Global ABS Portal's aim is to provide a free centralized access point for public deal information enabling easy access to investors and regulators alike. Prior to Lewtan Technologies' initiative, finding this kind of deal-specific information could only be done via commercial vendors and, hence, this is a great step towards more transparency and simpler access to deal-related information.

According to Lewtan Technologies' commercial website, the company utilizes its commercial platform ABSNet and leverages its sourcing infrastructure in order to supply the original OC as well as remittance reports via Global ABS Portal. The information on the portal is updated in real time (i.e., as soon as new reports become available).

This particular initiative helps to bridge the gap between Europe and the U.S., which uses the SEC's EDGAR database to provide similar information on U.S. transactions paired with increased disclosure requirements under RegAB.

EDGAR database
http://www.sec.gov/edgar.shtml

Irish Stock exchange
http://www.ise.ie/app/specSecList.asp

Irish Stock Exchange Transparency Initiative

Some of the stock exchanges that are more involved in the structured finance market than others—due to taxation laws, jurisdiction, and regulation—realized that they can play their part in increasing transparency and providing all the transaction documentation of deals that are listed by them on the exchange's website. The underlying idea is to create a centralized information repository (sometimes referred to as a "one stop shop" for transaction documentation) which can be used by issuers and investors alike and, hence, can help in reducing perceived opaqueness.

An example of such an exchange-driven project is the development of a transaction data portal by the Irish Stock Exchange as part of its transparency initiative, the result of which can be found by visiting the internet link above.

As a consequence of this project, the Irish Stock Exchange, together with a select number of representatives from both issuers and investors, has significantly enhanced its website, ensuring that it is suitable and usable for investors wishing to gain more information on issued securities and deal-related information. This offering is available to all issuers whose securities are listed on the Irish Stock Exchange. It enables issuers to publish electronic versions of investor reports, transaction documents, and other related financial information on the site.

"Transaction documents" that can be made publicly available in such a way include trust deeds, agency agreements, subscription agreements, servicing agreements, sale agreements, security agreements, investment or collateral agreements, and swap documentation.

"Investor reports" include, for instance, post-issuance reports, collateral reports, etc.; whereas "financials" include annual financial statements, half-yearly financial statements, quarterly financial statements, etc.

Further information including the annual fee schedule by the issuer for this service, how to submit reports for upload, and the relevant contact details can be found on the Irish Stock Exchange website.

23.3 VENDORS

ABSNet
www.absnet.net

Corporate Headquarters
Lewtan 400-2 Totten Pond Rd, 4th Fl.
Waltham, MA 02451
Tel.: 781-895-9800
Fax: 781-890-3684
www.lewtan.com

United Kingdom Office
Lewtan
15 St. Mary at Hill
London EC3R 8EE
Tel.: +44-(0)-20-7621-2000
Fax: +44-(0)-20-7623-8793

ABSXchange

For questions regarding ABSXchange, please contact:

David Pagliaro
EMEA Regional Director
Tel.: +44-20-7176-3522
Mobile: +44-7799-866-447
Email: *david_pagliaro@standardandpoors.com*

Bloomberg
www.bloomberg.com

Main
The Americas +1-212-318-2000
EMEA +44-20-7330-7500
Asia-Pacific +65-6212-1000

Fitch Solutions
www.fitchsolutions.com

U.S.
One State Street Plaza
New York, NY 10004
Tel.: +1-212-908-0500 +1-800-75-FITCH

U.K.
30 North Colonnade, Canary Wharf
London E14 5GN, U.K.
Tel.: +44-203-530-1000

Intex
www.intex.com

North America
Intex Solutions, Inc.
110 A Street
Needham, MA 02494
Tel.: +1-781-449-6222
Fax: +1-781-444-2318
Email: *sales@intex.com*

Europe
Intex Solutions, Inc.
60 Cannon Street
London EC4N 6NP
United Kingdom
Tel.: +44-20-7002-1055
Fax: +44-20-7002-1100
Email: *europesales@intex.com*

Moody's Analytics
http://www.wsainc.com/

London
One Canada Square
Canary Wharf
London E14 5FA
Tel.: +44-(0)-207-772-1000
Email: *info@wsainc.com*

New York
7 World Trade Center
250 Greenwich St.
New York, NY 10007
Tel.: +1-212-553-1100
Email: *info@wsainc.com*

Principia Partners
http://www.ppllc.com/

New York
Principia Partners
156 William Street - 11th Floor
New York, NY 10038
Tel.: +1-(212)-480-2270
Email: *info@ppllc.com*

London
Principia Partners
Queen's House
8-9 Queen Street
London EC4N 1SP, UK
Tel.: +44-(0)-20-7618-1350
Fax: +44-(0)-20-7618-1351
Email: *info@ppllc.com*

Trepp
www.trepp.com

North America
477 Madison Avenue
New York, NY 10022
Tel.: +1-212-754-1010

United Kingdom
15 St. Mary at Hill
London EC3R 8EE
Tel.: +44-(0)-20-7621-2075
Fax: +44-(0)-20-7623-8793

23.4 STRUCTURED FINANCE PERIODICALS AND OTHER USEFUL RESOURCES

Asset-Backed Alert
http://www.abalert.com/index.php

Securitization professionals rely on each weekly issue of *Asset-Backed Alert* for hard-to-get news and statistics on asset-backed and mortgage-backed securitization activities throughout the world.

The newsletter's coverage takes a forward-looking approach, routinely tipping off subscribers to emerging risks and opportunities in securitization. Coverage includes:

- Asset-backed and mortgage-backed securitization activity in the U.S., Europe, Asia, Australia, Latin America, and Canada.
- Hush-hush issuance plans, including those involving assets that are new to asset-backed securitization.
- Investor strategies for maximizing returns and minimizing risk in structured-finance investments.
- Career openings for securitization professionals.
- Shifts in the supply/demand balance of the asset-backed securitization market.
- New developments in the booming markets for collateralized debt obligations.

Subscribers to *Asset-Backed Alert* get free online access to the ABS Database, which captures information on all asset-backed and mortgage-backed securitization issues sold worldwide. The database, compiled by the editors of *Asset-Backed Alert*, is—according to the newsletter—the only comprehensive listing of public and private asset-backed and mortgage-backed securitizations—including collateralized debt obligations.

Relying on its database, *Asset-Backed Alert* regularly publishes rankings of key participants in asset-backed securitization such as underwriters, issuers, trustees, law firms, bond insurers, and rating agencies. It also provides readers with a steady flow of statistical summaries showing securitization trends in all of the world's asset-backed securities markets.

Asset Securitization Report
http://www.structuredfinancenews.com/

Anchored by *Asset Securitization Report*, StructuredFinanceNews.com was launched in April 2008 as one of the premier online destinations for the structured finance industry.

In addition to news and commentary on topics like asset-backeds, covered bonds, mortgage-backeds, and derivatives, StructuredFinanceNews.com offers an extensive news archive and a proprietary people database that offers hard-to-find information on the industry's top players.

Backed up by an experienced team of journalists across the globe, *Asset Securitization Report* provides a full range of news, people coverage, analysis, and expert commentary, as well as a weekly aggregation of Wall Street's securitization research.

The ASR Scorecards Database provides exhaustive and accurate transaction information on U.S. deals not available anywhere else. Sourced by the firm's research team with the help of experienced editors, ASR Scorecards serves as an exhaustive resource for historical and current U.S. deals inside scorecard data with deals and rankings.

IFR European Securitization Briefing
http://www.ifrbriefings.com/eurosec.php

The *IFR European Securitization Briefing* is written every evening after the markets have closed and is emailed to subscribers before the markets reopen. The briefing is broadcast in text with a PDF attachment and can be printed, viewed on your PC, or read on your wireless handheld device as you travel to work. The briefing contains:

- A forward-looking daily summary of the most important developments in the European securitization markets, including deals launched, pricings, mandates, and other news with the potential to impact the MBS, ABS, CDO, and CLO markets.
- A full listing of the deals that have been launched and priced recently, with spreads for the most significant tranches; there are also details of guidance released on upcoming deals.
- A pipeline of the main deals yet to release guidance, with details of likely deal timing, size, and leads.

Lexology
http://www.lexology.com/

Lexology is an innovative, web-based service that provides company law departments and law firms with a depth of free practical know-how that would be impossible to produce internally. By collaborating with the world's leading commercial law firms, *Lexology* is able to deliver fully tailored intelligence to the desktops of business lawyers worldwide on a daily basis.

It is free to subscribe to *Lexology*. Simply register and create your own legal newsfeed service—geared to your practice or business interests. *Lexology* will immediately begin to deliver the most recent legal analysis to you.

Securitization.net
http://www.securitization.net/

Securitization.net was developed to provide an open-platform website offering free structured finance information to a global audience. This internet resource not only expands the online availability of relevant industry information, but also encourages and increases industry participation in information exchange.

Securitization.net provides the premier forum for this exchange. Since early 2000 its sponsor, Mayer Brown, has continued to develop *Securitization.net* to meet the information needs of this market.

Structured Credit Investor (SCI)

http://www.structuredcreditinvestor.com/

SCI is a specialist publisher of news and analysis on all aspects of the structured credit and ABS markets. It publishes daily news items and a weekly news edition on Wednesdays that features in-depth analysis. *SCI*'s coverage is split into news channels, including CLO, RMBS, CMBS, CDO, CDS, or insurance-linked securities (ILS). There are several other news categories besides, covering all aspects of structured finance.

SCI is aimed at the buy side; its mission is to provide deeper and more accurate coverage of structured finance to market participants than is available elsewhere. The readership includes portfolio managers, broker-dealers, hedge funds, CDO managers, banks and CFOs.

Journal of Structured Finance

http://www.iijournals.com/toc/jsf/current

The *Journal of Structured Finance* (*JSF*) offers insightful, comprehensive research and commentary on all aspects of structured finance. It provides detailed analysis on structuring and investing in products such as ABSs, CDOs, CLOs, and MBSs. *JSF* covers such topics as:

- Credit derivatives and synthetic securitization
- Secondary trading in the CDO market
- Securitization in emerging markets and intellectual property
- Trends and developments in mortgage and home equity, credit card, auto loan and lease, student loan, and trade-receivable securitization
- Accounting, regulatory, and tax issues.

You get four printed issues a year plus online access to archived articles. *JSF* is ideal for commercial and investment bankers, lawyers, institutional investors, regulators involved in structured finance, librarians, and academics.

Total Securitization

http://www.totalsecuritization.com/

Total Securitization, the news service dedicated to the securitization, loan, bond, and distressed debt credit markets, covers the following:

- Today's news—the most recent stories the *Total Securitization* editorial staff has reported across all asset classes. These stories are posted throughout the day.
- Excess spread—*Total Securitization* scours the web and provides summaries of stories in other media that are of interest to the global credit market.
- Learning curves—an in-depth look at some aspects of the credit market including analysis of structures, details about new regulations, or other topics, written by industry practitioners.
- Archive search—archived articles from *Credit Investment News*, *Securitization News*, *BondWeek*, *Loan Market Week*, and *Structured Finance International* have been added to create a robust archive.
- News section—this feature allows you to view the most recent news for individual asset classes.
- Borrowing strategies—this feature contains stories detailing corporate borrowing strategies.

- EOD Scorecard—this downloadable Excel spreadsheet within "EOD Scorecard" tracks CDOs that have triggered events of default.
- Distressed fund tracker—an Excel spreadsheet that details fund launches with distressed investing startegies.
- Regulatory tracker—outlines pending regulatory and legislative actions and monitors the status on a weekly basis.
- League tables—quarterly securitization league tables supplied by Dealogic.
- Events—a listing of industry events.
- Buyers' guides—directories for different segments of the financial markets.

23.5 RATING AGENCIES

DBRS
www.dbrs.com

DBRS Limited
DBRS Tower
181 University Avenue, Suite 700
Toronto, ON M5H 3M7
Tel.: +1-416-593-5577
Fax: +1-416-593-8432

Fitch Ratings
www.fitchratings.com

New York
One State Street Plaza
NY 10004
Tel.: +1-212-908-0500

London
30 North Colonnade, Canary Wharf
London E14 5GN, U.K.
Tel.: +44-203-530-1000

Moody's Investor Services
www.moodys.com

New York, NY
Moody's Investors Service
7 World Trade Center
at 250 Greenwich Street
New York, NY 10007
U.S.A.
Tel.: +1-212-553-1653
Email: *clientservices@moodys.com*

London, U.K.
Moody's Investors Service Ltd.
Registered Office:
One Canada Square
Canary Wharf
London E14 5FA, U.K.
Tel.: + 44-20-7772-5454

Standard & Poor's
www.standardandpoors.com

New York
55 Water Street, New York, NY 10041
Tel.: 001-212-438-2000

Appendix A
Glossary

Tip

If you come across a certain term, whilst reading this book, that is not covered in the following glossary, I suggest you Google the term or take a look at Wikipedia—it's surprising how much information you can find on the internet nowadays—most of it is pretty accurate.

ABCP Asset-backed commercial paper whose principal and interest payments receipts come from the cash flows of the underlying assets. ABCP carries the risk that outstanding commercial paper cannot be reissued in order to repay maturing commercial paper and, usually, a so-called "back-stop" liquidity facility may be available to provide sufficient cash in order to repay investors.

API An application programming interface is in the broadest sense an interface between two (or more) software programs or applications that enable them to communicate with each other and to exchange information.

ARM (option ARM) Adjustable mortgage rate loan (i.e., a mortgage loan with an interest rate that is periodically adjusted and based on a specified index rate).

Advance rate The advance or loan advance rate is typically calculated by taking the loan balance and dividing it by the value of the underlying collateral. Advance rates are usually used in auto loan transactions and are equivalent to the loan-to-value (LTV) ratio used for residential mortgage loans. Consequently and similar to the LTV ratio, the higher the advance rate , the less equity is at stake by the borrower and, as a result, the less loan protection for the lender.

Adverse selection Adverse selection describes the changes to a collateral pool (e.g., a mortgage pool) whereby the pool's risk profile is assumed to worsen over time. This is based on presuming that borrowers who are more creditworthy than others are likely to repay their obligations earlier than weaker borrowers, which over time can lead to adverse selection.

Agency securities or agency deals Mortgage-backed bond instruments that enjoy credit protection based on either an explicit (for securities issue by Ginnie Mae securities) or an implicit guarantee (for bonds issued by Fannie Mae and Freddie Mac) by the U.S. government.

Alt-A loan An alternative A loan is a first-lien residential mortgage conforming with traditional credit guidelines and underwriting standards for prime mortgage. However, certain loan parameter such as LTV ratio, occupancy status, property type, limited loan documentation, and other factors do not qualify under a lender's standard underwriting criteria.

Amortization Amortization describes the process of reducing the principal amount of a liability gradually over time. An amortizing bond regularly returns principal as well as interest payments to investors in the securities. The timeline throughout which this repayment occurs is also known as an "amortization period". Depending on the individual structure, some amortizations can happen on a "pass-through" basis whereby principal receipts are frequently passed on to the investors. Some transactions follow a predetermined amortization schedule or adhere to amortization windows whereby principal receipts are collected in an escrow account and only paid to investors following the predetermined payment schedule. If the funds are collected throughout the transaction's life and repaid to the investors on maturity of the bond, then amortization is replaced by a so-called "bullet repayment".

Annuity or annuity mortgage loan Also known as a "repayment loan", the principal balance of such an annuity mortgage loan amortizes over the loan's life. Whilst frequent payments (usually monthly) are fixed, the makeup of each payment changes according to the loan's amortization schedule.

Arbitrage CDO A collateralized debt obligation which makes use of an imbalance between a higher aggregate yield received for the underlying assets and a lower yield that is payable on transaction securities.

Arrears If a borrower fails to pay on his debt obligation by a specified due date then he is said to be "in arrears".

ABS Asset-backed securitization is the process of issuing notes or bonds that are backed by a pool of financial assets that produce predictable cash flows for the repayment of principal as well as of interest.

Asset trigger event If the performance of underlying assets do not meet certain expectations or minimum requirements, as outlined in the transactions documents, such an event is triggered and the priority of payments will change as a consequence.

Assignment The legal transfer of a right, claim, interest, or property from one party to another.

Average life This is a crude measure of the expected duration of an investment or loan used to ascertain the average time required to repay the principal loan amount or to recoup the investment amount. Most importantly for structured finance bonds, the actual average life of such bonds depends heavily on the repayment rate of the underlying assets since their cash flow receipts are used in turn to repay the investors of the issued notes. A securities expected average life (or, by derivation, the expected maturity) is calculated by using a constant prepayment rate (CPR) for underlying assets that have a variable repayment rate (in contrast to assets that have a fixed repayment rate). This permits peer analysis of ABS instruments and benchmarking against other fixed income securities.

Backstop facility This is a loan facility agreement entered into by a highly rated entity (typically, a bank or other financial institution) guaranteeing payment in case the entity that first entered into the underlying loan is not able to deliver on its obligations.

Balance sheet CDO A collateralized debt obligation securitization of obligations owned by the sponsor of the transaction—as opposed to a managed CDO whereby the sponsor actively manages a portfolio of obligations which he or she does not already own and hence "ramps up" over a period of time.

Balloon repayment Loans with a balloon repayment have a considerable part of the original loan's principal outstanding until the final maturity of the loan when it becomes due. This in turn represents a refinancing risk as the borrower may not be able to repay such a large portion once the loan matures.

Bankruptcy remote One of the key (legal) concepts behind securitization is that assets transferred from an originator to an SPV are considered to be bankruptcy remote. This means the creditors of the originator cannot utilize or access those assets in case of the originator's bankruptcy as they are ring-fenced. For this reason, SPVs are sometimes also referred to as bankruptcy-remote vehicles or bankruptcy-remote SPVs. Note that not all securitization transactions utilize such vehicles: for instance, in the case of some synthetic transactions, the assets would remain in the originator's book(s) and the credit risk attached to those assets would be transferred to a third party via a credit default swap (CDS). From an investor's perspective, it is crucial to understand the deal structure and, if there are bankruptcy-remote vehicles involved, to gain confidence that the bankruptcy-remote status could be relied upon in case of an originator's insolvency. This is easier said than done as this status is only actually tested when an originator becomes insolvent. Other than that, investors can only rely on a legal opinion and possibly some comments/analysis from the credit rating agencies.

Buy-to-let loans These are mortgages extended to investors who are buying a property to rent. Hence, such investors rely on rental payments for the payback of the mortgage loan and, as such, buy-to-let loans (BTL) tend to carry a higher risk. In fact, a homeowner who is living in his or her own mortgaged property is expected to save "the roof over his family's head" whereas this may not necessarily apply to a BTL property investor.

CDR A constant default rate is, typically, the annualized rate of defaults on a group of loans or mortgages for collateralized products such as mortgage-backed securitizations. The CDR represents the percentage of outstanding loan or mortgage balances of the securitized mortgage pool that are in default.

Chinese wall Chinese walls are also known as information barriers. The purpose of these barriers is to assist in preventing the unauthorized disclosure of sensitive information and the misuse (or perceived misuse) of such. Information barriers are designed to help ensure that sensitive information is communicated only to authorized staff members of a specific firm who have a legitimate business need to know or have access to that information. Additionally, by assisting in the prevention of unauthorized disclosure of sensitive information, information barriers assist in the management of perceived or actual conflicts of interest and allow such firm to continue their normal sales, trading, and research activities despite other areas being in possession of sensitive information.

Churn rate (of assets) Churn rate (opposite: growth rate) is typically a measure of customer and/or asset attrition and is expressed as a percentage. It can be calculated by dividing the number of customers or loans (assets) for a given segment (i.e., retail business banking) that cease activity in a given period by the total active number of customer or loans for the given segment. If the churn rate is greater than the growth rate for new customers or loans, this would indicate that the customer or loan base is declining. Churn rates can be used to develop customer or loan retention policies.

Click-through transparency This describes a system functionality that enables users to click on a reported value for a certain key-specific key performance indicator (KPI) and, subsequently, an electronic version of the relevant investor report will open at the appropriate page with the key performance indicator value highlighted in the report. Also sometimes referred to as "drilldown' capability.

CPR Constant prepayment rate or conditional prepayment rate is the annual repayment rate on a pool of underlying assets (i.e., loans or mortgages) expressed as a percentage.

Commercial paper CPs are short-term promissory notes with maturities usually less than 270 days—most commonly between 30 and 50 days.

Commingling risk The risk that one entity's cash (e.g., cashflow receipts of an SPV) is mixed up with another entity's cash. It may also mean that one entity's cash goes into another entity's account and cannot be separately identified in case of bankruptcy of the other entity.

CRA Credit rating agency, such as Standard & Poor's, Moody's Investor Services, Fitch Ratings, Dominion Bond Ratings Service—to name a few.

Credit risk The risk that a counterparty or borrower will not acknowledge and service payment obligations and, hence, either pay not at all or over a longer period than was originally agreed.

Cross-collateralization This is a feature usually seen in relation to commercial real estate loans, whereby a borrower pledges assets that secure an individual mortgage loan as security for other loans made by the same borrowing entity. As such it is a credit protection technique.

CSV Comma-separated value is a popular electronic file format used to store tabular data in which numbers and text are stored in plain textual form—separated by commas, hence the name—which can be read in a text editor.

CUSIP number A Committee on Uniform Security Identification Procedures number is a 9-character alphanumeric code for North American securities. A unique securities identification number assigned to either a stock or bond issuance in order to facilitate clearing operations.

Default Failure/Breach by a counterparty to fulfill its obligations under a contractual agreement. This could be failure to pay, failure to deliver goods or assets, failure to hand over collateral, etc.

Delinquency Failure by a contractual counterparty to make a payment on a debt obligation or deliver goods or assets by the specific due date. Delinquencies can be used as early warning indicators for defaults; however, sometimes they resolve themselves and the obligation becomes "current" again.

Detachable coupon (DAC) or interest-only (IO) note A detachable coupon or interest-only note is the interest-only tranche of a structured finance tranche (typically, RMBS) with its notional value usually expressed as a proportion of the most senior note class within the transaction's capital structure. As it is an interest-only tranche, noteholders of a DAC will only receive interest payments but no principal payments.

Detachment point DP is the level above which a credit protection seller (e.g., a credit default swap) would cover losses.

Drilldown capability (see also *Click-through transparency*) The ability in a software application to drill down from a high data aggregation level (e.g., geographical region) into lower and more granular information that contributes to region data (i.e., countries, counties, zip codes, and so on). This capability permits switching from a high-level to a low-level data view (and back if necessary) enabling detailed analysis of what contributes to certain portfolios.

DSCR The so-called debt service coverage ratio is also known as the debt coverage ratio. It is a popular benchmark to assess an entity's ability to generate sufficient cash to cover its debt payments. DSCRs are often used by CRAs as part of their analysis when looking at cash flows of companies and in corporate banking as minimum DSCRs which often are covenant features of commercial loans.

Enforcement of security This means taking foreclosure on, for instance, a property that secures a mortgage loan or any other asset granted as collateral for debt, with a view to realize the value of this security or collateral—typically after default of the debtor.

Equity piece Also known as equity tranche. See *First-loss piece*.

Exposure at default Exposure at default (EAD) reflects, for example, the forecast amount that a borrower will draw on a commitment or other type of credit facility.

Expected losses ELs are losses that can reasonably be anticipated to occur. Banks that are able to estimate EL typically cover this exposure either through reserves or pricing. In statistical terms, ELs are represented by the amount of loss equal to the mean of the distribution, while unexpected losses (UL) are the difference between mean loss and potential loss represented by the assumed confidence interval of 99.9%.

Excess spread Excess spread is a form of structural credit enhancement. It generally represents the difference between revenues generated by securitized assets—usually, interest cash flows—and transaction expenses, such as interest payable to noteholders, servicing and operating fees, and losses on the underlying assets.

Expected maturity Expected maturities are typically between 12 and 18 months earlier than the final maturity (also known as legal maturity) of issued securities. At this date, issued securities are expected to have been repaid in full based on the original base case for the transaction and taking deal-specific assumptions into account, for instance, on the repayment speed and cash flow generation capabilities of the underlying notes.

FICO score A credit scoring system that is used in the U.S.

First-loss piece Also known as first-loss tranche, equity piece, or equity tranche. This typically describes the tranche in either a structured finance transaction or a synthetic note structure that absorbs losses incurred by the underlying collateral (e.g., mortgage losses of the underlying loan pool) or of the reference portfolio or index (e.g., caused by defaults of one or more referenced entities in an underlying credit default swap).

Flagging state This indicates how mortgages in an originator's booking system have been earmarked or identified. For instance, if a particular mortgage or, more generically, an asset has been securitized it no longer legally belongs to the originator and may carry a so-called hard flag in the system. This identifies the mortgage as belonging to a mortgage trust managed by a special purpose vehicle (SPV).

Floating rate notes FRNs are securities that carry an interest rate that is not fixed but, typically, has a margin above a market index (e.g., LIBOR + 23 basis points).

Fonds commun de créance An FCC is a funding vehicle typically used in France, usually in the form of a closed end mutual debt fund.

Foreclosure Foreclosure is a legal term which means that a lender is taking legal action against a real estate property owner who has pledged the property as collateral for the mortgage or loan. In doing so, the lender seeks the right to dispose of the property and use the resulting forced sale proceeds to satisfy the borrower's outstanding payments (principal, interest, fees, and other penalties).

Gearing A term that originated from the accounting space and is often used to describe the ratio of debt to equity for a given company.

Guaranteed investment contract A GIC is a financial contract involving a deposit account that guarantees a minimum rate of return. It is typically used to mitigate interest rate risk for a structured finance transaction.

HELOC Home equity lines of credit are loans for which the collateral provided to lenders is the borrower's equity in the property.

Hybrid ARM Also known as a hybrid adjustable rate, this occurs when the interest rate on a mortgage loan is fixed for a certain period and then changes to a variable or floating interest rate.

ICR The interest coverage ratio is a financial ratio used to determine an entity's ability to service its interest payments on its outstanding debt.

IRG Issuer report grades were introduced by Fitch Ratings in 4Q04. They are used by the rating agency to evaluate the quality of issuer's investor reports.

Legal final maturity Sometimes referred to as legal final, this is the date of a transaction when all principal balances of the securities must be repaid. As opposed to expected maturity, legal final maturity is solely driven by the transaction's legal documentation.

Loss given default LGD is the amount of losses a bank expects to incur on each defaulted asset.

Loss severity The actual level of loss suffered on a defaulted asset and after taking collateral (i.e., potential recovery of some of your funds) into account. It is usually expressed as a proportion or percentage of the original loan amount.

Mark-to-market Marking-to-market an asset or bond instrument states its value at today's market price.

MiFID The Markets in Financial Instruments Directive is a European Union law that provides harmonized regulation for investment services across the European Economic Area. Its main objectives are to increase competition and consumer protection in investment services. It came into force on November 1, 2007 and replaced the Investment Services Directive.

Monte Carlo simulation This is a statistical method approach—named for the famous race track—which performs a very large number of so-called model iteration or paths (usually a minimum number of 10,000 simulation runs, an optimum number of 250,000, or in some cases even more) using values from given distributions for variables that are not certain. After completion of all such simulation runs, the results' distribution can be used to see whether, for instance, the likelihood of default is in line with certain expectations such as an expected credit rating, etc.

Negative carry Negative carry occurs when assets repay or mature but the proceeds of these repayments have not yet been reinvested. As a consequence, the portfolio may not yield lower than originally expected and, in doing so, is creating a shortfall of cash compared with the liabilities which continue to repay.

Priority of payments See *Waterfall.*

Principal deficiency ledger PDL is simply an accounting or booking method to record losses experienced in the securitized pool in one principal and interest distribution cycle and carry them over to the next distribution cycle if they cannot be covered sufficiently in the first cash flow distribution cycle.

Probability of default Probability of default is the likelihood of a borrower defaulting over a specified time horizon.

Provisional pool Provisional pool activities are focused on assembling a pool of assets to the required standard and quality to execute and issue the transaction.

Re-REMIC Resecuritisation of a real estate mortgage investment conduit. Generally speaking, this is an investment-grade bond that separates mortgage pools into different maturity profiles and risk classes. Technically, it is really a new form of CDO or collateralized debt obligation that surfaced after the credit crisis and has been used to access the various government repo facilities.

Retention mechanism This is a structural feature of a transaction (e.g., a reserve account) that enables the structure to trap cash. Alternatively, in the sense of treatment of securitization under Basel II/III, it can refer to different ways to ensure that the originator retains an economic interest (also referred to as "skin in the game") in the transaction.

Secondary market New securities are usually traded in a primary market. The secondary market, on the contrary, is a market in which already existing securities are retraded.

Split rating A transaction that is rated by more than one external credit rating agency—say, rated Aa1 by Moody's, BBB by Standard & Poor's, and AA− by Fitch—is said to have split ratings (i.e., the agencies' opinion of the credit quality of this instruments differs). One way of overcoming the issues that can arise from having differing rating opinions is to assign internal ratings which can then be used instead of three different external ratings.

Waterfall Also known as priority of payments, this is the order in which notes are repaid. There are two types of waterfalls: the principal payment waterfall and the interest rate payment waterfall.

Appendix B
Ratings

B.1 FITCH RATINGS

B.1.1 Asset class generic

Rating Criteria for Repackaged Senior Structured Finance Notes (Cross-Sector Criteria Report)	07/10/2009	Global
Rating Criteria for Repackaged Senior Structured Finance Notes (Cross-Sector Criteria Report)	07/10/2009	Global
Rating Criteria for Repackaged Senior Structured Finance Notes (Cross-Sector Criteria Report)	07/10/2009	Global
Colombian RMBS Rating Criteria	01/10/2009	South America
Critério de Calificación para RMBS en Colombia	01/10/2009	South America
Criteria for Model Management	30/09/2009	Global
Global Rating Criteria for Structured Finance Servicers	30/09/2009	Global
Global Structured Finance Rating Criteria	30/09/2009	Global
Guidelines for Developing and Revising Criteria	30/09/2009	Global
Criteria for Model Management	30/09/2009	Global
Global Rating Criteria for Structured Finance Servicers	30/09/2009	Global
Guidelines for Developing and Revising Criteria	30/09/2009	Global
Global Structured Finance Rating Criteria	30/09/2009	Global
Global Rating Criteria for Structured Finance Servicers	30/09/2009	Global
Criteria for Model Management	30/09/2009	Global
Guidelines for Developing and Revising Criteria	30/09/2009	Global
Criteria for Model Management	30/09/2009	Global
Guidelines for Developing and Revising Criteria	30/09/2009	Global
EURIBOR Stresses	17/09/2009	Global
GBP LIBOR Stresses	17/09/2009	Global
Special-Purpose Vehicles in Structured Finance Transactions	17/09/2009	Global
Rating Criteria for Japanese Servicers	04/09/2009	Asia
Criteria for Structured Finance Recovery Ratings	17/08/2009	Global
USD LIBOR Stresses	31/07/2009	Global
Criteria for Partial-Credit Guarantees in Emerging Markets	30/07/2009	EMEA
USD MTA Stresses	30/06/2009	Global
Coercive Debt Exchange Criteria for Structured Finance	03/06/2009	Global
Exposure Draft: Counterparty Risk in Structured Finance Transactions	30/03/2009	Global
Exposure Draft: Counterparty Risk in Structured Finance Transactions	30/03/2009	Counterparty
Coercive Debt Exchange Criteria	03/03/2009	Global
Revisions to Rating Definitions—March 2009	03/03/2009	Global
Coercive Debt Exchange Criteria	03/03/2009	Global
Criteria for Structured Finance Loss Severity Ratings	17/02/2009	Global
Dutch Loss Severity Ratings	17/02/2009	Global
Mexican Low-Income Housing Construction Bridge Loan Securitization Rating Criteria	20/01/2009	South America
Global Rating Criteria for Structured Finance CDOs	16/12/2008	Global
Proposed Fully Updated Approach for Structured Finance CDOs and Placed Transactions under Analysis	14/10/2008	Global
Life Insurance Reserve Financing (Ratings Criteria)	08/07/2008	Global
Thai Servicers Rating Criteria (Thailand RMBS/CMBS/ABS)	27/06/2008	Asia
Catastrophe Bonds (Ratings Criteria)	11/03/2008	Global
Insurance—Linked Securities: Ratings Criteria (Global)	04/02/2008	Global
Criteria for Rating Currency Swap Obligations of an SPV in Structured Finance Transactions	10/01/2008	Global
Criteria for the Application of Recovery Rates to Future Flow Transactions	26/10/2007	Global

Future Flow Securitization Rating Criteria	26/10/2007	Global
Relatório de Metodología: Critério de Avaliação para RMBS no Brasil	24/10/2007	South America
Counterparty Risk in Structured Finance: Qualified Investment Criteria	27/09/2007	Global
Counterparty Risk in Structured Finance: Qualified Investment Criteria	27/09/2007	Counterparty
Thai Servicers Rating Criteria	02/08/2007	Asia
Counterparty Risk in Structured Finance Transactions: Hedge Criteria	01/08/2007	Global
Counterparty Risk in Structured Finance Transactions: Hedge Criteria	01/08/2007	Counterparty
Revised MVD Assumptions for Italian RMBS (Italy RMBS)	20/04/2007	EMEA
Australian RMBS Presale Model Notes	01/11/2006	Aus/Nwz
Interest Rate Risk in Structured Finance Transactions—Euribor	01/11/2006	Global
Rating Australian and New Zealand Sellers, Servicers, and Trust Managers	20/04/2006	Global
Taking Stock of German Multifamily Housing—Criteria and Rationale of Analysis	28/03/2006	EMEA
Rating Japanese Structured Finance Trustees	13/01/2006	Asia
Commingling Risk in Structured Finance Transactions	09/06/2004	Global

B.1.2 Counterparty related

Rating Criteria for Japanese Servicers	04/09/2009	Asia
Criteria to Analyze Legal Uncertainty in Emerging Market Securitizations—Amended (ABS/RMBS)	10/07/2009	EMEA
European Residential Mortgage Originator Review Criteria (Europe RMBS)	09/07/2009	EMEA
U.S. Commercial Mortgage Servicer Rating Criteria	19/06/2009	U.S.
U.S. Commercial Mortgage Originator Review Criteria	24/04/2009	U.S.
U.S. Residential Mortgage Originator Review Criteria	02/12/2008	U.S.
U.S. Residential Mortgage Third-Party Loan-Level Review Criteria	02/12/2008	U.S.
Rating Criteria for European Mortgage Loan Servicers—The Netherlands Market Addendum (Netherlands ESF)	14/02/2008	EMEA
Rating Criteria for European Mortgage Loan Servicers—U.K. Market Addendum (U.K. European Structured Finance)	28/01/2008	EMEA
Rating Criteria for European Mortgage Loan Servicers—German Market Addendum (Germany European Structured Finance)	14/12/2007	EMEA
Rating Criteria for European Mortgage Loan Servicers—Italian Market Addendum (Italy European Structured Finance)	01/11/2007	EMEA
Rating Criteria for European Mortgage Loan Servicers—Italian Market Addendum (Italy European Structured Finance)	01/11/2007	EMEA
Rating Criteria for European Mortgage Loan Servicers—Spanish Market Addendum (Spain European Structured Finance)	25/09/2007	EMEA
Rating Criteria for European Mortgage Loan Servicers—Russian Market Addendum (Russia European Structured Finance)	07/09/2007	EMEA
Thai Servicers Rating Criteria	02/08/2007	Asia
Criteria for Rating U.S. ABS Seller/Servicers	01/08/2007	U.S.
Criteria for Rating U.S. Auto Loan ABS Seller/Servicers	01/08/2007	U.S.
Criteria for Rating U.S. Credit Card ABS Seller/Servicers	01/08/2007	U.S.
Criteria for Rating U.S. Student Loan Seller/Servicers	01/08/2007	U.S.
Rating Japanese Servicers (Japan RMBS/CMBS/Unsecured Consumer Loans)	11/07/2007	Asia
Rating U.S. Small Balance Commercial Mortgage Servicers	09/07/2007	U.S.
Rating Australian and New Zealand Construction Loan Servicers	26/04/2007	AUS/NWZ
Rating U.S. Residential Mortgage Servicers	29/11/2006	Asia
Rating Australian and New Zealand Sellers, Servicers and Trust Managers	20/04/2006	AUS/NWZ
Rating Japanese Structured Finance Trustees	13/01/2006	

B.1.3 Asset-backed securitization

EMEA Consumer ABS Rating Criteria	01/09/2009	EMEA
U.S. Private Student Loan ABS Criteria	24/08/2009	U.S.
Rating Criteria for Indian Asset-Backed Securitizations (India ABS)	14/07/2009	Asia
Proposed Fully Updated Approach for Structured Finance CDOs; Placed Transactions Under Analysis	14/10/2008	Global
Criteria for Assessing Tax Risk in German Structured Finance Transactions	25/07/2008	EMEA
Criteria for Rating Transaction-Specific Support Facilities Provided to ABCP Conduits	10/07/2008	Global
Rating U.S. Equipment Lease and Loan Securitizations	16/06/2008	U.S.
Rating Criteria for U.S. Dealer Floorplan ABS	14/05/2008	U.S.

Rating Criteria for U.S. Timeshare Loans	02/05/2008	U.S.
Rating U.S. Federal Family Education Loan Program Student Loan ABS Criteria	11/04/2008	U.S.
Rating Criteria for U.S. Auto Lease-Backed Securitizations	12/03/2008	U.S.
U.S. Credit Card ABS Rating Criteria	10/03/2008	U.S.
European Auto Dealer Floorplan ABS Criteria	06/02/2008	EMEA
Global Rating Criteria for Trade Receivables Securitizations	28/01/2008	Global
Residual Values in European Auto ABS—Securitizing Market Risk	11/04/2006	EMEA

B.1.4 Collateralized debt obligations and related products

Rating Criteria for Repackaged Senior Structured Finance Notes (Cross-Sector Criteria Report)	07/10/2009	Global
Reviewing and Rating Credit Asset Managers	27/07/2009	Global
European SME CLOs Data Template (Europe CDOs) (Excel file)	23/07/2009	EMEA
Rating Criteria for European Granular Corporate Balance-Sheet Securitizations (SME CLOs) (Europe CDOs)	23/07/2009	EMEA
Global Rating Criteria for Single- and Multi-Name Credit-Linked Notes	13/04/2009	Global
Global Rating Criteria for Synthetic CDOs	09/03/2009	Global
Global Rating Criteria for Collateralized Debt Obligations with Emerging Market Exposure	02/03/2009	Global
Global Rating Criteria for Structured Finance CDOs	16/12/2008	Global
Global Rating Criteria for Project Finance Collateralized Debt Obligations	18/08/2008	Global
Global Criteria for Cash Flow Analysis in Corporate CDOs	30/04/2008	Global
Global Rating Criteria for Corporate CDOs	30/04/2008	Global
Rating Market Value Structures	18/04/2008	Global
Rating Methodology for U.S. Revolving Commercial Real Estate Loan CDOs	20/12/2007	U.S.
Rating Criteria for U.S. Bank and Insurance Trust Preferred CDOs	02/02/2005	U.S.

B.1.5 Commercial mortgage-backed securitization and real estate investment trusts

Global Structured Finance Rating Criteria	30/09/2009	Global
Criteria for Japanese CMBS Surveillance	02/09/2009	Asia
Surveillance Methodology for Recent Vintage U.S. CMBS	07/07/2009	U.S.
U.S. CMBS Criteria for Reviewing Post-Closing Actions	24/04/2009	U.S.
Coercive Debt Exchange Criteria	03/03/2009	Global
Revisions to Rating Definitions—March 2009	03/03/2009	Global
Criteria for European CMBS Surveillance (Europe CMBS)	12/11/2008	EMEA
Proposed Fully Updated Approach for Structured Finance CDOs and Placed Transactions under Analysis	14/10/2008	Global
U.S. CMBS Surveillance Criteria	07/10/2008	EMEA
Criteria for Assessing Tax Risk in German Structured Finance Transactions	25/07/2008	EMEA
Thai Servicers Rating Criteria (Thailand RMBS/CMBS/ABS)	27/06/2008	Asia
U.S. CMBS Loan Default Study: 1993–2007	09/06/2008	Global
U.S. PMM Scores: Measuring Property Type and Market Volatility	07/05/2008	U.S.
Rating Criteria for Fitch's U.S. CMBS Multiborrower Rating Model	04/01/2008	U.S.
Securitization of European Non-Performing Loans Criteria (Europe NPL)	22/10/2007	EMEA
Criteria for European CMBS Asset Analysis (Europe CMBS)	12/09/2007	EMEA
Criteria Regarding the Application of the Refinancing Register in German CMBS and RMBS Transactions (Germany RMBS/CMBS)	28/08/2007	EMEA
Rating Criteria for Japanese Real Estate Investment Trusts (Japan ABS)	18/06/2007	Asia
SMARTView (Fitch U.S. Structured Finance Monthly Public Reviews)	03/05/2007	U.S.
Taking Stock of German Multifamily Housing—Criteria and Rationale of Analysis	28/03/2006	EMEA
Rating Japanese Structured Finance Trustees	13/01/2006	Asia

B.1.6 Residential mortgage-backed securitization

SART—Foreclosure Detail Template	10/09/2009	U.S.
SART—Monthly Recovery Sources Template	10/09/2009	U.S.
SART—Pledged Deals Summary Template	10/09/2009	U.S.
SART—Recovery Rates Template	10/09/2009	U.S.
U.S. Residential Mortgage Servicer Advance Receivables Securitization Rating Criteria	10/09/2009	U.S.
National Risk Index, State- and MSA-level Risk Multipliers in ResiLogic	01/09/2009	U.S.

U.S. RMBS Cash Flow Analysis Criteria	20/08/2009	U.S.
U.S. RMBS Cash Flow Assumptions Workbook	20/08/2009	U.S.
U.S. Residential Mortgage Re-REMIC Criteria	20/08/2009	U.S.
ResiLogic: U.S. Residential Mortgage Loss Model Criteria—Amended	11/08/2009	U.S.
Revised Market Value Decline Assumptions for German Residential Mortgage-Backed Transactions (Germany RMBS)	09/06/2009	U.S.
EMEA RMBS Cash Flow Analysis Criteria	06/05/2009	EMEA
EMEA RMBS Surveillance Criteria	09/04/2009	EMEA
U.S. Prime RMBS Surveillance Criteria	30/03/2009	U.S.
Dutch Residential Mortgage Default Model Criteria (Netherlands RMBS)	02/02/2009	EMEA
U.S. RMBS Alt-A Surveillance Criteria	15/12/2008	U.S.
U.S. Residential Mortgage Loan Representations and Warranties Criteria	02/12/2008	U.S.
Addendum—Criteria for Automated Valuation Models in EMEA RMBS	20/11/2008	EMEA
Criteria for Automated Valuation Models in EMEA RMBS	20/11/2008	EMEA
Updated Surveillance Criteria for U.S. Subprime RMBS	19/11/2008	U.S.
Criteria for Rating Residential Mortgage Securitizations in Emerging Markets—EMEA	30/09/2008	EMEA
Criteria for Assessing Tax Risk in German Structured Finance Transactions	25/07/2008	EMEA
Australian Residential Mortgage Default Criteria	03/04/2008	AU.S.
UK Residential Mortgage Default Criteria	08/02/2008	EMEA
Spanish Residential Mortgage Default Model Criteria (Spain RMBS)	21/12/2007	EMEA
Brazilian RMBS Rating Criteria	08/11/2007	South America
Mexican RMBS Rating Criteria	26/10/2007	South America
Criteria Regarding the Application of the Refinancing Register in German CMBS and RMBS Transactions (Germany RMBS/CMBS)	28/08/2007	EMEA
Rating U.S. Small Balance Commercial Mortgage Servicers	09/07/2007	U.S.
Revised MVD Assumptions for Italian RMBS (Italy RMBS)	20/04/2007	EMEA
Revised MVD Assumptions for French RMBS Transactions (France RMBS)	28/03/2007	EMEA
Rating Guidelines for Financial Guarantors	09/01/2007	General
Revised MVD Assumptions for Belgian RMBS Transactions (Belgium RMBS)	08/01/2007	EMEA
Greek RMBS Rating Criteria (Greece RMBS)	13/12/2006	EMEA
Revised MVD Assumptions for U.K. RMBS Transactions (U.K. RMBS)	09/08/2006	EMEA
Criteria for NHG Guarantee Mortgage Loans in Dutch RMBS	08/06/2006	EMEA
European Criteria for Mortgage Insurance in RMBS Transactions	18/04/2006	EMEA
Irish Residential Mortgage Default Model 2006	07/03/2006	EMEA
Portuguese Residential Mortgage Default Model	16/12/2005	EMEA
Italian Residential Mortgage Default Model II—Amended	02/11/2005	EMEA
Repay My Mortgage? Over My Dead Body!—Fitch's Reverse Mortgage Criteria	19/09/2005	EMEA
Belgian Residential Mortgage Default Model 2005 (Belgium RMBS)	10/05/2005	EMEA
German Residential Mortgage Default Model 2004	01/12/2004	EMEA

B.2 MOODY'S

B.2.1 Asset class generic

Evaluating Distressed Exchanges	24/03/2009	Global
Incorporation of Joint-Default Analysis into Bank Ratings: A Refined Methodology	30/03/2007	Global
Updated Servicer Quality Rating Scale and Definitions	10/05/2005	Global
The Application of Joint Default Analysis to Government Related Issuers	27/04/2005	Global
Guidelines for the Withdrawal of Ratings	21/01/2004	Global
Analytical Implications of Employee Stock-Based Compensation	30/12/2002	Global
Two Party Pay Approach—Structure and Mechanics	30/04/2002	Global
Another Perspective on Risk Transference and Securitization	23/09/1999	Global
Assessing the Strength of a Liquidity Facility	16/06/1999	Global
Weighing the Added Credit Risks of Credit-Linked Securities: Update on Rating Approach	15/01/1996	Global

B.2.2 Counterparty related

Financial Guaranty Policies—What Is Needed for Credit Substitutions	02/03/2009	Global
Rating Methodology for the Financial Guaranty Insurance Industry	25/09/2006	Global
Portfolio Risk Model for Financial Guarantors	01/07/2000	Global

B.2.3 Miscellaneous other criteria

The Temporary Use of Cash in Structured Transactions: Eligible Investment Guidelines	09/12/2009	Global
Rating Methodology for Rating Debt Issuances of Certified Capital Companies	20/08/2009	Global
Mitigating Voluntary Bankruptcy Risk of U.S.-Domiciled Termination Derivative Product Companies and Assessing the Effectiveness of Continuation Derivative Product Companies	16/07/2009	U.S.
V Scores and Parameter Sensitivities in the Global Cash Flow CLO Sector 1	06/07/2009	Global
V Scores in the Global Corporate Super-Senior CDPC Sector	06/07/2009	Global
V Scores and Parameter Sensitivities in the Latin American Cross-Border Future Flows Sector	11/05/2009	Global
Rating Diversified Payment Rights Securitizations	17/03/2009	Global
Revising Default/Loss Assumptions over the Life of an ABS/RMBS Transaction	18/12/2008	EMEA
Updated: V Scores and Parameter Sensitivities for Structured Finance Securities	03/12/2008	Global
Assigning Structured Finance Common Representative Quality Ratings	12/12/2007	Global
Framework for De-Linking Hedge Counterparty Risks from Global Structured Finance Cashflow Transactions Methodology	10/05/2007	Global
Rating Japanese Whole Business Securitizations	16/04/2007	Asia
Rating Hedge Fund Gap Risk Products	16/11/2006	Global
Securitization in New Markets: Perspective	05/09/2006	EMEA
Re-examined Trustees' Role in ABS and RMBS	04/02/2003	U.S.
Rating Institutional-to-Retail Repackagings: An Application of Structured Notes Methodology	28/05/2002	Global
Rating *i*th-to-Default Basket Credit-Linked Notes	17/04/2002	Global
Repackaged Securities	28/09/2001	Global
Understanding the Risks in Credit Default Swaps	14/03/2001	Global
Rating Contingent Perfection Structures	17/04/1998	Asia
Rating Structured Notes—Refined	03/07/1997	Global
Evaluating Derivative Products Subsidiaries	15/10/1993	Global
Servicer Quality National Scale Ratings and Updated EMEA Servicer Quality Rating Scores	25/03/2008	EMEA
National Scale Ratings in South Africa	26/11/2007	EMEA
Mapping National Scale Ratings to Global Scale Ratings	20/09/2007	Global
National Scale Ratings in Kazakhstan	28/02/2007	Asia
The U.S. Municipal Bond Rating Scale: Mapping to the Global Rating Scale and Assigning Global Scale Ratings to Municipal Obligations	28/02/2007	Americas
National Scale Ratings in Indonesia	12/02/2007	Asia
National Scale Ratings in Ukraine	22/05/2006	EMEA
National Scale Ratings In Russia	12/07/2005	EMEA
National Scale Ratings	24/05/2004	Global
National Scale Ratings in Taiwan	16/10/2003	Asia

B.2.4 Asset-backed commercial paper related

Eligible Liquidity in Securities Arbitrage Programs	09/01/2006	Global
Analyzing Mortgage Warehouse Financing in EMEA ABCP Conduits	17/10/2005	EMEA
Analyzing Mortgage Warehouse Financing in ABCP Conduits	04/02/2005	Global
Floating-Rate ABCP: Covering the Risks	17/03/2003	Global
The Fundamentals of Asset-Backed Commercial Paper	03/02/2003	Global
Pros, Cons, and Considerations in Introducing an ABCP Conduit	09/10/2002	Global
Evaluating Credit Arbitrage ABCP Programs	22/08/2002	Global
Comparing and Contrasting Credit Arbitrage ABCP Programs and Structured Investment Vehicles	25/01/2002	Global
Floating Rate ABCP: Issues and Answers	10/12/1999	Global
Rating Commercial Paper Programs Backed by Maturity-Matched Loans	07/09/1999	Global
Jointly Supported Prime-1 Liquidity Facilities	18/08/1999	Global
On Being a Prudent Investor: Understanding the Nuts and Bolts of Australian ABCP Structures	04/08/1998	Global
Serialized ABCP: the Hidden Dangers	20/04/1998	Global
Jointly Supported Obligations	13/01/1998	Global
Achieving Post Review Status for Partially Supported ABCP Programs	09/10/1997	Global
Asset-Backed CP: Overview of Structures and Focus on Japan	04/12/1996	Global

Samurai Asset-Backed Commercial Paper: Rating Analysis	03/07/1996	Global
Importance of Liquidity Support in Asset-Backed Commercial Paper (The)	18/03/1994	Global

B.2.5 Asset-backed securitization

Trustee Quality Ratings for Latin America	07/08/2009	U.S.
Cash Flow Analysis of Synthetic ABS/RMBS Transations	07/08/2009	Global
Rating Australian Asset-Backed Securities	30/07/2009	Australia
Data Requirements for Australian ABS	30/07/2009	Australia
V Scores and Parameter Sensitivities in the Brazilian Consigned Loan ABS Sector	06/07/2009	Americas
Moody's Rating Obligations Backed by Future International Credit and Debit Card Merchant Voucher Receivables	30/06/2009	Global
Moody's Rating Transactions Backed by Guaranteed SME Loans in Argentina	26/06/2009	Americas
V Scores and Parameter Sensitivities in the EMEA Small-to-Medium Enterprise ABS Sector	15/06/2009	EMEA
Updated Cash Flow Analysis for Variable Rate Transactions Backed by Federal Family Education Loan Program (FFELP) Student Loans: Call for Comments	21/05/2009	U.S.
V Scores and Parameter Sensitivities in the Global Consumer Loan ABS Sector	14/05/2009	Global
Methodology Update on Interest Rate Assumptions in Student Loan-Backed Securitizations	31/03/2009	U.S.
Refining the ABS SME Approach: Moody's Probability of Default assumptions in the rating analysis of granular Small and Mid-sized Enterprise portfolios in EMEA	17/03/2009	EMEA
Rating Diversified Payment Rights Securitizations	17/03/2009	Global
V Scores and Parameter Sensitivities in the U.S. Student Loan ABS Sector	05/02/2009	U.S.
V Scores and Parameter Sensitivities in the U.S. Equipment Lease and Loan ABS Sector	22/01/2009	Americas
V Scores and Parameter Sensitivities in the non-U.S. Vehicle ABS Sector	20/01/2009	EMEA
V Scores and Parameter Sensitivities in the Global Credit Card ABS Sector	19/12/2008	Global
V Scores and Parameter Sensitivities in the U.S. Vehicle ABS Sector	16/12/2008	U.S.
Adjusting for the Seasoning of Pools in Projecting Auto Loan Losses	05/12/2008	U.S.
Methodology Update on Basis Risk in FFELP Student Loan-Backed Securitizations	19/11/2008	U.S.
Rating Mexican States' Securitizations Backed by Future Flows of Own-Source Revenues	18/09/2008	Americas
Updated: Transactions Backed by Real Estate Collateralized SME Loans in Japan: Focal Points in Rating Analysis	23/07/2008	Asia
NPL Securitization and Moody's Rating Methodology—Italian Technology for Export	18/02/2008	EMEA
The Role of Trustees in Japanese ABS Transactions Part III; Rating Implications under Japan's new Trust Law	18/12/2007	Asia
Japanese Consumer Finance Loan ABS: Expansion of Overpaid Interest Risk	21/11/2007	Asia
Rating U.S. Auto Loan-Backed Securities	29/06/2007	U.S.
Rating Securitizations of Lease Receivables in Japan	22/05/2007	Asia
U.S. Auto-Backed Securities: Using Stratified Data to Improve the Precision of Loss Analysis in Auto Loan Securitizations (Mix-Neutral Analysis)	08/05/2007	U.S.
Rating Credit Card Receivables-Backed Securities	16/04/2007	Global
Rating Securities Backed by Equipment Leases and Loans	02/04/2007	U.S.
Information on EMEA SME Securitizations Moody's view on granular SME loan receivable transactions and information guidelines	12/03/2007	EMEA
Monitoring ABS Ratings in Japan Volume 4: Revolving Diversified Pool ABS Backed by Card Receivables	15/12/2006	Asia
Backup Servicing in Consumer Finance Loan ABS in Japan	15/12/2006	Asia
Revised Cash Flow Assumptions for FFELP Student Loan-Backed Transactions	30/11/2006	Global
Cash Commingling Risk in EMEA ABS and RMBS Transactions: Moody's Approach	07/11/2006	EMEA
The Role of Trustees in Japanese ABS Transactions Part II; Controlling Measures of Mandatory Termination Risk	16/10/2006	Asia
Monitoring ABS Ratings in Japan, Volume 3: Revolving Diversified Pool ABS Backed by Auto Loans and Installment Sales Loans	15/08/2006	Asia
Multi-Pool Financial Lease-Backed Transactions in Italy	12/06/2006	EMEA
The Role of Trustees in Japanese ABS Transactions Part I	25/05/2006	Asia
Securitization of Non-performing Tax Receivables in Europe: Bridging the Gap between Structuring and Modeling	19/04/2006	EMEA
Historical Default Data Analysis for ABS Transactions in EMEA	29/11/2005	EMEA
Consumer Finance Loan ABS in Japan (Series 2: An Overview of the Attributes and Points of Analysis)	28/11/2005	Asia
Monitoring ABS Ratings in Japan, Volumes 1 and 2: Static Diversified Pool ABS Backed by Auto Loans and Installment Sales Loans	21/11/2005	Asia
Analyzing Default Rates and Principal Payment Rates of Japan's Credit Card Receivables	02/11/2005	Asia
Rating Obligations Backed by Future Export Receivables	24/10/2005	Global

Rating Wireless Towers-Backed Securitizations: A Path to Clear Reception in the ABS Market	19/09/2005	U.S.
Credit Enhancement for Commingling Risk in Japanese ABS: Updated Methodology	04/08/2005	Asia
View on Servicer Replacement Clause in Japanese ABS Transactions Part II	27/07/2005	Asia
View on Servicer Replacement Clause in Japanese ABS Transactions Part I	19/07/2005	Asia
Rating Securitizations Backed by Medical Service Fee Receivables in Japan	01/07/2005	Asia
Unsecured Non-Performing Loan Pool Modeling: An Update on Moody's Approach	14/04/2005	Global
Asset-Backed Servicer Quality ("SQ") Ratings in EMEA: Methodology	12/04/2005	EMEA
Addressing Risks Specific to Institution-to-Retail Trust Certificates	13/01/2005	U.S.
Understanding Metrics for Performance Monitoring, Volume 1: Credit Card-Backed Securities	01/12/2004	U.S.
Evaluating Unrated and Non-Investment-Grade Originators in EMEA ABS Transactions	24/11/2004	EMEA
Credit Card Servicer Quality Rating Methodology	29/06/2004	U.S.
Rating Securitization of Auto Lease Receivables with Maintenance Clauses in Japan	01/03/2004	Asia
Importance of Auditing Procedures for Monetary Receivables Securitizations in Japan	21/08/2003	Asia
The Fourier Transform Method: A New Method to Compute Portfolio Default and Loss Distributions	31/03/2003	Global
The Fourier Transform Method—Overview	15/01/2003	Global
Moody's Rating European Auto ABS: More Rubber Set to Hit European Roads	19/11/2002	EMEA
Monitoring Italian Non-Performing Loan Transactions	18/11/2002	EMEA
Rating Trade Receivables Backed Transactions	08/07/2002	Global
Debut of Inventory Securitization in Europe: Rating Approach	21/05/2002	EMEA
Rating Operating Company Securitizations	08/02/2002	U.S.
Consumer Finance ABS: Approach with a Focus on the Italian Market	08/01/2002	EMEA
Credit Enhancement Analysis in Japanese Auto Loan-Backed Securitization	07/12/2001	Asia
Rating Tobacco Settlement Revenues Securitizations	04/05/2001	U.S.
Franchise Loan ABS: An Adaptive Methodology for an Evolving Asset Class	25/08/2000	U.S.
The Lognormal Method Applied to ABS Analysis	20/07/2000	Global
Rating Obligations Backed by International Credit and Debit Card Receivables	11/02/2000	U.S.
Rating Music Royalty and Intellectual Property-Backed Transactions: There's No Business Like Show Business	01/07/1999	U.S.
Rating Obligations Backed by International Airline Ticket Receivables: The Sky's the Limit	09/04/1999	U.S.
Pooled Aircraft-Backed Securitization	12/03/1999	U.S.
Rating Mezzanine Securities in Structured Finance Transactions: The Impact of an Expected Value Approach	22/02/1999	Global
Rating Obligation Backed by International Telephone Settlement Payments	14/01/1999	U.S.
Auto Lease Securitization: Rating Approach	13/11/1998	Global
Bankruptcy Risk Analysis in Student Loan-Backed Securities Structures: Approach	28/09/1998	Global
Rating Agricultural and Construction Equipment Securitizations: The Securitization Market "Sprouts"	07/08/1998	U.S.
Rating Mutual Fund Fee Securitizations	24/04/1998	U.S.
Rating Structured Settlement Transactions	02/02/1998	U.S.
Trade Receivables Update: Concentrating on Dilution—Focus on Capital Goods and Consumer Products Receivables	18/02/1997	Global
Rating SBA Loan-Backed Securitizations	29/03/1996	U.S.
Credit Card Master Trusts: Assessing the Risks of Cash Flow Allocations	30/05/1995	Global
Retailers Learn Their ABCs: Addressing the Risk of Dilution With a Subordinate Tranche	30/05/1995	Global
Credit Card Master Trusts: The Risks of Account Additions	16/12/1994	Global
The Rating of Catastrophe-Linked Notes	19/09/1997	Global

B.2.6 Collateralized debt obligations and related products

Rating Collateralized Loan Obligations	12/08/2009	Global
Modified its Modeling Assumptions for Market-Value Collateralized Loan Obligations	09/07/2009	Global
V Scores and Parameter Sensitivities in the Global Cash Flow Structured Finance CDO Sector	30/04/2009	Global
V Scores and Parameter Sensitivities in the Global Corporate Synthetic CDO Sector	29/04/2009	Global
Corporate Asset Correlations Update: A Summary of Changes and Their Rationale	24/04/2009	Global
Updated: Rating Corporate Collateralized Synthetic Obligations	20/03/2009	Global
Rating SF CDOs	02/03/2009	Global
A Description of Tools for Monitoring Leveraged Super Senior Transactions	20/08/2008	Global
A description of Tools for Monitoring CPDO Transactions	23/07/2008	Global
CDO Rating Factors Analyzing Interest Rate Asset Specific Hedges	31/03/2008	Global

Collateral Manager Incentives, CDS Trading, and Value Extraction in Synthetic CDOs	21/11/2007	Global
Japan's SME CDOs: Focal Points in Rating Analysis and Monitoring	08/11/2007	Asia
Rating Granular SME Transactions in Europe, Middle East, and Africa	08/06/2007	EMEA
Revised Its Methodology for Emerging Market CDOs	11/04/2007	South America
Adapting U.S. Cash-Flow CLO Rating Methodology to PDR/LGD Initiative	16/02/2007	U.S.
Modeling "Exotic" Synthetic CDOs with CDOROM™	01/02/2007	EMEA
Rating the CDOs of SMEs in Europe	01/02/2007	EMEA
Rating Collateralized Debt Obligations with Pay-As-You-Go Credit Default Swaps	13/11/2006	Global
CDO Rating Factors Including TRUPS CDO Tranches in ABS CDOs	15/06/2006	Global
CDO Rating Factors Vol. III, No. 2 UPDATE: Post-Reinvestment Period Reinvesting in Actively-Managed CDOs	20/04/2006	Global
Rating U.S. REIT CDOs	04/04/2006	U.S.
CDO Rating Factors Vol. III, No. 1 Pro Rata Amortization in Synthetic Resecuritizations	22/03/2006	Global
Credit Derivative Product Companies	03/03/2006	Global
Rating Taiwanese CDO Transactions	15/02/2006	Asia
CDO Rating Factors Vol. II, No. 5 Implementing Par Haircuts in Structured Finance CDOs	25/01/2006	Global
Periodic Reports for Rated Credit Derivative Product Companies	21/12/2005	Global
CDO Rating Factors Vol. II, No. 4 Assigning Market Value to CDO Assets	14/12/2005	Global
Rating U.S. Middle Market CLOs: Part II	01/12/2005	U.S.
Modeling Rating Structured Finance Cash Flow CDO Transactions	26/09/2005	Global
Moody's Rating Multi-Currency CDOs	15/09/2005	Global
Revisited its Assumptions Regarding Structured Finance Default (and Asset) Correlations for CDOs	27/06/2005	Global
Initial Views On the Dealer Form of Confirmation for Pay-As-You-Go Credit Derivative Transactions	21/06/2005	Global
Rating Methodology: A Framework for Understanding Structured Financial Operating Companies	14/04/2005	Global
CDO Rating Factors Vol. II, No. 3 Notching Watchlisted Structured Finance Securities in CDOs	10/03/2005	Global
Collateralized Debt Obligations: A Primer	07/03/2005	Global
CDO Rating Factors Vol. II, No. 2 Quotation Amount in Synthetic CDOs	01/03/2005	Global
CDO Rating Factors Vol. II, No. 1 Rating U.S. SME CLOs: Using Credit Tools to Expand Manager Flexibility	01/02/2005	Global
Tax Event upon Merger in Synthetic CDO Transactions	11/01/2005	Global
Revisited Its Assumptions Regarding Corporate Default (and Asset) Correlations for CDOs	30/11/2004	Global
Moody's Correlated Binomial Default Distribution	10/08/2004	Global
CDO Rating Factors Vol. I, No. 6 Rating Digital Credit Default Swaps	15/07/2004	Global
CDO Rating Factors Vol. I, No. 5 Haircuts for Excess Caa Assets and Deep Discount Obligations	24/06/2004	Global
Rating Japanese CLOs Backed by Secured Sub-Performing Loans	25/05/2004	Asia
CDO Rating Factors Vol. I, No. 4 New Defined Terms for U.S. Cash Flow CBOs/CLOs: "Default Probability Rating" and "Obligation Rating"	21/05/2004	Global
Rating U.S. Bank Trust Preferred Security CDOs	14/04/2004	U.S.
Rating Insurance Trust Preferred Security CDOs	01/04/2004	U.S.
CDO Rating Factors Vol. I, No. 3 Recovery Rate Assumptions for U.S. Corporate Loans and Bonds: Picking up the Pieces	17/03/2004	Global
Rating U.S. Middle Market CLOs: Part I 16/03/2004 U.S.		
CDO Rating Factors Vol. I, No. 2 Current Pay Obligations in Cash Flow CDOs	02/03/2004	Global
Rating CDOs of Japanese Equity Default Swaps	25/02/2004	Asia
Rating CDO Repacks: An Application of the Structured Note Methodology	20/02/2004	Global
Using the Structured Note Methodology to Rate CDO Combo-Notes	20/02/2004	Global
Rating Synthetic Resecuritizations	29/10/2003	Global
Approach for Determining Positive Definite Correlation Matrices: A Tool for Modeling Correlated Defaults	16/09/2003	Global
Rating Market-Value CDOs: Volatility and Jump Probability Table Supplement	08/09/2003	Global
Rating Synthetic CDOs	29/07/2003	Global
Rating Collateralized Funds of Hedge Funds Obligations	10/07/2003	Global
Assessing Secondary Risks in Synthetic CDOs	17/03/2003	Global
Moody's Japanese Corporate Credit Pools in ABS/CLO Deals	17/01/2003	Asia
Rating Methodology: An Alternative Evaluating Market Value CDOs	05/12/2002	Global
U.S. Municipal Cash-Flow CDOs	26/11/2002	U.S.
Approach: The CDO Monitoring Process	27/09/2002	Global
Rating Distressed-Asset CDOs	16/11/2001	Global

Rating Multisector CDOs	15/09/2000	Global
Binomial Expansion Method Applied to CBO/CLO Analysis (The)	13/12/1996	Global
Rating Cash Flow Transactions Backed by Corporate Debt 1995 Update	10/04/1995	Global

B.2.7 Commercial mortgage-backed securitization and real estate investment trusts

V Scores and Parameter Sensitivities in the EMEA CMBS Sector	29/04/2009	EMEA
Updated: Surveillance Assumptions for Japanese CMBS	14/04/2009	Asia
V Scores and Parameter Sensitivities in the Asian CMBS Sector	02/04/2009	Asia
V Scores and Parameter Sensitivities in the U.S. CMBS Sector	25/03/2009	U.S.
Updated on its Surveillance Approach for EMEA CMBS	17/03/2009	EMEA
Update: U.S. CMBS Review Prompted by Declining Property Values and Rising Delinquencies	05/02/2009	U.S.
Australian SME CMBS Methodology	29/01/2009	Australia
Japan CMBS Supplemental Series 7: Analyzing CMBS Backed by Office Buildings	18/09/2008	Asia
Updated: Japan CMBS Supplemental Series 6: Analyzing Residential Properties	01/08/2008	Asia
Japan CMBS Supplemental Series 5: Analyzing CMBS that include Non-Recourse Loans to REITS	17/07/2008	Asia
Rating Japanese Commercial Real Estate CDOs	04/02/2008	Asia
Updated: Rating CMBS Transactions in Japan, Supplemental Series 4: Rating CMBS in Japan Backed by Hotel Properties	24/01/2008	Asia
Updated: Rating CMBS Transactions in Japan, Supplemental Series 3: Rating Considerations on Fixed-Term Leasehold and Lease-Free Loans in Japanese CMBS	17/12/2007	Asia
Monitoring CMBS Ratings in Japan, Supplemental Series 1: Key Issues in the CMBS Monitoring Process	14/11/2007	Asia
Updated: Rating CMBS Transactions in Japan, Supplemental Series 2: Rating CMBS in Japan Backed by Distribution Facilities	01/08/2007	Asia
Updated: Rating CMBS Transactions in Japan, Supplemental Series 1: Overview of Property Level Analysis	11/06/2007	Asia
Key Ratios for Rating REITs and Other Commercial Property Firms	03/05/2007	U.S.
Updated: Rating CMBS Transactions in Japan	09/04/2007	Asia
U.S. CMBS and CRE CDO: Rating Commercial Real Estate Mezzanine Loans	29/03/2007	U.S.
Rating EMEA Commercial Real Estate CDOs	24/01/2007	EMEA
Methodology for Assigning Real Estate Cash Flow Volatility Ratings	12/12/2006	Asia
Rating Commercial Land Loans	07/06/2006	U.S.
Real Estate Analysis for CMBS in EMEA: Portfolio Analysis (Portfolio)	24/04/2006	EMEA
Surveillance of Large Loan Transactions	08/03/2006	U.S.
Surveillance of Large Loan Transactions	08/03/2006	U.S.
Non-Sequential Payment Structures in European CMBS Transactions	28/02/2006	EMEA
Rating Methodology for REITs and Other Commercial Property Firms	24/01/2006	U.S.
Rating Commercial Real Estate Construction Loans	20/01/2006	U.S.
Analyzing Transitional Hotel Properties	08/12/2005	U.S.
Real Estate Tax Abatements	30/11/2005	U.S.
Monitoring CMBS Ratings in Japan	03/10/2005	Asia
Update on Real Estate Analysis for CMBS in EMEA	30/06/2005	EMEA
Updated on Real Estate Analysis for CMBS Transactions in EMEA	20/06/2005	EMEA
U.S. Moody's Rating Loans Secured by Nursing Facilities	06/04/2005	U.S.
Rating Real Estate Asset Trust Transactions in Taiwan	30/03/2005	Asia
Office Loans—Sustainable Rents and Tenant Ratings Are Key to Credit Quality	22/03/2005	U.S.
Rating Condo Conversion Loans	03/03/2005	U.S.
Moody's European Country Tiering for CMBS Recovery Rate Assumptions: Focus on Key Jurisdictions	28/01/2005	EMEA
Borrower-Affiliates Owning Their Related B-Notes	10/09/2004	U.S.
Rating Finance Transactions of Real Estate Development Projects in Japan	06/09/2004	Asia
Revolving Facilities in CDOs Backed by Commercial Real Estate Securities	29/07/2004	U.S.
Rating Static CDOs Backed by Commercial Real Estate Securities	17/06/2004	U.S.
Pari-Passu Notes in CMBS: Some "A"-Notes Are More Equal than Others	08/01/2004	U.S.
Rating Loans Secured by Manufactured Home Communities	20/10/2003	U.S.
Rating Loans Secured by Parking Facilities	20/10/2003	U.S.
Rating Loans Secured by Self-Storage Facilities	20/10/2003	U.S.
Rating Liquidating CMBS Transactions in Japan	30/05/2003	Asia
When Are Cap Rates Too High, Too Low, or Just Right?	11/03/2003	Global
Rating Loans Secured by Multi-Family Properties	26/02/2003	U.S.

Terrorism Insurance after the Federal Backstop	06/01/2003	U.S.
Occupancy Cost Ratio Is Key to Analysis of Mall Credit Risk	09/12/2002	U.S.
Assessing Loan Credit Quality at a Cyclical Trough	03/10/2002	U.S.
Surveillance	30/09/2002	U.S.
Rating CMBS Sale and Lease-Back Transactions in Japan	03/09/2002	Asia
Rating Recourse Loans in Canadian and U.S. Conduits	13/02/2002	U.S.
Positive and Negative Pooling: Tranching Large Loan CMBS	18/12/2001	U.S.
Rating Loans Secured by Industrial Properties	23/03/2001	U.S.
The Evolution of A-B Loans—Enhanced Rights of B Notes Lower Credit Quality of A Notes	26/01/2001	Global
Whole Business Securitizations: A Unique Opportunity for U.K. Assets?	16/10/2000	EMEA
Rating U.S. Conduit Transactions	15/09/2000	U.S.
Rating Large Loan/Single Borrower Transactions	07/07/2000	U.S.
Rating Canadian CMBS	25/05/2000	U.S.
Rating Floating Rate Transactions	12/05/2000	U.S.
Replacement Cost	09/03/2000	U.S.
A-B Notes and Other Forms of Subordinate Debt	04/02/2000	U.S.
Small Commercial Real Estate Loans	21/09/1999	U.S.
Rating Loans Secured by Office Properties	16/07/1999	U.S.
Secured Creditor Environmental Insurance	03/06/1999	U.S.
Rating Assisted Living Facilities	11/03/1999	U.S.
Rating Credit Tenant Lease (CTL) Backed Transactions	02/10/1998	U.S.

B.2.8 Covered bonds criteria

Assessing Swaps as Hedges in the Covered Bond Market	17/09/2008	EMEA
Timely Payments in Covered Bonds Following Sponsor Bank Default	18/03/2008	EMEA
European Covered Bond Legal Frameworks: Legal Checklist	08/12/2005	EMEA
Rating European Covered Bonds	13/06/2005	EMEA

B.2.9 Hybrid securities

Hybrid Tool Kit: An Update on Hybrid Analysis for U.S. Real Estate Investment Trusts (REITs)	20/03/2008	Global
Hybrid Tool Kit: Revised Treatment of Surplus Notes for Mutual Insurers	19/03/2008	Global
Hybrid Tool Kit: Limiting Equity Credit in the Capital Structure	11/03/2008	Global
Refinements to Tool Kit: Evolutionary, Not Revolutionary!	25/02/2005	Americas
Hybrid Securities Analysis—New Criteria for Adjustment of Financial Ratios to Reflect the Issuance of Hybrid Securities Product of the New Instruments Committee	10/11/2003	Americas
Tool Kit: Hybrid Securities Analysis	08/06/2000	Americas
Moody's Tool Kit: A Framework for Assessing Hybrid Securities	15/12/1999	Global
Monitoring Residential Mortgage-Backed Securitizations in Mexico	31/08/2009	U.S.
Rating Low-Income Residential Construction Loan Securitizations in Mexico	24/08/2009	U.S.
MILAN Methodology for Rating Korean RMBS	08/08/2009	Asia

B.2.10 Residential mortgage-backed securitization

Cash Flow Analysis of Synthetic ABS/RMBS Transations	07/08/2009	Global
FHA—VA RMBS Loss Projection Methodology: July 2009	20/07/2009	U.S.
V Scores and Parameter Sensitivities in the Mexican RMBS Sector	12/05/2009	U.S.
V Scores and Parameter Sensitivities in the U.S. RMBS Sector	01/05/2009	U.S.
V Scores and Parameter Sensitivities in the Major EMEA RMBS Subsectors	20/04/2009	EMEA
MILAN Methodology for Rating Irish RMBS	20/04/2009	EMEA
Updated MILAN Methodology for Rating German RMBS	07/04/2009	EMEA
Methodology for U.S. RMBS Master Servicer Quality Ratings	02/04/2009	U.S.
Prime Jumbo RMBS Loss Projection Update: March 2009	25/03/2009	U.S.
V Scores and Parameter Sensitivities in the Asia/Pacific RMBS Sector	24/03/2009	Asia
Updated NHG Mortgages in Rating Dutch RMBS	17/03/2009	EMEA
Updated MILAN Methodology for Rating Dutch RMBS	17/03/2009	EMEA
Subprime RMBS Loss Projection Update: March 2009	05/03/2009	U.S.
Option ARMs RMBS Loss Projection Update: February 2009	05/02/2009	U.S.

Alt-A RMBS Loss Projection Update: January 2009	22/01/2009	U.S.
Updated: Rating Spanish Government Sponsored Housing (VPO) RMBS	20/01/2009	EMEA
Rating U.S. Residential Mortgage-Backed Securities	31/12/2008	U.S.
Methodology for Rating RMBS in Europe, Middle East, and Africa	14/10/2008	EMEA
Automated Valuation Models in Rating U.K. RMBS	21/08/2008	EMEA
Methodology for Rating Russian RMBS	29/07/2008	EMEA
A Framework for Stressing House Prices in RMBS Transactions in EMEA	24/07/2008	EMEA
Updated Methodology for Rating Spanish RMBS	22/07/2008	EMEA
RMBS Master Trust Cash Flow Analysis	28/04/2008	EMEA
Updated Methodology for Rating U.K. RMBS	05/11/2007	EMEA
Rating Residential Mortgage-Backed Securities in Japan, Supplemental Series 13: Loan-by-Loan Model and Loss Rate Distribution Assumptions	19/10/2007	Asia
Monitoring Residential Mortgage-Backed Securities in Japan: Factors Affecting Credit Enhancement	04/10/2007	Asia
Interest Rate Risks in U.K. RMBS—Approach	02/10/2007	EMEA
Rating U.S. Option ARM RMBS—Updated Rating Approach	04/09/2007	U.S.
U.S. Alt-A RMBS—Updated Its Methodology: August 2007	21/08/2007	U.S.
U.S. Alt-A RMBS—Updated Its Methodology: August 2007	21/08/2007	U.S.
Update to Analyzing Delinquent Loans Included in Performing Subprime U.S. RMBS	21/08/2007	U.S.
Rating Residential Mortgage-Backed Securities in Japan, Supplemental Series 11: Waterfall (Part 1): Sequential Pay and Pro-Rata Pay	09/08/2007	Asia
Rating Residential Mortgage-Backed Securities in Japan, Supplemental Series 12: Waterfall (Part 2): Excess Spread and Credit Enhancement	09/08/2007	Asia
U.S. Subprime—Overview of Recent Refinements to Methodology: July 2007	02/08/2007	U.S.
U.S. Subprime—Overview of Recent Refinements to Methodology: July 2007	02/08/2007	U.S.
Rating RMBS in Emerging Securitization Markets—EMEA	08/06/2007	EMEA
U.S. RMBS: 40-year Mortgages in Subprime RMBS	09/01/2007	U.S.
Coding Subprime Residential Mortgage Documentation Programs: Updated Methodology	28/11/2006	U.S.
Closed End Seconds Residential Mortgage Securitization Cashflow Assumptions	02/11/2006	U.S.
Rating Methodology: Home Equity Lines of Credit ("HELOC") Securitizations	03/10/2006	U.S.
Rating Belgian RMBS	25/09/2006	EMEA
Rating Residential Mortgage-Backed Securities in Japan, Supplemental Series 10: Factors for Estimating CPR of Residential Mortgage Pools	27/06/2006	Asia
Rating Residential Mortgage-Backed Securities in Japan, Supplemental Series 9: Loss Curve Assumptions	16/06/2006	Asia
Coding Jumbo and Alt-A Residential Mortgage Documentation Programs	15/06/2006	U.S.
Rating Residential Mortgage-Backed Securities in Japan, Supplemental Series 8: Estimating Gross Loss for Bank Non-conforming Loan Pools	01/06/2006	Asia
Mortgage Insurance in EMEA RMBS Transactions: Potential Advantages and Analytical Considerations	01/06/2006	EMEA
Enhanced Step-down Test in Subprime Home Equity Transactions Earlier Performance Tests Provide Additional Protection for Investors	19/04/2006	U.S.
Updated Loss Coverage Methodology and Cashflow Assumptions for Closed End Second Lien Mortgage Loans	19/04/2006	U.S.
An Update—A Guideline for Sizing the Risk of Super Senior Support Classes in Home Equity and Alternative A Over-collateralization Transactions	20/03/2006	U.S.
Rating Residential Mortgage-Backed Securities in Japan, Supplemental Series 7: Loan-by-Loan Model and Gross Loss Estimation	16/03/2006	Asia
Sizing RMBS Large Loan Concentration Risk	24/02/2006	U.S.
Cashflow Assumptions for RMBS Alt-A Transactions	09/02/2006	U.S.
Cash Flow Analysis in EMEA RMBS: Testing Structural Features with the MARCO Model (Analyzer of Residential Cash Flows)	24/01/2006	EMEA
Update to Subprime Residential Mortgage Securitization Assumptions	02/12/2005	U.S.
Understanding Metrics for Performance Monitoring, Volume 3: Residential Mortgage-Backed Securities	14/10/2005	U.S.
Moody's Rating French RMBS	06/10/2005	EMEA
Rating Residential Mortgage-Backed Securities in Japan, Supplemental Series 6: Cash Flow Analysis/Rating Approach Based on Expected Loss	09/09/2005	Asia
Rating Investment-Purpose Condominium Loan-Backed Securitizations in Japan	08/08/2005	Asia
An Update to Analysis of Payment Shock Risk in Sub-Prime Hybrid ARM Products	12/05/2005	U.S.
Rating U.K. RMBS	06/04/2005	EMEA
The Importance of Representations and Warranties in RMBS Transactions	14/01/2005	U.S.
Rating Single Seller Mortgage Warehouse Structures	05/01/2005	U.S.

Rating Residential Mortgage-Backed Securities in Japan, Supplemental Series 5: Estimating Gross Loss Rate based on Index Pool	17/12/2004	Asia
Rating Residential Mortgage-Backed Securities in Japan, Supplemental Series 4: RMBS Interest Rate Risk	13/12/2004	Asia
Rating Residential Mortgage-Backed Securities in Japan, Supplemental Series 3: Servicing Risks upon Occurrence of Servicer Financial Institution's Credit Events	11/11/2004	Asia
Rating Portuguese RMBS	14/10/2004	EMEA
Loan Modifications and Forbearance Plans Impact on Home Equity Securitizations	24/09/2004	U.S.
Residential Mortgage Servicer Quality ("SQ") Ratings in Australia: Methodology	16/08/2004	Australia
Rating Residential Mortgage-Backed Securities in Japan: Supplemental Series 2 "Analyzing Multi-Party Guaranteed Pools"	10/08/2004	Asia
Rating Swiss RMBS	30/06/2004	EMEA
Rating Apartment Loan-Backed Securities in Japan	24/06/2004	Asia
Summary of and Introduction to: Rating Italian Residential Mortgage-Backed Securities	09/06/2004	EMEA
Rating Italian RMBS	09/06/2004	EMEA
Rating Dutch RMBS	01/06/2004	EMEA
Rating Initial Period, Interest-Only Mortgages in Prime RMBS	05/05/2004	U.S.
Rating Residential Mortgage-Backed Securities in Japan: Supplemental Series 1 "Recovery from Defaulted Receivables"	26/04/2004	Asia
Rating South African RMBS	20/04/2004	EMEA
Lender-Paid Mortgage Insurance	11/09/2003	U.S.
AU-MILAN—The Scoring Formula Revisited—Individual Loan Analysis for Australian RMBS	26/08/2003	EMEA
Overview of RMBS Monitoring Process	13/08/2003	U.S.
Rating Residential Mortgage-Backed Securities in Japan	12/05/2003	Asia
Mortgage Metrics: A Model Analysis of Residential Mortgage Pools	01/04/2003	U.S.
Analyzing Non-performing and Reperforming FHA and VA Residential Mortgage Loans	03/03/2003	U.S.
Rating Residential Mortgage Servicers	18/01/2001	EMEA
The Impact of Mortgage Insurance on the Subordination Level of Australian MBS	15/05/2000	Australia

B.2.11 Structured investment vehicles

FAQs Regarding Current State of Structured Investment Vehicle (SIV) Market	15/01/2008	Global
SIV Management Quality Ratings	18/01/2006	Global
Moody's Capital Model	28/01/2004	Global

B.3 STANDARD AND POOR'S

B.3.1 Asset-class generic

Updated Calibration of the Hedge Fund Evaluator V2.2 Model	22/09/2009	Global
Update to Global Methodologies and Assumptions for Corporate Cash Flow and Synthetic CDOs	17/09/2009	Global
Application of Supplemental Tests for Rating Global Corporate Cash Flow and Synthetic CDOs	17/09/2009	Global
General Criteria: Methodology and Assumptions: Approach to Evaluating Letter of Credit-Supported Debt	06/07/2009	Global
Revised Criteria Methodology for Servicer Risk Assessment	28/05/2009	Global
Methodology for Rating Structured Finance Securities with Call Provisions at Less than Par	14/05/2009	Global
General Criteria: Joint-Support Criteria Update	22/04/2009	Global
Reclassified REITS and REOCS that Issue Debt Securities Owned or Referenced by Rated CDOs and CDS	19/01/2009	Global
Reclassifies Insurance Companies that Issue Debt Securities Owned or Referenced by Rated CDOs and CDS	23/12/2008	Global
Probability of Default Correlation Assumptions Revised for Global CDOs/CDS Exposed to REITs/REOCs	06/11/2008	Global
Correlation Assumptions Revised for Rating Global CDOs/CDS Exposed to Insurance Companies	06/11/2008	Global
Cut Minimum Reinvestment Rate Assumptions for U.S. Structured and Muni Housing Bonds	31/10/2008	U.S.
Revised Correlation Assumptions for Rtng CDO/CDS Exposed to Financial Intermediaries	03/10/2008	Global

Overview of Japan's New Trust Law and Its Implications for Securitization Schemes	17/03/2008	Asia
Revising U.S. Municipal CDO Modeling Assumptions in CDO Evaluator Version 3.3	24/07/2007	Global
An Introduction to CDOs and Global CDO Ratings	08/06/2007	Global
Principles-Based Rating Methodology for Global Structured Finance Securities	29/05/2007	Global
Bankruptcy Remoteness of Special-Purpose Vehicles in Japanese Securitization Transactions	17/10/2006	Asia
Eligibility of New SPV Entities in Japanese Structured Finance Market	26/06/2006	Asia
Modified Structured Finance Default Assumptions In CDO Evaluator	19/06/2006	Global
Joint-Support Criteria Refined	03/02/2006	Global
CDO Evaluator Version 3.0: Technical Document	19/12/2005	Global
Credit Criteria for Triggers to Mitigate Commingling Risk in Japanese Structured Finance Transactions	28/10/2005	Asia
Credit Criteria for Triggers to Mitigate Commingling Risk in Japanese Structured Finance Transactions	28/10/2005	Asia
Credit Policy Update: Criteria on Use of Creditwatch and Outlooks Clarified	30/09/2005	Global
Criteria for Trustee and Common Representative Evaluation Services in Mexico	26/04/2005	South America
Interest-Only Rating Methodology for U.S. Assets Reviewed	20/04/2005	U.S.
Global Interest Rate and Currency Swaps: Calculating the Collateral Required Amount	26/02/2004	Global
Rating Methodology Refined for Canadian Real Estate First Mortgage Bonds	22/12/2003	U.S.
Use of Chukan Hojin Entities as Shareholders of SPVs in Japanese Structured Finance Transactions	17/11/2003	Asia
Refined Account Eligibility Criteria for Japanese Structured Finance Transactions	06/08/2003	Asia
Modified Approach to Reviewing AAA Rated Structured Transactions	26/04/2002	Global
Account Eligibility Criteria for Japanese Structured Finance Transactions Refined	03/02/2002	Asia
CDO Evaluator Applies Correlation and Monte Carlo Simulation to Determine Portfolio Quality	13/11/2001	Global
Eligible Investment Criteria for "AAA" Rated Structured Transactions	25/06/2001	Global
Distressed Debt CDOs: Spinning Straw into Gold	07/05/2001	Global
Implications of Insurer Financial Enhancement Ratings for Structured Finance	04/08/2000	Global
Adopted Revised Structured Finance Capital Charge Methodology	09/02/2000	Global
Securitization of Commercial and Asset-Based Lending Portfolios	18/10/1996	Global

B.3.2 Counterparty related

Revised Criteria for Including RMBS, CMBS, and ABS Servicers on Select Servicer List	16/04/2009	Global
Update and Clarification to Counterparty Criteria for Interest Rate Swap Counterparties in Rated Transactions	01/04/2009	Global
Updated Counterparty Criteria for Derivatives: Eligibility of "A-2" Counterparties Removed in "AAA" Transactions	22/10/2008	Global
Servicer Evaluation Criteria: Australia and New Zealand	07/08/2008	Australia/NWZ
Are CMBS Servicers Ready for a Spike in Maturing Loans and More Defaults?	17/04/2008	Global
Analysis of Loan Modifications and Servicer Reimbursements for U.S. RMBS Transactions with Senior/Subordinate Structures	10/04/2008	Miscellaneous
Legal Framework for Japan Business Securitization: Governance of Operating Company and Bankruptcy Remoteness	06/08/2007	Global
Methodology for Evaluating and Ranking Small-Balance Commercial Mortgage Servicers	23/07/2007	Miscellaneous
Revised Framework for Applying Counterparty and Supporting Party Criteria	08/05/2007	Global
In Servicer Evaluations Financial Strength Plays an Important (and Often Misunderstood) Role	14/03/2007	Miscellaneous
Weighing Country Risk in Our Criteria for Asset-Backed Securities	11/04/2006	Global
Criteria for Rating Global Credit Derivative Product Companies	04/11/2005	Global
Comments on Outsourcing Fee Disclosure Practices within the Mortgage Servicing Industry	03/03/2005	Miscellaneous
Global Methodology for Rating Capital Notes in SIV Structures	11/02/2005	Global
Servicer Evaluation Ranking Criteria	21/09/2004	Miscellaneous
Criteria Regarding "Prudent Servicing Practices" in CMBS Outlined	08/06/2004	Miscellaneous
Rating Criteria for U.S. REITs and REOCs	06/05/2004	Global
Global Interest Rate and Currency Swaps: Calculating the Collateral Required Amount	26/02/2004	Global
Global Interest Rate and Currency Swap Counterparty Rating Criteria Expanded	17/12/2003	Global
Structured Investment Vehicle Criteria: New Developments	04/09/2003	Global
Structured Investment Vehicle Criteria	13/03/2002	Global
Operating Companies: Rating Policy for Japanese Real Estate Investment Trusts	09/05/2001	Global
Achieving Dynamic Liquidity Requirements in Structured Investment Vehicles	13/09/2000	Global
Swap Counterparty Requirements Expanded for Interest Rate Swaps	19/05/2000	Global
Rating Derivative Product Companies	27/01/2000	Global

Derivative Product Companies: Risks and Future Directions	24/01/2000	Global
AAAt' Swaps Approved in Structured Finance Transactions	06/01/1999	Global
Assessing Sovereign Risk in Structured Finance In Emerging Markets	15/06/1998	Emerging markets
Role of the Backup Servicer	18/10/1996	Miscellaneous

B.3.3 Legal criteria

Anti-Predatory Lending Law Update Table in Revised U.S. Residential Mortgage Input File Format Glossary and Appendices to the Glossary for EVELS Version 7.0	16/09/2009	U.S.
Revised Assumptions for U.S. Tobacco Settlement-Backed Transactions	23/02/2009	U.S.
Methodology for "Springing" True Sale Opinions in U.S. RMBS Transactions	12/02/2009	U.S.
Standard & Poor's Criteria for Analyzing Loans Governed by Anti-Predatory Lending Laws	05/11/2008	U.S.
Standard & Poor's Announces Its Anti-Predatory Lending Law Criteria for New York Subprime Home Loans	05/11/2008	U.S.
European Legal Criteria for Structured Finance Transactions	28/08/2008	EMEA
Criteria for Rating Structured Finance Transactions that Include Loans Originated by Federal Thrifts Revised	05/03/2008	U.S.
Responded to Maine's Anti-Predatory Lending Law Amendments	28/01/2008	U.S.
Standard & Poor's Addresses Maine's New Anti-Predatory Lending Law	04/01/2008	U.S.
Revised Framework for Applying U.S. Tobacco Securitization Criteria	18/05/2007	U.S.
Legal Brief: The Impact of the Expanded Texas Tax on Securitizations	16/01/2007	U.S.
Independent Directors' Role Clarified for English SPEs	06/12/2006	EMEA
Addressed Tennessee Anti-Predatory Lending Law	20/10/2006	U.S.
Revised and Clarified Its Criteria Under Indiana Anti-Predatory Lending Law	20/10/2006	U.S.
Addressed Rhode Island Anti-Predatory Lending Law	20/10/2006	U.S.
Clarified Its Criteria in Ohio Due to Amendments to Ohio Law	20/10/2006	U.S.
Legal Criteria for U.S. Structured Finance Transactions: Overview of Legal Criteria for U.S. Structured Finance Transactions	01/10/2006	U.S.
Legal Criteria for U.S. Structured Finance Transactions: Securitizations by Code Transferors	01/10/2006	U.S.
Legal Criteria for U.S. Structured Finance Transactions: Securitizations by SPE Transferors and Non-Code Transferors	01/10/2006	U.S.
Legal Criteria for U.S. Structured Finance Transactions: Special-Purpose Entities	01/10/2006	U.S.
Legal Criteria for U.S. Structured Finance Transactions: Select Issues Criteria	01/10/2006	U.S.
Legal Criteria for U.S. Structured Finance Transactions: Criteria Related to Asset-Backed Securities	01/10/2006	U.S.
Legal Criteria for U.S. Structured Finance Transactions: Criteria Related to Securities Backed by Residential Mortgage Home Equity and Manufactured Housing Loans	01/10/2006	U.S.
Legal Criteria for U.S. Structured Finance Transactions: Criteria Related to Commercial Paper Conduits	01/10/2006	U.S.
Legal Criteria for U.S. Structured Finance Transactions: Criteria Related to Collateralized Debt Obligations	01/10/2006	U.S.
Legal Criteria for U.S. Structured Finance Transactions: Criteria Related to Global Synthetic Securities	01/10/2006	U.S.
Legal Criteria for U.S. Structured Finance Transactions: Criteria Related to New Asset-Backed Securities	01/10/2006	U.S.
Legal Criteria for U.S. Structured Finance Transactions: Criteria Related to Hybrid Asset-Backed Securities	01/10/2006	U.S.
Legal Criteria for U.S. Structured Finance Transactions: Criteria Related to Trustees, Servicers, Custodians, and Eligible Deposit Accounts	01/10/2006	U.S.
Legal Criteria for U.S. Structured Finance Transactions: Appendix I: Typical Factors Considered by Courts in Determining Existence of a True Sale	01/10/2006	U.S.
Legal Criteria for U.S. Structured Finance Transactions: Appendix II: Select Opinion Criteria/Language	01/10/2006	U.S.
Legal Criteria for U.S. Structured Finance Transactions: Appendix III: Revised UCC Article 9 Criteria	01/10/2006	U.S.
Legal Criteria for U.S. Structured Finance Transactions: Appendix IV: ABCP Officer's Certificate	01/10/2006	U.S.
Legal Criteria for U.S. Structured Finance Transactions: Appendix V: Model Representations and Warranties for Collateral Assignments of Funding Agreements	01/10/2006	U.S.
Legal Issues of Securitized Auto Loans in an E-Contract World	10/07/2006	U.S.
New Option for Addressing Transferor Preference Risk under the U.S. Bankruptcy Code	10/07/2006	U.S.

Standard & Poor's Addresses Massachusetts Regulations Regarding High-Cost Loans	21/12/2005	U.S.
Amended Structured Finance Legal Criteria for English and Welsh SPEs	16/12/2005	EMEA
Addressed Arkansas House Bill 1008 Regarding Reverse Mortgage Loans	14/07/2005	U.S.
Analyzing Operating Lease Risks in U.S. ABCP Seller Transactions	12/07/2005	U.S.
U.S. Bankruptcy Act Revisions May Favor Creditors but Won't Affect Rating Criteria	06/07/2005	U.S.
Rating Affirmations and Their Impact on Investors	20/04/2005	Global
Legal Criteria Applicable to European Transactions	17/03/2005	EMEA
Guide to Legal Issues in Rating Australian Securitization	01/03/2005	Asia
Standard & Poor's Eliminates Additional Credit Enhancement Requirements for Indiana Home Loans	07/02/2005	U.S.
Addressed Indiana Anti-Predatory Lending Law	18/10/2004	U.S.
Addressed Massachusetts' Predatory Home Loan Practices Act	20/09/2004	U.S.
Standard & Poor's Eliminates New Jersey Covered Home Loan Criteria	07/07/2004	U.S.
Legal Issues in Mexican Asset-Backed Securitizations	27/05/2004	South America
Anti-Predated Lending Alert: Revised Criteria Related to Anti-Predatory Lending Laws	13/05/2004	U.S.
Implemented Credit Enhancement Criteria and Revised Representations and Warranty Criteria for Including Anti-Predatory Lending Law Loans in U.S. Rated Structured Finance Transactions	13/05/2004	U.S.
Standard & Poor's Addresses Various Anti-Predatory Lending Laws Enacted Prior to January 2003	12/05/2004	U.S.
Standard & Poor's Addresses OCC Rule Regarding Preemption of State Anti-Predatory Lending Laws	03/03/2004	U.S.
Investors Benefit from the Legal/Structural Review of U.S. CMBS Transactions	26/02/2004	U.S.
Credit Where Credit Is Due: Examining the Legal Landscape of Structured Finance Transactions	23/02/2004	Global
New Criteria for Representations and Warranties for Collateral Assignments of Funding Agreements Issued by U.S. Life Insurance Companies	09/02/2004	U.S.
New Opinion Criteria for Rating Notes Secured by Funding Agreements Issued by a U.S. Life Insurance Company	09/02/2004	U.S.
Legal Criteria for Withholding Tax Issues in Structured Finance Transactions	04/02/2004	Global
Legal Criteria for Withholding Tax Issues in Structured Finance Transactions	04/02/2004	EMEA
Rejected Contracts in Bankruptcy and the Effect on Certain U.S. Securitizations	06/01/2004	U.S.
Reaffirmed Tax Opinion Criteria for U.S. Credit Card Transactions	05/12/2003	U.S.
Reaffirmed Certain Opinion Criteria for U.S. Credit Card Transactions	05/12/2003	U.S.
Standard & Poor's Announces Position on OTS Preemption Pronouncements	25/11/2003	U.S.
Criteria for Trust Issuers in U.S. Structured Finance Transactions	20/11/2003	U.S.
Announced Position on OCC's Preemption Order for the GFLA	03/10/2003	U.S.
Standard & Poor's Addresses New Jersey Predatory Lending Law	02/05/2003	U.S.
Evaluating Predatory Lending Laws: Standard & Poor's Explains Its Approach	15/04/2003	U.S.
Structured Finance Criteria for Installment Sales Contracts Leasing Contracts (Credit-Bail) and Leases in Quebec	26/11/2002	U.S.
State Statutes for the Securitization of Tobacco Settlement Revenues	24/10/2002	U.S.
U.S. Legal Criteria for "Recycled" Special-Purpose Entities	19/09/2002	U.S.
No Additional U.S. Legal Criteria Required for Electronic Contracts	17/09/2002	U.S.
Structured Finance Criteria for Canadian Special-Purpose Entities	26/08/2002	U.S.
What if a Servicer in a Securitized Transaction Becomes Insolvent?	20/08/2002	U.S.
Revised Article 9 of the Uniform Commercial Code: New Criteria	06/06/2001	U.S.
NIMS Analysis: Valuing Prepayment Penalty Fee Income	03/01/2001	U.S.
Behind the Ratings: Multiple-Use SPE Criteria for U.S. Transactions; Exceptions to Limitations on SPEs' Ability to Issue Additional Debt	10/03/2000	U.S.
Revised Legal Criteria for Multi- and Single-Member LLCs	01/09/1999	U.S.

B.3.4 Miscellaneous other criteria

Revised Assumptions for U.S. Tobacco Settlement-Backed Transactions	23/02/2009	Miscellaneous
Methodology and Assumptions for U.S. Structured Settlement Payment Securitizations	11/12/2008	Miscellaneous
Introduced U.S. Small-Business Portfolio Model	06/11/2007	Global
Revised Framework for Applying U.S. Tobacco Securitization Criteria	18/05/2007	Miscellaneous
U.S. Tobacco Securitization Cash Flow Assumptions Updated	16/02/2007	Miscellaneous
Two Rating Approaches Converge to Create Small-Balance Commercial Real Estate Loan Securitization Criteria	25/10/2006	Global
Updated U.S. Hurricane Catastrophe Bond Ratings Criteria	02/06/2006	Miscellaneous
Updated Tobacco Securitization Cash Flow Stress Tests	16/03/2006	Miscellaneous

Updated Its Approach to Rating U.S. Insurance Premium Loan Securitizations	28/04/2005	Miscellaneous
Securitizations of New Asset Classes: A Rating Approach	27/09/2004	Miscellaneous
Securitizing Vacation Homes In Mexico	01/09/2004	Miscellaneous
Aircraft Securitization Criteria: The Rating Process for Aircraft Financings	01/09/2004	Miscellaneous
Aircraft Securitization Criteria: The Rating Process for Aircraft Portfolio Securitizations	01/09/2004	Miscellaneous
Aircraft Securitization Criteria: Rating Considerations for Lease Pools	01/09/2004	Miscellaneous
Aircraft Securitization Criteria: Special Considerations for Aircraft Loan Portfolios	01/09/2004	Miscellaneous
Aircraft Securitization Criteria: The Servicer's Roles and Responsibilities	01/09/2004	Miscellaneous
Aircraft Securitization Criteria: Maintenance and Related Issues	01/09/2004	Miscellaneous
Aircraft Securitization Criteria: Surveillance	01/09/2004	Miscellaneous
Criteria for Securitization of U.S. Small and Middle-Market Enterprise Loans	30/01/2004	Global
Rating Criteria for U.S. Timeshare Loan Securitizations	08/10/2003	Miscellaneous
Global Timber Property Securitizations	01/05/2003	Miscellaneous
Mapping Internal Credit Scores to Ratings for CDOs	11/11/2002	Global
State Statutes for the Securitization of Tobacco Settlement Revenues	24/10/2002	Miscellaneous
Securitizing Stranded Costs	18/01/2001	Miscellaneous
Overview of the Tobacco Securitization Rating Methodology	25/10/2000	Miscellaneous
Marine Cargo Container Lessors Look to Securitize Fleets	27/07/2000	Miscellaneous
Rating Mutual Fund Fee-Backed Securities	30/03/2000	Global
Rating Hybrid Securitizations	13/09/1999	Miscellaneous
New Structured Finance Interest Rate and Currency Swap Criteria Broadens Allowable Counterparties	06/01/1999	Miscellaneous
Rating Operating Asset Transactions	20/05/1998	Miscellaneous
Franchise Loans Rating Criteria	04/03/1998	Miscellaneous

B.3.5 Asset-backed commercial paper related

Analysis of ABCP Ratings Following Changes to Ratings on Support Providers	18/12/2008	U.S.
Rating Methodology and Process for U.S. Asset-Backed Medium-Term Notes	23/01/2007	U.S.
What Is "Limited Liquidity/Illiquid Basket" and What Goes In It?	20/07/2006	U.S.
Updated Rating Approach as Popularity of Cash Flow-Based Extendible Note Programs Grows	11/07/2006	U.S.
ABCP Criteria: New Option for Addressing Transferor Preference Risk under the U.S. Bankruptcy Code	10/07/2006	U.S.
Credit Enhancement Levels Established for U.S. ABCP Eligible Bank Liquidity	07/09/2005	U.S.
Analyzing Operating Lease Risks in U.S. ABCP Seller Transactions	12/07/2005	U.S.
Rating U.S. Residential Asset-Backed Mortgage Warehousing Conduits	09/09/2003	U.S.
Revised Asset-Backed Commercial Paper Criteria for Liquidity Banks	07/03/2003	U.S.
Behind the Ratings: Approach for ABCP Liquidity Expanded	07/03/2000	U.S.
Revised Its Approach for Backup of Commercial Paper	02/11/1999	U.S.
New Credit Enhancement Approach to Loan-Backed Commercial Paper	15/04/1999	U.S.
Loan-Backed Commercial Paper Criteria Revised to Match Industry Changes	03/12/1997	U.S.
Loan-Backed Commercial Paper Criteria, June 1, 1999	n.a.	U.S.

B.3.6 Aseet-backed securitization

Methodology for Assessing Servicer Transfer Risk in Global Auto Dealer Floorplan ABS	07/10/2009	Global
Methodology and Assumptions for Rating Construction Loan Securitizations in Mexico	06/10/2009	South America
Methodology and Assumptions for Rating Short-Term U.S. Money Market-Eligible Notes Backed by Credit Card Receivables	02/07/2009	U.S.
Revised Global Methodology for Rating Rental Fleet ABS	29/06/2009	Global
Revised Global Methodology for Rating Rental Fleet ABS	29/06/2009	U.S.
Methodology and Assumptions for Rating Brazilian Trade Receivables Securitizations	13/05/2009	South America
Revised Assumptions for Auto Dealer Floorplan ABS Applied to European Transactions	08/04/2009	EMEA
Revised Criteria Assumptions for Auto Dealer Floorplan ABS	05/02/2009	U.S.
Methodology and Assumptions for Rating Brazilian Electric Power Receivables Future Flow Securitizations	05/02/2009	South America
Update to the Criteria for Rating European SME Securitizations	06/01/2009	EMEA
General Methodology and Assumptions for Rating U.S. Credit Card Securitizations	15/12/2008	U.S.
Approach to Rating Microfinance Securitizations	06/11/2008	South America
U.S. Auto Lease Return Rate and Loss Stresses	09/10/2008	U.S.
How Credit Card Bank Downgrades Could Affect Ratings on U.S. Credit Card ABS	07/10/2008	U.S.

Future Flow Cash Enhancement Reserves in Diversified Payment Rights Transactions	14/05/2008	South America
ABCP Conduit Ratings Are Not Materially Affected by Bond Insurance Exposure	16/04/2008	Global
Methodology for Rating and Surveilling European Corporate Securitizations	23/01/2008	EMEA
Update of Corporate Market Value Securitization Methodology and Assumptions	17/01/2008	EMEA
Rating Methodology and Assumptions for Auto Loan-Backed ABS Transactions in Japan	10/01/2008	Asia
In Mexico Local Governments Turn to Future Tax Revenue Securitization to Free Up Funds	26/10/2007	South America
Legal Framework for Japan Business Securitization; Governance of Operating Company and Bankruptcy Remoteness	06/08/2007	Asia
Corporate Performance Assessment for Global Structured Finance Transactions Backed by Future Receivables	26/07/2007	South America
Rating Methodology and Assumptions for Consumer Loan ABS in Japan	27/06/2007	Asia
Key Elements in Analysis of Corporate Split-type Japan Business Securitization Transactions	05/03/2007	Asia
Overview of Legal and Analytical Challenges in Rating U.K. Corporate Securitizations	18/01/2007	EMEA
CMBS and Corporate Securitizations—The Use of Unrated Fees in English Issuer SPE Structures	11/12/2006	EMEA
U.S. Corporate Securitization Transactions	24/10/2006	Global
Legal Issues of Securitized Auto Loans in an E-Contract World	10/07/2006	U.S.
Rating Methodology for Japan Business Securitization	04/07/2006	Asia
Rating Leasing Securitizations in Italy	03/05/2006	EMEA
Rating Methodology for CLOs Backed by German Participation Rights	25/04/2006	EMEA
Global Asset-Backed Commercial Paper Criteria	29/09/2005	Global
The Three Building Blocks of an Emerging Markets Future Flow Transaction Rating	16/11/2004	South America
The Main Legal and Analytical Rating Issues of Pub Securitizations	11/10/2004	EMEA
Debt Tranching and Ratings Caps in Global Insurance Securitization	06/10/2004	EMEA
The Role of Regulation and Government Support in Rating European Corporate Securitizations	04/10/2004	EMEA
Student Loan Criteria: Student Loan Programs	01/10/2004	U.S.
Student Loan Criteria: The Rating Process for Student Loan Transactions	01/10/2004	U.S.
Student Loan Criteria: Evaluating Risk in Student Loan Transactions	01/10/2004	U.S.
Student Loan Criteria: Structural Elements in Student Loan Transactions	01/10/2004	U.S.
Student Loan Criteria: Rating Methodology for Student Loan Transactions	01/10/2004	U.S.
Student Loan Criteria: Legal Considerations for Student Loan Transactions	01/10/2004	U.S.
Guidelines to the Release of Excess Cash in European Corporate Securitizations	28/09/2004	EMEA
Survey of Life Embedded Value Securitization in the U.K.	20/09/2004	EMEA
Auto Loan Criteria: the Rating Process for Auto Loan-Backed Transactions	01/09/2004	U.S.
Auto Loan Criteria: Credit Analysis for Auto Loan-Backed Transactions	01/09/2004	U.S.
Auto Loan Criteria: Structural Analysis for Auto Loan-Backed Transactions	01/09/2004	U.S.
Auto Loan Criteria: Legal Considerations in Rating Auto Loan-Backed Transactions	01/09/2004	U.S.
Manufactured Housing Criteria: The Rating Process for Manufactured Housing Transactions	01/09/2004	U.S.
Manufactured Housing Criteria: Credit Analysis of Manufactured Housing Transactions	01/09/2004	U.S.
Manufactured Housing Criteria: Structural Analysis of Manufactured Housing Transactions	01/09/2004	U.S.
Manufactured Housing Criteria: Cash Flow Modeling for Manufactured Housing Transactions	01/09/2004	U.S.
Manufactured Housing Criteria: Legal Criteria for Manufactured Housing Transactions	01/09/2004	U.S.
Equipment Leasing Criteria: The Rating Process for Lease-Backed Transactions	01/09/2004	U.S.
Equipment Leasing Criteria: Credit Risks Evaluated in Lease-Backed Securitizations	01/09/2004	U.S.
Equipment Leasing Criteria: Structural Considerations in Rating Lease-Backed Transactions	01/09/2004	U.S.
Equipment Leasing Criteria: Legal Considerations in Rating Lease-Backed Transactions	01/09/2004	U.S.
Trade Receivable Criteria: The Rating Process for Trade Receivables	01/09/2004	U.S.
Trade Receivable Criteria: Evaluating Trade Receivable Credit-Related Risks	01/09/2004	U.S.
Trade Receivable Criteria: Measuring Performance: the Sales-Based Approach for Trade Receivables	01/09/2004	U.S.
Trade Receivable Criteria: Calculating Credit Enhancement for Trade Receivables	01/09/2004	U.S.
Trade Receivable Criteria: Special Considerations for Health Care Receivable-Backed Transactions	01/09/2004	U.S.
Trade Receivable Criteria: Structural Considerations for Trade Receivables	01/09/2004	U.S.
Emerging Markets Criteria: Existing Assets: General Criteria Overview	01/09/2004	South America
Securitization in Latin America 1999: Existing Assets: Asset-Specific Rating Criteria	01/09/2004	South America
Securitization in Latin America 1999: Existing Assets: General Criteria Overview	01/09/2004	South America
Securitization of International Telephone Settlement Payments	01/09/2004	South America
Emerging Markets Criteria: Credit Card Merchant Voucher Securitization	01/09/2004	South America

Securitization in Latin America 1999: Credit Card Merchant Voucher Securitization	01/09/2004	South America
Assessing the Risk of Pension Plan Terminations on U.S. Auto Lease Securitizations	17/08/2004	U.S.
Credit Risk Tracker Strengthens Rating Analysis of CLOs of European SME Loans	10/06/2004	EMEA
Legal Issues in Mexican Asset-Backed Securitizations	27/05/2004	South America
U.S. Trade Receivable Securitization: Offset Risk under Long-Term Contracts	15/01/2004	U.S.
Reaffirmed Tax Opinion Criteria for U.S. Credit Card Transactions	05/12/2003	U.S.
Reaffirmed Certain Opinion Criteria for U.S. Credit Card Transactions	05/12/2003	U.S.
Principles for Analyzing Corporate Securitizations: Update	18/09/2003	Global
Corporate Securitizations: The Role of Risk Capital in Aligning Stakeholder Interests	18/09/2003	Global
Corporate Securitizations: The Role of Risk Capital in Aligning Stakeholder Interests	18/09/2003	EMEA
Default Modeling for European Consumer Asset-Backed Securitizations	23/06/2003	EMEA
Rating Methodology for CLOs Backed by European Small- and Midsize-Enterprise Loans	30/01/2003	EMEA
Innovative Financing in the Social Housing Market	10/10/2002	EMEA
Partial Credit Guarantees Accepted on Structured Finance Emerging Market Transactions	24/10/2001	South America
New Perfection Criteria for Auto Lease Structured Transactions	27/06/2001	U.S.
New Perfection Criteria for Alternative Student Loan Structured Transactions	27/06/2001	U.S.
New Perfection Criteria for Manufactured Housing Mortgage Loan Structured Transactions	27/06/2001	U.S.
Securitization of Federal Tax Participations by Mexican States and Municipalities	17/05/2001	South America
Facing Up to the Rating Challenges of Whole Company Securitizations	15/12/2000	Global
New Bank Survivability Criteria Should Aid Emerging Market Financial Future Flow Issuers	13/09/2000	South America
European Consumer Finance Criteria	10/03/2000	EMEA
CAPCO Structured Financings Surge	23/02/2000	U.S.
Revised Surveillance Policies for Expiring Letters of Credit	13/07/1999	U.S.
Global Synthetic Securities Criteria, June 1, 1999	01/06/1999	Global
Global Synthetic Securities Criteria: Synthetic Securities Match Investor Preferences, June 1, 1999	01/06/1999	Global
Global Synthetic Securities Criteria: The Rating Process, June 1, 1999	01/06/1999	Global
Global Synthetic Securities Criteria: Structural Considerations, June 1, 1999	01/06/1999	Global
Global Synthetic Securities Criteria: Legal Considerations, June 1, 1999	01/06/1999	Global
Global Synthetic Securities Criteria: Custodians and Book Entry Clearing Systems, June 1, 1999	01/06/1999	Global
Global Synthetic Securities Criteria: Third-Party Roles in Synthetic Securities, June 1, 1999	01/06/1999	Global
Global Synthetic Securities Criteria: Swap Agreement Criteria, June 1, 1999	01/06/1999	Global
Global Synthetic Securities Criteria: Swap-Independent Synthetic Securities, June 1, 1999	01/06/1999	Global
Global Synthetic Securities Criteria: Investor Considerations in Swap Agreements, June 1, 1999	01/06/1999	Global
Global Synthetic Securities Criteria: Swap Counterparty Payments in Synthetic Securities, June 1, 1999	01/06/1999	Global
Global Synthetic Securities Criteria: Investor Awareness through Disclosure, June 1, 1999	01/06/1999	Global
Tax Issues Present Risky Challenges for C Pieces	28/10/1998	U.S.
Rating Future Flow Dollar-Denominated Airline Ticket Receivables	28/10/1998	South America
Securitization of Future Emerging Surpluses on Life Insurance Policies	30/09/1998	EMEA
Securitization of Future Emerging Surpluses on Life Insurance Policies	30/09/1998	EMEA
Premium Proceeds Catching on for Auto ABS	01/04/1998	U.S.
Sizing Credit Enhancement in Manufactured Housing Transactions	17/12/1996	U.S.
Role of the Backup Servicer	18/10/1996	U.S.
New Assets Enter Securitization Market	16/10/1996	U.S.
Criteria for Rating Nonperforming Loans	19/09/1996	U.S.
Rating Swap-Independent Synthetic Securities	22/07/1996	U.S.

B.3.7 Collateralized debt obligations and related products

Revised Assumptions for Rating Global Multiple-Credit-Dependent Obligations	06/10/2009	Global
Surveillance Methodology for Global Cash Flow and Hybrid CDOs Subject to Acceleration or Liquidation after an EOD	02/09/2009	Global
Surveillance Methodology for Global Cash Flow and Hybrid CDOs Subject to Acceleration or Liquidation after an EOD	02/09/2009	Global
Methodology for Analyzing Rating Confirmation Requests to Replace Collateral Managers in Global CDOs	13/08/2009	Global
Revised CDO Current-Pay Criteria Assumptions for Corporate Debt when Issuers Announce a Distressed Exchange or Buyback	18/05/2009	Global
Methodology for Analyzing CDO Transactions that Purchase Their Own Discounted Debt	29/04/2009	Global

Revised Assumptions for Structured Finance Assets with Ratings on Credit Watch and Held within CDO Transactions	06/04/2009	Global
Revised Assumptions for Structured Finance Assets with Ratings on Credit Watch and Held within CDO Transactions	06/04/2009	Global
Proposed Changes to Global Methodologies and Assumptions for Rating Corporate Cash Flow and Synthetic CDOs	19/03/2009	Global
Proposed Changes to Global Methodologies and Assumptions for Rating Corporate Cash Flow and Synthetic CDOs	19/03/2009	Global
Summary and Highlights of Proposed Changes to Our Global Rating Methodology for Corporate Cash Flow and Synthetic CDOs	17/03/2009	Global
Summary and Highlights of Proposed Changes to Our Global Rating Methodology for Corporate Cash Flow and Synthetic CDOs	17/03/2009	Global
Risk Profile of Global Private Equity Securitizations No Longer Supports "AAA" Ratings	13/02/2009	Global
Advance Notice of Proposed Criteria Change: Market Conditions Negatively Impact CDOs of Structured Finance Securities	30/12/2008	Global
Advance Notice of Proposed Criteria Change: Market Conditions Negatively Impact CDOs of Structured Finance Securities	30/12/2008	Global
Advance Notice of Proposed Criteria Change: Price Declines and Volatility in the Leveraged Loan Market Test Market Value CLOs	21/12/2008	Global
Retranching CDOs of ABS with Substantial Exposure to Certain U.S. RMBS and CDO Securities	18/12/2008	Global
Methodology and Assumptions: Retranching CDOs of ABS with Substantial Exposure to Certain U.S. RMBS and CDO Securities	18/12/2008	Global
Global Methodology for Rating Trust Preferred/Hybrid Securities Revised	21/11/2008	Global
Recovery Assumptions Revised for U.S. RMBS Collateral Backing ABS CDO Transactions	17/10/2008	Global
Risk Profile of Hedge Fund Securitizations Does Not Support "AAA" Ratings	18/09/2008	Global
Recovery Assumptions Revised for Certain CDOs Backed Predominantly by U.S. RMBS	28/04/2008	Global
The Use of Rating-Based Haircuts in Event of Default Overcollateralization Tests for CDOs	19/03/2008	Global
The Use of Rating-Based Haircuts in Event of Default Overcollateralization Tests for CDOs	19/03/2008	Global
Revised Guidelines on Rating New CDOs with Certain U.S. RMBS Exposure	20/10/2007	Global
CDO Spotlight: Methodology Update for Rating Global CDOs of Trust Preferred Securities Surplus Notes and Non-Perpetual Hybrid Securities	03/10/2007	Global
Updated Global Recovery Rates for Use in Cash Flow CDOs	23/07/2007	Global
Comments on Process for Rating New CDOs with U.S. RMBS Exposure	18/07/2007	Global
Qualification and Treatment of Current-Pay Obligations in Global Cash Flow CLOs	11/07/2007	Global
Application of Revised Counterparty and Supporting Party Framework to Hybrid CDOs	10/07/2007	Global
The Covenant-Lite Juggernaut Is Raising CLO Risks and Is Responding	12/06/2007	Global
Quantitative Modeling Approach to Rating Index CPDO Structures, March 22, 2007	22/03/2007	Global
Announced Criteria for Holders of Loan Participations in U.S. CRE CDOs	11/01/2007	Global
Spotlight: Global Rating Approach to CDOs of Reinsurer Obligations	18/12/2006	Global
Global Rating Approach to CDOs of Reinsurer Obligations	18/12/2006	Global
Using Recovery Ratings in Cash Flow CDOs	17/10/2006	Global
Update to General Cash Flow Analytics Criteria for CDO Securitizations	17/10/2006	Global
Update to General Cash Flow Analytics Criteria for CDO Securitizations	17/10/2006	Global
Update to General Cash Flow Analytics Criteria for CDO Securitizations	17/10/2006	Global
Refinements to Synthetic CDOs CreditWatch and Upgrade Policy	15/09/2006	Global
Updated Portfolio Level Approach for Rating U.S. Market Value CDOs	12/06/2006	Global
CDO Spotlight: Rating Approach to Synthetic CDOs of Sovereigns or Local and Regional Governments	03/05/2006	Global
Revised Criteria for U.S. Market Value Structures Offer Collateral Managers More Flexibility	21/03/2006	Global
CDO Spotlight: Global Criteria for Securitizations of Funds of Hedge Funds, Januaay 18, 2006	18/01/2006	Global
Global MCDO Criteria Are a Natural Extension of Established Rating Methodologies	10/01/2006	Global
ISDA's CDS of ABS Templates Scrutinized	01/12/2005	Global
Updated U.S. Leveraged Closed-End Fund Criteria for Hedging Transactions	26/10/2005	Global
CDO Spotlight: Pro Rata Payment of Liabilities in Global CDOs Introduce Certain Risks	19/10/2005	Global
CDO Spotlight: How to Analyze and Differentiate U.S. Middle Market Loan CLOs	06/10/2005	Global
Criteria for Rating Market Value CDO Transactions	15/09/2005	Global
U.S. Cash Flow CDOs Increasingly Turn to CP Funding; Criteria Provided	13/07/2005	Global
New Nomenclature for Rating Global Notes with Credit-Contingent Coupons	24/11/2004	Global
CDO Spotlight: General Cash Flow Analytics for CDO Securitizations	25/08/2004	Global
CDO Spotlight: General Cash Flow Analytics for CDO Securitizations	25/08/2004	Global

CDO Spotlight: Rating Approach to Synthetic CDO Transactions Referencing U.S. Municipal Credits	19/07/2004	Global
CDO Spotlight: Issues in Rating Combination Notes in Cash Flow CDOs	04/03/2004	Global
Drill-Down Approach for Synthetic CDO Squared Transactions	10/12/2003	Global
Structured Investment Vehicle Criteria: New Developments	04/09/2003	Global
Criteria for Rating Synthetic CDO Transactions/Credit Derivative Criteria, September 2, 2003	02/09/2003	Global
Criteria for Rating Synthetic CDO Transactions/Credit Derivative Criteria: Section 1: Description of a Synthetic CDO Transaction, September 2, 2003	02/09/2003	Global
Criteria for Rating Synthetic CDO Transactions/Credit Derivative Criteria: Section II: CDO Documentation, September 2, 2003	02/09/2003	Global
Criteria for Rating Synthetic CDO Transactions/Credit Derivative Criteria: Section III: Sizing of Defaults and Recoveries and Calculating the Credit Enhancement, September 2, 2003	02/09/2003	Global
Criteria for Rating Synthetic CDO Transactions/Credit Derivative Criteria: Section IV: Timely Payment of Interest and Ultimate Payment of Principal, September 2, 2003	02/09/2003	Global
Criteria for Rating Synthetic CDO Transactions/Credit Derivative Criteria: Section IV: Timely Payment of Interest and Ultimate Payment of Principal, September 2, 2003	02/09/2003	Global
Criteria for Rating Synthetic CDO Transactions/Credit Derivative Criteria: Section VI: Trading and Management, September 2, 2003	02/09/2003	Global
Criteria for Rating Synthetic CDO Transactions/Credit Derivative Criteria: Section VII: Legal Analysis and Surveillance, September 2, 2003	02/09/2003	Global
Criteria for Rating Synthetic CDO Transactions/Credit Derivative Criteria: Section VIII: Other Synthetic Structures, September 2, 2003	02/09/2003	Global
Criteria for Rating Synthetic CDO Transactions/Credit Derivative Criteria: Section IX: Concluding Remarks, September 2, 2003	02/09/2003	Global
Surveillance Policy Clarified for Events of Default in Synthetic CDO Transactions	18/08/2003	Global
Mapping Internal Credit Scores to Ratings for CDOs	11/11/2002	Global
Global Cash Flow and Synthetic CDOs of Structured Finance Securities	11/11/2002	Global
Mapping Internal Credit Scores to Ratings for CDOs	11/11/2002	Global
Global Cash Flow and Synthetic CDOs of Structured Finance Securities	11/11/2002	Global
Rated Overcollateralization Benchmark: A New Tool for Primary and Secondary Market CDOs	02/10/2002	Global
Global Cash Flow and Synthetic CDO Criteria: The CDO Product, March 21, 2002	21/03/2002	Global
Global Cash Flow and Synthetic CDO Criteria: Standard & Poor's CDO Rating Process, March 21, 2002	21/03/2002	Global
Global Cash Flow and Synthetic CDO Criteria: CDO Transaction Structural Basics, March 21, 2002	21/03/2002	Global
Global Cash Flow and Synthetic CDO Criteria: CDO Evaluator and Portfolio Benchmarks, March 21, 2002	21/03/2002	Global
Global Cash Flow and Synthetic CDO Criteria: CDO Manager Quality: A Critical Consideration, March 21, 2002	21/03/2002	Global
Global Cash Flow and Synthetic CDO Criteria: CDO Recovery Levels and Timing, March 21, 2002	21/03/2002	Global
Global Cash Flow and Synthetic CDO Criteria: CDO Structural and Collateral Considerations, March 21, 2002	21/03/2002	Global
Global Cash Flow and Synthetic CDO Criteria: Cash Flow Analytics, March 21, 2002	21/03/2002	Global
Global Cash Flow and Synthetic CDO Criteria: Hedging Consideration, March 21, 2002	21/03/2002	Global
Global Cash Flow and Synthetic CDO Criteria: Legal Considerations for CDO Transactions, March 21, 2002	21/03/2002	Global
Global Cash Flow and Synthetic CDO Criteria: CDO Surveillance, March 21, 2002	21/03/2002	Global
Global Cash Flow and Synthetic CDO Criteria: Special Topics, March 21, 2002	21/03/2002	Global
Global Cash Flow and Synthetic CDO Criteria: Appendix A: Mapping Bank Loan Scoring Models, March 21, 2002	21/03/2002	Global
Global Cash Flow and Synthetic CDO Criteria: Appendix B: Structured Finance Interest Rate and Currency Swap Criteria, March 21, 2002	21/03/2002	Global
Global Cash Flow and Synthetic CDO Criteria: Appendix C: 'AAA' Swaps Approved in Structured Finance Transactions, March 21, 2002	21/03/2002	Global
Global Cash Flow and Synthetic CDO Criteria: Appendix D: Swap Agreement Criteria for CBO/CLO Transactions , March 21, 2002	21/03/2002	Global
Global Cash Flow and Synthetic CDO Criteria: Appendix E: Interest Rate Assumptions for Structured Ratings, March 21, 2002	21/03/2002	Global
Global Cash Flow and Synthetic CDO Criteria: The CDO Product, March 21, 2002	21/03/2002	Global

Global Cash Flow and Synthetic CDO Criteria: Standard & Poor's CDO Rating Process, March 21, 2002	21/03/2002	Global
Global Cash Flow and Synthetic CDO Criteria: CDO Transaction Structural Basics, March 21, 2002	21/03/2002	Global
Global Cash Flow and Synthetic CDO Criteria: CDO Evaluator and Portfolio Benchmarks, March 21, 2002	21/03/2002	Global
Global Cash Flow and Synthetic CDO Criteria: CDO Manager Quality: A Critical Consideration, March 21, 2002	21/03/2002	Global
Global Cash Flow and Synthetic CDO Criteria: CDO Recovery Levels and Timing, March 21, 2002	21/03/2002	Global
Global Cash Flow and Synthetic CDO Criteria: CDO Structural and Collateral Considerations, March 21, 2002	21/03/2002	Global
Global Cash Flow and Synthetic CDO Criteria: Cash Flow Analytics, March 21, 2002	21/03/2002	Global
Global Cash Flow and Synthetic CDO Criteria: Hedging Consideration, March 21, 2002	21/03/2002	Global
Global Cash Flow and Synthetic CDO Criteria: Legal Considerations for CDO Transactions, March 21, 2002	21/03/2002	Global
Global Cash Flow and Synthetic CDO Criteria: CDO Surveillance, March 21, 2002	21/03/2002	Global
Global Cash Flow and Synthetic CDO Criteria: Special Topics, March 21, 2002	21/03/2002	Global
Global Cash Flow and Synthetic CDO Criteria: Appendix A: Mapping Bank Loan Scoring Models, March 21, 2002	21/03/2002	Global
Global Cash Flow and Synthetic CDO Criteria: Appendix B: Structured Finance Interest Rate and Currency Swap Criteria, March 21, 2002	21/03/2002	Global
Global Cash Flow and Synthetic CDO Criteria: Appendix C: "AAA" Swaps Approved in Structured Finance Transactions, March 21, 2002	21/03/2002	Global
Global Cash Flow and Synthetic CDO Criteria: Appendix D: Swap Agreement Criteria for CBO/CLO Transactions, March 21, 2002	21/03/2002	Global
Global Cash Flow and Synthetic CDO Criteria: Appendix E: Interest Rate Assumptions for Structured Ratings, March 21, 2002	21/03/2002	Global
Commodities Futures and Swaps Contracts: Set-Off and Bankruptcy	10/12/2001	Global
Market Value Advance Rates for U.S. Treasury Securities	19/09/2001	Global
New Rating Criteria for Multiple-Credit-Dependent Obligations	21/05/2001	Global
Actively Managed Market Value CBOs: A New Market Sector Emerges	06/05/1999	Global
Market-Value Transactions: Volatility Factors Used to Calculate Dividends	03/02/1999	Global
Overcollateralization Methodology for Market Value Transactions Focus on Security's Pricing History	03/02/1999	Global
Index Overcollateralization Levels for Market Value Transactions: Guidelines and Applications	03/02/1999	Global
Market Value Transactions: Assumptions and Overcollateralization Levels for Bank Loans	03/02/1999	Global
Market Value Transactions: Criteria and Assumptions for Development of Bank Loan Overcollateralization Levels	03/02/1999	Global

B.3.8 Commercial mortgage-backed securitization and real estate investment trusts

Methodology and Assumptions for Rating Resecuritizations of U.S. Super-Senior Conduit/Fusion CMBS Classes	14/08/2009	U.S.
U.S. CMBS "AAA" Scenario Loss and Recovery Application	21/07/2009	U.S.
U.S. CMBS Rating Methodology and Assumptions for Conduit/Fusion Pools	26/06/2009	U.S.
FDIC TLGP Debt May Be Included as Defeasance Collateral in Rated U.S. CMBS Transactions	19/03/2009	U.S.
Requests Additional Information for Monitoring U.S. CRE CDOs	04/02/2009	U.S.
Advance Notice of Proposed Criteria Change: Economic Stress and Liquidity Constraints Take a Toll on U.S. CMBS	16/12/2008	U.S.
Qualified Transferees in U.S. CMBS Transactions	16/09/2008	U.S.
Minimum Tail Period for Australian and New Zealand CMBS Transactions	08/07/2008	Asia
Recovery Rates for CMBS Collateral in Resecuritization Transactions	28/05/2008	U.S.
Framework for Credit Analysis in European CMBS Transactions	21/05/2007	EMEA
Methodology for Japanese CMBS Loan Analysis	12/03/2007	Asia
Methodology for Japanese CMBS Real Estate Evaluation	12/03/2007	Asia
CMBS and Corporate Securitizations: The Use of Unrated Fees in English Issuer SPE Structures	11/12/2006	EMEA
Rating U.S. CMBS in the Face of Interest Shortfalls	23/02/2006	U.S.
Technical Challenges in European CMBS Structures	16/02/2006	EMEA
CMBS Property Evaluation Criteria: The Rating Process for CMBS Transactions	01/09/2004	U.S.

CMBS Property Evaluation Criteria: Commercial Property Cash Flow Analysis	01/09/2004	U.S.
CMBS Property Evaluation Criteria: Guidelines for Analysis of Major Property Types	01/09/2004	U.S.
CMBS Property Evaluation Criteria: Insurance Criteria for CMBS Transactions	01/09/2004	U.S.
CMBS Property Evaluation Criteria: Ground Lease Requirements in CMBS Transactions	01/09/2004	U.S.
European CMBS Loan Level Guidelines	01/09/2004	EMEA
Investors Benefit from the Legal/Structural Review of U.S. CMBS Transactions	26/02/2004	U.S.
U.S. Secured Creditor Environmental Insurance Policy Provider Rating Criteria Updated	04/11/2003	U.S.
Global CMBS Rating Methodology: Standing Tall in Falling Markets	16/10/2003	Global
U.S. CMBS Legal and Structured Finance Criteria: Property-Specific and Large Loan Transactions	01/05/2003	U.S.
U.S. CMBS Legal and Structured Finance Criteria: Pool Transactions	01/05/2003	U.S.
U.S. CMBS Legal and Structured Finance Criteria: Credit Tenant Loan Transactions	01/05/2003	U.S.
U.S. CMBS Legal and Structured Finance Criteria: Special-Purpose Bankruptcy-Remote Entities	01/05/2003	U.S.
U.S. CMBS Legal and Structured Finance Criteria: Legal Opinions	01/05/2003	U.S.
U.S. CMBS Legal and Structured Finance Criteria: Appendix I: Insurance Criteria for U.S. CMBS Transactions	01/05/2003	U.S.
U.S. CMBS Legal and Structured Finance Criteria: Appendix II: Eligible Investment Criteria for "AAA" Rated Structured Transactions	01/05/2003	U.S.
U.S. CMBS Legal and Structured Finance Criteria: Appendix III: Revised Article 9 of the Uniform Commercial Code: New Criteria	01/05/2003	U.S.
U.S. CMBS Legal and Structured Finance Criteria: Appendix IV: Defeasance Criteria for U.S. CMBS Transactions	01/05/2003	U.S.
U.S. CMBS Legal and Structured Finance Criteria: Appendix V: Form of Notice Regarding Defeasance of Mortgage Loans	01/05/2003	U.S.
U.S. CMBS Legal and Structured Finance Criteria: Appendix VI: Intercreditor Agreement	01/05/2003	U.S.
U.S. CMBS Legal and Structured Finance Criteria: Appendix VII: The Credit Impact of Secured Creditor Environmental Insurance of CMBS Transactions	01/05/2003	U.S.
U.S. CMBS Legal and Structured Finance Criteria: Appendix VIII: Large Loan Summary	01/05/2003	U.S.
U.S. CMBS Legal and Structured Finance Criteria: Appendix IX: Questionnaire for Interest Rate Cap Agreements	01/05/2003	U.S.
U.S. CMBS Legal and Structured Finance Criteria: Appendix X: Foreign Law Real Estate Issues Summary	01/05/2003	U.S.
U.S. CMBS Legal and Structured Finance Criteria: Appendix XI: Credit-Tenant Loans in Pool Transactions	01/05/2003	U.S.
U.S. CMBS Legal and Structured Finance Criteria: Appendix XII: Sample Guarantee Language	01/05/2003	U.S.
U.S. CMBS Legal and Structured Finance Criteria: Appendix XIII: Revised Legal Criteria for Multi- and Single-Member LLCs	01/05/2003	U.S.
U.S. CMBS Legal and Structured Finance Criteria: Appendix XIV: U.S. Legal Criteria for "Recycled" Special-Purpose Entities	01/05/2003	U.S.
U.S. CMBS Legal and Structured Finance Criteria: Appendix XV: Typical Factors Considered by Courts in Determining Existence of a True Sale	01/05/2003	U.S.
U.S. CMBS Legal and Structured Finance Criteria: Appendix XVI: Select Specific Opinion Criteria/Language	01/05/2003	U.S.
Defeasance Criteria for U.S. CMBS Transactions	04/04/2003	U.S.
Industrial Special Risks Insurance Requirements Change for Australian CMBS Transactions	27/11/2002	Asia
The Credit Impact of Secured Creditor Environmental Insurance on CMBS Transactions	04/05/2000	U.S.
Credit-Tenant Loans in Pool Transactions	03/11/1999	U.S.
Earthquake Insurance Requirements for U.S. CMBS Transactions	28/10/1998	U.S.

B.3.9 Covered bonds criteria

Applying the Derivative Counterparty Framework to Covered Bonds	26/02/2008	Global
New Italian Covered Bond Law Allows for Ratings Higher than Issuing Bank	30/05/2007	EMEA
Criteria for Rating Swedish Covered Bonds	20/06/2006	EMEA
Rating Methodology for Spanish Covered Bonds Considers Enhanced Post-Insolvency Treatment	19/04/2005	EMEA
Expanding European Covered Bond Universe Puts Spotlight on Key Analytics	16/07/2004	EMEA
Rating Pfandbriefe: The Analytical Perspective	08/04/2004	EMEA
German Pfandbriefe Framework Further Improved	30/03/2004	EMEA
Surviving Stress Scenarios: Assessing Asset Quality of Public Sector Covered Bond Collateral	23/09/2003	EMEA

Criteria for Rating Danish Covered Bonds (*Realkreditobligationer*)	10/07/2003	EMEA
Irish Covered Bonds Eligible for a Delinked Ratings Approach	19/02/2003	EMEA
Criteria for Rating Luxembourg *Lettres De Gage Publiques*	20/11/2001	EMEA
Developed Criteria for Rating *Obligations Foncières*	05/05/2000	EMEA

B.3.10 Residential mortgage-backed securitization

Standard & Poor's Revised Representations and Warranties Criteria for U.S. RMBS Transactions	28/09/2009	U.S.
Revised U.S. Residential Mortgage Input File Format Glossary and Appendices to the Glossary for LEVELS Version 7.0	16/09/2009	U.S.
Methodology and Assumptions for Rating U.S. RMBS Prime Alternative-A and Subprime Loans	10/09/2009	U.S.
Methodology and Assumptions for Rating U.S. RMBS Prime Alternative-A and Subprime Loans	10/09/2009	U.S.
Methodology and Assumptions for Rating U.S. RMBS Prime Alternative-A and Subprime Loans	10/09/2009	U.S.
Revised Loss Severity Methodology and Assumptions for U.S. Prime Subprime and Alternative-A RMBS Transactions Issued before 2005	19/08/2009	U.S.
Revised Loss Severity Methodology and Assumptions for U.S. Prime Subprime and Alternative-A RMBS Transactions Issued before 2005	19/08/2009	U.S.
Revised Loss Severity Methodology and Assumptions for U.S. Prime Subprime and Alternative-A RMBS Transactions Issued before 2005	19/08/2009	U.S.
Revised U.S. RMBS Interest Rate Assumptions for October 2009	06/08/2009	U.S.
Methodology for Loan Modifications that Include Forbearance Plans for U.S. RMBS	23/07/2009	U.S.
Revised U.S. Subprime and Alternative-A RMBS Loss Assumptions for Transactions Issued in 2005	06/07/2009	U.S.
Revised U.S. Subprime and Alternative-A RMBS Loss Assumptions for Transactions Issued in 2005 2006 and 2007	06/07/2009	U.S.
Revised U.S. Prime Jumbo RMBS Lifetime Loss Projections for Transactions Issued in 2005	16/06/2009	U.S.
Methodology: U.S. RMBS Servicer Advance Transactions	06/04/2009	U.S.
Rating Assumptions for U.S. Second-Lien HCLTV Home Improvement and Home Improvement/Title One RMBS Transactions	02/04/2009	U.S.
Rating Assumptions for U.S. First-Lien High Loan-To-Value RMBS Transactions	30/03/2009	U.S.
Standard & Poor's Rating Methodology and Assumptions for Australian RMBS Net Interest Margin Securities	30/03/2009	Asia
Methodology and Assumptions: Resecuritization of U.S. RMBS	17/03/2009	U.S.
Surveillance Methodology for U.S. RMBS Net Interest Margin Securities	17/03/2009	U.S.
Methodology and Assumptions for U.S. RMBS Issued before 2005	12/03/2009	U.S.
Revised Loss Assumptions for 2005 Vintage Prime Jumbo U.S. RMBS Transactions	11/03/2009	U.S.
Surveillance Methodology and Assumptions for U.S. RMBS "Scratch and Dent" Transactions	23/02/2009	U.S.
Methodology for "Springing" True Sale Opinions in U.S. RMBS Transactions	12/02/2009	U.S.
Revised Surveillance Default Curve for U.S. Prime Jumbo RMBS Issued in 2006 and 2007	11/02/2009	U.S.
Revised Methodology and Assumptions for Automated Valuation Models in U.S. RMBS	06/02/2009	U.S.
U.S. RMBS Synthetic Risk Transfers	06/02/2009	U.S.
Revised Definitions and Assumptions for Documentation Types in U.S. RMBS	06/02/2009	U.S.
Revised Methodology and Assumptions for Primary Mortgage Insurance in U.S. RMBS	06/02/2009	U.S.
Methodology and Assumptions: Guidelines for Reviewing U.S. RMBS Loan Modification Amendments	29/01/2009	U.S.
LEVELS Mexico Estimates the Risk of Defaults and Recoveries for Mexican RMBS	20/01/2009	South America
Update to the Cash Flow Criteria for European RMBS Transactions	06/01/2009	EMEA
Update to the Criteria for Rating Spanish Residential Mortgage-Backed Securities	06/01/2009	EMEA
Update to the Criteria for Rating U.K. Residential Mortgage-Backed Securities	06/01/2009	EMEA
Update to the Criteria for Rating French Residential Mortgage-Backed Securities	06/01/2009	EMEA
Update to the Criteria for Rating Portuguese Residential Mortgage-Backed Securities	06/01/2009	EMEA
Update to the Criteria for Rating Italian Residential Mortgage-Backed Securities	06/01/2009	EMEA
Update to the Criteria for Rating German Residential Mortgage-Backed Securities	06/01/2009	EMEA
Methodology for the Surveillance of U.S. RMBS Re-REMIC Transactions	23/12/2008	U.S.
German Law Change Affects Mortgage Foreclosure Period Stresses	28/11/2008	EMEA
Incorporating Third-Party Due Diligence Results into the U.S. RMBS Rating Process	25/11/2008	U.S.
Enhanced Mortgage Originator and Underwriting Review Criteria for U.S. RMBS	25/11/2008	U.S.
Approach to Evaluating U.S. RMBS Distressed Collateral	19/11/2008	U.S.

Revised Italian RMBS High Constant Payment Rate Assumption	14/10/2008	EMEA
Criteria Assumptions: Default and Loss Assumptions for U.S. Fixed Alt-A RMBS Transactions	25/09/2008	U.S.
Standard & Poor's Makes Enhancements to the U.S. RMBS Ratings Process	12/09/2008	U.S.
Published Revised Projected Losses for '06/'07 U.S. Alt-A Short-Reset Hybrid	20/08/2008	U.S.
Revised U.S. Subprime Prime and Alternative-A RMBS Loss Assumptions	30/07/2008	U.S.
Revised U.S. Subprime Prime and Alternative-A RMBS Loss Assumptions	30/07/2008	U.S.
Revised U.S. Subprime Prime and Alternative-A RMBS Loss Assumptions July 30	20/07/2008	U.S.
Credit FAQ: Standard & Poor's Rating Methodology and Assumptions for U.S. RMBS Resecuritizations	02/07/2008	U.S.
Assessing the NHG Guarantee in Dutch RMBS Transactions: A Prudent Approach	11/06/2008	EMEA
Methodology and Assumptions for Rating U.S. RMBS Re-REMICs Clarified	02/05/2008	U.S.
Halted Rating Process for U.S. Closed-End Second-Lien Mortgage Loans	01/05/2008	U.S.
Application of Revised Cash Flow Assumptions for U.S. Residential Mortgage-Backed Securities	30/04/2008	U.S.
Recovery Assumptions Revised for Certain CDOs Backed Predominantly by U.S. RMBS	28/04/2008	U.S.
U.S. RMBS HECM Reverse Mortgage Analysis Assumptions Revised	11/04/2008	U.S.
Analysis of Loan Modifications and Servicer Reimbursements for U.S. RMBS Transactions with Senior/Subordinate Structures	10/04/2008	U.S.
Enhanced Version of SPIRE U.S. Residential Mortgage Cash Flow Model Released	07/04/2008	U.S.
Glossary of Terms for Requested Additional Loan-Level Fields for New U.S. RMBS Ratings	02/04/2008	U.S.
Revising Foreclosure-Frequency and Loss-Severity Assumptions for Rating U.S. RMBS	20/03/2008	U.S.
U.S. RMBS Nonconforming (Jumbo) Reverse Mortgage Analysis Assumptions Revised	20/03/2008	U.S.
Criteria for Rating Structured Finance Transactions that Include Loans Originated by Federal Thrifts Revised	05/03/2008	U.S.
Rating Methodology and Assumptions for Russian RMBS	31/01/2008	EMEA
Summary of Findings and Response to Request for Comment on Providing U.S. RMBS Monthly Loan-Level Performance Data	21/01/2008	U.S.
Proposed File Format: Standard & Poor's Request for Ongoing U.S. Residential Loan-Level Information	23/10/2007	U.S.
Standard & Poor's Revised Default and Loss Curves for U.S. Subprime RMBS	19/10/2007	U.S.
Rating Methodology for Residential Mortgage-Backed Securities in Japan	19/08/2007	Asia
Australia and New Zealand RMBS: Analyzing Credit Quality	21/02/2007	Asia
Changes to the Treatment of Potential Set-Off Risk in the Dutch RMBS Market	08/09/2006	EMEA
Deposit Insurance Limits Commingling Risk in Japan RMBS Deals	07/02/2006	Asia
Dutch RMBS Market Overview and Criteria	16/12/2005	EMEA
Guidelines for the Use of Automated Valuation Models for U.K. RMBS Transactions	15/09/2005	EMEA
Treatment of Flexible Mortgage Loans in U.K. RMBS Transactions	06/04/2005	EMEA
Methodology behind European RMBS Indices	08/11/2004	EMEA
Italian Mortgage Default Estimation: Incorporating the CRIF Decision Solutions Mortgage Risk Scale	16/09/2004	EMEA
Securitization in Latin America: Rating Criteria for Argentine Mortgage-Backed Securities	01/09/2004	South America
Rating Methodology for Apartment Loan Securitizations in Japan	11/07/2004	Asia
Cash Flow Criteria for European RMBS Transactions	20/11/2003	EMEA
Criteria for Rating French Residential Mortgage-Backed Securities	16/07/2003	EMEA
Criteria for Rating U.K. Reverse Mortgage-Backed Securities	08/08/2002	EMEA
Criteria for Rating Portuguese Residential Mortgage-Backed Securities	06/08/2002	EMEA
Criteria for Rating Italian Residential Mortgage-Backed Securities	16/07/2002	EMEA
Criteria for Rating Spanish Residential Mortgage-Backed Securities	01/03/2002	EMEA
Criteria for Rating German Residential Mortgage-Backed Securities	31/08/2001	EMEA
Revised Criteria for Rating U.K. Residential Mortgage-Backed Securities	05/07/2001	EMEA
U.S. Residential Subprime Mortgage Criteria: Appendix F: Criteria for FICO Scores, May 1, 2000	10/05/2000	U.S.
U.S. Residential Subprime Mortgage Criteria: Appendix E: Liabilities and Other Debt, May 1, 2000	09/05/2000	U.S.
U.S. Residential Subprime Mortgage Criteria: Servicer Evaluation Criteria, May 1, 2000	08/05/2000	U.S.
U.S. Residential Subprime Mortgage Criteria: Servicer Requirements, May 1, 2000	07/05/2000	U.S.
U.S. Residential Subprime Mortgage Criteria: Legal Criteria for Subprime Mortgage Transactions, May 1, 2000	06/05/2000	U.S.
U.S. Residential Subprime Mortgage Criteria: Structural Considerations for Subprime Mortgage Transactions, May 1, 2000	05/05/2000	U.S.
U.S. Residential Subprime Mortgage Criteria: Credit Analysis for Subprime Mortgage Transactions, May 1, 2000	04/05/2000	U.S.

U.S. Residential Subprime Mortgage Criteria: Loan Quality Guidelines for Subprime Mortgage Transactions, May 1, 2000	03/05/2000	U.S.
U.S. Residential Subprime Mortgage Criteria: The Rating Process for Subprime Mortgage Transactions, May 1, 2000	02/05/2000	U.S.
U.S. Residential Subprime Mortgage Criteria, May 1, 2000	01/05/2000	U.S.
Preliminary Rating Criteria for Singapore Residential Mortgage-Backed Securities	20/10/1999	Asia
New Assets 1998: Securitizing Municipal Revenues	01/03/1998	U.S.
New Assets 1998: Are the Cameras Ready to Roll on Securitizing "The Movies"? October 17	17/10/1997	U.S.
Small Multifamily Transaction Analyzed	22/07/1996	U.S.

Appendix C
List of abbreviations

ABCP	Asset-Backed Commercial Paper
ABS	Asset-Backed Securitization
AFME	Association for Financial Markets in Europe
API	Application Programming Interface
D,B&D	Doubtful, Bad and Dormant account
CDO	Collateralized Debt Obligation
CPR	Constant Prepayment Rate
CDR	Cumulative Default Rate
CRA	Credit Rating Agency
CSV	Comma-Separated Values
DSCR	Debt Service Coverage Ratio
DTC	Depository Trust Corporation (U.S.)
EST	Eastern Standard Time
FC	Foreclosure
FTP	File Transfer Protocol
GAAP	Generally Accepted Accounting Principles
GSE	Government-Sponsored or Government-Supported Entity
HE	Home Equity
HELOC	Home Equity Line Of Credit
ICR	Interest Coverage Ratio
IOSCO	International Organization of Securities COmmissions
IRP (and E-IRP)	Investor Reporting Package and European Investor Reporting Package, respectively
ISDA	International Swaps and Derivatives Association
LIBOR	London InterBank Offered Rate
LLP	Limited Liability Partnership
OC	Offering Circular
RATC	Rating Action Tool Code on Bloomberg
REO	Real Estate Owned
Repos	Representations and warranties
RMBS	Residential Mortgage-Backed Securitization
RW	Risk Weight
SEC	U.S. Securities and Exchange Commission
SF	Structured Finance
SIV	Structured Investment Vehicle
SME CDO	Small-to-Medium Enterprise Collateralized Debt Obligation
SPV	Special Purpose Vehicle
STP	Straight Through Processing
TRUPS	TRUst Preferred Security
XBRL	eXtensible Business Reporting Language

WAC	Weighted Average Coupon
WAL	Weighted Average Life
WARF	Weighted Average Rating Factor
WALS	Weighted Average Loss Severity
WAPI	Function on Bloomberg to access the API menu

Appendix D
Bibliography

Alexander, C. and Sheedy, E. (2004). *The Professional Risk Managers' Handbook: A Comprehensive Guide to Current Theory and Best Practices*, Wilmington, DE: Prima Publications.

Allman, K. A. (2007). *Modeling Structured Finance Cash Flows with Microsoft Excel: A Step-by-step Guide*, Hoboken, NJ: John Wiley & Sons.

Ashcraft, A. B. and Schuermann, T. (2008). *Understanding the Securitization of Subprime Mortgage Credit*, New York, Federal Reserve Bank of New York.

Banks, E. (2006). *Synthetic and Structured Assets: A Practical Guide to Investment and Risk*, Chichester, U.K.: John Wiley & Sons.

Blumke, A. (2009). *How to Invest in Structured Products: A Guide for Investors and Investment Advisors*, Hoboken, NJ: John Wiley & Sons.

Brand, A. (2009). *Risk in Financial Services*, London: Chartered Institute for Securities & Investments.

Bruyère, R. and Cont, R. (2006). *Credit Derivatives and Structured Credit: A Guide for Investors*, Chichester, U.K.: John Wiley & Sons.

Capital Markets (electronic resource). "The law and leading lawyers worldwide" (online), London: Practical Law Co.

Carlson, J. H. and Fabozzi, F. J. (1992). *The Trading and Securitization of Senior Bank Loans*, Chicago, IL: Probus.

Caselli, S. and Gatti, S. (2005). *Structured Finance: Techniques, Products and Market*, Berlin: Springer-Verlag.

Cavenagh, A. (2008). *New Frontiers in European Securitisation: Opportunities in Troubled Times*, London, Thomson Reuters.

Cherubini, U. and della Lunga, G. (2007). *Structured Finance: The Object Oriented Approach*, Chichester, U.K.: John Wiley & Sons.

Choudhry, M. (2004). *Structured Credit Products: Credit Derivatives and Synthetic Securitisation*, Singapore: John Wiley & Sons (Asia).

CISI (2007). *IT in Investment Operations: The Official Learning and Reference Manual*, London: Chartered Institute for Securities & Investment.

Cox, D. (2007). *Frontiers of Risk Management: Key Issues and Solutions*, London: Euromoney.

Das, S. (2001). *Structured Products and Hybrid Securities*, Singapore: John Wiley & Sons.

Das, S. (2005). *Credit Derivatives: CDOs and Structured Credit Products*, Singapore: John Wiley & Sons (Asia).

Davidson, A. S. (2003). *Securitization: Structuring and Investment Analysis*, New York: John Wiley & Sons.

EII (2010). *The Euromoney Securitisation and Structured Finance Handbook*, Colchester, U.K.: Euromoney Institutional Investor.

Fabozzi, F. J. (1997). *The Handbook of Nonagency Mortgage-backed Securities*, New Hope, PA: Frank J. Fabozzi Associates.

Fabozzi, F. J. (1998a). *Handbook of Structured Financial Products*, New Hope, PA: Frank J. Fabozzi Associates.

Fabozzi, F. J. (1998b). *Issuer Perspectives on Securitization*, New Hope, PA: Frank J. Fabozzi Associates.

Fabozzi, F. J. (1998c). *Advances in the Valuation and Management of Mortgage-backed Securities*, New Hope, PA: Frank J. Fabozzi Associates.

Fabozzi, F. J. (2001). *Accessing Capital Markets through Securitization*, New York: Frank J. Fabozzi Associates/Chichester, U.K.: John Wiley & Sons.

Fabozzi, F. J. (2006). *The Handbook of Mortgage-backed Securities*, New York: McGraw-Hill.

Fabozzi, F. J. and Choudhry, M. (2004). *The Handbook of European Structured Financial Products*, Hoboken, NJ: John Wiley & Sons.

Fabozzi, F. J. and Modigliani, F. (1992). *Mortgage and Mortgage-backed Securities Markets*, Boston, MA: Harvard Business School Press.

Fabozzi, F. J. and Molay, R. P. (1998). *Trends in Commercial Mortgage-backed Securities*, New Hope, PA: Frank J. Fabozzi Associates.

Fabozzi, F. J., Fabozzi, T. D., and Pollack, I. M. (1991). *The Handbook of Fixed Income Securities*, Homewood, IL: Business One Irwin.

Fabozzi, F. J., Bhattacharya, A. K., and Berliner, W. S. (2007). *Mortgage-backed Securities: Products, Structuring, and Analytical Techniques*, Hoboken, NJ: John Wiley & Sons.

Fender, I. and Mitchell, J. (2009). *Incentives and Tranche Retention in Securitisation: A Screening Model*, London: Centre for Economic Policy Research.

Hansen, M. K. R., Linell, I., van Vuuren, G., Mitropopulos, A., Jennings, S., d'Albert, K., Cromartie, J., Brewer, A. (2009). *Basel II and Securitisation: A Guided Tour through a New Landscape* (global special report), London: Fitch Ratings.

Huff, D. (1978). *How to Lie with Statistics*, Pelican Books.

IOSCO (2009). *Transparency of Structured Finance Products* (consultation report), International Organization of Securities Commissions.

Kendall, L. T. and Fishman, M. J. (1996). *A Primer on Securitization*, Cambridge, MA: MIT Press.

Kiff, J. (2010). *The Regulatory Overkill (?) of Global Securitization Markets: Opportunities in the Italian Funding Market*, Rome.

Knop, R. (2002). *Structured Products: A Complete Toolkit to Face Changing Financial Markets*, Chichester, U.K.: John Wiley & Sons.

Kothari, V. (2006). *Securitization: The Financial Instrument of the Future*, Singapore: John Wiley & Sons (Asia).

Kothari, V. (2009). *Credit Derivatives and Structured Credit Trading*, Singapore: John Wiley & Sons (Asia).

Lancaster, B. P., Schultz, G. M., and Fabozzi, F. J. (2008). *Structured Products and Related Credit Derivatives: A Comprehensive Guide for Investors*, Hoboken, NJ: John Wiley & Sons.

Pagano, M. and Volpin, P. (2008). *Securitization, Transparency and Liquidity*, London: Centre for Economic Policy Research.

Peachey, A. N. (2006). *Great Financial Disasters of Our Time*, Berlin: BVW Verlag.

PLC (2009). *Structured Finance and Securitisation Handbook: The Law in Key Jurisdictions Worldwide*, London: Practical Law Company.

Preinitz, W. (2009). *A Fast Track to Structured Finance Modeling, Monitoring, and Valuation: Jump Start VBA*, Hoboken, NJ: John Wiley & Sons.

Rajan, A., McDermott, G., and Roy, R. (2007). *The Structured Credit Handbook*, Hoboken, NJ: John Wiley & Sons.

Raynes, S. and Rutledge, A. (2003). *The Analysis of Structured Securities: Precise Risk Measurement and Capital Allocation*, Oxford, U.K.: Oxford University Press.

Reynolds, G. (2008). *Presentation Zen: Simple Ideas on Presentation Design and Delivery*, Berkeley, CA: New Riders.

Rutledge, A. and Raynes, S. (2010). *Elements of Structured Finance*, New York: Oxford University Press.

Schwarcz, S. L. (1993). *Structured Finance: A Guide to the Principles of Asset Securitization*, New York: Practising Law Institute.

SEC (2010). *Asset-backed Securities* (RIN 3235-AK37), Securities & Exchange Commission.

Servigny, A. D. and Jobst, N. J. (2007). *The Handbook of Structured Finance*, New York: McGraw-Hill.

Stone, C. A. and Zissu, A. (2005). *The Securitization Markets Handbook: Structures and Dynamics of Mortgage- and Asset-backed Securities*, Princeton, NJ: Bloomberg.

Tanega, J. and Curtin, E. (2009). *Securitisation Law: EU and US Disclosure Regulations*, London: LexisNexis.

Tavakoli, J. M. (2001). *Credit Derivatives and Synthetic Structures: A Guide to Instruments and Applications*, New York: John Wiley & Sons.

Tavakoli, J. M. (2008). *Structured Finance and Collateralized Debt Obligations: New Developments in Cash and Synthetic Securitization*, Hoboken, NJ: John Wiley & Sons.

Tick, E. (2007). *Structured Finance Modeling with Object-oriented VBA*, Hoboken, NJ: John Wiley & Sons.

Watson, R. and Carter, J. (2006). *Asset Securitisation and Synthetic Structures: Innovations in the European Credit Markets*, London: Euromoney Books.

Index